BUILDING OBJECT
CATEGORIES IN
DEVELOPMENTAL TIME

Carnegie Mellon Symposia on Cognition
David Klahr, Series Editor

Anderson • Cognitive Skills and Their Acquisition

Carroll/Payne • Cognition and Social Behavior

Carver/Klahr • Cognition and Instruction: Twenty-Five Years of Progress

Clark/Fiske • Affect and Cognition

Cohen/Schooler • Scientific Approaches to Consciousness

Cole • Perception and Production of Fluent Speech

Farah/Ratcliff • The Neuropsychology of High-Level Vision: Collected Tutorial Essays

Gershkoff-Stowe/Rakison • Building Object Categories in Developmental Time

Granrud • Visual Perception and Cognition in Infancy

Gregg • Knowledge and Cognition

Just/Carpenter • Cognitive Processes in Comprehension

Kimchi/Behrmann/Olson • Perceptual Organization in Vision: Behavioral and Neural Perspectives

Klahr • Cognition and Instruction

Klahr/Kotovsky • Complex Information Processing: The Impact of Herbert A. Simon

Lau/Sears • Political Cognition

MacWhinney • The Emergence of Language

MacWhinney • Mechanisms of Language Acquisition

McClelland/Siegler • Mechanisms of Cognitive Development: Behavioral and Neural Perspectives

Reder • Implicit Memory and Metacognition

Siegler • Children's Thinking: What Develops?

Sophian • Origins of Cognitive Skills

Steier/Mitchell • Mind Matters: A Tribute to Allen Newell

VanLehn • Architectures for Intelligence

BUILDING OBJECT CATEGORIES IN DEVELOPMENTAL TIME

Edited by

Lisa Gershkoff-Stowe
Indiana University

David H. Rakison
Carnegie Mellon University

32nd Carnegie Mellon Symposium
on Cognition

LEA LAWRENCE ERLBAUM ASSOCIATES, PUBLISHERS
2005 Mahwah, New Jersey   London

Lawrence Erlbaum Associates, Inc., Publishers
10 Industrial Avenue
Mahwah, New Jersey 07430
www.erlbaum.com

Cover art by Rachel Wu

Cover design by Kathryn Houghtaling Lacey

Library of Congress Cataloging-in-Publication Data

Carnegie Symposium on Cognition (32nd : 2002 : Carnegie-Mellon University)
    Building object categories in developmental time / edited by Lisa Gershkoff-Stowe
and David H. Rakison.
        p.   cm.
    "32nd Carnegie Mellon symposium series on cognition."
    Includes bibliographical references and index.
    ISBN 0-8058-4490-2
    ISBN 0-8058-4491-0 (pbk.)
    1. Categorization (Psychology) in children—Congresses.   I. Gershkoff-Stowe, Lisa.
II. Rakison, David H., 1969–   III. Title.

BF723.C27C37   2005
155.4′13—dc22
                                                              2004052068
                                                                  CIP

Books published by Lawrence Erlbaum Associates are printed on acid-free paper,
and their bindings are chosen for strength and durability.

Printed in the United States of America
10 9 8 7 6 5 4 3 2 1

To my children, Ben and Sarah.
—L. G.-S.

To those closest to me,
Caro, Michael, Jon, and Nic.
—D. H. R.

Contents

Contributors

Woo-kyoung Ahn, Department of Psychology, Yale University, 2 Hillhouse Avenue, New Haven, CT 06511-6814

Lawrence W. Barsalou, Department of Psychology, Emory University, 532 N. Kilgo Circle, Atlanta, GA 30322

Melissa Bowerman, Max Planck Institute for Psycholinguistics, Postbus 310, 6500 AH, Nijmegen, The Netherlands

Dedre Gentner, Department of Psychology, Northwestern University, 2029 Sheridan Road, Evanston, IL 60208

Lisa Gershkoff-Stowe, Department of Speech and Hearing Sciences and Cognitive Science Program, Indiana University, 200 South Jordan Avenue, Bloomington, IN 47405-7002

Frédéric Gosselin, Department of Psychology, University of Montreal, C.P. 6128, succ. Centre-ville, H3C 3J7, Montreal, QC Canada

Scott P. Johnson, Department of Psychology, New York University, 6 Washington Place, New York, NY 10003

Frank C. Keil, Department of Psychology, Yale University, 2 Hillhouse Avenue, New Haven, CT 06511-6814

Christian C. Luhmann, Department of Psychology, Vanderbilt University, 301 Wilson Hall, 111 21st Avenue South, Nashville, TN 37203

Brian MacWhinney, Department of Psychology, Carnegie Mellon University, 5000 Forbes Avenue, Pittsburgh, PA 15213

James L. McClelland, Center for the Neural Basis of Cognition and Department of Psychology, Carnegie Mellon University, 5000 Forbes Avenue, Pittsburgh, PA 15213

Charles A. Nelson, Institute of Child Development, 51 East River Road, Minneapolis, MN 55455-0345

Paul C. Quinn, Department of Psychology, University of Delaware, Wolf Hall, Newark, DE 19716-2577

David H. Rakison, Department of Psychology, Carnegie Mellon University, 5000 Forbes Avenue, Pittsburgh, PA 15213

Timothy T. Rogers, Department of Psychology, University of Wisconsin, 524 WJ Brogden Hall, Madison, WI 53706

Philippe G. Schyns, Department of Psychology, University of Glasgow, Room 416, 58 Hillhead Street, Glasgow, Scotland, UK G12 8QB

Robert Siegler, Department of Psychology, Carnegie Mellon University, 5000 Forbes Avenue, Pittsburgh, PA 15213

Linda B. Smith, Department of Psychology and Cognitive Science Program, Indiana University, 1101 E. 10th Street, Bloomington, IN 47405

Kelly Snyder, Department of Psychology, University of Denver, Frontier Hall, 2155 S. Race Street, Denver, CO 80208

Fei Xu, Department of Psychology, University of British Columbia, 2136 West Mall, Vancouver, BC Canada V6T 1ZA

Preface

In 1987, the 21st Carnegie Symposium on Cognition was organized by colleagues David Klahr and Kenneth Kotovsky. Its purpose was to examine and celebrate the far-reaching impact of H. A. Simon's work on the field of cognitive psychology. As they noted in the accompanying volume that followed from the conference, Herb Simon played an influential role in the scientific agenda of nearly all of the symposia since its inception in 1965 (Klahr & Kotovsky, 1989). In the years since that observation was made, Herb's authority and vision have continued to inspire the many outstanding scientists who regularly meet in Pittsburgh to present their work, reflect on issues of common concern, and identify remaining challenges in the study of human cognition. Herb Simon died before the start of the 32nd Carnegie Symposium held in June 2001, but his impact continues to sharpen and deepen our understanding of human behavior, as this volume attests.

This book concerns the way in which developmental processes work. It presents the current state of research in the area of early category development. The contributors to the volume attempt to answer the question of how children build object categories, beginning with the basic architecture of the brain and with the constraints or biases that provide the foundation of early perceptual experience. These advances are further considered in view of subsequent growth of language and other higher-order cognitive processes that guide the formation of coherent systems of knowledge.

The importance of categorization and concept formation to cognitive development, and to cognition in adults, cannot be underestimated. Categorization is the primary means of coding experience, which in turn reduces demands on inherently limited memory storage and perceptual and reasoning processes. Categorization is also inextricably linked to language processes. Words have the power to expand and sharpen category boundaries, to encourage category inductions beyond surface similarity, and to shift attention to less salient but potentially relevant properties of objects. The early classification abilities of infants and young children, and the mechanisms underlying those abilities, are of intense interest not only to developmental scientists, but also to investigators in fields as wide-ranging as neuroscience, visual perception, computational modeling, and linguistics.

As the title of this volume suggests, the ultimate aim of this collection is to account for the progressive elaboration of categorization in developmental time—age-related changes that appear globally stable over the time span of months and years. To investigate development over the long term, however, many of the contributors have focused their lens on the days, minutes, and even seconds of time over which change also occurs. A basic message of the 32nd Annual Symposium is that both local and global levels of analysis are essential to understanding the processes by which children's knowledge of categories develops.

There is no single point of view that inhabits the chapters of this volume. Rather, the chapters reflect the diverse backgrounds and rich theoretical perspectives of the particular set of invited speakers. Topics range from the neural substrates for face and object recognition to basic perceptual skills to the role of language and conceptual development in the transformation of emerging categories. The methods for exploring these topics are varied as well, and include both behavioral and neural approaches and computational models. Despite these differences, the reader will find much common ground across the chapters, particularly in their recurring reference to landmark studies in the developmental and adult categorization literature.

The book is divided into three Parts. Part I comprises six chapters and a commentary, which center on the fundamental processes of perception, memory, and attention. In the opening chapter, Charles Nelson and Kelly Snyder explore the neural bases for the development of categorization of face and nonface objects. They develop a cognitive neuroscience framework for categorization based on the human and nonhuman animal literature. They then apply this framework, in conjunction with Nelson's well-established model of face recognition, to the development of object processing more generally. Their aim is to show that face recognition offers a model system for other aspects of development.

In the next chapter, Johnson examines a critical precursor to object categorization, namely the ability to represent objects. Johnson tackles one of the thorniest debates in the developmental literature—the relative role of innate versus learned knowledge—by focusing on evidence from studies on object unity and occlusion. He proposes the *sensitivity-first* hypothesis, which stipulates that object knowledge arises from ontogenetic processes over developmental time, processes that are rooted in relatively low-level, perceptual-cognitive capacities. In support of this hypothesis, Johnson presents compelling behavioral and imaging data from studies with infants, adults, and nonhuman animals.

In the third chapter, Xu investigates the notion of individuation as another important precursor to object categorization. Individuation, as defined by Xu, is the process of representing numerically distinct individuals that can be tracked through time and space. She suggests a theory of *kind representations* that accounts for both categorization and individuation. Furthermore, she proposes that not all categories are created equal; some categories are kinds, and some kinds are "essence sortals." To support her view, Xu presents evidence of both an early developing object-based system of individuation and a relatively late developing kind-based system, the latter driven, perhaps, by advances in language learning.

Next, Gosselin and Schyns provide a user's guide to *Bubbles*, a technique that reveals the information that drives a measurable response. Bubbles is a technique that can resolve the credit assignment problem of attributing the determinants of a response to the parametric subspace of a carefully specified information search space. Gosselin and Schyns illustrate the technique with a complete example, the Face Inversion Effect, and discuss the six basic decisions that must be made to set up a Bubbles experiment (i.e., the stimulus set, the generation space, the "bubbles," the task, the group of observers, and the response). They describe methods to analyze the data and provide practical advice for the researcher intending to use the technique.

In his chapter, Quinn describes recent research with the familiarization/novelty preference procedure that investigates young infants' categorization of humans and nonhuman animals. At issue is whether category representations are formed online or constructed prior to the experiment. The evidence Quinn presents reveal that young infants use an online summary representation to categorize nonhuman animals at a basic level of exclusivity. In contrast, they use an exemplar representation, formed through previous experience, to categorize humans at a global level of exclusivity. In the former instance, infants appear to rely on part information to categorize; in the latter case, they rely on holistic–configural information. Quinn uses these data to develop further his perceptual learning model of early categorization.

Finally, Rakison examines the phenomenon known as the *perceptual to conceptual shift*. This phrase refers to the findings that younger children and infants tend to rely on perceptual properties as the basis for categorization, whereas older children weigh more heavily the nonobvious or conceptual properties of objects in category membership decisions. Based on a review of the literature, Rakison concludes that there is little evidence to support the notion that representational development undergoes some kind of transitional shift either in infancy or the preschool years. Rather, he presents a theoretical model and evidence that suggests that perceptual information provided by the different sensory input systems—including language—is continually added to the earliest representations through associative learning, and as sensitivity to different sorts of information emerges, so this gradual process gives the appearance of qualitative, representational change.

Smith's commentary on these chapters summarizes the field of early category development and points out that the field is very much in transition. She addresses the major themes highlighted by the chapters by focusing on a number of key questions: How are categories represented? Are general or special processes involved? Are categories based on percepts or concepts? Smith suggests that these issues are irresolvable but points out that the field is moving in new directions, toward fundamentally different ideas about what categories and category development might be. She describes these new directions in relation to several of the chapters presented throughout the volume.

Part II of the book comprises four chapters plus commentary, concerning how linguistic and conceptual advances transform children's developing category knowledge. Gershkoff-Stowe applies the principles of dynamic systems theory to the study of object category development. At the core of this approach is the idea that change is a function of converging forces that operate at multiple levels of time. Gershkoff-Stowe offers a mechanistic account of how large-scale developments in children's category behavior are specified in the real-time processes of seeing, manipulating, and naming objects. Her findings support the view that children are inherently flexible and adaptive in their ability to classify objects in response to variations in context.

Bowerman's chapter deals with covert or action-related object categories, for example, verbs like *open, cut,* or *break* that apply to events involving objects of a certain kind. She offers a cross-linguistic perspective, showing how different languages partition events differently according to the properties of the objects involved. The developmental question Bowerman asks is how children acquire covert object categories through the words they select to encode them. Her analysis of the errors young children produce reveal that extension patterns vary according to the language they learn and that these variations are systematically related to the semantic structure of the target language.

Gentner's chapter provides new insights into the acquisition of relational categories such as *predator* as well as the relational aspects of ordinary object categories such as *tiger.* She elaborates her theory of structural alignment as a general learning mechanism available to young children—one that promotes the learning of relational structure through the process of comparison. According to Gentner, the role of language is to encourage such comparison by guiding attention beyond surface-level commonalities to deep conceptual similarity. Such relational commonalities are thought to provide the "theory-like aspects of concepts and categories" that Ahn and Luhmann investigate in the next chapter.

Ahn and Luhmann analyze the rich conceptual structures of natural kinds and artifacts within which feature relations exist. They show that the critical role of features is not their specific content, for example, the shape of an object or its color; but rather the feature's position within a given conceptual structure. In particular, adults and children show a preference to attend to causes over effects. This processing bias is referred to as the *causal status hypothesis* and presents a plausible alternative to theory-based accounts of early category development, and in addition, to the enduring debate about whether children prefer form or function as a basis for object name generalization.

MacWhinney's commentary on these four chapters centers on the question of how extensively do the methods and findings reported here reflect real-world category learning in the everyday lives of children. Using examples from Web-related sources such as the Child Language Data Exchange System (CHILDES) and TalkBank, he advocates the need for researchers to explore, in addition, the rich social context in which concept and word learning is clearly embedded.

Part III is organized around the formation of system-based category knowledge, and in particular, how complex conceptual structure might be the emergent result of the fundamental cognitive processes discussed in previous chapters. In the first of the three chapters that comprise this last section, Keil remarks on the failing of prevalent theories of cognitive development in accounting for the nature and development of representational states that enable categorization. He describes empirical work showing how individuals track and use abstract causal patterns in category reasoning. The data reveal that not only children, but also adults have a shallowness of theory with which they think about the world. Keil interprets this "illusion of explanatory depth" as support for a revised concepts-as-theories view in which structural properties of causal systems are encoded and linked implicitly to domain-specific categories of knowledge.

Rogers and McClelland describe a number of simulations with a simple PDP model of semantic memory. They show that representations are organized with respect to certain especially useful or salient properties, regardless of whether such properties can be directly observed. They claim that in many cases this salience may be acquired through domain-general learning mechanisms that are sensitive to the high-order coherent covariation of directly observed stimulus properties across a breadth of experience. When trained with backpropagation to complete queries about the properties of different objects, the model's internal representations differentiate in a coarse-to-fine manner. As a consequence, different sets of properties come to be especially "salient" to the model at different points during development. Such dynamics, they claim, provide a simple account of the acquisition of conceptual structure from perceptual experience.

Barsalou's chapter considers the idea of abstraction as a central construct in cognitive science. Challenging established notions of how knowledge is represented, Barsalou presents an alternative theory known as *Dynamic Interpretation in Perceptual Symbol Systems* (DIPSS). According to the theory, conceptual structure is captured in loose collections of properties and relations of specific simulators. These simulators are applied dynamically across different contexts in an online and highly flexible manner. Barsalou provides convincing evidence consistent with this general account, applying his theory to a variety of abstraction phenomenon in categorization and learning.

The final commentary is offered by Siegler. He observes that all three chapters in this last section establish conclusions regarding categorization that are applicable to other cognitive domains including language, memory, and scientific thinking. As suggested by Newell (1973), a major goal in cognitive science is to develop broad, encompassing models that integrate results across a wide range of experimental tasks and that specify a small but precise set of mechanisms. Siegler commends these authors for making contributions toward this goal. In addition, however, he suggests that future work be directed toward constraining such models to identify the boundary conditions to which they apply and to search for new mechanisms beyond those currently specified.

ACKNOWLEDGMENTS

We are grateful to the many contributors who generously agreed to participate in the 32nd Annual Symposium on Cognition and whose work increases our understanding of the complex processes involved in building object categories in developmental time.

Thanks are due to the support staff and students in the department of psychology at Carnegie Mellon University for giving generously of their time: Kathy Majors, Bridget Boring, Margaret Kinsky, Tim Carroll, Annika Fasnacht, and Erin Hahn. We would also like to extend a special note of appreciation to Rochelle Sherman for her outstanding job of coordinating the behind-the-scenes details, and to Audrey Russo for her invaluable assistance in handling the many arrangements for the conference.

Marlene Behrmann provided valuable advice on how to organize the symposium. Jay McClelland and Heidi Feldman kindly opened up their beautiful home for a delightful evening of food and conversation. David Klahr provided priceless counsel in his role as series editor, and the quality of this volume owes much to his input. Finally, we would like to thank Bill Webber, editor at Lawrence Erlbaum Associates, for his guidance and especially his patience in bringing the book to publication. Sarah Wahlert, Senior Production Editor at LEA, was also fundamental in transforming many typewritten pages into the book that you now hold in your hands.

Funding for the 32nd Annual Symposium was provided by the psychology department at Carnegie Mellon University, the National Institute of Mental Health (1R13MH666370), and the National Science Foundation (BCS-0132328); we gratefully acknowledge their support.

—*Lisa Gershkoff-Stowe*
David Rakison

REFERENCES

Klahr, D., & Kotovsky, K. (1989). *Complex information processing: The impact of H. A. Simon.* Hillsdale, NJ: Lawrence Erlbaum Associates.

Newell, A. (1973). You can't play 20 questions with nature and win: Projective comments on the papers of this symposium. In W. G. Chase (Ed.), *Visual information processing* (pp. 283–308). New York: Academic.

Chapter 1

The Segregation of Face and Object Processing in Development: A Model System of Categorization?

Charles A. Nelson
University of Minnesota

Kelly Snyder
University of Denver

In our day-to-day existence we typically take for granted our ability to parse the world into categories. Thus, although we easily distinguish between cars and buses, we recognize that both are vehicles and thus both are forms of transportation. Similarly, with the exceptions of patients such as the protagonist in Oliver Sack's story, *The Man Who Mistook His Wife for a Hat* (Sacks, 1990), most of us readily distinguish among different types of hats, and know the function of hats, and thus, recognize that most hats are a form of apparel. Finally, a category we often take for granted concerns faces and objects; thus, although we are all expert at discriminating among different faces and among different objects, we never fail to distinguish between these two broad classes; that is, we do not generally confuse our colleague's face as a vehicle or as apparel. Suffice to say, then, that discriminating between and within the classes of stimuli we call faces and objects is fundamentally a process of categorization.

As other chapters in this volume make clear, the ability to parse the world into structured categories makes its appearance within the first months of life. Much development remains, however, as experience and learning gradually lay the foundation for an increasingly sophisticated ability to categorize the world. In this chapter we attempt to explore the neural bases for the development of this ability, focusing specifically on the categorization of face and nonface objects. We only briefly review the behavioral literature on categorization in infancy and childhood, as others contributing to this volume have far more expertise in this area than we do. Because

1

there are currently few data that describe the neural mechanisms that may underlie these developments, we turn instead to a discussion of what is known about this relation—that is, between brain and behavior—in the adult. Having drawn on the adult literature to establish a cognitive neuroscience framework on categorization, we next return to the developmental literature, focusing our attention on the segregation of objects and faces. We do so on the pretext that there is now a substantial literature concerning the neural mechanisms of object/face processing in infants and children; we also do so on the premise that such segregation may provide a model system for other aspects of development. During this discussion we draw the distinction between the neural processes putatively involved in segregating faces and objects, and the *acquisition* of these processes. This discussion foreshadows our strong developmental bias toward cognitive neuroscience generally.

BEHAVIORAL DEVELOPMENT LITERATURE

Imagine the world confronted by the infant who cannot recognize the boundaries between and within categories. Thus, the infant who must learn anew his mother's face each time he is presented with a new orientation of this face, simply because the infant cannot detect the constancy across exemplars. Or, the infant who sees different cats or different dogs and yet fails to recognize that these belong to different groups of mammals. Work by a number of investigators, including several contributing to this volume, have elegantly established some solid footing on the development of categorization.

Perceptual Versus Conceptual Categorization

Mandler (2000) argued that categorization consists of two different processes: perceptual categorization and conceptual categorization. Perceptual categorization is characterized as an automatic process that occurs as a result of mere exposure to visual information. The perceptual system is thought to abstract the principal components of a set of visual stimuli (Posner & Keele, 1968), resulting in the formation of a perceptual prototype or schema. This process is considered to be independent of awareness (Moscovitch, Goshen-Gottstein, & Vriezen, 1994). For example, although we are very good at categorizing human faces by gender, the information or criteria we use to do so is inaccessible to our explicit or conscious evaluation. Mandler argued that perceptual categories are used for object identification and recognition.

Conceptual categorization, on the other hand, is based on the functional properties of objects rather than on perceptual similarities between class exemplars. Functional properties consist of information such as how objects interact with other objects (e.g., a cat chases a mouse), and what objects can and cannot do (e.g., a dog can run but it can't fly). Conceptual categorization, according to Mandler (2000), creates the notion of kinds (e.g., animals, plants, vehicles). In contrast to the automatic, unconscious processing of perceptual information in perceptual categorization, conceptual information is thought to be acquired by attentive, conscious analysis and a "redescription" of perceptual information into conceptual form. Thus, the process of conceptual categorization gives meaning to objects, and is part of the creation of a central, accessible representational system.

In short, perceptual categorization leads to knowledge about what something looks like, whereas conceptual categorization leads to knowledge about what something is (i.e., its meaning). In extending these definitions to faces, we might speculate that facial discrimination or identification likely reflects examples of perceptual categorization (e.g., discriminating male faces from female faces, "old" faces from "young" faces). In contrast, assigning functional significance to faces (e.g., recognizing the feeling state of a particular facial expression, such as "that person is angry with me") may reflect a process of conceptual categorization. A major question in developmental research on categorization, then, is how one negotiates the transition from perceptually based to conceptually based categories (for elaboration, see Rakison, chap. 6, this volume).

The Development of Conceptual Categories

There are at least two competing views on the development of conceptual categories. According to one view (Eimas, 1994; Madole & Oakes, 1999; Mervis & Rosch, 1981; Quinn, 2002; Rakison & Poulin-Dubois, 2001), perceptual categories (i.e., dogs, cats) are the foundation on which conceptual categories are built. For example, infants first learn to discriminate the physical characteristics of dogs from the physical characteristics of cats (e.g., dogs are generally larger and have longer snouts than cats), and then they learn to associate various behaviors (i.e., barks vs. meows) with these perceptual categories. An alternative view (Mandler & McDonough, 1993, 1998) posits that conceptual categorization does not consist of adding conceptual information onto perceptual categories, but is rather an independent and parallel process. In this view, concepts form at an early age from experienced contingencies between objects, but early concepts tend to be abstract, general, vague, and global in nature (e.g., things with legs are self-movers). This view predicts that more global levels of categorization (e.g., superordinate) will precede basic-level categorization.

Thus, much of the developmental research on categorization has centered on a debate over which develops first, basic-level (dogs vs. cats) or global-level (animals vs. furniture) categories?

The Development of Basic-Level Categories

Infants appear to be capable of forming representations of basic-level categories from a very early age. For instance, when habituation and preferential-looking procedures are used, infants as young as 3 and 4 months have been shown to form categories of geometric forms (i.e., triangle, square) from distorted dot patterns (Bomba & Siqueland, 1983), categories of cats and dogs that exclude birds (Quinn, Eimas, & Rosenkrantz, 1993), categories of horses that exclude cats, giraffes, and zebras (Eimas & Quinn, 1994), categories of cats that exclude horses and tigers (Eimas & Quinn, 1994), and categories of tables that exclude couches and chairs (Behl-Chadha, 1996). Thus, young infants appear to be able to form basic-level categories for various animals, furniture, and geometric forms.

The categories that young infants form, however, appear to lack some specificity. For example, Quinn and colleagues found that 3- and 4-month-old infants only formed a category of dogs that excluded cats when the infants were familiarized with a set of highly similar looking dogs (Quinn et al., 1993), and that the category of cat that young infants formed did not exclude female lions (Eimas & Quinn, 1994). Infants were able to differentiate categories of cats and female lions by 6 to 7 months (Eimas & Quinn, 1994), and were also able to do so at 3 and 4 months when they were administered a familiarization procedure that involved initial presentation of cat–cat pairs, followed by presentations of cat–lion pairs along with cat–cat reminders (Eimas, Quinn, & Cowan, 1994). These findings indicate that the categories that infants form are dependent, to a large extent, on the degree of within- and across-category variability present in the familiarization stimuli. That is, when presented with the same category exemplars, older but not younger infants were sensitive to perceptual information that resulted in a more specific prototype of a cat. Younger infants, on the other hand, were only sensitive to this perceptual information when they received experience with exemplars from a perceptually similar yet different category (i.e., female lions). An important direction for future research may be to determine the mechanisms underlying this developmental difference in sensitivity to perceptual information in forming category prototypes.

The Development of Superordinate-Level Categories

A much-debated question in the literature on the development of superordinate-level categories is whether global categories are perceptually or conceptually based. When habituation and preferential-looking procedures are used to assess categorization, infants appear to be capable of forming superordinate-level categories at a very young age. For example, 3- and 4-month-olds have been found to form categories of furniture that exclude vehicles, and a category of mammals (including exemplars of deer, cats, elephants, horses, rabbits, squirrels, tigers, and zebras) that excluded birds, fish, and furniture (Behl-Chadha, 1996). Furthermore, 2-month-olds have been found to form categories of mammals that exclude furniture (Quinn & Johnson, 1998). Quinn (1998) argued that these findings support the idea that global categories are not necessarily conceptually based; in contrast, Mandler (2000) argued that the categories for which superordinate-level categorization has been demonstrated in young infants have a high degree of perceptual similarity, and so may not be representative of global categories in general.

When object examination, sequential touching, and sorting tasks are used to assess categorization, different patterns of findings emerge. In these tasks, superordinate-level categorization appears to precede basic-level categorization. Using the object examination task, Mandler and McDonough (1993) demonstrated that 7- to 11-month-old infants differentiated animals from vehicles, but failed to differentiate dogs from either rabbits or fish. Furthermore, 9-month-olds were shown to differentiate furniture from both animals and vehicles, and 11-month-olds were shown to differentiate animals and vehicles from plants, yet 7- to 11-month-olds failed to differentiate basic-level categories of tables, chairs, and beds (Mandler & McDonough, 1998). Likewise, using the sequential-touching task, 18-month-olds differentiated between animals and vehicles, but did not differentiate between basic-level categories of animals until 24 to 30 months (Mandler, Bauer, & McDonough, 1991; for elaboration on the processes underlying superordinate categorization in infancy, see Rakison & Butterworth, 1998).

How Are Categories Formed?

Another important issue in categorization research is to understand what information infants are using to distinguish categories from one another. Some researchers have argued that overall shape information is the basis for basic-level categorization (Marr, 1982) whereas others have argued that basic-level categories are distinguished on the basis of sets of correlated attributes (Rosch, Mervis, Gray, Johnson, & Boyes-Braem, 1976). There is some evidence to indicate that infants' categorization of animals depends importantly on facial features, thus favoring Rosch et al.'s position. For instance, Quinn and Eimas (1996) found that young infants' categorization of dogs and cats was based on facial features and not body shape. In addition, Mareschal, French, and Quinn (2000) demonstrated that the asymmetry in categorization of dogs and cats in young infants is due to the greater variability in the facial features of dogs (also see Quinn, chap. 5, this volume).

There is also evidence to suggest that infants are, indeed, sensitive to the correlations among features. For instance, Younger (1985) found that the prototype formed during familiarization depends on the correlations between features among the exemplars. Specifically, she found that when correlations between features of animals were linear (e.g., long legs were always correlated with short necks), infants formed multiple, more narrowly defined prototypes. In contrast, when correlations between features of animals were nonlinear (e.g., long legs were correlated with both long and short necks), infants formed a single prototype for the entire group of animals. In addition, infants between 4 and 10 months develop sensitivity to the correlated attribute structure of faces (Younger, 1992; Younger & Cohen, 1986). Thus, the findings of Quinn and colleagues with regard to the importance of facial features, and variability in the facial features of class exemplars to categorization of animals, may in fact reflect infants' sensitivity to correlated attributes of faces.

Methodological Issues

One important issue in the developmental categorization literature is the extent to which different measures produce different patterns of results. For example, the age at which infants first appear to classify objects into superordinate and basic-level categories depends on the task used to assess categorization. For instance, using the object examination task, Mandler and McDonough (1993) found that 7-month-olds differentiated the categories of animals from vehicles, but did not differentiate between different categories of animals (e.g., dogs vs. fish). Using habituation and preferential-looking techniques, on the other hand, Quinn and colleagues (Eimas & Quinn, 1994; Quinn et al., 1993) have demonstrated that infants as young as 3 and 4 months can differentiate between different categories of animals (e.g., cat vs. dog, dog vs. rabbit). Similarly, Oakes, Plumert, Lansink, and Merryman (1996) found that 10-month-olds differentiated animals from people in a familiarization, but not a sequential-touching task.

Mandler (1988, 2000) argued that different tasks reflect different kinds of categorization. In her view, habituation and preferential-looking tasks reflect perceptual categorization, whereas sequential touching and object examination reflect conceptual categorization. Oakes and Madole (2000), on the other hand, noted that different tasks place different demands on processes such as attention and memory, and that this may account for some of the differences in the pattern of results (also see Rakison & Butterworth, 1998). Furthermore, Oakes and Madole argued that preferential-looking tasks may not assess categories already possessed by infants, but may instead induce infants to form a category based on the objects presented during familiarization and, in this way, are different from tasks which do not contain a familiarization phase but present all of the objects for classification simultaneously.

WHAT IS KNOWN ABOUT THE NEURAL BASES OF CATEGORIZATION IN THE ADULT?

Unfortunately, there has been little research examining the neural bases of the *development* of categorization. This is in contrast to the now voluminous literature on categorization in the adult, a topic to which we next direct our attention.

Neuropsychological data have proved useful in shedding light on the multiple views about the acquisition of category knowledge. For instance, "prototype" models of categorization posit that information about category prototypes is acquired and represented separately from category exemplars, whereas "exemplar" models posit that category knowledge is an emergent property of memory for specific exemplars (i.e., a function of the similarity between novel items and specific exemplars stored in memory; Nosofsky, 1992; Pickering, 1997). Thus, if categorization depends on comparisons between novel items and remembered exemplars, then subjects with impaired ability to form new memories (i.e., amnesic patients) should be impaired at learning new categories.

Category Acquisition in Amnesic Patients

There is now a good deal of evidence to suggest that category acquisition is a nondeclarative process. Multiple studies have found that amnesic patients, who are impaired in tasks requiring declarative memory, nevertheless exhibit normal acquisition of category knowledge. This has been shown for tasks in which category membership is defined by (a) the rules of an artificial grammar system (Knowlton, Ramus, & Squire, 1992), (b) probabilistic classification learning (Filoteo, Maddox, & Davis, 2001), and (c) perceptual similarity or family resemblance of category members (Knowlton & Squire, 1993). As the last of these is most relevant to object and face categorization, we focus our review of the cognitive neuroscience literature on it.

Categorization Based on Perceptual Similarity.   Research with amnesic patients has shown, in general, that the acquisition of category-knowledge does not depend on normal declarative memory. The basic finding from multiple studies is that amnesic patients are as accurate at classifying novel patterns as controls, but are impaired at recognizing the specific stimuli presented during training.

Knowlton and Squire (1993) were among the first to provide neuro-psychological evidence for a dissociation between categorization and recognition memory. In this study, amnesic patients and controls studied a series of 40 training items. The patterns consisted of dot patterns that were all "high distortions" of a nonstudied prototype. After viewing all of the training patterns, subjects were told that the patterns belonged to the same category. Subjects then made yes/no judgments regarding whether novel test patterns belonged to the same category as the training items. Amnesic patients and controls did not differ in their categorization accuracy (mean categorization accuracy was ~60% for amnesic patients and ~64% for controls), yet control subjects were significantly more accurate than amnesic patients at recognizing previously seen items (mean recognition accuracy was ~65% for amnesic patients and ~80% for controls). The authors concluded that category knowledge can develop in the absence of declarative memory for specific category exemplars.

The possibility that some residual declarative memory in the amnesic patients tested might be sufficient to support normal classification performance was tested in a study of E.P., a patient who developed severe anterograde and retrograde amnesia following herpes simplex encephalitis (Squire & Knowlton, 1995). E.P. suffered extensive bilateral damage to the amygdaloid complex, the hippocampal region (CA fields, dentate gyrus, and subicular complex), and the entorhinal, perirhinal, parahippocampal, and inferiotemporal cortices, structures believed to be important for normal declarative memory.

Using the dot pattern classification task described earlier, Squire and Knowlton (1995) found a dissociation in E.P.'s performance on classification and recognition tasks. As expected, E.P. did not differ from controls in categorization accuracy, yet E.P.'s recognition memory for the same stimuli was severely impaired. When asked to make a recognition memory judgment about a single dot pattern that had been presented 40 times, E.P. was significantly impaired and performed at chance (E.P.'s mean recognition accuracy was 49.4%), whereas control subjects were very accurate (control subjects' mean recognition accuracy was 95.2%). Furthermore, the use of two different classification tasks, one based on experience with multiple exemplars of a category and one based exclusively on repeated exposure to the category prototype, demonstrated an additional dissociation in E.P.'s classification performance. When classification was based on experience with multiple novel exemplars of a category-prototype, E.P. did not differ from controls in categorization accuracy (mean categorization accuracy was ~62% for both E.P. and controls). On the other hand, when classification was based on experience with a single category-prototype (even though the prototype was repeated 40 times), E.P. was significantly impaired and performed at chance (mean categorization accuracy was 55%), whereas control subjects were accurate (mean categorization accuracy was ~65.4%). These results suggest that the ability to classify items in the absence of declarative memory depends on exposure to variability in members of the category.

Because dot patterns are perceptually similar to one another, are difficult to describe verbally, and have no discrete features that distinguish one category from another, it is possible that category-knowledge is acquired implicitly only when category members meet these criteria, but that category knowledge may be acquired explicitly when exemplars are easily verbalized stimuli that exhibit discrete features. In other words, the acquisition of category knowledge could differ depending on what "defines" a category.

Reed, Squire, Patalano, Smith, and Jonides (1999) tested this hypothesis by presenting amnesic patients and healthy volunteers with cartoon animals composed of nine discrete features (viz., head, face, head ornaments, neck, legs, tail, body, body markings, and feet). Each feature could take one of two values (e.g., head could be facing up or down). One value was defined as the prototypic value, the other comprised the nonprototypic value (by default). Subjects studied 40 "low" distortions (i.e., containing either seven or eight of the nine prototypic features) of the prototypic animal during training. Immediately following training, subjects were asked to make a yes or no judgment as to whether novel test animals belonged to the same category as the training animals. Immediately following the classification task, the names of the nine features were presented one at a time and subjects were asked to identify the possible values of the feature. As in previous studies, the results showed that amnesic patients were just as accurate at classifying novel category exemplars as controls (mean categorization accuracy was ~69% for amnesic patients and ~74% for controls), but were impaired at recalling the specific features of the training items (mean recall accuracy was ~49% for amnesic patients and ~81% for controls). Of special interest were the results of patient E.P., the same patient described in Squire and Knowlton (1995) previously. Patient E.P.'s overall endorsement rate was 70.8%, reflecting high discrimination between the two categories, yet his pattern of responding was the opposite of that found for both the controls and the other amnesic patients. That is, E.P. always endorsed the nonprototype, yet he was unable to provide *any* accurate answers on the cued-recall test. This pattern of results suggests that E.P. was able to learn about the prototype during training, but was unable to remember which category (i.e., the prototype or nonprototype) to respond to during the classification task. The results of this study suggest that category knowledge about items that have discrete, verbalizable features can also be acquired implicitly, in the absence of declarative memory for the training items.

Taken together, the findings reviewed here suggest that category knowledge can develop in the absence of declarative (and thus conscious) memory for category members, and likely involves implicit learning about the category prototype via exposure to multiple category exemplars. The finding that amnesic patients exhibit normal classification despite impaired recognition of category exemplars further suggests that category acquisition does not depend on the limbic-diencephalic structures necessary for declarative memory. Knowlton and Squire (1993) suggested that category acquisition may depend, instead, on either (a) corticostriatal systems involved in habit learning, or (b) "gradual changes intrinsic to the neocortex by which the neocortex can gradually accrue knowledge independently of the hippocampus and related structures" (p. 1749).

Category Acquisition in Parkinson's Patients

An alternative possibility is that category knowledge can be acquired, and classification performance can proceed, in multiple ways: (a) in the absence of declarative memory (amnesics), and (b) via declarative memory. It is possible that these two systems operate in parallel, and somewhat redundantly, with respect to the acquisition of category-knowledge. Thus, it has been demonstrated that category-knowledge can be acquired in the absence of declarative memory, but it must also be demonstrated that category-knowledge *cannot* be acquired via declarative memory to support a single-system view of category learning. This would require a double-dissociation, and a demonstration that patients with intact declarative and impaired nondeclarative memory are unable to acquire category-knowledge. An example of patients meeting the latter criterion are those with Parkinson's disease (PD).

In fact, Knowlton, Mangels, and Squire (1996) and Knowlton, Squire, et al. (1996) reported that Parkinson's patients were impaired in a probabilistic classification learning task, while Reber and Squire (1999) found intact category learning in Parkinson's patients for both artificial grammars and dot patterns. The fact that Parkinson's patients were found to be impaired in probabilistic classification, but not artificial grammar and dot pattern classification, may be due to any of several differences between these tasks. For example, probabilistic classification requires subjects to acquire category knowledge by learning cue-outcome relations through trial-by-trial feedback, whereas in artificial grammar and dot pattern classification, subjects acquire category knowledge via simple exposure to members of the category. In addition, categorization rule complexity may differ across these tasks.

THE NEURAL BASIS OF CATEGORY JUDGMENTS

Knowlton and Squire (1993) proposed that categorization may depend on corticostriatal systems involved in habit learning, or "gradual changes intrinsic to the neocortex by which the neocortex can gradually accrue knowledge independently of the hippocampus and related structures" (p. 1749). One source of evidence for this proposal comes from neuroimaging studies of healthy adult subjects.

Reber, Stark, and Squire (1998a) used functional MRI (fMRI) to identify cortical areas involved in the classification of novel dot patterns. Subjects initially studied a series of 40 dot patterns that were distortions of a nonstudied prototype and then subsequently made yes/no judgments regarding whether novel dot patterns belonged to the same category as the previously studied patterns. The processing of category versus noncategory patterns was associated with a large decrease in activation of posterior occipital cortical areas (BA 17/18), including visual cortical areas V1 and V2, and a significant increase in activity in the left and right anterior frontal cortex (BA 10) and the right inferior lateral frontal cortex (BA 44/47). Due to the fact that decreases in activity in posterior cortical areas have been reported in studies of visual priming (Schacter & Buckner, 1998; Squire et al., 1992; Wiggs & Martin, 1998), the authors argued that decreases in occipital areas in response to category patterns reflect enhanced perceptual facilitation for a previously encountered (or highly similar) visual stimulus, and thus nondeclarative memory for the category. Activity in the right inferior frontal gyrus has been implicated in tasks requiring spatial working memory (Courtney, Ungerleider, Kell, & Haxby, 1997; Smith et al., 1995), suggesting that the increase in activity in this region in the present study may reflect greater demands on spatial working memory (i.e., examination of a greater proportion of dots in the pattern) required to calculate a successful match versus a nonmatch. Finally, the authors suggest that the increase in prefrontal activity (BA 10) may reflect processes involved in attempts to intentionally retrieve information about learned exemplars, as previous studies have implicated BA 10 in the intentional retrieval of nonverbal material (Moscovitch, Kapur, Kohler, & Houle, 1995; Schacter et al., 1995; Tulving, Markowitsch, Craik, Habib, & Houle, 1996), but also noted that work with amnesic patients suggests that such strategies do not confer a performance advantage.

In a related study, Reber, Stark, and Squire (1998b) used fMRI to contrast cortical areas involved in classification versus recognition of dot patterns. The stimuli and classification task were identical to that used in Reber et al. (1998a). For the recognition task, subjects first studied five dot patterns that were repeated eight times each, and then made yes/no judgments regarding whether test patterns had been presented previously. As in the previous study, judgments of categorical versus noncategorical patterns were associated with a significant reduction in activity in posterior occipital cortical areas (BA 17/18). In contrast, an increase in activity in right occipital cortex (BA 17/18) was observed during the recognition task, consistent with previous studies of visual recognition memory (Nyberg et al., 1995; Rugg, Fletcher, Frith, Frambach, & Dolan, 1996; Tulving, Markowitsch, Craik, Habib, & Houle, 1996). Although the specific occipital areas exhibiting changes were not completely identical in the two tasks, increased activation during the recognition task occurred in the same region that had exhibited decreased activation during the classification task. Thus, this study provides evidence for a dissociation in activation in posterior occipital areas for categorization versus recognition tasks, and that stimuli are represented in a fundamentally different way during recognition than during categorization.

The findings just reviewed provide evidence that categorization involves reductions in the activity of posterior occipital areas much like visual priming, and that categorization and recognition are associated with qualitatively different patterns of neural activity in the same cortical region. One limitation of these findings is that they may reflect processes and neural activity associated with only one type of categorization, as the same task was used in both studies. In other words, the process of judging category membership may differ for different kinds of categories and different levels of categorization. For example, judging category membership for a category characterized by reliable, visual-perceptive features (i.e., all dogs have four legs and a tail) may rely heavily on similarity-based visual comparisons, whereas judging category membership for categories that are not primarily defined by perceptual information (i.e., a hammer and a drill are both tools) may rely more on evaluating propositional information about the category and its exemplars. Furthermore, the processes of identifying defining features of a concept (e.g., what defines a tool?), ignoring irrelevant information (e.g., a hammer and a drill both have handles), and tracking the evaluation of multiple propositions to arrive at a decision may be especially dependent on executive processes such as selective attention, working memory, and inhibition (Grossman et al., 2002). One way to address these questions is to investigate differences in neural activation during categorization of objects at different levels of categorization.

Functional Neuroanatomy of Superordinate-Level Categorization of Visual Objects

In general, superordinate-level categorization appears to be heavily dependent on semantic knowledge (Jolicoeur, Gluck, & Kosslyn, 1984). Thus, the brain systems that mediate superordinate-level categorization should be closely aligned with the brain systems mediating semantic memory. One approach to investigating the neural systems associated with superordinate-level categorization has been to compare processing of objects belonging to different superordinate-level categories (e.g., natural objects vs. artifacts).

Gerlach, Law, Gade, and Paulson (2000) presented subjects with pictures of familiar objects and asked them to decide whether the object was a natural object (e.g., a bear) or an artifact (e.g., a hammer). Categorization, in general, was associated with increased regional cerebral blood flow (rCBF) in the left inferior temporal gyrus (BA 20), a region thought to be associated with semantic processing of pictures and words (Binder et al., 1997; Vandenberghe, Price, Wise, Josephs, & Frackowiak, 1996). Furthermore, categorization of artifacts compared to natural objects was additionally associated with activation of the left premotor cortex, left anterior cingulate gyrus (BA 24), orbitofrontal parts of the cortex (BA 11 and 47), and the left inferior frontal gyrus (BA 46). The left premotor cortex is thought to be associated with action knowledge associated with artifacts (Grafton, Fadiga, Arbib, & Rizzolatti, 1997), suggesting that increased activity in this region reflects the use of action knowledge in the categorization of artifacts. Because the anterior cingulate gyrus has been associated with motor inhibition (Devinsky, Morrell, & Vogt, 1995), the authors suggested that the activity in this area during the categorization of artifacts reflects the suppression of movement associated with the artifact. Finally, as dorsolateral prefrontal areas have been found to be associated with the retrieval of knowledge, activation in this region is thought to reflect the retrieval of semantic/action knowledge (Kapur, Rose, & Liddle, 1994).

Using a similar approach, Grossman et al. (2002) used fMRI to identify cortical areas associated with different categories of knowledge in semantic memory. They presented subjects with words for animals, implements, and abstract nouns, and asked subjects to make a "pleasant"/"not pleasant" judgment of each object. This task is thought to engage semantic knowledge while avoiding the problems associated with requiring different responses or requesting item-specific information. Compared with pleasantness judgments of pseudowords, the processing of words for implements was associated with activation of left postereolateral temporal cortex (BA 37 and 21) and left prefrontal cortex (BA 10 and 9); the processing of words for animals was associated with activation of left ventral-medial temporal-occipital association cortex (BA 17, 18 and 19); and the processing of abstract nouns was associated with activation of left postereolateral temporal cortex (BA 37, 39, 21, 22), left prefrontal cortex (BA 10 and 9), and right prefrontal cortex (BA 10 and 32). Activation associated specifically with Animals was observed in left medial temporal-occipital cortex, and activation associated specifically with Implements was observed in left postereolateral temporal and left prefrontal cortices. The authors hypothesize that activation associated with processing of Animals is early in the visual processing stream (i.e., left medial temporal-occipital cortex) due to the fact that the features of animals are stable (e.g., all horses have four legs) and highly intercorrelated (e.g., objects with four legs also typically have a tail), lending category judgments to similarity-based visual comparisons. Implements and Abstract Nouns, on the other hand, have "unstable perceptual features and complex functional associations" (p. 945), requiring the integration of distributed, multimodal representations. Thus, the prefrontal activation may reflect the recruitment of executive processes "that contribute to complex reasoning about definition-like criteria for categorization" (p. 945), whereas the postereolateral temporal activation may reflect "the integration of sensory-motor or prepositional knowledge represented in multiple association cortices" (p. 945).

Functional Neuroanatomy of Basic-Level Categorization of Visual Objects

To provide but a single example (of many) of the neural bases of basic-level categorization, consider a recent study by Op de Beeck, Beatse, Wagemans, Sunaert, and Van Hecke (2000). These authors asked subjects to judge whether two familiar pictures, presented sequentially, belonged to the same basic-level category (i.e., are both chairs?). They found bilateral activation in the fusiform gyrus (BA 19/37), striate and extrastriate cortex (including the lingual gyrus), and the intraparietal sulcus for this categorization task compared to a condition in which subjects judged whether or not two nonsense objects matched in orientation.

Functional Neuroanatomy of Subordinate-Level Categorization of Visual Objects

The fusiform gyrus appears to play an important role in subordinate-level categorization tasks. For instance, Gauthier, Anderson, Tarr, Skudlarski, and Gore (1997) found increased activation in the fusiform and inferotemporal gyri when subjects performed a subordinate compared to a basic-level categorization task. In addition, Op de Beeck et al. (2000) found bilateral activation in the fusiform gyrus (BA 19/37), striate and extrastriate cortex (including the lingual gyrus), the intraparietal sulcus, and BA 8 and BA 45 for a task in which subjects were asked to judge whether two familiar pictures, presented sequentially, were exactly the same compared to a condition in which subjects judged whether or not two nonsense objects matched in orientation. Furthermore, they compared this exemplar-matching task with a basic-level category-matching task (i.e., subordinate-level categorization–basic-level categorization) and found only bilateral activation of the intraparietal sulcus. Thus, basic-level and subordinate-level categorization activates much of the same cortical areas in this task. The authors hypothesized that enhanced activity in the intraparietal sulcus may reflect the increased spatial attention required to make finer discriminations (i.e., exemplar match) between stimuli.

Summary and Discussion

In general, categorization judgments are associated with a highly distributed pattern of neural activity, reflecting multiple processes associated with: (a) the specific kind of knowledge required to make the decision (i.e., areas associated with semantic knowledge in general, and action knowledge in particular for artifact categories), (b) spatial attentional demands for making visual discriminations, (c) perceptual facilitation for a previously encountered (or highly similar) visual stimulus, (d) spatial working memory, (e) intentional retrieval of verbal and/or nonverbal knowledge, and (f) suppression of movement associated with the action knowledge. Furthermore, different kinds of categories and different levels of categorization are associated with different patterns of neural activation.

THE ABILITY TO SEGREGATE FACES AND OBJECTS: A COGNITIVE NEUROSCIENCE PERSPECTIVE

Thus far in our review we have discussed the literature on categorization broadly defined. We now turn away from this general literature and turn our attention instead to the categorization of faces and objects. We begin by briefly reviewing the adult literature on this topic, and then turn to the developmental literature.

The Categorization of Faces and Objects—Adults

Distinguishing between faces and nonfaces likely involves making a distinction between stimuli that exist at the subordinate or basic level versus the superordinate level. For example, objects typically exist at the superordinate (e.g., vehicles), basic (e.g., cars), and subordinate (e.g., BMWs) levels. In contrast, it is harder to force faces into this scheme. Indeed, most studies of face recognition operate at only a single level: for example, discriminating one face from another or one facial expression from another (i.e., two subordinate-level judgments). One must keep this distinction in mind as we review the literature on the "specialness" of faces, as it may be the case that faces are perceived as a special class of objects because of the constraints on the level at which they are represented.

Most of what is known about the segregation of faces and objects can be found in the adult cognitive neuroscience literature and the basic neuroscience literature with animals. After summarizing the main take-home points from both literatures, we turn our attention to the developmental literature.

Is Face Recognition a Special Case of Object Perception?

We begin by talking a bit about the literature that supports the assertion that face recognition is subserved by specialized neural tissue, orthogonal to that subserving object recognition.

Neuropsychological Literature

Experimental studies performed with neurologically normal samples have suggested that faces are perceived as a special class of stimuli, distinct from other patterned objects. For example, Farah and colleagues, among others, have suggested that face recognition differs from object recognition in that the former involves representing a face as a single, complex whole, whereas the latter typically involves decomposition into constituent elements (e.g., Farah, Wilson, Drain, & Tanaka, 1998; for review, see Farah, Humphreys, & Rodman, 1999). In support of this hypothesis are demonstrations that normal adults are far better at recognizing faces presented right side up (i.e., in their normal orientation) than upside down.

A second line of evidence that faces are "special" comes from individuals with *prosopagnosia.* Prosopagnosia is a rather specific impairment in the ability to recognize familiar faces (for representative examples of this literature, see Damasio, Damasio, & Van Hoesen, 1982; DeRenzi, 1986; Farah, Wilson, Drain, & Tanaka 1995; Farah et al., 1999; McNeil & Warrington, 1993). Another way to think of this is that an entire category of objects is selectively knocked out. Prosopagnosia is generally accompanied by damage to the ventral occipitotemporal and temporal cortex. An illustrative example of prosopagnosia can be found in patients who are very impaired in recognizing familiar faces although general object perception is typically intact. Intriguingly, even more specific deficits have been observed in patients with highly focal lesions. For example, one such patient, S.M. (who incurred bilateral calcification of the amygdala), was impaired in her ability to judge facial expressions, particularly negative expressions (e.g., fear; see Adolphs, Tranel, Damasio, & Damasio, 1994; Adolphs, Tranel, Damasio, & Damasio, 1995). Finally, further evidence for the segregation of faces and objects comes from a case report by Moscovitch, in which a patient is reported to have intact face perception but impaired object perception (Moscovitch, Winocur, & Behrmann, 1997).

Neuroimaging Studies With Humans.   Research with patients has increasingly been complemented by neuroimaging studies with neurologically intact adults and with single unit work with monkeys (the latter, of course, provides even greater spatial localization than human neuroimaging). With regard to the former, Kanwisher and colleagues (using fMRI) have reported increased activation in the fusiform gyrus to faces in general (Kanwisher, Tong, & Nakayama, 1998), with less activation observed to faces presented upside down (Kanwisher, McDermott, & Chun, 1997). This same group has reported greater activation in this region to faces than to human or animal heads. From this pattern of findings, Kanwisher, like Farah, proposed that faces are accorded special status by the brain. A slightly different perspective on this problem has been studied by Gauthier and colleagues, who have reported that as naive subjects acquired expertise in recognizing artificial stimuli (e.g., "greebles") at a subordinate level of categorization, the middle fusiform gyrus in the right hemisphere is recruited and shows a pattern of activation that is indistinguishable from that elicited by faces (Gauthier, Tarr, Anderson, Skudlarski, & Gore, 1999). Similarly, under passive viewing, activation in this area is greater in a single subject with expertise in viewing greeble faces versus individuals lacking such expertise. Overall, these results suggest that the fusiform "face area" becomes specialized with experience, a point to which we return later.

Electrophysiological Work With Animals.   Turning to the work with nonhuman primates, face-responsive cells have been found in several areas of the temporal cortex, particularly the superior temporal polysensory area (area TPO), the inferior temporal cortex (areas TEa and Tem), and along the ventral bank of the superior temporal sulcus (STS) (for examples of this literature, see Baylis, Rolls, & Leonard, 1987; Perrett, Rolls, & Caan, 1982; Perrett et al., 1984; Perrett et al., 1985; Perrett & Mistlin, 1990; Rolls & Baylis, 1986; Yamane, Kaji, & Kawano, 1988). And, using a combination of optical imaging and single unit recordings, regional clustering of cells in the anterior inferior temporal (IT) cortex of monkeys are activated during the time faces are presented (Wang, Tanaka, & Tanifuji, 1996). Finally, neurons responsive to faces have also been observed in the amygdala (Leonard, Rolls, Wilson, & Baylis, 1985; Rolls, 1984), and within the amygdala, some nuclei have been found to be responsive to individual faces, whereas others respond to individual expressions (Aggleton, Burton, & Passingham, 1980; Nahm, Albright, & Amaral, 1991). (This latter finding is consistent with human neuroimaging and lesion studies, in which the amygdala has been observed to play a particularly important role in recognizing particular facial expressions, such as fear [see Adolphs et al., 1994, 1995]).

Summary of Neuroimaging and Single Unit Work

For a variety of reasons, it is difficult to compare the single unit work with monkeys to the functional imaging work with humans. For example, there are species differences and differences in the spatial resolution of single unit and optical recordings relative to fMRI and PET. Nevertheless, the *general* findings from both programs of research collectively suggest that regions within the inferior temporal cortex play an important role in face recognition, and the amygdala appears to play an important role in assigning affective significance to faces (e.g., facial emotion).

From the literature reviewed thus far it appears that faces may be accorded special status by the brain; however, what is unclear is on what basis face specialization develops. From an evolutionary perspective, recognizing faces and facial expressions would be adaptive, and thus selected for through evolution. For example, distinguishing between a caregiver's face and the face of a stranger, or recognizing that a given face looks afraid or angry, may have survival value. The adaptive value of face recognition, then, should result in face recognition (a) being present in nonhuman primates to a comparable degree as in humans, (b) appearing early in life, and (c) being subserved by specialized neural tissue.

Behavioral Studies With Monkeys

Both human *and* nonhuman primates use their faces to produce a range of social signals. Thus, it is not surprising that monkeys are quite good at both face and emotion recognition. For example, Pascalis and Bachevalier (1998) tested both human adults and mature Rhesus monkeys on their ability to discriminate a range of human and monkey faces and objects. Both groups did equally well in recognizing objects. However, humans did better than monkeys in recognizing human faces, whereas the converse was true for monkeys. This species-specific effect suggests that experience viewing faces played an important role in the findings.

Studies of Human Development

Before reviewing the human developmental literature on face recognition, it is important to stress one caveat to this work: Most such studies only directly examine *discrimination* of faces; face *recognition* is often inferred but not directly evaluated. Thus, for example, one deduces discrimination based on longer looking at a novel face relative to a familiar face, and *infers* recognition of the former by this same pattern of looking; yet, such studies do not directly test for recognition, for obvious reasons—for example, one cannot ask an infant to "push this button whenever you see a familiar face." To continue this example, an infant may be "asked" to discriminate one male face from another, or even to categorize male faces and females faces, but we do not know from such work if they "know" what constitutes "maleness" or "femaleness" or what it means to be a male or female.

Behavioral Studies in Newborns

The study of development has played an important historical role in understanding the "special" nature of faces given early speculation that this ability was innate. For example, Bowlby (1969), among others, argued that because it is adaptive for the young infant to be able to recognize potential caregivers and/or emotional signals carried by the face, experience with faces should be unnecessary for this ability to develop. Although there were, in fact, early reports that newborns (who would by default lack experience with faces) preferred to look at faces over other patterned stimuli (e.g., Goren, Sarty, & Wu, 1975), there were other reports that failed to find such preferences (e.g., Hershenson, 1965; Thomas, 1965). Over the years, however, the pendulum has swung back to supporting the view that newborns are capable of recognizing faces. For example, in an extension of an early and oft-cited study by Goren et al. (1975), Johnson and colleagues reported that newborns (Johnson, Dziurawiec, Ellis, & Morton, 1991) and 10-week-old infants (Johnson, Dziurawiec, Bartrip, & Morton, 1992) show a visual preference (as inferred from eye and head movements) for a moving face-like stimulus than for a scrambled or nonface stimulus, although this effect failed to obtain at 5 weeks. Subsequent research has replicated this basic finding (e.g., Valenza, Simion, Macchi-Cassia, & Umilta, 1996). However, debate continues as to whether it is "facedness" per se that is responsible for the visual preference; for example, more recent work by Simion and colleagues (e.g., Simion, Valenza, Macchi-Cassia, Turati, & Umilta, 2002; Turati, Simion, Milani, & Umilta, 2002) have revealed that a stimulus with an oval perimeter and internal features situated in the upper half of the oval are preferred over the same oval with features situated in the lower half; moreover, these features do not need to resemble faces, they can also simply be dot patterns. Thus, the extent to which the original findings by Goren et al. and Johnson et al. are due to preferences for faces qua faces is unclear (for reviews, see deHaan, 2001; Johnson & Morton, 1991; Nelson, 2001).

Behavioral Studies in Infants

There is rapid development in the sophistication with which infants respond to faces after the first few months of life. For example, Fagan (1972) demonstrated that beginning at around 4 months of age infants' recognition of upright faces is superior to the recognition of upside down faces, suggesting that at this age infants have developed a face "schema." Between 3 and 7 months infants also grow more adept at recognizing and categorizing faces, particularly facial expressions. For example, in a very early study in this area, Nelson, Morse, and Leavitt (1979) demonstrated that 7-month-old infants were capable of categorizing happy faces and distinguishing happy from fear; thus, if infants were presented with multiple exemplars of happy faces, and then presented with a new exemplar of happy and the same new exemplar of fear, they would show a novelty preference for fear. Interestingly, this same finding was not observed when infants were first presented with fearful faces; here, and in many subsequent studies, there is no evidence that infants can categorize fearful faces (for review, see Nelson & de Haan, 1996b).

Over the years this basic finding—of categorizing some facial expressions and not others—has been replicated many times, with increasingly more challenging tasks. Thus, one can present 7-month-olds with both male and female models posing happy expressions, and still observe them generalize their discrimination across yet other (novel) models posing happy, and discriminate happy from another expression (e.g., Nelson & Dolgin, 1985). And, in an impressive recent demonstration of categorization, Kotsoni, de Haan, and Johnson (2001) morphed happy and fear facial expressions and examined the boundary at which infants recognized fear. Not only were 7-month-old infants able to categorize the fear face, but also their category boundary (i.e., the point in the continuum where happy is judged to switch to fear) was comparable to adults.

Collectively, the recognition of faces appears to develop rapidly over the course of the first 6 to 12 months, and is far more robust than it is in the newborn period.

We now turn to the literature that speaks to the neural basis of the development of face and emotion recognition.

Neuropsychological Studies.

De Schonen and her colleagues have demonstrated that 4- to 9-month-old infants show a right hemisphere (left visual field; LVF) bias toward processing faces, similar to what is observed in the adult. For example, de Schonen and Mathivet (1989) have reported that infants recognize a face faster if the face is initially presented in the LVF as opposed to the RVF.

Neuroimaging-Type Studies.   Our group (e.g., de Haan & Nelson, 1997) has used event-related potentials (ERPs) to examine the recognition of familiar faces in 6-month-old infants by contrasting mothers' faces to strangers' faces under a variety of conditions. We reported no ERP differences when two strangers' faces were used, but clear ERP differences when mother was paired with stranger; importantly, the specific ERP components that distinguished the two faces differed depending on whether the stranger was similar or dissimilar looking to the mother. In both cases, greater ERP activity was observed at the right versus left temporal scalp, consistent with the right hemisphere bias for face processing observed by de Schonen and colleagues.

In a follow-up study, these same authors (de Haan & Nelson, 1999) examined the recognition of familiar and novel faces and objects in 6-month-old infants. We observed ERP differences that distinguished familiar from novel events (faces and objects), and importantly, faces versus objects. For example, a P400 component was observed over occipital scalp that had a shorter latency to faces than to objects whereas the positive slow wave (PSW) was larger for novel than familiar stimuli, independent of whether the stimulus was a toy or a face. The NC was generally larger for familiar than for novel stimuli; for faces, however, the difference was seen at midline and right temporal scalp sites, whereas for objects it was more widespread and bilaterally distributed over the surface of the scalp.

Recently, Tzourio-Mazoyer et al. (2002) reported a very unusual study in which neurologically compromised 2-month-old infants were studied using PET. Infants were presented with faces or flashing red and green diodes. Although a rather broad array of areas were activated to faces that seemingly had little to do with face processing per se (e.g., left superior temporal and inferior frontal gyri, areas typically associated with language processing), activity was also observed in the fusiform gyrus, similar to what has been observed in adults. Activation of the fusiform gyrus would also be consistent with behavioral reports of infant preferences for face-like stimuli, although activation in other cortical regions is inconsistent with adult findings.

NEURAL CORRELATES OF EMOTION RECOGNITION

There is a rich and extensive literature on infants' discrimination of facial emotion. In categorization terms, we might argue that this involves discriminating stimuli at the subordinate level. Specifically, in most tasks infants are presented with two identical faces that differ only in the arrangement of facial features (e.g., those denoting discrete expressions). For example, Nelson and de Haan (1996a) reported that the amplitude of the PSW was greater to happy than to fearful faces, whereas the amplitude of the NC was greater to fearful than to happy faces. No ERP differences were observed when fear and anger were contrasted. The observation that the amplitude of the NC was greater to fear than to happy is consistent with the behavioral findings that infants attend more to fear than to happy. And, the failure to observe ERP differences to fear and anger are consistent with the behavioral findings that infants have difficulty discriminating between two negative emotions.

In terms of older children, Nelson and Nugent (1990) presented 4- to 6-year-old children with happy and angry faces. Across two conditions subjects were asked to attend and keep track of either the happy face or the angry face. As expected, the task-relevant stimulus (be it happy or angry) invoked a P300 response, as would be expected in the adult. However, regardless of task instructions, the N400 (an attentional component) was larger to angry faces.

Thus, even when subjects showed a P300 to the task-relevant happy face, their obligatory attentional response (N400) was greatest to angry faces. These findings are similar to those observed to other negative emotions (e.g., fear) in the adult neuroimaging literature reviewed earlier.

In an intriguing line of work concerned with the extent to which experience viewing facial emotion influences the neural correlates of such processing, Pollak and colleagues have been studying children who have experienced child maltreatment. For example, Pollak, Klorman, Thatcher, and Cicchetti (2001) reported that maltreated children showed larger P300 amplitude when angry faces appeared as targets than did control children; the two groups did not differ when targets were either happy or fearful facial expressions. The authors interpreted these findings to suggest that aberrant emotional experiences associated with maltreatment appears to influence how particular facial emotions are processed.

Face Recognition in Infants and Children
With Brain Damage

There are only a handful of studies conducted with children suffering from damage to the areas of the brain implicated in face recognition. For example, Ellis and Young (1988) reported on a prosopagnosic 9-year-old girl, K.D., who contracted meningitis at the age of 14 months. K.D. was studied extensively and showed no signs of being able to recognize faces as she grew older. Similarly, Mancini and colleagues (Mancini, de Schonen, Deruelle, & Massoulier, 1994) reported on a series of 6 patients ranging in age from 7 to 11 years, 3 of whom sustained damage to the left hemisphere and 3 to the right (in most cases the damage occurred prenatally). Children varied enormously in their face and speech perception abilities (none were formally prosopagnosic). Finally, Farah and colleagues reported on the case of a 16-year-old boy who developed meningitis at 1 day of age, with CT at age 6 revealing bilateral occipital and occipitotemporal lesions. "Adam" showed no overt object agnosia when real objects were used, but did have difficulty with photographs of objects. Adam is, however, impaired in recognizing faces, including those he encounters in everyday life. Collectively, given that all these children had had years of experience with faces raised the possibility that the circuits that subserve face recognition are relatively rigid and unable to reorganize and/or that the surrounding regions are unable to take over this function.

Summary and Discussion of Developmental Findings

First, face recognition develops rapidly in the first months of life, and under a number of conditions is observed as early as a few hours after birth. Second, there is evidence that faces are processed differently than objects (even when familiarity is controlled for). Third, the right hemisphere (and possibly right temporal lobe) appears specialized for processing faces. Fourth, we know that processing facial expressions develops on a similar time frame as processing other aspects of faces, although what structures/circuits subserve this ability are unknown. Finally, there are some data to suggest that early damage to the regions of the brain that would normally subserve face recognition results in a long-term impairment, suggesting a lack of plasticity in this system.

Less is known about categorizing faces than nonface objects. For example, unlike the object categorization literature, much of the literature on categorizing faces involves discriminating stimuli that exist only at the subordinate or basic levels (e.g., discriminating one face from another or one facial expression from another). Moreover, only infrequently has the infant's ability to generalize from a subordinate level stimulus to a basic level stimulus (e.g., to recognize the same person despite changes in facial expression) been investigated. These limitations are unfortunate, as it precludes us from really addressing the fundamental issue of whether the processes underlying face recognition are similar to or different from those underlying object recognition.

With respect to methodological issues in facial categorization, again, little is known, primarily because one dependent measure—looking time—dominates the literature. Finally, with respect to whether categorizing facial stimuli reflects perceptual versus conceptual (or perceptual *to* conceptual) processes, again, little is known. For all these reasons, then, it is difficult to draw parallels between the extensive literature on object categorization (see many of the chapters comprising this volume) and face categorization. As trite as the saying has become, clearly there is a need for additional research.

How are we to account for the development of a face processing "system" in light of the data reviewed herein (and the gaps in the literature)? In the remainder of this chapter we provide a possible answer to this question.

A MODEL OF FACE RECOGNITION

For a number of years one of us has been developing a model of face recognition that bears some similarity to models of speech perception (Nelson, 1993, 2001). For example, with regard to speech perception, we know that very young infants are able to discriminate a range of speech sounds and even recognize their mother's voice (perhaps similar to the reports of newborns recognizing their mother's face). Second, nonhuman species, such as monkeys and chinchillas, are able to categorize human speech (see Doupe & Kuhl, 1999, for review), comparable, perhaps, to how monkeys are able to discriminate human faces from one another. Third, in both human infants and in birds, experience appears to play a crucial role in recruiting cortical areas that specialize in speech perception, which in turn leads to increased perceptual proficiency. Like faces, then, there appears to be the *potential* for cortical specialization for speech perception that is dependent on experience. Finally, and perhaps most importantly, there appears to be a narrowing of the perceptual window with increased exposure to speech. For example, prior to approximately 6 to 8 months of age, infants throughout the world are able to discriminate the phonemes from languages other than the one in which they are being reared. However, as infants approach 1 year, the perceptual window begins to narrow and they behave more like adults; that is, they are best at discriminating those sounds that are native to their own language.

There are several examples of a similar phenomenon with faces. Pascalis, de Haan, and Nelson (2002) recently reported that whereas 6- and 9-month-old infants and adults are all very good at discriminating different human faces, only 6-month-olds are also good at doing so with monkey faces. We interpreted this finding to suggest that distributed and prolonged exposure to human faces in the older infants and adults led to a perceptual narrowing of the types of faces that could be easily discriminated, whereas in the youngest infants the perceptual window was broadly tuned so as to support a range of perceptual discriminations. Second, as reviewed earlier, adults have difficulty discriminating inverted faces, a phenomenon that appears to emerge by about 4 to 5 months of age. Third, there is the well-known "other race" effect, in which adults, more so than children, find it easier to recognize faces from their own race (O'Toole, Deffenbacher, Valentin, & Abdi, 1994). Fourth, there is the finding that expertise recognizing Greebles leads to recruitment of the fusiform gyrus (Gauthier et al., 1999). And, this phenomenon is not limited to Greebles; for example, Gauthier and colleagues (e.g., Gauthier, Skudlarski, Gore, & Anderson, 2000) have also reported similar effects with cars and birds. Thus, these data suggest it is the development of expertise in recognizing (presumably) any class of object that recruits the fusiform gyrus. Fifth, as discussed previously both monkeys and human adults are better at recognizing faces from their own species. Finally, as previously discussed, maltreated children respond differentially to certain facial expressions (e.g., anger) relative to nonmaltreated children, presumably due to their greater experience viewing such expressions.

Let us assume, then, that like language, selection pressures have led to the genetic specification for neural tissue that has the *potential* to become specialized for face recognition. However, there must be input into this system in order to set it correctly (whether there is a critical or sensitive period for doing so is unknown, although recent data from children with congenital cataracts suggest there may be; see Le Grand, Mondloch, Maurer, & Brent, 2001). Over time, different portions of the temporal lobe are "captured" by these early experiences, with the result that the face recognition system becomes fine tuned.

What is assumed here is simply that evolutionary pressures have led to a cortex that is flexible and open to learning during development. In terms of the development of face recognition, then, all one need posit is that (a) regions within the inferior temporal cortex have the *potential* to become specialized for face recognition (much as our brains possess tissue that can *become* specialized for speech and language), (b) the face perception apparatus becomes tuned with exposure to faces, which in turn leads to increased specification and parcellation of neural tissue, and (c) this specification includes the many types of information conveyed by faces, including recognizing gender, age, and emotional information. The developmental literature reviewed herein suggests that the time frame for the development of general face perception abilities occurs rapidly within the first months of life, with fine tuning (e.g., in recognizing negative emotions like fear and anger) taking place later in the first and second years. Indeed, given the general changes in infants' visual abilities that occur over this time period, coupled with how relatively few negative emotions typically developing infants see over the first 1 to 2 years of life, we would expect that the recognition of certain facial expressions to be delayed relative to that of more general face recognition abilities.

IMPLICATIONS FOR PERCEIVING OBJECT
CATEGORIES

On the whole, it appears that faces are indeed perceived as a separate class of objects, a phenomenon that is also associated with neural circuits that reside in the inferior temporal cortex. However, it is our contention that such specialized processing is experience- and activity-driven; presumably, for example, if infants or young children were never exposed to faces, they would not develop such a specialized ability.[1] (To our knowledge, such a study has never been reported, for obvious reasons.)

It is difficult to speculate what the implications this model has for the development of object recognition. Unlike faces, which exist primarily at the subordinate (e.g., facial expression) or basic level of categories (e.g., facial identity), objects exist at many levels, that is, subordinate, basic, and superordinate. Early in development, of course, infants are bombarded with both face and nonface objects. However, faces likely begin to stand out for three reasons: First, unlike objects, faces possess adaptive significance, which in turn may have led to the evolution of neural tissue that has the potential to become dedicated to face recognition. Second, as previously stated, the levels at which faces are represented are more constrained than the levels at which nonface objects are represented. Accordingly, the task of recognizing faces may develop on a different time frame than for recognizing objects. Thus, for example, if there is neural tissue that has the potential to become specialized for face recognition, and given how ubiquitous faces are in the infant's life, face recognition skills should acquire sophistication sooner than object recognition skills. (Although conversely, one might argue that the sheer abundance of and similarity among faces might make for slower acquisition and delayed expertise.) Third, unlike objects, faces are associated with care giving and social discourse, and thus may acquire affective significance. As infants accumulate more experience with faces, perceptual tuning occurs, the perceptual window narrows, and neural tissue specialized for face recognition develops. But, what about object recognition? Perhaps at first nonface objects are perceived as just that: anything that is not a face. Once this binary rule is established, infants can then begin

---

[1]Of course, an alternative way to compromise the development of this ability would be to knock out the areas that will become specialized for face recognition early enough in life so that even when faces are available for viewing, this tissue cannot become specialized. The literature reviewed on child prosopagnosia is consistent with this prediction. The fact that so little recovery of function is observed is intriguing, and suggests that face recognition may be fundamentally different from some aspects of language acquisition; with regard to language, of course, Bates and others have shown that despite marked damage to left frontal or temporal areas early in life, children typically develop fairly normal language abilities (for review, see Bates & Roe, 2001).

the process of learning about the different types of objects that exist, and the different levels on which objects are represented. Although surely there will be some cortical specialization for this ability (by virtue of constraints on the assembly of the visual system), our predictions are that (a) this specialization should occur on a much slower time course that that observed for face recognition, (b) the areas involved will partially overlap those involved in face recognition (an observation supported by the adult neuroimaging literature) but will also extend beyond the boundaries of the fusiform gyrus, and (c) there will be greater plasticity in the object recognition system, larger because of the greater range in levels on which objects can be represented. Alas, as there are currently no active research programs exploring the ontogeny of the neural bases of object recognition, these predictions await confirmation, and until then we sit precariously perched on the proverbial tree limb.

REFERENCES

Adolphs, R., Tranel, D., Damasio, H., & Damasio, A. (1994). Impaired recognition of emotion in facial expressions following bilateral damage to the human amygdala. *Nature, 372,* 669–672.

Adolphs, R., Tranel, D., Damasio, H., & Damasio, A. (1995). Fear and the human amygdala. *Journal of Neuroscience, 15,* 5879–5891.

Aggleton, J. P., Burton, M. J., & Passingham, R. E. (1980). Cortical and subcortical afferents to the amygdala of the rhesus monkey (Macaca mulatta). *Brain Research, 190,* 347–368.

Bates, E., & Roe, K. (2001). Language development in children with unilateral brain injury. In C. A. Nelson & M. Luciana (Eds.), *Handbook of developmental cognitive neuroscience* (pp. 281–307). Cambridge, MA: MIT Press.

Baylis, G. C., Rolls, E. T., & Leonard, C. M. (1987). Functional subdivisions of the temporal lobe neocortex. *The Journal of Neuroscience, 7,* 330–342.

Behl-Chadha, G. (1996). Superordinate-like categorical representations in early infancy. *Cognition, 60,* 104–141.

Binder, J. R., Springer, J. A., Bellgowan, P. S. F., Swanson, S. J., Frost, J. A., & Hammeke, T. A. (1997). A comparison of brain activation patterns produced by auditory and visual lexical–semantic language tasks. *NeuroImage, 5,* 588.

Bomba, P. C., & Siqueland, E. R. (1983). The nature and structure of infant form categories. *Journal of Experimental Child Psychology, 35,* 294–328.

Bowlby, J. (1969). *Attachment and loss.* New York: Basic Books.

Courtney, S. M., Ungerleider, L. G., Kell, K., & Haxby, J. V. (1997). Transient and sustained activity in a distributed neural system for human working memory. *Nature, 386,* 608–611.

Damasio, A. R., Damasio, H., & Van Hoesen, G. W. (1982). Prosopagnosia: Anatomic basis and behavioral mechanisms. *Neurology, 32,* 331–341.

de Haan, M. (2001). The neuropsychology of face processing in infancy and childhood. In C. A. Nelson & M. Luciana (Eds.), *Handbook of developmental cognitive neuroscience* (pp. 381–398). Cambridge, MA: MIT Press.

de Haan, M., & Nelson, C. A. (1997). Recognition of the mother's face by 6-month-old infants: A neurobehavioral study. *Child Development, 68,* 187–210.

de Haan, M., & Nelson, C. A. (1999). Electrocortical correlates of face and object recognition by 6-month-old infants. *Developmental Psychology, 35,* 1113–1121.

DeRenzi, E. (1986). Current issues in prosopagnosia. In H. Ellis, M. A. Jeeves, F. Newcombe, & S. Young (Eds.), *Aspects of face processing* (NATO ASI Series, 0 28, pp. 243–252). Hingham, MA: Martinus Nijhoff.

de Schonen, S., & Mathivet, E. (1989). First come first served: A scenario about the development of hemispheric specialization in face processing in infancy. *European Bulletin of Cognitive Psychology, 9,* 3–44.

Devinsky, O., Morrell, M. J., & Vogt, B. A. (1995). Contributions of anterior cingulated cortex to behavior. *Brain, 118,* 279–306.

Doupe, A. J., & Kuhl, P. K. (1999). Birdsong and human speech: Common themes and mechanisms. *Annual Review of Neuroscience, 22,* 567–631.

Eimas, P. D. (1994). Categorization in early infancy and the continuity of development. *Cognition, 50,* 83–93.

Eimas, P. D., & Quinn, P. C. (1994). Studies on the formation of perceptually based basic-level categories in young infants. *Child Development, 65,* 903–917.

Eimas, P. D., Quinn, P. C., & Cowan, P. (1994). Development of exclusivity in perceptually based categories of young infants. *Journal of Experimental Child Psychology, 58,* 418–431.

Ellis, H. D., & Young, A. W. (1988). Training in face-processing skills for a child with acquired prosopagnosia. *Developmental Neuropsychology, 4,* 283–294.

Fagan, J. (1972). Infants' recognition memory for faces. *Journal of Experimental Child Psychology, 14,* 453–476.

Farah, M., Humphreys, G. W., & Rodman, H. R. (1999). Object and face recognition. In M. J. Zigmond, F. E. Bloom, S. C. Landis, J. L. Roberts, & L. R. Squire (Eds.), *Fundamental neuroscience* (pp. 1339–1361). San Diego, CA: Academic Press.

Farah, M. J., Wilson, K. D., Drain, H. M., & Tanaka, J. R. (1995). The inverted face inversion effect in prosopagnosia: Evidence for mandatory, face-specific perceptual mechanisms. *Visual Research, 14,* 2089–2093.

Farah, M. J., Wilson, K. D., Drain, H. M., & Tanaka, J. R. (1998). What is "special" about face perception? *Psychological Review, 105,* 482–498.

Filoteo, J. V., Maddox, W. T., & Davis, J. D. (2001). Quantitative modeling of category learning in amnesic patients. *Journal of the International Neuropsychological Society, 7,* 1–19.

Gauthier, I., Anderson, A. W., Tarr, M. J., Skudlarski, P., & Gore, J. C. (1997). Levels of categorization in visual recognition studied using functional magnetic resonance imaging. *Current Biology, 7,* 645–651.

Gauthier, I., Skudlarski, P., Gore, J. C., & Anderson, A. W. (2000). Expertise for cars and birds recruits brain areas involved in face recognition. *Nature Neuroscience, 3*(2), 191–197.

Gauthier, I., Tarr, M. J., Anderson, A. W., Skudlarski, P., & Gore, J. C. (1999). Activation of the middle fusiform 'face area' increases with expertise in recognizing novel objects. *Nature Neuroscience, 2,* 568–580.

Gerlach, C., Law, I., Gade, A., & Paulson, O. B. (2000). Categorization and category effects in normal object recognition: A PET study. *Neuropsychologia, 38,* 1693–1703.

Goren, C., Sarty, M., & Wu, P. (1975). Visual following and pattern discrimination of face-like stimuli by newborn infants. *Pediatrics, 56,* 544–549.

Grafton, S. T., Fadiga, L., Arbib, M. A., & Rizzolatti, G. (1997). Premotor cortex activation during observation and naming of familiar tools. *NeuroImage, 6,* 231–236.

Grossman, M., Koenig, P., DeVita, C., Glosser, G., Alsop, D., Detre, J., & Gee, J. (2002). The neural basis for category-specific knowledge: An fMRI study. *NeuroImage, 15,* 936–948.

Hershenson, M. (1965, June). *Form perception in the human newborn.* Paper presented at the Second Annual Symposium, Center for Visual Science, University of Rochester, NY.

Johnson, M. H., Dziurawiec, S., Bartrip, J., & Morton, J. (1992). The effect of movement of internal features on infants' preferences for face-like stimuli. *Infant Behavior and Development, 15*, 129–136.

Johnson, M. H., Dziurawiec, S., Ellis, H., & Morton, J. (1991). Newborns' preferential tracking of face-like stimuli and its subsequent decline. *Cognition, 40*, 1–19.

Johnson, M. H., & Morton, J. (1991). *Biology and cognitive development: The case of face recognition.* Cambridge, MA: Blackwell.

Jolicoeur, P., Gluck, M. A., & Kosslyn, S. M. (1984). Pictures and names: Making the connection. *Cognitive Psychology, 16*, 243–275.

Kanwisher, N., McDermott, J., & Chun, M. M. (1997). The fusiform face area: A module in human extrastriate cortex specialized for face perception. *Journal of Neuroscience, 17*, 4302–4311.

Kanwisher, N., Tong, F., & Nakayama, K. (1998). The effect of face inversion on the human fusiform face area. *Cognition, 68*, 1–11.

Kapur, S., Rose, R., & Liddle, P. F. (1994). The role of the left prefrontal cortex in verbal processing: Semantic processing or willed action? *NeuroReport, 5*, 2193–2196.

Knowlton, B. J., Mangels, J. A., & Squire, L. R. (1996). A neostriatal habit learning system in humans. *Science, 273*, 1399–1402.

Knowlton, B. J., Ramus, S. J., & Squire, L. R. (1992). Intact artificial grammar learning in amnesia: Dissociation of classification learning and explicit memory for specific instances. *Psychological Science, 3*, 172–179.

Knowlton, B. J., & Squire, L. R. (1993). The learning of categories: Parallel brain systems for item memory and category knowledge. *Science, 262*, 1747–1749.

Knowlton, B. J., Squire, L. R., Paulsen, J. S., Swerdlow, N. R., Swenson, M., & Butters, N. (1996). Dissociations within nondeclarative memory in Huntington's disease. *Neuropsychology, 10*, 169–181.

Kotsoni, E., de Haan, M., & Johnson, M. H. (2001). Categorical perception of facial expressions by 7-month-old infants. *Perception, 30*, 1115–1125.

Le Grand, R., Mondloch, C. J., Maurer, D., & Brent, H. P. (2001). Neuroperception: Early visual experience and face processing. *Nature, 410*(6831), 890.

Leonard, C. M., Rolls, E. T., Wilson, F. A., & Baylis, G. C. (1985). Neurons in the amygdala of the monkey with responses selective for faces. *Behavioral Brain Research, 15*, 159–176.

Madole, K. L., & Oakes, L. M. (1999). Making sense of infant categorization: Stable processes and changing representations. *Developmental Review, 19*, 263–296.

Mancini, J., de Schonen, S., Deruelle, C., & Massoulier, A. (1994). Face recognition in children with early right or left brain damage. *Developmental Medicine and Child Neurology, 36*, 156–166.

Mandler, J. M. (1988). How to build a baby: On the development of an accessible representational system. *Cognitive Development, 3*, 113–136.

Mandler, J. M. (2000). Perceptual and conceptual processes in infancy. *Journal of Cognition and Development, 1*, 3–36.

Mandler, J. M., Bauer, P. J., & McDonough, L. (1991). Separating the sheep from the goats: Differentiating global categories. *Cognitive Psychology, 23*, 263–298.

Mandler, J. M., & McDonough, L. (1993). Concept formation in infancy. *Cognitive Development, 8*, 291–318.

Mandler, J. M., & McDonough, L. (1998). On developing a knowledge base in infancy. *Developmental Psychology, 34*, 1274–1288.

Mareschal, D., French, R. M., & Quinn, P. (2000). A connectionist account of asymmetric category learning in early infancy. *Developmental Psychology, 36*, 635–645.

Marr, D. (1982). *Vision.* San Francisco: Freeman.

McNeil, J., & Warrington, E. K. (1993). Prosopagnosia: A face-specific disorder. *Quarterly Journal of Experimental Psychology, 46A*, 1–10.

Mervis, C. B., & Rosch, E. (1981). Categorization of natural objects. *Annual Review of Psychology*, *32*, 89–115.

Moscovitch, M., Goshen-Gottstein, Y., & Vriezen, E. (1994). Memory without conscious recollection: A tutorial review from a neuropsychological perspective. In C. Umilta & M. Moscovitch (Eds.), *Attention and performance XV: Conscious and nonconscious information processing*. Cambridge, MA: MIT Press.

Moscovitch, M., Kapur, S., Kohler, S., & Houle, S. (1995). Distinct neural correlates of visual long-term memory for spatial location and object identity: A positron emission tomography study in humans. *Proceedings of the National Academy of Sciences USA*, *92*, 3721–3725.

Moscovitch, M., Winocur, G., & Behrmann, M. (1997). What is special about face recognition? Nineteen experiments on a person with visual object agnosia and dyslexia but normal face recognition. *Journal of Cognitive Neuroscience*, *9*, 555–604.

Nahm, F. K., Albright, T. D., & Amaral, D. G. (1991). Neuronal responses of the monkey amygdaloid complex to dynamic visual stimuli. *Society for Neuroscience Abstracts*, *17*, 473.

Nelson, C. A. (1993). The recognition of facial expressions in infancy: Behavioral and electrophysiological correlates. In B. de Boysson-Bardies, S. de Schonen, P. Jusczyk, P. MacNeilage, & J. Morton (Eds.), *Developmental neurocognition: Speech and face processing in the first year of life* (pp. 187–193). Hingham, MA: Kluwer Academic Press.

Nelson, C. A. (2001). The development and neural bases of face recognition. *Infant and Child Development*, *10*, 3–18.

Nelson, C. A., & de Haan, M. (1996a). Neural correlates of infants' visual responsiveness to facial expressions of emotion. *Developmental Psychobiology*, *29*, 577–595.

Nelson, C. A., & de Haan, M. (1996b). A neurobiological approach to the recognition of facial expressions in infancy. In J. A. Russell (Ed.), *The psychology of facial expression* (pp. 176–204). New York: Cambridge University Press.

Nelson, C. A., & Dolgin, K. (1985). The generalized discrimination of facial expressions by 7-month-old infants. *Child Development*, *56*, 58–61.

Nelson, C. A., Morse, P. A., & Leavitt, L. A. (1979). Recognition of facial expressions by 7-month-old infants. *Child Development*, *50*, 1239–1242.

Nelson, C. A., & Nugent, K. (1990). Recognition memory and resource allocation as revealed by children's event-related potential responses to happy and angry faces. *Developmental Psychology*, *26*, 171–179.

Nosofsky, R. M. (1992). Exemplar-based approach to relating categorization, identification, and recognition. In F. G. Ashby (Ed.), *Multiple dimensional models of perception and cognition* (pp. 363–393). Hillsdale, NJ: Lawrence Erlbaum Associates.

Nyberg, L., Tulving, E., Habib, R., Nilsson, L., Kapur, S., Houle, S., Cabeza, R., & McIntosh, A. (1995). Functional brain maps of retrieval mode and recovery of episodic information. *NeuroReport*, *7*, 249–252.

Oakes, L. M., & Madole, K. L. (2000). The future of infant categorization research: A process-oriented approach. *Child Development*, *71*, 119–126.

Oakes, L. M., Plumert, J. M., Lansink, J. M., & Merryman, J. D. (1996). Evidence for task-dependent categorization in infancy. *Infant Behavior and Development*, *19*, 425–440.

Op de Beeck, H., Beatse, E., Wagemans, J., Sunaert, S., & Van Hecke, P. (2000). The representation of shape in the context of visual object categorization tasks. *NeuroImage*, *12*, 28–40.

O'Toole Deffenbacher, K. A., Valentin, D., & Abdi, H. (1994). Structural aspects of face recognition and the other-race effect. *Memory and Cognition*, *22*, 208–224.

Pascalis, O., & Bachevalier, J. (1998). Face recognition in primates: A cross-species study. *Behavioral Processes*, *43*, 87–96.

Pascalis, O., de Haan, M., & Nelson, C. A. (2002). Is face processing species specific during the first year of life? *Science*, *296*, 1321–1323.

Perrett, D. I., & Mistlin, A. J. (1990). Perception of facial characteristics by monkeys. In W. C. Stebbins & M. A. Berkley (Eds.), *Comparative perception: Vol. 2. Complex signals* (pp. 187–215). New York: Wiley.

Perrett, D. I., Rolls, E. T., & Caan, W. (1982). Visual neurons responsive to faces in the monkey temporal cortex. *Experimental Brain Research, 47,* 329–342.

Perrett, D. I., Smith, P. A. J., Misturi, A. J., Chitty, A. J., Head, A. S., Potter, D. D., Broennimann, R., Milner, A. D., & Jeeves, M. A. (1985). Visual analysis of body movements by neurons in the temporal cortex of the macaque monkey: A preliminary report. *Behavioural Brain Research, 16,* 153–170.

Perrett, D. I., Smith, P. A. J., Potter, D. D., Mistlin, A. S., Head, A. S., Milner, A. D., & Jeeves, M. A. (1984). Neurons responsive to faces in the temporal cortex: Studies of functional organization, sensitivity to identity and relation to perception. *Human Neurobiology, 3,* 197–208.

Pickering, A. D. (1997). New approaches to study of amnesic patients: What can a neurofunctional philosophy and neural network methods offer? *Memory, 5,* 255–300.

Pollak, S. D., Klorman, R., Thatcher, J. E., & Cicchetti, D. (2001). P3b reflects maltreated children's reactions to facial displays of emotion. *Psychophysiology, 38,* 1–8.

Posner, M. I., & Keele, S. W. (1968). On the genesis of abstract ideas. *Journal of Experimental Psychology, 77,* 353–362.

Quinn, P. C. (1998). Object and spatial categorization in young infants: "What" and "where" in early visual perception. In A. Slater (Ed.), *Perceptual development: Visual, auditory, and speech perception in infancy* (pp. 131–165). East Sussex, England: Psychology Press (Taylor & Francis).

Quinn, P. C. (2002). Beyond prototypes: Asymmetries in infant categorization and what they teach us about the mechanisms guiding early knowledge acquisition. *Advances in Child Development and Behavior, 29,* 161–193.

Quinn, P. C., & Eimas, P. D. (1996). Perceptual cues that permit categorical differentiation of animal species by infants. *Journal of Experimental Child Psychology, 63,* 189–211.

Quinn, P. C., Eimas, P. D., & Rosenkrantz, S. L. (1993). Evidence for representations of perceptual similar natural categories by 3-month-old and 4-month-old infants. *Perception, 22,* 463–475.

Quinn, P. C., & Johnson, M. H. (1998, April). *Global before perceptual category representations in connectionist networks and 2-month-old infants.* Paper presented at the International Conference on Infant Studies, Atlanta, GA.

Rakison, D. H., & Butterworth, G. E. (1998). Infants' attention to object structure in early categorization. *Developmental Psychology, 34*(6), 1310–1325.

Rakison, D. H., & Poulin-Dubois, D. (2001). Developmental origin of the animate-inanimate distinction. *Psychological Bulletin, 127*(2), 209–228.

Reber, P. J., & Squire, L. R. (1999). Intact learning of artificial grammars and intact category learning by patients with Parkinson's disease. *Behavioral Neuroscience, 113,* 235–242.

Reber, J. M., Stark, C. E. L., & Squire, L. R. (1998). Contrasting cortical activity associated with category memory and recognition memory. *Learning and Memory, 5,* 420–428.

Reed, J. M., Squire, L. R., Patalano, A. L., Smith, E. E., & Jonides, J. (1999). Learning about categories that are defined by object-like stimuli despite impaired declarative memory. *Behavioral Neuroscience, 113,* 411–419.

Rolls, E. T. (1984). Neurons in the cortex of the temporal lobe and in the amygdala of the monkey with responses selective for faces. *Human Neurobiology, 3,* 209–222.

Rolls, E. T., & Baylis, G. C. (1986). Size and contrast have only small effects on the responses to faces of neurons in the cortex of the superior temporal sulcus of the monkey. *Experimental Brain Research, 65,* 38–48.

Rosch, E., Mervis, C. B., Gray, W., Johnson, D., & Boyes-Braem, P. (1976). Basic objects in natural categories. *Cognitive Psychology, 3,* 382–439.

Rugg, M. D., Fletcher, P. C., Frith, C. D., Frambach, M., & Dolan, R. J. (1996). Differential activation of the prefrontal cortex in successful and unsuccessful memory retrieval. *Brain, 119,* 2073–2083.

Sacks, O. W. (1990). *The man who mistook his wife for a hat and other clinical tales.* New York: Harper Perennial.

Schacter, D. L., & Buckner, R. L. (1998). Priming and the brain. *Neuron, 20,* 185–195.

Schacter, D. L., Reiman, E., Uecker, A., Polster, M. R., Yung, L. S., & Cooper, L. A. (1995). Brain regions associated with retrieval of structurally coherent visual information. *Nature, 376,* 537–539.

Simion, F., Valenza, E., Macchi-Cassia, V., Turati, C., & Umilta, C. (2002). Newborns' preferences for up-down asymmetrical configurations. *Developmental Science, 5*(4), 427–434.

Smith, E. E., Jonides, J., Keoppe, R. A., Awh, E., Schumache, E. H., & Minoshima, S. (1995). Spatial versus object working memory: PET investigations. *Journal of Cognitive Neuroscience, 7,* 337–356.

Squire, L. R., & Knowlton, B. J. (1995). Learning about categories in the absence of memory. *Proceedings of the National Academy of Sciences, 92,* 12470–12474.

Squire, L. R., Ojemann, J. G., Miezin, F. M., Petersen, S. E., Videen, T. O., & Raichle, M. E. (1992). Activation of the hippocampus in normal humans: A functional anatomical study of memory. *Proceedings of the National Academy of Science, 89,* 1837–1841.

Thomas, H. (1965). Visual-fixation responses of infants to stimuli of varying complexity. *Child Development, 36,* 629–638.

Tulving, E., Markowitsch, H. J., Craik, F., Habib, R., & Houle, S. (1996). Novelty and familiarity activations in PET studies of memory encoding and retrieval. *Cerebral Cortex, 6,* 71–79.

Turati, C., Simion, F., Milani, I., & Umilta, C. (2002). Newborns' preference for faces: What is crucial? *Developmental Psychology, 38*(6), 875–882.

Tzourio-Mazoyer, N., de Schonen, S., Crivello, F., Reutter, B., Aujard, Y., & Mazoyer, B. (2002). Neural correlates of woman face processing by 2-month-old infants. *NeuroImage, 15,* 454–461.

Valenza, E., Simion, F., Macchi-Cassia, V., & Umilta, C. (1996). Face preference at birth. *Journal of Experimental Psychology: Human Perception and Performance, 22,* 892–903.

Vandenberghe, R., Price, C., Wise, R., Josephs, O., & Frackowiak, R. S. (1996). Functional anatomy of a common semantic system for words and pictures. *Nature, 383,* 254–256.

Wang, G., Tanaka, K., & Tanifuji, M. (1996, June). Optical imaging of functional organization in the monkey inferotemporal cortex. *Science, 272*(5268), 1665–1668.

Wiggs, C. L., & Martin, A. (1998). Properties and mechanisms of perceptual priming. *Current Opinions in Neurobiology, 8,* 227–233.

Yamane, S., Kaji, S., & Kawano, K. (1988). What facial features activate face neurons in the inferotemporal cortex of the monkey? *Experimental Brain Research, 73,* 209–214.

Younger, B. A. (1985). The segregation of items into categories by 10-month-old infants. *Child Development, 56,* 1574–1583.

Younger, B. (1992). Developmental change in infant categorization: The perception of correlations among facial features. *Child Development, 63,* 1526–1535.

Younger, B. A., & Cohen, L. B. (1986). Developmental changes in infants' perception of correlations among attributes. *Child Development, 57,* 803–815.

Chapter 2

Building Knowledge From Perception in Infancy

Scott P. Johnson
New York University

That all our knowledge begins with experience there can be no doubt. For how is it possible that the faculty of cognition should be awakened into exercise otherwise than by means of objects which affect our senses, and partly of themselves produce representations, rouse our powers of understanding into activity, to compare, to connect, or to separate these, and so to convert the raw materials of our sensuous impressions into a knowledge of objects, which is called experience? In respect of time, therefore, no knowledge of ours is antecedent to experience, but begins with it.

But, though all our knowledge begins with experience, it by no means follows that it all arises out of experience. For, on the contrary, it is quite possible that our empirical knowledge is a compound of that which we receive through impressions, and that which the faculty of cognition supplies from itself (sensuous impressions giving merely the occasion*), in addition to which we cannot distinguish from the original element given by sense, till long practice has made us attentive to, and skilful in separating it. It is, therefore, a question which requires close investigation, and is not to be answered at first sight—whether there exists a knowledge altogether independent of experience, and even of all sensuous impressions?*

—Kant (1787/1934, p. 25)

Kant sketched out a framework for explorations of a fundamental question of cognitive science: the origins of knowledge in humans. He presents in lucid form the empiricist viewpoint, taken up also by philosophers such as Hume and Locke, holding the position that much human knowledge necessarily arises from direct experience with objects and events in the world:

33

registering their components, retaining them in memory, integrating them across space and time, and forming associations among them as experience accrues. An alternative view expressed in the quote, shared by philosophers such as Descartes, held that some kinds of knowledge must have origins in unobservable concepts, because sensory impressions were thought to be inadequate to determine fully the rich nature of human cognitive skills. The final part of the quote is a call for empirical work to resolve the issue, which to this day resists a purely philosophical answer.

This debate has continued, and inspires the subject of this chapter. One exceptionally controversial argument concerns origins of object knowledge, an argument that is often centered on the question of infants' representations of occluded objects. I suggest that the term *representation* in this context implies two interrelated components: first, some neural activity that registers the presence of a hidden object or hidden object part in the absence of direct perceptual support, and second, some outward (i.e., observable) behavioral manifestation of the internal activity. At the present time, few researchers have access to the first component of representation in infancy, due to difficulties in direct recording of cortical activity. Reports describing such activity are beginning to emerge, however, some of which are recounted subsequently. The second component has received more extensive investigation, yet until recently, data were unavailable to provide firm conclusions about object knowledge in the youngest postnatal humans. Movement toward a resolution comes from research with infants at birth and across the next several months, experiments that examine infants' behavioral responses to partly or fully hidden objects. These experiments, many of which are described subsequently, provide convincing evidence that infants are born with sensory systems sufficient to ascertain the boundaries and motions of many visible surfaces, but there is no evidence of any ability to detect more than what is directly visible. That is, infants are born without any means to perceive occlusion, and therefore, on my definition, no knowledge of objects. Perceptual "filling-in" of the missing parts of objects develops across the first 6 months after birth, and constitutes the earliest evidence of knowledge of objects in the world beyond direct perception. The rest of this chapter recounts some of this recent evidence, following a description of some early empirical efforts and theories. The chapter concludes with speculation concerning mechanisms of development and potential avenues for further research.

ORIGINS OF OBJECT KNOWLEDGE: TWO VIEWS

Piaget (1954) described the first systematic investigations of how infants, beginning at birth and extending across the next several years, respond to objects in the external world and their spatial relations. He considered the development of object knowledge to be a problem of construction of dual, corresponding concepts: first, that objects have permanence and constancy across time and space, and second, that objects exist external to the self in a particular spatial arrangement. Piaget did not have at his disposal the wealth of methods that researchers use today, but he did manage to devise a series of clever manipulations of objects, generally involving occlusion, and he provided detailed accounts of infants' and children's overt responses to them. These observations revealed a developmental sequence of behaviors that were taken to reflect underlying knowledge of objects and their spatial relations, and led to Piaget's account of the emergence of object permanence. Initially, infants provided no responses to indicate knowledge of object permanence, although there was early recognition of familiar objects. Between 3 and 6 months after birth, however, infants began to show evidence of veridical responses to occlusion, such as search for the hidden part of an object that was partly visible, or direction of gaze toward the (presumably) expected emergence point of a moving object that became obstructed. Later, at around 8 months of age, infants searched for fully hidden objects; later still (around 18 to 24 months) infants solved somewhat complex hiding tasks involving more than one location, at which point Piaget ascribed them full object permanence. Initially, then, the infant experiences no objects per se, but rather surfaces that appear and disappear inconsistently, and the infant experiences no objective environment, but rather fleeting images that are arbitrary and subjective (i.e., produced through self-initiated movements). Piaget argued that throughout this sequence, the principal mechanism of development was rooted in the infant's own behavior: engaging with objects, following their motions, and taking note of the consequences of self-directed actions.

Piaget's observations and descriptions have enjoyed strong support from repeated replications over the past several decades, but his interpretation of infants' behavior has come under fire, mostly from researchers who use methods that are claimed to be more sensitive in tapping underlying cognitive constructs. Three cardinal examples are found in reports by Baillargeon, Spelke, and Wasserman (1985), by Spelke, Breinlinger, Macomber, and Jacobson (1992), and by Kellman and Spelke (1983). In the Baillargeon et al. experiment, 5-month-olds were shown two objects: a box and a screen, arranged such that the screen rotated around and, apparently, through the space occupied by the box (a so-called "impossible" event that was accomplished with one-way mirrors). In the Spelke et al. experiment, 2.5-month-olds were shown a ball rolling behind an occluder. The top of a barrier, perpendicular to the ball's path of motion, was visible protruding from behind the occluder. The occluder was then raised, and the ball was revealed apparently to have rolled past the barrier (again, an impossible event, accomplished by surreptitiously moving the ball). Infants were reported to have shown heightened interest in these impossible events relative to possible or control displays. This led the researchers to conclude that the infants were somehow surprised by the apparent violation of object solidity (i.e., an object cannot move through the space occupied by another object) and the violation of location under occlusion. In the Kellman and Spelke experiment, 4-month-olds were familiarized with a moving rod whose center was occluded by a box. Infants subsequently looked longer at a "broken rod" display (with a gap in the space formerly occupied by the box) than at a complete rod, although both these stimuli resembled the visible portions of the rod presented during familiarization. This result, assumed to reflect a postfamiliarization novelty preference, implies that the infants experienced the partly occluded rod as more similar to the complete test stimulus: as a single, coherent object.

These three studies, and others, have been viewed as providing support for a nativist theory of cognitive development stressing an innate knowledge component (i.e., independent of experience) that guides infant responses to objects, a suggestion that I call the *knowledge-first* hypothesis. This hypothesis rests on three key assumptions. First, object knowledge may be innate because veridical responses to occlusion are observed at an early age, and there may be inadequate opportunities over the first several postnatal months for infant learning of fundamental concepts, such as persistence across occlusion (Baillargeon, 1995). Second, object knowledge may be constrained by the physics and ecology of the world, such that early perceptual rules tend to be biased toward environmental regularities (Kellman, 1993). Third, some kinds of object knowledge ("core principles") may be unchanged across development because, among other reasons, it makes little sense to develop a concept that must later be overturned (Spelke, 1994). On the knowledge-first account, Piaget underestimated infants' object knowledge, most likely because of the inadequacy (i.e., insensitivity) of his methods. His methods have been thought to rely too heavily on overt manual responses, such as coordinated reaching; difficulties with reaching may mask latent cognitive capacities.

The contributions of manual activity to origins of object knowledge is beyond the scope of this chapter, but there is strong evidence of many veridical responses to occlusion prior to 5 to 6 months of age, when many infants begin to manipulate objects systematically with their hands. Nevertheless, I argue in subsequent sections that the three nativist assumptions discussed previously are incorrect when subjected to empirical investigation: The youngest postnatal humans (i.e., neonates) do not perceive occlusion, early object knowledge does not accord with many environmental regularities, and several fundamental perceptual "rules" are, in fact, overturned in the course of development. Moreover, when the measure of object knowledge is not manual reaching but is an overt oculomotor response, a motor system that is largely mature shortly after birth (Johnson, 2001a), infants' responses accord well with those from experiments that examine looking times only.

In place of the Piagetian and knowledge-first (nativist) views, I offer the *sensitivity-first* hypothesis, which stipulates that object knowledge arises from ontogenetic processes over developmental time, processes that are rooted in three relatively low-level perceptual-cognitive capacities: The first is a facility to detect separate regions of visual space that constitute visible surface fragments (e.g., figure–ground segregation), the second is the ability to retain information for short intervals, and the third is a system of inherent visual preferences (e.g., for moving over stationary objects). All three capacities are available to infants at birth (Slater, 1995). The sensitivity-first hypothesis is to be favored over the knowledge-first hypothesis on the basis of parsimony, because the sensitivity-first view assumes less that is necessary for the emergence of knowledge in humans; in particular the necessity for innate knowledge is obviated. Yet arguments from parsimony are no substitute for evidence. The next two sections of the chapter describe two literatures that furnish such evidence. The two literatures concern perception of the unity of partly occluded objects, and perception of the continuity of a partly occluded object trajectory. The evidence is clear: Infants first detect visible surface fragments, and subsequently link them across space and time to provide veridical percepts of occlusion. This shift from perception of surface fragments to perception of objects marks one of the most important developmental events to occur in ontogeny, and represents a revolutionary change in how infants must experience the world. How this might be accomplished is considered in subsequent sections of this chapter.

PERCEPTION OF OBJECT UNITY

Kellman and Spelke (1983) tested for perception of object unity with a paradigm that assumes a novelty preference after habituation to a rod-and-box display, as depicted in Fig. 2.1. Four-month-olds were found to perceive unity when the rod parts underwent a common translatory motion above and below the occluder (as revealed by a posthabituation preference for a broken rod display), but failed to show a test display preference after viewing a static rod-and-box arrangement (cf. Jusczyk, Johnson, Spelke, & Kennedy, 1999). Kellman and Spelke concluded that "Humans may begin life with the notion that the environment is composed of things that are coherent, that move as units independently of each other, and that tend to persist, maintaining their coherence and boundaries as they move" (1983, p. 521). Kellman (1993) has since argued that young infants are "edge-insensitive," meaning that only motion information contributes to unity

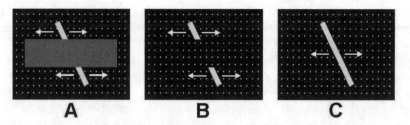

FIG. 2.1.   Displays used to probe infants' perception of object unity. After habituation to A, longer looking at B implies perception of the rod parts' unity during habituation. Longer looking at C, in contrast, implies perception of disjoint objects. These conclusions are based on the assumption of posthabituation novelty preferences.

perception, perhaps due to its high ecological utility and reliability. Static information (such as edge alignment of the rod parts across the occluder) is insufficient to specify unity until later than 6 months.

Two recent lines of evidence present a more complex picture. The first comes from experiments with younger infants, and calls into question the claim that coherent object perception is innate. When neonates were examined for perception of object unity in occlusion stimuli, they showed a strong posthabituation preference for a complete test display, implying that they responded solely on the basis of what was directly visible and did not perceive occlusion (Slater, Johnson, Brown, & Badenoch, 1996; Slater, Morison, Somers, Mattock, Brown, & Taylor, 1990). Two-month-olds have been found to perceive unity when the occluder is made relatively narrow (Fig. 2.2A) or contains gaps (Johnson & Aslin, 1995; Johnson, Cohen, Marks, & Johnson, 2003), but not when the occluder is wider, as in Fig. 2.1A (Johnson & Náñez, 1995). The second line of evidence comes from further

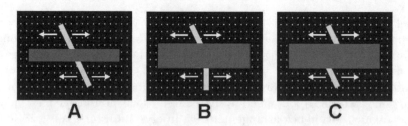

FIG. 2.2.   A: Two-month-olds perceive unity when the occluder is relatively narrow (as shown) but not when it is wide. B: The rod edges are misaligned, meaning they would meet to form a "bent" object were they to be extended behind the occluder. C: The rod edges would not meet if extended. Four-month-olds' unity percepts are indeterminate in B, and in C, 4-month-olds appear to perceive the rod parts as disjoint. These results obtain despite the common motion of rod parts, which should serve to support unity percepts.

experiments with 4-month-old infants, and calls into question the claim that edge alignment has no bearing on young infants' perception of object unity. Four-month-olds were presented with rod-and-box displays in which the rod parts were misaligned, or arranged such that they would meet at an obtuse angle (i.e., a single deflection) if extended behind the occluder (Fig. 2.2B), and showed no test display preference. When 4-month-olds viewed displays in which the rod parts were nonaligned, and would meet with two deflections if extended, the infants looked longer subsequently at a complete rod display (Johnson & Aslin, 1996; Smith, Johnson, & Spelke, 2003). (In both cases, the broken and complete test displays in this case matched the visible rod parts viewed during habituation; i.e., they were "bent" and "crooked," respectively.) These results obtained even when common motion of the rod parts would have been expected to specify unity, and therefore imply a kind of "edge sensitivity" in 4-month-olds. That is, the infants were not led by motion to perceive unity: Instead, the nonaligned rod parts appear to have been perceived as disjoint objects, and determinations of unity versus disjoint objects in the misaligned rod display were indefinite.

The knowledge-first and sensitivity-first views offer opposing accounts of these patterns of data. On the knowledge-first hypothesis, infants are predisposed from the start of postnatal life to experience objects as bounded, coherent, and continuous across time and space; common motion is a reliable indicator of these object properties (Spelke & Van de Walle, 1993). This account appeals to the possibility of limitations in motion sensitivity as responsible both for the failure of neonates to perceive object unity, and the effects of misalignment and occluder size on 2- and 4-month-old infants' unity percepts. Motion sensitivity refers to the registration of patterns of visual motion, as opposed to a mechanism that codes merely for differences in position, observed across time (as in, say, a strobe-lit environment). Veridical perception of motion in random-dot displays, for example, requires true motion discrimination. A mechanism limited to position-sensitivity cannot detect such motion because individual "snapshots" (such as frames of an animation sequence) are too similar to discriminate consistently (Johnson & Mason, 2002). Wattam-Bell (1996a, 1996b) has reported evidence that infants younger than 6 to 8 weeks are insensitive to motion in random-dot displays, implying a lack of motion discrimination. If neonates are insensitive to the common motion of the visible rod parts, then it is unlikely the infants would perceive unity. Furthermore, on the knowledge-first hypothesis, detectability of common motion by 2- and 4-month-olds is modulated by both edge relations and spatial distance. Specifically, misaligned rod edges, or rod parts separated by a large spatial gap, are less likely to be perceived as undergoing common motion (see Smith et al., 2003, for further discussion of these possibilities). On the knowledge-first account, therefore, latent object knowledge precedes complete sensitivity to the visual information specifying unity, and when sensitivity emerges in ontogeny, object knowledge can be more fully expressed.

The sensitivity-first hypothesis presents a contrasting account. On this view, infants discriminate differences in movement and position of the moving rod segments in a rod-and-box display, and detectability of motion is unaffected by distance or orientation of object edges. The limitation on unity percepts in the youngest infants instead reflects a general impairment in veridical object perception. In particular, very young infants are unable to form representations of hidden objects or object parts. In other words, occlusion perception develops, not sensitivity to visual information specifying objects and their arrangements. The roles of alignment and occluder width are more direct on this account: Perception of unity of edges that are not aligned across a spatial gap is unlikely unless there is other evidence to support this percept (such as global form, as when a circular object is partly occluded; see Johnson, Bremner, Slater, & Mason, 2000). (Adults, likewise, are more liable to perceive the unity of edges that are aligned, and unity judgments drop off as the relative angle departs from 180°; Jusczyk et al., 1999; Kellman & Shipley, 1991.) Finally, evidence to date reveals that the ability to perceive occlusion begins to emerge at about 2 months, and this ability is fragile initially. Two-month-olds, therefore, are more likely to perceive unity in a narrow-occluder display than when unity percepts are challenged by a wider spatial gap. With development, infants become more facile at integrating object parts over increasing spatial distances.

Until recently, extant published data could not determine whether the knowledge-first or the sensitivity-first hypothesis is the better account of the development of object perception. I have completed a series of experiments designed to settle the issue (Johnson, in press). The knowledge-first hypothesis predicts that in any display that supports unity perception in infants, the infants are necessarily sensitive to the motions of the visible surfaces. Conversely, in any display that does not support unity percepts, infants are necessarily insensitive to the motions of the surfaces. In contrast, the sensitivity-first hypothesis predicts that there will be displays in which infants perceive the motions of visible object surfaces, yet are unable to perceive unity due to other limitations, such as an inability to link disparate surfaces across a spatial gap.

These predictions were tested in two experiments, both with 2-month-old infants. In the first experiment, infants were tested for perception of object unity in one of three displays: a narrow-occluder display, a wide-occluder display, and a bent rod display (Fig. 2.3). In the first two displays, the rod parts were aligned across the occluder. In the third, the rod parts were misaligned, and would meet at an angle of 154° if extended behind the occluder. After habituation to one of these three displays, infants were

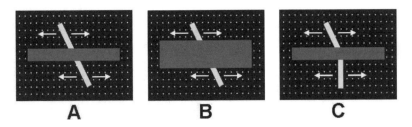

FIG. 2.3.   Displays used to probe perception of object unity in 2-month-olds. The infants perceived unity in A, but not in B or C.

shown two test displays (broken and complete rod), as per the standard object unity paradigm. Infants habituated to the narrow-occluder stimulus exhibited a reliable and consistent preference for the broken rod, but infants habituated to the wide-occluder and bent rod stimuli exhibited the opposite preference. These results imply that only infants in the first group perceived the rod parts' unity, a result that replicated Johnson and Aslin (1995).

I next asked if the 2-month-olds who were habituated to the wide-occluder and bent rod displays failed to perceive unity because the increased spatial distance of interpolation, or the rod parts' misalignment, prevented them from perceiving the common motion in the display. This was accomplished by habituating separate groups of infants to one of six displays. In three of the displays, the rod parts underwent a common translatory motion, as in the first experiment (the *corresponding motion* displays; Fig. 2.4, A, B, C). In the other three displays, the rod parts maintained their orientations relative to one another as in the corresponding motion displays, but moved in opposite directions (the *converse motion* displays; Fig. 2.4, D, E, F). After habituation, infants were presented with the same display, alternating with the display with the same occluder size and rod part orientation, but the opposite motion pattern. I reasoned that if occluder width and rod segment alignment have an influence on infants' motion discrimination, then only infants habituated to the narrow occluder displays with aligned rod parts would show increased interest during test, in accord with the knowledge-first view. Alternatively, if occluder width and edge alignment are irrelevant to motion discrimination, then infants habituated to corresponding motion would tend to look longer at the converse motion display, and infants habituated to converse motion would look longer at the corresponding motion display, despite the spatial distance and orientation of the rod segments. This outcome would provide support for the sensitivity-first view.

The results were unambiguous: Infants showed a reliable preference for the opposite motion pattern, regardless of occluder width and rod segment

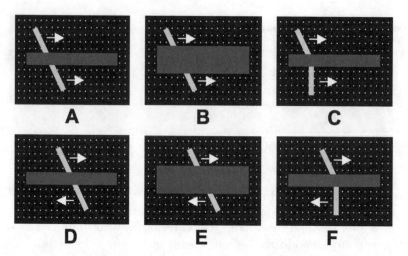

FIG. 2.4.   Displays used to probe motion sensitivity in 2-month-olds as a function of distance and orientation of moving rod segments. Infants habituated to A showed subsequent increased interest in D, and vice versa, as well as stimulus pairs B and E, and C and F. These results suggest that failure to perceive unity in the displays depicted in Fig. 2.3B and 2.3C was not a result of an insensitivity to the rod parts' motions.

orientation. These findings, alongside those of the first experiment, are consistent with predictions of the sensitivity-first hypothesis in their suggestion that 2-month-olds' perception of object unity are not limited by restrictions in discrimination of the motions and orientations of visible surfaces leading behind the occluder. Why, then, did infants in the first experiment fail to perceive unity in the wide occluder and bent rod displays? On the sensitivity-first account, spatial distance challenges the likelihood of perception of connectedness, as does misalignment, but for different reasons. A wide occluder can restrict infants' ability to integrate across too great a spatial gap, a restriction that is overcome with developmental improvements in spatiotemporal integration. Edge misalignment impedes perception of connectedness for all observers, infant and adult, because misaligned edges simply are less likely than aligned edges to be connected behind an occluder (Kellman & Shipley, 1991). These conclusions were verified in a third experiment, in which 4-month-old infants were tested for perception of object unity in the wide occluder and bent rod displays (Fig. 2.3B and Fig. 2.3C, respectively). A reliable preference for the broken rod was obtained from infants in the first, but not the second, condition, suggesting unity perception in the wide occluder display, but not the bent rod stimulus (replicating results reported by Johnson & Aslin, 1996). The older infants, therefore, were able to perceive unity despite the greater distance of interpolation relative to the narrow occluder. However, the misaligned edges of the bent rod blocked unity percepts, even with the reduced spatial distance of the rod parts (i.e., the narrow occluder in the bent rod display).

In summary, experiments that probe development of perception of object unity provide support for the thesis that young infants analyze the motions and arrangements of visible surfaces, and only later come to integrate these surfaces into percepts of coherent, partly occluded objects. On this view, therefore, development of object knowledge begins with perception of visible object components, and proceeds with increasing proficiency at representation of those object parts that cannot be discerned directly. In the next section I consider new evidence from experiments with moving objects that become briefly fully occluded, evidence that corroborates this developmental progression.

PERCEPTION OF OBJECT TRAJECTORIES

Veridical perception of partly occluded objects, discussed in the previous section, involves filling in a spatial gap. In the case of a moving object whose trajectory is partly hidden, as when a rolling ball becomes occluded by a nearer surface and then re-emerges, an observer must fill in a spatiotemporal gap, or a gap across space and time. Because the moving object is completely hidden from view temporarily, spatiotemporal filling-in might impose a greater challenge to developing perceptual/cognitive systems than does spatial filling-in, in which case we might expect that perceptual completion of a spatiotemporal gap would be achieved only by older infants.

My colleagues and I recently conducted a series of studies that examined infants' perception of object trajectories, asking whether young infants perceive a trajectory as continuous if a moving object is out of view for a short time (Johnson, Bremner, Slater, Mason, Foster, & Cheshire, 2003). Infants were first habituated to a ball translating back and forth along a horizontal, center-occluded trajectory (Fig. 2.5A), and were then presented with two test displays designed to match the habituation stimulus in different ways. The *discontinuous trajectory* display (Fig. 2.5B) matched the directly visible portions of the object trajectory, whereas the *continuous trajectory* display (Fig. 2.5C) matched the continuity of object motion as the ball traveled. We reasoned that if infants perceived the ball's trajectory as continuous in the habituation display, they would prefer the discontinuous trajectory stimulus at test, because it would be more novel, relative to the continuous trajectory stimulus. Alternately, if infants responded only on the basis of what was directly visible, the continuous trajectory test display would be perceived as more novel and would garner increased attention. This is because the discontinuous trajectory is more similar to the visible portions of the trajectory: a ball moving to a vertical edge, going out of sight, and then reappear-

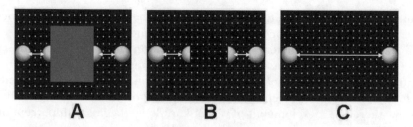

FIG. 2.5.   Displays used to probe infants' perception of trajectory continuity.
After habituation to A, longer looking at B implies perception of the persistence of the ball during habituation, despite becoming occluded for a short
interval. Longer looking at C, in contrast, implies perception of disjoint motion segments.

ing at another edge, reversing course and going out of and into view
repetitively.

We conducted three experiments (Johnson, Bremner, et al., 2003). In
the first, 4- and 6-month-olds were habituated to a small ball moving behind
an occluder 17.7 cm wide (total occlusion time 667 ms) which then re-
emerged and reversed direction in a repetitive cycle. Following habituation, the infants viewed the two test displays (discontinuous and continuous
trajectories) in alternation (see Fig. 2.5). The 4-month-olds looked reliably
longer at the continuous display, but the 6-month-olds preferred the discontinuous display. (Age-matched controls exhibited no reliable test display preference in all three experiments.) We concluded that the older infants perceived the continuity of the trajectory during habituation, but the
younger infants appeared to perceive only the visible segments of the trajectory, and did not integrate them across the spatiotemporal gap imposed by
the occluder.

We next asked if 4-month-olds would perceive trajectory continuity if
spatiotemporal demands of the task were eased, which we accomplished
by reducing the occluder width to 7.0 cm (total occlusion time 67 ms), as
depicted in Fig. 2.6A. We also tested 2-month-olds; test displays were identical to those employed in the first experiment, except the gap size in the
discontinuous display was reduced to correspond to the reduced-gap habituation stimulus. Here, the 4-month-olds showed a reliable preference
for the discontinuous trajectory, suggesting perception of trajectory continuity during habituation. These results indicate, moreover, that 4-month-
olds' responses to moving object displays depend strongly on spatiotemporal characteristics of the stimulus. In particular, time out of sight
and distance of interpolation appear to determine whether continuity is
perceived. The 2-month-olds, however, preferred neither test display, providing no evidence of perceiving trajectory continuity, even with a minimal occlusion time.

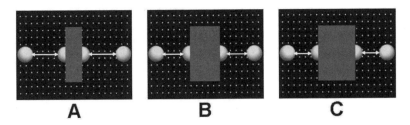

FIG. 2.6.   Displays used to examine 4-month-olds' perception of trajectory continuity as a function of occluder width. In general, the longer the ball was out of sight, the less likely the infants were to perceive its persistence on occlusion.

In the third experiment, we explored further the possibility that 4-month-olds' continuity percepts are determined by the size of the spatiotemporal gap. We varied occlusion time with two intermediate occlusion widths between those used in the first two experiments: 12.1 cm (total occlusion time 400 ms) and 14.8 cm (total occlusion time 533 ms), as depicted in Figs. 2.6B and 2.6C, respectively. Ball size and speed remained the same. The infants looked longer reliably at the discontinuous trajectory subsequent to habituation to the 12.1 cm occluder width display, but infants habituated to the slightly wider display showed no consistent preference. We concluded that infants perceived continuity in the former display (as they did in the narrow occluder display of the second experiment) but in the latter display the percept was indeterminate, neither one of continuity nor one of discontinuity. Perception of trajectory continuity in 4-month-olds, therefore, appears to be determined in a fairly straightforward manner by spatiotemporal characteristics of the stimulus: time out of sight and distance of interpolation.

In summary, experiments that examine development of perception of trajectory continuity in infancy corroborate outcomes of experiments that probe perception of object unity: Veridical responses to object occlusion emerge subsequent to a time when infants appear to perceive only what is directly visible. A key difference between these two kinds of perceptual filling-in, however, is found in the age at which this transition occurs. In the case of object unity, the pivotal age is 2 months, and in the case of trajectory continuity, the pivotal age is 4 months. The age difference is likely due to increasing demands placed on the visual system by the necessity of representing an object that is fully hidden in our trajectory displays. When these demands are eased by reducing the spatiotemporal gap, 4-month-olds can be induced to perceive a trajectory as continuous despite partial occlusion. When demands are increased, 4-month-olds appear to revert to a "default" response (perception of visible segments only), and continuity percepts are abolished.

A ROLE FOR EXPERIENCE IN THE DEVELOPMENT
OF OBJECT REPRESENTATIONS

The work discussed previously highlights fundamental changes in the nature of infants' object knowledge: Our experiments document a clear progression across the first several postnatal months from perception of surface fragments only to veridical representations of partly and fully occluded objects. (Much remains to be learned about objects, of course: Older infants show marked limitations in guiding manual reaches toward locations of hidden objects under many circumstances; see Bremner, 1985, for review, and Berthier, DeBlois, Poirier, Novak, & Clifton, 2000, for evidence of search limitations in preschoolers.) To this point, however, this work remains principally descriptive, both in terms of the age at which infants achieve competence at these perceptual tasks, and the kinds of stimulus events that are most likely to lead to success or failure at occlusion perception. What remains to be discovered are the underlying mechanisms responsible for the age-related behavioral changes. In this section, I describe some preliminary data that may move us closer to this goal, and in the next section, I sketch out suggestions for speculation concerning neurophysiological developments that may be responsible for the developmental changes.

In our trajectory continuity work, we found that occlusion perception is fragile at 4 months, but that veridical percepts can be prompted with reduced spatiotemporal demands (Johnson, Bremner, et al., 2003). This finding leads to the prediction that other kinds of added support might also induce veridical percepts of object occlusion, such as additional experience viewing objects. To test the role of experience, we examined young infants' responses to object trajectory displays by measuring anticipatory eye movements (Johnson, Amso, & Slemmer, 2003). We reasoned that a veridical representation of a moving object trajectory would be evinced as a consistent pattern of fixations toward the far side of the occluder on the ball's occlusion, indicating some level of expectation of its re-emergence. We had two predictions. First, 6-month-olds were expected to produce more anticipations than would 4-month-olds when viewing a ball-box display (Fig. 2.5A), because object representations are more robust in the older age group (Johnson, Bremner, et al., 2003). The second prediction concerns age differences in infants' reaction to experience. Four-month-olds were expected to benefit from initial experience viewing unoccluded object trajectories, because infants at this age are in a transition from perception of surface fragments to perception of occlusion in trajectory displays, and are therefore "prepared" for an enhancement in performance toward veridical percepts. Six-month-olds, however, were expected to receive no additional benefit from supplementary experience, because they are more facile at the task to begin with.

Infants were tested in one of four conditions. In the *baseline* condition, infants were shown the ball-box display depicted in Fig. 2.5A as eye movements were recorded with a corneal-reflection eye tracker. The display was presented for eight 30-s trials. In the *random* condition, infants viewed eight presentations of displays that were identical to the ball-box stimulus except the ball's point of re-emergence after occlusion was randomized (left or right). In this case, anticipation offers no gain to the observer, who is just as likely to make perceptual contact with the ball if the point of gaze remains where the object moved out of view. (We reasoned that anticipations in the random condition might be random eye movements themselves.) In the *training* condition, infants were first presented with four trials of the ball only, fully visible on its lateral trajectory (no occluder), followed by four trials with the ball-box display, as in the predictable condition. Finally, in the *generalization* condition, infants first viewed four trials with a vertical unoccluded trajectory, followed by four trials with a partly occluded horizontal trajectory.

In all conditions, an eye movement toward the opposite side of the box that was initiated 150 ms or less subsequent to the ball's re-emergence was coded as an anticipation. The 150 ms criterion was chosen to allow sufficient time to code the eye movement (see Glimcher, 2001); an eye movement initiated after this time was coded as a "response." (Other eye movements were coded as "off task," if the point of gaze was directed elsewhere relative to locations where the ball appeared, or as a "wait," if the point of gaze remained directed toward the location that the ball left. These eye movements were not entered into the analyses.)

In general, infants appeared to be interested in seeing the ball, producing an anticipation, a response, or a wait (i.e., a behavior that assures perceptual contact) on an average of 74.3% of trials ($SD = 15.3$). Recall that we hypothesized that 4-month-olds would produce relatively fewer anticipations than would 6-month-olds in the baseline condition. This hypothesis was supported: 4-month-olds anticipated on 20.1% of trials ($SD = 2.5$), whereas 6-month-olds anticipated on 37.2% of trials ($SD = 1.8$) (see Fig. 2.7). Additional analyses revealed that the 4-month-olds' anticipation behavior in the baseline condition did not differ reliably relative to the random condition (M anticipations = 22.5%, $SD = 3.4$). Moreover, performance did not improve across trials (as would be expected if the infants learned the repetitive sequence). In fact, there was a significant *decline* in anticipations across trials. These results indicate that eye movement patterns may have been driven more in the older age group by a veridical representation of the object on its path behind the occluder. Object trajectory

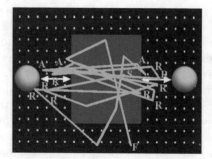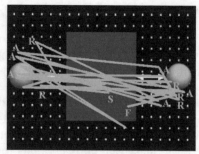

FIG. 2.7. Examples of infants' scanning patterns while viewing displays in which a ball repeatedly moved behind a box and then re-emerged. Left: A 4-month-old. Right: A 6-month-old. S = start of scan, F = finish of scan, A = anticipation (moving the point of gaze toward the opposite edge of the ball's place of occlusion prior to its re-emergence), R = response (looking at the ball after it re-emerged). Note that the 6-month-old's tracking pattern shows more anticipations than responses, whereas the 4-month-old's pattern is the opposite.

representations seem to have played a reduced role in the younger infants, as predicted, although overall anticipation levels were somewhat higher than reports of anticipation performance in the visual expectation paradigm (e.g., Canfield, Smith, Brezsnyak, & Snow, 1997).

Recall that we hypothesized also that 4-month-olds would benefit from experience in the form of prior exposure to a ball moving on an unoccluded trajectory, if they subsequently viewed the ball-box stimulus, but that 6-month-olds would not benefit to the same extent. This hypothesis, too was supported: 4-month-olds in the training condition anticipated on 36.5% of trials when the ball-box stimulus was presented ($SD = 2.9$), reliably more robust performance relative to 4-month-olds in the baseline condition. Comparisons of the two 6-month-old groups, in contrast, revealed no significant differences (M anticipations in the training condition = 26.7%, $SD = 2.5$). Finally, the improvement in anticipation performance seen in the 4-month-old training group generalized from exposure to a different trajectory orientation (M anticipations in the training condition = 37.2%, $SD = 3.9$), implying that infants in the training condition were not simply trained for facilitation of horizontal eye movements, but instead true representation-based anticipations.

In summary, these results provide corroborative support for the outcomes of our habituation experiments, described previously (Johnson, Bremner, et al., 2003), in their suggestion that there are consequential changes around 4 months after birth in representations of occluded objects. Such representations are sufficiently strong by 6 months to guide anticipatory looking behaviors consistently when viewing predictable moving object event sequences. Four-month-olds' anticipations under these conditions provided little evidence of veridical object representations. However, a short exposure to an unoccluded object trajectory induces markedly superior performance in our tracking task in this age group. Oculomotor experience, therefore, may play a key role in development of object knowledge in infancy, as proposed by Piaget (1954): "Visual accommodation to rapid movements makes possible the anticipations of future positions of the object and consequently endows it with a certain permanence" (p. 14). The precise mechanisms underlying these changes, nevertheless, remain unknown. This question is considered in the next two sections of the chapter.

NEURAL MECHANISMS

A complete account of perceptual filling-in in infancy requires an understanding of the cortical mechanisms in the adult that support veridical perception of partly and fully occluded surfaces and objects, as well as an understanding of developmental processes leading to this end state. What, then, is known about the neurophysiological bases of object representations?

In the adult primate, information flows from subcortical structures (i.e., retina and thalamus) to a part of the occipital lobe known as the primary visual area, or V1. (The majority of the research on cortex relies on animal models because many tools available to examine anatomy and function, such as single-unit recordings, are not amenable for use with humans. Fortunately, some monkey species, such as macaques, have visual systems that provide close analogues to human brain function; see Felleman & Van Essen, 1991.) Reciprocal connections carry information to secondary visual areas (e.g., V2, V3, V4, and MT). From these primary and secondary visual areas, visual information diverges to two partly segregated, yet interconnected streams (Goodale & Milner, 1992; Schiller, 1996). The first, known as the ventral stream, flows to the temporal cortex. This pathway is specialized for object recognition, which is largely realized in an area known as the inferotemporal cortex, or IT (Tanaka, 1997). IT, in turn, projects to the perirhinal cortex and other areas involved in categorization of visual stimuli and formation of visual memories (e.g., entorhinal cortex and hippocampus). It projects as well to a part of the frontal lobe, the lateral prefrontal cortex, which is implicated in learning contingencies among stimuli as well as planning and behavioral consequences (Miller, 2000; Miyashita & Hayashi, 2000; see Fig. 2.8). The second visual pathway, which is responsible for coding spatial information (object location and object-oriented action), flows from primary and secondary visual areas to parietal structures. Parietal cortex also receives reciprocal connections to and from IT and

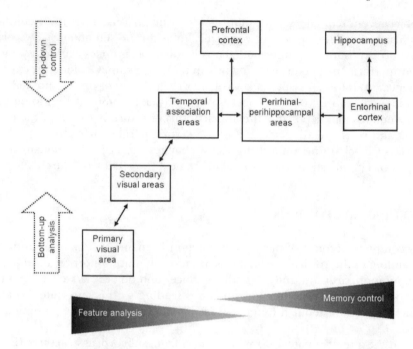

FIG. 2.8. Schematic depiction of cortical areas in the ventral visual processing stream that code for object features and memory formation. Adapted
from Miyashita and Hayashi (2000).

prefrontal cortex. Because IT is so richly interconnected with lower-level areas responsible for feature analysis, in addition to higher-level areas responsible for object memory and behavior, IT is sometimes referred to as an "association cortex." IT, therefore, is a central locus of object-oriented cortical
activity.

There is evidence that spatial filling-in may be accomplished in part with
relatively low-level mechanisms whose origins are centered in cortical areas
V1 and V2, and send information about edge connectedness to downstream ventral locations, including IT. Synaptic connections between individual visual neurons allow information about edge orientation and motion
to be passed to neighboring neurons, and these cell-to-cell activations are
most strong within and across cell groups that code similar orientations
(Roelfsema & Singer, 1998). There are two mechanisms that appear to
maximize the effectiveness of these activations. The first is the general size
of the networks of neurons that respond preferentially to each orientation.
Network size is augmented by "long-range" connections, the extended
growth of axons and dendrites of individual cells. Long-range interactions
may extend across several millimeters of cortex, and can provide informa-

tion about edge connectedness across a span of at least several degrees of visual field, even across a spatial gap (cf. Heydt, Peterhans, & Baumgartner, 1984). The second mechanism is geared toward the spreading of activation across networks via a cooperative response process, synchronized oscillatory activity in the gamma range (~40 Hz; Singer & Gray, 1995). Neighboring cells that code for similar orientations, then, are connected both by virtue of their intrinsic wiring patterns and by firing with coordinated bursts of activity. This scheme is very effective at detecting connectedness, so much so that an area somewhat higher in the processing hierarchy (the lateral occipital complex, which straddles secondary visual areas and IT in humans), known to contribute to segmentation of salient regions of the visual scene (Stanley & Rubin, 2003), responds just as strongly to partly occluded line drawings of familiar objects as to unoccluded views of the objects (Lerner, Hendler, & Malach, 2002). Partial edge occlusion in the adult, therefore, poses little difficulty to cortical object identification processes, at lower and middle levels of the ventral pathway.

In addition to participation in spatial filling-in, IT plays a central role in maintaining representations of objects, participating in spatiotemporal filling-in. It has long been known that IT proper and adjacent areas provide analysis of global shape (e.g., Kanwisher, Woods, Iacoboni, & Mazziotta, 1997) and visual features (Tanaka, 1997). There is some evidence as well for specialized circuits (in and around the fusiform gyrus) that code for such stimuli as faces (Perrett, Rolls, & Caan, 1982), hands (Desimone, Albright, Gross, & Bruce, 1984), and locations in space (Epstein & Kanwisher, 1998). Most neurons in the ventral stream, however, are tuned more broadly, and respond to a variety of objects and features (see Grill-Spector, Kourtzi, & Kanwisher, 2001). Recently, evidence has emerged that some neurons appear to be specialized for occlusion *qua* occlusion. Baker, Keysers, Jellema, Wicker, and Perrett (2001) discovered a set of neurons in monkey temporal lobe (specifically, in the superior temporal sulcus) that responded most strongly *after* a stimulus of interest (e.g., an experimenter, walking across the room) had gone out of view. When the experimenter again came into view, these "occlusion neurons" returned to baseline activity levels. In other words, these cells exhibited their most vigorous activity *subsequent to occlusion*. Similar results were found in response to moving occlusion stimuli when recording from parietal cortex (Assad & Maunsell, 1995). It is unknown at present whether input from other areas (such as those involved in working memory) drives these cells. Whether cells or circuits, however, such mechanisms may provide the neurophysiological substrate for the perceptual capacity to track objects across a short interval out of sight.

In summary, cortical mechanisms that code for perceptual completion exist in both early and mid-level stages of the visual processing stream.

These mechanisms provide feed information about object coherence and permanence to subsequent stages for further processing. The revealing of such neural schemes in nonhuman primates corroborates psychophysical evidence from adult humans for preattentive completion of image fragments from both binocular (He & Nakayama, 1992) and monocular cues (Rensink & Enns, 1998), and other occlusion phenomena such as transparency (Watanabe & Cavanaugh, 1992) and illusory contours (Davis & Driver, 1994). Occlusion, therefore, is a perceptual challenge with which the visual system deals effectively by devoting cortical resources to the problem at its earliest possible opportunity, reflecting the importance of the problem to veridical perception (see Nakayama, He, & Shimojo, 1995).

WHAT DEVELOPS? OR, PLASTICITY AND PREPAREDNESS

Two facts are important for a theoretical account of the development of object knowledge, with the present emphasis on neurophysiology. First, the cortex is partly functional from birth in humans, and second, the cortex remains plastic and subject to change with experience throughout the lifespan. Each is discussed in turn next.

Little direct evidence is available concerning contributions of neural development to veridical object perception in human infants. However, it is notable that certain behaviors characteristic of human neonates may reflect limited cortical function. For example, as discussed previously, neonates will habituate to repetitive visual stimuli, and subsequently recover interest to novel stimuli (Slater, 1995). Decrement of interest and novelty preferences are elicited even when the two eyes are patched alternately between habituation and test (Slater, Morison, & Rose, 1983), a key finding that obviates an account of recognition memory based strictly on contributions of subcortical structures. This is because inputs to the eyes are segregated until they reach cortex (see Atkinson, 1992, for further discussion of cortical function in neonates). In human adults, repeated exposure to a set of stimuli has been found to lead to a reduction in responses of visual areas within temporal lobes (Chao, Weisberg, & Martin, 2002). Taken together, these findings imply a common mechanism underlying recognition memory in infant and adult human, centered in the ventral stream. The fundamental cortical basis of recognition memory, therefore, may be largely unchanged across postnatal development, although marked improvements in flexibility occur with age (Alvarado & Bachevalier, 2000).

The rudiments of a functional recognition memory in neonates, nevertheless, should not be taken as evidence for full cortical maturity. On the contrary: Anatomical investigations of temporal cortex in infant monkeys reveal little evidence of fully mature circuits subserving object recognition (Rodman, 2003). Nearly all neurons in humans develop by the seventh month after gestation, and the majority of neurons occupy appropriate target regions prior to birth (see Johnson, 1997, for review of anatomical development of primate cortex). The precise patterns of connectivities among neural networks, however, undergo considerable development across infancy, in terms of generation and pruning of synaptic connections, and growth of axons and dendrites (Goldman-Rakic, 1987; Rakic, Bourgeois, Eckenhoff, Zecevic, & Goldman-Rakic, 1986). Neurotransmitter function and myelination also undergo substantial postnatal development (see Webb, Monk, & Nelson, 2001, for review). IT appears to receive input from essentially the same ventral structures in infant monkeys (2 to 18 weeks of age) as in adults, although many connections to and from some nonvisual higher areas were found to be absent in infancy (Rodman, 1994; Rodman & Consuelos, 1994). Despite heavy innervation from lower visual areas, however, responses of individual cells in IT are immature: Strength of response (i.e., firing rates) was reported as significantly reduced relative to that of adult monkeys viewing identical stimuli, and response latencies were more variable in the infants (Rodman, O Scalaidhe, & Gross, 1993). Interestingly, stimulus selectivity was observed for many IT neurons, some of which responded most strongly, for example, to faces or specific shapes. Given the extremely complex nature of the myriad processes involved in constructing cortex, it is impossible to pinpoint any single developmental cause that tips the infant monkey or human toward veridical object perception, but I provide speculation subsequently toward this goal.

The Chao et al. (2002) findings of flexibility of temporal lobe responses as a function of experience introduce the second important aspect of the neural account of development of object representations presented here: the fact that cortex is plastic throughout life. Plasticity is evinced, for example, by experiments that examined responses of single cells in IT of the macaque monkey in a task in which the animal was rewarded for locating a set of pre-exposed targets in a cluttered scene (Sheinberg & Logothetis, 2001). With experience, the neurons became highly sensitized to objects in the training set, firing at a significantly higher rate just before the animal made a saccade toward the target. Two important conclusions emerge as a result of this work. First, temporal neurons adapt to the immediate task, suggesting that response flexibility is an inherent characteristic of normal IT activity. Second, an important function of temporal neurons lies in connecting learned targets to actions (in this case, locating the targets via saccades), and, perhaps, the formation of other, more complex associations among objects, and between objects and behavior.

Experiments in which responses of neurons in perirhinal cortex are recorded lead to similar conclusions (Erickson, Jagadeesh, & Desimone,

2000). On exposure to a set of training stimuli, anatomical changes occurred in perirhinal tissue: the formation of clusters of neurons exhibiting similar responses to preferred targets. These structural changes required only a few dozen exposures to each object. (Perirhinal cortex receives reciprocated input from IT, and serves as a conduit to structures involved in formation of long-term memories; i.e., entorhinal cortex and hippocampus.) Experiments in which prefrontal neurons were recorded in a categorization task corroborate and extend these findings (Freedman, Riesenhuber, Poggio, & Miller, 2001). Individual neurons developed selectivity for one of two categories (cats vs. dogs), and generalized responses to new stimuli not seen during training.

Taken together, these results provide evidence for plasticity in mature ventral stream function, suggesting a possible neural basis for learning new categories throughout life. However, such flexibility is not characteristic of all perceptual and cognitive systems. It is well-known that for some systems, high levels of response flexibility are limited to a particular window of time, early in life, the so-called critical or sensitive period. For example, infants younger than about 6 months have been found to be sensitive to vowel and consonant contrasts produced in all the world's languages, but the ability to discriminate some non-native contrasts is lost after this time. This has been taken as evidence of a change in perception as a result of experience, a retention of some discrimination and representation skills at the expense of others (Kuhl, 2000). There is evidence from a face perception paradigm suggesting a similar developmental phenomenon in visual development (Pascalis, de Haan, & Nelson, 2002).

Examples of critical periods abound in the literature on visual development as well. Normal visual experience, shortly after initial exposure to patterned light, is necessary for optimal development of acuity, stereopsis, motion discrimination, and contrast sensitivity, among other visual functions (see Daw, 2003, for review). A general principle encompassing the literature on plasticity (in mature function) and the literature on critical periods (in immature function) might be that for higher-level cognitive skills, such as learning and memory for new stimuli and complex associations, continued flexibility assures the ability to respond appropriately to unexpected and novel input (Nelson, 2000). For lower-level perceptual skills, in contrast, perceptual systems become tuned to the input that remains constant across development.

The literatures reviewed in this and the previous sections lead to the following conclusions concerning development of object knowledge in humans, in terms of success at tasks that tap perceptual filling-in:

- *Spatial filling-in* may be accomplished with relatively low- and mid-level mechanisms (i.e., prior to IT in the ventral processing stream). On this account, development consists of two kinds of neural maturation. First, long-range cell-to-cell interactions that connect neural circuits coding for common edge orientations reach sufficient maturity at about 2 months of age to support perception of object unity under some circumstances (cf. Burkhalter, 1993; Burkhalter, Bernardo, & Charles, 1993). Second, firing patterns of these cell assemblies come to be synchronized, in part via reduction of neural "noise" intrinsic to all cortical circuits, but especially prevalent in infancy (Singer, 1995; Skoczenski & Norcia, 1998; cf. Csibra, Davis, Spratling, & Johnson, 2000). Maturation of both mechanisms continues over the first postnatal year, reflected in continued progress in unity perception under more demanding conditions (e.g., Craton, 1996), and perhaps even into childhood (Kovács, 2000). Other possible developmental mechanisms include general improvements in information-processing skills, such as self-directed eye movements under free viewing conditions (Johnson & Johnson, 2000), and associative learning, such as matching unoccluded and partly occluded views of identical objects (Mareschal & Johnson, 2002). See Johnson (2001b) for further discussion of these possibilities.

- *Spatiotemporal filling-in* may be accomplished by higher-level mechanisms, centered in IT and perirhinal cortex, that support neural activity coding for objects that have become occluded, and that guide overt behavioral responses. These behaviors include, in young infants, novelty responses to fragments of object surfaces and paths (i.e., perception of object unity and perception of trajectory continuity, respectively), anticipatory eye movements, and appropriate reaching behaviors in older infants. This progression toward more complex behaviors in the face of increasingly elaborate hiding tasks is consistent with a view positing age-related strengthening of neural representations, such that with development, stronger representations support success at enacting appropriate behaviors across a wide range of situations involving occlusion (Munakata, 2001).

- Four months of age in human infants constitutes a *critical period* in development of object representations. Our training condition induced object-oriented behavior typical of an older age group, but infants at the older age (6 months) provided no evidence of benefit from enrichment (Johnson, Amso, & Slemmer, 2003). This may be because 4-month-olds are maximally prepared to take advantage of the assistance brought by short-term experience. Six-month-olds, in contrast, come to the task enabled to form representations without additional aid. In other words, the kind of plasticity seen in some of the paradigms reviewed previously (e.g., Chao et al., 2002; Erickson et al., 2000) is characteristic of a limited time span during development of object knowledge.

- The object tracking system relies on exposure to moving object events to reach maturity, highlighting *the importance of experience* in development of object knowledge. There is no evidence from our paradigm, however, that additional experience beyond what infants would normally receive in the everyday environment has any beneficial long-term effect.

QUESTIONS OUTSTANDING

The claims outlined in the previous section, in some respects, raise more questions than are answered by the work from which they are derived:

• *Why is motion necessary for young infants' perception of object unity?* I argued that a principal developmental mechanism is rooted in long-range interactions between cell assemblies coding for colinearity; how does edge motion fit into this scheme? Notably, there have been recent findings from my own laboratory that would seem to contradict this account, findings providing evidence that young infants can perceive unity in displays without any aligned edges above and below the occluder (Johnson et al., 2000; Johnson, Bremner, Slater, Mason, & Foster, 2002; Johnson, Cohen, et al., 2003). It seems likely that unity perception cannot be reduced to a limited set of principles. It may be that for infants, as for adults, perception of the unity of partly occluded objects relies on a range of visual information, including, but not limited to, motion and edge orientation. The contribution of motion may lie in its salience, or in some unknown, lower-level interaction with edge detection mechanisms in primary or secondary visual areas.

• *What is the role of eye movements in perceiving object unity or trajectory continuity?* A considerable proportion of the literature on infant cognitive development relies on measures of preferential looking toward two or more displays presented simultaneously or sequentially. Yet we know nearly nothing about the precise patterns of eye movements produced by infants as they participate in our tasks, in terms of self-directed exploration of the stimulus. At a descriptive level, we know that scanning patterns change with age, encompassing, for example, a wider array of visual features that are examined during search (Bronson, 1994; Haith, 1980; Johnson & Johnson, 2000). The scope of our knowledge of perceptual and cognitive development will be expanded substantially when we have more information about how infants actually perform the tasks we set before them. Progress toward answering these questions is being made. For example, my colleagues and I found that 3-month-olds who provided evidence of unity perception in a rod-and-box display (i.e., longer looking at a broken rod test display) exhibited systematic differences in scanning patterns relative to infants who apparently failed to perceive unity, such as more frequent fixations in the vicinity of the rod parts and their paths of motion (Johnson, Slemmer, & Amso, in press).

- *What makes a representation stronger?* Munakata (e.g., 2001) has argued for a view of cognitive development based on "graded representations," a view that resonates with the account I present in this chapter. Theories based on graded representations have a potent intuitive appeal. Missing from these theories, however, is a mechanistic explanation of how a "weak" representation is transformed into a "strong" one, and precisely why strong representations are better able to guide, for example, correct reaches toward object hiding locations, whereas weak representations may be capable of directing looking behaviors only.

- *How flexible are newly-formed representations?* The 4-month-olds we observed who viewed unoccluded object trajectories (i.e., the training group) subsequently showed a pattern of visual anticipation in response to partly occluded trajectories that matched the behavior of older infants (Johnson, Amso, & Slemmer, 2003). Would this experience generalize to a new set of stimuli, say a new occluder and a new moving object? If so, this would provide further evidence that the infants learned a true concept (i.e., objects move along linear paths, and emerge in a predictable fashion from behind an occluding surface). If not, this might suggest that learning is relatively context-dependent, and that establishment of true concepts awaits further experience. This paradigm might be used to address, in addition, the current, heated controversy regarding infants' knowledge of object identity: whether individuation of objects as separate entities stems from spatiotemporal information (i.e., object motion and location) exclusively or from featural information (i.e., surface colors and patterns) as well (see Needham & Baillargeon, 2000; Wilcox, 1999; Xu, Carey, & Welch, 1999, for discussion).

CONCLUSIONS

Despite many interesting, unanswered questions that arise from this work, we are now in an excellent position to answer, with conviction, Kant's queries of the origins of knowledge. The evidence recounted above from infant psychophysics experiments provides a clear picture of the postnatal starting point and the transition toward development of object knowledge in humans subsequent to birth. Notably, the developmental foundations for these processes begin well before birth: Infants are born with a partly functional visual system, but no means to represent objects or object parts in the absence of directly perceivable information. Object representations are anchored in initial abilities to detect motions and features of constituent parts, and are triggered by a combination of neural maturation and experience. The scope of this proposal is broadened and strengthened by appeal to evidence for the neurophysiological mechanisms that code for object

58

representations in humans and nonhuman primates. This evidence yields, among other information, the cortical loci of object representations and some of the vital characteristics of these areas, such as their development and plasticity. The advantage of this supportive evidence lies in its suggestion that the problem of origins of object knowledge is a tractable one. When put to the test, it is a problem that is sure to yield more and more vital data concerning the developmental foundations of human cognition, if we ask the right questions, use the right tools, and look in the right places.

REFERENCES

Alvarado, M. C., & Bachevalier, J. (2000). Revisiting the maturation of medial temporal lobe memory functions in primates. *Learning & Memory, 7*, 244–256.
Assad, J. A., & Maunsell, J. H. R. (1995). Neuronal correlates of inferred motion in primate posterior parietal cortex. *Nature, 373*, 518–521.
Atkinson, J. (1992). Early visual development: Differential functioning of parvocellular and magnocellular pathways. *Eye, 6*, 129–135.
Baillargeon, R. (1995). A model of physical reasoning in infancy. In C. Rovee-Collier & L. P. Lipsitt (Eds.), *Advances in infancy research* (Vol. 9, pp. 305–371). Norwood, NJ: Ablex.
Baillargeon, R., Spelke, E. S., & Wasserman, S. (1985). Object permanence in five-month-old infants. *Developmental Psychology, 20*, 191–208.
Baker, C. I., Keysers, C., Jellema, T., Wicker, B., & Perrett, D. I. (2001). Neuronal representation of disappearing and hidden objects in temporal cortex of the macaque. *Experimental Brain Research, 140*, 375–381.
Berthier, N. E., DeBlois, S., Poirier, C. R., Novak, M. A., & Clifton, R. K. (2000). Where's the ball? Two- and three-year-olds reason about unseen events. *Developmental Psychology, 36*, 394–401.
Bremner, J. G. (1985). Object tracking and search in infancy: A review of data and a theoretical evaluation. *Developmental Review, 5*, 371–396.
Bronson, G. W. (1994). Infants' transitions toward adult-like scanning. *Child Development, 65*, 1243–1261.
Burkhalter, A. (1993). Development of forward and feedback connections between areas V1 and V2 of human visual cortex. *Cerebral Cortex, 3*, 476–487.
Burkhalter, A., Bernardo, K. L., & Charles, V. (1993). Development of local circuits in human visual cortex. *Journal of Neuroscience, 13*, 1916–1931.
Canfield, R. L., Smith, E. G., Brezsnyak, M. P., & Snow, K. L. (1997). Information processing through the first year of life: A longitudinal study using the visual expectation paradigm. *Monographs of the Society for Research in Child Development, 62*(2), Serial No. 250.
Chao, L. I., Weisberg, J., & Martin, A. (2002). Experience-dependent modulation of category-related cortical activity. *Cerebral Cortex, 12*, 545–551.
Craton, L. G. (1996). The development of perceptual completion abilities: Infants' perception of stationary, partially occluded objects. *Child Development, 67*, 890–904.
Csibra, G., Davis, G., Spratling, M. W., & Johnson, M. H. (2000). Gamma oscillations and object processing in the infant brain. *Science, 290*, 1582–1585.
Davis, G., & Driver, J. (1994). Parallel detection of Kanizsa subjective figures in the human visual system. *Nature, 371*, 791–793.
Daw, N. W. (2003). Critical periods in the visual system. In B. Hopkins & S. P. Johnson (Eds.), *Neurobiology of infant vision* (pp. 43–103). Westport, CT: Praeger.

Desimone, R., Albright, T. D., Gross, C. G., & Bruce, C. (1984). Stimulus-selective properties of inferior temporal neurons in the macaque. *Journal of Neuroscience, 4,* 2051–2062.

Epstein, R., & Kanwisher, N. (1998). A cortical representation of the local visual environment. *Nature, 392,* 598–601.

Erickson, C. A., Jagadeesh, B., & Desimone, R. (2000). Clustering of perirhinal neurons with similar properties following visual experience in adult monkeys. *Nature Neuroscience, 3,* 1143–1148.

Felleman, D. J., & Van Essen, D. C. (1991). Distributed hierarchical processing in the primate cerebral cortex. *Cerebral Cortex, 1,* 1–47.

Freedman, D. J., Riesenhuber, M., Poggio, T., & Miller, E. K. (2001). Categorical representation of visual stimuli in the primate prefrontal cortex. *Science, 291,* 312–316.

Glimcher, P. W. (2001). Making choices: The neurophysiology of visual-saccadic decision making. *Trends in Neurosciences, 24,* 654–659.

Goldman-Rakic, P. S. (1987). Development of cortical circuitry and cognitive functions. *Child Development, 58,* 642–691.

Goodale, M. A., & Milner, A. D. (1992). Separate visual pathways for perception and action. *Trends in Neurosciences, 15,* 20–25.

Grill-Spector, K., Kopurtzi, Z., & Kanwisher, N. (2001). The lateral occipital complex and its role in object recognition. *Vision Research, 41,* 1409–1422.

Haith, M. M. (1980). *Rules that babies look by: The organization of newborn visual activity.* Hillsdale, NJ: Lawrence Erlbaum Associates.

He, Z. J., & Nakayama, K. (1992). Surfaces versus features in visual search. *Nature, 359,* 231–233.

Heydt, R. von der, Peterhans, E., & Baumgartner, G. (1984). Illusory contours and cortical neuron responses. *Science, 224,* 1260–1262.

Johnson, M. H. (1997). *Developmental cognitive neuroscience.* London: Blackwell.

Johnson, S. P. (2001a). Neurophysiological and psychophysical approaches to visual development. In A. F. Kalverboer & A. Gramsbergen (Series Eds.) & J. B. Hopkins (Section Ed.), *Handbook of brain and behaviour in human development: IV. Development of perception and cognition* (pp. 653–675). Amsterdam: Elsevier.

Johnson, S. P. (2001b). Visual development in human infants: Binding features, surfaces, and objects. *Visual Cognition, 8,* 565–578.

Johnson, S. P. (in press). Development of perceptual completion in infancy. *Psychological Science.*

Johnson, S. P., Amso, D., & Slemmer, J. A. (2003). Development of object concepts in infancy: Evidence for early learning in an eye tracking paradigm. *Proceedings of the National Academy of Sciences (USA), 100,* 10568–10573.

Johnson, S. P., & Aslin, R. N. (1995). Perception of object unity in 2-month-old infants. *Developmental Psychology, 31,* 739–745.

Johnson, S. P., & Aslin, R. N. (1996). Perception of object unity in young infants: The roles of motion, depth, and orientation. *Cognitive Development, 11,* 161–180.

Johnson, S. P., Bremner, J. G., Slater, A., & Mason, U. (2000). The role of good form in young infants' perception of partly occluded objects. *Journal of Experimental Child Psychology, 76,* 1–25.

Johnson, S. P., Bremner, J. G., Slater, A., Mason, U., & Foster, K. (2002). Young infants' perception of unity and form in occlusion displays. *Journal of Experimental Child Psychology, 81,* 358–374.

Johnson, S. P., Bremner, J. G., Slater, A., Mason, U., Foster, K., & Cheshire, A. (2003). Infants' perception of object trajectories. *Child Development, 74,* 94–108.

Johnson, S. P., Cohen, L. B., Marks, K. H., & Johnson, K. L. (2003). Young infants' perception of object unity in rotation displays. *Infancy, 4,* 285–295.

Johnson, S. P., & Johnson, K. L. (2000). Early perception-action coupling: Eye movements and the development of object perception. *Infant Behavior and Development, 23*, 461–483.

Johnson, S. P., & Mason, U. (2002). Perception of kinetic illusory contours by 2-month-old infants. *Child Development, 73*, 22–34.

Johnson, S. P., & Náñez, J. E. (1995). Young infants' perception of object unity in two-dimensional displays. *Infant Behavior and Development, 18*, 133–143.

Johnson, S. P., Slemmer, J. A., & Amso, D. (in press). Where infants look determines how they see: Eye movements and object perception performance in 3-month-olds. *Infancy.*

Jusczyk, P. W., Johnson, S. P., Spelke, E. S., & Kennedy, L. J. (1999). Synchronous change and perception of object unity: Evidence from adults and infants. *Cognition, 71*, 257–288.

Kant, I. (1934). *Critique of pure reason* (J. M. D. Meikeljohn, Trans.). London: J. M. Dent and Sons, Ltd. (Original work published 1787)

Kanwisher, N., Woods, R. P., Iacoboni, M., & Mazziotta, J. C. (1997). A locus in human extrastriate cortex for visual shape analysis. *Journal of Cognitive Neuroscience, 9*, 133–142.

Kellman, P. J. (1993). Kinematic foundations of infant visual perception. In C. E. Granrud (Ed.), *Visual perception and cognition in infancy* (pp. 121–173). Hillsdale, NJ: Lawrence Erlbaum Associates.

Kellman, P. J., & Shipley, T. F. (1991). A theory of visual interpolation in object perception. *Cognitive Psychology, 23*, 141–221.

Kellman, P. J., & Spelke, E. S. (1983). Perception of partly occluded objects in infancy. *Cognitive Psychology, 15*, 483–524.

Kovács, I. (2000). Human development of perceptual organization. *Vision Research, 40*, 1301–1310.

Kuhl, P. K. (2000). Language, mind, and brain: Experience alters perception. In M. S. Gazzaniga (Ed.), *The new cognitive neurosciences* (pp. 99–115). Cambridge, MA: MIT Press.

Lerner, Y., Hendler, T., & Malach, R. (2002). Object-completion effects in the human lateral occipital complex. *Cerebral Cortex, 12*, 163–177.

Mareschal, D., & Johnson, S. P. (2002). Learning to perceive object unity: A connectionist account. *Developmental Science, 5*, 151–185.

Miller, E. K. (2000). Organization through experience. *Nature Neuroscience, 3*, 1066–1068.

Miyashita, Y., & Hayashi, T. (2000). Neural representation of visual objects: Encoding and top-down activation. *Current Opinion in Neurobiology, 10*, 187–194.

Munakata, Y. (2001). Graded representations in behavioral dissociations. *Trends in Cognitive Sciences, 5*, 309–315.

Nakayama, K., He, Z. J., & Shimojo, S. (1995). Visual surface representation: A critical link between lower-level and higher-level vision. In D. N. Osherson (Series Ed.) & S. M. Kosslyn & D. N. Osherson (Vol. Eds.), *Visual cognition: Vol. 2. An invitation to cognitive science* (2nd ed., pp. 1–70). Cambridge, MA: MIT Press.

Needham, A., & Baillargeon, R. (2000). Infants' use of featural and experiential information in segregating and individuating objects: A reply to Xu, Carey and Welch (2000). *Cognition, 74*, 255–284.

Nelson, C. A. (2000). Neural plasticity and human development: The role of early experience in sculpting memory systems. *Developmental Science, 3*, 115–130.

Pascalis, O., de Haan, M., & Nelson, C. A. (2002). Is face processing species-specific during the first year of life? *Science, 296*, 1321–1323.

Perrett, D. I., Rolls, E. T., & Caan, W. (1982). Visual neurones responsive to faces in the monkey temporal cortex. *Experimental Brain Research, 47*, 329–342.

Piaget, J. (1954). *The construction of reality in the child* (M. Cook, Trans.). New York: Basic Books. (Original work published 1937)

Rakic, P., Bourgeois, J. P., Eckenhoff, M. E. F., Zecevic, N., & Goldman-Rakic, P. S. (1986). Concurrent overproduction of synapses in diverse regions of the primate cerebral cortex. *Science, 232*, 232–235.

Rensink, R. A., & Enns, J. T. (1998). Early completion of occluded objects. *Vision Research, 38,* 2489–2505.

Rodman, H. R. (1994). Development of inferior temporal cortex in the monkey. *Cerebral Cortex, 5,* 484–498.

Rodman, H. R. (2003). Development of temporal lobe circuits for object recognition: Data and theoretical perspectives from nonhuman primates. In B. Hopkins & S. P. Johnson (Eds.), *Neurobiology of infant vision* (pp. 105–145). Westport, CT: Praeger.

Rodman, H. R., & Consuelos, M. J. (1994). Cortical projections to anterior inferior temporal cortex in infant macaque monkeys. *Visual Neuroscience, 11,* 119–133.

Rodman, H. R., O Scalaidhe, S. P., & Gross, C. G. (1993). Response properties of neurons in temporal cortical visual areas of infant monkeys. *Journal of Neurophysiology, 70,* 1115–1136.

Roelfsema, P. R., & Singer, W. (1998). Detecting connectedness. *Cerebral Cortex, 8,* 385–396.

Rovee Collier, C., Schechter, A., Shyi, G. C., & Shields, P. J. (1992). Perceptual identification of contextual attributes and infant memory retrieval. *Developmental Psychology, 28,* 307–318.

Schiller, P. H. (1996). On the specificity of neurons and visual areas. *Behavioural Brain Research, 76,* 21–35.

Sheinberg, D. L., & Logothetis, N. K. (2001). Noticing familiar objects in real-world scenes: The role of temporal cortical neurons in natural vision. *Journal of Neuroscience, 21,* 1340–1350.

Singer, W. (1995). Development and plasticity of cortical processing architectures. *Science, 270,* 758–764.

Singer, W., & Gray, C. M. (1995). Visual feature integration and the temporal correlation hypothesis. *Annual Review of Neuroscience, 18,* 555–586.

Skoczenski, A. M., & Norcia, A. M. (1998). Neural noise limitations on infant visual sensitivity. *Nature, 391,* 697–700.

Slater, A. (1995). Visual perception and memory at birth. In C. Rovee-Collier & L. P. Lipsitt (Eds.), *Advances in infancy research* (Vol. 9, pp. 107–162). Norwood, NJ: Ablex.

Slater, A., Johnson, S. P., Brown, E., & Badenoch, M. (1996). Newborn infants' perception of partly occluded objects. *Infant Behavior and Development, 19,* 145–148.

Slater, A., Morison, V., & Rose, D. (1983). Locus of habituation in the human newborn. *Perception, 12,* 593–598.

Slater, A., Morison, V., Somers, M., Mattock, A., Brown, E., & Taylor, D. (1990). Newborn and older infants' perception of partly occluded objects. *Infant Behavior and Development, 13,* 33–49.

Smith, W. C., Johnson, S. P., & Spelke, E. S. (2003). Motion and edge sensitivity in perception of object unity. *Cognitive Psychology, 46,* 31–64.

Spelke, E. S. (1994). Initial knowledge: Six suggestions. *Cognition, 50,* 431–445.

Spelke, E. S., Breinlinger, K., Macomber, J., & Jacobson, K. (1992). Origins of knowledge. *Psychological Review, 99,* 605–632.

Spelke, E. S., & Van de Walle, G. (1993). Perceiving and reasoning about objects: Insights from infants. In N. Eilan, R. A. McCarthy, & B. Brewer (Eds.), *Spatial representation: Problems in philosophy and psychology* (pp. 132–161). Oxford: Blackwell.

Stanley, D. A., & Rubin, N. (2003). fMRI activation in response to illusory contours and salient regions in the human lateral occipital complex. *Neuron, 37,* 323–331.

Tanaka, K. (1997). Mechanisms of visual object recognition: Monkey and human studies. *Current Opinion in Neurobiology, 7,* 523–529.

Watanabe, T., & Cavanaugh, P. (1992). The role of transparency in perceptual grouping and pattern recognition. *Perception, 21,* 133–139.

Wattam-Bell, J. (1996a). Visual motion processing in 1-month-old infants: Habituation experiments. *Vision Research, 36,* 1679–1685.

Wattam-Bell, J. (1996b). Visual motion processing in 1-month-old infants: Preferential-looking experiments. *Vision Research, 36,* 1671–1677.

Webb, S. J., Monk, C. S., & Nelson, C. A. (2001). Mechanisms of postnatal neurobiological development: Implications for human development. *Developmental Neuropsychology, 19,*
147–171.

Wilcox, T. (1999). Object individuation: Infants' use of shape, size, pattern, and color. *Cognition, 72,* 125–166.

Xu, F., Carey, S., & Welch, J. (1999). Infants' ability to use object kind information for object
individuation. *Cognition, 70,* 137–166.

Chapter 3

Categories, Kinds, and Object Individuation in Infancy

Fei Xu
University of British Columbia

INTRODUCTION

Psychologists and philosophers have been debating about the nature of categories, kinds, and the role of language in concept representation and concept acquisition for decades if not centuries. When studying the nature of kind representations, much of the literature in cognitive and developmental psychology has focused on the important process of categorization (see the many chapters in this volume). In this chapter, I focus on a less studied aspect of kind representations, namely the process of individuation. I suggest that a theory of kind representations should account for both categorization and individuation.

What is a category and what is a kind? To begin, I use a taxonomy to clarify the relationship between the various terms and to pinpoint the focus of this chapter (Fig. 3.1).

I adopt a very broad construe of categories. Any group of objects that is minimally coherent will be considered a category, for example, dog, chair, person, passenger, girl, baby, water, gold, red things, things to take to the beach, anything that is bigger than an elephant, all instances of the verb "walk," all instances of the preposition "in," and so on. These categories make intuitive sense because all members of each category have some attributes in common, but how coherent or how "tight" these categories are differ dramatically (see Markman, 1989; Millikan, 1998, among others, for discussions). For instance, the category *dog* is intuitively a paradigmatic example of a category, whereas the category *red things* is a more peripheral example. A subset of categories is kinds. Kinds are categories with rich inductive potential, for example, *dog, chair, person, girl, baby, water, gold.* Some kind concepts provide not only the basis for categorization (which all kind concepts do by virtue of being a subset of all categories) but also the basis of individuation.

What is the process of individuation? It is the process for establishing numerically distinct individuals that can be tracked through time and space, for example, objects, people, events. A subset of all kind concepts, dubbed "sortals" by philosophers of language, provides the criteria for categorization and individuation. To avoid terminological confusion, I call these concepts "sortal-kinds," which include *dog, chair, person, girl,* and *baby* (Fig. 3.1), in contrast with "substance-kinds," which include *water, gold,* and so on. Within sortal-kinds, some individuate and trace the identity of an entity through all of its existence, such as *dog, person, chair.* These are what I call "essence sortals." Other sortal-kinds only individuate and trace the identity of an entity for part of its existence, such as *baby, girl, passenger.* These I call "stage sortals."

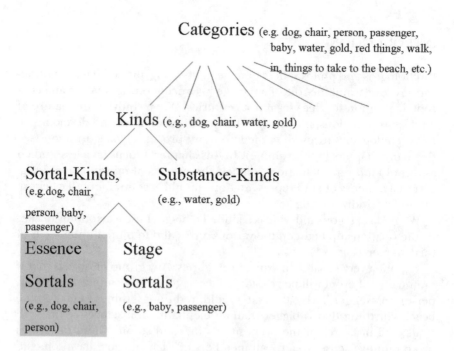

FIG. 3.1.   A taxonomy of categories, kinds, kind-sortals, substance sortals, and essence sortals.

Why is individuation important and why should a theory of concepts account for both categorization and individuation? Perhaps one way to put the issue simply is that categorization is the process of *identification*, and individuation is the process of *re-identification* (Millikan, 1996). Our conceptual system represents categories and these groupings allow us to *identify* specific instances of categories; our conceptual system also represents kinds and *re-identifies* instances of categories over time. For example, if we identify that a dog (a specific instance of the category *dog*) walked into a cabin, then a few minutes later, we again identify that a dog (as opposed to a cat) came out of the cabin. We ask ourselves: Was that a single dog going in and coming out, or was that two distinct dogs, one went in and the other came out? That is, re-identification takes place in our conceptual system, most of the time automatically. Re-identification or individuation has consequences in whether our visual system interprets the event as having one or two dogs in the scene, whether the same proper name, Fido, can be applied, and whether we should run faster for our lives should we happen to be afraid of dogs of a particular breed. "Sortal-kinds" are the subset of our categories that provide criteria for both categorization and individuation, that is, identification and re-identification (Millikan, 1998). One reason why the study of individuation is importantly complementary to the study of categorization is because human adults are committed to a world populated with individuals (people, objects, or events) that persist: We may encounter Joe Schmoe on both Monday and Wednesday; we may sit in the same office chair every day of the week; and we may go to the first and ninth innings of the same baseball game. Most studies of categorization are concerned with how we group and identify instances, leaving open the question whether it was the same object or objects that are categorized each time. The study of individuation is concerned with precisely the problem of persistence, of objects, people, and events.

Issues of object individuation are relatively new to the study of cognitive and language development, but it has a long history in the study of object perception and attention. Several related phenomena have been studied extensively. For example, the phenomenon of apparent motion has generated a rather large literature of its own and the issue at hand is whether an object is perceived as one and the same, and under what conditions human observers would trade off path of motion information and perceptual property information in tracking objects over time and space. Another example is the "tunnel effect" (e.g., Burke, 1952). Consider the following event: A blue circle goes behind an occluder and a red square comes out the other side (Fig. 3.2). We know that if the spatiotemporal parameters are set within a certain range, adults perceive that the blue circle has turned into a red square. In other words, a single object has persisted through space and

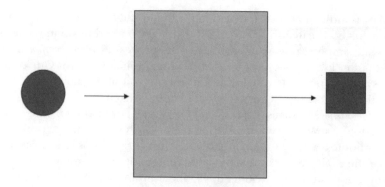

FIG. 3.2.   Diagram demonstrating the tunnel effect.

time and it has different properties (blue vs. red, circle vs. square) on the two sides of the occluder.

Now consider a similar event. A dog goes behind an occluder and a cat comes out the other side (Fig. 3.3). Under conditions identical to the circle/square event, we would perceive the event as involving two distinct objects, namely a dog and a cat. If the occluder were removed, we would expect to find the dog behind it. Our representations of kinds such as *dog* and *cat* include a belief that dogs and cats are of different kinds and have different essences therefore dogs do not turn into cats (e.g., Gelman, 2003; Medin & Ortony, 1989). For adults, these two systems of individuation operate together, the former being the object-based attention system and the latter being the kind-based system.

"DOG"   "CAT"

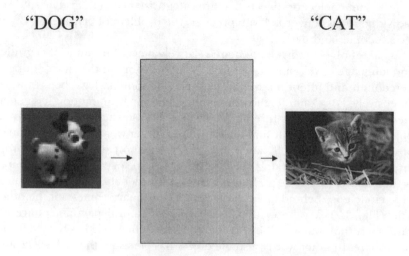

FIG. 3.3.   Diagram demonstrating the role of kind membership.

This chapter presents a review of the development of object individuation in infancy. I argue that two systems of individuation are present: an early developing object-based individuation system (by about 4 months of age), and a later developing kind-based individuation system (starting at around 9–12 months of age). Furthermore, I argue that learning labels for object kinds plays an important, perhaps causal, role in the development of the second, kind-based system of individuation.

What Are the Initial Criteria for Object Individuation in Infancy?

Use of Spatiotemporal Information for Object Individuation.   In recent years, a number of researchers have shown that even very young infants employ spatiotemporal criteria in the service of object individuation. Spelke, Kestenbaum, Simons, and Wein (1995; see also Moore, Borton, & Darby, 1978, and Spelke & Kestenbaum, 1986) asked whether infants had any criteria for deciding whether an object is the same one as a previously seen object, using the violation-of-expectancy looking time paradigm. The question about criteria for numerical distinctness is a step beyond object permanence; not only did these researchers ask whether infants represent objects when they are out of sight, but also whether infants have any means for establishing and representing a world that is populated with multiple distinct objects, all of which are permanent. In their studies, 4-month-old infants were seated in front of a puppet stage. Two opaque screens sat on the stage, with some space in between. A rod appeared from behind the left screen and moved to the left side of the stage, then returned behind the left screen. After a short pause, an identical-looking rod appeared from behind the right screen, moved to the right side of the stage, and returned behind the right screen (see Fig. 3.4 for a variant of the procedure with toy objects). The mature understanding of the physical world includes the generalization that objects travel on spatiotemporal continuous paths such that no object can go from point A to point B without traveling through the space in between. Therefore the spatiotemporal information in the event—no object traveled through the space between the two screens—informs adults that there must be two distinct objects involved in this event. What about young human infants? Does their mental faculty also possess such understanding of how the physical world works? To answer this question, Spelke et al. (1995) removed the screens on the test trials, revealing to the infants either an event in which a single rod moved back and forth, or an event in which two identical rods moved back and forth. Infants' looking times were recorded. By the logic of this experimental paradigm, if the infants had established a representation of two objects in the event and habituated to it, they should look longer at the single rod event on the test trials.

68

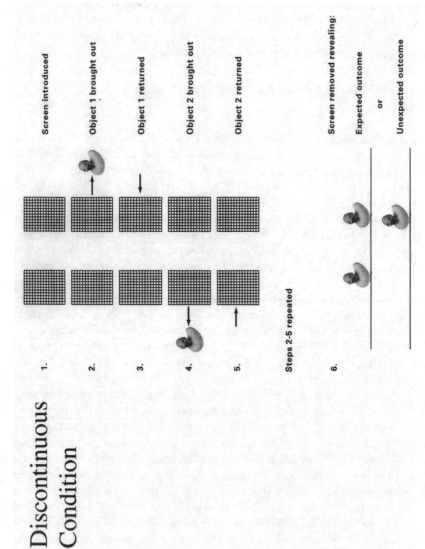

Discontinuous Condition

1. Screen introduced

2. Object 1 brought out

3. Object 1 returned

4. Object 2 brought out

5. Object 2 returned

Steps 2-5 repeated

6. Screen removed revealing:

Expected outcome

or

Unexpected outcome

FIG. 3.4. Schematic representation of the experimental procedure in Spelke et al. (1995).

Four-month-old infants did so. This finding has been replicated with 10-month-old infants using a variant of the procedure and a variety of small objects such as toy trucks, balls, and toy ducks (Xu & Carey, 1996). Furthermore, by 10 months, if the object does travel through the space in between the two screens, infants establish a representation of a single object in the event. That is, not only does spatiotemporal discontinuity lead to a representation of two distinct objects, but also spatiotemporal continuity leads to a representation of a single, persisting object. Other laboratories have also replicated this basic finding using somewhat different procedures (e.g., Aguiar & Baillargeon, 1999; Simon, Hespos, & Rochat, 1997; Wynn, 1992, among others).

Thus, even young infants have some criteria for establishing representations of distinct objects. These criteria are spatiotemporal in nature, including generalizations such as objects travel on spatiotemporally connected paths, two objects cannot occupy the same space at the same time, and one object cannot be in two places at the same time (for empirical evidence for the latter two generalizations, see Baillargeon, 1995; Baillargeon & Graber, 1987; Baillargeon, Spelke, & Wasserman, 1985, among others).

Use of Property Information for Object Individuation. Do infants use other types of information in the service of object individuation? Adults use at least two other types of information: perceptual property information (contrasts in color, size, texture, such as a red triangle and a green disc) and object kind information (membership in different kinds, e.g., a cat seen on the window sill at Time 1 and a cup seen on the same window sill at Time 2). Wilcox and Baillargeon (1998a; Experiments 7 & 8) first showed that 9-month-old infants were able to use property information for establishing a representation of two distinct objects. In their study, two conditions were contrasted. In the box-ball condition, a box (e.g., blue, square/cube-shaped) moved behind an occluder, and then a ball (e.g., red, round) came out the other side. The occluder was removed to reveal nothing behind it (see Fig. 3.5). In the ball-ball condition, a ball moved behind an occluder, and then a ball came out the other side. The occluder was then removed to reveal nothing behind it. These researchers reasoned that if the infants had used the property differences between the box and the ball to establish a representation of two distinct objects, they should look longer at the ball outcome in the box-ball condition than in the ball-ball condition. This was indeed what they found.

Inspired by the studies of Wilcox and Baillargeon (1998) and employing a procedure devised by other researchers (LeCompte & Gratch, 1972; Tinkelpaugh, 1928; Uller, Leslie, & Carey, 2000), Xu and Baker (in press) used a manual search methodology to address the question whether infants

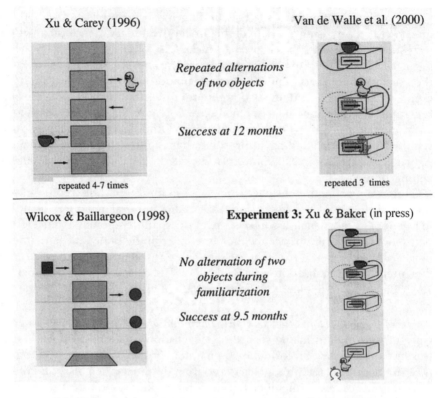

FIG. 3.5. Schematic representations of the experimental procedures in Wilcox and Baillargeon (1998a), Xu and Baker (in press), Xu and Carey (1996), and Van de Walle et al. (2000).

can use perceptual property information for object individuation. Because of the high task demands of a manual search procedure, they tested 10-month-old infants. Infants saw a single object, say a cup, removed from and replaced in the box. On half the trials, the object that the infant retrieved was the same as the object she was shown (No-Switch trials). On the other half of trials, the object that the infant retrieved was different from the object she was shown, say a toy duck (Switch trials; Fig. 3.5). The retrieved object was then taken away. If the infants had used property information to establish two distinct objects, they should then search more persistently inside the box on the Switch trials than on the No-Switch trials. This pattern of search was obtained at 10 months. Thus by 10 months of age, infants are able to use perceptual property information for object individuation in both a looking time paradigm and a manual search paradigm.

In summary, studies from various laboratories have shown that infants are able to use spatiotemporal information and perceptual property information for object individuation as early as 4 months of age.

What Develops Over Time? A Kind-Based Individuation System

Strong Spatiotemporal Evidence for a Single Object Overrides Property Information. What about object kind information? Can infants use kind membership as a source of evidence for establishing distinct objects in an event? Xu and Carey (1996) and Wilcox and Baillargeon (1998; Experiments 1 & 2) found that strong spatiotemporal evidence for a single object changing properties overrides property information. In Xu and Carey's experiments, 10- and 12-month-old infants were shown the following event: One screen is put on a puppet stage. A toy duck emerges from behind the screen and returns behind it. After a short pause, a ball emerges from behind the same screen to the other side and returns behind it (Fig. 3.6). The event is repeated a number of times, thus presenting the infants with multiple alternations of the objects: duck, ball, duck, ball, duck, ball, and so on. Adults, who understand that ducks and balls are two different kinds of objects and that they do not typically turn into each other behind screens, conclude that there must be two distinct objects. On the test trials, the screen was removed to reveal either the expected outcome of two objects or the unexpected outcome of only one object. If infants are able to use object kind information for object individuation, they should look longer at the unexpected outcome. The results, however, were surprising: 10-month-old infants did not look longer at the unexpected outcome of one object. Their looking-time pattern for the one- and two-object outcomes was not different from their baseline preference, which was measured by showing infants just the two outcomes without familiarization and, not surprisingly, the infants looked longer at two objects than one object. In contrast, 12-month-old infants looked longer at the one-object, unexpected outcome, overcoming their baseline preference for two objects. In other words, 10-month-old infants failed to draw the inference that there should be two distinct objects behind the screen, whereas 12-month-old infants succeeded in doing so.

Two critical control conditions established that the method was sensitive. When 10-month-old infants were shown the two objects *simultaneously* for 2 or 3 seconds at the beginning of the experiment (Fig. 3.7), they looked longer at the unexpected, one-object outcome, overcoming a baseline preference for two objects. Thus when clear spatiotemporal evidence was provided, these infants were able to establish a representation of two distinct objects behind the screen.

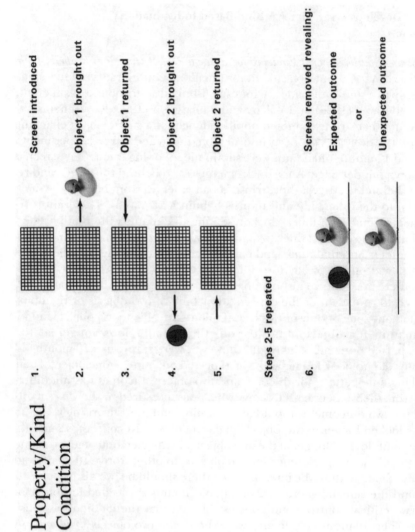

FIG. 3.6. Schematic representations of the experimental procedure of the property/kind condition of Xu and Carey (1996).

72

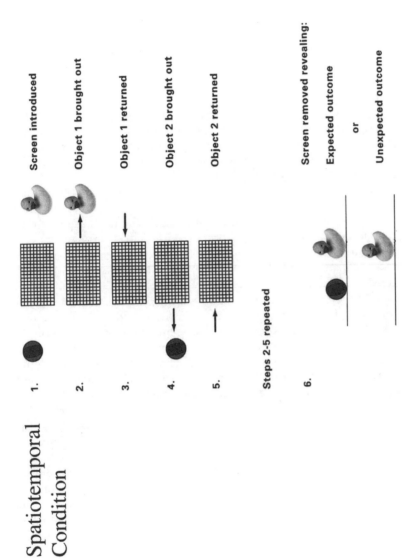

Spatiotemporal Condition

1.

Screen introduced

2.

Object 1 brought out

3.

Object 1 returned

4.

Object 2 brought out

5.

Object 2 returned

Steps 2-5 repeated

6.

Screen removed revealing:

Expected outcome

or

Unexpected outcome

FIG. 3.7. Schematic representations of the experimental procedure of the spatiotemporal condition of Xu and Carey (1996).

73

Furthermore, Xu and Carey (1996) showed that the 10-month-old infants in their experiments were not blind to the perceptual differences between the two objects.[1] During familiarization, one group of infants was shown the two objects alternating, for example, duck, ball, duck, ball, and their looking times on these four trials were recorded. A second group of infants was shown one object repeatedly, for example, duck, duck, duck, duck, and their looking times were recorded. The results showed that the looking times declined less for the first group of infants compared to the second group. That is, it took the first group of infants longer to habituate than the second group, presumably because the first group encoded the perceptual property differences between the two objects. This was an important control condition because it replicated the results of infant categorization studies in which 3- or 4-month-old infants were shown to be able to distinguish dogs from cats (e.g., Eimas & Quinn, 1994). These results also allowed us to better characterize the failure of the 10-month-old infants: Their difficulty did not lie in not being able to encode the perceptual property differences between the objects. Instead, their failure was due to not being able to take these perceptual property differences or object kind information into account when computing how many objects were involved in an event. Wilcox and Baillargeon (1998a) replicated this developmental change using a variant of the procedure.

A third line of convergent evidence comes from Van de Walle, Carey, and Prevor (2000). In these studies, a manual search procedure was used instead of the violation-of-expectancy looking-time procedure. Ten- and 12-month-old infants were trained to reach through a spandex slit into a box to retrieve objects; the box was constructed such that the infants could not see what was inside (Fig. 3.5). Two types of trials were included: one-object and two-object trials in which individuation must be based on kind contrasts. In a one-object trial, the experimenter pulled out an object (e.g., a toy telephone), and replaced it into the box. This was repeated once. In a two-object trial, the experimenter pulled out an object (e.g., a toy telephone), and replaced it into the box. Then the experimenter pulled out a second object (e.g., a toy car), and replaced it into the box. This event was repeated several times; thus as in the Xu and Carey studies, it presented infants with multiple alternations of the objects. The box was then pushed within the infant's reach, and patterns of search were measured. After the infant had retrieved one object from the box, the experimenter surrepti-

---

[1]It is important to note that the phenomenon we see here in infants is not the same as the phenomenon of change blindness in adults. The infants in our studies were not blind to the property differences, as was shown in Xu and Carey (1996) and Xu et al. (in press). The difficulty lies in the step beyond detecting perceptual differences in which further computations of numerical distinctness must draw on the perceptual information. In contrast, "change blindness" is a failure in detecting any perceptual differences between two scenes. It does not involve the further computation of establishing numerically distinct objects.

tiously removed the second object through a back flap of the box on the two-object trial. Thus the box was empty on both the one- and two-object trials. The first object was taken away from the infant; therefore, she was expected to reach into the box again on both types of trials. The question was: How persistently would the infant search in the box on the one- and two-object trials when she found the box empty? If the infant has established a representation of two objects based on the kind contrasts (e.g., a telephone and a car), she should search more persistently on the two-object trials than the one-object trials. Twelve-month-old infants, but not 10-month-old infants, showed this pattern of results.

In addition, Krøjgaard (2000) found that even when infants were presented with objects with personal significance that were brought from home (e.g., the child's own rattle), 10-month-old infants failed at this task with the same procedure as Xu and Carey (1996). Similarly, Bonatti, Frot, Zangl, and Mehler (2002) found the same failure with simple objects (e.g., a blue box vs. a yellow cylinder).

Kind Information Overrides Strong Spatiotemporal Evidence for a Single Object

What accounts for the differences in performance between the studies of Wilcox and Baillargeon (1998a; Experiments 7 & 8) and Xu and Baker (in press) on the one hand, and the studies of Xu and Carey (1996), Wilcox and Baillargeon (1998a; Experiments 1 & 2), Krøjgaard (2000), and Bonatti, et al. (2002) on the other? The simplification of the procedure seems to allow infants to succeed a few months earlier. But why? I suggest that the more complex procedures provided stronger evidence that the event involved a single object with different sets of properties at different times. The key difference between the more complex procedures and the simpler ones was that between multiple alternations of objects and a single alternation of objects. The former, akin to an apparent motion display with a square and a circle alternating several times, induced a stronger perception of a single object. This is characteristic of the object-based attention system. That is, strong spatiotemporal evidence can override perceptual property information (see Xu, 2003; Xu & Baker, in press, for discussions).

If this is the correct interpretation, what about 12-month-old infants and adults who represented two distinct objects behind the screen even with the complex procedures? One possibility is that the emergence of the second, kind-based system of individuation operates independently of the object-based attention system, and it is this system that allowed for the inference of two objects. In other words, representations of object kinds can override strong spatiotemporal evidence for a single object. However, another possible interpretation is that by 12 months, strong spatiotemporal evidence can no longer override perceptual property information. This second interpretation is at first glance more parsimonious, because it does not posit a new construct, namely the representation of kinds. How can we empirically test these two interpretations?

In one series of experiments, information about object kind, conveyed by shape, was compared with information about perceptual properties, conveyed by color, size, and a combination of color, size, and surface pattern (Xu, Carey, & Quint, 2004). Using the paradigm of Xu and Carey (1996), 12-month-old infants were shown an event in which an object (e.g., a red ball) emerged from behind a screen and returned behind it, followed by an object (e.g., a green ball of the same size and material) that emerged from behind the screen from the other side and returned (Fig. 3.8). On the test trials, the screen was removed. Infants were shown two objects (a red ball and a green ball, the expected outcome) or just a single object (a red ball or a green ball, the unexpected outcome) and looking times were recorded. We found that 12-month-old infants did not look longer at the unexpected, one-object outcome, suggesting that they did not use the color differences to establish a representation of two distinct objects.

Two control conditions were included to ensure that our method was sensitive. To ensure that the infants encoded the color differences, we compared a group of infants who saw the two objects alternating (e.g., red ball, green ball, red ball, green ball, etc.) with another group of infants who saw the same object over and over again (e.g., red ball, red ball, red ball, etc.). We found that it took the first group longer to habituate, thus providing evidence that infants at this age were able to encode the color differences in our experiment. In addition, we tested yet another group of infants for whom spatiotemporal evidence of two objects was provided, that is, the two objects, the red ball and the green ball, were shown *simultaneously*. In this case, the infants did look longer at the unexpected, one-object outcome on the test trials.

In two other experiments, infants were shown perceptual property differences involving size alone (e.g., a small red ball and a large red ball) or a combination of size, color, and surface pattern (e.g., a small green and purple glittery tennis ball and a large glittery red ball), and they failed to establish two distinct objects based on these contrasts, just as in the color experiment. Again, control conditions found that the infants encoded the perceptual property contrasts, but they did not use them for the purpose of object individuation.

In the last experiment of this series, infants were shown two types of shape contrasts (holding color, size, and surface pattern of objects constant): a within-kind shape contrast (e.g., a sippy cup with two handles and a top vs. a regular cup with one handle) or a cross-kind shape contrast (e.g., a regular cup and a bottle). During familiarization trials, we found that the infants were roughly equally sensitive to both types of shape difference. That is, the rate of habituation was the same in the two conditions. On the test trials, the

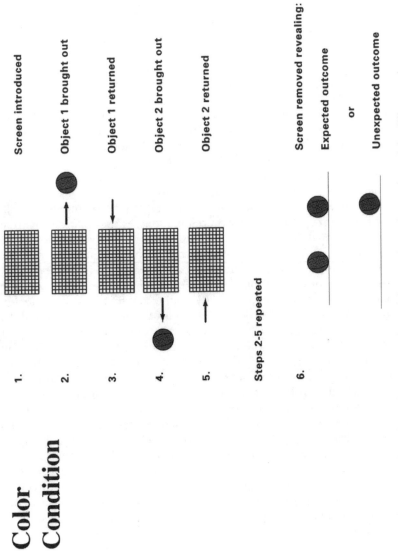

FIG. 3.8. Schematic representations of the experimental procedure of the different color condition of Xu et al. (2004).

screen was removed to reveal one or two objects. Only the infants who saw the cross-kind shape contrast looked longer at the unexpected, one-object outcome; the infants who saw the within-kind shape contrast did not look longer at the unexpected, one-object outcome. Together with the results of the first three experiments when property contrasts alone were shown, these findings provide evidence that kind representations (and not just perceptual property representations) underlie the success at 12 months.

A second series of experiments conducted by Bonatti et al. (2002) provided converging evidence for this claim. They found that when an extremely salient and important contrast was given to 10-month-old infants, that is, a doll head versus a toy dog head, they succeeded in positing two distinct objects with the more complex procedure of Xu and Carey (1996). In contrast, showing a female doll head versus a male doll head did not lead to a representation of two distinct objects. The authors concluded, and I agree, that it was the kind distinction between human and nonhuman that explained the success and failure in this case.

In summary, these studies support the claim that kind representations are distinct from perceptual property representations, as they play distinct roles in object individuation at 12 months. These studies also lend support to the conceptual distinction between object-based individuation and kind-based individuation, for this latter system emerges markedly later in development.

Other laboratories have found results consistent with the interpretation that kind representations emerge at the end of the first year. In a categorization task, Waxman and Markow (1995) and Waxman (1999) showed that by 12 to 13 months, infants are sensitive to the distinction between property and kind, as is marked by the linguistic distinction between count nouns (e.g., a dog, a spoon) and adjectives (e.g., it is red, it is square). In these studies, infants were shown a set of objects to play with, one at a time. On hearing each of the objects being described by a count noun ("Look, it's a blicket"), infants showed a preference to play with an object of a different kind on the test trial, suggesting that they had extracted kind similarity during familiarization. In contrast, on hearing each of the objects being described by an adjective ("Look, it's a blickish one"), infants showed a preference for an object that differed in some perceptual property (e.g., color or texture) on the test trial, suggesting that they had extracted a perceptual property similarity during familiarization. As count nouns typically denote kinds whereas adjectives typically denote properties, these results corroborate with the findings of Xu et al. (2004).

Characteristics of the Object-Based and Kind-Based Systems of Individuation

In terms of cognitive architecture, the studies just reviewed provide some initial evidence that two individuation systems are operative: an early developing object-based system, and a later developing kind-based system. Each system has its own characteristics with respect to the types of information used in establishing distinct objects.

The object-based system of individuation has the following characteristics:

1. Primary criteria for establishing individual objects: spatiotemporal information;
2. Secondary criteria for establishing individual objects: perceptual property information;
3. Strong spatiotemporal information can override perceptual property information.

The kind-based system of individuation has the following characteristics:

1. Primary criteria for establishing individual objects: kind information;
2. Secondary criteria for establishing individual objects: perceptual property information;
3. Perceptual property information is secondary because it is kind-relative (e.g., size contrast may indicate the presence of two chairs, one small and one large, but it does not necessarily indicate the presence of two plants, since a small plant at Time 1 can grow into a large plant at Time 2).[2]

Object Individuation Studies and Infant Categorization Studies

The findings of Bonatti et al. (2002), Van de Walle et al. (2000), Wilcox and Baillargeon (1998a; Experiments 1 & 2), and Xu and Carey (1996) seem to contradict the findings of many infant categorization studies (e.g., Cohen & Younger, 1983; Eimas & Quinn, 1994; Quinn, Eimas, & Rosenkrantz, 1993). The following paradigm was often used in infant categorization studies: 3- and 4-month-old infants were familiarized with different pairs of exemplars from a given category, for example, cat, then they were shown a pair of pictures consisting of a new exemplar from the old category (another cat) and an exemplar from a different category (e.g., a dog). The results showed that infants preferentially looked more at the picture with the exemplar from the new category, suggesting that they had extracted the category similarity during familiarization. These results were sometimes interpreted as evidence that infants represent basic-level kind concepts (e.g.,

---

[2]The third characteristic of the kind-based system has not been tested directly with infants. Studies are underway to address this issue.

Macnamara, 1986). The Xu and Carey, Wilcox and Baillargeon, and others' findings, however, suggest that perhaps these infant categorization studies show early sensitivity to cat-shape (or cat-properties) and dog-shape (or dog-properties). The infants in the categorization studies did not encode the habituation stimuli as a series of distinct individuals (e.g., a cat, another cat, a third cat that is numerically distinct from the first two) then dishabituate to an object that is numerically distinct from the cats (e.g., a dog). Instead, infants may have discriminated the individual exemplars then extracted the commonalities among the habituation stimuli as cat-shape or cat-properties and dishabituated to dog-shape or dog-properties (as was also suggested by Quinn, Eimas, and colleagues). It is only when infants represent distinct individuals, such as cats and dogs, are we warranted to conclude that they represent kind concepts. After all, sortal-kinds provide both the basis for categorization and individuation.

Thus there is no contradiction per se between the infant categorization studies and the results of Xu and Carey (1996) and others. The suggestion here (see also Xu, 1997, 1999, 2003; Xu & Carey, 1996) is that the categories revealed by many of the infant categorization studies are perceptual categories. In order to address the issue of kind representations (which are conceptual by definition), more stringent tests may be needed, namely object individuation tasks.[3]

What is the Mechanism That Underlies the Development of the Kind-Based System of Individuation?

I argued for the existence of two systems of object individuation in adults: the object-based system of individuation and the kind-based system of individuation. Furthermore, I presented evidence that the object-based system of individuation develops as early as 4 months of age in infancy, whereas the kind-based system of individuation begins to develop toward the end of the first year. As developmental psychologists, we are not only interested in documenting developmental changes, but also the mechanisms that allow changes to happen over time. Thus the key question is: How do these two systems of individuation develop? Some have argued that the object-based system may be largely hard-wired (e.g., Spelke, 1990; Spelke et al., 1992; but

---

[3]The study of object segregation, most notably the work of Needham and colleagues, is related to the inquiry in this chapter. The respective roles of spatiotemporal, perceptual property, and kind information have been discussed in detail elsewhere (e.g., Needham & Baillargeon, 2000; Xu, 2003; Xu, Carey, & Welch, 1999). The problem of object segregation is related but not identical to the problem of object individuation (i.e., tracking individual objects over time and space), although some of the same issues arise. I have suggested elsewhere that in the case of object segregation, kind information is very important when perceptual information is ambiguous.

see Johnson, 2000, for a different view). What about the second, kind-based system of individuation? Many have noted that infants begin to comprehend and produce their first words toward the end of the first year, and many of their first words are nouns for object categories. I suggest that it is not a coincidence that along with acquiring their first words, infants also begin to develop a kind-based system of individuation. Some recent studies from my laboratory provide some initial evidence that perhaps language plays a causal role in this process.

Xu (2002) presented 9-month-old infants with the same object individuation task as in Xu and Carey (1996), with the following crucial manipulation: As each object emerged from behind the screen, the infants heard a label for it in infant-directed speech on some of the trials. In the two-word condition, the infants heard two distinct labels in infant-directed speech, "Look, a duck" (when the duck was shown) and "Look, a ball" (when the ball was shown, Fig. 3.9). In the one-word condition, the infants heard a single label applied to both objects (the duck and the ball), "Look, a toy." On some of the familiarization trials, the object was left stationary on the stage and the infant's looking time was recorded. Half of these trials were labeled and half were silent. On the test trials, the screen was removed to reveal either both objects (the duck and the ball; the expected outcome) or one of the two objects (the duck or the ball; the unexpected outcome). If the infants had established a representation of two objects, they should look longer at the unexpected outcome of one object. The results showed that in the two-word condition, but not in the one-word condition, infants looked longer at the unexpected outcome. Thus upon hearing two distinct labels, even 9-month-old infants were able to use the differences in object kind to establish a representation of two distinct objects. Furthermore, this effect was not simply due to hearing some words, because the infants failed the task when a single label was provided. Fineberg (2003) has replicated this basic finding with a different set of objects and words.

One may wonder whether the presence of two distinct words heightened the infants' attention to the objects whereas the presence of a single word did not, and whether perhaps more attention led to a fuller encoding of object properties that accounted for the success in the two-word condition. I analyzed the looking time data during familiarization, comparing the silent and the labeled trials. In both the two-word and the one-word conditions, infants' looking times were longer when the objects were labeled than when not labeled. Therefore, the presence of labels did increase the infants' attention to the objects but it increased their attention *to the same extent* in the two conditions. It appeared to be the presence of two distinct labels per se that led to the earlier success on this task at 9 months.

An immediate question arises: Are the facilitation effects language specific? Would other types of auditory information help as well? In the next

Two-word Condition

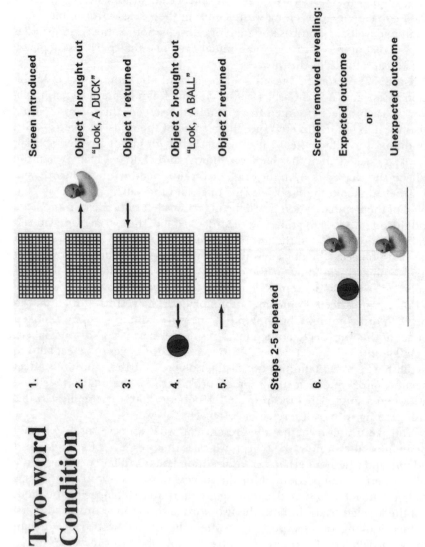

1. Screen introduced

2. Object 1 brought out
   "Look, A DUCK"

3. Object 1 returned

4. Object 2 brought out
   "Look, A BALL"

5. Object 2 returned

Steps 2-5 repeated

6. Screen removed revealing:

   Expected outcome

   or

   Unexpected outcome

FIG. 3.9. Schematic representations of the two-word condition of Xu (2002).

two experiments, instead of using two words, I used two tones or two distinct sounds (e.g., a car alarm sound or a spaceship sound produced by a gadget). As each object emerged from behind the screen, a tone/sound was played (e.g., "Look, [Tone/Sound 1] or "Look, [Tone/Sound 2]"). Under these conditions, 9-month-old infants did not look longer at the one-object, unexpected outcome on the test trials. I also replicated the positive finding of the first experiment, using another pair of familiar objects (a cup and a shoe) as well as a pair of unfamiliar objects labeled with nonsense words (e.g., "a fendle" and "a toma"). In the last experiment of this series, I used two emotional expressions to contrast with words. Emotional expressions provide a particularly good contrast with words because both kinds of expressions are intentional and are produced by the human vocal tract. However, only words are symbolic; they stand in for the objects or object categories. Each of us may have our likes and dislikes, for example, you may say "Ah" when you see broccoli on the dinner table and I may say "Eww," but we both call the stuff "broccoli." Using the same object individuation task, we presented 9-month-old infants with unfamiliar objects and provided either two distinct words ("a blicket" and "a tupa") or two emotional expressions ("Ah," signaling approval or satisfaction, and "Eww," signaling dislike or disgust). Infants looked longer at the unexpected outcome of one object on the test trials in the word condition but not in the emotional expression condition. These results suggest that infants can use distinct labels to help them succeed earlier in an object individuation task, and these facilitation effects may be language specific.

To investigate further how powerful words are in facilitating object individuation in infancy, three lines of investigation are currently underway in my laboratory. In the first series of experiments, we asked whether the presence of labels could override conflicting perceptual information (Xu, 2004a). Nine-month-old infants were asked to solve the same object individuation task in which words were pitted against perceptual information. Four conditions were included, crossing two variables: number of objects (one or two unfamiliar objects) and number of labels (one or two nonsense words). That is, infants were shown either a single object emerging from both sides of the screen or two different objects emerging alternately from behind the screen, accompanied by either a single label or two distinct labels. On the test trials, the screen was removed to reveal a single object. The One-word/one-object condition served as a baseline and the looking times of the other conditions were compared with it. The infants in the One-word/two-object condition did not look reliably longer than those infants in the One-word/one-object condition. In contrast, the infants in both the Two-word/one-object and the Two-word/two-object conditions looked reliably longer than those infants in the One-word/one-object condition. In other words, the number of words appeared to have driven the infants' expectations of how many objects were behind the screen: If two words were used, the infants expected two objects behind the screen; if one word was used, the infants expected one object behind the screen. These findings suggest that words are powerful in guiding object individuation at 9 months, so powerful that they can override perceptual information.

In a second series of experiments, I asked if language is the only mechanism that allows infants to construct object kind representations. Instead of labeling the objects as each of them emerged from behind the screen, each of the two objects made a distinct, internally generated sound, for example, one object was a bell mounted vertically on a base, so turning it makes it go "ding;" the other object was a cylinder and when turned upside down, it goes "moo." The sounds were distinct from each other, and the actions for producing the sounds were also distinct from each other. When given the same amount of information as in the two-word conditions, however, 9-month-old infants failed to establish a representation of two objects, that is, they did not look longer at the unexpected, one-object outcome when the screen was removed on the test trials (Xu, 2004b).

In a third series of experiments, we began to ask whether the act of referring, using labels, would guide the process of establishing object representations in infants. We employed the same manual search procedure with 12-month-old infants as Van de Walle et al. (2000). Instead of showing the infant objects being pulled out of the box, we simply looked into the box and referred to what's inside, "Look, a fep!" In the two-word trials, two different labels were used; in the one-word trials, the same label was used twice. Then the box was presented to the infant and search behavior was measured. Infants spontaneously reached into the box and they always retrieved one object. Then the critical part of the experiment began. The box was empty and it sat within reach of the infant. The question was whether subsequent search behavior was correlated with the number of labels heard during the demonstration period. An adult would reach in a second time to look for another object if they had heard two distinct labels, but not if they had only heard a single label. Infants behaved similarly: They reached in more on the two-word trials and when they found the box empty, they searched more persistently on the two-word trials than on the one-word trials. Even without having seen any of the objects, the acts of referring led the infant to posit objects inside the box, and the number of labels appears to tell the infant the number of distinct objects to be expected inside the box.

These ongoing studies provide preliminary evidence that language in the form of labeling is a powerful tool in shaping infants' representations of objects and language may be a particularly efficient way in solving the problem of object individuation for young infants.

What Is the Role of Labeling?
Words as "Essence Placeholders"

What is the mechanism by which labeling could impact on infants' object representations? I suggest that words for object categories are "essence placeholders" (Gelman, 2003; Medin & Ortony, 1989). Hence the term "essence sortals" (see Fig. 3.1). By virtue of being called "a dog," the infant learns that this is a kind, and the word "dog" becomes the placeholder for a distinct dog-essence. If an object, seen on a different occasion, is called "a cup," the infants assume that the word refers to a different kind, and it will have a different set of properties from the dogs that are referred to by the word "dog." Although infants cannot learn the concept *dog* from linguistic input alone, the "dubbing event" may allow the infant to posit a placeholder in his or her conceptual system.

Two other lines of research provide further support for this idea that words are "essence placeholders." In a series of categorization studies, Balaban and Waxman (1997) showed that labeling can facilitate categorization in infants as young as 9 months. In their studies, the infants were familiarized with a set of pictures of a given category, say, rabbits. One group of infants heard a word when shown the picture, that is, "a rabbit," on some trials. For a second group of infants, a tone accompanied the presentation of the picture on some trials. The results showed that although both words and tones heightened the infants' attention to the objects, it was only in the label condition that the infants categorized the objects. That is, they preferentially looked at an exemplar from a new category (e.g., a pig) compared to an exemplar from the old category (e.g., a new rabbit). These results suggest that in the presence of a label, infants group together the exemplars into a single category more readily than in the absence of a label.

In a series of experiments with 16- to 21-month-old infants, Welder and Graham (2001) found that labeling guides infants' inductive inference, and it sometimes overrides perceptual similarity. In their studies, the experimenter modeled a non-obvious property of an unfamiliar target object, e.g., an object making a rattling sound when shaken, and the infant was given other test objects that were perceptually similar or dissimilar to the target object. In addition, one group of infants heard a label applied to both the target object and the test objects, whereas a second group did not hear a label. The question of interest was whether infants would predict that the test objects would also possess the nonobvious property by reproducing the action, for example, they should shake the object if they expected it to rattle. The results showed that labeling had a powerful effect on inductive inference, often overriding perceptual similarity.

These results suggest that even early in language development, labeling may exert influence on several aspects of cognition. Infants may expect that words for objects map onto distinct kinds in their environment; words are "essence placeholders." Given this expectation, if each of several objects is labeled as "a rabbit," it provides evidence to the infant that they belong to the same kind. Similarly, the very fact that one object is called "a duck" and one object seen on a different occasion is called "a ball" is sufficient evidence for infants to posit two distinct kinds or essences. According to one of the basic tenets of psychological essentialism (Gelman, 2003; Medin & Ortony, 1991), essences determine the surface features and properties of objects. Three consequences follow. First, if two objects share a label, they should belong to the same kind and their perceptual property similarities should be analyzed, as in the categorization task. Second, if two kinds of objects are indeed behind an occluder because two distinct labels are heard, there must be two distinct tokens of objects, as in the object individuation task. Third, if two objects share a label, they should have the same non-obvious properties, as in the inductive inference task. The assumption that words are essence placeholders may be a mechanism by which infants first establish what *kinds of things* are in their environment.

CONCLUSION

I focused on a less studied aspect of kind representations in this chapter, namely the process of individuation. I argued that not all categories are created equal, some categories are kinds, some kinds are sortal-kinds, and some sortal-kinds are essence sortals. I have also presented evidence that there is an early developing object-based system of individuation, and a relatively late developing kind-based system of individuation. The development of kind-based system is perhaps driven by language learning. My hope is that this line of inquiry will complement the research on infant categorization, and we will be able to have a more complete theory of kind representations that accounts for both categorization and individuation. In this last section, I briefly consider the implications of the current research in terms of broader questions in cognitive development and language acquisition.

The conceptual claim that is the foundation of this research is the distinction between kind and property. The basic idea is that representations of kinds define our ontology, and generally speaking, kinds are lexicalized as nouns in natural language. Some of these kinds are sortal-kinds, which provide criteria for individuation and identity and which are lexicalized as count nouns (in languages that make the count/mass distinction). Other kinds are substance-kinds, which are lexicalized as mass nouns, and their role in individuation and identity is a matter of dispute (see, e.g., Hirsch, 1982). Whether these kinds are in the head or in the world is not critical; suffice to say that I suspect there is a reasonable correspondence between our representations and what's out there in the world (loosely based on evolutionary arguments). Properties, on the other hand, are a different species. Properties are properties of kinds; they are predicates that correspond to lexical categories such as adjectives and verbs. The studies reviewed previously are concerned with properties that can be expressed by adjectival phrases.

A second major claim in this work is a claim about cognitive architecture: an object-based system of individuation and a second, kind-based system of individuation. Each system has its own developmental course and its own characteristics. Each system uses several sources of information and weighs them differently in its operation. The studies reviewed in this chapter focus on the interplay between spatiotemporal information, perceptual property information, and kind information.

The third major claim has to do with the role of language in conceptual development. I am inclined to endow the human infant with certain expectations about words at the beginning of language acquisition such that in a "dubbing event" (e.g., "That's a dog!"), a word (in this case, "dog") serves as a pointer to a particular sortal-kind in the environment. Via such dubbing events, the infant begins to represent some sortal-kinds, that is, essence sortals.

The overall view of development I subscribe to here is one that has both continuity and discontinuity components. On the one hand, I am sympathetic to the view that human infants are born with a mechanism—the object-based attention system—that carves up the world into distinct units. On the other hand, I also suggest that infants' worldview undergoes fundamental changes: They begin with a world populated with objects and substances. By the end of the first year of life, they begin to conceptualize a world populated with sortal-kinds (and perhaps substance-kinds as well). In this new world, objects are thought of not as "qua object" but rather "qua dog" or "qua table." This developmental story makes good sense in terms of learnability, I suggest, because it starts the child on solid ground with the concept of an object (à la Spelke, 1990) and it allows the child to work with these individuated objects, and, with the help of language, ultimately develop a new ontology of sortal-kinds.

ACKNOWLEDGMENTS

I wish to thank Allison Baker, Paul Bloom, Susan Carey, Frank Keil, Ellen Markman, James Putsjevsky, Cristina Sorrentino, Elizabeth Spelke, and Joshua Tenenbaum for many helpful discussions, and David Rakison for comments on an earlier draft of the paper. This research was supported by NSF grant (SBR-9910729).

REFERENCES

Aguiar, A., & Baillargeon, R. (1999). 2.5-month-old infants' reasoning about when objects should and should not be occluded. *Cognitive Psychology, 39,* 116–157.

Baillargeon, R. (1995). A model of physical reasoning in infancy. In C. Rovee-Collier & L. P. Lipsitt (Eds.), *Advances in infancy research* (Vol. 9, pp. 305–371). Norwood, NJ: Ablex.

Baillargeon, R., & Graber, M. (1987). Where's the rabbit? 5.5-month-old infants' representation of the height of a hidden object. *Cognitive Development, 2,* 375–392.

Baillargeon, R., Spelke, E. S., & Wasserman, S. (1985). Object permanence in 5-month-old infants. *Cognition, 20,* 191–208.

Balaban, M., & Waxman, S. (1997). Words may facilitate categorization in 9-month-old infants. *Journal of Experimental Child Psychology, 64,* 3–26.

Bonatti, L., Frot, E., Zangl, R., & Mehler, J. (2002). The human first hypothesis: Identification of conspecifics and individuation of objects in the young infant. *Cognitive Psychology, 44*(4), 388–426.

Burke, L. (1952). On the tunnel effect. *Quarterly Journal of Experimental Psychology, 4,* 121–138.

Cohen, L. B., & Younger, B. A. (1983). Perceptual categorization in the infant. In E. K. Scholnick (Ed.), *New trends in conceptual representation* (pp. 197–220). Hillsdale, NJ: Lawrence Erlbaum Associates.

Eimas, P., & Quinn, P. (1994). Studies on the formation of perceptually based basic-level categories in young infants. *Child Development, 65,* 903–917.

Fineberg, I. A. (2003). *Phonological detail of word representations during the earliest stages of word learning.* Unpublished doctoral dissertation, New School University, New York.

Gelman, S. A. (2003). *The essential child: Origins of essentialism in everyday thought.* London: Oxford University Press.

Hirsch, E. (1982). *The concept of identity.* New York: Oxford University Press.

Johnson, S. P. (2000). The development of visual surface perception: Insights into the ontogeny of knowledge. In C. Rovee-Collier, L. P. Lipsitt, & H. Hayne (Eds.), *Progress in infancy research* (Vol. 1, pp. 113–154). Mahwah, NJ: Lawrence Erlbaum Associates.

Krøjgaard, P. (2000). Object individuation in 10-month-old infants: Do significant objects make a difference? *Cognitive Development, 15,* 169–184.

LeCompte, G. K., & Gratch, G. (1972). Violation of a rule as a method of diagnosing infants' levels of object concept. *Child Development, 43,* 385–396.

Macnamara, J. (1986). *A border dispute: The place of logic in psychology.* Cambridge, MA: MIT Press.

Markman, E. (1989). *Categorization and naming in children.* Cambridge, MA: MIT Press.

Medin, D., & Ortony, A. (1989). Psychological essentialism. In S. Vosniadou & A. Ortony (Eds.), *Similarity and analogical reasoning* (pp. 179–195). New York: Cambridge University Press.

Millikan, R. (1998). A common structure for concepts of individuals, stuffs, and basic kinds: More mama, more milk and more mouse. *Behavioral and Brain Sciences, 22*(1), 55–65.

Moore, M. K., Borton, R., & Darby, B. L. (1978). Visual tracking in young infants: Evidence for object identity or object permanence? *Journal of Experimental Child Psychology, 25,* 183–198.

Needham, A., & Baillargeon, R. (2000). Infants' use of featural and experiential information in segregating and individuating objects: A reply to Xu, Carey, & Welch (1999). *Cognition, 74,* 255–284.

Quinn, P., Eimas, P., & Rosenkrantz, S. L. (1993). Evidence for representations of perceptually similar natural categories by three- and four-month-old infants. *Perception, 22,* 463–475.

Simon, T., Hespos, S., & Rochat, P. (1995). Do infants understand simple arithmetic? A replication of Wynn (1992). *Cognitive Development, 10,* 253–269.

Spelke, E. S. (1990). Principles of object perception. *Cognitive Science, 14,* 29–56.

Spelke, E. S., Brelinger, K., Macomber, J., & Jacobson, K. (1992). Origins of knowledge. *Psychological Review, 99,* 605–632.

Spelke, E. S., & Kestenbaum, R. (1986). *Les origines du concept d'object* [The origins of the concept of object]. *Psychologie Francaise, 31,* 67–72.

Spelke, E. S., Kestenbaum, R., Simons, D. J., & Wein, D. (1995). Spatio-temporal continuity, smoothness of motion and object identity in infancy. *British Journal of Developmental Psychology, 13,* 113–142.

Tinkelpaugh, O. L. (1928). An experimental study of representative factors in monkeys. *Journal of Comparative Psychology, 8*(3), 197–236.

Uller, C., Leslie, A., & Carey, S. (2000). *Reaching for objects in a box: Further evidence for the 10- to 12-month shift in the bases of object individuation.* Poster session presented at the 12th biennial meeting of the International Conference on Infant Studies, Brighton, England.

Van de Walle, G. A., Carey, S., &. Prevor, M. (2000). Bases for object individuation in infancy: Evidence from manual search. *Journal of Cognition and Development, 1,* 249–280.

Waxman, S. R. (1999). Specifying the scope of 13-month-olds' expectations for novel words. *Cognition, 70,* B35–B50.

Waxman, S. R., & Markow, D. R. (1995). Words as invitations to form categories: Evidence from 12- to 13-month-old infants. *Cognitive Psychology, 29,* 257–302.

Welder, A. N., & Graham, S. A. (2001). The influence of shape similarity and shared labels on infants' inductive inferences about nonobvious object properties. *Child Development, 72,* 1653–1673.

Wilcox, T., & Baillargeon, R. (1998a). Object individuation in infancy: The use of featural information in reasoning about occlusion events. *Cognitive Psychology, 37,* 97–155.

Wilcox, T., & Baillargeon, R. (1998b). Object individuation in young infants: Further evidence with an event-monitoring paradigm. *Developmental Science, 1,* 127–142.

Wynn, K. (1992). Addition and subtraction by human infants. *Nature, 358,* 749–750.

Xu, F. (1997). From Lot's wife to a pillar of salt: Evidence that physical object is a sortal concept. *Mind and Language, 12,* 365–392.

Xu, F. (1999). Object individuation and object identity in infancy: The role of spatiotemporal information, object property information, and language. *Acta Psychologica, 102,* 113–136.

Xu, F. (2002). The role of language in acquiring kind concepts in infancy. *Cognition, 85,* 223–250.

Xu, F. (2003). The development of object individuation in infancy. In H. Hayne & J. Fagen (Eds.), *Progress in infancy research* (Vol. 3, pp. 159–192). Mahwah, NJ: Lawrence Erlbaum Associates.

Xu, F. (2004a). *The effects of labeling on object individuation in 9-month-old infants.* Manuscript under review.

Xu, F. (2004b). *Is language the only mechanism that helps construct object kind concepts in infancy?* Manuscript in preparation.

Xu, F., & Baker, A. (in press). Object individuation in 10-month-old infants using a simplified manual search method. *Journal of Cognition and Development.*

Xu, F., & Carey, S. (1996). Infants' metaphysics: The case of numerical identity. *Cognitive Psychology, 30,* 111–153.

Xu, F., Carey, S., & Quint, N. (2004). The emergence of kind-based object individuation in infancy. *Cognitive Psychology, 49,* 155–190.

Xu, F., Carey, S., & Welch, J. (1999). Infants' ability to use object kind information for object individuation. *Cognition, 70,* 137–166.

Xu, F., Cote, M., & Baker, A. (in press). Labeling guides object individuation in 12-month-old infants. *Psychological Science.*

Chapter 4

Bubbles: A User's Guide

Frédéric Gosselin
Université de Montréal

Philippe G. Schyns
University of Glasgow

INTRODUCTION

The herring gull chick begs for food by pecking at its mother's beak. In a seminal experiment, Nobel-prizewinning ethologist Nikko Tinbergen and co-worker (Tinbergen & Perdeck, 1950) sought to discover the stimulus that maximized this response. This enterprise led to the remarkable discovery of the *super-stimulus*: an artificial stimulus that evokes a stronger response than the original, natural stimulus. For example, a white stick with three red annuli moving up and down produces a stronger pecking response than the head of the herring gull's mother.

At an abstract level, the search for the super-stimulus can be framed as a generic search problem. Given a measurable dependent variable (e.g., the pecking rate response), the problem is to find the specific parameters of the independent variable(s) (e.g., the characteristics of the mother's head) that optimize the dependent variable. Obviously, this approach is not limited to ethology. An approach similar in spirit is that of Nobel prize winners Hubel and Wiesel who searched for the stimulus that optimizes the response of cells in the primary visual cortex (see Hubel, 1988, for a review). Much to their surprise, they discovered that small spots of light, which are so effective in the retina and Lateral Geniculate Nucleus (LGN) were much less effective in visual cortex. Instead, simple cells in primary visual cortex responded optimally to inputs with linear properties, such as a line with a specific width and orientation in the plane. At the next level of cortical integration, optimal inputs become more complicated. For example, complex cells tend to respond better to a stimulus with a critical orientation, but also with a characteristic speed and direction, adding to the width and orientation search space a third dimension. Further up the integration ladder, cells in temporal cortex respond to complex object properties (Kobatabe & Tanaka, 1994) such as orientation in depth (Perrett, Mistlin, & Chitty, 1987), object similarities (Vogels, 1999), and the information responsible for visual object categorization (Sigala & Logothetis, 2002; Vogels, 1999).

However, even though IT cells are just "a few synaptic connections away" from primary visual cortex, their optimal stimuli are hidden in a much more complex search space: the physical world. With its many faces, objects, and scenes, this space does not comprise just the few degrees of freedom required to represent the little spots of light positioned within the visual field, or the moving orientated bars. Instead, IT cells respond to structured information that varies in 2D retinal position, 2D rotation in the image plane, 3D rotation in depth, illumination, articulation, and so forth. Among these multiple degrees of freedom, different subspaces of parameters represent the effective stimuli of IT cells. The challenge is to understand what these subspaces are.

And it is still one of the greatest methodological challenges in Cognitive Science: When dealing with complex visual stimuli, how can a brain event (e.g., an ERP response, or an fMRI measurement) or a human behavior (e.g., a categorization response) be attributed to a specific object category (e.g., a beach scene), a specific object (e.g., a deck chair), a specific feature (e.g., the texture of the deck chair), or a specific function (e.g., a beach, deck chair, or texture detector)? In the absence of a principled method, the specificity of the response (e.g., to the beach) is determined by contrast with responses from carefully chosen contrast categories (e.g., roads, cities, mountains, fields, and so forth), and informal hypotheses tested. Unfortunately, a dense correlative structure exists in the low-level visual properties of category members (e.g., luminance energy, main directions of orientation, spatial frequency composition, and so forth), only a small subset of which can be controlled with a finite number of carefully chosen contrast categories. Consequently, the specificity of the brain or behavioral response might be due to incidental input statistics and not to the category per se (Schyns, Jentzsch, Johnson, Schweinberger, & Gosselin, 2003).

In this chapter, we present *Bubbles* (Gosselin & Schyns, 2001), a method designed to solve the problem of finding the effective stimulus in the complex search spaces that are characteristic of visual categorization. From the outset, it is important to stress that the method can be scaled down and applied to simpler search spaces. However, the originality of Bubbles is that it can handle search spaces that have so far proven to be elusive (e.g., the information responsible for face recognition, Gosselin & Schyns, 2001,

Schyns, Bonnar, & Gosselin, 2002; scene recognition, Nielsen, Rainer, Brucklacher, & Logothetis, 2002; or the perception of complex figures, Bonnar, Gosselin, & Schyns, 2002). The chapter is organized as a user's guide. First, we introduce a typical research problem never before addressed with Bubbles: the Face Inversion Effect. We then discuss the six main decisions that must be made to set up a Bubbles experiment, discussing critical issues with examples from our own research.

The Problem: The Face Inversion Effect

In a seminal article, Yin (1969) reported that the recognition of face pictures was disproportionately affected by a 180 deg rotation in the image plane from the normal, upright viewing condition. This phenomenon is now commonly called the Face Inversion Effect (FIE). Since then, the FIE has been replicated in multiple experimental situations (e.g., Carey, Diamond, & Woods, 1980; Philips & Rawles, 1979; Scapinello & Yarmey, 1970; Carey & Diamond, 1977; Diamond & Carey, 1986; Freire, Lee, & Symons, 2000; Leder & Bruce, 2000; Tanaka & Farah, 1993; Valentine & Bruce, 1986; Yarmey, 1971).

There is now agreement among most face recognition researchers that the FIE does not arise from long-term memory interferences, but instead from a greater difficulty to perceptually encode inverted face information (e.g., Farah, Wilson, Drain, & Tanaka, 1998; Moscovitch, Behrmann, & Winocur, 1997; Phelps & Roberts, 1994; Searcy & Bartlett, 1996; Freire et al., 2000). Therefore, recent studies have examined more closely the encoding differences that occur when experiencing an upright or an inverted face. However, the specification of these differences has so far remained largely unknown (Rossion & Gauthier, 2002).

To address the FIE with Bubbles, we need to make six basic decisions: (a) what is the stimulus set, (b) in which space will stimuli be generated, (c) what is the "sample," (d) what is the observer's task, (e) what are the observer's possible responses, and (f) is the analysis per observer, or per group of observers. In resolving all of these, we set up a search space and vary the parameters of the independent variables (upright and inverted face information) that determine the measurable dependent variable (the observer's response). The Bubbles solution should specify the difference between the information subspaces driving the processing of upright and inverted faces.

Stimulus Set?

In a Bubbles experiment, the stimulus set is crucial because it critically bounds what will be tested. Here, we used a total of 10 greyscale faces (5 males, 5 females), each one of which displayed 3 different expressions (neutral, angry, and happy). Hairstyle was normalized, and so were global orientation and the location of the light source. Stimuli could be upright or inverted, but when inverted, we flipped the image so as to keep the light source to the right of the face.

Generally speaking, the larger the stimulus set, the better the Bubbles solution should be. A large stimulus set will tend to prevent observers from adopting strategies atypical of natural processing. In the FIE example, the stimulus set restricts the search space for differences in upright and inverted face encodings to a few males and females with a limited set of expressions in highly restricted conditions of presentation (only one light source, three poses, and static images). Although this also applies in most face recognition experiments, it is important to point out that the Bubbles solution will be tied to these limitations. In our research we have already used faces in other experiments with human participants (Gosselin & Schyns, 2001; Schyns, Bonnar, & Gosselin, 2002; Schyns, Jentzsch, Schweinberger, Johnson, & Gosselin, 2003), but also in animals experiments (Gibson, Gosselin, Wasserman, & Schyns, 2002). Other stimuli used ranged from 3D models of Gouraud shaded animals (Schyns & Gosselin, 2002) to a painting of Dali (Bonnar, Gosselin, & Schyns, 2002). Other researchers have also applied Bubbles to natural scenes (Nielsen, Rainer, Brucklacher, & Logothetis, 2002). Although these applications only involved visual stimuli, the technique should straightforwardly generalize to auditory and tactile stimulus sets, or to cross-modal combinations of these.

Stimulus Generation Space?

The choice of a proper stimulus generation space is one of the most important decisions when setting up a Bubbles experiment. Remember that we are searching for the parameters of the independent variables (upright and inverted face information) that determine the FIE. Each independent variable considered constitutes one independent dimension whose parametric values will be searched. To illustrate, our face stimuli are 2D pictures. The axes of the 2D plane could be searched to find the (x, y) coordinates of face information that determine upright versus inverted performance. The stimulus generation space would then be two-dimensional, and the solution would be a subset of the plane.

However, there is evidence that early vision does analyze the input at multiple spatial scales (or spatial frequencies, see de Valois & de Valois, 1990, for a review), and that mechanisms of face recognition rely on this input (see Morrison & Schyns, 2001, for a review). Thus, a better space to search for the determinants of FIE could include a third dimension of spatial scales. Specifically, we segmented the third dimension into five independent bands of fine to coarse spatial frequencies of one octave each, with cutoffs at 90, 45, 22.5, 11.25, 5.62, and 2.81 cycles per face. The solution subspace becomes an interaction between the two dimensions of face feature location, and the third dimension of spatial scale.

In setting up this search space, we are making a number of assumptions that are worth pointing out. We are assuming that the face pictures are normalized for the position of their main features (i.e., the x, y locations of the eyes, nose, mouth, chin, cheeks, and forehead are roughly similar across face pictures). This is necessary because the selected search space is not invariant to translation in the image plane. Similarly, we are assuming that the faces in the pictures will have the same size, because the search space is not invariant to scale changes. Note that these constraints on the search space are not constraints on the technique itself. It is possible to set up translation invariant search spaces (see Schyns & Gosselin, 2002, for a Fourier implementation), and it is also possible to set up scale invariant search spaces. However, the experimental question (the nature of face features that determine FIE) suggested a search space where the location of face features would be known.

In our research, we have used a variety of stimulus generation spaces, ranging from the 2D image plane (Gibson, Gosselin, Wasserman, & Schyns, 2002; Gosselin & Schyns, 2001; O'Donnell, Gosselin, & Schyns, 2002; Schyns, Jentzsch, Schweinberger, Johnson, & Gosselin, 2003), the 3D space used here (2D image × spatial scales, Bonnar, Gosselin, & Schyns, 2002; Gosselin & Schyns, 2001; Schyns, Bonnar, & Gosselin, 2002), a translation invariant 1D scale space (Schyns & Gosselin, 2002), and a 3D space comprising the standard 2D image plane and time (Vinette, Gosselin, & Schyns, 2004).

From this discussion, it should be clear that the number of dimensions making up the stimulus generation space is critical to the number of trials required to reach a stable Bubbles solution. Generally speaking, to visit each point of a search space, there is a combinatorial explosion of steps with the increasing number of dimensions. Note, however, that if the dimensions of the search can be collapsed for the analyses, then the search space itself can be large. For example, one could decide that spatial scales are, after all, not that important for FIE, collapse the data along this dimension, and analyze feature use in the 2D image plane.

The Samples?

At this stage, two important decisions have been made and the search can almost begin. In the search, information is sampled from the set-up space, and the next decision to make concerns the unit of sampling. This unit depends on a number of factors, including the stimuli, the nature of the search space, and the task to be performed.

To bring the observer away from ceiling and chance performance, relevant information must sometimes be sampled, and sometimes not be sampled. The parameters of the sampling unit must be adjusted to ensure this modulation of performance. A first parameter is the geometry of the sampling unit. An information sample is effectively a cut in the search space. A sampling unit with different "punch-hole" geometries will change the information sampled and displayed to the observer. Our research has mostly used a Gaussian-shaped geometries, either in 2D (Gibson, Gosselin, Wasserman, & Schyns, 2002; Gosselin & Schyns, 2001; Nielsen et al., 2002; O'Donnell, Gosselin, & Schyns, 2002; Schyns, Jentzsch, Schweinberger, Johnson, & Gosselin, 2003) or in 3D (Bonnar, Gosselin, & Schyns, 2002; Gosselin & Schyns, 2001; Schyns, Bonnar, & Gosselin, 2002). This choice was motivated by two main factors: Gaussian functions produce a *smooth* cut (producing a sample that does not introduce hard-edge artifacts), without orientation biases of the sampled information (i.e., a Gaussian is *circularly symmetric*).

A different search space could require geometries other than Gaussian. For example, if orientation information was searched as an independent dimension, the sampling unit would need to introduce orientation biases. For example, a Gabor function could be designed to sample information at several orientations (e.g., 0, 45, 90, and 135 deg). More abstract geometries can also be used, when the search space is itself abstract. For example, in Schyns and Gosselin (2002), the bubble was a dot sampling Fourier coefficients in a Fourier Transform search space.

Another important parameter of the sampling unit is its size. The size is largely determined by considering the scale of the stimulus and the expected size of the relevant information for the task at hand. To illustrate, we know that the eyes, the mouth, and the nose are the most useful features to make face decisions. It would therefore be advisable that the size of the sampling unit in a FIE task be similar to the size of the important features. A very small sampling unit (e.g., the pixel of an image) provides a precise sample of the search space, but many trials are required to converge on a solution of the search. Clearly, the size of the sampling unit must be chosen with a priori considerations of the expected scale of the solution.

For the reasons just discussed, the bubble of our FIE example has a Gaussian geometry. The scale of the bubble was chosen to sample three cycles per face (i.e., STDs of .13, .27, .54, 1.08, and 2.15 deg of visual angle, from fine to coarse scales, see Fig. 4.1). On any given trial, information is sampled from the search space by a number of bubbles. The sampling is typically performed randomly and is thus nonbiased. Figure 4.1 a–e illustrates the sampling procedure. In Fig. 4.1b, the face shown in Fig. 4.1a is decomposed into five independent scales. In Fig. 4.1c bubbles with a Gaussian geometry sample the information space at random locations (overlap is permitted). In Fig. 4.1d the bubbles in Fig. 4.1c are applied to the appropri-

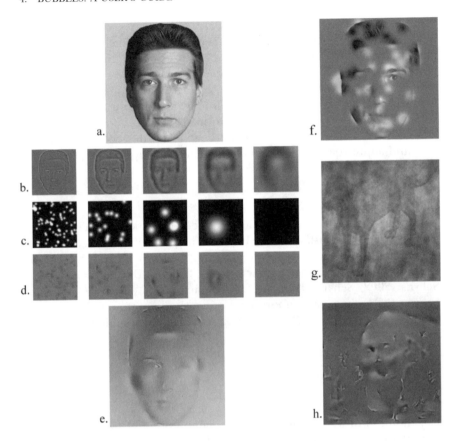

FIG. 4.1. Pictures in (b) decompose (a) in five scales; (c) illustrate the "bubbles" applied to each scale; (d) are the revealed information of (b) by the bubbles of (c). Note that on this particular trial there is no revealed information at the fifth scale. By integrating the pictures in (d) we obtain (e), a sample stimulus (Gosselin & Schyns, 2001; Schyns, Bonnar, & Gosselin, 2002). Picture (f) is (a) sampled in the image plane (Gosselin & Schyns, 2001; Gibson, Gosselin, Wasserman, & Schyns, 2002; Jentzsch et al., 2002; O'Donnell, Schyns, & Gosselin, 2002). Picture (g) is a 3D shape model of a dog sampled in phase space (Schyns & Gosselin, 2002). Finally, picture (h) is the ambiguous area of a Dali painting sampled in the same generation space as (e) (Bonnar, Gosselin, & Schyns, 2002).

ate scales in Fig. 4.1b. Finally, in Fig. 4.1e the pictures of Fig. 4.1d are added together to produce a subsample of the face information in Fig. 4.1a.

One important point about bubbles: their number. It can either be adjusted on-line to maintain performance at a given level (e.g., Gosselin & Schyns, 2001; Schyns, Bonnar, & Gosselin, 2002), or be kept constant throughout the experiment (i.e., Gibson, Gosselin, Wasserman, & Schyns,

2002; Jentzsch, Gosselin, Schweinberger, & Schyns, 2003). The technique will work so long as performance is between floor and ceiling. The advantage of adjusting bubble numbers to equate performance is that Bubbles solutions are comparable. In the FIE example, we maintained categorization of sampled face information at about 75% correct by adjusting the number of bubbles using a gradient descent algorithm on a trial per trial basis. The initial bubble number resulted from an informed guess (i.e., between 50 and 60 bubbles for a first session), and we let the gradient descent algorithm take over and adjust the bubble number to maintain performance at 75%.

The Task?

At this stage, the sampling procedure has been fully specified. The final decision is that of the task. We have explored a variety of face categorizations in humans and animals (Gibson, Gosselin, Wasserman, & Schyns, 2002; Gosselin & Schyns, 2001; Jentzsch et al., 2003; O'Donnell, Gosselin, & Schyns, 2002; Schyns, Bonnar, & Gosselin, 2002; Vinette, Gosselin, & Schyns, 2004), basic and subordinate categorizations of models of animals (Schyns & Gosselin, 2002), and discriminations of an ambiguous painting by Dali (Bonnar, Gosselin, & Schyns, 2002). In the FIE example, observers will identify the faces in the upright and inverted conditions.

Observers?

Depending on the objectives of the research, different types of observers can interact with the Bubbles algorithm. For example, we have applied the technique to groups of human observers (Bonnar, Gosselin, & Schyns, 2002; Gosselin & Schyns, 2001; Schyns, Bonnar, & Gosselin, 2002) just like here, individual observers to track down effects of expertise acquisition (Jentzsch et al., 2003; O'Donnell, Gosselin, & Schyns, 2002; Vinette, Gosselin, & Schyns, 2004), infants to tackle issues in development (Humphreys, Gosselin, Schyns, Kaufman, & Johnson, 2002), pigeons (Gibson, Gosselin, Wasserman, & Schyns, 2002), and ideal observers, which are models providing a benchmark of the information available in a task (Gosselin & Schyns, 2001). We have several ongoing research projects involving brain-damaged patients.

Response?

The response is an interesting parameter of a Bubbles experiment because the technique is in principle sensitive to any measurable dependent variable. Here, observers pressed labeled keys corresponding to the names of

10 individuals. We have used such key-press responses to derive correct and incorrect responses (Bonnar, Gosselin, & Schyns, 2002; Gibson et al., 2002; Gosselin & Schyns, 2001; O'Donnell, Gosselin, & Schyns, 2002; Schyns, Bonnar, & Gosselin, 2002; Vinette, Gosselin, & Schyns, 2004) and response latencies (Schyns, Bonnar, & Gosselin, 2002). In addition, we also used preferential looking (Humphreys et al., 2002) and N170 amplitudes (Schyns, Bonnar, & Gosselin, 2002). Other responses could be the firing rate of single cells, fMRI, galvanic skin response, plethysmograph, eye movements, and so forth. To the extent that Bubbles is essentially an empirical tool, it is useful to record as many different responses as possible (e.g., correct/incorrect, latencies, and N170 in a face-recognition experiment). It is difficult to predict before the experiment how responses will correlate with the parameters of the search space.

ANALYSES

Now that the search has been run, the data are collected, and the analyses can be performed. Remember that the goal of the search is to isolate a subspace of information that determines the measured response(s). Technically, a multiple linear regression on the samples (explanatory variable) and the responses (predictive variable) provides this solution. This reduces to summing all the bubble masks in different response bins, where the number of responses is a function of the nature of the response itself.[1] For example, two bins are sufficient to tease apart correct and incorrect responses, but more bins are necessary to cover the range of electric activity (or cell firing rate) of a brain response. To reveal the most important information, we can perform a linear operation on the bins (e.g., subtracting the wrong response from the correct response bin; divide the correct response bin by the sum of the correct and incorrect response bins). The result of this operation is usually transformed into Z-scores, and thresholded (e.g., at 1.65, $p < .05$, or 2.33, $p < .01$). The outcome of this analysis is the product of Bubbles, revealing the effective subspace of input information. In the visual domain, this outcome is a filtering function that can be applied on the original stimulus to reveal the information that drives the task.

In the FIE example, three observers learned to criterion (perfect identification of all faces twice in a row) the name attached to each of the 10 faces from printed pictures with corresponding name at the bottom. During the experiment, observers had to determine the identity of each sparse face (from 10 possibilities). The experiment comprised 6 sessions of 780 trials

---

[1]However, it is also useful to keep all the sampled information of each trial to be able to do more detailed analysis such as the conjunctive use of information (see Schyns, Bonnar, & Gosselin, 2002).

(i.e., 13 presentations of the 30 faces upright and inverted), but we only used the data of the last five sessions (for a total of 3,900 trials per subject), when observers were really familiar with the faces and experimental procedure. In a trial, one sparse face computed as described earlier appeared on the screen either upright or inverted. To respond, observers pressed labeled computer keyboard keys (self-paced, and with correct vs. incorrect feedback). A chin-rest maintained subjects at a 100 cm constant viewing distance. Stimuli subtended 5.72 × 5.72 deg of visual angle on the screen.

On average, observers required 46 and 126 bubbles to reach the 75% performance criterion in upright and inverted conditions, respectively. The number of bubbles (between 197 and 30 bubbles, depending on observers and condition) and average performance (between 86% and 75%) did vary across the six experimental sessions, to stabilize in the last session. In this session, observers in upright and inverted respectively required an average of 30 and 65 bubbles for performance levels 75% and 76%. The comparatively higher number of bubbles in the inverted condition suggests a higher requirement of visual information, suggesting a more difficult inverted condition, diagnosing a FIE.

We can now turn to a comparison of the required information in each condition to attain the same level of performance. To this end, we first perform a linear multiple regression. Practically, for each spatial scale, we computed two independent sums: We added together all the information samples leading to correct responses in one sum, and all the information samples leading to incorrect responses in another sum. At each spatial scale, we then subtracted these two sums to construct an image that discriminates the information leading to correct and incorrect responses (see the first row of Fig. 4.2 for the discrimination images at each scale). If all regions of the search space were equally effective at determining the response, the image would be a uniform gray. To pull out the most effective region, we computed Z-scores for each discrimination image, and indicated in red the regions that are 1.65 STD away from their mean (corresponding to a $p < .05$). These regions circumscribe the subspace driving upright and inverted face classification responses. If we project the original face in Fig. 4.1a into this diagnostic subspace, we obtain the effective stimuli displayed at the extreme right of the rows in Fig. 4.2. Technically, each effective stimulus is obtained by multiplying the face information at each scale in Fig. 4.1b with the corresponding thresholded coefficients in the rows of Fig. 4.2.

For upright faces, the eyes are the most important local features. The only scales with diagnostic information are the second and the third. This is consistent with the results of Gosselin and Schyns (2001) and Schyns, Bonnar, and Gosselin (2002). However, these experiments did not include an inverted condition. Observers saw two, not three, expressions, and they were less familiar with the faces (i.e., 1,000 rather than 3,900 trials).

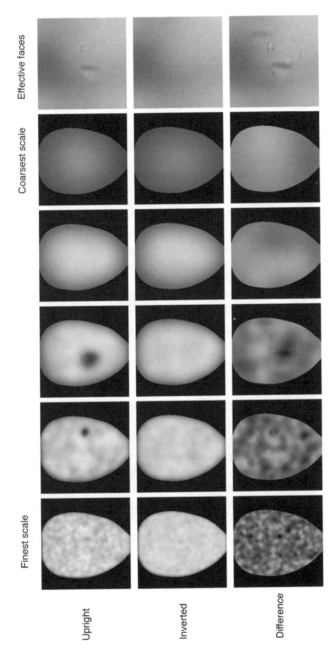

FIG. 4.2.   The first row of this figure applies to the upright condition. It gives the five classification images at each scale, from finest to coarsest. The red areas revealing a face are significantly above chance ($p < .05$). The rightmost picture is the effective face. The second and third rows are the same as the first one, except that they apply to the inverted condition and the difference between the upright and inverted conditions, respectively.

For inverted faces, observers do not seem to rely on any specific features to perform the task. They all seem equally good, or bad. This is reflected in the second row of Fig. 4.2. As the number of bubbles was unequal in upright and inverted, we computed the discrimination image on the normalized Z-score images. Here, the first three scales contain diagnostic information. The eyes, the nose, and the right part of the mouth are the most important local features that explain the difference between inverted and upright information use in face processing.

DISCUSSION

We started this problem with a generic methodological question: Given a dependent measurable response (behavioral, electrophysiological, or other) of an organism, how can we determine the optimal subset of parameters from the independent variables that determine the response? With simple stimuli (e.g., Gabor functions, or sinewaves), this is not much of a challenge, because they can only vary along a few degrees of freedom, limiting the complexity of the task. With the stimuli that are typical of realistic face, object, and scene categorizations, the task had proven so far intractable.

Bubbles is a technique that can resolve the credit assignment problem of attributing the determinants of a response to the parametric subspace of a carefully specified information search space. Using the Face Inversion Effect as an example, we reviewed the six basic decisions to be made to set up a Bubbles experiment. They are, in order, deciding the stimulus set, the dimensions within which to search for information, the geometry of the unit to sample information, the task, the observers, and the response(s) to measure. Applying these to the FIE, we revealed that differences in local face information use (the eyes, nose, and mouth) represented at the scales between 90 and 22.5 cycles per face, determined the effect. This subspace, at least in the visual realm, takes the shape of a diagnostic filtering function that can be applied to render the effective stimulus of the task.

Applications of Bubbles are not restricted to the developed cognitive system. In fact, applications are currently underway to compare how systems at different stages of development use (possibly differentially) the information that is available from a set of stimuli. For example, Humphreys et al. (2002) have adapted the preferential looking paradigm ubiquitous in the development literature to apply Bubbles to a sample of 7-month-old infants. Infants were shown pairs of faces, their mother's face and that of a stranger with similar coloring (with hairlines occluded by a shower cap). On each 5 sec trial, both faces in the pair were covered by the same random bubble mask, and the bubble mask differed across trials. On each trial (of up to 20), they recorded how long the infants looked at their mothers' faces, and how long at the strangers' faces. Results were amalgamated across infants and used to produce diagnostic masks, which are diagnostic of the identity of the mother (using the looking times to the mother) and of the facial information that attracts infant attention (using the overall looking time to both faces on the trials). In both cases, the results were very much similar to those of adults, with a bias to the eyes.

Despite a wide range of applications, there are obvious shortcomings to Bubbles. The first main shortcoming is the combinatorial explosion in number of trials that are required to exhaustively explore the search space. Practically, Bubbles is tractable within low-dimensional search spaces, and users are advised to restrict the dimensionality of the search space to be as low as possible. High-dimensional problems are made tractable with heuristics that guide the search toward regions of more promising solutions, leaving aside less promising regions of the space. Heuristic search can be performed with adaptive statistical sampling, or their implementations. However, any heuristic search introduces biases, resulting in a trade-off between speed and suboptimal solutions, that is, local minima. In any case, the number of trials in Bubbles will need to be reduced to apply the techniques to brain-damaged patients, children, or when learning is itself a factor of the experiment. To illustrate, with a Gaussian of sigma = 10 pixels and a 256×256 pixels image, the search space comprises minimally 25×25 different locations to visit, and the solution should converge within less than 500 trials. If 5 scales are added as a third dimension, the solution converges within about 5,000 trials. There is little doubt that significant learning occurs during these 5,000 trials. We are currently developing several heuristic searches to minimize these numbers (e.g., Leclerc & Gosselin, 2002).

A second shortcoming of Bubbles is the relationship between the scale and geometry of the sample, and the scale of the solution. The scale and geometry of the sample impose biases on the search space. If the scale is too small with respect to that of the solution, important information will not be revealed within one sample, and the same situation occurs when the geometry of the punch-hole sampling unit does not fit that of the solution. Remember that the Bubbles algorithm adaptively adjusts the number of bubbles to maintain the observer at a given performance criterion (e.g., 75% correct). Thus, a higher sampling density, leading to sample overlap, can partially overcome the problems just discussed. However, there is always the possibility that observers will adopt strategies that enable performance to criterion, but are nevertheless atypical of natural human categorization.

At a more theoretical level, one could ask the question "What is the information revealed by the Bubbles algorithm?" The safe response is "the information required to drive a response at a given performance level." However, to the extent that this information is processed somewhere between the input and the response, it has interesting implications for psychological processing. To illustrate, consider the high-level task of face categorization, and its underlying face features. One interesting property of Bubbles is that the researcher can set up a search space that subsumes that of the assumed categorization features (e.g., the eyes, the nose, and the mouth). For example, the 3D search space discussed earlier (2D image × spatial scales) formally represents any face feature as a linear combination of information from the scales. Consequently, task-specific face features can emerge in the Bubbles solution from the use of information at one, or several of these scales (see Gosselin & Schyns, 2001; Schyns, Bonnar, & Gosselin, 2002, for examples). Thus, while not applying the search directly to the features, but in a space that represents these features, Bubbles can reveal the subspace in which important features are actually represented. It is in such spaces that Bubbles solutions tend to be most interesting.

To illustrate, some would argue that the subspace in which important features are represented is in fact the information subspace to which attention is allocated. Earlier, we argued that this diagnostic subspace could be used as a diagnostic filtering function to reveal the effective stimulus. Future research will need to characterize this filtering function, enabling bridges to be erected between cognition, attention, and perception.

REFERENCES

Bonnar, L., Gosselin, F., & Schyns, P. G. (2002). Understanding Dali's slave market with the disappearing bust of Voltaire: A case study in the scale information driving perception. *Perception, 31*, 683–691.

Carey, S., & Diamond, R. (1977). From piecemeal to configurational representation of faces. *Science, 195*, 312–314.

Carey, S., Diamond, R., & Woods, B. (1980). The development of face recognition: A maturational component. *Developmental Psychology, 16*, 257–269.

De Valois, R. L., & De Valois, K. K. (1990). *Spatial vision.* New York: Oxford University Press.

Diamond, R., & Carey, S. (1986). Why faces are and are not special: An effect of expertise. *Journal of Experimental Psychology: General, 115*, 107–117.

Farah, M. J., Wilson, K. D., Drain, M., & Tanaka, J. N. (1998). What is "special" about face perception? *Psychological Review, 105*, 482–498.

Freire, A., Lee, K., & Symons, L. A. (2000). The face-inversion effect as a deficit in the encoding of configural information: Direct evidence. *Perception, 29*, 159–170.

Gibson, B. M., Gosselin, F., Wasserman, E. A., & Schyns, P. G. (2002). Pigeons use specific and consistent features to discriminate human faces. *Abstracts of the Psychonomics Society, 7*, 108.

Gosselin, F., & Schyns, P. G. (2001). Bubbles: A technique to reveal the use of information in recognition. *Vision Research, 41*, 2261–2271.

Gosselin, F., & Schyns, P. G. (2002). RAP: A new framework for visual categorization. *Trends in Cognitive Science, 6*, 70–77.

Hubel, D. H. (1988). *Eye, brain and vision.* New York: Scientific American Library.

Humphreys, K., Gosselin, F., Schyns, P. G., Kaufman, J., & Johnson, M. H. (2002, April). Do 7-month-old infants use the same information as adults to process facial identity? *International Conference on Infant Studies*, Toronto, Canada, 18–21.

Kobatabe, E., & Tanaka, K. (1994). Neuronal selectivities to complex object features in the ventral visual pathway of the macaque cerebral cortex. *Journal of Neurophysiology, 71*, 856–867.

Leclerc, J., & Gosselin, F. (2002). Adaptative Bubbles. *Perception, 31*(Suppl.), 146.

Leder, H., & Bruce, V. (2000). When inverse faces are recognized: The role of configural information in face recognition. *Quarterly Journal of Experimental Psychology A, 53*, 513–536.

Morrison, D., & Schyns, P. G. (2001). Usage of spatial scales for the categorization of faces, objects and scenes. *Psychological Bulletin and Review, 8*, 454–469.

Moscovitch, M., Behrmann, M., & Winocur, G. (1997). What is special about face recognition? Nineteen experiments on a person with visual object agnosia and dyslexia but normal face recognition. *Journal of Cognitive Neuroscience, 9*, 555–604.

Nielsen, K. J., Rainer, G., Brucklacher, V., & Logothetis, N. K. (2002). Studying the representation of natural images with the use of behavioural reverse correlation. *25th European Conference on Visual Perception*.

O'Donnell, C., Gosselin, F., & Schyns, P. G. (2002). The acquisition of facial expertise and how that mediates the information utilized to recognize the face. *Journal of Vision, 2*(7), Abstract 692.

Perrett, D. I., Mistlin, A. J., & Chitty, A. J. (1987). Visual neurons responsive to faces. *Trends in Neuroscience, 10*, 358–364.

Phelps, M. T., & Roberts, W. A. (1994). Memory for pictures of upright and inverted primate faces in humans, squirrel-monkeys, and pigeons. *Journal of Comparative Psychology, 108*, 114–125.

Philips, R. J., & Rawles, R. E. (1979). Recognition of upright and inverted faces: A correlational study. *Perception, 43*, 39–56.

Rossion, B., & Gauthier, I. (2002). How does the brain process upright and inverted faces? *Behavioral & Cognitive Neuroscience Reviews, 1*(1), 63–75.

Scapinello, K. F., & Yarmey, A. D. (1970). The role of familiarity and orientation in immediate and delayed recognition of pictorial stimuli. *Psychonomic Science, 21*, 329–331.

Schyns, P. G., Bonnar, L., & Gosselin, F. (2002). Show me the features! Understanding recognition from the use of visual information. *Psychological Science, 13*, 402–409.

Schyns, P. G., & Gosselin, F. (2002). A natural bias for basic-level object categorizations. *Journal of Vision, 2*(7), Abstract 407.

Schyns, P. G., Jentzsch, I., Johnson, M., Schweinberger, S. R., & Gosselin, F. (2003). A principled method for determining the functionality of brain responses. *Neuroreport, 14*, 1665–1669.

Searcy, J. H., & Bartlett, J. C. (1996). Inversion and processing of component and spatial-relational information in faces. *Journal of Experimental Psychology: Human Perception and Performance, 22*, 904–915.

Sigala, N., & Logothetis, N. (2002). Visual categorization shapes feature selectivity in the primate temporal cortex. *Nature, 415*, 318–320.

Tanaka, J. W., & Farah, M. J. (1993). Parts and wholes in face recognition. *Journal of Experimental Psychology, 46A*, 225–245.

Tinbergen, N., & Perdeck, A. C. (1950). On the stimulus situation releasing the begging response in the newly hatched herring gull chick (Larus argentatus Pont.). *Behaviour, 3*, 1–39.

Valentine, T., & Bruce, V. (1986). Recognizing familiar faces: The role of distinctiveness and familiarity. *Canadian Journal of Psychology, 40*, 300–305.

Vinette, C., Gosselin, F., & Schyns, P. G. (2004). Spatio-temporal dynamics of face recognition in a flash: It's in the eyes! *Cognitive Science, 28*, 289–301.

Vogels, R. (1999). Categorization of complex visual images by Rhesus monkeys. Part 2: Single-cell study. *European Journal of Neuroscience, 11,* 1239–1255.

Yarmey, A. D. (1971). Recognition memory for familiar "public" faces: Effects of orientation and delay. *Psychonomic Science, 24*(6), 286–288.

Yin, R. K. (1969). Looking at upside-down faces. *Journal of Experimental Psychology, 81,* 141–145.

Chapter 5

Young Infants' Categorization of Humans Versus Nonhuman Animals: Roles for Knowledge Access and Perceptual Process

Paul C. Quinn
University of Delaware

INTRODUCTION

At some point during development, humans must come to recognize discriminably different objects with important common characteristics as members of the same category. When and how category representations become available have been enduring issues for several generations of investigators, and a traditional view had it that category representations were a late achievement, dependent on the emergence of language, logic, and instruction (e.g., Bruner, Olver, & Greenfield, 1966). However, in the last 20 years, the results of a number of studies are consistent with the conclusion that at least some of the abilities needed for category formation are functional in preverbal infants (Mandler, 2000; Mareschal & Quinn, 2001).

This chapter examines what we know about the determinants of categorization during the first half-year of life. The emphasis is on how young infants categorize humans and nonhuman animals in studies that measure infant looking time responses to visually presented exemplars. One issue that receives particular focus while discussing the evidence is whether the category representations are formed online during the course of each experiment, or whether the experiments tap into category representations that were constructed on the basis of previous experience. It is argued that although the results on how infants categorize nonhuman animals may be explainable in terms of online category formation processes that are deployed during the course of an experiment, the findings on how infants categorize humans are suggestive of representations being activated that were constructed prior to participation in the experiment. Indeed, the data imply that infants as young as 3 to 4 months of age are already "experts" at representing humans, and more generally that "expert" representations can arise quite early in development with sufficient experience.

THE MEASURE

To empirically establish categorization in young infants, one can use a familiarization/novelty-preference procedure that capitalizes on the preference that infants from birth onward display for novel stimulation (Slater, 1995). In this procedure, infants in an experimental group are presented with a number of different exemplars, all of which belong to the same category, during a series of familiarization trials. Subsequently, during a novel category preference test, infants are presented with two novel stimuli, one from the familiar category, and the other from a novel category. Generalization of familiarization to the novel instance from the familiar category and a preference for the novel instance from the novel category are taken as evidence that the infants have on some basis grouped together or categorized the instances from the familiar category (including the novel one) and recognized that the novel instance from the novel category does not belong to this grouping (or category representation). Another way of describing infant performance is to say that the infants have formed a category representation of the exemplars presented during familiarization that includes the novel exemplar of the familiar category, but excludes the novel exemplar from the novel category.

To infer category formation by infants, two additional empirical criteria need to be met. First, it must be shown that the preference for the novel category instances in the experimental group did not occur because of an a priori preference. The category formation study should thus be repeated with a control group of infants with one important difference: The preference test exemplars are presented without the familiarization exemplars. In this way, one measures spontaneous preference for the exemplars that were presented in the novel category preference test of the category formation study. An inference of category formation is permitted if the novel category preference observed in the experimental group is significantly greater than the spontaneous preference (for the same category) observed in the control group.

Second, because categorization denotes equivalent responding to a set of discriminably different instances, one needs to confirm that infants can discriminate items within categories. If infants do not discriminate between the individual instances from the familiar category, then the category formation study would simply demonstrate between-category discrimination, a process that may be considerably simpler than a categorization process that requires grouping of discriminably different instances together (see Quinn & Eimas, 1998, for further comment on the dissociation between processes of categorization and discrimination). To demonstrate within-category discrimination, each infant in a separate control group is presented with an exemplar from the familiar category and subsequently presented with a novelty preference test pairing the familiar exemplar and a novel exemplar from the same category. A reliable preference for the novel member of each pair permits the inference that infants in the category formation study had grouped together a class of discriminably different entities.

CATEGORY REPRESENTATIONS FOR NONHUMAN ANIMAL SPECIES

Category representations may exist at different levels of inclusiveness and form hierarchically organized systems of knowledge representation (Rosch, Mervis, Gray, Johnson, & Boyes-Braem, 1976). Human adults can, for example, represent mammal or animal at a global or superordinate level of inclusiveness, dog at an intermediate or basic level of inclusiveness, and beagle at a specific or subordinate level of inclusiveness. Likewise, in the domain of furniture items, furniture is superordinate, chair is basic, and lawn chair is subordinate. With respect to the emergence of category representations during early development, we have been able to show that young infants can form category representations for basic-level classes chosen from the same superordinate category (Eimas & Quinn, 1994; Quinn, Eimas, & Rosenkrantz, 1993; reviewed in Quinn, 2002c). For example, 3- and 4-month-old infants familiarized with colored photographic exemplars of domestic cats, representing a variety of breeds, stances, and orientations, generalized their familiarization to novel cats and displayed a novel category preference for birds, dogs, horses, and tigers. Examples of the cat and dog stimuli are presented in Fig. 5.1. In addition, infants familiarized with colored photographic exemplars of horses, generalized their familiarization to novel horses, and showed a novel category preference for cats, giraffes, and zebras. These results indicate that the category representation for cats included novel cats, but excluded birds, dogs, horses, and tigers, and the category representation for horses included novel horses, but excluded cats, zebras, and giraffes.

The findings of early categorization of nonhuman animal species are noteworthy because they suggest young infants possess abilities to divide the world of objects appropriately into perceptual clusters that approximate a basic level of exclusivity. Moreover, these perceptual cluster representations may later come to have conceptual significance for adults. That is, the category distinctions made by quite young infants appear to consis-

FIG. 5.1. Examples of the cat and dog stimuli used in Quinn, Eimas, and Rosenkrantz (1993).

tently map onto the same distinctions that later in life come to have a conceptual nature. As such, this early veridical parsing of the world could permit infants to begin to connect new knowledge with their category representations. For example, if young infants possess abilities to form a category representation for cats (e.g., one that is based on observable surface attributes including body shape, parts, markings, face information, communicative sounds, and motion), then more abstract information that is learned later (e.g., that cats are meat eaters, make good pets, possess cat DNA, and give birth to kittens) can be used to enrich the early perceptually based category representation and allow for the development of a conceptually based representation (i.e., a concept) for cats. The conceptual representations found later in life might thus be viewed as informational enrichments of young infants' category representations (Eimas, 1994; Quinn, 2002b; Quinn & Eimas, 1997, 2000). By this view, the abilities that young infants have to form perceptual category representations form the primitive base from which adult conceptions of objects develop.

One clarification that may be helpful at this point in the chapter is to acknowledge that the infants who are presented with exemplars of nonhuman animals (e.g., cats or horses) and form category representations in the laboratory are not necessarily leaving the laboratory with long-term representations for cats and horses that will themselves represent the start-up structures into which subsequent experience and knowledge can be incorporated. The claim is more that the infants are demonstrating parsing skills in the laboratory that may be successfully deployed to form representations for classes of real objects when those objects are encountered in the natural environment. It is the latter group of representations that may serve as the actual supports for further knowledge acquisition.

INFORMATION USED BY INFANTS TO FORM CATEGORY REPRESENTATIONS FOR NONHUMAN ANIMAL SPECIES

An issue raised by the findings of early categorization concerns the attributes that young infants use to form category representations for nonhuman animal species. Given the static nature of the stimuli and the young age of the infants, the attributes are undoubtedly perceptual in nature and detectable from the surfaces of the stimuli. For example, the representation of cats may exclude birds on the basis of the number of legs. In addition, the representation for horses may exclude horses and giraffes on the basis of distinctive body markings. However, in the case of perceptually similar nonhuman animal species such as cats and dogs, the diagnostic cues are not obvious inasmuch as the categories are marked by four legs, eyes, ears, tails, and comparable body shapes. The literature on basic-level categorization by adults suggests that subtle differences in a particular attribute, the pattern of correlation across a number of attributes, or overall shape, might provide bases for differentiating object classes with perceptual overlap (Marr, 1982; Murphy, 1991; Rosch et al., 1976).

In a series of experiments, we showed that information from a particular part or attribute may supply the infants with a sufficient basis to form category representations for perceptually similar nonhuman animal species. In particular, information from the head and face region of the animal exemplars has been shown to provide a means by which infants form a category representation for cats that excludes dogs (Quinn & Eimas, 1996). In one experiment, 3- and 4-month-old infants were randomly assigned to one of three groups: Whole Animal, Head Only, or Body Only. In the Whole Animal group, infants were presented with domestic cats and tested with a novel cat paired with a novel dog. The Head Only group was presented with the same cats and dogs as the Whole Animal group, but now only their faces were visible; the body information had been occluded. The third group, the Body Only group, was also familiarized with the same animals shown to the Whole Animal group, but, in this instance, the face information had been occluded and only the body information was available. The critical finding was that only infants in the Whole Animal and Head Only groups displayed reliable novel category preferences; the Body Only group divided their attention between the novel cat and dog bodies.

Infants were also found to form the category representations based on the head region (and not the body region) when presented with whole cats or dogs during familiarization, and preference tested with a pair of hybrid stimuli: a novel cat head on a novel dog body and a novel dog head on a novel cat body (Spencer, Quinn, Johnson, & Karmiloff-Smith, 1997). In this case, the novel category preference was found for the stimuli containing the novel category head. These studies thus suggest that information from the head region provides the infants with a sufficient basis to form individuated category representations for cats and dogs.

The findings that young infants' category representations of perceptually overlapping nonhuman animal species are based on perceptual part or attribute information that can be detected from the surfaces of the exemplars fits well with findings that have been reported for older infants' categorization of nonhuman animals. Using the sequential touching procedure to measure categorization of toy objects, Rakison and Butterworth (1998) showed that 14- to 22-month-old infants rely on perceptual part information to form separate category representations for nonhuman animals and vehicles. For example, when intact animal and vehicle toys were used to depict the categories, the infants were able to divide the two classes into separate groupings; however, when the categorization was repeated, but with the legs removed from the animals and the wheels from the vehicles, the infants no longer formed differentiated representations of the categories, indicating that these featural attributes were important for the category distinction. The set of findings taken together (Quinn & Eimas, 1996; Rakison & Butterworth, 1998; Spencer et al., 1997) indicate that both younger and older infants categorically represent nonhuman animals on the basis of perceptual part or feature information.

INFANTS' CATEGORIZATION OF NONHUMAN ANIMALS: ONLINE PROCESSING VERSUS PRIOR EXPERIENCE

As observed in the introductory section of the chapter, an important issue regarding the category representations of infants is whether they are formed online, during the course of an experiment (a case of *category formation*), or whether the experiment is simply tapping into category representations that were constructed (presumably on the basis of real-life experience) *before* the experiment began (an instance of *category possession*). The design of the familiarization/novelty-preference procedure lends itself to an interpretation that can be understood in terms of category formation. Infants are presumed to construct the category representation as more and more exemplars from the familiar category are presented (see Mareschal, French, & Quinn, 2000, and Mareschal, Quinn, & French, 2002, for an explicit computational model of the online category formation process).

It is, however, difficult to completely rule out the possibility that knowledge access does not facilitate the performance of infants participating in the familiarization-novelty preference procedure. Consider, for example, the performance of young infants (3 to 4 months of age) presented with cats or horses and then tested with exemplars from contrasting animal categories such as birds, dogs, tigers, giraffes, and zebras. Given that such young infants are not likely to have observed (at least directly) mammals such as giraffes or zebras or the particular cat and horse exemplars depicted in the task, one might be tempted to say that the participating infants rely exclusively on perceptual processing, and that they are forming the category representation during the course of the familiarization trials. However, parents are known to read to their infants from picture books that may contain pictorial exemplars of animals. In addition, even young infants may be able to recognize that mammals like giraffes and zebras are more like other animals (including humans) than furniture items (Quinn & Eimas, 1998). Thus, even in an experiment that is designed as a study of concept formation, it is possible that young infants may recruit from a preexisting knowledge base that at least in part determines their preference behavior.

We have approached this issue in two ways. First, during the past 10 years, in numerous experiments, we investigated whether infants form separate category representations for cats and dogs. Because many families have cats or dogs or both as pets, it is possible to compare the categorization performance of infants that have been exposed to pets at home with those that have not. A variety of analyses have been performed, and none have revealed a facilitative effect of a home pet on categorization performance. These null results thus fail to support the suggestion that infant categorization of nonhuman animals in the laboratory is assisted by real-world experience with nonhuman animals occurring prior to arrival at the laboratory.

Another way to think about the contributions of perceptual process and knowledge access in infant categorization performance is to argue that if infants possess, for example, preformed representations for nonhuman animal species that are simply being tapped into as a basis for performance during an experiment conducted with the familiarization/novelty-preference procedure, then it should prove difficult to manipulate categorization performance via perceptual perturbations to the stimuli. That is, via knowledge access, cats should be recognized as cats, and dogs should be recognized as dogs. However, in a series of experiments, we have shown that it is possible to manipulate infant categorization performance for the classes of cats and dogs. This was possible because of an asymmetry in categorization performance that was detected in our initial investigation (Quinn et al., 1993). Al-

though infants familiarized with cats displayed a subsequent novelty preference for dogs compared with novel cats, infants familiarized with dogs did
not display a subsequent preference for cats over novel dogs. This asymmetric outcome can be interpreted as follows: Infants familiarized with cats
formed a category representation for cats that included novel cats, but excluded dogs, whereas infants familiarized with dogs formed a category representation for dogs that included both novel dogs as well as cats.

In follow-up investigations designed to determine the basis for the asymmetry, we established that the cat versus dog novel category preference results could not be explained via a spontaneous preference for dogs: Infants
presented with cats versus dogs without prior familiarization did not have
an a priori preference for the dogs (Quinn et al., 1993). However, we were
able to demonstrate that the initial asymmetry reflected the fact that the
dogs were more variable than the cats, causing the cats to be subsumed under the broader class of dogs (French, Mermillod, Quinn, Chauvin, &
Mareschal, 2002; Mareschal et al., 2000; Mareschal et al., 2002; Quinn et al.,
1993). The variability explanation was supported by two pieces of evidence.
First, we obtained typicality ratings of the stimuli to determine if the internal structure of the dog category had greater breadth relative to the internal structure of the cat category. Mothers of our infant research participants were asked to indicate how representative an item was of its particular
category. The results were consistent with our expectations: The variability
of the ratings for the dogs was reliably higher than the variability of the ratings for the cats. Second, we measured the values of 10 surface dimensions
of the cat and dog stimuli. The dimensions included geometric and head/
face extents: vertical extent, horizontal extent, leg length, head width, head
length, ear separation, eye separation, ear length, nose width, and nose
length. The physical measurements further supported the idea of greater
perceptual variability of the dogs because the ranges of perceptual features
of the cats were found to be largely included in those of the dogs. Thus, an
infant familiarized on the less variable category, cat, would, in general, view
an exemplar of a dog as a novel stimulus, whereas an infant familiarized on
the more variable and inclusive category, dog, would tend to perceive a cat
exemplar as simply belonging to the already-familiar dog category.

Several experimental results provide additional support for this interpretation of the cat versus dog asymmetry. For example, in one experiment
conducted with 3- to 4-month-olds, when the variability of the dog class was
reduced, thereby removing the inclusion relation of cats within dogs, the
asymmetry was removed (Quinn et al., 1993). In another experiment carried out with the same age group, the inclusivity relation of the categories
was reversed through a combination of stimulus selection (i.e., selection of
a highly varied set of cats and a set of dogs with low variability) and minor
image processing, and the asymmetry was reversed (French, Mareschal,

Mermillod, & Quinn, 2004; French, Mermillod, Quinn, & Mareschal, 2001). In other words, the infants formed a category representation for cats that included dogs, and a category representation for dogs that excluded cats. Finally, in a third experiment conducted with 3- to 4-month-olds, a low-variance category of cats and a high-variance category of dogs were presented to the infants, as in the original Quinn et al. (1993) study, but in this instance the stimuli were preselected and their images were slightly modified so that the inclusion relation was removed, and there was no asymmetry observed (French et al., 2004). Positive evidence for categorization was observed in both familiarization conditions.

The studies of categorization of cat and dog images by young infants make the important point that the infants are forming their category representations for nonhuman animals over the course of the familiarization trials, rather than tapping into pre-existing concepts that had been formed prior to arriving at the laboratory. If infants in the cat versus dog categorization studies had simply been tapping into category representations established before participation in the experiments, then infant responsiveness should not have varied with the variations in the category information presented. The fact that infant responsiveness did vary across experiments suggests that the categories were being formed during the familiarization experience and that the boundaries can be manipulated depending on the information presented during familiarization.

A CATEGORY REPRESENTATION FOR HUMANS

Although the data just described inform us about the skills of young infants to categorize nonhuman animals, they do not tell us about early abilities to categorize humans. Clearly, any theory of knowledge acquisition about animals would be incomplete without accounting for how a category representation for humans arises. Given the data indicating that infants could form category representations for nonhuman animal species, and the perceptual differences between nonhuman animals and humans (e.g., presence vs. absence of clothing, canonical orientation of body torso—vertical vs. horizontal, arms vs. no arms), we believed it would be a straightforward matter to demonstrate that infants would form a category representation for humans that excluded exemplars of nonhuman animal species. We therefore presented 3- and 4-month-old infants with photographic exemplars of 12 humans (male and female) depicted in a variety of standing, walking, or running poses and in earth tone (i.e., non-pastel) clothing (Quinn & Eimas, 1998). Examples of the human stimuli are presented in Fig. 5.2. The infants were then preference tested with a novel human paired with a cat, and a different novel human paired with a horse. To our surprise, no novel category preferences for either the cats or horses were observed. In addition, we

FIG. 5.2.   Examples of the human stimuli used in Quinn and Eimas (1998).

found that there was no spontaneous preference among the infants for humans over nonhuman animals, a preference that if present, could have interfered with (i.e., masked) a preference for cats and horses over humans. Moreover, we found that the human pictures were not judged by undergraduate research participants to be more variable than the pictures of cats or horses.

The initial result on how infants represent humans, in particular, the generalization of familiarization from humans to cats and horses, leaves open the question of whether infants did not categorize the human exemplars or whether the infants formed a broad category representation for humans, one that included novel humans, cats, and horses. In subsequent experiments, we were able to provide evidence that infants categorize humans, but the representation for humans is quite broad (Quinn & Eimas, 1998). In particular, we found that the representation for humans by 3- and 4-month-old infants included novel humans, cats, horses, and even fish; however, it excluded cars. The broad global-level representation for humans stands in contrast to the narrower basic-level representations for nonhuman animal species (i.e., cats, horses) that were found to exclude humans, exemplars from related nonhuman animal species, and cars. There is thus a clear asymmetry in the level of exclusivity of the category representations formed by young infants for humans versus nonhuman animal species.

CATEGORY REPRESENTATIONS FOR HUMANS VERSUS NONHUMAN ANIMALS: EXAMINING THE NATURE OF THE REPRESENTATION

The demonstrated asymmetry in the representations for humans and non-human animal species in terms of categorical exclusivity raises the question of whether humans are represented differently from other nonhuman animal species. Because of the greater experience that most 3- to 4-month-olds have with humans (even if limited to repeated presentations of just a few humans—parents, older siblings, caregivers) relative to nonhuman animal species, we have hypothesized that humans might be represented by infants as *individual exemplars* belonging to the same category (Quinn & Eimas, 1998). Also reasonable is the possibility that the less frequently experienced nonhuman animal species might be represented by *category-level information*, possibly a summary prototype representing an average of the exemplars presented in the laboratory, rather than exemplar-specific details, that is, details about each individual instance or member of a category (Bomba & Siqueland, 1983). These proposals link with the idea that young infants may be at a more advanced stage of processing humans relative to nonhuman animals. In effect, over the course of a time span as short as 3 to 4 months of life, the differential experience that infants have with humans versus non-human animal species may have the inductive effect of driving infants to become human "experts."

To examine the nature of the representations infants form for humans versus nonhuman animal species, Quinn and Eimas (1998) presented one group of 3- to 4-month-olds with 12 humans and another with 12 cats. As schematically presented in Fig. 5.3, both groups were administered two

	Preference Tests	
Familiar Category	Categorization	Exemplar Memory
Cats	Novel Human versus Novel Cat	Novel Cat versus Familiar Cat
Humans	Novel Cat versus Novel Human	Novel Human versus Familiar Human

Experimental Design Used to Test Categorization and Exemplar Memory for Humans vs. Cats in 3- to 4-Month-Old Infants

FIG. 5.3. Schematic depiction of the experimental design used by Quinn and Eimas (1998) to investigate infant categorization and exemplar memory for humans and nonhuman animals.

preference tests: in one, a novel cat was paired with a novel human (the test of categorization); in the other, a novel member of the familiar category was paired with a familiar category member (the test of exemplar memory). The latter pairing is based on the assumption that if individual exemplars are represented, then the novel member of the familiar category should be preferred. If individual exemplars are not represented, and the category representation is of a summary nature, then looking times to both stimuli should be approximately equal.

The results revealed a significant interaction: Infants familiarized with cats preferred a novel human to a novel cat, but not a novel cat over a familiar one; infants familiarized with humans did not prefer a novel cat over a novel human, but did prefer a novel over a familiar human. This interaction provides further support for the claim that the young infant's category representation for humans includes many other animals (at least cats, horses, and fish), whereas the category representations for nonhuman animal species (cats, horses) exclude humans as well as other animal species (Eimas & Quinn, 1994; Quinn et al., 1993). The data also support the suggestion that the category representation of humans is exemplar-based, whereas the category representation of nonhuman animal species is based on summary information on the order of a prototype that represents an averaging of the familiar exemplars.

The data correspond with recently proposed ideas regarding the representation of expertise that have emerged in the perceptual learning and categorization literatures in adults (Gauthier & Tarr, 1997; Smith & Minda, 1998). In particular, the possibility that humans may be represented at a more advanced stage of processing than nonhuman animals is consistent with a hypothesized representational shift from a summary-based structure to exemplar-based memory during the time-course of category learning. A developmental marker for expertise with a particular category might thus be the presence of an exemplar-based representation for that category.

AN ACCOUNT OF THE DIFFERENCES IN THE REPRESENTATION OF HUMANS VERSUS NONHUMAN ANIMALS BY YOUNG INFANTS

How does one explain the differences in the way that infants represent humans versus nonhuman animals? Moreover, how does one account for the fact that the representation for humans appears to be both global in its level of exclusiveness and exemplar-based in its nature? Quinn and Eimas (1998) argued that a broad representation for humans may be based on a wide range of individual exemplars as a result of young infants' considerable familiarity with humans. The suggestion is that infants may develop an exemplar-based representation of humans (i.e., subordinate-like representations for individual humans clustered together in a representation of humans in general) in some n-dimensional space where each dimension represents quantitative variation of an animal attribute (e.g., eye separation, leg length). This broad representation is in opposition to some form of relatively narrow summary representation for other species. For example, in the n-dimensional space, the exemplar nature of the human representation could be taken as a cluster of exemplar points defining a human region, rather than a single summary (i.e., prototype) point defining nonhuman animal species (e.g., cats, horses).

An extensive representation for humans may form a cognitive reference region (Rosch, 1975) for infants. Because of the size difference between the human region and the cat (or horse) point, the representation for humans would be more accepting of a wide range of values along each dimension, and thus more likely to incorporate nonhuman animal species. In effect, a category representation for humans could behave as a powerful attractor, somewhat like a perceptual magnet (e.g., Kuhl, 1991), that acts to include (i.e., pull in) stimuli that have at least some common attributes (e.g., faces, skeletal appendages, elongated bodies). The asymmetry with respect to the categories of nonhuman animals and humans is significant because it foreshadows Carey's (1985) results showing that 4-year-old children classify a number of nonhuman animals by their similarity to humans. In addition, Pauen (2000), using a habituation–dishabituation procedure, reported corroborating evidence for a broadly inclusive category representation for humans that includes nonhuman animals in 5-month-old infants. Both the infant and child data thus suggest that humans may function as an organizing structure for information acquired about other animals.

The representation of humans and nonhuman animals by infants is likely to represent a kind of other-species effect that results from perceptual learning due to differential experience, rather than a case of humans being "special." For example, Humphrey (1974; see also Pascalis & Bachevalier, 1998) has reported that monkeys represent other monkeys at the level of individual exemplars, but represent exemplars of other species (i.e., cats, dogs, horses, pigs, and sheep) at the category level. These findings imply that the observed asymmetry in human infants' representation of humans versus nonhuman animals is mediated by general learning mechanisms rather than human-specific mechanisms.

MODELING THE ASYMMETRY IN THE CATEGORIZATION OF HUMANS VERSUS NONHUMAN ANIMALS BY YOUNG INFANTS

It is important to mention that the simple neural network that can simulate the cat versus dog asymmetry (i.e., a model that embodies within-task learning) cannot simulate the human versus nonhuman animal asymmetry.

However, a model that adds a long-term memory structure along with previous training on humans can simulate the human versus nonhuman animal asymmetry (Mermillod, French, Quinn, & Mareschal, 2003). These simulations show that a "dual-network" connectionist architecture that incorporates both bottom-up (i.e., short-term memory) and top-down (i.e., long-term memory) processing is sufficient to account for the empirical results on categorization of humans versus nonhuman animals obtained with the infants. The dual-network memory model was able to reproduce the results of Quinn and Eimas (1998) because the LTM network contained a representation of humans that influenced processing in the STM network. In particular, this LTM information had the effect of increasing the attractor basin for humans, causing it to largely include nonhuman animals (i.e., horses), thereby giving rise to the asymmetry reported by Quinn and Eimas (1998). The computational data are thus consistent with the descriptive account of human versus nonhuman animal asymmetry offered by Quinn and Eimas (1998).

INFORMATION USED BY INFANTS TO FORM A GLOBAL CATEGORY REPRESENTATION FOR HUMANS

The chapter has thus far included a discussion of evidence indicating that young infants' representations for nonhuman animals are basic-level in their exclusivity, structured with summary-level information, and anchored by part information. In contrast, young infants' representation for humans is global in its exclusivity, and based on exemplar information. What has not yet been considered is the information used by infants to form a category representation for humans. However, a recent study investigated this issue and examined in particular the perceptual information that was the basis for the human versus nonhuman animal asymmetry (Quinn, 2004).

The experiment followed from the investigation of whether infants formed category representations for nonhuman animal species based on information from the head, body, or whole animal (Quinn & Eimas, 1996). Three- and 4-month-old infants were familiarized with 12 exemplars of humans or 12 exemplars of cats, and tested with a novel human versus a novel cat. Within the human and cat conditions, the infants were randomly assigned to one of three experimental groups: Whole Animal, Head Only, and Body Only. Examples of the stimuli from the different groups are displayed in Fig. 5.4. In the Whole Animal Group, infants were familiarized and tested with entire, intact stimuli (head + body). In the Head Only group, only the heads of the stimuli were visible; the body information had been occluded. In the Body Only group, only the bodies of the stimuli were

FIG. 5.4. Examples of the nonhuman animal and human exemplars in the Whole Stimulus, Head Only, and Body Only depictions of Quinn (2004).

visible; the head information had been occluded. The particular form of the asymmetry, a category representation for cats that excludes humans and a category representation for humans that includes cats, was observed only with the Whole Animal stimuli. Neither head nor body information alone were sufficient to produce the asymmetry.

The results suggest that the incorporation of nonhuman animal species into a broadly inclusive category representation of humans may be based on the overall structure of the stimuli (e.g., a head region adjoining an elongated body axis with skeletal appendages). The finding that the human representation is based on holistic information contrasts with the findings that representations for nonhuman animal species may be based on part or attribute (i.e., featural) information—heads in the case of cats versus dogs.

The data correspond well with the notion that young infants may be representing humans at an "expert" level and recently proposed ideas regarding the representation of expertise that have emerged in the cognitive neuroscience literature (Gauthier & Nelson, 2001; Gauthier, Skudlarski, Gore, & Anderson, 2000; Gauthier & Tarr, 2002). In particular, Gauthier and colleagues have argued that an area of the fusiform gyrus in the brains of adults, once believed to represent faces specifically, actually represents expert knowledge more generally. Moreover, these researchers have demonstrated that expert object recognition by this brain area is characterized by holistic–configural processing. The results reported here indicate that young infants may already possess an "expert" representation for humans that is based on holistic information, and imply that "expert" representations may occur early in development with sufficient experience. As neuroimaging techniques are developed for use with infants, it will be interesting to learn whether convergent evidence for this speculation can be obtained.

ARE YOUNG INFANTS' REPRESENTATIONS FOR HUMANS INFLUENCED BY EXPERIENCE OCCURRING PRIOR TO THE EXPERIMENT?

Thus far in the chapter, it has been argued that the representation of humans by young infants is based on experience occurring prior to the experiment. In this section, direct evidence for this suggestion is discussed. The experiments to be reviewed examine, in particular, how infants categorize a human attribute, namely, the gender of human faces. In past work that relied on the habituation–dishabituation procedure, Leinbach and Fagot (1993) investigated the categorization of face gender by 5- to 12-month-old infants and reported an unexpected asymmetry: Infants habituated to males looked more to a novel female than a novel male, whereas infants habituated to females did not look more to a novel male relative to a novel female. This pattern of results could be taken as evidence that the infants had formed a representation for male that excluded female, but not a representation for female that excluded male. The findings were intriguing and led Leinbach and Fagot to speculate that "young infants simply prefer to look at a female face" (p. 330). A spontaneous preference for female over male faces would facilitate any novel category preference for female faces after familiarization with male faces, but would interfere with any novel category preference for male faces after familiarization with female faces.

In a series of experiments, Quinn, Yahr, Kuhn, Slater, and Pascalis (2002) further investigated the male versus female face asymmetry reported by Leinbach and Fagot (1993). We were interested in: (a) whether the asymmetry could be replicated, (b) whether it generalized to other stimulus sets, age groups, and procedures, and (c) the basis for the asymmetry. To begin to answer these questions, we used the familiarization/novelty-preference procedure to examine the representation of the gender of human faces by 3- to 4-month-olds. The faces, presented alone, were color photographs of female and male models. The female and male faces had neutral to slightly positive emotional expression, were judged to be of comparable attractiveness, and were matched for direction of gaze. Examples are shown in the left half of Fig. 5.5. In the first experiment, infants were administered familiarization trials with eight male or female faces and then given test trials with a novel male face paired with a novel female face. The

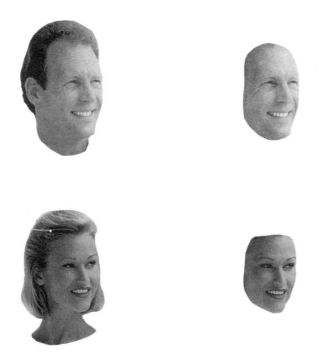

FIG. 5.5.   Examples of the human face stimuli (with and without hair) used in Quinn, Yahr, Kuhn, Slater, and Pascalis (2002).

asymmetry reported by Leinbach and Fagot was replicated: Infants familiarized with males preferred females, but infants familiarized with females did not prefer males.

In a second experiment, we explored the explanation for the asymmetry suggested by Leinbach and Fagot (1993), namely, that infants might spontaneously prefer female faces. To investigate this possibility, a group of 3- to 4-month-olds was presented with a series of paired-preference trials, each of which presented a different male face with a different female face. A mean preference for females was observed. The asymmetry reported in the categorization experiment thus appears to be the result of a spontaneous preference for female faces. This spontaneous preference could have facilitated a novel category preference for females after familiarization with males, and interfered with a novel category preference for males after familiarization with females.

In additional experiments, we pursued two low-level sensory explanations for the spontaneous preference for female faces. First, we asked whether the spontaneous preference for female faces might be attributable to higher external contrast information resulting from a greater amount of hair surrounding the internal face region of the stimulus. The experiment assessing spontaneous preference was thus repeated, but in this instance with face stimuli without external hair cues. Examples are shown in the right half of Fig. 5.5. Here, the infants still preferred the female faces, indicating that the preference for female faces is not the result of higher contrast created by a greater amount of hair.

Second, we questioned whether the spontaneous preference for female faces was due to higher contrast of the internal features, possibly resulting from females' greater use of cosmetics. We repeated the first control experiment with faces without hair, but in this instance, the faces were inverted. We reasoned that if the female preference was due to higher contrast of the internal features, then the preference should be preserved with the inversion manipulation, because the internal features are present in both upright and inverted faces. The result was that the infants no longer preferred the female faces, suggesting that the spontaneous preference depends on processing of the internal features in their upright orientation.

Given that the evidence did not support sensory explanations for the female face preference displayed by young infants, we began to examine a cognitive explanation for the preference, namely, that infants might prefer female over male faces because of greater familiarity with female faces. It is known that young infants will display a spontaneous preference for mother's face over a strange female face, even in the absence of external hair cues (Bartrip, Morton, & de Schonen, 2001). Also, female faces differ structurally from male faces, albeit in complex ways (Burton, Bruce, & Dench, 1993; O'Toole, Vetter, Troje, & Bulthoff, 1997). Finally, a majority of infants in the first 3 months of life are reared with female primary caregivers, and this was true for all the infants thus far described for the experiments of Quinn et al. (2002). Therefore, we suggested that infants might generalize their experiences with primary caregivers who are female to female faces more generally. The argument is that young infants reared with a female primary caregiver may become more expert at processing female faces relative to processing male faces. Adult participants display an other-race effect in identification of human faces that may be the result of differential experience (O'Toole, Deffenbacher, Abdi, & Bartlett, 1991), and we have hypothesized that young infants may display an other-gender effect in the processing of human faces that results from early differential experience.

If young infants reared with female primary caregivers become "female experts," then it should be possible to reverse the gender preference in infants reared with male primary caregivers. Although far fewer infants are reared primarily by their fathers, Quinn et al. (2002) and Quinn (2003) tested eight such infants, between 3 and 4 months of age. On the spontaneous preference test between upright male and female faces without hair, seven of the eight infants preferred the male faces. This outcome is not definitive because of the small sample, but it is consistent with the idea that infant attention to human stimuli may be biased toward the gender with which the infant has greater experience.

An implication of female expertise for infants raised with female primary caregivers is that young infants may become more efficient at processing the exemplar-specific details of individual female faces relative to male faces (Gauthier & Tarr, 1997; Gauthier, Williams, Tarr, & Tanaka, 1998). This suggestion follows from the earlier arguments and evidence that infants may be more expert at processing human versus nonhuman animal stimuli, and may be more likely to process individual humans as subordinate-level exemplars as opposed to the basic-level summaries observed for nonhuman animals. To test the processing of female versus male face information by infants, 3- to 4-month-old infants were presented with eight male or female faces. Infants familiarized with males were then preference tested with a novel versus familiar male face, and infants familiarized with females were preference tested with a novel versus familiar female face. The findings were that infants familiarized with male faces did not display a differential preference between a familiar and novel male face. In contrast, infants familiarized with females displayed a preference for the novel female face. The results are consistent with the idea that infants were representing the male faces in terms of a summary structure (i.e., a male prototype), whereas the female faces were represented as individual exemplars. These findings provide further confirmation that infants reared with female primary caregivers are more expert at processing the details that define individual female faces relative to male faces.

It is interesting to consider the findings of Quinn et al. (2002) on infant categorization of male versus female in relation to the results of Quinn and Eimas (1998) on categorization of humans (in general) versus nonhuman animals. Quinn and Eimas (1998) reported that 3- to 4-month-olds were more likely to represent individual humans than nonhuman animals at the expert, exemplar level. The results of Quinn et al. (2002) extend the Quinn and Eimas (1998) findings by demonstrating that within the category of humans, there may be an *additional* expert advantage for the gender with which the infants have more experience (as determined by the gender of the primary caregiver). This suggestion receives support when one reanalyzes the investigation of human exemplar memory in Quinn and Eimas (1998) in light of the findings of Quinn et al. (2002). In particular, there was a trend for stronger exemplar memory in Quinn and Eimas (1998) when the familiar exemplar presented in the preference test was female rather than male.

One other point of comparison between Quinn and Eimas (1998) and Quinn et al. (2002) that deserves comment centers on the issue of spontaneous preference. In Quinn and Eimas (1998), there was no spontaneous preference for the human over nonhuman animal stimuli. In Quinn et al.

(2002), there was a spontaneous preference for female over male. We believe that this difference in the two studies, the lack of spontaneous preference in the one case, and its presence in the other, may reflect differences in the way the human stimuli were presented. In Quinn and Eimas (1998), the human stimuli were whole, fully clothed, and depicted with head, arms, legs, and the body torso in their correct spatial arrangement. In contrast, in Quinn et al. (2002), the human stimuli were enlarged faces, and may have tapped into a cognitive–emotional process that is related to attachment (i.e., similar to the one that gets activated when young infants prefer mother's to stranger's face). Such a process, when stimulated, may direct infants to maintain fixation on the triggering stimulus.

As was the case with the human/nonhuman animal asymmetry, we believe the male/female face asymmetry to be theoretically significant because it indicates that infants' categorization of humans in laboratory tasks is influenced by experience occurring prior to participation in the tasks. The asymmetries are also significant because they imply that knowledge acquisition does not proceed along an equivalent developmental course for all classes of stimulation. Rather, frequently experienced perceptual inputs (e.g., humans vs. nonhuman animals, male vs. female caregivers) create cognitive reference regions in the overall representational scheme of young infants.

CONCLUSION

The evidence reviewed in this chapter suggests that there are differences in the way young infants categorize humans and nonhuman animals. In particular, young infants categorize nonhuman animals: (a) at a basic-level of exclusivity, (b) on the basis of part information, (c) with a summary representation, and (d) because of learning occurring within the experimental task. In contrast, young infants categorize humans: (a) at a global-level of exclusivity, (b) on the basis of holistic–configural information, (c) with an exemplar representation, and (d) by recruiting from a pre-existing knowledge base about humans that arises from experience with humans.

One may ask on the basis of this data review whether the differences in the way that young infants represent humans and nonhuman animals are qualitative or quantitative. One way to think about the differences is that they are quantitative and reflect the effects of experience and the development of expertise. The collection of findings, taken together, lays the foundation for a perceptual learning model of early knowledge acquisition (Quinn, 2002a). This model is sketched out schematically in Fig. 5.6. Young infants, during the course of early experience over the first few months of life, begin to experience numerous objects from various categories. Initially, as shown in Panel a of Fig. 5.6, because of limited experience with a small number of exemplars, the infants' system of representation is likely to consist of individual en-

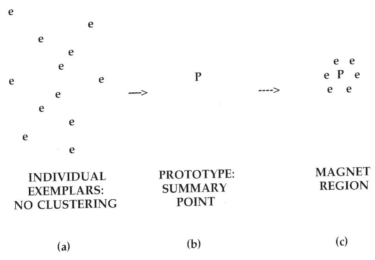

FIG. 5.6. Schematic depiction of the perceptual learning model of early knowledge acquisition.

tities, loosely clustered. However, as is illustrated in Panel b of Fig. 5.6, with sufficient experience, and aided by core abilities to represent within-category similarity and between-category dissimilarity, the infant may begin to form structured representations organized around summary-level prototypes. The expectation is that such representations (a) would be formed for a variety of generic object categories and (b) could serve as perceptual placeholders for the acquisition of knowledge beyond infancy.

The learning of certain categories may proceed beyond prototypes if infants are provided with additional experience that might come in the form of large numbers of exemplars or rich or lengthy interaction with a smaller number of exemplars. As is depicted in Panel c of Fig. 5.6, the summary structure might then become elaborated by the addition of information about individual exemplars. This information serves to both enrich and empower the summary structure, in effect, giving rise to the beginnings of an "expert" representation or cognitive reference region. In the infant's overall system of category representation, this region might come to consist of a relatively large number of points in mental space, one point for each exemplar as well as the summary structure. The representational magnification that occurs around these regions of mental space may give rise to psychophysical magnet-like properties. Such regions may be the cognitive equivalents of the "attractor basins" described in the dynamic systems literature (Thelen & Smith, 1994).

Early category representations that serve as magnet regions in psychological space may have considerable significance for knowledge acquisition in general because of their potential to organize large portions of experience. For example, the incorporation of nonhuman animal species into a category representation for humans may be the process that allows for the development of a broad domain-level category representation for animals. By this view, humans may be the "glue" that provides the coherence for a category representation of animals.

As research inquiring into the beginnings of knowledge acquisition continues, one question that remains for the perceptual learning account is to determine more precisely how long-term experiential knowledge for a variety of generic object classes, including humans and their attributes (i.e., gender), interacts with short-term experiential knowledge acquired during a series of familiarization trials to produce a particular pattern of looking on preference test trials. However this question is resolved, the proposed perceptual learning model of infant category formation can accommodate much of the data on early categorization, including the differences in the way infants represent humans and nonhuman animals, and may represent a viable framework for thinking about the early course of knowledge acquisition in general.

ACKNOWLEDGMENTS

The author thanks Lisa Gershkoff-Stowe and David Rakison for organizing the symposium and inviting this chapter contribution. Preparation of the chapter was supported by NSF Grant BCS-0096300 and by NIH Grant HD-42451. The chapter is dedicated to Peter D. Eimas.

REFERENCES

Bartrip, J., Morton, J., & de Schonen, S. (2001). Responses to mother's face in 3-week to 5-month-old infants. *British Journal of Developmental Psychology, 19,* 219–232.

Bomba, P. C., & Siqueland, E. R. (1983). The nature and structure of infant form categories. *Journal of Experimental Child Psychology, 35,* 294–328.

Bruner, J. S., Olver, R. R., & Greenfield, P. M. (1966). *Studies in cognitive growth.* New York: Wiley.

Burton, A. M., Bruce, V., & Dench, N. (1993). What's the difference between men and women? Evidence from facial measurement. *Perception, 22,* 153–176.

Carey, S. (1985). *Conceptual change in childhood.* Cambridge, MA: MIT Press.

Eimas, P. D. (1994). Categorization in early infancy and the continuity of development. *Cognition, 50,* 83–93.

Eimas, P. D., & Quinn, P. C. (1994). Studies on the formation of perceptually based basic-level categories in young infants. *Child Development, 65,* 903–917.

French, R. M., Mareschal, D., Mermillod, M., & Quinn, P. C. (2004). The role of bottom-up processing in perceptual categorization by 3- to 4-month-old infants: Simulations and data. *Journal of Experimental Psychology: General, 133,* 382–397.

French, R. M., Mermillod, M., Quinn, P. C., Chauvin, A., & Mareschal, D. (2002). The importance of starting blurry: Simulating improved basic-level category learning in infants due to weak visual acuity. In W. Gray & C. Schunn (Eds.), *Proceedings of the 24th Annual Conference of the Cognitive Science Society* (pp. 322–327). Mahwah, NJ: Lawrence Erlbaum Associates.

French, R. M., Mermillod, M., Quinn, P. C., & Mareschal, D. (2001). Reversing category exclusivities in infant perceptual categorization: Simulations and data. In K. Stenning & J. Moore (Eds.), *Proceedings of the 23rd Annual Conference of the Cognitive Science Society* (pp. 307–312). Mahwah, NJ: Lawrence Erlbaum Associates.

Gauthier, I., & Nelson, C. A. (2001). The development of face expertise. *Current Opinion in Neurobiology, 11,* 219–224.

Gauthier, I., Skudlarski, P., Gore, J. C., & Anderson, A. W. (2000). Expertise for cars and birds recruits brain areas involved in face recognition. *Nature Neuroscience, 3,* 191–197.

Gauthier, I., & Tarr, M. J. (1997). Becoming a "Greeble" expert: Exploring mechanisms for face recognition. *Vision Research, 37,* 1673–1681.

Gauthier, I., & Tarr, M. J. (2002). Unraveling mechanisms for expert object recognition: Bridging brain activity and behavior. *Journal of Experimental Psychology: Human Perception and Performance, 28,* 431–446.

Gauthier, I., Williams, P., Tarr, M. J., & Tanaka, J. (1998). Training "Greeble" experts: A framework for studying object recognition processes. *Vision Research, 38,* 2401–2428.

Humphrey, N. K. (1974). Species and individuals in the perceptual world of monkeys. *Perception, 3,* 105–114.

Kuhl, P. K. (1991). Human adults and human infants show a "perceptual magnet effect" for the prototypes of speech categories, monkeys do not. *Perception & Psychophysics, 50,* 93–107.

Leinbach, M. D., & Fagot, B. I. (1993). Categorical habituation to male and female faces: Gender schematic processing in infancy. *Infant Behavior & Development, 16,* 317–332.

Mandler, J. M. (2000). Perceptual and conceptual processes. *Journal of Cognition and Development, 1,* 3–36.

Mareschal, D., French, R. M., & Quinn, P. C. (2000). A connectionist account of asymmetric category learning in early infancy. *Developmental Psychology, 36,* 635–645.

Mareschal, D., & Quinn, P. C. (2001). Categorization in infancy. *Trends in Cognitive Sciences, 5,* 443–450.

Mareschal, D., Quinn, P. C., & French, R. M. (2002). Asymmetric interference in 3- to 4-month-olds' sequential category learning. *Cognitive Science, 26,* 377–389.

Marr, D. (1982). *Vision.* San Francisco: W. H. Freeman.

Mermillod, M., French, R. M., Quinn, P. C., & Mareschal, D. (2003). The importance of long-term memory in infant perceptual categorization. In R. Alterman & D. Kirsh (Eds.), *Proceedings of the 25th Annual Conference of the Cognitive Science Society* (pp. 804–809). Mahwah, NJ: Lawrence Erlbaum Associates.

Murphy, G. L. (1991). Parts in object concepts: Experiments with artificial categories. *Memory and Cognition, 19,* 423–438.

O'Toole, A. J., Deffenbacher, K. A., Abdi, H., & Bartlett, J. C. (1991). Simulating the "other-race" effect as a problem in perceptual learning. *Connection Science, 3,* 163–178.

O'Toole, A., Vetter, T., Troje, N. F., & Bulthoff, H. H. (1997). Sex classification is better with three-dimensional head structure than with image intensity information. *Perception, 26,* 75–84.

Pascalis, O., & Bachevalier, J. (1998). Face recognition in primates: A cross species study. *Behavioral Processes, 43,* 87–96.

Pauen, S. (2000). Early differentiation within the animate domain: Are humans something special? *Journal of Experimental Child Psychology, 75,* 134–151.

Quinn, P. C. (2002a). Beyond prototypes: Asymmetries in infant categorization and what they teach us about the mechanisms guiding early knowledge acquisition. In R. Kail & H. Reese

(Eds.), *Advances in child development and behavior* (Vol. 29, pp. 161–193). San Diego: Academic Press.

Quinn, P. C. (2002b). Category representation in infants. *Current Directions in Psychological Science, 11*, 66–70.

Quinn, P. C. (2002c). Early categorization: A new synthesis. In U. Goswami (Ed.), *Blackwell handbook of childhood cognitive development* (pp. 84–101). Oxford, England: Blackwell.

Quinn, P. C. (2003, April). Why do young infants prefer female faces? In M. S. Strauss (Organizer), *Development of facial expertise in infancy*. Symposium conducted at the meeting of the Society for Research in Child Development, Tampa, FL.

Quinn, P. C. (2004). Is the asymmetry in young infants' categorization of humans versus nonhuman animals based on head, body, or global gestalt information? *Psychonomic Bulletin & Review, 11*, 92–97.

Quinn, P. C., & Eimas, P. D. (1996). Perceptual cues that permit categorical differentiation of animal species by infants. *Journal of Experimental Child Psychology, 63*, 189–211.

Quinn, P. C., & Eimas, P. D. (1997). A reexamination of the perceptual-to-conceptual shift in mental representations. *Review of General Psychology, 1*, 271–287.

Quinn, P. C., & Eimas, P. D. (1998). Evidence for a global categorical representation of humans by young infants. *Journal of Experimental Child Psychology, 69*, 151–174.

Quinn, P. C., & Eimas, P. D. (2000). The emergence of category representations during infancy: Are separate perceptual and conceptual processes required? *Journal of Cognition and Development, 1*, 55–61.

Quinn, P. C., Eimas, P. D., & Rosenkrantz, S. L. (1993). Evidence for representations of perceptually similar natural categories by 3- and 4-month-old infants. *Perception, 22*, 463–475.

Quinn, P. C., Yahr, J., Kuhn, A., Slater, A. M., & Pascalis, O. (2002). Representation of the gender of human faces by infants: A preference for female. *Perception, 31*, 1109–1121.

Rakison, D., & Butterworth, G. (1998). Infants' use of object parts in early categorization. *Developmental Psychology, 34*, 49–62.

Rosch, E. (1975). Cognitive reference points. *Cognitive Psychology, 7*, 532–547.

Rosch, E., Mervis, C. B., Gray, W. D., Johnson, D. M., & Boyes-Braem, P. (1976). Basic objects in natural categories. *Cognitive Psychology, 8*, 382–439.

Slater, A. M. (1995). Visual perception and memory at birth. In C. Rovee-Collier & L. P. Lipsitt (Eds.), *Advances in infancy research* (Vol. 9, pp. 107–162). Norwood, NJ: Ablex.

Smith, J. D., & Minda, J. P. (1998). Prototypes in the mist: The early epochs of category learning. *Journal of Experimental Psychology: Learning, Memory, and Cognition, 24*, 1411–1430.

Spencer, J., Quinn, P. C., Johnson, M. H., & Karmiloff-Smith, A. (1997). Heads you win, tails you lose: Evidence for young infants categorizing mammals by head and facial attributes (Special Issue: Perceptual Development). *Early Development and Parenting, 6*, 113–126.

Thelen, E., & Smith, L. B. (1994). *A dynamic systems approach to the development of cognition and action*. Cambridge, MA: MIT Press.

Chapter 6

The Perceptual to Conceptual Shift in Infancy and Early Childhood: A Surface or Deep Distinction?

David H. Rakison
Carnegie Mellon University

> *Categorization abilities in infancy are perceptual skills, based on the correlations between object features. Categorization skills in childhood also involve perceptual analyses of objects, but in addition are based on naïve theories about category membership and knowledge about characteristic or defining category features. The key point is whether we should interpret this to mean that categorization in infancy is qualitatively different from categorization in childhood.*
> —Goswami (1998, p. 289)

INTRODUCTION

Of all the ongoing debates within the early cognitive developmental literature, perhaps none is more hotly disputed and ill-defined than the transition known as the *perceptual to conceptual shift*. This phrase is generally used to describe the phenomenon whereby younger children and infants tend to rely on perceptual properties as the basis for categorization, whereas older children, typically toddlers and preschoolers, weigh more heavily the nonobvious or conceptual properties of objects in category membership decisions (Gelman & Markman, 1986, 1987; Mandler, 1992; Keil, 1991; Murphy & Medin, 1985; Piaget, 1952; Wellman & Gelman, 1988). In other words, it is believed that to determine which things "belong together," infants use surface properties such as facial features, shape, parts, or texture, but older children and presumably adults use deeper properties that are less often available in the perceptual array such as labels, internal biological components, or motion capabilities.

A classic example of this developmental phenomenon can be found in a study by Keil (1989; see also Rips, 1989) who presented children with stories in which various objects underwent an appearance transformation but retained their nonobvious properties. In one such story, children were shown a picture of a raccoon and told that it possessed the blood, bones, and reproductive properties of a skunk. From around 4 years of age, but not earlier, children judged that in such cases it was the nonobvious properties rather than the perceptual appearance of things that determine what they are, or more specifically, how they should be labeled. A similarly powerful illustration comes from work by Gelman and colleagues (e.g., Gelman & Markman, 1986, 1987; Davidson & Gelman, 1990) who found that 2½- to 3-year-old children, but not those around 2 years of age, make inductions to perceptually dissimilar pictures of objects of the same category (e.g., a cobra after being shown a brown snake) rather than to perceptually similar objects from a different category (e.g., a worm). Other examples that attest to young children's appreciation for nonobvious properties abound in the cognitive developmental literature. It has been found, for instance, that by preschool age children become sensitive to invisible properties such as germs (Au, Sidle, & Rollins, 1993; Kalish, 1996), aspects of the reproductive process (Springer, 1996), and features of growth, inheritance, and illness (e.g., Backscheider, Shatz, & Gelman, 1993; Springer & Keil, 1991). These data are often used to support the *theory view*, by which is meant that children of preschool age and older categorize and make inferences on the basis of information about ontology, causation, function, and other properties that are not directly observable (Carey, 1985; Gelman & Koenig, 2003; Gopnik & Wellman, 1994).

In light of recent work with infants it might also be argued that a similar transition occurs prior to the preschool years with regard to the knowledge acquisition of motion properties. For example, infants as young as 3 months can form categorical representations for cats, dogs, people, animals, and furniture and it is assumed that this behavior is grounded in perceptual information alone (for reviews see Quinn, chap. 5, this volume; Quinn & Eimas, 1996a, 1997). However, according to some researchers, by around 9 to 11 months of age infants categorize as equivalent those same classes of objects through *conceptual* categorization whereby things are grouped because they share a *meaning* (e.g., grouping animals because they are self-propelled) (Mandler & Bauer, 1988; Mandler, Bauer, & McDonough, 1991; Mandler & McDonough, 1998a). Moreover, it has been suggested that infants in the same age range can make inductive inferences such that they can generalize behaviors like drinking and sleeping to animals rather than to vehicles, and behaviors like starting with a key and giving people rides to vehicles rather than to animals (Mandler & McDonough, 1996, 1998b). Is it possible that this development in infancy reflects the same kind of shift observed in preschoolers?

The developmental change just outlined—namely, the acquisition of, and reliance on, information not consistently available in the perceptual array—is clearly a landmark in infants' and young children's evolving representations for objects in the world. Over and above being able to categorize things on the basis of their surface appearance, children following this transition can appropriately attribute various biological, psychological, and physical characteristics to different object kinds. But why, one might ask, is this latter state preferable? Perceptual cues, it is argued, are inherently unreliable as the basis for categorization because they are generally epiphenomenal in relation to the "true" or essential properties that characterize category membership. Perceptually given features such as "has four legs" or "has a long tail" are thought to be misleading in category membership decisions—not all dogs have a long tail—but deeper, nonobvious properties tend not to be (e.g., all dogs have hearts and dog DNA) (Murphy & Medin, 1985). Moreover, it is assumed that representations that include nonobvious information of objects are more abstract and more complex, which ultimately allows them more flexibly to be applied in cognitive functions such as induction, language, and memory.

Despite this portrayal of the tendency toward conceptual categorization in early development, things are not quite so cut and dry. I refer not to minor disputes over the interpretation of children's performance in one task or another but rather a questioning of the fundamental definitions of the terms involved and the content and structure of early representations. Relatively recent advances in developmental experimental methodology as well as the emergence of new theoretical perspectives, for example, have allowed researchers to examine more directly the nature of perceptual and conceptual categorization (e.g., Eimas, 1994; Jones & Smith, 1993; Oakes & Madole, 1999; Quinn & Eimas, 1997; Rakison & Poulin-Dubois, 2001; Rakison, 2003). At issue is not only the nature of conceptual structure but also its content; that is, the form in which concepts are represented, and the information about things in the world that is included within these concepts. The questions posed are, therefore, not trivial and are put forward mainly at a theoretical level. As will become apparent, there are also currently wildly diverging views on each of these issues within the developmental literature, and there are data that can be taken to support each side of the argument.

For the purposes of confining the scope of the chapter I focus predominantly on five separate but very much interrelated issues that pertain to the *perceptual to conceptual shift* (hereafter labeled the P2CS). The themes to be addressed are:

1. What is the difference between perceptual and conceptual information;

2. Whether children undergo a stage-like "perceptual to conceptual" shift;

3. Whether children rely on perceptual information rather than conceptual information in category membership decisions;

4. Whether perceptual information is inherently less reliable than nonobvious properties as a basis for categorization; and

5. What mechanism or mechanisms underlie the acquisition of knowledge about perceptual properties and nonobvious properties?

By concentrating on these themes my aim is to provide a detailed description of the P2CS, to discuss the pivotal claims concerning the nature of representational change in infancy and early childhood, and to supply a (hopefully) cohesive theoretical perspective on what is considered to be a fundamental yet rather opaque area of cognitive development.

What Is Perceptual Information and Conceptual Information?

One of the problems with the notion of the perceptual to conceptual shift is that the very terms *perceptual* and *conceptual* are tricky to delineate, and in many cases individual researchers characterize them quite differently. Generally, the terms "perceptual information" and "perceptual cues" refer to properties or features of an object, entity, or event that are consistently available in the sensory array. Thus perceptual information is often used to describe the surface properties or features of things such as size, color, shape, parts, and so on. In contrast, the terms "conceptual," "nonobvious," or "nonobservable" information generally refer to those properties or features of an object, entity, or event that are not often if at all available in the sensory array. Such properties are generally taken to include internal biological and technological components of animates and inanimates (e.g., brains, hearts, engines, silicon chips), psychological states (e.g., beliefs, intentions, and goals), and motion capabilities (e.g., self-propulsion, agency, and contingent action).

These general definitions are also often followed in describing categorization in infants and young children. The terms "perceptual representation" and "perceptual categorization" are used to convey the idea that children attend to, and have knowledge of, the surface properties of objects and rely on these properties to classify things, and the terms "conceptual representation" and "conceptual categorization" imply that children have knowledge of, and presumably use, the nonobvious properties of objects, category relations (e.g., "this thing is an animal"), or what the *meaning* of something is (Mandler, 1992). According to a number of researchers (e.g., Quinn & Eimas, 1997; Mandler, 1992), a crucial difference between perceptually and conceptually based representations is that the latter allows inferences about the behavior and properties of objects or entities that are not available in the sensory array. This is not to say, however, that conceptual categorization excludes altogether any reference to perceptual cues. It seems difficult, if not impossible, to envisage a process whereby infants or children access conceptual knowledge about an object or entity without first identifying that object or entity on the basis of its perceptual appearance. This view is most vehemently argued by Mandler (1992, 1998, 2000, 2003) who posits two separate but connected processes in categorization. One of these processes involves perceptual categorization whereby an object or entity is identified based on its surface appearance, and the other involves conceptual categorization whereby the same object or entity is classified on the basis of its nonobservable properties (e.g., motion characteristics).

There are, however, a number of problems with the creation of a simple dichotomy of surface properties on the one hand and nonobservable properties on the other. Most importantly, to label perceptual properties as such based on their accessibility in the sensory array leaves questionable the identity of those only intermittently available to the perceptual system. Even though properties such as "acts as an agent" or "meows" are not continually present when one observes a cat, these properties become part of the representation for a cat through the visual and auditory systems. Thus it is possible, if not necessary, to ask at what point on the continuum between observable and nonobservable should a property be considered perceptual or conceptual? The resolution of this issue is crucial in determining the nature of the P2CS, but has thus far been generally overlooked in the developmental literature. My view, which is delineated in detail later in this chapter, is that a strong case can be made for considering all properties of objects perceptual in the sense that they enter the representational system through one or more of the sensory input systems and that the same basic associative learning mechanism underlies most, if not all aspects of this early knowledge acquisition. The consequence of this view is that there is no qualitative difference between representations for perceptual and so-called nonobservable information. For now, however, I think it important to bear in mind that in considering the P2CS one must not make staunch assumptions about the nature of perceptual and nonobvious information, their role in categorization at different ages, and the mental structures in which they are represented.

Do Children Undergo a Stage-Like "Perceptual to Conceptual" Shift?

Although Piaget (1952) failed to provide a coherent explanation for how a sensorimotor infant develops into a conceptual infant, his influence on early cognitive developmental research led to an initial bias whereby any transition from a reliance on perceptual information to nonobvious information was viewed as a qualitative change in behavior (see also Bruner, Olver, & Greenfield, 1966). This assumption is without doubt understandable given the data that suggest that young infants are perceptually bound and older infants and preschool children are conceptually bound when making category membership decisions. For example, as highlighted at the beginning of this chapter there is evidence that children as young as 2½ years of age make inductions to perceptually dissimilar objects of the same category rather than to perceptually similar objects from a different category (Davidson & Gelman, 1990; Gelman & Coley, 1990; Gelman & Markman, 1987), and from around 4 years of age judge that nonobvious properties rather than the perceptual appearance of things determine what they are, or more specifically, how they should be labeled (Keil, 1989; see also Rips, 1989).

Despite this evidence of perhaps two (or more) transitions in behavior—one in infancy and one around 3 to 4 years of age—many researchers no longer believe that a "shift" from perceptual to conceptual categorization occurs; however, the reasons for this stance varies from researcher to researcher. Mandler (1992, 1998, 2003) argued that there is no need for a PC2S because although perceptual cues are important in the classification process, the "conceptual interpretation of perceptual arrays begins either at birth or as soon as stable perceptual schemas are formed in the first month or two" (Mandler, 2003, p. 106). According to Mandler, therefore, the primary basis for categorization is conceptual rather than perceptual virtually throughout the lifespan. A quite different view is taken by Oakes and Madole (1999, 2003) who claimed that perceptual and conceptual categorization essentially involve similar basic processes and are therefore intrinsically related. They argued that the observed change in infants' categorizing behavior emerges not because of the development of new categorization processes but instead is a result of ever-increasing access to different types of information via general development in cognitive, motor, and linguistic skills. For example, Oakes and Madole (2003) argued that the emerging ability to integrate spatiotemporal information allows infants to learn about functional properties at around 14 to 18 months of age. Similarly, Smith and Heise (1992) proposed that infants' experience with correlations in the environment causes them to pay greater attention to the attributes that are a part of those correlations. In this way, infants move from an unstructured "similarity space" to a distorted or structured similarity space that is weighted toward particular features and correlations of features.

Finally, it has been proposed that categorization is grounded in perceptual information not only during infancy but also throughout the lifespan. Elsewhere I have argued (Rakison, 2003; Rakison & Poulin-Dubois, 2001) as have Quinn and Eimas (e.g., Eimas, 1994; Quinn & Eimas, 1997, 2000) that concept acquisition is a process of continuous representational enrichment that relies on a perceptual system that is sufficiently sensitive and robust to allow infants to form categories that cohere because of similarity relations. Thus, young infants categorize on the basis of object features such as shape and texture (e.g., Jones, Smith, & Landau, 1991), functional parts (e.g., Rakison & Butterworth, 1998a; Rakison & Cohen, 1999), or facial features (e.g., Quinn & Eimas, 1996b), and later learn about many non-observable properties of objects through language (Quinn & Eimas, 1997, 2000; Rakison, 2003; Rakison & Poulin-Dubois, 2001).

Quinn and Eimas and I differ, however, in our view of the very nature of perceptually and conceptually based representations. According to Quinn and Eimas (1997), perceptual categorization involves complex information but "does not include inferential information unavailable to the perceptual system" (p. 273). In contrast, conceptual representations are informative about object kinds and "presumably support numerous inferences about the nature and behavior of the thing represented" (p. 273). The implication of these statements is that although the general processes underlying the acquisition of representations remains constant throughout development, the very nature of perceptual and conceptual representations are fundamentally different. Although I agree with the general notion advanced in these statements, my stance is that infants' representations are "perceptual" throughout development in the sense that all information concerning things in the world is derived from sensory input. Moreover, I claim that these representations are capable of supporting some kind of inferences about the properties of objects or their behaviors at virtually all points in their evolution (Rakison, 2003; Rakison & Poulin-Dubois, 2001). For instance, there is evidence that infants as young as 3 months of age can develop *expectations* about the appearance of items on a screen (see Haith, Wentworth, & Canfield, 1993; Roberts, 1998). I present additional evidence from my laboratory later in the chapter to support this view.

As a more broad comment on the nature of the PC2S, it is worth pointing out that the movement away from a view of a stage-like shift in early category and concept development coincides with similar claims about developmental change in general. Siegler (1996) has forcefully argued that classic stage-based theories such as those of Piaget and Kohlberg, as well as more recent accounts such as those by Carey (1985) and Wellman (1990), sit uncomfortably with a good deal of developmental data. As an alternative, Siegler argued that developmental change is better described and explained as continuous, with different strategies competing with each other as a series of overlapping waves. In this way, development is not a set of discrete "jumps" from one state to another but rather is best viewed as an increase and decrease in the frequency with which certain strategies, information, or processes are relied on.

In summary, although there is evidence that preschoolers and older children have knowledge about the nonobvious properties of objects, it is far from clear whether this knowledge results from a perceptual to conceptual shift of any kind. Certainly there is little support for the notion of a stage-like transition, and according to a number of theorists it is questionable whether a representational shift of any kind actually occurs. A number of important issues remain, however. Most notably it is unclear at what point in development, if at all, the change is made from perceptual to conceptual representations. Moreover, what causes this developmental change also remains moot. These issues are discussed, at least in part, in the following sections.

Do Infants and Children Rely on Perceptual Information or Nonobvious Information to Categorize?

Thus far in this chapter it has been taken for granted that infants tend to rely on surface properties to categorize—that is, have perceptual representations—and that older children tend to rely on nonobvious properties to categories—that is, have conceptual representations. I have already suggested that the distinction between perceptual and conceptual representations is more opaque than is generally assumed, mainly because of the argument that all information enters the representational system via one or more of the perceptual systems. At a different level of analysis, however, it is possible to examine the available evidence to assess whether it supports the claim that infants and young children categorize conceptually rather than perceptually.

Evidence of Conceptual Categorization and Induction in Infants. The notion that infants' representations involve conceptual information has been most strikingly argued by Mandler (1992, 1998, 2000, 2003; Mandler & McDonough, 1996, 1998b). According to Mandler, by around 12 months of age, infants no longer categorize objects because of their appearance but rather because of a shared *meaning*. For example, by around the end of the first year of life infants will group together various mammals because they are understood to be self-propelled entities that can act as agents. These conceptual categories are based on *image-schemas*, or *conceptual primitives*, that encapsulate crucial abstract characteristics of objects' spatial structure and movement (see also R. Gelman, 1990; R. Gelman, Durgin, & Kaufman, 1995). For instance, image-schemas that summarize animate entities represent self-motion, animate-motion (moving nonlinearly), causing action at a distance, and agency. Mandler (1992, 2000) proposed that these image-schemas are constructed through an innate process of *perceptual analysis* that recodes aspects of the perceptual display into a more abstract, accessible form.

The evidence that Mandler used to support this theory comes from three separate experimental procedures used with infants. Data from sequential-touching and object-examining tasks revealed that infants in the second year of life formed categories when stimuli possessed low within-class perceptual similarity—for example, animals, vehicles, or furniture (Mandler & Bauer, 1988; Mandler et al., 1991)—and infants as young as 9 months of age categorized as different items that were perceptually similar such as planes and birds (Mandler & McDonough, 1993). In the inductive generalization task infants observe an action and are allowed to repeat that action with two objects, one drawn from the same category and one drawn from a different category than the model exemplar (Mandler & McDonough, 1996, 1998b). As outlined earlier, using this methodology it has been shown that infants as young as 9 to 11 months generalize behaviors like drinking and sleeping to animals and behaviors such as "starting with a key" and "gives rides" to vehicles. Moreover, when infants were presented with two objects from the same superordinate category to repeat an action (e.g., a dog and a cat after seeing a dog "drink" from a cup), they were just as likely to use either exemplar, a finding that was interpreted to mean that infants understand that both objects were capable of that action.

There are, nevertheless, both empirical and theoretical grounds to question Mandler's view that infants categorize conceptually within the first year of life. At a theoretical level, Mandler's (1992, 1998, 2000) theory has been questioned for its failure to specify how the process of perceptual analysis—whereby information available in the perceptual array is translated into a simpler, conceptual image-schema—might operate. This process, which is the crux of Mandler's theory, is as yet laid out only in general terms that fail to provide sufficient information to allow for a direct empirical test to be made. An additional problem with Mandler's formulation is that as a consequence of the notion that there are distinct mechanisms that deal with perceptual and conceptual categorization, the appearance of objects is represented separately from their meaning. That is, "image schemas representing biological motion, self-motion, and contingent motion would be independent of the actual appearance of the movement of any particular object" (Mandler, 2000, p. 20). One cannot help but wonder whether it is necessary to posit such a dual-process framework when a single, integrated representational mechanism offers a more parsimonious and just as viable framework for concept development in infants and adults (Goldstone & Barsalou, 1998; Quinn, Johnson, Mareschal, Rakison, & Younger, 2000). Finally, it is questionable whether the process of perceptual analysis differs from perceptual categorization of movement patterns (Quinn & Eimas, 2000). There is no compelling reason why movement patterns of objects need to be abstracted in the way formulated by Mandler (1992, 2000): It is just as reasonable to suppose that these perceptually available patterns of movement are associated with individual exemplars, and then later are generalized to other category members.

At an empirical level, it is unclear why it is necessary to posit that infants have early conceptual knowledge about objects' meaning in order to explain the sequential touching, object examining, and generalized imitation data that Mandler presents (e.g., Mandler & Bauer, 1988; Mandler et al., 1991; Mandler & McDonough, 1993, 1996, 1998a, 1998b). In many cases there is evidence that perceptual similarity can play the role ascribed to conceptual knowledge in such experiments. For example, evidence from sequential touching studies by Rakison and Butterworth (1998a) revealed that 14- to 18-month-old infants' ability to form superordinate categories such as animals, vehicles, and furniture is guided by the presence or absence of object parts such as legs and wheels. For example, infants as old as 14 and 18 months categorize animals that possess legs as different from vehicles with wheels but they are unable to do so when animals possess no legs and vehicles possess no wheels or when animals and vehicles possess both legs and wheels.

There are also data to suggest that infants' inductive generalizations in the task used by Mandler and McDonough (1996, 1998b) may be guided more by perceptual similarity than knowledge about the specific actions of animates and inanimates. Using the same general procedure as that in the studies by Mandler and McDonough (1996, 1998b), I have found that infants will repeat the observed actions with a category exemplar from the "wrong" category if the experimenter models the action with an exemplar from that "wrong" category (Rakison, 2003). For example, if an experimenter models a cat going up a set of stairs, 14- and 18-month-olds will repeat the action with a novel animal; but if the experimenter models a car going up a set of stairs infants in the same age groups will repeat the action with a novel vehicle (Rakison, 2003).

To investigate further infants' knowledge of motion properties and their behavior in the task, I recently developed a novel version of the inductive generalization procedure and tested infants with two simple motions of animates (a dog walking/hopping and a bird flying) and two simple motions of inanimates (a car rolling and a plane flying) (Rakison, 2004). In the modified version of the task, infants were presented with four objects rather than two in the baseline and generalization phases. One of the stimuli was drawn from the same superordinate domain as the model and shared over-all similarity and functional parts with that exemplar (SPSC: same parts, same category). For example, when the cat was the model exemplar the SPSC exemplar was a dog. Another test stimulus was drawn from the same superordinate domain as the model but did not share overall similarity or functional parts (DPSC: different parts, same category). For example, when the cat was the model exemplar the DPSC exemplar was a dolphin. A third stimulus was drawn from a different superordinate domain than the model but had the same functional parts as the model (SPDC: same parts, differ-ent category). For example, when the cat was the model exemplar the SPDC exemplar was a table (with four legs). Finally, one stimulus was drawn from a different superordinate domain and shared no obvious functional parts with the model (DPDC: different category different parts); when the cat was the model the DPDC exemplar was a car. A full list of the stimuli used in the task is presented in Table 6.1, and the stimuli from the cat "rolling" condition can be seen in Fig. 6.1.

This experimental design made it possible to explore the basis for in-fants' choice of objects to generalize the observed actions as well as whether knowledge for motion properties develops in parallel for the domains of land- and air-movement. Moreover, in separate experiments the motions were modeled to infants with either the appropriate exemplar (as in Table 6.1) or a simple U-shaped block (see Fig. 6.2). The idea behind the use of a U-shaped block as a model was to give infants as little information about the identity or category of the objects that performed the motions in question and thereby test more stringently their knowledge of those motions.

To simplify matters, I discuss infants' behavior only in conditions in which land-based motions were modeled (i.e., hopping and rolling). In the experiment in which the events were modeled with the appropriate exem-plar, it was found that infants at 14 months repeated the observed action with the SPSC exemplar only marginally more than any other exemplar, suggesting that they would choose only those stimuli that were perceptually

TABLE 6.1
Stimuli Used in Inductive Generalization Studies in Which Events
Were Modeled With an Appropriate Exemplar (as Shown Here)
or an Ambiguous U-Shaped Block (Rakison, 2004)

Motion Events	Model	Test Stimuli			
		SPSC	*SPDC*	*DPSC*	*DPDC*
Vehicle rolling	Car	RV	Stroller	Boat	Cow
Animal walking	Cat	Dog	Table	Dolphin	Truck
Vehicle flying	Plane	Space shuttle	Dragonfly	Car	Duck
Animal flying	Eagle	Parrot	Plane	Dog	Grasshopper

FIG. 6.1. Example of stimuli used in the cat "rolling" condition (Rakison, 2004).

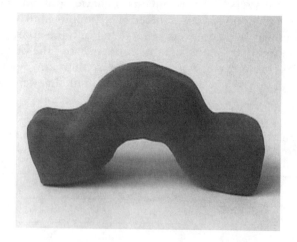

FIG. 6.2. The ambiguous block stimulus used to model events.

142

(or conceptually) similar to the model. In contrast, infants at 18 months chose the SPSC exemplar and SPDC exemplars to demonstrate the actions. Infants at 22 months, however, tended to repeat the observed motions only with the perceptually and conceptually similar exemplar (SPSC). These findings imply a developmental trend whereby infants at 14 months have little or no basis for generalization, infants at 18 months relate object parts with specific motions, and infants at 22 months have generalized motion properties to whole objects but only those that are similar overall to the model (e.g., from a cat to a dog but not a dolphin).

The experiment in which the actions were modeled by the experimenter with the block exemplar were even more revealing about 18- and 22-month-old infants' developing representations for animates and inanimates (Rakison, 2004). In the experiment in which the land tasks were modeled with a U-shaped block, 18-month-olds chose the SPSC and SPDC exemplars to repeat the observed action, whereas 22-month-olds chose the SPSC and DPSC exemplars to hop or roll. This pattern of results suggests that infants brought some knowledge of the motion characteristics of animates and inanimates with them to the task: Infants were able to demonstrate actions even when no information was presented about the items that engage in those actions. That the 22-month-olds behaved differently in this experiment in comparison to those of the same age who saw an appropriate exemplar model the same action suggests that infants are affected somewhat by the stimulus used in the experimental situation (see also Rakison, 2003). That is, infants may have been directed to imitate only actions with the exemplars that were similar to the model, and when no information was given about the model, infants were more unconstrained in their choice.

In my view these studies have a number of implications for the discussion at hand. First, they support the notion that infants at least as old as 18 months do not generalize the actions they observe in the inductive generalization procedure on the basis of nonobservable properties or category membership. Instead, the data presented here, which are consistent with my earlier work (see Rakison, 2003; Rakison & Poulin-Dubois, 2002), suggest that 14- and 18-month-old infants' knowledge of the motion properties of objects may be based primarily in an association between an action or motion and the causally relevant functional parts involved in that action or motion. In contrast, older infants, those around 22 months, appear to have extended this association to whole objects or categories of objects (see also Jones & Smith, 1993; Quinn & Eimas, 1997). This conclusion is supported by infants' behavior across the two experiments described here, but the most compelling evidence was found in the block-model study. In that task infants at 18 months in the land-task chose the objects that possessed the appropriate parts for the motion (e.g., they made the cat and table "walk"), whereas infants at 22 months chose the two objects that belong to the appropriate category for the motion (e.g., they made the cat and dolphin "walk"). Ongoing research in my laboratory is exploring how infants start to generalize motion cues from causally relevant parts to other object features or whole objects.

Evidence of Conceptual Categorization and Induction in Preschoolers. The notion that older children base their categorization and inductions on knowledge about nonperceptual properties has also come under scrutiny in recent years. In particular, Smith and her colleagues (e.g., Jones & Smith, 1993; Smith & Samuelson, 1997; Thelen & Smith, 1994) argued that in studies like those conducted by Gelman, in which perceptual properties are pitted against category membership, perceptual aspects of the stimuli are impoverished compared to their real world appearance. This, in addition to the fact that the objects are typically labeled with familiar names— snake, worm, cat, skunk, for example—means that children have to make a category induction either on the basis of nonobvious properties and a label or on the basis of a line drawing. Similarly, in the transformation studies by Keil (1989), children are presented with a line drawing and a considerable amount of information about the entity's nonobvious properties. Perhaps children interpret this bias in the amount of information given as a suggestion that, in fact, the object is defined by its nonperceptual properties, and therefore they tend to choose nonobvious properties to decide what kind of thing something is. Indeed, there is evidence that children 8 years and younger will generalize a trait to a perceptually identical drawing rather than one with the same label (Farrar, Raney, & Boyer, 1992). Finally, Jones and Smith (1993) suggested that children and adults in the induction and transformation studies may use general knowledge about biology, the validity of stories, and even the psychology of experiments, rather than knowledge about skunks, raccoons, or worms per se. In other words, judgments about category membership in such tasks may be "assembled from multiple kinds of knowledge that include perceptual, nonperceptual, linguistic and even social referents" (p. 137).

The crux of Jones and Smith's (1993) claim is that perception and language play roles equal to nonperceptual information in naming, categorization, and conceptual knowledge. It should be borne in mind, however, that although the arguments by Smith and colleagues are forceful, there is little in the way of data to support or refute them. Jones and Smith (1993; see also Jones et al., 1991) presented evidence that features such as overall shape, eyes, and texture are important cues in categorization and label extension; however, whether there is some stable representational core that predominates in categorization, induction, and language, and what information is stored at that core, remains unknown. And indeed, an inherent problem with studies in which perceptual and conceptual information are pitted against each other is that it is difficult, if not impossible, to balance the presentation of such cues. As a result, for any given finding that falls on one side of the argument or the other—that is, data that suggest that young children use perceptual information or nonobvious information to categorize—it is possible to make the case that the different types of information were not equally salient in the task. Nonetheless, it is important to consider seriously the empirical data and theoretical arguments outlined here because they at least bring into question whether infants and preschoolers rely on nonobvious properties in categorization, induction, and language.

Is Perceptual Information Less Reliable Than Nonobvious Properties as a Basis for Categorization?

The discussions in the previous sections highlight three points: First, it is difficult to discern or argue for a qualitative difference at a representational level between perceptual and nonobvious properties; second, there is little evidence of a qualitative "shift" from one kind of representation to the other; and third, it should not be tacitly assumed that infants and children rely on nonobvious properties to classify, or in other words, that they engage in what has been called conceptual categorization (Mandler, 1992). But what of the claims that conceptual representations must underlie categorization because nonobvious properties are more reliable and less misleading about category membership than perceptual, surface properties? The theoretical argument for this claim rests on the representational structure of information. It is putatively held that the core of concepts are stable in that they are built from a list of propositions that are unchanging, static representations (Medin & Ortony, 1989); for instance, any number of people would know that dogs give birth to puppies rather than kittens. A corollary is that perceptual similarity is inherently unstable in that the aspect of similarity to which adults attend varies depending on the context (e.g., Barsalou, 1989; Jones & Smith, 1993); thus in one context kittens might be considered more like lions, and in another they might be considered more like puppies. If both of these premises are accepted, then, according to some, it logically follows that perceptual information cannot be at the core of stable representations and therefore nonobvious properties must play such a role (Medin & Ortony, 1989).

Within this framework, it has been claimed that there is a nonarbitrary, causal relationship between surface and deep properties whereby the central nonobvious attributes of a thing constrain and even generate its surface attributes. According to Medin and Ortony (1989; see also Brown, 1989; Rips, 1989; E. E. Smith, Medin, & Rips, 1984), this causes children and adults to be drawn to surface similarities that in turn lead them to more central conceptual properties. For example, a child might find animal legs perceptually salient and consequently be guided to internal properties such as animacy, support, and so on. Thus, despite perceptual similarities, objects are judged to be members of a larger category by virtue of qualities that are invariably not perceptual, or they are defined by some underlying nature that makes them what they are. The result is what Medin and Ortony (1989) called *psychological essentialism*. They defined it as the belief that objects of a category share some sort of common essence or are "the same kind of thing," and claimed that it is at the core of concepts and therefore category membership decisions. In support of such a view one could refer to the work of Gelman, Keil, and others that was discussed earlier in the chapter.

This line of reasoning is certainly persuasive and has been highly influential within the field. Nevertheless, there are a number of reasons why this theoretical view may not accurately describe the nature of developing representations. First, that adults will attend to different aspects of surface similarity depending on contextual cues should not be considered as an inherent weakness—as appears to be Medin and Ortony's (1989) view—but instead can be viewed as a strength in terms of the dynamic and flexible way in which perceptual information (as well as other kinds of information) can be used differently in a variety of situations (see also Jones & Smith, 1993; L. B. Smith, 2000; Thelen & Smith, 1994). Second, it remains to be seen whether the claim that the core of representations are a stable list of propositions is a veridical one. Although this view is probably held implicitly by many of those within Cognitive Science who study concepts and concept acquisition, there is no direct evidence that it is an accurate portrayal of representational content. Indeed, in combining both of these last two points, Jones and Smith (1993) claimed that: "What we call 'categories' and 'concepts' are the emergent products of multiple knowledge sources in specific task contexts. By this view, there is no set intension (definition in the head) or extension (category in the world). Both are transient and emergent in the task at hand" (p. 136).

Finally, and somewhat more problematic for Medin and Ortony's view, it is important to reflect on the advantage of attention to nonobvious properties, or in other words, to think about categorization in terms of a simple cost-benefit analysis. I do not doubt that surface properties are constrained and caused by nonobvious properties or that such nonobvious properties are in some sense a more reliable cue of category membership. Thus it is beyond argument that tigers' stripes have a genetic foundation and that tiger DNA is a better predictor than stripes that an animal is a tiger rather than, say, a zebra. However, my claim is that although as adults we may know the causal relation between deeper, nonobservable properties and surface properties, there is no reason to access this knowledge when surface properties will suffice in category membership judgments.

Instead, I propose that perceptual cues provide sufficient information for accurate categorization in all but a few cases, and the cost of accessing information about conceptual properties generally outweighs the benefits. To return to the example I just used, if a tiger-looking big cat were to walk into my office would it be more parsimonious to decide from its appearance—large, striped, with big teeth—that this animal has the potential to attack and kill me or would it be necessary for me to refer my knowledge of nonobvious properties such as whether it has tiger DNA or its parents were tigers? I think that few would argue that accessing nonobvious properties would be helpful in such a situation. Let us consider a more everyday example. My Honda Prelude looks very much like a car. It has four wheels, windows, seats, furry dice, and all the other amenities that a car should have. Would you need to determine that it has an engine, requires gas, and can actually function as a car in order to call it a car? Or would you assume that if it looks like a car, it is, most likely, a car?

So why is it that in studies such as those by Gelman and Keil, children are more likely to use nonobvious properties than surface properties to make category membership judgments? I propose that what emerges around the preschool years is not a perceptual to conceptual shift at all but rather an understanding that nonobvious properties—those that cannot be seen—are more highly correlated with category membership than surface features. This does not mean that surface features are poor predictors of what kind of thing an object is, but instead that nonobvious properties are more strongly, if not perfectly, related to category membership. This newfound knowledge does not mean, however, that the default basis for categorization becomes nonobvious properties; surface properties, for the reasons given in the previous paragraph, continue to play a primary role in everyday category decisions. But, when perceptual cues are directly pitted against nonobvious properties—as they are in the studies by Keil, Gelman, and others—children will chose the latter over the former because of this newly developed assumption about their ontological predictive power. This interpretation of preschooler's behavior is consistent with Siegler's (1996) view of conceptual change as overlapping ways. Thus, it is not that one representational content or structure replaces another but rather that a new strategy emerges for categorizing objects, events, and properties, and this strategy competes with those already available to the young child and is deemed most productive under certain conditions. To test this hypothesis, I have recently investigated the role of similarity and nonobvious properties (e.g., has a round heart, likes people) on inductive inference by preschoolers and adults (Hahn & Rakison, 2003). Hahn and I examined category membership decisions in the context of varied statistical information about the distribution of surface and nonobvious properties. Participants were taught new categories of animals, birds, and insects that varied in the degree to

which nonobvious or perceptual properties predicted category membership. The results showed that preschoolers as well as adults use distribu-
tional information to inform their inductive inferences; that is, both groups
used surface properties or nonobvious properties when each was the better
predictor of category membership, and they did so whether or not labels
were present.

Some critics of this view may argue that what is at issue here is the difference between judging something to be a member of a category and recognizing it as an exemplar of a category. In other words, it could be claimed
that perceptual cues are used to determine what something is whereas
nonobvious cues are used to determine what the meaning of something is
(e.g., Mandler, 1992, 2000, 2003). In many cases, however, these two aspects of object processing are difficult, if not impossible, to discriminate,
and it is unclear whether it is necessary to access knowledge of nonobvious
properties in everyday category membership decisions.

What Mechanisms Underlie the Acquisition of Knowledge
About Perceptual Properties and Nonobvious Properties?

A final issue that is integral in any discussion of the perceptual to conceptual shift, and in any discussion of cognitive development in general, concerns the mechanisms that underlie the acquisition of representations early
in life. I use the term *mechanism* here to refer to the mental processes that allow or cause developmental change (see Siegler, 1996). Somewhat surprisingly, a focus on the mechanism underlying change is commonly absent
from discussion of conceptual developmental. For example, those who support the theory theory view often overlook the issue of developmental
change because it is believed that relatively sophisticated concepts are present early in life (Gelman & Koenig, 2003).

In recent years, however, a focus on mechanism has become more prominent in the work of those who study infants' representations. Leslie (1984,
1988, 1995), for example, presented a nativist and *modular* view of infants'
developing representations of objects. He proposed that infants are born
with a three-part theory of Agency, with separate brain mechanisms for
each, which process the mechanical, intentional, and cognitive properties
of agents. Thus, distinct mental modules direct infants' attention toward
different kinds of events and allow them to interpret those events; for example, a *theory of body*, or *ToBy*, biases infants to interpret agents as having an
internal and renewable source of energy, and a *theory of mind mechanism*
(ToMM) interprets an agents' action as goal directed or involving intentionality. Elsewhere, I have argued that there are a number of problems
with such a modular view (Rakison & Poulin-Dubois, 2001). First, it is not
clear why these modules are not initially functional but instead must be

"triggered" at some, generally unspecified, point in the first years of life. For example, infants do not perceive actions as causal or goal-directed until around 6 to 7 months of age (Oakes & Cohen, 1990; Leslie & Keeble, 1987; Woodward, 1999). Second, it remains an open question how distinct modules deal with information that involves both mechanical and intentional action such as when a hand reaches for a toy. Mandler (1992, 1998, 2000, 2003) offered perhaps the most influential proposal of the representational change in infancy. As was outlined earlier, Mandler posited that from very early in life infants possess two representational systems, one that supports perceptual categorization and one that supports conceptual categorization. The perceptual categorization system is involved more in object recognition whereas the conceptual categorization system allows infants to classify objects based on their meaning.

A third view concerning the mechanism for representational change, which was also outlined earlier, is that the information incorporated into infants' and children's concepts is inherently perceptual in nature and that representational development occurs through gradual, incremental learning (Eimas, 1994; Quinn & Eimas, 1997, 2000; Rakison & Poulin-Dubois, 2001; Rakison, 2003). The claim is that concept acquisition is a process of continuous representational enrichment that relies on a perceptual system that is sufficiently sensitive and robust to allow infants to form categories that cohere because of similarity relations. The development of language allows the acquisition of knowledge about the nonobservable characteristics of objects—in particular, biological functions like reproduction and other internal properties—through formal and informal tuition. Moreover, it has been postulated that children are able to acquire information about objects through language after very few exposures, and this information may be generalized broadly across category members (Rakison, 2003). This is a form of what has been labeled *fast mapping* (see Bloom, 2000) although in the case outlined here it is not that infants connect a label to a referent but rather they connect an object property to a category. For instance, children may learn that dogs have hearts after hearing this proposition only once or twice, and they would assume that many, if not all dogs possess hearts. In combination, these processes lead, ultimately, to a representation for animals that include shape, texture, parts, facial features, and less obvious, nonobservable properties.

As discussed earlier, my view differs from that of Quinn and Eimas in a number of ways. Most notably, Quinn and Eimas argued that only conceptual representations, and not perceptual ones, can support inferential processes whereby infants can use information unavailable to the perceptual system. In contrast, I do not support the distinction, either at a semantic or theoretical level, between perceptual and conceptual representations, and I believe that even the earliest representations can support inferential processes in the form of *expectations* that result from the association between static and dynamic cues. Thus, the perception of one component of the relationship activates an expectation about the existence of the other component (Rakison, 2003; see also Haith et al., 1993; Roberts, 1998). In the case of properties that are available only intermittently in the perceptual array such as motion properties, the result is a representation of an associative link that embodies what has come to be labeled "nonobvious" knowledge; however, there is no need to apply the kind of rich description to these representations that has been suggested in previous formulations of concept development (e.g., Leslie, 1995; Mandler, 1992). For the kind of expectations outlined here, what is associated is a perceptual feature—legs, for instance—with an intermittently available motion characteristic such as self-propulsion.

An additional divergence from Quinn and Eimas' (1997, 2000) theory is that I have proposed the early presence of a number of *attention biases*— though other terms such as *constraints* or *learning enablers* could just as easily describe them—that direct infants to causally relevant information available in the perceptual array. The presence of these attention biases means that not all information available in the perceptual array is equally salient to infants, and consequently the theory is not undermined by the argument of Original Sim (Keil, 1981). These biases include, but are not limited to, attention to motion, both at a global and a local level, and attention to the static and dynamic features of entities and objects. An attentional system that is drawn to motion is most likely an evolutionary adaptation that helps humans, as well as other species, to detect the presence of potential prey or a potential predatory threat. Indeed, there is evidence that newborns prefer moving objects over static objects (Slater, 1989), that 4-month-olds' perception of object unity for a partly occluded object depends on common motion (Kellman & Spelke, 1983), and that by 3 months of age infants prefer a human moving point-light display to an unstructured point-light display (Bertenthal, 1993). Moreover, motion cues continue to play an important role throughout the lifespan. It has been found that adults and infants detect an object's properties more easily when it moves than when it is stationary (Burnham & Day, 1979), and that 4- and 7-year-olds as well as adults base their category judgments for animals on motion characteristics rather than shape when those two attributes are pitted against each other (Mak & Vera, 1999).

Support for this view of representational development in infancy comes from a number of studies with a variation of the Switch design (Gentner, 1978; Younger & Cohen, 1986) within the habituation procedure. In the basic Switch design, infants are habituated to two events, one in which feature A^1 is paired with feature B^1 and one in which feature A^2 is paired with feature B^2. Once habituated to these stimuli, infants are presented with a trial in which the feature pairings are switched—for example, feature A^1 is shown with feature B^2—and a trial in which the feature pairings remain unchanged from that shown during habituation. This design is especially ideal for examining infants' ability to learn correlations because relatively long looking time to the "switch" test trial compared to a familiar trial can only be caused by infants' detection of a novel feature pairing and not because of the introduction of a novel feature. Using this basic design, it has been shown that 7-month-olds can detect correlations among the static features of schematic animals (Younger & Cohen, 1986), 14-month-olds can associate a label with a moving object (Werker, Cohen, Lloyd, Casasola, & Stager, 1998), and 14- to 18-month-olds can associate an object's form with its function (Madole, Oakes, & Cohen, 1993; Madole & Cohen, 1995). In the novel variation of this design described here, infants were habituated to events in which there were three variables rather than two (Rakison & Poulin-Dubois, 2002). Thus, infants were habituated to pairings $P^1B^1M^1$ and $P^2B^2M^2$ (P = parts, B = body, M = motion path) and then presented with test events that violated these correlations. The strength of such a design is that it allows investigation of infants' ability to detect and encode correlations as well as their predilection to attend to certain correlations and ignore others.

In one series of studies, 10-, 14-, and 18-month-old infants' were habituated to two events in which an object moved across a screen. Each object consisted of a unique body (red oval-shape or blue pot-shape), a pair of unique moving parts (yellow cigar shapes that moved horizontally or green diamond shapes that moved vertically), and a unique motion path (rectilinear or curvilinear). Infants might see during habituation, for example, a blue-bodied object with yellow horizontally moving parts travel along a linear trajectory and a red-bodied object with green vertically moving parts travel along a curvilinear trajectory. During the test phase of the experiment, infants were shown one trial in which the parts were switched in relation to the pairing seen during habituation (e.g., $P^2B^1M^1$), one trial in which the body was switched in relation to the pairing seen during habituation (e.g., $P^1B^2M^1$), one trial in which the motion was switched compared to that seen earlier (e.g., $P^1B^1M^2$), and one trial that was the same as that seen during habituation. For example, given the two habituation stimuli just described, in the parts switch infants might see the blue-bodied object travel linearly but with green horizontally moving parts, in the object switch they might see the blue-bodied object with green vertically moving parts travel along a curvilinear trajectory, and in the motion switch they might see the red-bodied object with green vertically moving parts travel along a linear trajectory.

The results of the experiments were not only consistent with previous research in this area (e.g., Madole & Cohen, 1995; Werker et al., 1998), but they also supported the idea that correlations in which one or both cues are dynamic are privileged in infants' processing of events. Infants at 10 months of age failed to learn any of the correlations, and a subsequent experiment revealed that they could process independently the static bodies of the objects but not the dynamic parts or motion trajectory of the object. In contrast, infants at 14 months attended to the correlation between an object's parts and its motion trajectory, as evidenced by a significant increase in looking time to the part switch in comparison to the familiar test trial. In addition, 18-month-old infants recovered visual attention to all three switch test trials suggesting that they had encoded all of the correlations among the features in the event; that is, they had learned that objects with particular parts and a particular body moved in a certain way.

To test whether the dynamic nature of features is crucial in capturing infants' attention to causally relevant relations involving those features, in a separate experiment 14- and 18-month-olds were presented with the same habituation and tests events as those previously described, but in these events the features of the objects did not move. The results of the experiment revealed that 14-month-old infants under these conditions no longer learned the correlation between object parts and motion trajectory (or any other correlations in the events) and 18-month-olds attended only to the correlation between parts and motion trajectory. The behavior of the 18-month-old group in this experiment suggested that they expected that the external parts of an object are related to the motion characteristics of that object. Finally, in more recent work in my laboratory (Rakison, in press), I used a similar design to examine the age at which infants can use the relationship between dynamic parts and a motion trajectory to form categories. This work has revealed that it is not until 22 months that infants form categories based on these correlations, and they will not form a category based on other, less salient correlations such as that between a motion path and a body type or a body type and part type.

Taken together, these studies suggest that the movement of causally relevant parts may help infants to distinguish such features from other, less significant features. Moreover, the data suggest that an associative learning mechanism underlying the ability to encode correlations among dynamic features may come online at some point early in the second year and is not limited to the linguistic domain (Werker et al., 1998). Perhaps more impressively, these data suggest that infants are selective in the correlations to which they will attend. In all likelihood, this selectivity acts as a learning constraint by directing infants to discover, and learn about, those relations that exist between features that are causally relevant. Infants would learn first, for example, that things with legs move one way and things with wheels move another way, and then later they would generalize this correlation to other object features possessed by the objects in question (e.g., faces, tails, seats, headlights, and so on).

SUMMARY AND CONCLUSIONS

In this chapter I examined five separate but interconnected themes concerning the perceptual to conceptual shift in early childhood. Based on a review of the literature of related theoretical and empirical work on these themes, a number of conclusions have been made about the nature of early representational development. I outline these conclusions as follows.

First and foremost, I argued that there is no logical or empirical reason to differentiate between perceptual information and that which is nonobservable because both are acquired through the same domain general associative learning mechanism (Rakison, 2003; Rakison & Hahn, in press). Thus, in my view the same processes are involved in learning that a dog has legs, that a dog is self-propelled, that a dog has a heart, and that a dog is called a "dog." In each case, the information is conveyed through a perceptual input system—in the examples given here, the visual and linguistic systems—and associative processes are sufficient to explain how each becomes part of the child's mental structures. Moreover, I have made the claim, and presented evidence to support this claim, that infants' earliest representations can support a simple sort of inference that is best thought of as an expectation. Once an infant learns that things with legs are also self-propelled, they would expect an object with legs to move on its own (even if it were not moving) and they would expect that things that move on their own have legs (even if those legs cannot be seen).

A direct implication of these claims is that no perceptual to conceptual shift occurs in infancy or early childhood. That is, it is redundant to think about a transition whereby infants and younger children possess perceptual representations—which do not support inference or carry any meaning about an object—and older children and adult possess conceptual representations—which do support inference and support meaning. Instead I argued that infants' earliest representations are fundamentally similar, though impoverished versions of the representations found in older children. Moreover, I have posited that the putative qualitative shift found in categorization studies such as those by Keil, Gelman, and others is observed for two reasons. First, it is the case that surface and nonobservable properties are presented in these studies in such a way that the latter is more salient with regard to the amount of information given and the quality of that information (Jones & Smith, 1993). Second, it may well be that nonobvious attributes, which can be considered perceptual in the sense that they are learned via one of the sensory modalities, are primary in the kinds of studies already mentioned because they are perfectly correlated with category membership whereas other, more surface attributes are less so. For instance, all birds have bird DNA but not all birds can fly. This is not to say, however, that the categories that children and adults form in the real world will cohere because of such "nonobvious" properties; after all, if something has wings and feathers it is a pretty good bet that it is a bird. But in studies where two attributes are pitted against each other—irrespective of the methodological issues discussed earlier—it is perhaps not surprising that children might favor the one that is more invariantly associated with category membership. What might emerge in the preschool years is not, therefore, a predilection to rely on nonobvious cues, but rather the assumption that nonobvious cues are more strongly correlated with category membership than are surface properties.

In summary, in this chapter I presented theory and evidence to support the notion that it is erroneous to think of representational development as undergoing some kind of transitional shift either in infancy or the preschool years. Rather, perceptual information provided by the different sensory input systems, including language, is continually added to the earliest representations through associative learning, and as sensitivity to different sorts of information emerges, so this gradual process gives the appearance of qualitative, representational change. The available evidence goes some way to support this position, though clearly further research is needed to substantiate the claims made here, including that from other disciplines within Cognitive Science such as computational modeling (see Rogers & McClelland, chap. 14, this volume). Nonetheless, the theory posited here is very much in line with current thinking in early cognition that stresses an infant who is reliant on information available in the perceptual array and uses that information during category and concept formation (e.g., Eimas, 1994; Jones & Smith, 1993; Mareschal & French, 2000; Quinn & Eimas, 1996a; Younger & Fearing, 1999, 2000). The next step, and one that I think is destined to prove fruitful, is to determine more explicitly how and when these early representations evolve into the more detailed and complex ones that we, as adults, possess.

REFERENCES

Au, T. K., Sidle, A. L., & Rollins, K. B. (1993). Developing an intuitive understanding of conservation and contamination: Invisible particles as a plausible mechanism. *Developmental Psychology, 29*(2), 286–299.

Backscheider, A. G., Shatz, M., & Gelman, S. A. (1993). Preschoolers' ability to distinguish living kinds as a function of regrowth. *Child Development, 64,* 1242–1267.

Barsalou, L. W. (1989). Intraconcept similarity and its implications for interconcept similarity. In S. Vosniadou & A. Ortony (Eds.), *Similarity and analogical reasoning* (pp. 76–121). Cambridge, England: Cambridge University Press.

Bertenthal, B. I. (1993). Infants' perception of biochemical motions: Intrinsic image and knowledge-based constraints. In C. Granrud (Ed.), *Visual perception and cognition in infancy: Carnegie-Mellon symposia on cognition* (pp. 175–214). Hillsdale, NJ: Lawrence Erlbaum Associates.

Bloom, P. (2000). *How children learn the meanings of words.* Cambridge, MA: MIT Press.

Brown, A. (1989). Analogical learning and transfer: What develops? In S. Vosniadou & A. Ortony (Eds.), *Similarity and analogical reasoning* (pp. 369–412). New York: Cambridge Press.

Bruner, J. S., Olver, R. R., & Greenfield, P. M. (1966). *Studies in cognitive growth.* New York: Wiley.

Burnham, D. K., & Day, R. H. (1979). Detection of color in rotating objects by infants and its generalization over changes in velocity. *Journal of Experimental Child Psychology, 6,* 191–204.

Carey, S. (1985). *Conceptual change in childhood.* Cambridge, MA: MIT Press.

Davidson, N. S., & Gelman, S. A. (1990). Inductions from novel categories: The role of language and conceptual structure. *Cognitive Development, 5,* 151–176.

Eimas, P. D. (1994). Categorization in infancy and the continuity of development. *Cognition, 50,* 83–93.

Farrar, M. J., Raney, G. E., & Boyer, M. E. (1992). Knowledge, concepts, and inferences in childhood. *Child Development, 63,* 673–691.

Gelman, R. (1990). First principles to organize attention to and learning about relevant data: Number and the animate–inanimate distinction as examples. *Cognitive Science, 14,* 79–106.

Gelman, R., Durgin, F., & Kaufman, K. (1995). Distinguishing between animates and inanimates: Not by motion alone. In D. Sperber & D. Premack (Eds.), *Causal cognition: A multidisciplinary debate* (pp. 150–184). Oxford, England: Clarendon Press.

Gelman, S. A., & Coley, J. D. (1990). The importance of knowing a dodo is a bird: Categories and inferences in 2-year-old children. *Developmental Psychology, 26,* 796–804.

Gelman, S. A., & Koenig, M. A. (2003). Theory-based categorization in early childhood. In D. H. Rakison & L. M. Oakes, (Eds.), *Early concept and category development: Making sense of the blooming, buzzing confusion* (pp. 330–339). New York: Oxford University Press.

Gelman, S. A., & Markman, E. M. (1986). Categories and induction in young children. *Cognition, 23,* 183–209.

Gelman, S. A., & Markman, E. M. (1987). Young children's inductions from natural kinds: The role of categories and appearances. *Child Development, 58,* 1532–1541.

Gentner, D. (1978). On relational meaning: The acquisition of verb meaning. *Child Development, 49,* 988–998.

Goldstone, R. L., & Barsalou, L. W. (1998). Studies on the formation of perceptually based basic-level categories in young infants. *Child Development, 65,* 903–917.

Gopnik, A., & Wellman, H. M. (1994). The theory theory. In L. A. Hirschfeld & S. A. Gelman (Eds.), *Mapping the mind: Domain specificity in cognition and culture* (pp. 257–293). Cambridge, England: Cambridge University Press.

Goswami, U. (1998). *Cognition in children.* East Sussex, UK: Psychology Press.

Hahn, E., & Rakison, D. H. (2003). *Perceptual versus nonobvious features in category membership decisions: A statistical learning account.* Poster presented at the Cognitive Development Society Conference, Park City, UT.

Haith, M., Wentworth, N., & Canfield, R. (1993). The formation of expectations in early infancy. In C. Rovee Collier & L. P. Lipsitt (Eds.), *Advances in infancy research* (Vol. 8, pp. 217–249). Norwood, NJ: Ablex.

Jones, S. S., & Smith, L. B. (1993). The place of perception in children's concepts. *Cognitive Development, 8,* 113–139.

Jones, S. S., Smith, L. B., & Landau, B. (1991). Object properties and knowledge in early lexical learning. *Child Development, 62,* 499–516.

Kalish, C. W. (1996). Preschoolers' understanding of germs as invisible mechanisms. *Cognitive Development, 11,* 83–106.

Keil, F. C. (1981). Constraints on knowledge and cognitive development. *Psychological Review, 88,* 197–227.

Keil, F. C. (1989). *Concepts, kinds, and cognitive development.* Cambridge, MA: MIT Press.

Keil, F. C. (1991). The emergence of theoretical beliefs as constraints on concepts. In S. Carey & R. Gelman (Eds.), *The epigenesis of mind* (pp. 133–169). Hillsdale, NJ: Lawrence Erlbaum Associates.

Kellman, P. J., & Spelke, E. S. (1983). Perception of partly occluded objects in infancy. *Cognitive Psychology, 15,* 483–524.

Leslie, A. M. (1984). Infant perception of a manual pick-up event. *British Journal of Developmental Psychology, 2,* 19–32.

Leslie, A. M. (1988). The necessity of illusion: Perception and thought in infancy. In L. Weiskrantz (Ed.), *Thought without language* (pp. 185–210). New York: Oxford University Press.

Leslie, A. M. (1995). A theory of agency. In D. Sperber & D. Premack (Eds.), *Causal cognition: A multidisciplinary debate* (pp. 121–149). Oxford, England: Clarendon Press.

Leslie, A. M., & Keeble, S. (1987). Do six-month-old infants perceive causality? *Cognition, 25,* 265–288.

Madole, K. L., & Cohen, L. B. (1995). The role of object parts in infants' attention to form–function correlations. *Developmental Psychology, 31,* 637–648.

Madole, K. L., Oakes, L. M., & Cohen, L. B. (1993). Developmental changes in infants' attention to function and form-function correlations. *Cognitive Development, 8,* 189–209.

Mak, B. S. K., & Vera, A. (1999). The role of motion in children's categorization of objects. *Cognition, 71,* 11–21.

Mandler, J. M. (1992). How to build a baby: II. Conceptual primitives. *Psychological Review, 99,* 587–604.

Mandler, J. M. (1998). Representation. In W. Damon (Series Ed.) & D. Kuhn & R. S. Siegler (Vol. Eds.), *Handbook of child psychology: Vol. 2. Cognition, perception, and language* (5th ed., pp. 255–308). New York: Wiley.

Mandler, J. M. (2000). Perceptual and conceptual processes in infancy. *Journal of Cognition and Development, 1,* 3–36.

Mandler, J. M. (2003). Conceptual categorization. In D. H. Rakison & L. M. Oakes (Eds.), *Early concept and category development: Making sense of the blooming, buzzing confusion* (pp. 103–131). New York: Oxford University Press.

Mandler, J. M., & Bauer, P. J. (1988). The cradle of categorization: Is the basic level basic? *Cognitive Development, 3,* 247–264.

Mandler, J. M., Bauer, P. J., & McDonough, L. (1991). Separating the sheep from the goats: Differentiating global categories. *Cognitive Psychology, 23,* 263–298.

Mandler, J. M., & McDonough, L. (1993). Concept formation in infancy. *Cognitive Development, 8,* 291–318.

Mandler, J. M., & McDonough, L. (1996). Drinking and driving don't mix: Inductive generalization in infancy. *Cognition, 59,* 307–335.

Mandler, J. M., & McDonough, L. (1998a). On developing a knowledge base in infancy. *Development Psychology, 34,* 1274–1288.

Mandler, J. M., & McDonough, L. (1998b). Studies in inductive inference in infancy. *Cognitive Psychology, 37,* 60–96.

Mareschal, D., & French, R. M. (2000). Mechanisms of categorization in infancy. *Infancy, 1,* 59–76.

Medin, D. L., & Ortony, A. (1989). Psychological essentialism. In S. Vosniadou & A. Ortony (Eds.), *Similarity and analogical reasoning* (pp. 179–195). Cambridge: Cambridge University Press.

Murphy, G. L., & Medin, D. L. (1985). The role of theories in conceptual coherence. *Psychological Review, 92,* 289–316.

Oakes, L. M., & Cohen, L. B. (1990). Infant perception of a causal event. *Cognitive Development, 5,* 193–207.

Oakes, L. M., & Madole, K. L. (1999). From seeing to thinking: Reply to Mandler. *Developmental Review, 19,* 307–318.

Oakes, L. M., & Madole, K. L. (2003). Principles of developmental change in infants' category formation. In D. H. Rakison & L. M. Oakes (Eds.), *Early concept and category development: Making sense of the blooming, buzzing confusion* (pp. 159–192). New York: Oxford University Press.

Piaget, J. (1952). *The origins of intelligence in the childhood.* New York: International Universities Press.

Quinn, P. C., & Eimas, P. D. (1996a). Perceptual organization and categorization in young infants. In C. Rovee-Collier & L. P. Lipsitt (Eds.), *Advances in infancy research* (Vol. 11, pp. 1–36). Norwood, NJ: Ablex.

Quinn, P. C., & Eimas, P. D. (1996b). Perceptual cues that permit categorical differentiation of animal species by infants. *Journal of Experimental Child Psychology, 63,* 189–211.

Quinn, P. C., & Eimas, P. D. (1997). A reexamination of the perceptual-to-conceptual shift in mental representations. *Review of General Psychology, 1,* 271–287.

Quinn, P. C., & Eimas, P. D. (2000). The emergence of category representations during infancy: Are separate perceptual and conceptual processes required? *Journal of Cognition and Development, 1,* 55–61.

Quinn, P. C., Johnson, M., Mareschal, D., Rakison, D., & Younger, B. (2000). Response to Mandler and Smith: A dual process framework for understanding early categorization? *Infancy, 1,* 111–122.

Rakison, D. H. (2003). Parts, categorization, and the animate–inanimate distinction in infancy. In D. H. Rakison & L. M. Oakes (Eds.), *Early concept and category development: Making sense of the blooming, buzzing confusion* (pp. 159–192). New York: Oxford University Press.

Rakison, D. H. (2004). *Developing knowledge of objects' motion properties in infancy.* Manuscript under review.

Rakison, D. H. (in press). Infants' sensitivity to correlation among static and dynamic features in a category context. *Journal of Experimental Child Psychology.*

Rakison, D. H., & Butterworth, G. (1998a). Infants' use of parts in early categorization. *Developmental Psychology, 34,* 49–62.

Rakison, D. H., & Butterworth, G. (1998b). Infant attention to object structure in early categorization. *Developmental Psychology, 34,* 1310–1325.

Rakison, D. H., & Cohen, L. B. (1999). Infants' use of functional parts in basic-like categorization. *Developmental Science, 2,* 423–432.

Rakison, D. H., & Hahn, E. (in press). The mechanisms of early categorization and induction: Smart or dumb infants? In R. Kail (Ed.), *Advances in Child Development and Behavior* (Vol. 32). New York: Academic Press.

Rakison, D. H., & Poulin-Dubois, D. (2001). Developmental origin of the animate–inanimate distinction. *Psychological Bulletin, 127,* 209–228.

Rips, L. J. (1989). Similarity, typicality and categorization. In S. Vosniadou & A. Ortony (Eds.), *Similarity and analogical reasoning* (pp. 21–59). Cambridge, England: Cambridge University Press.

Roberts, K. (1998). Linguistic and nonlinguistic factors influencing infant categorization: Studies of the relationship between cognition and language. In C. Rovee-Collier & L. P. Lipsitt (Eds.), *Advances in infancy research* (Vol. 11, pp. 45–107). London: Ablex.

Siegler, R. S. (1996). *Emerging minds.* New York: Oxford University Press.

Slater, A. M. (1989). Visual memory and perception in early infancy. In A. Slater & G. Bremner (Eds.), *Infant development* (pp. 43–72). Hove, UK: Lawrence Erlbaum Associates.

Smith, E. E., Medin, D. L., & Rips, L. J. (1984). A psychological approach to concepts: Comments on Rey's "Concepts and stereotypes." *Cognition, 17,* 265–274.

Smith, L. B. (2000). From knowledge to knowing: Real progress in the study of infant categorization. *Infancy, 1,* 91–97.

Smith, L. B., & Heise, D. (1992). Perceptual similarity and conceptual structure. In B. Burns (Ed.), *Percepts, concepts, and categories* (pp. 233–273). Amsterdam: Elsevier.

Smith, L. B., & Samuelson, L. K. (1997). Perceiving and remembering: Category stability, variability and development. In K. Lamberts & D. Shanks (Eds.), *Knowledge, concepts, and categories* (pp. 161–195). Cambridge, MA: MIT Press.

Springer, K. (1996). Young children's understanding of a biological basis for parent–offspring relations. *Child Development, 67*, 2841–2856.

Springer, K., & Keil, F. C. (1991). Early differentiation of causal mechanisms appropriate to biological and nonbiological kinds. *Child Development, 62*, 767–781.

Thelen, E., & Smith, L. B. (1994). *A dynamic systems approach to the development of cognition and action.* Cambridge, MA: MIT Press/Bradford Books.

Wellman, H. M. (1990). *The child's theory of mind.* Cambridge, MA: MIT Press.

Wellman, H. M., & Gelman, S. A. (1988). Children's understanding of the non-obvious. In R. Sternberg (Ed.), *Advances in the psychology of human intelligence* (Vol. 4, pp. 99–135). Hillsdale, NJ: Lawrence Erlbaum Associates.

Werker, J. F., Cohen, L. B., Lloyd, V. L., Casasola, M., & Stager, C. L. (1998). Acquisition of word-object associations by 14-month-old infants. *Developmental Psychology, 34*, 1289–1309.

Woodward, A. L. (1999). Infants' ability to distinguish between purposeful and non-purposeful behaviors. *Infant Behavior and Development, 22*, 145–160.

Younger, B. A., & Cohen, L. B. (1986). Developmental change in infants' perception of correlations among attributes. *Child Development, 57*, 803–815.

Younger, B. A., & Fearing, D. D. (1999). Parsing items into separate categories: Developmental change in infant categorization. *Child Development, 70*, 291–303.

Younger, B. A., & Fearing, D. D. (2000). A global-to-basic trend in early categorization: Evidence from a dual-category habituation task. *Infancy, 1*, 47–58.

Chapter 7

Emerging Ideas About Categories

Linda B. Smith
Indiana University

INTRODUCTION

The study of human categorization is contentious because it matters. How we understand the processes that give rise to categories is at the very core of how we understand human cognition. Over the past several decades, there has been growing concern that the assumptions that define and distinguish competing theories may not be quite right. These assumptions are based on the traditional metaphor that views categories as discrete, bounded things that are stable over time and context. In this view, categories are enduringly real, object-like, truly out there in the world and also in our heads. Thus, theorists in this tradition write about categories being *acquired, discovered,* and *possessed.* The boundedness and stability expected of categories is well exemplified in the following quote from Keil (1994):

> Shared mental structures are assumed to be constant across repeated categorizations of the same set of instances and different from other categorizations. When I think about the category of dogs, a specific mental representation is assumed to be responsible for that category and roughly the same representation for a later categorization of dogs by myself or by another. (p. 169)

The problem with these traditional ideas is the fluidity of human categories that appear to be exquisitely malleable, adapting to fit the idiosyncrasies of the moment (e.g., Barsalou, 1993a, 1993b; Bransford & Johnson,

1972; Malt, 1994). We do not, it turns out, think *exactly* the same thing each time we think about a dog. Moreover, if you and I have different histories, we may well—even in the same context—think differently about the very same dog (e.g., Yoshida & Smith, 2003a, 2003b).

The chapters in this volume have been written in the midst of shifting assumptions about the fundamental nature of categories. There is not yet a well-accepted new framework, never mind a new theory, but research on these issues is clearly in flux. The goal of this commentary is to provide perspective on emerging ideas as represented in this volume.

A Brief History of Categories

The traditional treatment of categories derives from logic. This conceptualization, the logic of classes, distinguishes between the *extension* of a class and the *intension* of a class. The extension is all the possible members of a class. Thus the extension of the class "triangle" is all possible triangles. The intension is the rule that picks out all and only members of the class, for example, the intensional definition of a triangle might be a "closed figure having three sides." Traditional psychological theories of categorization reflect these ideas of fixed extensions and intensions. In psychology, the extension is the "repeated categorizations" that people make, that is, the data to be explained. The intension is the hypothesized concept that determines the extension, the mental structure that proposed to cause people to categorize the way they do. Although this view has dominated theorizing and research on categories for nearly half a century, its theoretical problems have been evident for some time.

In the 1960s, theories of categorization attempted to explain the assumed fixed category extensions by internally represented intensive definitions that were lists of necessary and sufficient features. This approach came to be rejected on both theoretical and empirical grounds. First, there was no psychological basis for determining the features that form the primitives for concepts (Murphy & Medin, 1985). Second, no successful version of the theory was ever formulated—no one could find the defining properties of such everyday categories as dog or cow or game (see Rosch & Mervis, 1975; Smith & Medin, 1981). Third, there were data that directly contradicted the idea of necessary and sufficient features. Specifically, if a category is defined by necessary and sufficient features, all members should be equally good members. But the data say otherwise; people reliably judge some members of a category to be better than others. For example, a robin is a better example of a bird than is a penguin (e.g., Rosch, 1973).

In the 1970s, the field turned to probabilistic theories (Smith & Medin, 1981). These theories sought to explain human category judgments by tying them to general cognitive processes of memory, attention, association, and generalization by similarity. There are two versions, alike in the processes they assume, but different in their internal representations. And indeed, it has been argued that these two versions may not be formally distinguishable (Estes, 1986). By one account, known as prototype theory, concepts became lists of characteristic rather than defining features—a move that readily elevated robins over penguins as examples of birds (see Smith & Medin, 1981). By another, more radical version known as exemplar theory, concepts do not really exist in the sense of intensional definitions that determine category membership. Instead, people remember instances and associated properties (including associated language), and then general processes of memory retrieval, association, and generalization by similarity give rise to the in-task category judgments (e.g., Nosofsky, 1984; see also Smith & Medin, 1981). These exemplar accounts readily explain typicality effects and other effects suggesting probabilistic category membership. These theories also explain a wide array of experimental results on category learning, recognition, recall, and generalization (e.g., Nosofsky, 1984; Zaki & Nosofsky, 2001). Probabilistic feature-based theories also have had considerable recent success in modeling adults' judgments of common categories and their organization into domains (McRae, Cree, Westmacott, & de Sa, 1999; Vigliocco, Vinson, Lewis, & Garrett, 2004). In these efforts, the statistical regularities in large normative studies of everyday object and action categories have been shown to closely predict adult category and semantic judgments in a variety of tasks. Normative studies of the statistical structure of the first 300 nouns learned by children have also been shown to be predictive of their category learning (Samuelson & Smith, 2000; Smith, Colunga, & Yoshida, 2003).

However, probabilistic theories—both prototype and exemplar—have difficulty accounting for how people reason about categories. Specifically, people sometimes make category judgments that are decidedly more in accord with a defining feature view than a probabilistic view. For example, people will maintain that an organism that has no properties anything at all like a bird other than bird DNA and bird parents is, nonetheless, a bird (e.g., Rips, 1989; Keil, 1994).

In light of these last results, a number of researchers in the 1980s and 1990s turned to theory-like accounts of categories (e.g., Murphy & Medin, 1985). The idea here is that the mental structures that determine categories are naïve theories about the causal relatedness of different kinds of properties, both observable and nonobservable. For example, such a theory might include the following: Birds have wings and are lightweight *because* they fly and these behavioral and physical properties arise *because* of the genetic structure of birds. Accordingly, many researchers began studying people's beliefs about "really makes something what it is" and their reasoning

about the causal relatedness of properties relevant to category membership. The results of these studies suggest a distinction between core characteristics of things (and often not directly observable properties such as
DNA) and the surface characteristics of things (for example, being bird
shaped). That is, within intuitive theories some features are more important, and have more causal force, than others.

One version of the intuitive-theory account posits that people's theories
about kinds are "essentialist" (see Gelman, 2003). The idea here is that people believe there is "an essence" that determines whether or not an instance
is a member of a category. By this account, the reason that an organism that
looks and acts nothing like a bird might still be judged to "really be a bird"
is because the subject believes the organism possesses the essential but
nonobvious properties that are true of all and only birds. These essentialist
ideas thus resurrect the criterial-property concepts of the 1960s and the
idea that a believed intension (a belief in an essential property) determines
the extension (the belief in what really is a bird). However, by the modern-
day essentialist perspective, it is not that instances actually share these properties or that these essential properties are even useful in recognizing instances in the world, but rather beliefs in the existence of these essential
properties govern how people *reason* about category members. Moreover,
these beliefs are organized by theory-like representations that causally relate instances and their properties.

Much contemporary research is devoted to the study of intuitive theories
and their development. The intuitive theory view of concepts has opened
new fields of study about categories—including induction, conceptual combination, and causal reasoning (E. Smith, 1989; Medin, 1989; Keil, 2003).
Research on intuitive theories has also led to interesting insights about how
reasoning differs in different domains (e.g., for biological versus nonbiological kinds, see Gelman, 2003).

Still, the naïve-theory view has its own problems. First, and as Ahn and
Luhmann discuss in their chapter (chap. 11, this volume), there is no consensus as to what a naïve theory is, the formal nature of the representations,
or the kinds of knowledge included. In general, naïve-theory theories are
not as well defined or formalized as the probabilistic-feature sort, making
rigorous testing of predictions difficult. Second, naïve theories clearly do
not explain the full range of data traditionally viewed as the province of a
theory of categorization. Instead, certain phenomena (induction, conceptual change, conceptual combination, and judgments of causal relatedness) are singled out as theoretically more important than phenomena concerning the recognition of instances. Thus, naïve theory accounts do not
explain how one knows a bird when one sees (or hears) one, nor do they
explain why robins are judged to be psychologically better birds than penguins. Moreover, the fact that people readily make these judgments is seen

as pretty much irrelevant to the intuitive-theory account of human categories (e.g., Armstrong, Gleitman, & Gleitman, 1983).

Third, naïve theories may not explain the very data they take to be their core phenomena. Keil (chap. 13, this volume; also Rozenblit & Keil, 2002) presents compelling data that even adults' naïve theories are often explanatorily inadequate and often quite incoherent. People believe they understand phenomena with greater precision and coherence than they really do. Keil (2003) suggested that people have at best coarse, not-quite right, and gap-filled understandings of the causal structure of even basic things. He provided evidence that their seeming causally based reasoning in laboratory experiments may derive from a combination of quite sketchy knowledge along with task-specific information. That is, causal reasoning appears to be made in the moment, ad hoc and on-the-fly, much like the ad hoc categories described earlier by Barsalou (1983). These in-the-moment temporary creations enable people to reason well, in ways adapted to the specific task—despite real gaps in their knowledge about causal relatedness. These results place naïve theories in the domain of situated cognition and real-time processes. In so doing, they forewarn that any complete theory of categories will require a specification of *both* knowledge (features correlations, theories) *and* the general cognitive processes on which they must depend.

General or Special Processes?

The dispute between probabilistic-feature accounts and naïve-theory accounts is also a debate about the fundamental nature of cognition. Is it based on general processes of perception, memory, attention, association, and generalization by similarity, or does it require other kinds of mechanisms and, in particular, propositional representations necessary to coherent and causal theories about how features are related? The differing positions are related to a disagreement about the most relevant data for a theory of categorization. The signature markers of domain general processes are frequency, instance, similarity, and typicality effects. These effects are ubiquitous throughout human (and animal) cognition. Yet some aspects of human cognition—category induction, conceptual combination, conceptual change—have been argued to be relatively immune from such effects (e.g., Barrett, Abdi, Murphy, & Gallagher, 1993; Murphy & Allopenna, 1994; Sloman, 1997; Gelman & Koenig, 2003). Proponents of the naïve theory view argue that phenomena that do not show these characteristic patterns are theoretically the most important, precisely because they cannot be easily explained by general processes and demand a special explanation in terms of propositional representations. Proponents of the naïve theory view admit that people do use general frequency and similarity-based processes to make some category decisions. Keil, for example, suggested that people use only general process solutions in "desperation" when the particular category decision lacks the "nurturance and support of beliefs and principles" (1994, p. 239). Thus on one side are naïve-theory theorists who contend that certain aspects of human categorization cannot be explained by domain general cognitive processes, and who maintain that these phenomena are therefore most critical to a theory of categorization. As a consequence, these researchers study for the most part how people verbally reason about categories.

On the other side are those who seek explanations in terms of general processes, the side that includes probabilistic feature theories. These researchers concentrate on the relation between category decisions and what they see as the foundational processes: memory, attention, perceptual learning, and similarity (e.g., Barsalou, 2003; Chater & Vitanyi, 2003; Hampton, 2001; Goldstone & Steyvers, 2001; Nosofsky & Palmeri, 1998). Accordingly, these researchers pick problems to study that do not overlap much with those studied by naïve-theory theorists, problems such as the perceptual properties critical to the recognition of instances, attention, and perceptual learning.

There have been, however, some attempts by naïve-theory researchers to directly pit the two approaches against each other. The goal is to support the naïve theory side by showing that people's category judgments do not depend strongly on similarity relations, the idea being that if similarity can be ruled out then propositional or theory-like beliefs are supported. The method used in these studies has not gone without criticism (see Jones & Smith, 1993). The experiments in this genre often present subjects with verbal descriptions of truly bizarre scenarios: animals that are magically transformed from one kind to another or the birth of babies with the DNA of one species and the appearance of another (e.g., Rips, 1989; Keil, 1991; Gelman & Coley, 1990). These fantastic scenarios are necessary because instances of the same real-world categories typically share deep conceptual similarities *and also* many perceptual and associative similarities, making it difficult with more ordinary scenarios to show that similarity does not matter (e.g., Jones & Smith, 1993).

Percepts or Concepts

In the developmental literature, this battle is fought over the issue of whether children's categories are based on perceptual similarities such as shape and features such as wheels or whether their categories are based on conceptual features such as "can be eaten" or "used to carry water." As Ahn points out in her chapter, this is a distortion of the larger theoretical issue that is not really about the kind of features but about the nature of the representations (feature correlations and counts vs. causal propositional structures). Ahn also notes that the perceptual–conceptual distinction is misleading in the developmental literature in that many of the "conceptual" features studied by developmental researchers are directly perceivable. Alternatively, these conceptual features could derive from direct associations among words (see, e.g., McRae et al., 1999; Vigliocco et al., 2004; Landauer & Dumais, 1997).

The developmental question has focused on the issue of percepts versus concepts primarily because of the developmental data themselves. A hundred years of research in developmental psychology suggests that preschool children often base their decisions on the static and currently perceptually available properties whereas older children base theirs on remembered properties or inferences. The fact of this general developmental trend is incontestable. What is contested is what it means. One possibility is that children have fundamentally different kinds of concepts than adults; what Keil (1994) suggested are "pseudoconcepts" whereas adults have theory-like or "true" concepts. The idea that children have different, more "illogical" concepts is one with a long history in developmental psychology (Bruner, 1986; Piaget, 1970; Wohwill, 1967).

For proponents of the naïve theory view, acceptance of this hypothesis would mean that developmentally immature categories based on perceptual similarity would have to change into developmentally mature categories based on intuitive theories. As Keil (1991) noted this would require "that coherent [intuitive] theories be able to develop out of something like networks of associations, that interconnected sets of explanatory beliefs can rise out of nothing more than probabilistic tabulations of features and relations" (p. 246). Keil went on to conclude, "This notion falters when one recognizes that there are not persuasive accounts in any domain showing how this might occur." Thus the idea of a qualitative shift in the very nature of concepts is rejected out-of-hand by contemporary proponents of the naïve-theory account. It is not a position widely supported by the other side either. (For a third position supporting the idea of potentially qualitative shifts in representation see Fischer, Kenny, & Pipp, 1990; Andrews & Halford, 2002; Karmiloff-Smith, 1999.)

A second possibility, then, is that children's concepts are like adult concepts but that both are based on general processes of association and generalization by similarity. This is the possibility that adherents of the naïve theory view must defend against and it has a number of supporters. These challenges to the naïve theory view attempt a direct assault by showing that the core phenomena assumed to be "conceptual" and *un*explainable by general psychological processes can, in fact, be explained by ordinary processes of perception, attention, and memory. Attacks of this kind are now rising on many fronts, for example, in powerful similarity-based models (e.g.,

Hampton, 2001), in statistical learners fed only text as input (Landauer & Dumais, 1997), in successful feature-based models of common categories (McRae et al., 1999; Vigliocco et al., 2004), in Bayesian models that explain conceptual coherence essentially through feature tabulation and statistical inference (Tenenbaum & Griffiths, 2001), in connectionist models of category development (Smith et al., 2003), in explanations of cross-linguistic differences in categories (Yoshida & Smith, 2003a, 2003b; Sera et al., 2002), and in studies of perceptual learning and perceptual symbol systems (Goldstone & Barsalou, 1998). Rogers and McClelland (chap. 14, this volume) take a particularly comprehensive approach. They systematically demonstrate that connectionist networks can mimic many of the phenomena believed to be diagnostic of naïve theories and thus *not* based on general processes. Connectionist networks are associative learners that generalize by similarity and produce graded, context dependent decisions. This challenge thus goes to the core premise behind the segregation of human categorization data into two separate kinds: those explainable by general processes and those said not to be so explainable.

The third possibility is that children's concepts are like adult concepts, and are fundamentally at their core propositional and theory-like. By this hypothesis, children may often make judgments using the surface similarities of things, but there are aspects of their reasoning about categories that cannot be explained by associative learning, the tabulation of instances, and perceptual similarity. This is the specific possibility adherents to the naïve-theory view must support. The evidence for this position is, again, category judgments that do not seem to depend on the immediate perceptual input and that seem not to be influenced by similarity effects or that involve causal relations assumed to be unexplainable by general cognitive processes (e.g., Sloman, 1997; Gelman, 2003).

Is It Resolvable?

How can one decide between these two opposing views? Progress on this question appears stalled. This may be because the logical structure of the argument is itself flawed. Consider the structure of the two opposing claims.

General Process. The claim here is that one set of processes (which we can call G for general) explains human categories.

Naïve Theories. The claim here is only that there are *some* phenomena not explainable by G but that require other special mechanisms and representations, or S.

Three discouraging consequences arise in this structure.

1. It is a necessary truth that naïve-theory theorists can explain everything that general process accounts can. Anything explainable by G is necessarily explainable by G + S. This means naïve theory accounts are more powerful whereas general process accounts are more constrained and more parsimonious. It's a matter of "I can do more than you" versus "I can do (almost) everything you do, more elegantly."

2. The critical evidence for distinguishing these two approaches is a negative, showing that there are at least some aspects of human categorization that cannot be explained by general processes. This claim can never be disproven.

3. There is no way out of the debate. Each phenomenon that a naïve-theory theorist points to as special has some potential of being explained by a more powerful model of general processes (as in Rogers & McClelland, chap. 14, this volume). But for every phenomenon so explained there are other, perhaps even more special phenomena to be discovered by the naïve-theory theorist.

Stepping Out of the Box

Nonetheless, there are many exciting new discoveries—discoveries that do not resolve the dispute between theory-based and general-process based controversies—but that suggest instead that the field is moving in new directions, toward fundamental ideas about what categories and category development might be.

Perceptual Learning. New evidence shows that category learning systematically alters perceptual processing, creating dimensions and features and thus the very way the world is perceived and remembered. Quinn, Nelson and Snyder, and Gosselin and Schyn (chaps. 5, 1, and 4, respectively) all provide relevant data, much of it concerning human face perception. This is a domain in which one might expect to find hardwired competencies unaffected by experience. However, face-specific processing appears to be a consequence of experience with faces. As Nelson and Snyder argued, infants' early experiences with faces consist of seeing a very few individuals in many, many contexts. This learning environment appears to teach infants to attend to the configural properties that distinguish individuals. In contrast, infants' early experiences with common objects such as spoons, cups, and toys consist of encounters with many different instances of each category. Moreover, unlike people, instances of common categories are substitutable, that is, functionally equivalent. This learning environment appears to teach infants to attend less to the details of common objects and more to their overall similarities. This conclusion is supported both by evidence from infants and from adult training experiments. In these studies, nonface stimuli were made to engage in face-perception processes by training participants to distinguish individuals (e.g., Tarr & Gauthier, 2000). Gosselin and Schyn's studies show that perceptual learning of this sort makes feature processing highly context- and task-specific. For example, adults process very different features when asked to judge the gender versus the emotion of a face.

Evidence in the literature suggests further that perceptual learning affects early as well as late stages of processing (see Goldstone & Barsalou, 1998, for a review). For example, effects of perceptual learning have been found in elementary perceptual tasks that precede decisions of category membership, including same–different judgment tasks (Goldstone, 1994) and part detection (e.g., Lin & Murphy, 1997). Other studies suggest that young children's attention to perceptual properties and perhaps even their parsing of object shape may change in fundamental ways as a product of learning object categories (see Smith, 2003; also Needham, Barrett, & Peterman, 2002).

Perceptual learning clearly complicates the traditional view (e.g., Keil, 1994) of perception (and perceptual similarity) as raw, unprocessed and "knowledge-less." If fundamental perceptual processes change, become tuned to specific tasks as a function of experience in those tasks, then those processes are themselves knowledge-laden. A visual system that processes faces and objects differently "knows" that these are different kinds. The task dependency of perceptual features challenges Murphy and Medin's (1985) idea that category-specific feature selection can only be explained by causal theories of category structure. In this way, findings about perceptual learning undermine a distinction between perception and knowledge.

Embodiment. The knowledge-laden and history-dependent nature of perceptual processes encourages new ideas about representation, and specifically the idea that these are transient emergent events that are close to the sensory surface (Barsalou, chap. 15, this volume). In this view, the internal language for thought, perception, and action are fundamentally the same and must be so if they are to mesh seamlessly in creating intentional acts. A now growing industry of results supports this view. These include findings that actions prime categories (Tucker & Ellis, 2001), that objects are recognized better when we put our bodies in positions consistent with our usual actions on those objects (Creem & Proffitt, 2001), and even that verb meanings are tied to eye movements (Richardson, Spivey, Barsalou, & McRae, 2003). Studies using fMRI and PET are also consistent with these ideas and show that the visual identification of artifacts engages cortical regions associated with the typical motor actions on those artifacts (Ishai, Ungerleider, Martin, & Haxby, 2000; Faillenot, Toni, Decety, Gregoire, & Jeannerod, 1997).

In developmental studies, Rakison (chap. 6, this volume) and Gershkoff-Stowe (chap. 8, this volume) also find evidence for the role of action and the context-dependency of the features that children process when categorizing. Both sets of studies show that young children are highly sensitive to the features that are relevant to acting on objects: to the wheels that allow things to be rolled, to the springs that make objects bounce. These studies suggest a way in which one might bring together the insights of naïve-theory theorists that some features matter more because of their causal status and insights about perceptual learning and the embodied nature of general memory processes. In addition, these findings along with those of Barsalou remind that categories are acquired and used in a physical world by physical beings who act in that world and perceive the consequences of their own actions.

Nested Time Scales. In one influential series of experiments, Quinn (chap. 5, this volume) showed that infants' categories of "cats" and "dogs" are the emergent product of the experiences in the task, and do not represent prior, represented knowledge about the two categories. Instead, transient memories formed in the real-time experiences in the task—the repeated presentations of seeing particular cats—create categories in *performance.* Further, Quinn has begun to trace how the contributions of the immediate input, the task, and long-term experiences change with development. As the long-term memory contribution becomes stronger, decisions become more stable across stimulus and context. In her chapter, Gershkoff-Stowe also traces how infants' actions on objects—their in-task experiences—combine with their previous experiences to create in-task categories.

These studies remind us that the behavior we see at any moment is the product of processes operating over nested times scales (Smith & Thelen, 2003). The processes relevant to a baby's pattern of looking in the Quinn experiments or to a child's pattern of sequential touching in Gershkoff-Stowe's experiments include the sensory input at the moment of the behavior. But they also include the immediately preceding events: the cats and dogs one has seen in the last several minutes in the experiment, the objects the infant has touched and made to bounce just previously. The longer history of the infant—the dogs and cats seen over a lifetime, the objects and actions experienced over a lifetime—also matter. The relevant time scale to understanding categorization will therefore be in seconds, in minutes, in days, and in years. A complete theory must not just consider processes at all these time scales, but also integrate them and understand they influence each other over time. This is the dynamic systems perspective heralded by Gershkoff-Stowe (see also Samuelson & Smith, 2000).

Johnson's research (chap. 2, this volume) also illustrates this integrative approach. Johnson begins with the assumption that infants possess a vast array of perceptual processes and that these tune and adjust themselves through their interaction with the world, and in so doing create higher level processes, what one might call, for example, object perception. Johnson notes findings parallel to those with human infants in infant monkeys and the correlated changes in the underlying neurophysiology. These neurophysiological studies make concrete the idea of many components interacting at many levels of analysis, from contrast receptors, to neural pathways, to the correlations among features in the world. The multicausality of developmental process is itself a challenge to the traditional framework for studying categories that demands a single answer to "what categories really are?" Johnson concludes that "It seems likely that unity perception cannot be reduced to a limited set of principles" (p. 56). It seems likely that human categories cannot be so reduced either.

SO WHAT IS NEXT?

It is always difficult to understand major change when one is in the midst of it. Further hindsight is always better than foresight. Thus, one cannot confidently make predictions about where the field is going. But it does seem to be going. The change is perhaps driven by the stale nature of the debates within the traditional metaphor: features or theories? But it is also driven by new advances in understanding neural processes and their plasticity, in computational approaches to learning, in large-scale analyses of the statistical structure of the learning environment, and in fundamental processes such as perceptual learning. It may not be clear where research on categories is going, but it *is* moving, and that is good.

REFERENCES

Andrews, G., & Halford, G. S. (2002). A cognitive complexity metric applied to cognitive development. *Cognitive Psychology, 45*(2), 153–219.

Armstrong, S. L., Gleitman, L. R., & Gleitman, H. (1983). What some concepts might not be. *Cognition, 13*(3), 263–308.

Barrett, S. E., Abdi, H., Murphy, G. L., & Gallagher, J. M. (1993). Theory-based correlations and their role in children's concepts. *Child Development, 64*(6), 1595–1616.

Barsalou, L. W. (1983). Ad hoc categories. *Memory & Cognition, 11*(3), 211–227.

Barsalou, L. W. (1993a). Flexibility, structure, and linguistic vagary in concepts: Manifestations of a compositional system of perceptual symbols. In A. Collins & S. Gathercole (Eds.), *Theories of memory* (pp. 29–101). Hillsdale, NJ: Lawrence Erlbaum Associates.

Barsalou, L. W. (1993b). Challenging assumptions about concepts. *Cognitive Development, 8*(2), 169–180.

Barsalou, L. W. (2003). Situated simulation in the human conceptual system: Conceptual representation [Special issue]. *Language & Cognitive Processes, 18*(5–6), 513–562.

Bransford, J. D., & Johnson, M. K. (1972). Contextual prerequisites for understanding: Some investigations of comprehension and recall. *Journal of Verbal Learning & Verbal Behavior, 11*(6), 717–726.

Bruner, J. (1986). *Actual minds, possible worlds.* Cambridge, MA: Harvard University Press.

Chater, N., & Vitanyi, P. M. B. (2003). The generalized universal law of generalization. *Journal of Mathematical Psychology, 47*(3), 346–369.

Creem, S. H., & Proffitt, D. R. (2001). Grasping objects by their handles: A necessary interaction between cognition and action. *Journal of Experimental Psychology: Human Perception & Performance, 27*(1), 218–228.

Estes, W. K. (1986). Memory storage and retrieval processes in category learning. *Journal of Experimental Psychology: General, 115*(2), 155–174.

Faillenot, I., Toni, I., Decety, J., Gregoire, M., & Jeannerod, M. (1997). Visual pathways for object-oriented action and object recognition: Functional anatomy with PET. *Cerebral Cortex, 7*(1), 77–85.

Fischer, K. W., Kenny, S. L., & Pipp, S. L. (1990). How cognitive processes and environmental conditions organize discontinuities in the development of abstractions. In C. N. Alexander & E. J. Langer (Eds.), *Higher stages of human development: Perspectives on adult growth* (pp. 162–187). London: Oxford University Press.

Gelman, S. A. (2003). *The essential child: Origins of essentialism in everyday thought.* London: Oxford University Press.

Gelman, S. A., & Coley, J. D. (1990). The importance of knowing a dodo is a bird: Categories and inferences in 2-year-old children. *Developmental Psychology, 26*(5), 796–804.

Gelman, S. A., & Koenig, M. A. (2003). Theory-based categorization in early childhood. In D. Rakison & L. Oakes (Eds.), *Early category and concept development: Making sense of the blooming, buzzing confusion* (pp. 330–359). London: Oxford University Press.

Goldstone, R. L. (1994). Influences of categorization on perceptual discrimination. *Journal of Experimental Psychology: General, 123*(2), 178–200.

Goldstone, R. L., & Barsalou, L. W. (1998). Reuniting perception and conception. *Cognition, 65*(2–3), 231–262.

Goldstone, R. L., & Steyvers, M. (2001). The sensitization and differentiation of dimensions during category learning. *Journal of Experimental Psychology: General, 130*(1), 116–139.

Hampton, J. A. (2001). The role of similarity in natural categorization. In U. Hahn & M. Ramscar (Eds.), *Similarity and categorization* (pp. 13–28). London: Oxford University Press.

Ishai, A., Ungerleider, L. G., Martin, A., & Haxby, J. V. (2000). The representation of objects in the human occipital and temporal cortex. *Journal of Cognitive Neuroscience, 12*(Suppl. 2), 35–51.

Jones, S. S., & Smith, L. B. (1993). The place of perception in children's concepts. *Cognitive Development, 8*(2), 113–139.

Karmiloff-Smith, A. (1999). Taking development seriously. *Human Development, 42*(6), 325–327.

Keil, F. C. (1991). The emergence of theoretical beliefs as constraints on concepts. In S. Carey & R. Gelman (Eds.), *The epigenesis of mind: Essays on biology and cognition. The Jean Piaget Symposium Series* (pp. 237–256). Hillsdale, NJ: Lawrence Erlbaum Associates.

Keil, F. C. (1994). Explanation, association, and the acquisition of word meaning. In L. Gleitman & B. Landau (Eds.), *The acquisition of the lexicon* (pp. 169–196). Cambridge, MA: MIT Press.

Keil, F. C. (2003). Categorisation, causation, and the limits of understanding: Conceptual representation [Special issue]. *Language & Cognitive Processes, 18*(5–6), 663–692.

Landauer, T. K., & Dumais, S. T. (1997). A solution to Plato's problem: The latent semantic analysis theory of acquisition, induction, and representation of knowledge. *Psychological Review, 104*(2), 211–240.

Lin, E. L., & Murphy, G. L. (1997). Effects of background knowledge on object categorization and part detection. *Journal of Experimental Psychology: Human Perception & Performance,* 23(4), 1153–1169.

Malt, B. C. (1994). Water is not H-sub-2O. *Cognitive Psychology,* 27(1), 41–70.

McRae, K., Cree, G. S., Westmacott, R., & de Sa, V. R. (1999). Further evidence for feature correlations in semantic memory: Visual word recognition [Special issue]. *Canadian Journal of Experimental Psychology,* 53(4), 360–373.

Medin, D. L. (1989). Concepts and conceptual structure. *American Psychologist,* 44(12), 1469–1481.

Murphy, G. L., & Allopenna, P. D. (1994). The locus of knowledge effects in concept learning. *Journal of Experimental Psychology: Learning, Memory, & Cognition,* 20(4), 904–919.

Murphy, G. L., & Medin, D. L. (1985). The role of theories in conceptual coherence. *Psychological Review,* 92(3), 289–316.

Needham, A., Barrett, T., & Peterman, K. (2002). A pick me up for infants' exploratory skills: Early simulated experiences reaching for objects using 'sticky' mittens enhances young infants' object exploration skills. *Infant Behavior & Development,* 25(3), 279–295.

Nosofsky, R. M. (1984). Choice, similarity, and the context theory of classification. *Journal of Experimental Psychology: Learning, Memory, & Cognition,* 10(1), 104–114.

Nosofsky, R. M., & Palmeri, T. J. (1998). A rule-plus-exception model for classifying objects in continuous-dimension spaces. *Psychonomic Bulletin & Review,* 5(3), 345–369.

Piaget, J. (1970). *Genetic epistemology* (E. Duckworth, Trans.). New York: Columbia University Press.

Richardson, D. C., Spivey, M. J., Barsalou, L. W., & McRae, K. (2003). Spatial representations activated during real-time comprehension of verbs. *Cognitive Science,* 27(5), 767–780.

Rips, L. J. (1989). Similarity, typicality, and categorization. In S. Vosniadou & A. Ortony (Eds.), *Similarity and analogical reasoning* (pp. 21–59). New York: Cambridge University Press.

Rosch, E. H. (1973). Natural categories. *Cognitive Psychology,* 4(3), 328–350.

Rosch, E., & Mervis, C. B. (1975). Family resemblances: Studies in the internal structure of categories. *Cognitive Psychology,* 7(4), 573–605.

Rozenblit, L., & Keil, F. (2002). The misunderstood limits of folk science: An illusion of explanatory depth. *Cognitive Science,* 26(5), 521–562.

Samuelson, L. K., & Smith, L. B. (2000). Grounding development in cognitive processes. *Child Development,* 71(1), 98–106.

Sera, M. D., Elieff, C., Forbes, J., Burch, M. C., Rodriguez, W., & Dubois, D. P. (2002). When language affects cognition and when it does not: An analysis of grammatical gender and classification. *Journal of Experimental Psychology: General,* 131(3), 377–397.

Sloman, S. A. (1997). Explanatory coherence and the induction of properties. *Thinking & Reasoning,* 3(2), 81–110.

Smith, E. E. (1989). Concepts and induction. In M. I. Posner (Ed.), *Foundations of cognitive science* (pp. 501–526). Cambridge, MA: MIT Press.

Smith, E. E., & Medin, D. L. (1981). *Concepts and categories.* Cambridge, MA: Harvard University Press.

Smith, L. B. (2003). Learning to recognize objects. *Psychological Science,* 14(3), 244–250.

Smith, L. B., Colunga, E., & Yoshida, H. (2003). Making an ontology: Cross-linguistic evidence. In D. Rakison & L. Oakes (Eds.), *Early category and concept development: Making sense of the blooming, buzzing confusion* (pp. 275–302). London: Oxford University Press.

Smith, L. B., & Thelen, E. (2003). Development as a dynamic system. *Trends in Cognitive Science,* 7, 343–348.

Tarr, M. J., & Gauthier, I. (2000). FFA: A flexible fusiform area for subordinate-level visual processing automatized by expertise. *Nature Neuroscience,* 3(8), 764–769.

Tenenbaum, J. B., & Griffiths, T. L. (2001). Generalization, similarity and Bayesian inference. *Behavioral & Brain Sciences,* 24(4), 629–640.

Tucker, M., & Ellis, R. (2001). The potentiation of grasp types during visual object categorization. *Visual Cognition, 8*(6), 769–800.

Vigliocco, G., Vinson, D., Lewis, W., & Garrett, M. (2004). Representing the meanings of object and action words: The Featural Unity and Semantic Space (FUSS) hypothesis. *Cognitive Psychology, 48,* 422–488.

Wohwill, J. F. (1967). The mystery of the pre-logical child. *Psychology Today, 1*(3), 24–34.

Yoshida, H., & Smith, L. B. (2003a). Shifting ontological boundaries: How Japanese- and English-speaking children generalize names for animals and artifacts. *Developmental Science, 6*(1), 1–17.

Yoshida, H., & Smith, L. B. (2003b). Response: Correlation, concepts and cross-linguistic differences. *Developmental Science, 6*(1), 30–34.

Zaki, S. R., & Nosofsky, R. M. (2001). Exemplar accounts of blending and distinctiveness effects in perceptual old-new recognition. *Journal of Experimental Psychology: Learning, Memory, & Cognition, 27*(4), 1022–1041.

Chapter 8

Imposing Equivalence on Things in the World: A Dynamic Systems Perspective

Lisa Gershkoff-Stowe
Indiana University

INTRODUCTION

The young child negotiates a world that is infinitely rich and structured in information. From birth, babies actively acquire this information and use it to organize experience and guide their behavior. Several recent studies have documented the infants' remarkable ability to learn the probabilistic patterns among variables in a wide range of perceptual and cognitive tasks (Kelly & Martin, 1994). In processing language, for example, 8-month-olds can track the statistical regularities in continuous speech to discover the boundaries of individual words (Saffran, Aslin, & Newport, 1996). Moreover, they appear sensitive not only to simple co-occurrences, but also to transitional probabilities (Aslin, Saffran, & Newport, 1998) and to multiple cues that are themselves probabilistic in nature (Johnson & Jusczyk, 2001).

No less remarkable are the range of capabilities that infants demonstrate in perceiving and organizing real-world objects. Younger (1985, 1990) found, for example, that infants under 1 year of age could detect clusters of correlated attributes among members of the same natural object category. Thus they treated perceptually discriminable stimuli as equivalent when the objects shared related features, such as the feet and tails of imaginary animals. More generally, studies of early categorization and naming indicate that children learn about the relations between properties of objects by selecting or abstracting their similarities. For example, they distinguish between animate and inanimate (Rakison & Poulin-Dubois, 2001; Yoshida &

Smith, 2003), shape and material (Imai & Gentner, 1997; Samuelson & Smith, 1999; Soja, Carey, & Spelke, 1991), and dimensions such as color and size (Sandhofer & Smith, 2001). Like adults, then, infants and young children groups things into meaningful and practical categories. These early capabilities underscore a perceptual system that is exquisitely sensitive to regularities and patterns in the world. As such they offer a useful starting point for understanding and explaining the problem of how categories develop.

This chapter concerns children's experience with objects—perceiving, manipulating, and naming them—and how such experience plays a critical role in the formation of category knowledge. The view I present is based on principles of dynamic systems theory; it emphasizes the interplay between multiple, cascading processes within a single developing system. Specifically, I show how a variety of perceptual, motor, cognitive, and linguistic supports operate in tandem to guide category development. In addition, I consider how these supports present children with alternative and often competing cues for determining category membership. Importantly, these cues shift in developmental significance as the child moves through time and space. By this dynamic view, categorization is a highly flexible process that operates along multiple scales of time. That is, new categories, in response to specific task demands, are assembled opportunistically into stable, developmentally characteristic patterns. As such, children's classifications are best understood as the product of both their lifetime history and the immediate experience of acting on and observing objects in a particular task context.

This chapter is organized into four sections. Section I provides a selective review of research findings that detail the nature and types of categories that children form and the specific features that drive their category decisions. Primary emphasis is given to the competing role of shape and function and the way in which naming can alter the context in which classification occurs. Section II presents dynamic systems theory as an alternative approach to the study of category development. Dynamic systems theory suggests a method for integrating the contribution of multiple influences and provides a mechanism for explaining the variability with which children assign objects to categories. In the third section, I report data from a series of experiments that examine the nature of children's flexibility across changing contexts and development. The key result from these studies is that children exploit information as a consequence of several converging influences, including (a) their existing knowledge about things in the world, (b) an emerging system of word-to-category mappings, (c) the relative salience of form and function, and (d) current and past exposure to objects within a specific task context. The findings suggest the adaptive character of children's categorization and demonstrate their ability to softly assemble information in a fluid, task-dependent manner. Additionally, the findings highlight the importance of studying classification behavior on-line, as it arises in response to multiple determining sources (Barsalou, 1993; Smith, 1995). Section IV concludes the chapter with a discussion of the value of dynamic systems theory and its potential for guiding inquiry into the processes that underlie the formation and development of children's categories.

CATEGORIZING BY MULTIPLE SIMILARITIES

In their everyday experience, children sometimes put together like objects in close spatial proximity. This behavior, spontaneous and to no apparent purpose, seems to be a commentary on the existence of kinds. Figure 8.1 depicts one such grouping made by a 3-year-old child in play. In this complex array, the child has linked together several different kinds of objects that vary on multiple perceptual dimensions. For example, as shown at the top left corner of the figure, the child has arranged a series of stacking dolls in size, from large to small, and trolls that vary in both size and hair color. Next to these is an assortment of underwater sea creatures (King Triton, a turtle, swordfish, and sting ray) that seem to bear little physical resemblance to one another, and so forth.

What inspires children to organize objects spatially in this manner? Many developmentalists have suggested that such activity is not merely a be-

FIG. 8.1. Spontaneous grouping of objects produced by a 3-year-old child in play.

havior, but an event through which children actually *discover* classification. For example, in reflecting on the product of her play as depicted in Fig. 8.1, the child described the objects as "families" of mommies, daddies, and babies. This grouping, and her justification for it, reveals much about what the child knows about objects and the type of relations she uses for categorizing them. Perhaps most importantly, such behavior offers insight into the general processes that give rise to children's categories.

Piaget (1962) considered this kind of early sensorimotor play a steppingstone to the *idea* of classification, namely, that objects can be grouped by multiple similarities. Motivated by Piaget's theory, Sugarman (1983) used simple contrasting sets of objects to investigate the development of children's classificatory play. She observed that "substantial changes occur in the kind of conceptual operation in which 1- to 3-year-old children are engaging when they manipulatively classify objects" (p. 147). Of particular note, Sugarman found that between 1 and 2 years of age, children's responses are limited to successive piecemeal groupings, such that they focus on only one perceptual feature at a time. For example, when presented with a mixed array of four blocks and four plates, 18-month-olds handled successively first one block and then another block and then a third, passing over the plates. Between 2 and 3 years of age, however, children began to construct class-consistent groupings that entailed the conceptual ability to link individual comparisons and to consider more than one class of things simultaneously. Thus, at 30 months of age, children separated the four blocks and four plates, placing them into two spatially distinct locations. Such changes are consistent with Piaget's stage-like characterization of development: Children form categories that are guided initially by appearance and only later do they form categories that reflect true conceptual understanding (Inhelder & Piaget, 1964).

The developmental story as conceived by Piaget is that categories are built, one-by-one, from sensorimotor experience; with age, infants and young children impose increasing structure on what they know about the objects and events around them. These ideas, though often criticized, seem to reflect a basic truth: Children's classifications do emerge from processes that involve noticing, exploring, and comparing the properties of things. One unresolved question, however, is how children know *what* information is most relevant to the formation of a category. For example, the fact that color is present in the world does not guarantee its psychological relevance or its uptake in processing and learning (Gelman, 1990). Instead, relevance seems to depend on structure that is *internal* to the child. An alternative view, therefore, is that children have and make use of abstract categories right from the start. This idea fits with a large body of research indicating that children can and often do pay attention to abstract, theoretical information rather than to properties directly perceivable by the senses (e.g.,

Carey, 1985; Diesendruck, 2003; Gelman & Koenig, 2003; Gopnik & Sobel, 2000; Keil, 1995; Markman, 1989; Massey & Gelman, 1988; Woodward, 1998).

For example, Gelman and Markman (1986, 1987) found that when 3-year-olds were given information about an insect that "breathes air" and then presented with a choice between a perceptually similar leaf and a perceptually dissimilar beetle, children overlooked appearance and chose the taxonomic match. Several researchers have interpreted this principled behavior as evidence that children's categories are structured according to innate, domain-specific concepts that define and guide attention to what is to be learned. For instance, the early ability to distinguish between animates and inanimates is believed to privilege, and hence promote, learning about motion, causality, and intentionality (Legerstee, 2001).

Other researchers assert, however, that children's use of top-down, conceptual modes of thinking—that is, behaviors that do not depend on information given in the immediate input—are best explained by domain-general processes. By this contrasting view, abstract knowledge does not pre-exist, but is made out of repeated interactions with the physical and social world through associative and attentional learning mechanisms (Smith, 1995; Smith, Jones, & Landau, 1996). Children attend to inputs that support the development of categories shared by adults because of richly correlated structures that are inherent in the perceived structure of the environment. Shape, in particular, is a readily perceptible feature of objects to which children initially appear to attend.

Categorizing by Shape

There is much evidence to suggest that object shape is a physical property relevant to the acquisition of children's earliest categories, particularly at the basic level (Rosch, Mervis, Gray, Johnson, & Boyes-Braem, 1976). For example, Quinn, Eimas, and Rosenkrantz (1993) found that 3- to 4-months-olds distinguished categories of cats and dogs from categories of birds based on the visible form properties of two-dimensional stimuli. Shape also appears to be especially relevant in the context of naming (Baldwin, 1989; 1992; Imai, Gentner, & Uchida, 1994; Landau, Smith, & Jones, 1988; 1998; Markman & Hutchinson, 1984). Even prelinguistic infants show increased attention to shape-based objects in the presence of labels (Baldwin & Markman, 1989). Among older children, a number of experiments with preschoolers have shown that shape is often the preferred dimension in novel noun generalization and similarity judgment tasks (Graham, Williams, & Huber, 1999; Landau et al., 1998; Merriman, Scott, & Marazita, 1993; Prawat & Wildfong, 1980; Tomikawa & Dodd, 1980). For example, in one classic study, 4- and 5-year-olds were told the names of two novel objects that varied either in form or function. These children later judged a hybrid object on the basis of similarities of shape rather than similarities of function (Gentner, 1978).

Although shape captures children's attention in a variety of circumstances, they do not apply it indiscriminately across context. Children often consider multiple sources of information in addition to shape, including knowledge of syntax and ontological kind. For instance, when asked to generalize novel names to novel objects, preschoolers attend to shape in the context of solid, rigid things and the syntactic frame for count nouns, and to material in the context of nonsolid, deformable things and the syntactic frame for mass nouns (Imai & Gentner, 1997; Samuelson & Smith, 2000; Smith, Jones, & Landau, 1996; Soja et al., 1991).

Smith (1995) and colleagues (Landau et al., 1988; Smith, Colunga, & Yoshida, 2003) suggested that an early preference for shape reflects a specific attentional bias that is created by statistical regularities in the beginning noun categories that children learn. This hypothesis is supported by several converging lines of evidence indicating that the shape bias is made increasingly robust by early noun learning. In particular, analysis of the first 100 nouns that children say demonstrates a temporal link between the strength of the shape bias and developments in early productive vocabulary (Gershkoff-Stowe & Smith, 2004; Samuelson & Smith, 1999). Additionally, experiments that train children to attend to shape in novel noun generalization tasks inside the laboratory are associated with accelerated vocabulary growth outside the laboratory (Smith, Jones, Landau, Gershkoff-Stowe, & Samuelson, 2002). Finally, children identified as late-talkers (those who rank below the 30th percentile on the MacArthur CDI) are significantly less likely to use shape consistently in extending a new word to name a novel object when compared to normally developing children (Jones, 2003).

Taken together, these findings are useful for explaining the possible origins of the shape bias and, more generally, for detailing the mechanisms of associative learning. However, such findings account for only one aspect of what is clearly a larger and more intricate developmental picture. After all, children acquire many different kinds of words in addition to nouns (e.g., Tomasello & Akhtar, 1995) and they categorize objects by criteria other than shape (e.g., Keil, 1989; Markman, 1989). One criterion that has generated particular interest as a basis of classification is function. The ability to classify by function presents a challenge to perceptually based accounts of category development because it implies, first, that young children are not automatically captured by "superficial" aspects of surface similarity. Second, it implies that children's early categories are based, at least partially, on information that goes beyond perceptible properties. These issues are

especially relevant to proponents of theory-based views of category development and have been the focus for much recent investigation and debate
(see, for example, Gelman & Koenig, 2003).

Categorizing by Function

Whereas it is well established that adults recognize function as a critical aspect of categorization (Barsalou, 1989; Malt & Johnson, 1992; Miller &
Johnson-Laird, 1976), it is less clear whether children share the same understanding, or how that understanding might change with development
(Landau et al., 1998). To apprehend function, children must be able to attend to the dynamic properties of objects and to integrate that information
over time (Oakes & Madole, 2003). Early studies by Nelson (1973, 1974)
suggest that children as young as 12 to 16 months of age show an appreciation for an object's function and use it as a basis of classification. Children's
sensitivity to function was believed to play an important role in their initial
understandings of word meaning. For example, children might first learn
that "a hole is to dig" and from this, learn to generalize new instances on
the basis of form (although see Clark, 1993, for a different view). More recently, evidence from Madole and Cohen (1995) indicates that prelinguistic infants are sensitive to the correspondences between the structural
features of objects and their apparent functions. Using a standard habituation paradigm, they found that 14- and 18-month-old infants who were exposed to a toy during a familiarization procedure (e.g., object with wheels)
later increased attention to a novel object during testing when the object violated the familiar form–function relationship (e.g., does not roll).

Other studies demonstrate, in addition, that young children use function information to extend novel words to novel objects, particularly when
they are allowed direct experience with the objects or when the relationship between the structure and function is made transparent (Baldwin,
Markman, & Melartin, 1993; Booth & Waxman, 2003; Corrigan &
Schommer, 1984; Kemler-Nelson, Russell, Duke, & Jones, 2000; McCarrell
& Callanan, 1995). However, preschool-aged children are also capable of
making use of functional information even when perceptual cues are not
readily apparent (Kemler-Nelson et al., 1995). Instead, they seem to rely on
nonobvious properties related to the intention or history of the user
(Bloom, 1996; Bloom & Markson, 1998; Gelman & Ebeling, 1998). For example, Gelman and Bloom (2000) asked 3- and 4-year-olds to identify artifacts that were described as either accidentally or intentionally created.
They found that children were more likely to classify and name an object if
they were told that it had been created by design (e.g., a knife) than if the

object had been formed by accident (e.g., a jagged piece of plexiglas). These findings are intriguing because they raise an important theoretical question: namely, what directs children to use abstract criteria, particularly in the presence of competing perceptual cues?

Effects of Context

One apparent answer to this question, of course, is context. Context is critically tied to how humans determine categories. In studies with adults, researchers have found that context affects people's judgments about which features are most relevant for classifying objects (Barsalou, 1982; Goldstone, 1998). For example, the features that come to mind when thinking about playing the piano are very different from the features that come to mind when thinking about *moving* a piano (Barclay, Bransford, Franks, McCarrell, & Nitsch, 1974). Children also show an influence of context. Thus, given a new fact about a familiar object (e.g., a pillow made out of wood), children can correctly use this new piece of information as a basis for category membership (e.g., the object is hard rather than soft) (Kalish & Gelman, 1992). Like adults, then, children readily adapt their classifications to fit the local conditions of the task.

Numerous studies have documented the various effects of context on children's object classifications (Fenson, Vella, & Kennedy, 1989; Oakes, Plumert, Lansink, & Merryman, 1996; Markman, Cox, & Machida, 1981; Younger & Furrer, 2003). Here I consider three of these factors: the experimental instructions, procedure, and stimulus materials, and refer the reader to Madole and Oakes (1999) for additional discussion.

Experimental Instructions. One important variable that appears to direct children away from more immediate perceptual influences are the particular instructions given by the experimenter. In one recent study, for example, 3- and 4-year-old children were shown a triad of objects consisting of a standard (triceratops) and two alternatives that were either perceptually similar (rhinoceros) or conceptually similar (stegosaurus) to the standard. The children heard one of two kinds of instructions (Deák & Bauer, 1995). Some children were asked to find the one "most like this one." In this context, the children showed a strong reliance on similarities of appearance. That is, they selected the triceratops and rhinoceros. Other children were asked to find the one that was "the same kind as this one." In this second context, children were more likely to select objects that were similar in taxonomy, in this case the triceratops and stegosaurus. Based on these results, the authors concluded, first, that different kinds of instructions do in fact convey different information and second, that children as young as 3-years-old are keenly sensitive to these differences.

Experimental Procedure.   Additional studies documenting the effects of context suggest that the type of procedure used by the experimenter impacts not only the kinds of classifications children produce, but also when and if they produce them. For example, object-examining tasks reveal surprisingly sophisticated category abilities in infants 12 months old and younger, including what appears to be the ability to consider abstract similarity. In one widely cited study, Mandler and McDonough (1993) reported that 9- to 12-month-olds distinguished between the superordinate categories of animals and vehicles, categories that are outwardly structured by few perceptually similar properties. However, contrary to these findings, a separate group of 12-month-old infants showed no evidence of classifying at the superordinate level when sequential-touching was used as a measure of performance (Mandler & Bauer, 1988). In interpreting this disparity, Oakes and colleagues (Madole & Oakes, 1999; Oakes et al., 1996) suggested that the two procedures might actually place very different demands on the infants. In an object-examining task, items from a single category are first presented sequentially and children are required to select one of two novel stimuli, one from a familiar category and the other from a novel category. In a sequential-touching task, multiple items from two categories are presented simultaneously and children are required to impose their own organization on the array.

To test their hypothesis, Oakes et al. (1996) provided a within-subject comparison of the classification performance of infants (10-, 13-, and 16-month-olds) in both an object-examining and sequential-touching task, using identical sets of plastic toy animals and people. As predicted, the youngest group of infants succeeded in the object-examining task, but failed to demonstrate superordinate grouping in the sequential-touching task. In contrast, the older infants performed successfully in both tasks. Together, the findings confirmed the authors' assertion that the two procedures were not equivalent: Infants with limited cognitive resources are most challenged in free sorting tasks that do not first specify the categories-to-be-learned.

Stimulus Materials.   A third factor related to the effects of context concerns the particular stimulus materials used in an object classification task. There is ample evidence to suggest that children have access to very different kinds of information when presented with real, three-dimensional objects as compared to simple line drawings or photographs (Deák & Bauer, 1996). Smith and Heise (1992) suggested that properties relevant to taxonomic kind—for example, texture, weight, and surface gradient—increase in salience when children are given the opportunity to interact with real physical objects. Information about function is also heightened when the objects are presented as dynamic rather than static displays (Corrigan &

Schommer, 1984; Deák, Ray, & Pick, 2002). Not only the nature of the stimuli, but the range of items to which children are exposed, appear to play a central role in the categories they form. For example, Younger and Fearing (2000) showed that when prelinguistic infants were familiarized with a broad range of exemplars such as animals and vehicles, they tended to form global categories that included other animals but excluded vehicles. When given a more narrow range of exemplars, however, for example, all cows and all cars, infants formed separate categories that included only cows or only cars. What appears to matter, then, is the degree of contrast between familiar categories.

In summary, the extant literature offers a wealth of evidence for the role of contextual factors in the similarities children perceive when deciding object category membership. Even very young children demonstrate a remarkable degree of complexity in their ability to consider a host of properties relevant to classification. Moreover, as discussed in the following section, language also plays a contributing role in determining which set of features is most relevant to the categorization task at hand.

Effects of Naming

Many studies of category development have shown that the extent to which certain features such as shape and function are used by children to classify objects is changed with the introduction of labels. Naming provides children with an additional source of information, though the precise nature of that information and its origin is extensively debated. Brown (1956) long ago noted that words are highly diagnostic for category membership:

> There are two important things to say about naming behavior. For one who has already acquired a category the meaningful utterance of another can provide evidence that the speaker possesses the same category. For one who has not yet acquired a given category the meaningful utterance of another *can function as an attribute of the category* to be acquired. (p. 275, italics added)[1]

Children may use words as attributes of categories in different ways. The most basic way is simply to match items that have the same name. For example, a child might learn that sharks at the aquarium and guppies at the pet store are members of the same kind because both are called "fish." Beyond the similarity of label, however, children are capable of using the *semantic* content of words to establish the relevant link between object and kind. Knowing that sharks and guppies breathe under water, for instance, but

---

[1]Although, for a different view, see Markman and Jaswal (2003) who contended that "words are not features of objects; words are symbols that refer" (p. 399).

dolphins do not, may direct children to look for specific properties that are shared in common, for example, whether or not they possess gills. In this sense, labels contribute to the process of categorization by invoking consideration of top-down, conceptual information (Wellman & Gelman, 1998).

The consequence of labels is most evident in studies that compare children's classifications in naming and no-naming tasks. Past research has documented that words highlight attention to categories of objects in systematic ways. For example, Waxman and Hall (1993) presented infants, 15- and 21-months-old, with a standard and choice of two test objects. One of the alternative objects was taxonomically related to the standard (e.g., carrot and tomato) and the other was thematically related (e.g., carrot and rabbit). Waxman and Hall found a reliable increase in taxonomic groupings when infants were told the name of the standard object. In contrast infants were more likely to pick the thematically related object in the absence of labels. Similar findings have also been obtained with novel rather than familiar words (Waxman & Booth, 2001). Waxman interpreted these results as evidence that infants possess a universal expectation that object names and object categories are fundamentally linked (for related ideas, see Golinkoff, Mervis, & Hirsh-Pasek, 1994; Markman & Hutchinson, 1984). Furthermore, she maintained that the expectation is present in children prior to the acquisition of words and only later does it become fine-tuned with advances in cognitive and linguistic development.

One difficulty with Waxman's interpretation, however, is that things in the world that are taxonomically related tend also to be related in appearance. This issue continues to be vigorously debated in the literature (for example, see Booth & Waxman, 2002; Smith, Jones, Yoshida, & Colunga, 2003). Smith (2000) argued for an alternative account, one that emphasizes learned over intrinsic biases. Support for Smith's argument is based on evidence suggesting that the majority of children's early vocabularies consist of count-noun words that refer to objects frequently similar in form (Samuelson & Smith, 1999). By this account, names serve, at least initially, to direct children's attention to objects that are perceptually similar in appearance. Thus, according to Smith, children's category knowledge is best conceived as a *product* rather than a prerequisite for word learning.

Summary

This section provided a selective review about the nature of early category acquisition and the ways in which young children obtain information about the relevant features of objects. It also provided an examination of the effects of variations in context on the outcome of children's classifications and, in particular, how labels intersect the relation between perceptual and conceptual bases for classification. Unresolved theoretical differences remain. Long-standing questions concerning the origins of children's category preferences—whether they are learned or innate, domain-general or domain-specific—continue to spur research and discussion. Regardless of the outcome of these debates, however, developmental considerations strongly suggest that children modify attention to the features of objects in response to underlying changes in the environment and to advances in cognitive and linguistic ability. These developments broaden the range of possible features available to children and alter the salience of significant cues (Oakes & Madole, 2003).

Together, the findings underscore the remarkable flexibility of children's classifications. They also testify to the idea that children exploit multiple sources of information as a consequence of both real-time factors—that is, the immediate demands of the task and environmental context—and the developmental status of the child. In the next section, a dynamic systems perspective is described. Dynamic systems theory provides a unique framework for conceptualizing the changing nature of children's category behavior and suggests a way to reconcile many of the differences between competing theoretical accounts. Key points of dynamic system theory are emphasized that invite a closer look at the processes underlying developmental change.

A DYNAMIC SYSTEMS PERSPECTIVE

Dynamic systems theory presents a mechanistic account of change and development that can be broadly applied to a diverse range of phenomena. Several recent studies have adopted a dynamical perspective to investigate problems of perception (Butterworth, 1993; Freyd, 1992), cognition (Smith & Samuelson, 2003; Smith, Thelen, Titzer, & McLin, 1999), emotion (Lewis, Lamey, & Douglas, 1999; Wolff, 1993), language (Tucker & Hirsch-Pasek, 1993; van Geert, 1991), and motor control (Goldfield, 1993; Thelen & Ulrich, 1991). Within a dynamic systems framework are a number of general principles that define a common approach to research. These principles are presented first. Following this, three experimental studies are described in which a dynamic systems approach is used to examine changes in early category behavior.

Multiple, Contingent Processes

Like other developmental theories, dynamic systems theory recognizes that there are many heterogeneous influences operating on development. Endogenous factors include those events related to the organic status of the child, for example, age-related improvements in memory and attention span, whereas exogenous factors refer to pressures, both from the surrounding physical and social environment, and from the conditions of the task itself. Dynamic systems theory departs from other approaches, however, in its primary focus on the *contingency* of outcome. That is, new forms are constructed out of the successive and mutually interacting influences of these many endogenous and exogenous forces. This cascading process, moreover, occurs at many levels of function, ranging from the neuroanatomical to the social.

According to Oyama (1985), the notion of contingency removes the need to distinguish between causes that are privileged or essential and those that are merely supporting or interfering. This is because change is the result of interactions that are always co-determined. Furthermore, the notion of contingency calls into question the argument that development is governed primarily by inherent constraints and merely modulated by the independent influence of context. Rather, by a dynamic systems view, development is mutually determined by parallel and interacting processes.

Self-Organizing Processes

A second related principle of dynamic systems theory is that development proceeds as a *self-organizing* process. This means that behavior emerges in a bottom-up fashion from the many cooperative elements that comprise the total system. This perspective differs from other theories in which behavior is largely striped from the elements that produce it. In a dynamical view, behavior changes as a result of existing patterns that lose stability. This process frees components to reorganize into *new* stable states (Thelen, 1989). Furthermore, the timing of this transition from one stable state to another stable state often occurs at critical points as a result of small changes in one or more elements. Such change may engender discontinuous leaps in behavior, thus giving development its stage-like character.

To understand how a developing system can generate its own change, it is first necessary to specify which of many potential elements play a contributing role and then map the concurrent pathways of those elements in relation to newly emerging patterns of behavior. In doing so, it becomes possible to detail how various links change over time as the individual elements that comprise the system themselves wax and wane. The value of this dynamical approach is to reveal the interdependencies among subsystems and to capture the nonstationary coupling and uncoupling of constituent parts.

Real-Time Processes

A third important principle invoked by dynamic systems theory concerns assumptions about temporality, specifically the idea that development is inseparable from the processes that take place in continuous time. In a dynamic systems account of development, behavior operates simultaneously over multiple scales of time (Thelen & Smith, 1994). Everyday perceptions, memories, and actions—processes occurring over the seconds and minutes of real time—are intimately connected to large-scale changes occurring over the months and years of ontogenetic time. This principle allows a solution to the long-standing puzzle in developmental science: how to explain the regularity and stability that characterizes long-term development and the flux and instability that characterizes behavior in the short term.

According to a dynamic systems account, the contributions of the here-and-now task context and the current and past state of the organism are equally important. New behavior arises flexibly as the developing system assembles and reassembles in response to changes at the local level. Because the developing system is multidetermined and open to influence from the surrounding environment, it is difficult to predict the precise behavior to emerge at any given point in time. However, local flexibility always occurs within the context of constraints that can potentially be specified. These constraints serve to introduce order and stability over longer durations of time.

Processes of Knowing

A final principle centers on how knowledge is conceived in a dynamic systems framework. Much research has been concerned with identifying the core knowledge structures that children possess. Presumably these mental structures prescribe the formulation and use of categories, which become increasingly more elaborated with age. By this view, knowledge is conceptualized as an all-or-nothing thing—static, enduring, and abstract in form (Thelen & Smith, 1994). Much of the current literature, however, seems to be at odds with this view. Rather, research consistently shows the flexibility and dependence of behavior across various tasks and contexts (Barsalou, 1989).

In contrast to the predominant view, dynamic systems theory conceptualizes knowledge as existing only in the processes of knowing, processes that are continuous, graded, and interactive. Information is not out there, waiting to be received by the child. Rather, "meaning is emergent in perceiving and acting in specific contexts and in a history of perceiving and acting in context" (Thelen & Smith, 1994). By this view there is no duality between structure and process or between competence and performance; there is only the child in context.

To summarize the key points of dynamic systems theory, this section has suggested a set of general principles that serve as guidelines for conceptualizing development and conducting empirical study. A dynamical view takes into account the multicausal nature of behavior; no single component has priority as a source of change. Because behavior is at all times softly assembled, it is possible to study the cooperative interactions of participating units to discover the conditions and constraints that result in specific behavioral outcomes. In a complex dynamical system such as the developing child, many heterogeneous influences combine to assemble behavior across *multiple* scales of time. The relevant units of study thus include the dimension of real time associated with the current context and demands of the task as well as the recent and long-term history of the child. In the next section, these time scales are applied to the investigation of object category development in young children.

CATEGORY DEVELOPMENT FROM A DYNAMIC SYSTEMS PERSPECTIVE

As suggested by the extant developmental literature, children's category behaviors, like many other behaviors they exhibit, resemble a dynamic system: They are fluid, opportunistic, locally unpredictable, and globally coherent and stable. Indeed, far from indexing the fixedness of children's categories, most studies reveal their extraordinary responsiveness to changing task demands. In light of this view, a dynamic systems approach is directed toward specifying how classification emerges in a task-specific context and at a particular moment in development. In the experiments that follow, I use an object manipulation task to capture changes in children's classification behavior and map those behaviors to a dynamic systems approach.

The Object Manipulation Task

Researchers have relied on a number of different procedures to obtain evidence of children's category knowledge. The object manipulation task is one procedure used primarily with children over 12 months of age. In a typical task, children are presented with a mixed array of objects from two contrasting categories, for example, four clay balls and four yellow cubes (Ricciuti, 1965). Children are allowed to play freely with the objects for several minutes and measures of their touching or grouping are obtained.

   The object manipulation task has a number of advantages that merit its use with very young children. First, it exploits the child's tendency to visually inspect objects by manipulating or touching them. Second, the verbal instructions associated with the procedure are kept to a minimum and require no verbal response on the part of the child. Third, the procedure yields two primary measures of category behavior: spatial grouping and sequential touching. These behaviors are developmentally related (Gershkoff-Stowe & Namy, 1995) and thus the same task is appropriate for a wide age-range of children. Finally, by manipulating the relatedness of the objects, the task can be used to explore the formation of children's concepts and the boundaries that define category membership.

Two questions are addressed in the following set of experiments. The first question is focused at the level of developmental time: How does children's experience with particular categories lead them to notice similarity and to discover that they can comment on it? The second question is aimed at real-time processes: How does children's activity within a particular task lead them to classify by multiple similarities? This question is motivated by the idea that if children can shift from one property to another through experience in the task itself, it must be because new categories are assembled opportunistically in response to specific task demands.

Changes Over Developmental Time

Gershkoff-Stowe, Thal, Smith, and Namy (1997) conducted a 5-month longitudinal study to examine the effects of familiarity and practice on children's sorting behavior. Twenty-four children visited the laboratory at 3-week intervals, from 16 to 21 months of age. At each experimental session, children saw 3 sets of objects, presented one at a time in random order. Half of the children were exposed to the same sets of objects at each session, while the other children were exposed to entirely novel sets. Children's behavior was coded for both spatial grouping and sequential touching for one-class and two-classes of objects. Following Piaget, the ability to organize a mixed array of eight objects into two spatially segregated groups by kind was used as an index of mature categorization.

Table 8.1 presents the mean age at which children in both groups demonstrated one-class grouping, two-class touching, and two-class grouping. The key result of this analysis is that the age at which children demonstrated advances in categorization varied as a function of practice. Specifically, familiarity mattered at each level of complexity; children who played with the same objects each time classified significantly earlier than children who played with different objects.

TABLE 8.1
Mean Age (in Months) Children Achieved Three Classification
Levels When Presented With the Same or Different
Objects at Each Laboratory Session

	Different	Same
One-class grouping	17.0	16.6
One-class touching	18.9	17.9
Two-class grouping	19.2	18.7

Further analysis revealed a strong, positive correlation ($r = .76$, $p < .05$) between the age of children at their first session and the age at which two-class grouping initially appeared. That is, children who started the experiment earlier also achieved advanced categorization earlier. This suggests that time in the experiment rather than age itself is the crucial variable. A third key result is displayed in Fig. 8.2. In this figure, classification data are shown in the sessions prior to the first session in which children exhibited exhaustive, two-category grouping. The results indicate a close developmental relation between the onset of spontaneous sequential touching and the separation of like objects into spatially distinct groups. More specifically, the figure reveals that sequential touching preceded the onset of spatial grouping by several weeks and, in addition, that the frequency of sequential touching increased steadily up to the session in which two-category grouping first appeared.

Together the findings suggest that repeated experience manipulating like objects from different classes leads children to understand that objects can be spatially organized by their similarities and differences. Put differently, the activity of sequential touching may actually help children to *create* the discovery of two-category object grouping.

In a second study, Namy, Smith, and Gershkoff-Stowe (1997) addressed more specifically what children learn in the process of playing with objects over the course of several months. In their everyday lives young children have repeated opportunities to handle objects directly—to apprehend not

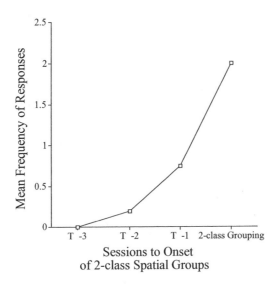

FIG. 8.2.   Mean frequency of spatial groupings by session prior to the onset of exhaustive, two-category object grouping.

only their static, visual properties, but to learn about their texture, weight, rigidity, how they move, and what they are used for. In this longitudinal experiment, the principle manipulation was the opportunity to organize objects spatially by kind. Sixteen children participated, beginning when they were 18-months-old. Children were tested at 3-week intervals until they were approximately 21 months of age. At each session, children were presented with a transparent shape-sorter in which only one of two kinds of stimuli would fit (e.g., 4 red wooden houses and 4 yellow plastic rings). Half of the children were given both kinds of objects to play with at the same time. Because only one of the two kinds would fit into the sorter, however, these children had the opportunity to compare the two kinds: those that they placed inside the shape sorter and those that remained outside. A second group of children was given the same amount of experience playing with both kinds of objects; however, they saw only one set at a time. Thus, these children did not have the opportunity to directly compare one kind of thing to another kind of thing. Following a brief distracter task, both groups of children were tested in a free play period in which the two object kinds were available. Assessment was based on the number of groupings children produced involving either one or two classes of objects.

The principal result is presented in Fig. 8.3. The figure shows the mean number of object groupings children produced by condition for privileged kinds (the class that fit the shape sorter) and nonprivileged kinds (the class that did not fit). The data reveal that opportunities to play with one kind (Compare condition), in the context of comparing and rejecting a second kind, led to an increase in the number and complexity of object groups relative to playing successively with only one kind (No Compare condition).

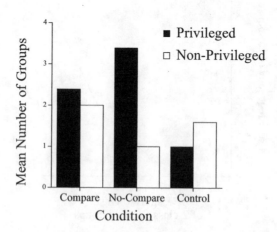

FIG. 8.3. Mean number of object groupings for privileged and nonprivileged kinds as a function of three conditions.

Thus, the shape sorter enabled children to reflect on the sameness of the objects, rather than simply recognizing in a successive, piecemeal fashion that one object is like or not like another. These findings suggest that children not only profit from the structure available in the world, but in addition, create structure through their own interactions with objects.

Together, the findings from both longitudinal experiments indicate that repeated practice with familiar sets of objects promotes the development of classificatory behavior through the active comparison of objects by kind. In the next experiment, I consider how stable developmental patterns may be altered in response to online changes in the visual, functional, and verbal components of a task. This research thus brings together the influence of *multiple* scales of time on children's classificatory behavior.

Changes Over Real Time

The purpose of this experiment was to test the effect of two highly salient, but competing properties on children's grouping behavior. Object sets were constructed to promote categorization in either of two ways: according to *shape* or *function*. An additional purpose was to assess children's ability to shift attention from one relevant feature to another in response to prior experience in the task. This was accomplished by comparing the object manipulations of children in a within-subject design to children in a between-subject design.

Participants were 3-year-old children enrolled in a university day care facility. Children were presented with two sets of novel objects. Each set contained eight objects from two contrasting categories. An example is shown in Fig. 8.4. In this figure, the experimental set consists of two shape groups and two function groups, both of which have overlapping features. One shape group contains four similarly shaped but non-identical objects made of multicolored pipe cleaners that project from a small styrofoam ball. The second shape group contains four similarly shaped but non-identical objects made of different colored faux fur wrapped around a small rounded knob.

Additionally in the figure are two function groups, each sharing a common part. Four of the objects have a flexible wire spring attached to the styrofoam ball; the other four have a shiny metal disk attached to the furry knob. When not disabled, the wire spring can be moved so that it wobbles back and forth; the metal disk can be pressed so that it produces a short chirping noise. In the Within-subject design, however, children's initial encounter with the objects consisted of an identical set in which the function was disabled on all of the objects. That is, pressing the metal disk did not produce a sound, and the spring was made rigid by a small rod inserted inside of it. Therefore, although the children could readily perceive the func-

FIG. 8.4. Sample object set used in Experiment 1.

tion-related parts of the objects, the actual functions themselves were not perceptible.

Sets of objects were presented on metal trays (28 cm × 43 cm). Additionally, two large transparent containers were used in the task. Previous research suggests that providing opportunities for containing objects encourages spatial grouping in young children (Markman et al., 1981; Namy et al., 1997). Accordingly, the experimenter presented two containers at the start of each presentation and explained that these were "for putting things in." She then placed the tray of eight objects between the two containers. No further reference was made to the containers, although the experimenter occasionally used nonverbal prompts to encourage their use, for example, touching or pushing them closer to the tray. However, children were free to use the containers or not.

In the Within-subject design, eight children were presented with the objects a total of three times. The first presentation served as a baseline or control. The experimenter presented all eight objects on a tray in a random arrangement and told the child, "These are for you. Can you fix them up?" In this Baseline condition, the function was not discernible for either class of objects. Children were encouraged to manipulate the objects for 1½ minutes, after which the experimenter removed the tray.

Children were then shown two exemplars and the previously hidden function was demonstrated for each class of objects. Figure 8.5 shows an example of two of the exemplars that children saw. Note that both objects share the same overall shape, but each has a unique function associated with a perceptually different part. The experimenter demonstrated each function, by pressing the round, flat part of the object shown on the right and causing it to produce a chirping sound, and by waving the wire part of

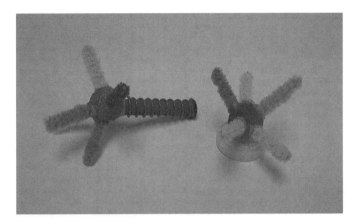

FIG. 8.5.   Function condition stimuli.

the object on the left and causing it to spring back and forth. The two exemplars were counterbalanced for order of presentation and left–right position. Also counterbalanced was the selection of the overall shape represented in the demonstration (spiky pipe cleaners vs. furry knobs). The children were again given the eight objects on a tray and told to "fix them up." Following another 1½ minutes, the tray was removed. This second presentation was known as the Function condition.

In the third and final encounter with the objects, children in the Within-subject design were again shown two exemplars, this time having the same function, but a different overall shape. The experimenter offered a novel name for each object (e.g., "zav" and "bard") and repeated the label several times. In addition, two placards were placed on the table. Each placard had the label of one object class on it, written in bold, lower-case letters (approximately 7.5 cm × 22.5 cm). The experimenter drew attention to the word by tapping the card and holding each object just above the card as she named it.[2] Children were also encouraged to say the names themselves. Figure 8.6 shows an example of two exemplars used to name each of the two classes of objects in the set. This third presentation was known as the Name condition.

An additional group of 20 3-year-olds participated in the Between-subject design of the experiment. The procedure was the same as the Within-subject design except that half of the children were randomly assigned to either a Function or Name condition and no baseline was included.

---

[2]We thank Sharon Carver, Director of the Children's School at Carnegie Mellon University, for this idea.

FIG. 8.6. Name condition stimuli.

All test sessions were videotaped and subsequently coded for whether children categorized the objects by shape or function, and for the number of total touches they produced for each set. This latter analysis indicated no reliable differences in the number of total touches children produced as a function of either design or condition. Children were credited with a classification if it involved the sequential manipulation or object grouping of three or four objects from one class (single classification) or from both classes (exhaustive classification).

The essential research question is to what features do children attend in response to online changes in context? Figure 8.7 presents the mean proportion of classifications that were shape-based by condition in the Within-subject design. Children demonstrated an initial bias for categorizing by shape, as suggested by the high rate of shape-based choices in the Baseline condition (.70). However, children readily shifted their basis for classification in response to the experimenter's demonstration of function. Thus they significantly reduced the proportion of shape-based groupings in the Function condition (.30). In addition, although there was a substantial rise in the rate of shape-based classifications with the introduction of object labels in the Name condition (.45), children's recent prior experience in the task appeared to affect their tendency to classify by shape. This conclusion is based on evidence comparing children in the Within-subject and Between-subject designs, as shown in Fig. 8.8.

In this figure, data from Fig. 8.7 are included for direct comparison. As shown, there is a similar trend in the rate of shape-based classifications for both the Within-subject and Between-subject designs. Children consistently produced significantly more groupings by shape when presented with the object label than when presented with the object function. More

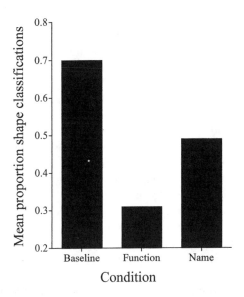

FIG. 8.7. Within-subject design: Proportion of shape-based classifications for Baseline, Function, and Name conditions.

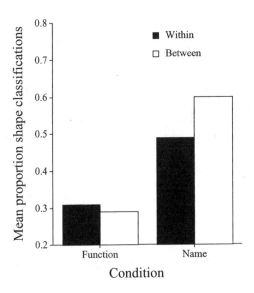

FIG. 8.8. Between-subject and within-subject comparison: Proportion of shape-based classifications for Function and Name conditions.

interestingly, however, are children's responses in the Name condition. Children were more likely to organize the objects by shape in the Between-subject design where they did not see the function demonstrated by the experimenter prior to hearing the object named (.60). These results demonstrate the short-term influence of prior experience in the task and highlight the importance of considering behavioral change over different scales of time.

A final piece of evidence concerns the effects of children's spontaneous naming on their performance in the task. Consider the proportion of shape-based choices in the Baseline condition, as shown in Fig. 8.7, and the two Name conditions shown in Fig. 8.8. If naming highlights attention to shape, as previous research suggests, then why is the rate of children's responses lower in both naming conditions relative to the Baseline condition? Although the carry over effect from the Function to the Name condition in the Within-subject design is a plausible explanation, there is an additional, uncontrolled factor operating in both conditions, namely, their spontaneous utterances in the task.

Fifty percent of the children in the Within-subject Baseline condition generated a label of their *own* invention, compared to 26% and 38% in the Function and Name conditions, respectively. In contrast, none of the children in the Between-subject Function condition offered a label, whereas 40% in the Name condition did. For example, one child examined the pipe cleaners and commented, "These are flowers." He then went on to sort the objects by shape. Another child stroked the fur-like knobs and said, "This feels like a dog," and also sorted the objects by shape. More frequently, however, children focused on the function-related aspect of the object, including functions that were not intended by the experimenter! For example, one child was apparently reminded of a camera when presented with the second set of objects. This child held up each object with a similar part and said, "Taking a picture." In this case, the child classified the objects by function.

Together, the findings from this study strongly suggest that 3-year-old children group objects by multiple similarities. Like adults, they are *flexible* classifiers, capable of modulating attention to cues by their usefulness in a specific task context. Moreover, children's classifications are simultaneously influenced at multiple scales of time, including the immediate input, prior task-specific events, and the child's accumulated experience in the everyday world. The results thus suggest an understanding of developmental change as the emergent product of processes that occur in real time. What happens in the day-to-day activity at the local level is inextricably related to global developments over the long term (Smith & Thelen, 2003).

CONCLUSION

This chapter extends the principles of dynamic systems theory to the domain of early categorization. As such, it demonstrates the wide utility of dynamic systems as a general theory of development. Dynamic systems theory predicts the facts of development by allowing for local flexibility in the form of changes in context and prior history, and global consistency in the form of the system's overall organization and processing. In addition, the theory contributes to the discovery of developmental process through the adoption of an epigenetic view. The concept of epigenesis is that new patterns of behavior arise from antecedent conditions that in themselves contain neither the behavior nor the prescription for behavior (Gottlieb, 1998; Thelen, 1989). Accordingly, to understand how behavior emerges, researchers need to characterize, in detail, the current and progressive state of the system, tying those developments to the changing context in which new behavior appears. This approach makes it possible to analyze the cooperativity of the elements within the system as they themselves change continuously over time (Gershkoff-Stowe & Thelen, 2004).

The findings reported in this chapter indicate that real-world experience with categories in everyday life—for example, the fact that cups can be stacked and spoons collected—leads children to notice similarity and to comment on it. In addition, this chapter suggests that the categories children themselves form arise from their direct perception and motor interaction with objects in a task-specific context. To illustrate the processes that take children to this point, we can return to the example in Fig. 8.1 involving the complex, spontaneous grouping produced by a 3-year-old child in play. How does the immediate input, events in the task, and the child's general experience with objects outside the task together create this kind of category behavior? The answer lies in the concept of soft-assembly: the on-line construction of categories in a manner that is flexible and open to learning.

Figure 8.9 suggests a schematic view from a dynamic systems perspective. It shows the interaction of forces at three different scales of time: the dimension of real-time associated with the current context and demands of the task, the recent past experience with task-specific objects, and the long-term experience with objects more generally. These three levels sometimes work together to influence behavior and sometimes compete, depending on the child's particular circumstance and point in development. Moreover, at each of these levels, multiple factors direct the child to attend selectively to certain object properties and not to others.

Consider first the task-dependent influences occurring in real time. Key among these factors is the multidimensional array of perceptual features.

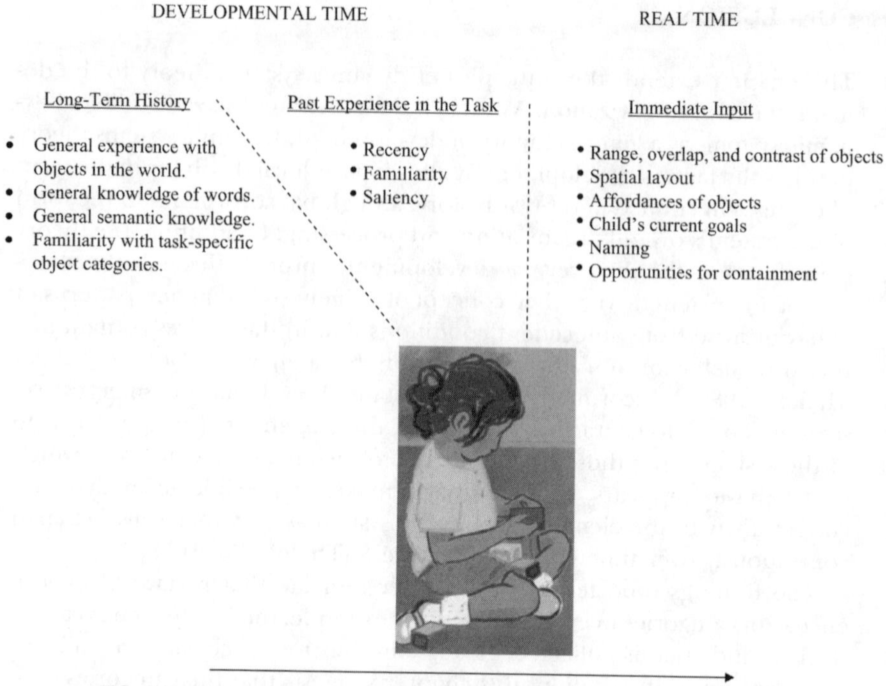

DEVELOPMENTAL TIME   REAL TIME

Long-Term History	Past Experience in the Task	Immediate Input
• General experience with objects in the world. • General knowledge of words. • General semantic knowledge. • Familiarity with task-specific object categories.	• Recency • Familiarity • Saliency	• Range, overlap, and contrast of objects • Spatial layout • Affordances of objects • Child's current goals • Naming • Opportunities for containment

FIG. 8.9.   A dynamic systems view of categorization at three time scales.

What information the child has available, however, is determined, in part, by the nature of the presentation, for example, whether the objects are presented in isolation or jointly, with similar or contrasting pairs, and with a wide or narrow range of exemplars. Such contextual factors help the child to notice the common structure among objects and to focus on different types of relationships (Gentner & Gunn, 2001). These influences are further mediated by the presence or absence of linguistic constructions (by the child or others); the idea being that language increases the pull toward similarity of shape (Landau et al., 1988). Finally, the current goals of the child, together with the particular affordances of the objects, have important consequences for how categories are assembled in real time (Pick, 1997).

At the second level of influence is the short-term effect of prior recent events. Here, activity within the task leads to shifts in attention through specific experiences in the task itself. Thus, what the child did just previously will influence performance in the future, for instance, through trial-by-trial updates of the similarity weightings between objects (Kruschke, 2003). In this critical sense, the conditions that lead the child to focus on some sources of information over others is affected by very general properties of memory and retrieval, namely, the frequency and recency of previously selected attributes (see also Barsalou, 1993).

A third and final level of influence concerns the child's long-term history, that is, what the individual brings to the task, both in the form of prior learning and processing capabilities. For example, the number of perceptual dimensions to which the child can simultaneously attend may account for some of the developmental differences we find when we compare 2-year-olds to 3-year-olds in tasks of categorization (e.g., Sugarman, 1983). Additionally, however, the child's general semantic or propositional knowledge, a rapidly expanding lexicon, and knowledge of specific category labels are factors that are also likely to constrain the search for common features. These ideas suggest that developing a rich, interconnected system of concepts may impact selective attention by emphasizing features that are not solely based on perceptual similarity.

As suggested by this example, there are a myriad of possible influences that might be relevant in a particular task context. Dynamic systems theory offers an approach for studying how these varied and mutually interacting factors line up to affect category behavior at a particular moment in time. The strength of dynamic systems theory is to emphasize the simultaneous influence of multiple variables. Each individual act of perceiving objects, operating on them, and naming them, changes the system—in the form of establishing new connections, strengthening existing ones, and providing the context for competitive learning. By this view, it is the activity of the system itself that is the causal force behind changes in the developing system. An additional strength of dynamic systems theory is to recognize the equifinality of development—the idea that children pursue a variety of routes toward mature behavior. Key to understanding this dynamic process is the accumulated experience and performance variability of individual children. Thus, the categories that children develop are the product of both a particular history and the immediate forces of perception and memory that occur within a specific task context.

In viewing behavior through the lens of dynamic systems theory, researchers have the potential to capture the complexity of development as it changes over different scales of time. In a dynamic account of category development, the real-time processes that underlie individual acts of classification and the long-term developmental history of organizing objects in everyday experience are unified into a single account.

REFERENCES

Aslin, R. N., Saffran, J. R., & Newport, E. L. (1998). Computation of conditional probability statistics by 8-month-old infants. *Psychological Science, 9*(4), 321–324.

Baldwin, D. A. (1989). Priorities in children's expectations about object label reference: Form over color. *Child Development, 60*(6), 1291–1306.

Baldwin, D. A. (1992). Clarifying the role of shape in children's taxonomic assumption. *Journal of Experimental Child Psychology, 54*(3), 392–416.

Baldwin, D. A., & Markman, E. M. (1989). Establishing word-object relations: A first step. *Child Development, 60*(2), 381–398.

Baldwin, D. A., Markman, E. M., & Melartin, R. L. (1993). Infants' ability to draw inferences about nonobvious object properties: Evidence from exploratory play. *Child Development, 64*(3), 711–728.

Barclay, J. R., Bransford, J. D., Franks, J. J., McCarrell, N. S., & Nitsch, K. (1974). Comprehension and semantic flexibility. *Journal of Verbal Learning & Verbal Behavior, 13*(4), 471–481.

Barsalou, L. W. (1982). Context-independent and context-dependent information in concepts. *Memory & Cognition, 10*(1), 82–93.

Barsalou, L. W. (1989). Intraconcept similarity and its implications for interconcept similarity. In S. Vosniadou & A. Ortony (Eds.), *Similarity and analogical reasoning* (pp. 76–121). New York: Cambridge University Press.

Barsalou, L. W. (1993). Flexibility, structure, and linguistic vagary in concepts: Manifestations of a compositional system of perceptual symbols. In A. F. Collins, S. E. Gathercole, M. A. Conway, & P. E. Morris (Eds.), *Theories of memory* (pp. 29–101). Hillsdale, NJ: Lawrence Erlbaum Associates.

Bloom, P. (1996). Intention, history, and artifact concepts. *Cognition, 60*(1), 1–29.

Bloom, P., & Markson, L. (1998). Intention and analogy in children's naming of pictorial representations. *Psychological Science, 9*(3), 200–204.

Booth, A. E., & Waxman, S. R. (2002). Object names and object functions serve as cues to categories for infants. *Developmental Psychology, 38*(6), 948–957.

Booth, A. E., & Waxman, S. R. (2003). Bringing theories of word learning in line with the evidence. *Cognition, 87*(3), 215–218.

Brown, R. W. (1956). Language and categories. In J. S. Bruner, J. J. Goodnow, & A. G. Austin (Eds.), *A study of thinking* (pp. 247–312). Oxford, England: Wiley.

Butterworth, G. (1993). Dynamic approaches to infant perception and action: Old and new theories about the origins of knowledge. In L. B. Smith & E. Thelen (Eds.), *A dynamic systems approach to development* (pp. 171–187). Cambridge, MA: MIT Press.

Carey, S. (1985). *Conceptual change in childhood.* Cambridge, MA: Bradford/MIT Press.

Clark, E. V. (1993). *The lexicon in acquisition.* Cambridge, England: Cambridge University Press.

Corrigan, R., & Schommer, M. (1984). Form versus function revisited: The role of social input and memory factors. *Child Development, 55*(5), 1721–1726.

Deák, G., & Bauer, P. J. (1995). The effects of task comprehension on preschoolers' and adults' categorization choices. *Journal of Experimental Child Psychology, 60*(3), 393–427.

Deák, G. O., & Bauer, P. J. (1996). The dynamics of preschoolers' categorization choices. *Child Development, 67*(3), 740–767.

Deák, G. O., Ray, S. D., & Pick, A. D. (2002). Matching and naming objects by shape or function: Age and context effects in preschool children. *Developmental Psychology, 38*(4), 503–518.

Diesendruck, G. (2003). Categories for names or names for categories? The interplay between domain-specific conceptual structure and language. *Language & Cognitive Processes: Conceptual Representation, 18*(5–6), 759–787.

Fenson, L., Vella, D., & Kennedy, M. (1989). Children's knowledge of thematic and taxonomic relations at two years of age. *Child Development, 60*(4), 911–919.

Freyd, J. J. (1992). Dynamic representations guiding adaptive behavior. In F. Macar, V. Pouthas, & W. J. Friedman (Eds.), *Time, action and cognition: Towards bridging the gap* (pp. 309–323). New York: Kluwer Academic/Plenum.

Gelman, R. (1990). First principles organize attention to and learning about relevant data: Number and the animate-animate distinction as examples. *Cognitive Science, 14*(1), 79–106.

Gelman, S. A., & Bloom, P. (2000). Young children are sensitive to how an object was created when deciding what to name it. *Cognition, 76*(2), 91–103.

Gelman, S. A., & Ebeling, K. S. (1998). Shape and representational status in children's early naming. *Cognition, 66*(2), B35–B47.

Gelman, S. A., & Koenig, M. A. (2003). Theory-based categorization in early childhood. In D. H. Rakison & L. M. Oakes (Eds.), *Early category and concept development: Making sense of the blooming, buzzing confusion* (pp. 330–359). London: Oxford University Press.

Gelman, S. A., & Markman, E. M. (1986). Categories and induction in young children. *Cognition, 23*(3), 183–209.

Gelman, S. A., & Markman, E. M. (1987). Young children's inductions from natural kinds: The role of categories and appearances. *Child Development, 58*(6), 1532–1541.

Gentner, D. (1978). A study of early word meaning using artificial objects: What looks like a Jiggy but acts like a Zimbo? *Papers & Reports on Child Language Development, 15*, 1–6.

Gentner, D., & Gunn, V. (2001). Structural alignment facilitates the noticing of differences. *Memory & Cognition, 29*(4), 565–577.

Gershkoff-Stowe, L., & Namy, L. L. (1995). Sequential touching and spatial grouping: A curvilinear developmental trend. Poster presented at the Society for Research in Child Development Biennial Meeting, Indianapolis, Indiana.

Gershkoff-Stowe, L., & Smith, L. B. (2004). Shape and the first hundred nouns. *Child Development, 75*(4), 1–17.

Gershkoff-Stowe, L., Thal, D. J., Smith, L. B., & Namy, L. L. (1997). Categorization and its developmental relation to early language. *Child Development, 68*(5), 843–859.

Gershkoff-Stowe, L., & Thelen, E. (2004). U-shaped changes in behavior: A dynamic systems perspective. *Journal of Cognition and Development, 1*(5), 11–36.

Goldfield, E. C. (1993). Dynamic systems in development: Action systems. In L. B. Smith & E. Thelen (Eds.), *A dynamic systems approach to development: Applications* (pp. 51–70). Cambridge, MA: MIT Press.

Goldstone, R. L. (1998). Perceptual learning. *Annual Review of Psychology, 49*, 585–612.

Golinkoff, R. M., Mervis, C. B., & Hirsh-Pasek, K. (1994). Early object labels: The case for a developmental lexical principles framework. *Journal of Child Language, 21*(1), 125–155.

Gopnik, A., & Sobel, D. M. (2000). Detecting blickets: How young children use information about novel causal powers in categorization and induction. *Child Development, 71*(5), 1205–1222.

Gottlieb, G. (1998). Normally occurring environmental and behavioral influences on gene activity: From central dogma to probabilistic epigenesis. *Psychological Review, 105*(4), 792–802.

Graham, S. A., Williams, L. D., & Huber, J. F. (1999). Preschoolers' and adults' reliance on object shape and object function for lexical extension. *Journal of Experimental Child Psychology, 74*(2), 128–151.

Imai, M., & Gentner, D. (1997). A cross-linguistic study of early word meaning: Universal ontology and linguistic influence. *Cognition, 62*(2), 169–200.

Imai, M., Gentner, D., & Uchida, N. (1994). Children's theories of word meaning: The role of shape similarity in early acquisition. *Cognitive Development, 9*(1), 45–75.

Inhelder, B., & Piaget, J. (1964). *The early growth of logic in the child: Classification and seriation.* New York: Harper & Row

Johnson, E. K., & Jusczyk, P. W. (2001). Word segmentation by 8-month-olds: When speech cues count more than statistics. *Journal of Memory & Language, 44*(4), 548–567.

Jones, S. S. (2003). Late talkers show no shape bias in a novel name extension task. *Developmental Science, 6*(5), 477–483.

Kalish, C. W., & Gelman, S. A. (1992). On wooden pillows: Multiple classification and children's category-based inductions. *Child Development, 63*(6), 1536–1557.

Keil, F. C. (1989). *Concepts, kinds and cognitive development.* Cambridge, MA: MIT Press.

Keil, F. C. (1995). The growth of causal understandings of natural kinds. In D. Sperber, D. Premack, & A. J. Premack (Eds.), *Causal cognition: A multidisciplinary debate* (pp. 234–267). New York: Clarendon Press/Oxford University Press.

Kelly, M. H., & Martin, S. (1994). Domain-general abilities applied to domain-specific tasks: Sensitivity to probabilities in perception, cognition, and language. *Lingua, 92*, 105–140.

Kemler-Nelson, D. G., and 11 Swarthmore College students. (1995). Principle-based inferences in young children's categorization: Revisiting the impact of function on the naming of artifacts. *Cognitive Development, 10*, 347–380.

Kemler-Nelson, D. G., Russell, R., Duke, N., & Jones, K. (2000). Two-year-olds will name artifacts by their functions. *Child Development, 71*(5), 1271–1288.

Kruschke, J. K. (2003). Attention in learning. *Current Directions in Psychological Science, 12*(5), 171–175.

Landau, B., Smith, L. B., & Jones, S. S. (1988). The importance of shape in early lexical learning. *Cognitive Development, 3*(3), 299–321.

Landau, B., Smith, L. B., & Jones, S. S. (1998). Object shape, object function, and object name. *Journal of Memory & Language, 38*(1), 1–27.

Legerstee, M. (2001). Domain specificity and the epistemic triangle: The development of the concept of animacy in infancy. In F. Lacerda, C. von Hofsten, & M. Heimann (Eds.), *Emerging cognitive abilities in early infancy* (pp. 193–212). Mahwah, NJ: Lawrence Erlbaum Associates.

Lewis, M. D., Lamey, A. V., & Douglas, L. (1999). A new dynamic systems method for the analysis of early socioemotional development. *Developmental Science, 2*(4), 457–475.

Madole, K. L., & Cohen, L. B. (1995). The role of object parts in infants' attention to form–function correlations. *Developmental Psychology, 31*(4), 637–648.

Madole, K. L., & Oakes, L. M. (1999). Making sense of infant categorization: Stable processes and changing representations. *Developmental Review, 19*(2), 263–296.

Malt, B. C., & Johnson, E. C. (1992). Do artifact concepts have cores? *Journal of Memory & Language, 31*(2), 195–217.

Mandler, J. M., & Bauer, P. J. (1988). The cradle of categorization: Is the basic level basic? *Cognitive Development, 3*(3), 247–264.

Mandler, J. M., & McDonough, L. (1993). Concept formation in infancy. *Cognitive Development, 8*(3), 291–318.

Markman, E. M. (1989). *Categorization and naming in children: Problems of induction.* Cambridge, MA: MIT Press.

Markman, E. M., Cox, B., & Machida, S. (1981). The standard object-sorting task as a measure of conceptual organization. *Developmental Psychology, 17*(1), 115–117.

Markman, E. M., & Hutchinson, J. E. (1984). Children's sensitivity to constraints on word meaning: Taxonomic versus thematic relations. *Cognitive Psychology, 16*(1), 1–27.

Markman, E. M., & Jaswal, V. K. (2003). Abilities and assumptions underlying conceptual development. In D. H. Rakison & L. M. Oakes (Eds.), *Early category and concept development: Making sense of the blooming, buzzing confusion* (pp. 384–402). London: Oxford University Press.

Massey, C. M., & Gelman, R. (1988). Preschooler's ability to decide whether a photographed unfamiliar object can move itself. *Developmental Psychology, 24*(3), 307–317.

McCarrell, N. S., & Callanan, M. A. (1995). Form–function correspondences in children's inference. *Child Development, 66*(2), 532–546.

Merriman, W. E., Scott, P. D., & Marazita, J. (1993). An appearance–function shift in children's object naming. *Journal of Child Language, 20*(1), 101–118.

Miller, G. A., & Johnson-Laird, P. N. (1976). *Language and perception.* Oxford, England: Harvard University Press.

Namy, L. L., Smith, L. B., & Gershkoff-Stowe, L. (1997). Young children's discovery of spatial classification. *Cognitive Development, 12*(2), 163–184.

Nelson, K. (1973). Structure and strategy in learning to talk. *Monographs of the Society for Research in Child Development, 38*(1–2, Serial No. 149), 136.

Nelson, K. (1974). Concept, word, and sentence: Interrelations in acquisition and development. *Psychological Review, 81*(4), 267–285.

Oakes, L. M., & Madole, K. L. (2003). Principles of developmental changes in infants' category formation. In D. H. Rakison & L. M. Oakes (Eds.), *Early category and concept development: Making sense of the blooming, buzzing confusion* (pp. 132–158). London: Oxford University Press.

Oakes, L. M., Plumert, J. M., Lansink, J. M., & Merryman, J. D. (1996). Evidence for task-dependent categorization in infancy. *Infant Behavior & Development, 19*(4), 425–440.

Oyama, S. (1985). *The ontogeny of information: Developmental systems and evolution.* New York: Cambridge University Press.

Piaget, J. (1962). *Play, dreams, and imitation in childhood* (C. Gattegno & F. M. Hodgson, Trans.). New York: Norton.

Pick, A. D. (1997). Perceptual learning, categorizing and cognitive development. In C. Dent-Read & P. Zukow-Goldring (Eds.), *Evolving explanations of development: Ecological approaches to organism-environment systems* (pp. 335–370). Washington, DC: American Psychological Association.

Prawat, R. S., & Wildfong, S. (1980). The influence of functional context on children's labeling responses. *Child Development, 51*(4), 1057–1060.

Quinn, P. C., Eimas, P. D., & Rosenkrantz, S. L. (1993). Evidence for representations of perceptually similar natural categories by 3-month-old and 4-month-old infants. *Perception, 22*(4), 463–475.

Rakison, D. H., & Poulin-Dubois, D. (2001). Developmental origin of the animate–inanimate distinction. *Psychological Bulletin, 127*(2), 209–228.

Ricciuti, H. N. (1965). Object grouping and selective ordering behavior in infants 12 to 24 months old. *Merrill-Palmer Quarterly, 11*(2), 129–148.

Rosch, E., Mervis, C. B., Gray, W. D., Johnson, D. M., & Boyes-Braem, P. (1976). Basic objects in natural categories. *Cognitive Psychology, 8,* 382–439.

Saffran, J. R., Aslin, R. N., & Newport, E. L. (1996, December). Statistical learning by 8-month-old infants. *Science, 274*(5294), 1926–1928.

Samuelson, L. K., & Smith, L. B. (1999). Early noun vocabularies: Do ontology, category organization and syntax correspond? *Cognition, 73*(1), 1–33.

Samuelson, L. K., & Smith, L. B. (2000). Children's attention to rigid and deformable shape in naming and non-naming tasks. *Child Development, 71*(6), 1555–1570.

Sandhofer, C. M., & Smith, L. B. (2001). Why children learn color and size words so differently: Evidence from adults' learning of artificial terms. *Journal of Experimental Psychology: General, 130*(4), 600–617.

Smith, L. B. (1995). Self-organizing processes in learning to learn words: Development is not induction. In C. A. Nelson (Ed.), *Basic and applied perspectives on learning, cognition, and development. The Minnesota Symposia on Child Psychology: Vol. 28* (pp. 1–32). Hillsdale, NJ: Lawrence Erlbaum Associates.

Smith, L. B. (2000). Learning how to learn words: An associative crane. In R. M. Golinkoff, K. Hirsh-Pasek, L. Bloom, L. B. Smith, A. L. Woodward, N. Akhtar, M. Tomasello, & G. Hollich (Eds.), *Becoming a word learner: A debate on lexical acquisition* (pp. 51–80). London: Oxford University Press.

Smith, L. B., Colunga, E., & Yoshida, H. (2003). Making an ontology: Cross-linguistic evidence. In D. H. Rakison & L. M. Oakes (Eds.), *Early category and concept development: Making sense of the blooming, buzzing confusion* (pp. 275–302). London: Oxford University Press.

Smith, L. B., & Heise, D. (1992). Perceptual similarity and conceptual structure. In B. Burns (Ed.), *Percepts, concepts and categories: The representation and processing of information* (pp. 233–272). Oxford, England: North-Holland.

Smith, L. B., Jones, S. S., & Landau, B. (1996). Naming in young children: A dumb attentional mechanism? *Cognition, 60*(2), 143–171.

Smith, L. B., Jones, S. S., Landau, B., Gershkoff-Stowe, L., & Samuelson, L. (2002). Object name learning provides on-the-job training for attention. *Psychological Science, 13*, 13–19.

Smith, L. B., Jones, S. S., Yoshida, H., & Colunga, E. (2003). Whose DAM account? Attentional learning explains Booth and Waxman. *Cognition, 87*, 209–213.

Smith, L. B., & Samuelson, L. K. (2003). Different is good: Connectionism and dynamic systems theory are complementary emergentist approaches to development. *Developmental Science, 6*(4), 434–439.

Smith, L. B., & Thelen, E. (2003). Development as a dynamic system. *TRENDS in Cognitive Science, 7*, 343–348.

Smith, L. B., Thelen, E., Titzer, R., & McLin, D. (1999). Knowing in the context of acting: The task dynamics of the A-not-B error. *Psychological Review, 106*(2), 235–260.

Soja, N. N., Carey, S., & Spelke, E. S. (1991). Ontological categories guide young children's inductions of word meaning: Object terms and substance terms. *Cognition, 38*(2), 179–211.

Sugarman, S. (1983). *Children's early thought: Developments in classification.* Cambridge, England: Cambridge University Press.

Thelen, E. (1989). Self-organization in developmental processes: Can systems approaches work? In M. R. Gunnar & E. Thelen (Eds.), *Systems and development* (Vol. 22, pp. 77–117). Hillsdale, NJ: Lawrence Erlbaum Associates.

Thelen, E., & Smith, L. B. (1994). *A dynamic systems approach to the development of cognition and action.* Cambridge, MA: MIT Press.

Thelen, E., & Ulrich, B. D. (1991). Hidden skills: A dynamic systems analysis of treadmill stepping during the first year. *Monographs of the Society for Research in Child Development, 56*(1, Serial No. 223), 104.

Tomasello, M., & Akhtar, N. (1995). Two-year-olds use pragmatic cues to differentiate reference to objects and actions. *Cognitive Development, 10*(2), 201–224.

Tomikawa, S. A., & Dodd, D. H. (1980). Early word meanings: Perceptually or functionally based? *Child Development, 51*(4), 1103–1109.

Tucker, M., & Hirsh-Pasek, K. (1993). Systems and language: Implications for acquisition. In L. B. Smith & E. Thelen (Eds.), *A dynamic systems approach to development* (pp. 359–384). Cambridge, MA: MIT Press.

van Geert, P. (1991). A dynamic systems model of cognitive and language growth. *Psychological Review, 98*(1), 3–53.

Waxman, S. R., & Booth, A. E. (2001). On the insufficiency of evidence for a domain-general account of word learning. *Cognition, 78*(3), 277–279.

Waxman, S. R., & Hall, D. G. (1993). The development of a linkage between count nouns and object categories: Evidence from 15- to 21-month-old infants. *Child Development, 64*(4), 1224–1241.

Wellman, H. M., & Gelman, S. A. (1998). Knowledge acquisition in foundational domains. In D. Kuhn & R. S. Siegler (Eds.), *Handbook of child psychology: Vol. 2. Cognition, perception, and language* (pp. 523–573). New York: Wiley.

Wolff, P. H. (1993). Behavioral and emotional states in infancy: A dynamic perspective. In L. B. Smith & E. Thelen (Eds.), *A dynamic systems approach to development* (pp. 189–208). Cambridge, MA: MIT Press.

Woodward, A. L. (1998). Infants selectively encode the goal object of an actor's reach. *Cognition, 69*(1), 1–34.

Yoshida, H., & Smith, L. B. (2003). Shifting ontological boundaries: How Japanese- and English-speaking children generalize names for animals and artifacts. *Developmental Science, 6*(1), 1–36.

Younger, B. A. (1985). The segregation of items into categories by ten-month-old infants. *Child Development, 56*(6), 1574–1583.

Younger, B. (1990). Infants' detection of correlations among feature categories. *Child Development, 61*, 614–621.

Younger, B. A., & Fearing, D. D. (2000). A global-to-basic trend in early categorization: Evidence from a dual-category habituation task. *Infancy, 1*(1), 47–58.

Younger, B. A., & Furrer, S. D. (2003). A comparison of visual familiarization and object-examining measures of categorization in 9-month-old infants. *Infancy, 4*(3), 327–348.

Chapter 9

Why Can't You "Open" a Nut or "Break" a Cooked Noodle? Learning Covert Object Categories in Action Word Meanings

Melissa Bowerman
Max Planck Institute for Psycholinguistics
Nijmegen, The Netherlands

INTRODUCTION

Psychologists interested in the development of object concepts have focused primarily on categories of objects that are labeled by nouns, such as *dog, animal, cup,* and *chair.* Named categories of objects are indeed critically important for language learners. But object classes are woven into the structure of language in a number of less obvious ways as well, for example, into the meanings of verbs, prepositions, particles, and other relational words. These concepts are often "covert": Speakers are typically not consciously aware of them, and they elude simple description. Yet children must master them to become fluent speakers of their native language. How do they do this?

As an informal introduction to the problem, let's look first at a relatively straightforward case. The felicitous use of the English verb *kick* requires that the action referred to involve a specific body part, a "foot" (generously defined so as to take in hooves, paws, and the like). It cannot be applied to otherwise "kick-like" actions using another body part (arm, wing, tail, etc.), much less no body part at all (except for certain metaphorical extensions). So "foot" is a covert object category lurking in *kick.* In this case the covert category coincides with a concept for which there is a nominal label, *foot.* Other examples of such verbs include *eat* ("food"), *drink* ("liquids"), and *neigh* ("horse"). Although the importance of "foot" for the concept *kick* may seem obvious, it is not necessarily so for children.

For example, between the ages of 1;6 and 1;8 a little girl, E, overextended *kick* to a variety of actions that were in some ways kick-like but did not involve a foot, such as throwing something, bumping her stomach up against a mirror on the wall, the fluttering of a moth on the table, and hitting a ball with the front wheel of her tricycle, making it roll (Bowerman, 1978a). Interestingly, this error ceased just as the noun *foot* appeared in her vocabulary.

Unlike *kick*, most covert object categories underlying non-nominal forms do not correspond directly to named object categories. Good examples are the objects relevant for actions English speakers call *open, cut,* or *break.* The existence of action-related object requirements becomes most apparent when these requirements are violated, as in the following child utterances (Bowerman, 1978a, and unpublished records):

1. OPEN
   a. *Open.* (Trying to separate two stuck-together Frisbees. C 1;4)
   b. *Open.* (Request for M[other] to crack nuts for her. E 1;6)
   c. *Mommy! Open!* (Wants M to take last pieces out of a wooden jigsaw puzzle. C 1;8)
2. CUT
   a. *Daddy cut ice.* (Watching F[ather] break ice cubes into chips with a rolling pin. C 1;10)
   b. *Me cutting.* (Pulling pieces of peach apart with her fingers. C 2;1)
   c. *Hey! I was about to cut mine!* (Getting ready to crack a nut with a mallet; upset when M puts her nut down in its place. C 7;7)
3. BREAK
   a. *Break it.* (Peeling a cooked noodle apart. E 1;8)
   b. *Don't break my coat.* (As someone pulls on the back of her coat. C 2;11)

In every instance the child's intention is clear, and the action is in many ways similar to an action that can felicitously be described as *open, break,* or *cut.* But it is strange to speak of "opening" objects like nuts or Frisbees, "cutting" things with instruments like rolling pins, fingers, or mallets, and "breaking" objects like cooked noodles and coats. What does the child have to know in order to be able to apply these verbs only to events involving objects of the "right kind"?

For adults who speak the same language as the child, the categories may seem obvious: Surely any self-respecting infant will come to identify "openables," "cutting instruments," and "breakables" in the course of his or her nonlinguistic interactions with the world! But there is striking variation across languages in the makeup of the covert object categories associated with verbs and other relational morphemes. For instance, the class of "openable objects" that is critical to the meaning of the English verb *open* is irrelevant in Korean, which partitions the domain covered by English *open* among at least six verbs (Bowerman & Choi, 2001).

The language-specificity of covert object categories raises an intriguing possibility: that children form object categories not only through their nonlinguistic experience with objects (and possibly their observations of how adults label them), but also through learning the semantics of action words. Roger Brown once suggested that "the requirement that a child learn to make correct referential use of a morpheme . . . is sufficient to cause the child to form the governing concept if the physical world has not already imposed it upon him" (1965, p. 317). In the cognitivist climate of the last 40 years, this idea has rarely been pursued. One goal of this chapter is to show why, after all, it must be taken seriously.

CROSSLINGUISTIC PERSPECTIVES ON COVERT OBJECT CATEGORIES

It is possible, as we have just seen, to illustrate covert object classification by non-nominal forms using English examples, but English in fact demands relatively little of its learners along these lines: In this language, information about objects *is* in fact heavily concentrated in nouns. In many other languages the task of imparting object information is far more extensively shared by other parts of speech, including special classifier morphemes, verbs, prepositions, particles, and verb affixes. The relative emphasis on nominals built into the structure of English and related languages—which is mirrored, incidentally, in the relative emphasis placed on learning nouns by English-speaking mothers (Choi, 2000)—is perhaps an important reason why investigations of object categorization in the Western world have revolved so closely around nouns and noun semantics. If the developmentalists interested in the acquisition of object concepts had been native speakers of, say, Cherokee, Navajo, or a Mayan language, the research in this field might have looked very different!

Classifiers

The best known linguistic devices with which languages express covert object category information are probably *numeral classifiers* (see Grinevald, 2000, and Aikhenvald, 2000, for good recent reviews). Characteristic of Southeast and East Asian languages, and also found in Mesoamerica and

Oceania, numeral classifiers are elements that are obligatory in noun phrases in the context of *quantifying* objects (e.g., counting them, or asking how many there are). These forms often have anaphoric (pronoun-like) uses as well. Numeral classifiers categorize the referents of noun exhaustively as members of one or another of a discrete set of classes, most typically on the basis of dimensionality and shape, often combined with secondary characteristics of consistency, size, or animacy. Paraphrases give the rough idea: "one *ROUND.CLASS* orange (ball, stone . . .)"; "two *LONG.RIGID.CLASS* pencils (boards, guns . . .)"; "three *FLAT.FLEXIBLE.CLASS* blankets (pants, pieces of paper . . .)"; "five *FOUR-LEGGED.CLASS* donkeys (cows, dogs . . .)."[1]

In real life, of course, the meanings of classifiers do not come pre-labeled for children: It is one thing to read a gloss like *ROUND.CLASS* or *LONG.RIGID.CLASS* (these sound deceptively simple), and another to arrive at such meanings through observing actual contexts of use. And although similar physical features of objects often play a role in the semantics of numeral classifiers across languages (E. Clark, 1976), the categories vary and can be quite idiosyncratic. For instance, Burmese has a numeral classifier for "long slender living or recently living things which are vertical or perpendicular to the object to which they are attached" (trees, plant, blades of grass, hair, strands of woolen yarn, etc.) (Burling, 1965). And Tzeltal Mayan has a classifier for "oblong, vertically erect solid objects slightly diminishing toward the apex" (Berlin, 1968).

There are several other less familiar types of classifiers as well (Grinevald, 2000; Aikhenvald, 2000).[2] For example, many Oceanic languages have *genitive classifiers*: bound morphemes that must be used in constructions specifying possession, as suggested by paraphrases like "my-*EDIBLE.CLASS* food,"

---

[1]In some languages each noun can be combined with only one classifier, while in others different classifiers can be used to highlight different aspects of a noun's referent. For example, in Japanese, T-shirts can be enumerated with a classifier for either *FLAT FLEXIBLE* objects or *CLOTHING ITEMS*, whereas in Burmese, knives can be counted as *LONG RIGID* objects (along with umbrellas, spoons, etc.), as *CUTTING INSTRUMENTS* (along with axes, scissors, etc.), or as *HUNTING INSTRUMENTS* (along with guns, bows and arrows, etc.) (Grinevald, 2003).

[2]In some cultures, *conventional gestures* may serve a function analogous to that of classifiers. For example, when indicating the height of something, it is conventional in much of Mexico to vary the orientation and shape of the hand according to the class of the object being measured (Foster, 1948): index finger pointing upward for humans (e.g., a child); hand extended sideways with palm vertical to the ground for nonhuman animates (e.g., a donkey); and hand flat with palm down for inanimates (e.g., a fence or table). The selection of the gesture is done outside the focus of awareness, and can sometimes lead to implicit dilemmas. When asked the size of the wooden statues of the saints in the church of a neighboring town, a village woman talked confidently, while her hand wavered uncertainly back and forth between the "inanimate" and the "human" gesture (Mary L. Foster, personal communication, 1975). (See Zavala, 2000, p. 144, and Wilkins, 2003, for additional examples of classification by gesture.)

"my-*TRANSPORT.CLASS* boat," "my-*WEAPON.CLASS* bow." These classifiers tend to pick out object categories defined by function, as shown, rather than shape. Still another classifier genre, *noun classifiers*, is found in many Mayan and Amazonian languages; these forms serve various syntactic functions such as determiner of a noun and third-person pronoun. For example, for Jakaltek Mayan: "*MAN.CLASS* John saw *ANIMAL.CLASS* snake" (John saw the snake); "ripe *PLANT.CLASS* tomato is red" (the ripe tomato is red); "*MALE.NON-KIN* saw *ANIMAL.CLASS* (he saw it [an animal])." Classifiers of this kind often pick out the material of which something is constituted.[3]

Some languages have only one set of obligatory classifiers, whereas others have two or three, often requiring speakers to classify the same object in multiple ways within the confines of a single sentence. For example, to report that "there are two avocados" in Akatek Mayan, one says roughly, "there are two-*INANIMATE.CLASS VEGETABLE.CLASS* avocados," thus indicating not only that these things are avocados (the noun), but also that they are inanimate entities (the numeral classifier), as well as vegetable entities (the noun classifier) (Zavala, 2000). But multiple classification of the same referent is not restricted to exotic languages. Notice, for example, that in the everyday English sentence *I put the apple in the bowl*, the object to which the apple is transferred is assigned not only (by the noun *bowl*) to the category of "bowls," but also (by the preposition *in*) to a more abstract class of containers and volumes that encompasses, for example, baskets, mugs, mouths, puddles, gopher holes, and clouds.

Classification by Verbs

Systematic categorizations of objects of the kind typically associated with classifiers are carried out in some languages by verbs (see Grinevald, 2000, and Aikhenvald, 2000). One kind of classification by verb involves a relatively transparent operation whereby an affix specifying a certain class of objects is inserted into the verb stem, with an effect suggested by paraphrases like "I *VEHICLE-have* a car" (I have a car) and "I *DOMESTIC.PET-have* a dog" (I have a dog). Another kind of verbal classification, particularly well developed in Athapaskan languages of North America such as Navajo and Chipewya, requires speakers to choose among multiple distinct verb stems,

---

[3]These classifiers apply not only to objects that are clearly, for example, "animals" or "plants," but also to objects that come from these sources (thus, *ANIMAL.CLASS* egg/milk/shoe; *ROCK.CLASS* bottle/can/pot) (Grinevald, 2000). Such systems evolve over time, and the introduction of nontraditional objects may force creative extensions and eventual changes in the category; for instance, modern Jakaltek speakers classify plastic sandals along with leather footwear under the *ANIMAL.CLASS* marker.

all expressing what from the English point of view is "the same" event or situation, but involving objects of different kinds. For example, to speak of the motion or location of an entity, a Navajo speaker must select from among 12 parallel "classificatory verb" stems according to whether X is a: ROUND OBJECT, LONG OBJECT, LIVING BEING, FABRIC-LIKE OBJECT, BULKY OBJECT, RIGID CONTAINER WITH CONTENTS, SET OF OBJECTS, SET OF PARALLEL OBJECTS, MASS, WOOL-LIKE MASS, MUD-LIKE MASS, ROPE-LIKE OBJECT (Hoijer, 1945).

These verb stems often define whole covert taxonomies of objects (Basso, 1968; Carter, 1976; Haas, 1967). For instance, to say "X is there" or "give me X," Chipewya speakers must not only distinguish animate referents from referents of all other kinds, but subdivide them by choice of verb stem according to whether they are AWAKE, SLEEPING, or DEAD (with the last-mentioned including not only dead people but, for example, a raw fish) (Carter, 1976). According to Carroll and Casagrande (1958), speakers of languages like these are not consciously aware of the systematic nature of the object classifications built into their verb system, and have no explicit labels for these object categories.

Although few languages build object classification into their verbs as pervasively as Athapaskan languages, every language has verbs that impose restrictions on the kinds of objects involved in the event.[4] The zeal with which languages differentiate among objects in their verbs is related in part to language family affiliation; for example, the Mayan languages dazzle speakers of English with their proliferation of verbs for seemingly "similar" events and situations involving different objects (Berlin, 1967; P. Brown, 1994, 2001; Pye, 1996). Degree of object differentiation is also influenced by broader typological differences among languages; for example, Plank (1985) showed that in domain after domain, German draws finer semantic distinctions with its verbs than English does, and he related this to the fact that German, but not English, distinguishes formally between types of grammatical objects (accusative vs. dative). An additional influence is the geographical area where a language is spoken: for example, verbs make fine object distinctions not only in Mayan languages but in many other unrelated languages of Mesoamerica as well. But even when languages agree in subdividing events according to the properties of the objects involved, they differ in how finely they partition the object categories, the object properties that are important, and which categories of objects are important for which kinds of events.

---

[4]The object with which the verb must "agree" is often the referent of the direct object of a transitive verb or the subject of an intransitive verb. Subjects of transitive verbs typically impose only very general constraints, for example, that the referent entity be animate (Keenan, 1986). These constraints have often been treated grammatically as "selection restrictions" on core arguments, but verbs can also constrain the referents of instruments, place noun-phrases, and other non-arguments: *kick* (foot) and *carry* (support by a body part) are examples.

Categorization of Objects Relevant to Early-Learned Action Words

Among the conceptual domains that are broken down differently by different languages, several are of particular interest from a developmental point of view because they include high-frequency verbs and other relational words that are learned very early, usually in the second year of life, and some comparative data are available on how children use them. These include verbs for dressing (putting on clothing), carrying and holding things, and consumption.

Dressing. For putting on clothing in English, one verb fits all: Regardless of the clothing item or body part, *put on* is the verb of choice (Fig. 9.1a).[5] Other languages require the speaker to choose from among a set of dressing verbs that distinguish between putting clothing onto various parts of the body. For example, Korean (Fig. 9.1b) distinguishes (among other dressing categories) between putting clothing on the head (*ssuta*, e.g., for hat, face mask, glasses, putting up umbrella), trunk or legs (*ipta*, e.g., for coat, shirt, pants, skirt), feet (*sinta*, e.g., for shoes, socks, roller skates), and wrist or waist (*chata*, e.g., for bracelet, belt, dagger) (Choi & Bowerman, 1991).

Japanese (Fig. 9.1c) also has a set of specialized "dressing" verbs, but the body regions and clothing sets that these verbs pick out are not identical to those of Korean (Kameyama, 1983); in common is a "head" verb (*kaburu*),[6] but below the neck the main partition falls not at the ankles but at the waist (*kiru* for the upper torso, *haku* for the lower torso on down through the feet) (compare Figs. 9.1b and 9.1c).

Still another approach is seen in the dressing verbs of two African languages (Schaefer, 1985). Tswana, a Bantu language of Botswana, distinguishes between putting clothing on the extremities (head, hands and arms, feet: *gòrwálà*) versus on the more central region of the body (*gòàpàrà*) (Fig. 9.1d), whereas Yoruba, a Niger–Congo language of Nigeria, has a special verb for putting clothing on the head (*dê*), but collapses all the other regions of the body into a single category (*wọ*) (Fig. 9.1e).

---

[5]English in fact treats putting on clothing as a subtype of a much broader concept: *put on* picks out controlled actions (typically by hand) of bringing one entity into contact with the exterior surface of another entity ("put the magnet on the refrigerator," "put the cup on the table," etc.). But the "dressing" version of *put on* is syntactically somewhat specialized, in that the goal object is routinely omitted: *put your coat on/?on your body*; compare with *put your cup *on/on the table*. Some languages have a special verb for "putting on clothing" (e.g., Tzeltal and Tzotzil Mayan; P. Brown, 2001; de León, 2001), but do not subdivide the domain further.

[6]The meanings of the two "head" verbs are not, however, identical: Korean *ssuta* can be used for donning anything that is conventionally worn on the head or face, including, for instance, glasses, whereas Japanese *kaburu* is used for covering the head with something—conventionally hats and the like, but also, for example, a blanket or coat.

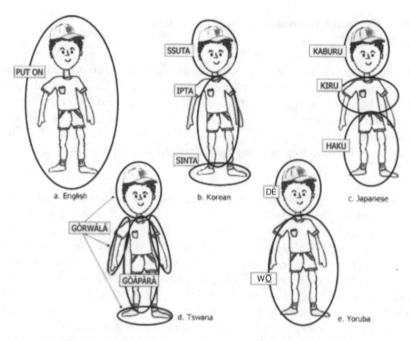

FIG. 9.1.   Categorization of acts of putting on clothing in several languages.

Carrying.   When someone moves along supporting an object above the ground, this is described as "carrying" by speakers of English. *Carry* is indifferent to both *what* is carried and *where* on the actor's body it is supported (Fig. 9.2a). We have already seen that when talking about the movement or location of objects, speakers of Athapaskan languages like Navajo must choose among verb stems on the basis of the nature of the object; the application of these roots to "carrying" events is shown in Fig. 9.2b. Events such as those shown in Fig. 9.2 are also distinguished in Tzeltal Mayan (P. Brown, 2001), Tzotzil Mayan (de León, 2001), and Korean (Choi & Bowerman, 1991), but differently in Navajo: not according to the carried object, but to the body part that supports this object; see Fig. 9.2c for the Tzeltal system.[7]

---

[7]There are other differences among these verbs in addition to those captured in Fig. 9.2. English *carry* requires the agent to be moving; *hold* is its usual static counterpart (Talmy, 1985): *Mary *carried/held the baby while she sat on the couch; Mary carried/*held the baby into the kitchen.* The Navajo forms are applied to both the motion and location of the specified kind of object across a wide range of event types distinguished in English (carrying, giving, throwing, putting, etc.). The Tzeltal and Korean forms are more similar to English *hold* than to *carry* in that they do not inherently specify motion. Toddlers often use them as requests to be picked up and supported by the specified body part.

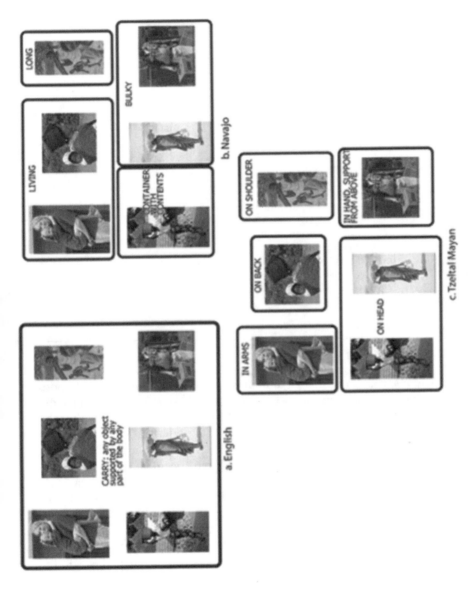

FIG. 9.2. Categorization of "carrying" in several languages.

217

TABLE 9.1
Verbs of Consumption in Different Languages

ENGLISH
- *eat* (solids)
- *drink* (liquids)
- *smoke* (smoke)

GERMAN
- *essen* (solids, by humans)
- *fressen* (solids, by animals)
- *trinken* (liquids)
- *rauchen* (smoke)

TURKISH (Slobin, personal communication, March 12, 2002)
- *yemek* (solids)
- *içmek* (liquids, smoke)

KALAM (New Guinea) (Pawley, 1993)
- *ñb-* (solids, liquids, smoke)

TZELTAL MAYAN (Berlin, 1967; P. Brown, 2001)
- *tun* (superordinate 'eat', used only in interrogative contexts, e.g., "What are you eating?")
- *lo'* (soft, mushy, or gelatinous objects, e.g., banana, potato)
- *ti'* (meat, chili, mushrooms)
- *k'ux* (individuated hardish objects, e.g., beans, radish, nut)
- *we'* (tortillas, breadstuffs)
- *tz'u'* (chewy object with pulp expectorated, e.g., sugarcane)
- *butz'* (foods that dissolve in mouth with little mastication, e.g., candy)
- *uch'* (liquids)
- *nuk'* (smoke)

Consumption. English discriminates between consuming solid foods (*eat*), liquids (*drink*), and tobacco smoke (*smoke*). German has similar distinctions, but obligatorily breaks down "eating" according to whether the actor is human (*essen*) or animal (*fressen*). Turkish has an "eat" verb similar to that of English, but it collapses the consumption of liquids and smoke into a single category ("fluids") (D. I. Slobin, personal communication, March 12, 2002). Kalam, a language of Papua New Guinea, has only a single verb root for consumption, which it applies to solids, liquids, and smoke alike (Pawley, 1993). Tzeltal Mayan has verbs comparable to English *drink* and *smoke*, but it obligatorily partitions "eating" into a large number of categories depending on the kind of food eaten, for example, *ti'* for meat, *we'* for tortillas and grain-based foods, *lo'* for soft things like bananas (Berlin, 1967; P. Brown, 2001).[8] These differences are outlined in Table 9.1.

---

[8]Tzeltal does have a superordinate verb for eating, *tun*, for situations in which the identity of the foodstuff is unknown, as in "What are you eating?," but one of the more specific verbs must be used when the identity is known.

ACQUIRING COVERT OBJECT CATEGORIES: SOME THEORETICAL QUESTIONS

Children learning a variety of languages begin to talk about acts of putting on clothing, carrying, and consumption well before the age of 2. How do they implicitly classify these events through the words they select to encode them? Before turning to the data, let us consider what we might expect.

Role of Nonlinguistic Object Concepts

Since the cognitive revolution of the early 1970s, there has been a pervasive assumption among developmentalists that in the early stages of language acquisition, children link words to concepts they have already formed on a nonlinguistic basis (Gleitman, 1990; Nelson, 1974; Piaget, 1954; Slobin, 1973; see Bowerman, 2000, for an overview). These concepts are, by hypothesis, the same all around the world, because they are shaped not by exposure to language but by infants' shared cognitive and perceptual predispositions (E. Clark, 1976), universal environmental and biological conditions (e.g., gravity, upright posture, possession of a human body) (H. Clark, 1973), and universal childhood experiences such as eating, sleeping, self-motion, and object manipulations.

This assumption of "cognitive priority" has been seriously challenged in recent years: A growing number of studies now shows that children are surprisingly sensitive to language-specific semantic categories in the input language by as early as 18 to 24 months (Bowerman, 1996; Bowerman & Choi, 2001, 2003; P. Brown, 2001; Choi & Bowerman, 1991; Choi, McDonough, Bowerman, & Mandler, 1999; de León, 2001). This work suggests that children attend to the distribution of forms across contexts in the linguistic input from at least as early as the one-word stage, and can use this information to *construct* semantic categories when necessary (i.e., when the concepts needed to guide the word's application are not already nonlinguistically present) (Bowerman & Choi, 2001, 2003; Casasola, in press; Casasola, Wilbourn, & Yang, in press).[9]

So far, the evidence for language specificity and for language-driven learning comes almost entirely from the domain of spatial relations; other kinds of meanings have yet to be systematically explored. When it comes to object categorization, the existing literature gives little reason to expect early sensitivity to language-specific categories. Infants have been shown to categorize objects at various levels of abstraction long before words are

---

[9]Whether these semantic categories, once formed, influence nonlinguistic cognition as well as language behavior (i.e., whether they have Whorfian effects) is controversial; see Bowerman and Choi (2003) and other chapters in Gentner and Goldin-Meadow (2003) for discussion.

comprehended or produced (Quinn & Eimas, 1996). Theorists differ on what is important in children's object categorization, with some emphasizing perceptual similarities, especially of shape, and others stressing higher-level conceptual knowledge about objects (see Landau, Smith, & Jones, 1998, for a review), but these processes are widely assumed to run off on a nonlinguistic basis, at least during the first couple of years of life.

Several recent studies have asked whether labeling might serve as a general stimulant to object categorization. Using a familiarity/novelty-preference procedure, these studies show that providing labels (compared to no labels) when introducing objects indeed prompts categorization in infants as young as 9 to 13 months (e.g., Balaban & Waxman, 1997; Waxman & Markow, 1995). But the categories tested tend to be ones that infants of this age already know, so the labels may have simply facilitated infants' display of their existing object category knowledge rather than prompting them to form new categories (Nazzi & Gopnik, 2001, although see Booth & Waxman, 2002, for evidence on novel categories). Further experiments on the role of language in categorization show that the way children generalize a novel word is influenced by its word class; in particular, count-noun syntax heightens attention to an object's *shape* (Landau, Smith, & Jones, 1988, 1998). For learners of Japanese, a language that does not make the mass–count distinction, the attention to shape is attenuated (Imai & Gentner, 1997).

What for our purposes is a critical limitation to the studies in these two paradigms is that none of them shows—or attempts to show—that toddlers will categorize a set of novel objects differently as a direct function of the way a training set of objects has been classified by the words used for them.[10]

---

[10]I am aware of only two studies examining whether very young children can form arbitrarily different object categories depending on the distribution of noun labels across exemplars. Nazzi and Gopnik (2001) presented 20-month-olds with object triads consisting of three perceptually and conceptually dissimilar objects. In play sessions some children heard one label for objects A and B and another for C, while others heard one label for A and C and another for B. When subsequently shown A and asked "Which one goes with this?," children's choice between B and C was consistent with the classification suggested by the verbal input. The children were tested only on the items that had been explicitly labeled in the training, so it is unclear whether these categories were productive (i.e., could be extended to new objects). Landau and Shipley (1996) taught children either a single label for two novel and perceptually dissimilar objects (the "standards"), or two different labels. Four additional novel objects, shape-morphed so as to fall perceptually along a line between the standards, were then presented. Two- and 3-year-olds in the "same label" condition accepted the label at ceiling for all the novel objects as well as the standards, "probably guided by the assumption that members lying on the hypothetical similarity line between standards are also members of the category" (Landau & Shipley, 1996, p. 446). Children in the "different label" condition generalized the labels only to the novel objects most similar in form to the standards. This study suggests that differences in the distribution of nouns across objects can indeed affect generalization to novel instances, at least in children over 2.

Overall, then, there is little reason to expect very young children to be sensitive even to those language-specific categories of objects that are labeled by the nouns of their target language, much less those that are defined only indirectly, by their association with action words.

Object Category Size and Ease of Learning

A second developmental question is whether children's ease of learning object-sensitive words for events is affected by the fineness with which the objects are partitioned. Is it easier to learn a single verb for "putting on clothing" or multiple verbs for putting more restricted classes of clothing on different regions of the body? A single verb for "eating" or multiple verbs for eating foods of different kinds? Ultimately this is a question about the level of abstraction at which infants spontaneously conceptualize events: Words that categorize at their preferred level should be easier to learn, or at least to extend to an appropriate range of actions, than those that pick out either bigger categories (thus neglecting distinctions that are salient to infants), or smaller categories (forcing attention to distinctions that are not salient).

According to one classical tradition, cognitive development progresses from global to differentiated (Gibson & Gibson, 1955; Werner, 1957). Thus, it should be easier to learn a single verb for a domain than a number of finer verbs. Recent studies supporting a "global to differentiated" progression in object-category formation include McDonough (2002) and Mandler and McDonough (1993, 2000). According to another classical tradition, it is *abstraction* that is difficult for children (Luria, 1930/1992; Saltz & Sigel, 1967): Early learning is at first concrete and context-bound, and generalization goes slowly stepwise from first-encountered exemplars to increasingly dissimilar exemplars. Modern adherents of this position suggest that it should be easier to learn a category revolving around a specific class of perceptually similar objects than a category applying across sets of dissimilar objects (Gentner & Boroditsky, 2001; Gentner & Rattermann, 1991; Quinn, 2003; Quinn & Eimas, 1996). Still other possibilities, of course, are that children initially do best at some intermediate level of abstraction (cf. the alleged, although controversial, primacy of the "basic level" in children's acquisition of noun taxonomies; Anglin, 1977; Rosch, Mervis, Gray, Johnson, & Boyes-Braem, 1976), or that the preferred level varies across different domains of events. Common to all these positions is the idea that the level of abstraction preferred by young language learners is determined by cognition, not by the semantic structure of the input language. But is this indeed the case?

ACQUIRING COVERT OBJECT CATEGORIES
FOR EVENTS OF DRESSING, CARRYING,
AND CONSUMPTION

In the crosslinguistic literature on early lexical development, there is by
now sufficient material to allow at least an informal exploration of these
questions. In this section we look at verbs of dressing, carrying, and consuming. A more complex set of cases—verbs of opening, cutting, and
breaking—is saved for later.

Dressing. In a comparison of how learners of English and Korean about
14 months to 3 years of age spontaneously encode motion events, Choi and
Bowerman (1991) reported that both sets of children get the hang of dressing verbs early. By around 17 to 20 months, Korean-speaking children distinguish appropriately between putting clothing on the head (*ssuta*), the
trunk or legs (*ipta*), and the feet (*sinta*), while English-speaking children
use a single form, *on* or *put on*, for all these actions.

To explore this pattern in a more controlled way, Bowerman and Choi
(2001; Bowerman, 1996) asked learners of Korean and English (age 2
yrs.–3½ yrs.) to describe eight specific actions of putting on clothing (along
with many other object manipulations). In the youngest age group, 2 years
to 2½ years, the Korean learners correctly used *ipta* for donning a dress, un-
dershirt, and underpants 100% of the time; they used *sinta* for putting on
shoes, slippers, and socks 97% of the time; and they said *ssuta* for putting on
a big loose hat and a tight wool cap 50% of the time. The corresponding
frequencies with which same-age learners of English produced *(put) on* for
these specific groups of events is 90%, 97%, and 100%. Most nontarget responses in Korean were acceptable uses of *kkita* 'fit tightly into/onto', a
more general verb not specialized to clothing (Choi & Bowerman, 1991),
for putting on shoes and socks and pulling on the wool cap.

In a study of the acquisition of clothing verbs in Japanese, Kameyama
(1983) found that children age 2 to 5 used *kaburu* appropriately for putting
on a hat 93% of the time, *kiru* for putting on a coat 64% of the time, and
haku for putting on shorts and shoes 71% of the time. Most nontarget responses in Japanese involved the "light" verb *yaru* 'do'. Recall that Korean
and Japanese differ in their classification of the lower body (Figs. 9.1b,
9.1c), so this means that the two sets of learners differed in whether they
treated putting on underpants/shorts like putting on shirts and dresses
(Korean) or like putting on shoes and socks (Japanese).[11]

---

[11]To determine whether the children linked clothing verbs more to clothing items or to
body parts, Kameyama also tested them on nonconventional actions like putting shorts over the
arms or a coat over the head. Responses were inconsistent, suggesting that verb meanings re-

There was no evidence that learners of Korean or Japanese initially associated any of their specific dressing verbs with a global meaning of "putting on clothing." Nontarget responses by Korean and Japanese children rarely involved overextensions of the dressing verbs to inappropriate body regions (e.g., Korean *ipta* [torso] to putting on a hat or shoes). Such errors—which would suggest reliance on a large, English-style concept like "put clothing item onto any body part"—constituted only 2.9% of the total relevant responses for the Korean children across the three age groups (2 yrs.–3½ yrs.); the comparable figure across the Japanese children from all three age groups (2½ yrs.–5 yrs.) is 8.9%.

These errors, although never frequent, actually increased over time rather than decreased, at least for the Korean children[12] (0% at 2 yrs.–2½ yrs., 2.5% at 2½ yrs.–3 yrs., and 6.3% at 3 yrs.–3½ yrs.); this is also counter to what we would expect if the children initially entertained a global concept of "putting on clothing," followed later by differentiation. In a previous study I documented a similar increase over time in substitution errors among a set of semantically related verbs, in that case verbs of caused motion such as *put, bring, take,* and *give* (Bowerman, 1978b). My interpretation for that pattern is also applicable here: The verbs are at first learned and used independently of one another, each for its own domain, but over time they draw together and become integrated into a common semantic domain, and so begin to compete with each other.

Carrying.   The comparative acquisition data is sparser for carrying and consumption than for putting on clothing, and it is limited to spontaneous speech. But it is compatible with the results for the dressing verbs. Choi and Bowerman (1991) reported that two learners of English began to use *carry* at 19 and 21 months. In inspecting the raw data for this study for purposes of this chapter, I found that the verb was extended during the first few weeks of use to a wide variety of carried objects (child, grocery bag, glass, bear, diaper, tricycle, etc.). It was, however, used in connection with support only by the arms (e.g., carrying a baby) or the hands (e.g., carrying a glass or a dirty diaper). Learners of Korean in this same age range distinguish appropriately between *anta* 'hold/carry in arms' and *epta* 'hold/carry on back' (Choi & Bowerman, 1991); by 24 months they add *tulta* 'carry in hands'. A child learning Tzotzil Mayan distinguished at 19 months between *pet* 'carry in arms' and *kuch* 'carry on back' (de León, 2001).

---

volved around prototypes in which clothing item and body part are combined in the conventional way.

[12]Figures broken down by age are difficult to derive from the Japanese data, but the data are at least compatible with a similar increase: The higher percentage of overextensions overall than in Korean (8.9% vs. 2.9%) may be because the Japanese children were on average older (2½ yrs.–5 yrs. as compared to 2 yrs.–3½ yrs.).

Differences in the frequency and manner of talking about carrying on different body parts is likely to be related to cultural practices as well as language categories. In Western industrial society, people carry babies and other entities on the back relatively rarely; in Mayan culture this is much more frequent. The two learners of English in Choi and Bowerman's (1991) study assimilated the concept of a child being carried on the back to the larger category of "riding." The word *ride* was used appropriately and frequently, from 16 months for one child and 19 months for the other, for events in which humans and other animates (including teddy bears, etc.) were supported and moved "for fun" by a wide range of objects (tricycle, spinning chair, rocking horse, wagon, toy train or car, bouncing parental shin, etc.). The assignment of acts of carrying children on the back to this larger category of "riding" events, as seen in the English data, is not found in the acquisition of Mayan or Korean.

Consumption.   According to P. Brown (2001), learners of Tzeltal Mayan begin to distinguish appropriately at around 18 to 24 months between *we'* 'eat corn- or grain-based food' (e.g., tortilla), *lo'* 'eat soft things' (e.g., banana), and *k'ux* 'eat crunchy things' (e.g., beans). A child learning Tzotzil, a sister Mayan language with a similar set of eating distinctions, used the "meat-eating" verb at 2 years when she first saw birthday cake, an unfamiliar food item, but switched spontaneously to the "corn-/grain-based-eating" verb as soon as she tasted it (Lourdes de León, personal communication, 2001).

Although it is clear that learners of English begin to produce the verbs *eat* (and *drink*) early, I am not aware of any published data on what kinds of consumables they use these verbs for. So I searched for these verbs in the longitudinal spontaneous speech records from the two English-speaking children studied by Choi and Bowerman (1991). *Eat* emerged at 17 to 18 months and was immediately extended to a wide range of solid foods; by 23 months the inventory included cake, French fries, sugar, crackers, cheese, yogurt, grass (said of a cow), hamburger, sandwich, cereal, apple, grapes, grapefruit, carrots, artichokes, popcorn, chocolate, lollipops, batter, cardamom seeds, and many more. *Drink* emerged at 17 and 20 months, and was likewise rapidly extended to beverages of many kinds (water, juice, milk, 7-Up, Coke, coffee, iced tea, liquid Jello, beer, wine, etc.), as well as to a variety of drinking techniques (from a glass, cup, bottle, bowl [said of a cat], straw, drinking fountain, spoon).[13]

---

[13]The covert categories associated with *eat* and *drink* are well enough understood by at least 26 months that learners of English can direct their gaze rapidly to an appropriate object in a visual array on the basis of the verb alone. For example, when asked "Which one do you *eat*?," they initiate an eye movement within 100 msec of the verb's offset to the cookie rather than the car (Chang & Fernald, 2003).

TAKING STOCK

One of the theoretical questions raised earlier was whether children's early action-word use revolves around a set of event concepts that is universally shared. In the data just examined, there is no evidence that children learning different languages apply a uniform set of concepts to events of dressing, carrying, and consuming. Well before 2 years of age, they have discovered some of the major covert object categories that their language uses in grouping or distinguishing such events. Of course, they do not necessarily learn all the words of a domain early. They start, not surprisingly, with the words that are frequent in the speech around them. But once they begin to produce a word, they extend it rather quickly across a range of appropriate or near-appropriate events.

A second question was whether children find it easier to learn "big" (global, abstract) event categories or "small" (differentiated, concrete) categories involving objects of specific types. Category size per se seems to make little difference (although category makeup does, as we see shortly). On the one hand, children can readily learn event categories that make few or no distinctions among objects; recall English *put on, carry,* and *eat,* and to this evidence we can add toddlers' use of path particles like *up, down, in, out, on, off* for the movements of essentially any object (Choi & Bowerman, 1991; Smiley & Huttenlocher, 1995). On the other hand, it takes children no longer to learn some finer subdivisions of these categories: In the same time frame (about 18–24 months), learners of Korean, Japanese, Tzeltal, and Tzotzil successfully differentiate among several subtypes of dressing, carrying, and/or eating events. Later, we consider what kind of learning procedure could account for these patterns.

Despite their striking overall attunement to the semantic categories of the input language, children inevitably make some errors in word use. These are important for two reasons. First, errors help establish that children are using the words productively, and so rule out an uninteresting reason for early language-specificity: that young children simply learn "what to say" for particular events they have often heard adults talk about. It is difficult to establish productivity with confidence when the available data are limited (as for Tzeltal and Tzotzil carrying and eating verbs), but for the English versus Korean contrasts we have considered, there is good evidence for productive categorization in both spontaneous and elicited speech (see Bowerman & Choi, 2001, and especially Choi & Bowerman, 1991, pp. 110–113, for discussion and evidence).

Errors are also important because they provide clues to the learning mechanisms that enable children to acquire language-specific covert object categories so early. If children displayed uniform accuracy across categories of all kinds from the beginning, we would not know where to look. But differential difficulty gives us a foot in the door to understanding the learning process. To the coarse-grained question whether "bigger" or "smaller" covert object categories are inherently easier, the answer was "children can learn both relatively accurately from the beginning." But some "big" categories do have special properties that give rise to telling errors.

"OPENING," "CUTTING," AND "BREAKING" IN ADULT AND CHILD LANGUAGE

Three such categories are picked out by the English verbs *open, cut,* and *break.* Children often overextend these verbs to objects of the wrong kinds, as illustrated at the beginning of this chapter. At one time I assumed that overextensions like these reflected children's spontaneous way of viewing the world; for instance, that when a child says *open* not only for opening doors and boxes but also for manipulations with Frisbees and jigsaw puzzles, she does so because she has mapped the word *open* to a concept of her own nonlinguistic devising, perhaps "separation."

With the benefit of hindsight and more crosslinguistic data, I now interpret these errors differently: as resulting from an *interaction* between, on the one hand, children's nonlinguistic capacity to recognize relational similarities across events involving objects of different kinds and, on the other, their implicit efforts to make sense of how words are used in the speech around them. The evidence is that extension patterns *vary* for children learning different languages, and these variations are *systematically related* to the way the domain is categorized in the target language.

The English Category of "Openable Objects"

Overextensions with *open* and its translation equivalents are common among young learners of English, French, German, Dutch, and other languages (Bowerman, 1978a, 1996; Clark, Carpenter, & Deutsch, 1995). If these errors were caused by toddlers' nonlinguistic way of conceptualizing the world, we could expect to see them in all children. But no word is used by learners of Korean for a similar range of events (Bowerman, 1996; Bowerman & Choi, 2003). Why not?

A first clue that the semantic structure of the target language is somehow involved is that Korean has no word that even begins to approximate the semantic range of English *open.* The conceptual glue that unifies, for example, "opening a door," "opening the mouth," "opening an envelope," and "opening a book" for speakers of English seems to be missing, and the domain is parceled out among a number of crosscutting categories that emphasize different aspects of the events (see Fig. 9.3). Many languages parti-

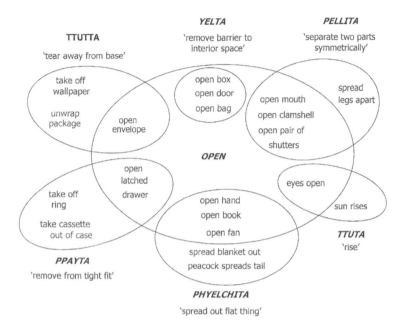

FIG. 9.3.   Categorization of "opening" in English and Korean.

tion the "opening" events of English among a number of different verbs, but the criteria used for this differ strikingly from one language to another.[14] An English-like category of "opening" events does not seem to be inevitable to human cognition.

Let us imagine, then, with Roger Brown, that a child takes a new word as a "lure to cognition" (1958, p. 206)—as an invitation to discover the meaning that governs adult use of the word "if the physical world has not already imposed it upon him" (1965, p. 317). How might learners go to work on words like *open* and, for instance, *yelta* (top center of Fig. 9.3), an early-learned Korean verb that is usually considered the translation equivalent of *open?*

Observing uses of *open* for actions on a wide variety of objects, learners of English are invited to generalize broadly, to look for an abstract relational

---

[14]For example, Japanese divides up most English "opening" events between two verbs: *akeru* is applied to opening doors, boxes, and many of the other objects in Fig. 9.3, but *hiraku* is needed for opening a hand, book, or fan. Some events—for example, opening the mouth, eyes, clamshell, or pair of shutters—can be described with either verb, depending on whether the speaker wishes to emphasize accessing an interior space or the separation of parts. In Lao, a language spoken in Laos, there is a special verb for opening the eyes, another for opening the hand, and still another for opening the mouth or spreading wings; manipulations with doors, boxes, books, fans, clamshells, and shutters all fall together. (For information about "opening" in Japanese, I am grateful to Megumi Kameyama, Sotaro Kita, and Ayumi Matsuo; for Lao, I thank Nick Enfield.)

meaning that is indifferent to the physical differences between a door, a pair of shutters, a mouth, a book, and an envelope. Learners of Korean, in contrast, are confronted with a different verb at every turn, and these verbs instruct them, in effect, to compare actions of opening a door, box, bag, and the like to discover what they share ('remove barrier to interior space': *yelta*), which is *not* shared by, say, opening a pair of shutters or a mouth; and, further, to determine what this latter set of actions share ('separate two parts symmetrically': *pellita*) that is not shared by opening a book, hand, or fan ('spread out a flat thing': *phyelchita*). These different "instructions" are associated with a broad pattern of overextensions for children learning English *open* (or a similar verb in French, German, etc.), but an essentially correct extension of Korean *yelta* 'open' from the beginning (Bowerman, 1996).[15]

Verbs associated with perceptually diverse classes of objects are not inevitably overextended; we saw that the English verbs *eat* and *put on* are used appropriately even though they require control of object categories such as "food," "clothing," and "body part." So why do children overshoot the target category for *open*?

There is reason to suppose that notions like "food," "clothing," and "body part" form relatively coherent categories for human beings regardless of how they are treated in specific languages. These categories are constituted by clusters of perceptual and functional features that correlate in the world of experience, just as features like wings, beaks, feathers, and flying correlate (Rosch et al., 1976). One bit of evidence that the categories are coherent is that they are usually dignified with a noun label that serves as a superordinate node in an object taxonomy ("food": bread, meat, fruit, etc.; "clothing": hat, coat, pants, etc.; "body parts": head, torso, legs, feet, etc.).[16] Another is that in the meanings of the "dressing" and "consump-

---

[15]Learners of Korean do often overextend *ppayta* 'remove from tight fit'. As suggested by the examples of this category in Fig. 9.3, *ppayta*, like English *open*, is a large category in adult speech that encompasses actions on a perceptually very diverse set of objects. Although the (over)extensions of *open* by English-speaking children and *ppayta* by Korean-speaking children overlap to some extent, the overall range of these two words is language-specific: Each word clearly has its core in the adult meaning of the target word—'separate to make something accessible' for *open*, and 'separate fitted or interlocked objects with a bit of force' (e.g., Lego blocks apart, top off pen) for *ppayta* (Bowerman & Choi, 2003).

[16]It would be useful to know more than we do about the developmental relationship between learning the covert object categories associated with verbs and learning the explicit nominal labels for these categories, where they exist. For adults, word pairs like *eat* and *food*, *put on* and *clothing*, are at least partially mutually defining (*food* is stuff that you can "eat"; *clothing* is the main category of things that you can "put on" or "wear," although these verbs also apply to makeup and jewelry). But the acquisition of verbs and their associated nominals do not necessarily run off in tandem. In particular, children as old as 5 to 6 years often underextend a superordinate nominal like *food* or *clothing*—for example, rejecting a lollipop or cookie as

tion" verbs in various languages, they behave as a set: for example, if the category "food" is collapsed with other categories under a higher node (as in Kalam's single verb for "consume": eat/drink/smoke), all its members go together; and if the category is subdivided (as in Tzeltal's multiple eating verbs), the daughter categories exhaustively partition the content of the mother node but do not go beyond it to pull in members that have nothing to do with eating.[17]

For English *open*—and also for *cut* and *break*, which we examine in a moment—the situation is different: The features that characterize the objects associated with these verbs do not cluster together in the real world, but instead are sprinkled about in a more "matrix-like" fashion (see Huttenlocher & Lui, 1979, on this useful notion). In cases like these, languages impose their own, somewhat arbitrary partitionings: They elect to go with certain features and feature combinations rather than others. Once conventionalized and shared within a speech community, these implicit choices seem natural and obvious to those who have learned them. But children have no way of knowing, independently of the linguistic input, how the partitioning will be done in their language (see Gentner, 1982, for discussion); the categories must be acquired on the basis of the linguistic input.

What properties of objects must English speakers be able to identify in order to extend *open* correctly? This is admittedly a complex question, but as an approximation, we can say that an entity that can be physically "opened" should have the following three properties (Bowerman, 1978a; Levison, 1993):[18] (a) it is a *unitary object* (although it may have separable parts, such as a pot with a lid); (b) it *separates along predetermined lines*, not unpredictably (hence actions of "opening" are usually reversible: objects that can be "opened" can also be "closed"); and (c) separation affords *access* to something (e.g., a "content," an interior space, or a previously concealed part of the object with which you can do something).

"food," or a shoe or glove as "clothing" (Anglin, 1977; Saltz, Soller, & Sigel, 1972)—even though children of this age and far younger routinely apply the verbs *eat* and *put on* to actions involving such objects.

[17]These remarks apply to the literal use of these terms. Of course, verbs for dressing and eating, like other verbs, often develop metaphorical extensions, and these may show considerable crosslinguistic variability (I am grateful to Cliff Pye for reminding me of this). For example, one "dresses" a turkey and a salad in English but not in Dutch; on the other hand, a nicely decorated party or a festively set table can be "well-dressed" (*mooi aangekleed*) in Dutch but not in English.

[18]In discussing the extensions of *open*, *break*, and *cut*, I limit myself to literal uses of the verbs for physical actions on objects, ignoring metaphorical extensions such as "open a meeting," "break your heart," and "cut through all the nonsense," which are learned much later by children. I also limit myself to transitive examples, and to "bare" instances of *open* alone as the main verb; its distribution as a particle in conjunction with a verb, as in *crack open* for a nut or *cut open* for an apple, is much more liberal; see also footnote 19 on the phrasal verb *open up*.

These features all come together in the objects for which *open* sounds fine, for example, a door, window, box, bag, mouth, umbrella, fan, or jack-knife. But the features do not have a strong affiliation with each other: They are widely distributed in the world of experience, and they often turn up alone or in pairs. For example, stuck-together Lego pieces and Frisbees separate in a predictable way, but they are neither unitary objects nor allow access to something. A jigsaw puzzle separates predictably and it *is* a unitary (multipart) object, but again, there is nothing to access. Nuts, eggs, and apples are units with something to access, but they do not come apart along predetermined lines. (Walnuts do, but the action cannot be reversed.) Electrical appliances such as television sets are also units with something to access (their functions, when turned on), but one does not access them by separating anything. In these situations adults do not normally say *open*, but children often do (Table 9.2).[19] Learning how to use *open* as fluent speakers do requires being able to combine the relevant features consistently, and this takes time; application across too broad a range of objects is still common even among children as old as 6 or 7 (Schaefer, 1979).

"Breaking" and "Cutting"

Like *open*, the verbs *break* and *cut* revolve around categories of objects that, in crosslinguistic perspective, can be seen as constructs of English. Many languages distinguish between, say, cutting something with a sharp instrument and breaking something with a blow, but this complex domain is carved up differently in different languages (Bowerman, Majid, Erkelens, Narasimhan, & Chen, 2004; Majid, van Staden, Boster, & Bowerman, 2004; Pye, 1994, 1996). Just as for "opening," there is a range of relevant features—for example, "degree of force, direction of force, instrument, type of object, spatial configuration of object, object's material" (Pye, 1996)—but these features are distributed independently across events, and do not cluster to delineate particular sets of actions that everyone agrees are somehow alike. Different languages make different implicit choices about which features must be attended to and how they should be combined.

Breaking. Although English *break* prototypically applies to material disruptions in rigid objects, it is also used for one-dimensional and (some) three-dimensional flexible objects (e.g., a rope or thread, a baguette). But

---

[19]When an entity meets the first and third criteria (being a unit with something to access), but not the second ("predicable lines of separation"), the acceptability of *open* improves with the addition of the particle *up*: (surgeon) "Let's ??open/open up the patient"; (plumber) "We need to ??open/open up the floor in that room." The restrictions discussed here are specific for English; many languages, including Spanish and Finnish, have a "big category" verb similar to English *open* that is also applied, for example, to turning on electrical appliances or water faucets.

TABLE 9.2
Some Overextensions of *OPEN* by C and E
From 1;4 to 3;2

Objects lacking predictable lines of separation
   cracking peanuts
   peeling paper off a book cover
   peeling skin off a hotdog
   peeling a banana
   peeling a hardboiled egg
   pulling apart a meatball
   pulling apart a grapefruit section
   breaking a roll (*"Will you open this?"*)
   unbending a flexible mommy doll (*"Open mommy"*)
Objects with parts designed to separate, but nothing to "access"
   pulling leg off doll
   taking pieces out of jigsaw puzzle
   pulling legs of nail scissors apart
   pulling removable tip off paintbrush
Separations of assemblies that are not unitary objects
   pulling pop-beads apart
   unscrewing stake from block
   pulling up shirt (*"Open your tummy . . . now close it"*)
   raising couch cushion to look under it
   taking wide, stubby candle out of shallow holder
   pushing chair back from table (*"I'm gonna open my chair"*)
   untangling pieces of yarn
   pushing M's knees apart (*"Open your knees"*)
Access but no separation involved
   turning on television set
   turning on lights
   turning on electric typewriter

Note. From "The Acquisition of Word Meaning: An Investigation Into Some Current Conflicts," by M. Bowerman, 1978a, in N. Waterson and C. Snow (Eds.), *The Development of Communication*, pp. 263–287. New York: Wiley. Also from M. Bowerman, unpublished records.

break sounds strange for inflicting material disruptions on flexible two-dimensional objects, for example, a sheet of paper, blanket, coat, or cooked noodle; *tear* (or *rip*) is needed instead.[20] The distinction between "breaking" and "tearing" in English also includes some information about the manner of the action. Separations in two-dimensional flexible entities like paper and cloth normally come about "bit by bit," and this manner is characteristic for *tear*; when the separation occurs all at once, *break* is often possible ("The heavy groceries broke the shopping bag"; "the high-pitched

---

[20]English *break* has another use not considered here, to do with objects becoming nonfunctional rather than coming apart ("I broke my watch"). Many languages have a special verb for this sense.

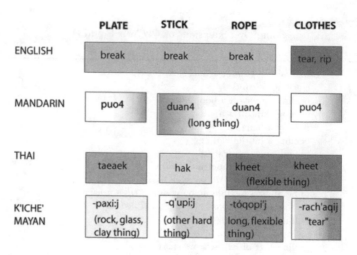

FIG. 9.4. Categorization of "breaking" in several languages (Pye et al., 1995).

sound broke the membrane"). Other languages dissect the "breaking" and "tearing" events of English differently, using various combinations of properties such as the object's shape, dimensionality, and material (see Fig. 9.4, based on Pye, 1994, 1996; Pye, Loeb, & Pao, 1995).

Cutting. English distinguishes strictly between separations in objects brought about with a sharp implement (*cut*) and those effected in other ways, such as by fist or hammer blows, or snapping or pulling apart with the hands (*break*). Many languages have a somewhat similar contrast, but with the boundary between events of "cutting" and events of "breaking" falling in different places. For example, in Sranan, an English-based creole of Surinam, the nature of the separation is more critical than the use of a sharp-edged implement: A clean, "cut-like" break qualifies for the "cut" verb, *koti*, regardless of how it is brought about. So whereas English implicitly groups (a) "breaking a thread by jerking on it" with (b) "breaking a pot with a hammer" (both called *break*), and distinguishes these from (c) "cutting bread with a knife" (*cut*), Sranan groups (a) with (c) (both *koti* 'effect a neat, "cut-like" fracture'), and distinguishes them from (b) (*broko* 'break a hard, brittle object') (Essegbey, 2003). Spanish *cortar*, which is usually translated as 'cut', patterns similarly to Sranan *koti*; for example, it is used for breaking thread and plucking flowers (Enrique Palancar, personal communication, June 2001).

The sharp implement presupposed by English *cut* is prototypically a knife or a pair of scissors, tools especially designed for this purpose. But "cutting" can be done with a much wider range of objects, for example, a cookie cutter, piece of broken glass or pottery, fingernail, wire or thread, blade of grass, or piece of paper. These objects are diverse both perceptually and in their usual functions, but they all have something in common: a *thin linear edge*. This edge is criterial for the literal use of *cut* in English, along with the "manner" specification that the separation in the object acted on must be caused by pressure from this edge, not, for example, by a blow from the handle of the cutting tool. Dutch and Mandarin also employ the notion of a thin linear edge, but they impose an obligatory distinction between actions of cutting with *two* opposing edges (scissors, gardening shears, nail clippers, etc.) versus with a *single* edge (knife, fingernail, grass blade, etc.) (*knippen* vs. *snijden* in Dutch, *jian3* vs. *qie1* in Mandarin [Bowerman et al., 2004; Chen, in progress; Erkelens, 2003]). So children acquiring these languages must learn a contrast that is irrelevant for learners of English.

Acquiring Verbs of Breaking and Cutting.   Like verbs for "opening," verbs for "breaking" and "cutting" are extended, and overextended, according to language-specific patterns. In an elicited production task comparing how children acquiring English, Mandarin, and K'iche' Mayan described various actions of "breaking" and "cutting," Pye et al. (1995) found far more overextensions among the learners of English than among the learners of Mandarin and K'iche'. For example, English learners age 3 to 5 said *break* not only—correctly—for "breaking a toothpick" (100%), but also in high numbers for dividing play dough (87%) and tearing paper (56%). Mandarin children often correctly used *duan4* 'break long thing' for the toothpick (64%), but extended it much less often to the play dough (25%) and not a single time to tearing paper.

The likelihood that children will overextend a particular "break" or "cut" verb is, as for *open*, related to the coherence of the associated covert object categories. "Small" categories revolving around perceptually rather similar objects seem to be readily acquired; for example, learners of both Dutch and Mandarin home in swiftly on their verbs for "double-bladed cutting," and rarely make errors (Bowerman et al., 2004; Chen, in progress; Erkelens, 2003). In contrast, certain kinds of "large," perceptually diverse categories—those involving language-specific and rather arbitrary choices about which features are important and how to combine them—give rise to many errors.

For example, English *break*, and related forms like *broke, broken*, are often used for events involving flexible two- and three-dimensional objects like cooked noodles and clothing. They are also overextended to actions of separating entities that are designed to be separated and rejoined, such as safety pins and overall straps (see Table 9.3). *Cut* is often overextended to actions involving instruments with no thin linear edge, such as crushing ice

TABLE 9.3
Some Overextensions of *BREAK/BROKEN* by C and E
From 1;5 to 1;10

Flat, flexible objects
   after tearing a magazine page
   after tearing a piece out of a pop-up book
   re: a wadded-up torn piece of Kleenex, a piece of chewed baloney, a torn playing card,
      a torn towel, a torn book
Objects designed to be separated/joined
   after overall straps come unbuckled and fall down
   after slip-on eraser comes off a pen
   pulling gently on a cloth chicken to unsnap it from a cloth book
   re: an open safety pin, an open broach, an open barrette, two donut-shaped magnets
      that have come apart, a picture of a boy assembling pieces of a model car

---

Note. From M. Bowerman, unpublished records.

with a rolling pin, pulling meatballs apart with the fingers, and cracking nuts with a mallet (see examples shown earlier).

Notice that the covert object categories associated with *break* and *cut*, like the one associated with *open*, encompass a vast range of perceptually and functionally diverse objects. (According to Pye, 1994, of the many languages he examined, "no other language has a ["breaking"] verb with as broad an extension as the English verb *break*," p. 15.) Although the objects involved are alike in some critical ways (e.g., the instruments associated with "cutting" all have a thin linear edge), these similarities play no particular role in a child's experience *except* insofar as they are relevant to adults' use of the verb. Identifying what the instances of the category have in common is not, then, a matter of finding out about the world, but of discovering the implicit criteria that adults weigh in choosing whether to say *cut*, *break*, or some other verb on a particular occasion.

Just as for *open*, it takes children a long time to completely work out the covert object categories associated with *break* and *cut*. Of the English-speaking 3- to 5-year-olds in Pye et al.'s (1995) elicited production task, 25% said *cut* for dividing play dough with a pencil, whereas none of the adults did. An average of 45% of these children said *break* across five actions of tearing paper with various instruments; adults never did. Similar results were obtained by Schaefer (1979) from even older children.

MECHANISMS FOR CONSTRUCTING COVERT
OBJECT CATEGORIES

We have seen that the ease or difficulty of learning a covert category of objects is not directly related to how finely the category is subdivided. Children can readily acquire action words associated with small, relatively specific object categories (e.g., the multiple clothing and holding/carrying verbs of Korean; the eating verbs of Tzeltal; the "double-bladed" cutting verbs of Dutch and Mandarin). But they are equally quick to acquire words revolving around large categories of objects, for example, "any object at all" (e.g., things that can go *up* or be *carried* in English), or large but relatively coherent classes like "food" (for *eat*) or "clothing" and "body part" (for *put on*). The action words that are troublesome, giving rise to overextension errors over a period of years, are those associated with perceptually and functionally very diverse objects that do share some properties, but that are classified and cross-classified differently by the action words of different languages. This pattern of evidence allows us to make some inferences about how children go about the task of acquiring covert object categories.

Generalizing to Fit the Attested Instances

First, it is clear that even very young children must pay close attention to associations between action words and objects in the speech around them. When they observe that a word is used for actions involving a sufficiently diverse set of objects, they generalize it quickly to "all objects" (cf. uses of spatial particles like *up, down, in, out*, and *away* between 18 and 24 months; Choi & Bowerman, 1991). But when the objects are closely similar in some way, children generalize conservatively, sticking to events involving the same sort of objects.

For instance, toddlers learning Dutch clearly register that uses of the verb *knippen* revolve tightly around events of cutting with a scissors(-like) implement, since they rarely extend it even to actions with knives, let alone rolling pins, fingers, and mallets. Learners of English often hear *cut* for events of cutting with scissors, but they quickly generalize this word to actions with knives and beyond (cf. the previously mentioned examples); this can be explained by reference to the broad range of instrument types associated with *cut* in the speech around them.

Comparison

Generalizing on the basis of attested instances involves not only *noticing* the objects involved in the events labeled by given action words, but also *comparing* them to discover what they have in common. Because the action words of different languages revolve around different sets of objects, comparisons lead to different results. A proposed mechanism that seems well-suited to capturing this process is *structure mapping* (Gentner, 1983, 2003, chap. 10, this volume; Gentner & Rattermann, 1991; Markman & Gentner, 1993).

According to structure mapping theory, learners try to align structured conceptual representations with each other and to identify how they are similar and different. At first alignments are based on perceptual similarities among the objects in the representations, but over time learners discover alignments based on more abstract relationships. Studies have suggested that comparison can call attention to relational similarities that otherwise go unnoticed.

Comparisons can be prompted in various ways. One important way, by hypothesis, is to hear different situations described by the same word (Bowerman & Choi, 2003; Gentner, 2003, chap. 10, this volume; see Casasola, in press; Casasola, Wilbourn, & Yang, in press, for experimental evidence). Exemplars of the concept encoded by a word such as *cut* or *break* are distributed haphazardly through a child's experience, and are often embedded in very different contexts (e.g., a hairdresser *cutting* the child's hair; mommy *cutting* a potato in the kitchen; the child *cutting* her foot on a piece of glass in the garden). Without language there is no reason to compare these events, but the shared word flags them as somehow "the same." Since words in different languages flag different, crosscutting sets of events, children are led to make different comparisons, and so to arrive at different sets of abstractions about relationships and the covert classes of objects that take part in them.[21]

Retreating From Overextensions

Some covert object categories are clearly difficult for children to form with precision. Although learners of English quickly get into the right semantic ballpark with *open, break,* and *cut,* it can take them years to rein in their categories to their adult boundaries. Why do overextensions eventually stop? Several factors are likely to play a role.

Competition and Contrast With Other Words.   A number of researchers have emphasized the importance of *competition* between semantically related forms in shaping children's lexical entries (e.g., MacWhinney, 1987). In a computational model of the acquisition of spatial words, Regier (1997) showed that overextended words will gradually retreat to their conventional adult boundaries if the learning model is equipped with a weak sensitivity to Mutual Exclusivity (Markman, 1989): the principle that a referent

---

[21]Another source of evidence that could facilitate children's cross-situational comparisons and discovery of the constrained set of objects associated with a verb is *frame talk*: "the other forms of talk which typically arise within the same exchange" (Wilkins, 2002). In an analysis of uses of *open* in the speech of one child and his mother, Wilkins found a high rate of frame talk—at first primarily from the mother but later increasingly from the child himself—containing the words *in, out,* and *close.* These words highlight features of "opening" events such as gaining access (put in, take out for boxes, etc.; go in, go out of doors), and the reversibility of the action, a property associated with the presence of "predetermined lines of separation."

cannot have more than one name. Applying this finding to the current problem, we can predict that an overextended semantic entry for *open*—for example, one that permits use of the word for separating Lego blocks and peeling oranges—will gradually be pruned back when the learner hears other people use verbs like *take apart* and *peel* for these events.

Precisely how these experiences change a child's semantic representation is uncertain, but the process is often assumed to involve progressive adjustments to the *weights* assigned to particular features (MacWhinney, 1987; Schaefer, 1979). For example, Schaefer found that children gave undue importance to the mere presence of a bladed tool in deciding whether an event could be described as "cutting"; they often accepted this verb even when the tool was used to break a bottle or a pot. Over time, encounters with other verbs such as *break* in these contexts presumably dilute the brute association of *cut* with bladed tools by tuning up sensitivity to the manner in which the tool is applied.

From Overall Similarity to Dimensional Similarity. Young children often rely on global resemblances among objects in categorizing, whereas older children and adults look for a match along specific dimensions (Smith, 1989; Sloutsky, Lo, & Fisher, 2001). For example, when asked to match a red ellipse to either a blue ellipse or an orange circle, preschoolers typically choose the orange circle (a partial match on both shape and color), whereas adults go for the blue ellipse (a full match on shape, no match on color). The isolation of dimensions, and the growing ability to hold one dimension constant while others vary, can be seen as a major conceptual achievement of the preschool years (Smith, 1989).

This framework offers a useful perspective on changes over time in children's use of verbs like *open, break,* and *cut.* Young children's overextensions of these verbs can be seen as "global matches" to the kinds of events for which they have heard adults use them: the child generalizes haphazardly on the basis of different dimensions or combinations of dimensions on different occasions. But to speak like an adult, children must isolate the *specific* dimensions that are important for a verb's meaning, and insist on a match in these, even though other aspects of the events may vary in myriad ways. This will often require them to override global similarity.

Consider a concrete example. In a nonlinguistic categorization task, Schaefer (1980) showed speakers of English (children age 2–8 years and adults) video clips showing someone opening, breaking, or cutting something, and for each clip he asked them to choose, from between two further clips, the one that showed the man "doing the same." Given the clip (a) "cutting an apple into pieces with a knife" and a choice between (b) "breaking a potato into pieces with the (vertically held) tines of a fork" and (c) "cutting out a cookie with a cookie cutter," subjects of all ages overwhelmingly chose (b)—a good global match, since both (a) and (b), but not (c), involve a roundish food object, an eating utensil, and the creation of bite-sized pieces for immediate eating. In a second task, adults were asked to judge the applicability of various verbs as descriptions of these same scenes (children were not tested on this). This time the "match" was unanimously between (a) and (c): Both events were deemed instances of "cutting" (involving separation by pressure from a linear edge), whereas (b) was "breaking."

To consistently apply a verb like *cut* correctly, then, children must be able to resist attractive global matches that maximize similarity on multiple properties and hold out for more austere matches along a single dimension or combination of dimensions. This may be possible only for children who have reached a certain level of cognitive maturity.

CONCLUSION

In the first few years of life children must learn to categorize objects in many different ways. The object categories we are most aware of are those associated with noun labels, such as *dog, apple, car,* and *furniture.* Presumably this is no accident: The reason these categories have labels is that they are useful constructs for us to think with, and to be able to communicate about.

Alongside this world of explicit object kinds is a shadow world of hidden object categories: ways of classifying objects that are woven subtly into the semantics of the verbs, classifiers, prepositions, and other relational words of the language we speak. Many of these categories play little or no role in our conscious mental life, and it is controversial whether they have any consequences for cognition outside of language (see footnote 9). But still we uncontrovertibly know them—the evidence is that we can use the language forms with which they are associated in the way that is normal within our speech community.

Children get to work on these covert categories remarkably early: As we have seen, they extend—and overextend—a number of words according to language-specific patterns well before the age of 2. The ability to ferret out patterns in the observed associations between words and objects so quickly attests to the power of the young child's learning mechanisms. Some categories are easy, whereas others can cause protracted difficulties. But in the end, every child winds up with firm intuitions, shared by other fluent speakers in the speech community, about the appropriate conjunction of action word and object:

(C, 7;11, and M are discussing a box of odds and ends, including broken toys and two scraps of felt)

C: What's in there now?

M: Some other broken things.

C: (smugly) *I* wouldn't call felt "*broken*," I would call it "*ripped.*"

The subject of this chapter has been to determine how children arrive at this state.

ACKNOWLEDGMENTS

I am grateful to Dedre Gentner and Cliff Pye for their valuable comments on an earlier draft of this chapter.

REFERENCES

Aikhenvald, A. Y. (2000). *Classifiers: A typology of noun classification devices.* Oxford, England: Oxford University Press.

Anglin, J. (1977). *Word, object, and conceptual development.* New York: Norton.

Balaban, M. T., & Waxman, S. R. (1997). Do words facilitate object categorization in 9-month-old infants? *Journal of Experimental Child Psychology, 64,* 3–26.

Basso, K. H. (1968). The Western Apache classificatory verb system: A formal analysis. *Southwestern Journal of Anthropology, 24,* 252–266.

Berlin, B. (1967). Categories of eating in Tzeltal and Navajo. *International Journal of American Linguistics, 33,* 1–6.

Berlin, B. (1968). *Tzeltal numeral classifiers: A study in ethnographic semantics.* The Hague, Netherlands: Mouton.

Booth, A. E., & Waxman, S. R. (2002). Object names and object functions serve as cues to categories for infants. *Developmental Psychology, 38,* 948–957.

Bowerman, M. (1978a). The acquisition of word meaning: An investigation into some current conflicts. In N. Waterson & C. Snow (Eds.), *The development of communication* (pp. 263–287). New York: Wiley.

Bowerman, M. (1978b). Systematizing semantic knowledge: Changes over time in the child's organization of word meaning. *Child Development, 49,* 977–987.

Bowerman, M. (1996). Learning how to structure space for language: A crosslinguistic perspective. In P. Bloom, M. Peterson, L. Nadel, & M. Garrett (Eds.), *Language and space: Language, speech, and communication* (pp. 385–436). Cambridge, MA: MIT Press.

Bowerman, M. (2000). Where do children's meanings come from? Rethinking the role of cognition in early semantic development. In L. P. Nucci, G. Saxe, & E. Turiel (Eds.), *Culture, thought, and development* (pp. 199–230). Mahwah, NJ: Lawrence Erlbaum Associates.

Bowerman, M., & Choi, S. (2001). Shaping meanings for language: Universal and language specific in the acquisition of spatial semantic categories. In M. Bowerman & S. C. Levinson (Eds.), *Language acquisition and conceptual development* (pp. 475–511). Cambridge, England: Cambridge University Press.

Bowerman, M., & Choi, S. (2003). Space under construction: Language-specific spatial categorization in first language acquisition. In D. Gentner & S. Goldin-Meadow (Eds.), *Language in mind: Advances in the study of language and thought* (pp. 387–427). Cambridge, MA: MIT Press.

Bowerman, M., Majid, A., Erkelens, M., Narasimhan, B., & Chen, J. (2004, April). *Learning how to encode events of 'cutting and breaking': A crosslinguistic study of semantic development.* Poster presented at the Child Language Research Forum, Stanford, CA.

Brown, P. (1994). The INs and ONs of Tzeltal locative expressions: The semantics of static descriptions of location. *Linguistics, 32,* 743–790.

Brown, P. (2001). Learning to talk about motion UP and DOWN in Tzeltal: Is there a language-specific bias for verb learning? In M. Bowerman & S. C. Levinson (Eds.), *Language acquisition and conceptual development* (pp. 512–543). Cambridge, England: Cambridge University Press.

Brown, R. (1958). *Words and things.* New York: The Free Press.

Brown, R. (1965). *Social psychology.* New York: The Free Press.

Burling, R. (1965). How to choose a Burmese numeral classifier. In M. Spiro (Ed.), *Context and meaning in cultural anthropology* (pp. 243–264). New York: The Free Press.

Carroll, J. B., & Casagrande, J. B. (1958). The function of language classifications in behavior. In E. E. Maccoby, T. M. Newcomb, & E. L. Hartley (Eds.), *Readings in social psychology* (pp. 18–31). New York: Holt, Rinehart & Winston.

Carter, R. M. (1976). Chipewyan classificatory verbs. *International Journal of American Linguistics, 42,* 24–30.

Casasola, M. (in press). Can language do the driving? The effect of linguistic input on infants' categorization of support spatial relations. *Developmental Psychology.*

Casasola, M., Wilbourn, M. P., & Yang, S. (in press). Can English-learning toddlers acquire and generalize a novel spatial word? *First Language.*

Chang, E., & Fernald, A. (2003, April). *Use of semantic knowledge in speech processing by 26-month-olds.* Paper presented at the biennial meeting of the Society for Research in Child Development, Tampa, FL.

Chen, J. (in progress). *The acquisition of verb compounds by Mandarin-speaking children.* Doctoral dissertation, Max Planck Institute for Psycholinguistics, Nijmegen, The Netherlands. Manuscript in preparation.

Choi, S. (2000). Caregiver input in English and Korean: Use of nouns and verbs in book-reading and toy–play contexts. *Journal of Child Language, 27,* 69–96.

Choi, S., & Bowerman, M. (1991). Learning to express motion events in English and Korean: The influence of language-specific lexicalization patterns. *Cognition, 41,* 83–121.

Choi, S., McDonough, L., Bowerman, M., & Mandler, J. (1999). Early sensitivity to language-specific spatial categories in English and Korean. *Cognitive Development, 14,* 241–268.

Clark, E. V. (1976). Universal categories: On the semantics of classifiers and children's early word meanings. In A. Juilland (Ed.), *Linguistic studies offered to Joseph Greenberg on the occasion of his sixtieth birthday* (Vol. 1, pp. 449–462). Saratoga, CA: Anna Libri.

Clark, E. V., Carpenter, K. L., & Deutsch, W. (1995). Reference states and reversals: Undoing actions with verbs. *Journal of Child Language, 22,* 633–662.

Clark, H. H. (1973). Space, time, semantics, and the child. In T. E. Moore (Ed.), *Cognitive development and the acquisition of language* (pp. 27–64). New York: Academic Press.

Craig, C. (1986). *Noun classes and categorization.* Amsterdam: John Benjamins.

de León, L. (2001). Finding the richest path: Language and cognition in the acquisition of verticality in Tzotzil (Mayan). In M. Bowerman & S. C. Levinson (Eds.), *Language acquisition and conceptual development* (pp. 544–565). Cambridge, England: Cambridge University Press.

Erkelens, M. (2003). The semantic organization of "cut" and "break" in Dutch. Master's thesis, Faculty of Letters, Free University of Amsterdam, Netherlands.

Essegbey, J. (2003). *CUT and BREAK verbs in Sranan.* Paper presented at meeting of the Society for Creole Languages, Trinidad.

Foster, G. M. (1948). *Empire's children: The people of Tzintzuntzan.* Smithsonian Institution Institute of Social Anthropology, Publication No. 6.

Gentner, D. (1982). Why nouns are learned before verbs: Linguistic relativity versus natural partitioning. In S. A. Kuczaj II (Ed.), *Language development: Vol. 2. Language, thought, and culture* (pp. 301–334). Hillsdale, NJ: Lawrence Erlbaum Associates.

Gentner, D. (1983). Structure mapping: A theoretical framework for analogy. *Cognitive Science, 7,* 155–170.

Gentner, D. (2003). Why we're so smart. In D. Gentner & S. Goldin-Meadow (Eds.), *Language in mind: Advances in the study of language and thought* (pp. 195–235). Cambridge, MA: MIT Press.

Gentner, D., & Boroditsky, L. (2001). Individuation, relativity, and early word learning. In M. Bowerman & S. C. Levinson (Eds.), *Language acquisition and conceptual development* (pp. 215–256). Cambridge, England: Cambridge University Press.

Gentner, D., & Goldin-Meadow, S. (2003). *Language in mind: Advances in the study of language and thought.* Cambridge, MA: MIT Press.

Gentner, D., & Rattermann, M. J. (1991). Language and the career of similarity. In S. A. Gelman & J. P. Byrnes (Eds.), *Perspectives on thought and language: Interrelations in development* (pp. 225–277). New York: Cambridge University Press.

Gibson, J. J., & Gibson, E. J. (1955). Perceptual learning: Differentiation or enrichment? *Psychological Review, 62,* 32–41.

Gleitman, L. (1990). The structural sources of verb meanings. *Language Acquisition, 1,* 3–55.

Grinevald, C. (2000). A morphosyntactic typology of classifiers. In G. Senft (Ed.), *Systems of nominal classification* (pp. 50–92). Cambridge, England: Cambridge University Press.

Grinevald, C. (2003). Classifier systems in the context of a typology of nominal classification. In K. Emmory (Ed.), *Perspectives on classifier constructions in sign languages* (pp. 91–109). Mahwah, NJ: Lawrence Erlbaum Associates.

Haas, M. R. (1967). Language and taxonomy in Northern California. *American Anthropologist, 69,* 358–362.

Hoijer, H. (1945). Classificatory verb stems in the Apachean languages. *International Journal of American Linguistics, 11,* 13–23.

Huttenlocher, J., & Lui, F. (1979). The semantic organization of some simple nouns and verbs. *Journal of Verbal Learning and Verbal Behavior, 18,* 141–162.

Imai, M., & Gentner, D. (1997). A crosslinguistic study of early word meaning: Universal ontology and linguistic influence. *Cognition, 62,* 169–200.

Kameyama, M. (1983). Acquiring clothing verbs in Japanese. *Papers and Reports in Child Language Development, 22.* Stanford, CA: Stanford University, Department of Linguistics.

Keenan, E. L. (1986). Semantic correlates of the ergative/absolutive distinction. *Linguistics, 22,* 197–223.

Landau, B., & Shipley, E. (1996). Object naming and category boundaries. In A. Stringfellow (Ed.), *Proceedings of the Boston University Conference on Language Development* (pp. 443–452). Brookline, MA: Cascadilla Press.

Landau, B., Smith, L., & Jones, S. (1988). The importance of shape in early lexical learning. *Cognitive Development, 3,* 299–321.

Landau, B., Smith, L., & Jones, S. (1998). Object perception and object naming in early development. *Trends in Cognitive Science, 2,* 19–24.

Levison, L. (1993). The topic is *open. Penn Review of Linguistics, 17,* 125–135.

Luria, A. R. (1992). The child and his behavior. In A. R. Luria & L. S. Vygotsky (Eds.), *Ape, primitive man, and child: Essays in the history of behaviour* (pp. 87–164). New York: Harvester Wheatsheaf. (Original work published 1930)

MacWhinney, B. (1987). The competition model. In B. MacWhinney (Ed.), *Mechanisms of language acquisition* (pp. 249–308). Hillsdale, NJ: Lawrence Erlbaum Associates.

Majid, A., van Staden, M., Boster, J. S., & Bowerman, M. (2004). Event categorization: A crosslinguistic perspective. *Proceedings of the Twenty-sixth Annual Meeting of the Cognitive Science Society,* pp. 885–890.

Mandler, J. M., & McDonough, L. (1993). Concept formation in infancy. *Cognitive Development*, *8*, 291–318.

Mandler, J. M., & McDonough, L. (2000). Advancing downward to the basic level. *Journal of Cognition and Development*, *1*, 379–403.

Markman, A. B., & Gentner, D. (1993). Structural alignment during similarity comparisons. *Cognitive Psychology*, *25*, 431–467.

Markman, E. (1989). *Categorization and naming in children: Problems of induction.* Cambridge, MA: MIT/Bradford.

McDonough, L. (2002). Basic-level nouns: First learned but misunderstood. *Journal of Child Language*, *29*, 357–377.

Nazzi, T., & Gopnik, A. (2001). Linguistic and cognitive abilities in infancy: When does language become a tool for categorization? *Cognition*, *80*, B11–B20.

Nelson, K. (1974). Concept, word, and sentence: Interrelations in acquisition and development. *Psychological Review*, *81*, 267–285.

Pawley, A. (1993). A language which defies description by ordinary means. In W. A. Foley (Ed.), *The role of theory in language description* (pp. 87–129). Berlin, Germany: Mouton de Gruyter.

Piaget, J. (1954). *The construction of reality in the child.* New York: Basic Books.

Plank, F. (1985). Verbs and objects in semantic agreement: Minor differences between English and German that might suggest a major one. *Journal of Semantics*, *3*, 305–360.

Pye, C. (1994). *Breaking concepts: Constraining predicate argument structure.* Unpublished manuscript, Department of Linguistics, University of Kansas.

Pye, C. (1996). K'iche' Maya verbs of breaking and cutting. *Kansas Working Papers in Linguistics*, *21*(Part II).

Pye, C., Loeb, D. F., & Pao, Y. (1995). The acquisition of breaking and cutting. In E. V. Clark (Ed.), *Proceedings of the Twenty-seventh Annual Child Language Research Forum* (pp. 227–236). Stanford: CSLI. (A longer, unpublished version of this paper including much more of the data exists as a manuscript.)

Quinn, P. C. (2003). Concepts are not just for objects: Categorization of spatial relation information by infants. In D. H. Rakison & L. M. Oakes (Eds.), *Early category and concept development: Making sense of the blooming, buzzing confusion* (pp. 50–76). Oxford, England: Oxford University Press.

Quinn, P. C., & Eimas, P. C. (1996). Perceptual organization and categorization in young infants. In C. Rovee-Collier & L. P. Lipsitt (Eds.), *Advances in infancy research* (Vol. 10, pp. 1–36). Westport, CT: Ablex.

Regier, T. (1997). Constraints on the learning of spatial terms: A computational investigation. In R. L. Goldstone, P. G. Schyns, & D. L. Medin (Eds.), *Psychology of learning and motivation* (Vol. 36, pp. 171–217). San Diego, CA: Academic Press.

Rosch, E., Mervis, C., Gray, W., Johnson, D., & Boyes-Braem, P. (1976). Basic objects in natural categories. *Cognitive Psychology*, *8*, 382–439.

Saltz, E., & Sigel, I. E. (1967). Concept overdiscrimination in children. *Journal of Experimental Psychology*, *73*, 1–8.

Saltz, E., Soller, E., & Sigel, I. E. (1972). The development of natural language concepts. *Child Development*, *43*, 1191–1202.

Schaefer, R. P. (1979). Child and adult verb categories. *Kansas Working Papers in Linguistics*, *4*(1), 61–76.

Schaefer, R. P. (1980). An experimental assessment of the boundaries demarcating three basic semantic categories in the domain of separation. Unpublished doctoral dissertation, Department of Linguistics, University of Kansas, Lawrence, KS.

Schaefer, R. P. (1985). Toward universal semantic categories for human body space. *Linguistics*, *23*, 391–410.

Slobin, D. I. (1973). Cognitive prerequisites for the development of grammar. In C. A. Ferguson & D. I. Slobin (Eds.), *Studies of child language development* (pp. 175–208). New York: Holt, Rinehart & Winston.

Sloutsky, V. M., Lo, Y.-F., & Fisher, A. V. (2001). How much does a shared name make things similar? Linguistic labels, similarity, and the development of inductive inference. *Child Development, 72,* 1695–1709.

Smiley, P., & Huttenlocher, J. (1995). Conceptual development and the child's early words for events, objects, and persons. In M. Tomasello & W. E. Merriman (Eds.), *Beyond names for things: Young children's acquisition of verbs* (pp. 21–66). Hillsdale, NJ: Lawrence Erlbaum Associates.

Smith, L. (1989). From global similarities to kinds of similarities: The construction of dimensions in development. In S. Vosniadou & A. Orthony (Eds.), *Similarity and analogical reasoning* (pp. 146–178). Cambridge, England: Cambridge University Press.

Talmy, L. (1985). Lexicalization patterns: Semantic structure in lexical form. In T. Shopen (Ed.), *Language typology and syntactic description: Vol. 3. Grammatical categories and the lexicon* (pp. 57–149). Cambridge, England: Cambridge University Press.

Waxman, S. R., & Markow, D. B. (1995). Words as invitations to form categories: Evidence from 12- to 13-month-old infants. *Cognitive Psychology, 29,* 257–302.

Werner, H. (1957). The concept of development from a developmental and organismic point of view. In D. B. Harris (Ed.), *The concept of development: An issue in the study of human development* (pp. 125–148). Minneapolis, MN: University of Minnesota Press.

Wilkins, D. (2002, April). On being "open": An ethno-semantic description of the English verb 'open' based on adult-child interactions. Paper presented at the Max Planck Institute for Psycholinguistics, Nijmegen, Netherlands.

Wilkins, D. (2003). Why pointing with the index finger is not a universal (in sociocultural and semiotic terms). In S. Kita (Ed.), *Pointing: Where language, culture, and cognition meet* (pp. 171–215). Mahwah, NJ: Lawrence Erlbaum Associates.

Zavala, R. (2000). Multiple classifier systems in Akatek (Mayan). In G. Senft (Ed.), *Systems of nominal classification* (pp. 114–146). Cambridge, England: Cambridge University Press.

Chapter 10

The Development of Relational Category Knowledge

Dedre Gentner
Northwestern University

Fish gotta swim and birds gotta fly. Robins eat worms, dogs chase cats, roses love sunshine. These kinds of relations are as much a part of our understanding of the world as are the direct properties of the entities themselves. Relational knowledge is a prominent feature of human categories—indeed, of human cognition in general. Nowhere is this clearer than in our ability to learn relational categories like *gift, weapon, predator,* or *central force system.* By *relational categories,* I mean categories whose meanings consist either of (a) relations with other entities, as in *predator* or *gift,* or (b) internal relations among a set of components, as in *robbery* or *central force system.*

My purpose here is, first, to discuss relational categories and how they are learned, and second, to discuss how children learn relational information about object categories. Relational categories contrast with object categories[1] (e.g., *tiger* or *cow*), whose members share intrinsic features, often including perceptual commonalities. Of course, object categories typically contain not only property information but also relational information. For example, that tigers hunt and eat animals is part of our concept of a tiger, along with intrinsic attributes such as their stripes. I return to the role of relational information in ordinary object categories later. For now, I make a strong contrast between object categories and relational categories, to better reveal the dimensions of difference.

---

[1]Elsewhere I have referred to this dichotomy as the entity category versus relational category distinction (Gentner & Kurtz, in press).

As noted by Gentner and Kurtz (in press; Kurtz & Gentner, 2001; see also Asmuth & Gentner, 2004), relational categories abound in ordinary language: for example, *gift, father, accident, priority, benefit, setback, symmetry,* and so on. Some are fairly restricted: for example, in the relational category *father(x, y)*, x and y must be animals of the same species (unless the term is metaphorically extended, an issue we consider later). But for many relational categories, the arguments can range widely. For example, a *goal* can be a physical hoop (for a basketball player), or a high mark on an exam, or a college degree, or a good marriage. Relational categories differ from object categories in that (as in the case of *goal*) the instances of a relational category do not need to have intrinsic properties in common. Gentner and Kurtz (in press), roughly following Markman and Stilwell (2001), divided relational categories into *relational role categories* (or *role categories*), and *relational schema categories* (or *schema categories*). Role categories, such as *thief*, are defined by *extrinsic relations*: Their members all play the same role in a relational schema. Schema categories, such as *robbery*, are defined by *internal relational structure*. Schema categories denote relational systems, and they generally take arguments. Role categories often serve as the arguments of implicit or explicit schema categories.

For example, *robbery* is a relational schema category with three conceptual arguments,[2] which are each relational role categories: *robbery (thief, goods-stolen, victim)*. The three role categories are *thief* (the agent who steals), *goods* (the things stolen), and *victim* (the one stolen from). As this example illustrates, not all the relational roles have to be specified on any given occasion. For example, one can refer to a *bank robbery* without explicitly specifying the thief.

The relations that enter into relational categories may include common function (e.g., *both are edible*), mechanical causal relations (e.g., *both are strong so they can bend things*), biological causal relations (e.g., *both need water to grow*), role relations (e.g., *both grow on trees*), and progeneration (e.g., *both have babies*). Relational categories can also be based on perceptual relations such as *symmetric in form*, mathematical relations such as *prime*, or logical relations such as *deductively sound*. It is these relational systems that provide the theory-like aspects of concepts and categories.

Although relational categories occur frequently in adult language, their acquisition poses a challenge to simple accounts of learning. Indeed, the human facility at learning relational categories has led many theorists to conclude that they are largely built in, or that there is innate preparation in the form of nascent belief structures or skeletal theories. Frank Keil (1994) gave a particularly clear statement of the position that general learning

---

[2]Syntactically, *robbery*'s argument structure includes *thief* and *victim*, but not *goods stolen*. Thus we can refer to *the thief's robbery of the bank*, but not to **the jewels' robbery* nor to **the robbery of the jewels*.

processes are insufficient to explain children's acquisition of relational categories: ". . . the extraordinary ease with which all of us do learn about functional objects, such as tools, relative to other species that exhibit sophisticated learning in so many other areas also argues against reduction to general learning procedures" (p. 251). This conclusion would surely be correct if the only general learning processes were elementary association and perceptual generalization. But at this point there is sufficient evidence to warrant examining a more sophisticated learning mechanism—analogical learning. As I will describe, analogical mapping, or more broadly, structural alignment and mapping[3] is a learning mechanism capable of abstracting relational structure.

A central claim of this chapter is that relational categories can be learned via experiential learning, guided by language. To preview the argument, I suggest that the simple, ubiquitous act of comparing two things is often highly informative to human learners. I suggest that human comparison processes involve structure-mapping—a process of structural alignment and mapping that naturally highlights relational commonalities, and that promotes the learning of connected relational systems. I begin by reviewing relational categories and contrasting them with object categories. Next, I briefly summarize structure-mapping theory and consider its role in learning. Then I show evidence that comparison processes are central in children's learning of relational knowledge in categories. A recurring theme throughout the chapter is the crucial role of relational language in inviting and shaping relational categories.

RELATIONAL CATEGORIES

The study of nominal relational categories is largely uncharted. With a few exceptions (e.g., Barr & Caplan, 1987; Markman & Stilwell, 2001), relational categories have been largely ignored in studies of concepts and categories. This is surprising, given their frequency. Informal ratings of the 100 highest and 100 lowest frequency nouns in the British National Corpus by Asmuth and Gentner (in preparation) revealed that a third to a half are defined primarily by common relational structure rather than by common object properties. Relational categories such as *spouse, contradiction, deviation,* and *symmetry* (from the low-frequency list) are nearly as common in adult discourse as object categories like *suitcase, garlic,* and *pigeon* (from the same list).

---

[3]The term "analogy" is typically restricted to nonliteral comparisons. Our evidence suggests that the same mechanisms are used in literal comparison (e.g., Markman & Gentner, 1993; Medin, Goldstone, & Gentner, 1993).

Relational categories named by nouns (like the ones we have been considering) have some commonalities with those named by verbs and prepositions, in that their meanings include relations between other concepts. The semantic similarity between nominal relational categories and verb categories carries over into other commonalities as well, leading Gentner and Kurtz (in press) to advance a speculative analogy (see also Asmuth & Gentner, 2004):

Relational categories : Object categories : : Verb categories : Noun categories

This analogy is only partial. As Croft (2001) pointed out, nouns differ from verbs not only in their semantic properties, but in their pragmatic functions: The function of nouns is reference and that of verbs is prediction. However, one way to gain insight into the contrast between relational categories and object categories is to explore the contrast between nouns and verbs.

Contrasting Verbs and Nouns

Gentner (1981; Gentner & Boroditsky, 2001) described a large set of interrelated processing differences between verbs and nouns. For instance, verbs are more cross-linguistically variable (Talmy, 1975; Langacker, 1987); harder to translate, less likely to be borrowed in language contact (Sobin, 1982; Morimoto, 1999); acquired later[4] in both first and second languages (Caselli et al., 1995; Gentner & Boroditsky, 2001; Tardif, Gelman, & Xu, 1999); and distributed at higher word frequencies than nouns (Gentner, 1981). Verbs are less hierarchically structured and more likely to show multiple branching (Graesser & Hopkinson, 1987) or matrix structure (Huttenlocher & Lui, 1979). In addition, verbs are less likely to be accurately remembered or recalled than nouns (Kersten & Earles, in press; Earles & Kersten, 2000) and are more polysemous, more context-sensitive, and more semantically mutable than nouns (Gentner, 1981; Gentner & Boroditsky, 2002; Gentner & France, 1988).

If this analogy is correct, relational categories should behave (relative to object categories) as verbs do relative to nouns. Although only a few of these predictions have been tested so far, the results are encouraging. For example, consider the related phenomena of mutability and memory. Gentner (1981) suggested that verbs fare more poorly in recognition and recall than nouns in part because they are more likely to adapt their meanings to the current context than are nouns (Gentner & France, 1988).

---

[4]Although it has been claimed that verbs are acquired as rapidly or more rapidly than nouns in languages whose input favors verbs, such as Mandarin (Tardif, 1996) and Korean (Gopnik & Choi, 1995), this claim has so far proved false when the vocabularies are explored more completely (Au, Dapretto, & Song, 1994; Pae, 1993; Tardif, Gelman, & Xu, 1999; see Gentner & Boroditsky, 2001, for a review).

Building on this hypothesis, Kersten and Earles (in press) gave participants a list of simple intransitive noun-verb sentences and asked them to recognize either the nouns or the verbs from a later list of four kinds of intransitive sentences (old/new noun × old/new verb). Two findings are of interest: First, recognition for nouns was better overall than recognition of verbs; and second, verb recognition was substantially (and significantly) better when the verb was paired with the same noun at test as at encoding. This effect of context was much smaller for nouns.

Asmuth and Gentner (2004) tested whether this pattern would hold for relational nouns vis-à-vis object nouns; that is, whether relational nouns would adapt more to context and therefore be less well recognized than object nouns. Participants read noun-noun combinations consisting of a relational noun and an object noun (randomly combined from controlled-frequency lists)—for example, *a mountain limitation*—and rated their comprehensibility. Later, participants were given a recognition test with four kinds of pairs: old/new relational nouns and old/new object nouns. Participants were more likely to accept as old a combination with an old object noun and a new relational noun than the reverse. When participants saw an old object noun in a phrase, they were likely to judge the whole phrase as old (regardless of whether the relational noun was old or new); but when they saw an old relational noun in a phrase, their judgment of new or old depended to a large extent on the familiarity of the object noun. These results suggest that relational nouns are more context sensitive than object nouns, mirroring the behavior of verbs relative to nouns.

In addition to this evidence that relational nouns are more context sensitive and poorer in recognition than object nouns, there is also evidence that they are more difficult to generate. Kurtz and Gentner (2001) compared relational categories (e.g., *barrier* and *target*) to superordinate object categories (e.g., *furniture* and *vegetable*) using an exemplar generation task. Both the total number of subcategories generated and the rate of generation were higher for object categories than for relational categories. Further, not surprisingly, the items generated for the object categories were independently rated as much more similar to each other than those generated for the relational categories. (This fits with the greater overlap in intrinsic properties for object categories.) Interestingly, when the task was run in the other direction, the pattern reversed. Asked to generate the categories to which dog could belong, people generated many times more relational categories than taxonomic object categories.[5] This low-level "bushi-

---

[5]In total, there were 6 object categories, and these could be hierarchically arranged: for example, *canine, mammal, animal, organism, living thing,* and *being.* There were 27 relational categories: *carnivore, pet, creature, guard, companion, friend, guide, hunter, racer, playmate, rescuer, fighter, showpiece, barrier, social parasite, threat, weapon, food, profit-maker, host for parasites, disease, carrier, cat chaser, swimmer, escapee, mess-maker,* and *transportation.*

ness" of relational categories—wherein a given item can have multiple upward branches—parallels the kinds of conceptual structures found for verbs (Graesser & Hopkinson, 1987; Pavlicic & Markman, 1997).

Acquiring Relational Categories

At some point in their first or second year, children catch on to the idea that words refer to things in the world. This first referential understanding centers around object and object categories. For these categories, the mapping from word → world is straightforward. The entities they refer to can readily be individuated on the basis of direct experience with the world (Gentner's [1982] Natural Partitions hypothesis). Often, the child has already individuated the referents prelinguistically, and has only to attach the word to the referent. I argued in my prior work that relational terms such as verbs and prepositions pose a greater challenge. Their referents are not simply "out there" in the experiential world; they are selected according to a semantic system. They have to be learned from the language as well as from the world. Indeed, as this line of theorizing predicts, names for entities—especially names for animate beings—are learned early in many languages (Gentner, 1982; Gentner & Boroditsky, 2001; Pae, 1993; Tardif et al., 1999). In this chapter I want to extend this argument to relational nouns. Just as concrete nouns predominate over relational-term verbs and prepositions in children's early vocabularies (because they refer to readily individuated things in the world), so object nouns should predominate over relational nouns. The same handicaps that make verbs hard to learn also make relational nouns hard to learn. Unlike object terms, they cannot be learned simply by correspondence to the world.

To see this, consider a highly simplified summary of the steps in initial word learning: (a) isolate part of the environment; (b) isolate part of the sound stream; (c) attach the sound segment to the environmental bit. For highly individuable entities and categories, step (a) is already done. To establish the word-to-world mapping, it only remains to find and attach the right speech segment. In contrast, for relational nouns, the parsing of the perceptual world into individual referents is not obvious. A child can tell which things in the room are *apples* by looking at them; but she cannot tell which things are *gifts*, or *goods-for-sale*, or *weapons*, without knowing something about their relations to other entities. The mapping from world-to-word is equally confusing: A carving knife is a *gift* if it is in a box under the Christmas tree, but a *kitchen implement* if it's used to carve a turkey, and a *weapon* if Mom uses it to scare away a burglar.

All this suggests that relational categories should be acquired later than object categories. One indication that this is the case comes from the Mac-

Arthur Communicative Developmental Inventory, which can be taken as a rough upper bound of the words children are likely to have in their vocabularies at a given age. For 8- to 16-month-olds, it lists 296 nouns, of which 93% are entity nouns (objects, animals, and people) and 7% are mixed entity-relational nouns, with no purely relational nouns. For 17- to 30-month-olds, the MCDI lists 411 nouns: 79% entity nouns, 13% mixed, and 8% relational nouns. Second, when children *do* learn relational terms, they often initially treat them as entity terms (Gentner & Rattermann, 1991). For example, a young child may describe a *brother* as a boy about 12 years old, and only later come to realize that it can be any male (however young or old) who is someone's sibling (E. Clark, 1993). For example, Hall and Waxman (1993) found that 3½-year-olds had difficulty learning novel relational nouns denoting concepts like *passenger*. Even when they were explicitly told (for example) "This one is a *blicket* BECAUSE IT IS RIDING IN A CAR," they tended to interpret the novel noun as referring to the object category. Likewise, Keil and Batterman (1984) found that 4-year-olds define a *taxi* as a yellow car. The relational knowledge that a taxi is a car that someone can hire to go where they want does not appear until a few years later. Eve Clark (1993) noted a similar pattern with kinship terms: Young children think of a *brother* as a young boy, and are surprised to see a middle-aged man described as someone's brother.

Having established the comparative difficulty of relational categories, we now turn to how they are acquired. I suggest that a major mechanism of relational learning is comparison—or more precisely, structure-mapping is a learning mechanism that can transmute experiential knowledge into abstract relational structures. I further suggest that abstract conceptual knowledge can be acquired by conservative initial learning followed by comparison processes that highlight common relational structure. Finally, I show that comparison can be invited by common language labels—*symbolic juxtaposition*—as well as by actual experiential juxtaposition. This gives humans immense flexibility in which relational structures are extracted and transmitted. Because a central issue in this work is mechanisms of learning, in the next section I review structure-mapping in comparison and discuss its role in children's learning.

The Role of Comparison in Learning Relational Categories.   Comparison is a general learning process that can promote deep relational learning and the development of theory-level explanations (Forbus, 2001; Gentner, 1983, 2003). According to structure-mapping theory, comparison acts to highlight commonalities, particularly relational commonalities that may not have been noticed prior to comparison (Gentner, 1983, 2003). This is because the structural alignment process operates to promote common systems of interconnected relations (as described further later). Thus when two representations are aligned, common structure is preferentially highlighted. This can result in the extraction of common higher order relational structure that was not readily evident within either item alone.

It is this property of comparison processing—that it heightens the salience of common structure—that is the key to how relational knowledge can develop via experiential learning. For example, there is considerable evidence that children and adults who compare two analogous cases are likely to derive a relational schema and to succeed subsequently at relational transfer to a greater degree than those who have seen the same materials but not compared them (Gentner, Loewenstein, & Thompson, 2003; Gick & Holyoak, 1983; Loewenstein, Thompson, & Gentner, 1999). This effect of alignment in promoting relational abstraction is evident across a wide span of ages and cognitive tasks (Gentner & Namy, 1999; Kotovsky & Gentner, 1996; Loewenstein & Gentner, 2001).

Structure-Mapping as a Domain-General Learning Mechanism

The defining characteristic of analogy is that it involves an alignment of relational structure. But it is not necessary to begin with a clear relational description in order for this process to operate. The simulation that embodies the process model of structure-mapping, SME (the Structure-Mapping Engine), begins by forming all possible identity matches, and gradually coalesces these to reach a global alignment (Falkenhainer, Forbus, & Gentner, 1989; Forbus et al., 1995). In the initial, local-match stage, SME typically has a large number of mutually inconsistent matches. Then it uses connections between the matched elements to impose structural consistency and to propose further matches, eventually arriving at one or a few global alignments that constitute possible interpretations of the comparison (for details, see Forbus, Gentner, & Law, 1995; Gentner & Markman, 1997; Markman & Gentner, 2000). The alignment must be structurally consistent; that is, it must be based on a *one-to-one correspondence* between elements of the representations, and it must satisfy *parallel connectivity* (i.e., if two predicates correspond, then their arguments must also correspond).

The final characteristic of analogy is *systematicity*: what tends to win out in an analogical match is a *connected system of relations* rather than an isolated set of matching bits (Gentner, 1983; Gentner & Markman, 1997). It is as though we had an implicit aesthetic built into our comparison process that likes connected systems better than lists of separate matches. Our penchant for systematicity seems to betoken a tacit preference for coherence and causal predictive power in analogical processing. Systematicity operates in several ways in the structure-mapping process. First, during the mapping itself, connected matches get more activation than do isolated matches (because match evidence is passed from a predicate to its arguments—one reason that interconnected matches win out). Second, systematicity influences whether a rerepresentation processes occur, as described later. Third, it influences which inferences are drawn: new inferences are only proposed if (a) there is an aligned common system; and (b) there is a predicate that is connected to the system in the base and not yet present in the target. In that case the predicate is projected into the target structure as a candidate inference. Finally, systematicity also influences the selection of an interpretation when more than one structurally consistent match exists between two situations. Assuming contextual relevance is equivalent, the largest and deepest, that is, the most systematic, relational match is preferred.

An important feature of the structure-mapping process—particularly if one intends to model learning in children—is that achieving a deep structural alignment does not require that the common schema be known in advance. Common structure can emerge through a comparison process that begins blind and local. This makes it an interesting candidate for a developmental learning process. For example, a child who notices a chance similarity may end up noticing common causal patterns without explicitly seeking to do so.

This process model suggests that comparison can promote learning in several different ways, including (a) highlighting common relational systems, thereby promoting the disembedding of subtle and possibly important structure; (b) projection of candidate inferences—inviting the importing of new knowledge about one domain on the basis of the other; and (c) rerepresentation—altering one or both representations so as to improve the match, as amplified later. It is clear that candidate inferences can qualify as learning. But at first glance it may seem that highlighting common structure is out of place on this list. I believe that highlighting does count as a learning process, based on the following assumptions. First, I suggest that human representations tend to be rich and contextually situated. Second, this is especially true of early domain learning, which tends to be conservative and specific to the initial context. In this case, focusing on a sparse common relational structure can be highly informative to the learner.

A third way that comparison fosters learning, in addition to highlighting common structure and inviting inferences, is by rerepresentation. Once a partial alignment has been built up, if two potentially corresponding relations do not match, and if their match would substantially improve the analogy, they can sometimes be rerepresented to match better (Falkenhainer, 1990; Yan, Forbus, & Gentner, 2003). For example, a group of participants asked to compare "George divorced Martha" and "Megacorp divested itself of Regal Tires" wrote out such commonalities as "Both got rid of something" or "Both ended an association." As in this example, rerepresentation can result in the extraction of common higher order relational structure that was formerly embedded in a specific domain. In Clement, Mawby, and Giles' (1994) terms, latent relational commonalities become manifest via rerepresentation.

Structure-Mapping in Development

This process model has implications for the course of comparison in learning and development. First, because matches at all levels enter into the maximal alignment, the easiest and most inevitably noticed similarity comparisons are those in which there is rich overall (literal) similarity between the situations. Thus, the match between a dachshund chasing a mouse and another dachshund chasing a mouse is inescapable; even a small child can see such a match. In this case the comparison process runs off easily, because the matching information is obvious and the object matches support the relational match. This means that a strong overall similarity match produces one clear dominant interpretation. In contrast, the match between a dachshund chasing a mouse and a shark chasing a salmon is not obvious on the surface. It is easy enough for a learner who understands ideas of predation and carnivorous behavior, but these ideas may not be available to a novice such as a small child. This suggests that novice learners and children should perceive overall similarity matches before they perceive partial matches, and indeed, this is the case (Gentner & Loewenstein, 2002; Halford, 1987, 1993; Kotovsky & Gentner, 1996; Smith, 1983, 1989).

Early in learning, children (and other novices) have rich knowledge of objects and sparse knowledge of relations; thus they initially make object matches and overall similarity matches. With increasing domain knowledge, children's relational representations become richer and deeper; it becomes possible to perceive and interpret purely relational matches. Thus, there occurs a relational shift with increasing knowledge (Gentner, 1988; Gentner & Rattermann, 1991). This shift is not linked to any particular Piagetian stage. Rather, the timing of the shift varies across domains and appears driven by changes in domain knowledge (Rattermann & Gentner, 1998a; see also Siegler, 1989). Evidence that the relational shift is due to gains in relational knowledge comes in three varieties: (a) the relational shift occurs at different ages for different domains and tasks; in particular, even very young children can show considerable analogical ability in highly familiar domains (Goswami & Brown, 1989; Gentner & Rattermann, 1991; Rattermann & Gentner, 1998a); (b) within a given age, children (and adults) who possess deep relational knowledge perform better in tasks than those who do not; and (c) children's analogical performance can be aided by the introduction of relational language.

It is much easier for young children to carry out a literal similarity comparison than to carry out a purely relational comparison, as just discussed.

But our research suggests that overall literal similarity, though it may seem obvious to adults, can be informative to children. We have repeatedly found that very close similarity comparisons potentiate relational insight and far transfer among children (Gentner & Namy, 1999, 2004; Kotovsky & Gentner, 1996; Loewenstein & Gentner, 2001). In particular, in some of our work, young children have shown substantial gains in relational insight after they were led to make close comparisons. Before describing the research, a brief introduction is in order.

Within this theoretical framework, we can contrast two kinds of analogical learning: *projective analogy* and *analogical encoding*. Both involve the same basic processes of alignment and projection. In *projective analogy*, the learning results chiefly from inference projection. A well-understood situation (the base) is aligned with a less understood situation (the target), and inferences are mapped from the base to the target (Gentner, 1983; Gentner & Markman, 1997; Holyoak & Thagard, 1995). Projective analogy plays an important role in learning and instruction (Bassok, 1990; Ross, 1987) as well as in scientific discovery (Dunbar, 1993; Gentner, 2002; Nersessian, 1992). But although projective analogy is important in learning, it cannot explain how the process gets started. If children learn by analogy with prior situations, then what happens in early learning, before the child has amassed a store of well-understood situations? A second limiting factor for projective analogy, even among adults, is the frequent failure of analogical remindings. When dealing with a given problem people often fail to think of a prior analogous case, even when it can be demonstrated that they have retained a memory of the case (Gentner, Rattermann, & Forbus, 1993; Gick & Holyoak, 1980, 1983). Thus even for adults, something more is needed to explain spontaneous relational learning.

This brings us to a second kind of analogical learning, *analogical encoding* or *mutual alignment* (Gentner, Loewenstein, & Thompson, 2003; Gentner & Namy, 1999; Loewenstein & Gentner, 2001; Loewenstein, Thompson, & Gentner, 1999; Namy & Gentner, 2002). Analogical encoding occurs when two analogous situations are present simultaneously and are compared to one another. Here the key process is not directional projection of information (though inferences can occur), but aligning, rerepresenting, and abstracting commonalities. If inferences are drawn they may be bidirectional, with both examples serving as bases as well as targets.

At first glance, it may seem that nothing new could come out of such a process. Indeed, it might seem that the result will simply be confusion, especially in early learning, when the two cases are only partially understood. On the contrary, the answer that emerges from our research is that comparison between two partially understood situations can lead to a better grasp of the relational structure and a deeper understanding of both situations. We have found this pattern with both children (Gentner & Namy, 1999;

Loewenstein & Gentner, 2001; Namy & Gentner, 2002; Waxman & Klibanoff, 2000) and adults (Loewenstein et al., 1999; Kurtz, Miao, & Gentner, 2001), in a variety of domains. Our results suggest that analogical encoding is a pervasive and important bootstrapping process. This process is initially quite conservative, particularly when driven by the child's own experience. Early in learning children spontaneously notice only very close matches, and spontaneously make only very small adjustments to the representations to achieve alignment. But a small gain in relational salience may pave the way for larger insights. In our research, we have found that even close alignments potentiate more distant (more analogical) alignments.

For example, in one line of studies, Kotovsky and Gentner (1996) showed that experience with concrete similarity comparisons can improve children's ability to detect cross-dimensional similarity. In these studies, 4-year-olds' ability to perceive cross-dimensional matches (e.g., a match between a size symmetry figure and a brightness symmetry figure) was markedly better when the cross-dimensional trials were presented *after* blocks of within-dimension trials (blocks of size symmetry and blocks of brightness symmetry) than when the two kinds of trials were intermixed. Note that this manipulation was extremely subtle. Both groups of children received the same trials, half within-dimension and half cross-dimension. Their task throughout was simply to choose which of two alternatives was most similar to the standard. No feedback was given at any time. Our intent was to mimic the results of experiential learning from fortuitous runs of examples that are either easy or difficult to compare.

The materials were all perceptual configurations, each made up of three geometric figures. A schematic example of a within-dimension size symmetry trial would be v-V-v (standard) with alternatives o-O-o versus O-o-o. In the cross-dimension trials, the alternatives were depicted along a different dimension as the standard (e.g., size vs. brightness): for example, v-V-v (standard) with ooo versus **o**oo (alternatives). In all cases, the two alternatives were made up of the same geometric figures (which were different from those in the standard), but only one alternative matched the standard's relational configuration. Thus the best answer could only be determined by a relational match.

The results showed that experience with concrete similarity comparisons can facilitate children's subsequent ability to detect cross-dimensional similarity. Specifically, 4-year-olds' ability to perceive cross-dimensional matches (e.g., size symmetry/brightness symmetry) was markedly better after experience with blocked trials of concrete similarity (blocks of size symmetry and blocks of brightness symmetry), as compared to a group who received the same set of trials intermixed. This result is perhaps surprising; it might have been supposed that comparing two highly similar examples would lead to the formation of a narrow understanding. After all, the rule of thumb in animal learning is "narrow training leads to fast learning, but narrow transfer." But in human learning, aligning highly similar examples can facilitate later perception of purely relational commonalities.

Kotovsky and Gentner (1996) suggested that the superior performance of the close-to-far sequence group results from *progressive alignment*: The within-dimension comparisons, being strong overall matches, are easy to align. But each time such an alignment occurs, the common structure is highlighted. Thus repeated experience on the within-dimension pairs acts to make the higher order relation of symmetry (or monotonic increase) more salient. When these children then encounter a cross-dimensional match, they experience a near-match of two highly salient relational structures, and this prompts a rerepresentation process, as discussed earlier. The remarks of one articulate 8-year-old in the mixed condition epitomize the process of alignment and rerepresentation.[6] On her first six trials, she responded correctly to all three within-dimension trials and incorrectly to all three cross-dimension trials. On the latter, she expressed a fair degree of frustration, with comments like "It can't be the size, because those two are the same size. It can't be color." Finally, on her seventh trial, she exclaimed excitedly, "Even though the smaller ones come first and the big one's in the middle, it's exactly the same—but different!" She went on to choose correctly for the remainder of the study. This comment "It's exactly the same—but different!" captures the essence of a rerepresentational insight.

These findings show that close alignment can potentiate far alignment. Making even very easy comparisons can increase children's insight into relational similarities. This pattern is consistent with research by Chen and Klahr (1999), who taught children the strategy of *control of variables*—normally a difficult idea to communicate—by giving them intensive practice in three different domains. Within each domain (e.g., pendulum motion), children naturally engaged in many close comparisons such as varying string length, weight, and so on. When children were transferred to a second, and especially to a third domain, they learned the strategy far faster than they had in the first domain. I speculate that one reason that children learned so well in this study was the concerted experience they received within each domain before encountering the next domain.

The claim that comparison enables spontaneous learning receives support from observations of young children's spontaneous learning. Many of the insights gained in this way are rather small, and to an adult may seem prosaic; but they are new to the child.

- Emma (at about 19 months) had a little cut on one hand. She looked back and forth between her two hands and then, looking at the hand with

---

[6]Unlike the 4-year-olds, 6- and 8-year-olds often succeeded at cross-dimensional matching even in the mixed condition.

the cut she said, "Yes booboo." Then she looked at the other hand and said "No booboo." She proceeded to look back and forth and say "Yes booboo; no booboo" at least half a dozen times, proud of herself for figuring this one out (J. Loewenstein, personal communication, January, 2003).

• Ricky (at about 22 months) was walking through the zoo with his mother and grandmother: "In the carnivore house we watched a magnificent Siberian tiger cleaning its paws with a huge pink tongue. Ricky stuck out his own tongue and handled it. Then he wanted to see my tongue and his mother's tongue in turn, as if to compare their sizes to his own and the tiger's. The tiger began to swing his tail slowly back and forth. Pointing to it, Ricky's mother said, 'Look at the tiger's long tail.' Ricky watched attentively, and then turned to look over his shoulder and felt his bottom to see the status of his tailedness" (M. Shatz, personal communication, April 1989; see also Shatz, 1994, p. 54).

• Sophie (3 years, 2 months) told that her father had gone to Jimmy's, at first thought it was a gym (as in "Gym-ies"). When her mother explained that Jimmy's was the name of a bar owned by a man named Jimmy, she said "Oh, I know. It's like Leona's (an Italian restaurant)." She later became interested in the fact that another restaurant, called Barbara Fritchie's, is *not* owned by Barbara Fritchie (A. Woodward, personal communication, March, 2003).

• At the same age, Sophie, having been told earlier that day about how baby teeth fall out and adult teeth grow in, advanced the theory that as she grows, her old "small" bones will leave her body and new "bigger" bones will grow in to replace them. She was very taken with the theory and resistant to correction. She also asserted that her small bones would be used by babies after she got her big bones—possibly by analogy to what happens with clothing she outgrows (A. Woodward, personal communication, March, 2003).

These examples illustrate several points: First, many of the early insights gained from spontaneous comparison are rather tiny from the adult point of view. Second, as with adults, candidate inferences may turn out to be wrong. Children do not have tails like tigers, and baby bones do not get discarded like baby teeth. But as in adult analogy, rejecting an analogical inference can be an occasion for learning. The child who checks to see whether he has a tail is following a precise morphological analogy; both the insight as to *where* his tail would have to be, if he had one, and the explicit noticing of the fact that he does not are advances in his understanding. In the restaurant case, by pursuing the analogy, Sophie learns the correct rule, that many, but not all, restaurants with human names are owned by the corresponding person. A third point, brought out by the tiger analogy, is that children do not have to discover all these useful comparisons by themselves. Adults often suggest a comparison, and the child then takes it further.

This raises the question of what kinds of situations invite children to engage in comparison process, especially early in learning, when (as just discussed) children's relational encodings are situated in specific contexts. One way that the "invitation to compare" can come about is through high surface similarity and spatiotemporal juxtaposition, as in the Kotovsky and Gentner studies. These kinds of close comparisons abound in some domains—for example, early object manipulation and support. In these domains, children naturally encounter closely juxtaposed high similarity pairs often enough to materially advance their understanding. For example, when young children repeat the same actions over and over (e.g., building and knocking down a block tower), this may reflect their delight at comparing and learning from small variations in the action.

Some relational categories may be helped along by this kind of experiential learning, with progressive alignment from close matches to less similar instances of the same relational structure. For example, the category *gift* may be initially learned by comparing literally similar exemplars at birthdays and holidays. The child's first representation of *gift* may typically include wrapping paper and a bow. Over time, further comparisons could lead the child to notice and extract the relational commonality that a gift must pass from one person to another. But many relational categories lack such "training wheels"—closely similar, frequently juxtaposed pairs that can seed the alignment of relational structure. Here culture and language step in. One way children notice nonobvious relational similarity is by receiving a direct signal to compare, as in "Look, these are alike" or "See this? It's kind of like a robin" (Callanan, 1990). Another way that children are invited to compare things that are not obviously similar is by their having the same linguistic label—what Gentner and Medina (1998) called "symbolic juxtaposition."

We have found evidence in our prior research that linguistic labels can invite relational concepts (Gentner & Loewenstein, 2002; Gentner & Rattermann, 1991; Loewenstein & Gentner, in press; Rattermann & Gentner, 1998b). For example, Rattermann and Gentner (1998b, 2001) found that introducing relational language helped 3-year-olds to carry out a relational mapping. In these studies, the relational pattern was *monotonic increase in size* across a line of objects; the correct answer was based on matching relative size and position. The mapping was made difficult by including a cross-mapping (Gentner & Toupin, 1986), such that the correct relational match was in conflict with a high-similarity local object match. We found that children who heard language conveying a monotonic relational structure (either *Daddy-Mommy-Baby* or *big-little-tiny*) performed far better than those who did not. The effect of language was dramatic: 3-year-olds in the

No-label condition performed at chance (32% correct); in contrast, a matched group given relational labels performed at 79% correct. Their performance was comparable to that of the 5-year-olds in the No-label condition. Further, children were able to transfer this learning to new triads even with no further use of the labels by the experimenters. Finally, children who receive relational language maintained high performance even 4 to 6 weeks later. Rattermann and Gentner suggested that the use of relational labels invited attention to the common relation of monotonic change and made it possible for the children to carry out a relational alignment (see Loewenstein & Gentner, in press, for related findings). These results are evidence for a facilitating effect of common language on children's appreciation of relational similarities.

The Role of Relational Language in Learning Relational Categories

The preceding discussion suggests that analogical comparison might provide a route by which children can learn relational categories—categories like *gift* and *accident*. For the many relational categories whose members do not share intrinsic similarity, I speculate that relational language plays a crucial role in acquisition, by inviting comparisons among exemplars of the categories (Gentner & Loewenstein, 2002). In this case, symbolic juxtaposition via common labels (rather than by spatiotemporal juxtaposition and overall similarity) is the impetus for comparison.

Gentner and Klibanoff (2001) investigated the acquisition of such categories by 3-, 4-, and 6-year-olds. As noted previously, relational categories (whose membership is determined by common relations rather than with common object properties) are learned rather late. This pattern fits with the general pattern of a relational shift in children's understanding, as discussed earlier (Gentner & Rattermann, 1991). More specifically, in the word learning task, children's well-documented focus on objects and object categories when learning nouns (E. Markman, 1989; Waxman, 1990) might be expected to interfere with their ability to learn relational nouns, which disregard the intrinsic properties of the object named. In a sense, children have to overcome their prior object-naming strategies to learn relational nouns.

Gentner and Klibanoff (2001) asked (a) whether children could derive a new relational abstraction over two examples; and (b) whether receiving a novel word to describe the common relation would help or hurt. We expected that older children—6-year-olds—would benefit from hearing a word used, while younger children—3-year-olds—would seek object reference meanings and would thus be less willing to derive a relational meaning if a word were used than without words.

We used a combination of comparison and labeling. Children aged 3, 4, and 6 were shown two pairs of picture cards (e.g., a knife and a watermelon, followed by an ax and a tree). In the Word condition, the experimenter used the same novel relational noun in both of these parallel contexts: for example, "Look, the knife is the *blick* for the watermelon. And see, the ax is the *blick* for the tree." Then the children were asked to choose the referent of the new relational term in a third context: for example, "What would be the *blick* for the paper?" They were given three alternative pictures: a pair of scissors (*relational response* [correct]), a pencil (*thematic response*), and another piece of paper (*object response*). A No-word control group saw the same series of analogous examples without the novel word: for example, "The knife goes with the watermelon, and the ax goes with the tree the *same way*. What would go with the paper the same way?" Note that the No-word group received overt comparison information (that the pairs go together in "the same way"), whereas the language group did not. If common labels are especially effective at encouraging deeper comparison processes, then children in the Word condition should outperform those in the No-word condition. However, if children take the word to be the name of an object, then children in the Word condition should perform worse than those in the No-word condition.

Not surprisingly, there was an effect of age: 4- and 6-year-old children gave many more relational responses than 3-year-olds, who performed at chance. More interestingly, as predicted, 6-year-olds, and also 4-year-olds, who heard novel relational nouns were more likely to choose the *same-relation* card than were their counterparts in the No-Word condition. In these studies, we did not see a depressive effect of a novel word; the youngest group (3-year-olds) performed at chance in both conditions. These studies suggest that at least by the age of four, (a) the meanings of novel relational categories can be learned through comparison by abstracting common relations across situations; (b) the use of a common label invites comparison processes; and (c) a direct statement that the situations are alike also prompts comparison, though (at least here) not as effectively as using the same word. These results show that common language can actually be a stronger invitation to compare than even direct statements like "this one goes with this one *in the same way*."

Learning Relational Aspects of Object Categories: Effects of Language and of Comparison

We have discussed children's learning of relational categories. But what about the relational aspects of object categories? Relational structure is central in adult category representation, and our relational knowledge about ordinary categories is often quite rich. For example, many studies have demonstrated the importance of causal structure in category learning and use. It has been shown that people's ability to learn and use categories is influenced by the number of causal links running in either direction (Rehder & Hastie, 2001) as well as by the causal status of properties as causes or effects (Ahn, 1998; Ahn, Gelman, Amsterlaw, Hohenstein, & Kalish, 2000). This work suggests that properties that enter into causal relations—perhaps especially those that cause other properties—take on greater salience and greater weight in membership judgments (Sloman, Love, & Ahn, 1998). Another indication of the importance of relational structure is that animate and artifactual categories appear to be differentiated in part by the nature of their causal relations (Carey, 1992; R. Gelman, Spelke, & Meck, 1983; S. Gelman, 1988; Keil, 1994). The importance of causal explanatory patterns in category representations is also underscored by the examples and arguments given in Murphy and Medin's (1985) theory view of categorization. For example, we classify a man in a tuxedo leaping into a swimming pool as a drunk person, even if that particular exemplar is entirely new, because our causal model of drunken partygoers fits his behavior.

How do children come to understand the relational aspects of ordinary entity categories—the causal and functional aspects of categories like *plate*, *tricycle*, and *umbrella*? Our research suggests that although preschool children may have considerable tacit knowledge of the relations that things participate in, this knowledge is often initially situationally embedded and difficult to access explicitly. To put it concretely, a child who knows that she can ride on a tricycle does not necessarily know that a tricycle can be categorized with other vehicles. Our research further suggests that comparison across examples is crucial in achieving a disembedded, portable knowledge of the relations that characterize ordinary categories.

Early in learning, children rely heavily on perceptual similarity in category extension (Baldwin, 1989; Imai, Gentner, & Uchida, 1994; Landau, Smith, & Jones, 1988). For example, they apply a novel word to objects that share shape or other distinctive features with the exemplar on which the label was learned; they call horses and cats "doggies," or any round shape a "ball" (Clark, 1973). This bias toward perceptual similarity as a basis for word extension might be a reasonable heuristic for young children, given their incomplete knowledge of causal and functional properties and how they enter into word meaning. The high correlation between perceptual similarity and conceptual similarity for basic level categories (which predominate in preschoolers' lexicons) means that perceptual similarity is often a good guide to a word's extension. However, this strategy is clearly not adequate over the long haul. Children must eventually come to appreciate the relational commonalities that loom large in the intensions of human categories. The question, then, is how children come to appreciate functional and relational aspects of categories.

Laura Namy and I proposed that structural alignment aids children's category learning by elevating the salience of relational knowledge that might otherwise remain situated and implicit (Gentner & Namy, 1999, 2004; Namy & Gentner, 2002). Specifically, we suggested (a) that hearing common labels applied to multiple entities invites children to engage in comparison processes; and (b) that the process of comparison highlights relational commonalities, including many that are not immediately evident on surface-level inspection. If comparison renders relations more salient, and if common labels encourage comparison, then this process might enable children to override compelling perceptual commonalities in favor of deeper conceptual ones.

To test these claims, we experimentally manipulated children's opportunity to compare objects from a given category and then tested their word extension, pitting a perceptual match against a perceptually dissimilar taxonomic match (Gentner & Namy, 1999). We used the standard word-extension method of applying a novel word (in "doggie language") to a standard, and asking the children to choose another exemplar from two (or three) alternatives. In our studies, we manipulated the opportunity to compare by presenting children with either a single instance or two perceptually similar instances of the category before eliciting their word extensions. The design of the materials allowed us to test whether comparison would highlight *relational* information or featural information. There were three groups of 4-year-olds: a comparison group and two solo (single-standard) groups. For example, children in the comparison group might see two instances of nonmotoric vehicles (a bicycle and a tricycle). One solo group would see the bicycle, and the other would see the tricycle. The task was a standard word-extension task. Children were told a novel puppet name for the standard(s) such as "blicket," and then asked to choose another blicket. The children chose from two alternatives: a perceptual alternative (a perceptually similar object from a different category, e.g., eyeglasses) and a taxonomic category alternative (a perceptually dissimilar object from the same category, e.g., a skateboard) (see Fig. 10.1).

Importantly, the standards were designed so that each of them was highly similar to the perceptual alternative. Indeed, when either standard was presented singly (in the solo conditions), the children chose the perceptually similar alternative. This allows a test of the structure-mapping account of the comparison process. If children compute similarity merely by concatenating surface commonalities, then if they select the perceptual match in the two solo conditions, they should be doubly likely to do so in the comparison condition. That is, on the behaviorist account of similarity, comparing two standards that are *both* more featurally similar to the perceptual choice than to the category choice should *increase* perceptual responding, relative to viewing a single standard. (Note also that the perceptual fea-

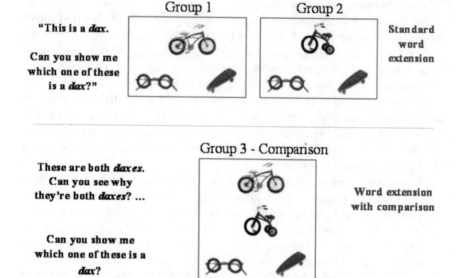

FIG. 10.1.   Sample materials in the Gentner and Namy (1999) study, showing solo conditions (above) and the comparison condition (below).

tures that the two standards both share are the *same* features they each
share with the perceptual alternative [e.g., two horizontally aligned circles].
Thus it is not a question of different matches diluting the featural predictions.) However, if comparing instances induces a structural alignment
process, then children who view two standards may be led to focus on previously implicit common relational structure, such as how the objects are
used and what causal activities they normally participate in. If so, then comparison should lead to a shift toward taxonomic category responding, despite the strong perceptual similarity between both of the standards and the
perceptual alternative.

This is precisely what we found. When shown both standards *together*,
children chose the conceptual match as the other "blicket" despite the fact
that their agemates preferred the perceptual match for *either* of the standards presented singly. These results show that comparison can facilitate
word extension on the basis of conceptual relations, and not merely perceptual features. More generally, at the theoretical level, these results provide critical evidence that comparison highlights common relations, *even
when common salient object features are also available*. Even when both standards
share salient perceptual commonalities, aligning the two can reveal a common relational structure that the child will then attend to. This suggests a
route by which early perceptually driven word extensions can give rise to

conceptual understanding. Structure-mapping processes may thus be instrumental in guiding children to adult-like category knowledge.

The Role of Language in Inviting Comparison. How important is language in this process? Gentner and Namy (2003) found that hearing a common label encouraged children to engage in comparison. We compared 4-year-olds' performance on the word extension task when they were either given a novel label for the two standards, as already shown, or were simply asked to compare them and find another: "See this one, and see this one? See how these are the same kind of thing? Can you find another one that's the same kind as these?" Children gave more category responses when common labels were used than in the no-label condition. This suggests that having a common label helps to invite comparison processes, that (to paraphrase Roger Brown, 1958), words are invitations to make comparisons.

In subsequent studies, Namy and Gentner (2002) further probed the relation between common labels and alignment processes. Children (again, 4-year-olds) were assigned to either a Unifying Label or Conflicting Label condition. In both conditions, children were shown two standard objects from the same category. Those in the Unifying Label condition heard both standards labeled with the same novel word (e.g., "This is a blicket and this is a blicket!"). Those in the Conflicting Label condition heard the two standards labeled with different novel words (e.g., "This is a blicket and this is a daxen!"). Then both groups were shown two alternatives (a perceptual alternative and a category alternative) and asked "Can you tell me? Which one is the same kind as these?" As in our previous studies, children who heard a Unifying label reliably selected the category alternative. In contrast, children who heard Conflicting labels chose the perceptual alternative; they resembled the children who had seen only a single standard object in the previous studies.

These results, like the Gentner and Klibanoff results, show that alignment can be invited by hearing a common label for two exemplars. Our results also show that alignment processes are used to extend novel words to new instances. Thus, we suggest that the relation between alignment and word-learning is a true boot-strapping relation. Hearing a common term invites an alignment that is then used to extend the term to new exemplars.

In addition to showing effects of language, these findings show that initial attention to perceptual similarities in word extension can actually serve to promote attention to deeper commonalities. Even though children's attention may be initially drawn to surface commonalities between two exemplars, the full process of comparison will result in highlighting any further relational commonalities that may be present. Add to this the fact that perceptual commonalities are often highly correlated with deeper relational commonalities, particularly for basic-level terms, which young children are most likely to be hearing and learning. (For example, fins and gills are correlated with a different type of breathing apparatus than are legs and fur [e.g., Murphy & Medin, 1985].) Gentner (1989) described this correlation between perceptual and conceptual information as fitting the "world is kind" hypothesis. Because of these correlations, perceptual commonalities are far more likely to be helpful than harmful in guiding young children to deeper understanding. Surface commonalities act as initial invitations to compare, and thus point the way to deeper commonalities that naturally become salient during comparison.

Such an explanation is consistent with the striking findings of Samuelson and Smith (2000). They showed experimentally that inducing a shape bias actually increases children's rate of vocabulary acquisition outside the lab. They taught children to attend to shape by teaching them object names that were organized by common shape. Children given this experimentally induced shape bias showed greater gains in vocabulary (as assessed by the Mac-Arthur CDI parental checklist) over the weeks following the training session than did matched children who either received no training or received training with varied patterns of input. These results would be baffling if we assumed that children stop at noticing perceptual commonalities. But in light of the earlier discussion, children's use of perceptual features as a basis for word extension may in fact be highly adaptive. When children lack knowledge about a category, perceptual commonalities may serve as way of gathering exemplars that can then be compared more deeply to extract relational commonalities[7] that can serve as core category knowledge.

Alignment in Early Learning

The analogical encoding process offers an escape from the conundrum that confronts us in trying to explain early experiential learning. Because it can lead to at least modest learning, even with only partially understood cases, it removes the need for a well-understood prior analog. Consistent with this line of reasoning, there is evidence that young infants can benefit from close comparisons. For example, Oakes and Ribar (in press) found that 4- to 6-month-old infants more readily form perceptual categories such as *dog* (and discriminate dogs from perceptually similar cats) when the infants are given the opportunity to view and compare objects in pairs than when the objects are presented one at a time. Namy, Smith, and Gershkoff-Stowe (1997) found that 18-month-old infants who were encouraged to directly compare items exhibited stronger categorical responding in a se-

---

[7]A similar interplay between initial perceptual object similarity and relational similarity has been observed in adult learning (Brooks, 1987; Ross, 1999; Ross, Perkins, & Tenpenny, 1990).

quential touching-type task than did infants who were not encouraged to compare the items. Finally, Oakes and her colleagues found that prior opportunities to compare items facilitated the performance of 13- and 16-month-old infants on a sequential-touching task (Oakes & Madole, 2003). When given multiple exemplars of *people* and *sea animals*, intermixed on the table, the infants were more likely to show category-related touching if they had previously been presented with the two categories separated (thus facilitating within-category comparison).

There is also evidence consistent with another claim made earlier: that early in development, comparison-based learning thrives on rich commonalities—both object commonalities and relational commonalities. Booth and Waxman (2002) showed that 14-month-olds given an optimal comparison sequence can learn better when given pairs characterized by both relational commonalities and property commonalities than when given pairs that only share object properties.[8] They taught infants categories like "oval green-blue objects with a loop on top, which can be swung from a hook." One group of infants had the opportunity to compare the objects carrying out their functions. Infants were first shown a pair of in-category objects, for each of which the experimenter demonstrated the function (swinging from a hook), saying, "Look what I can do with this one." After repeating this sequence, the experimenter showed another pair of in-category objects and repeated the same procedure. The experimenter next showed a contrasting object, a spool-shaped object with no loop on top, and demonstrated that the object could not perform the function. Next, the experimenter brought out the target object (another member of the initial category), demonstrated its function, and asked the child to "find another one." There were two alternatives, one from the initial category and one from a contrasting category. Under these rich comparison conditions, the 14-month-olds (and also a group of 18-month-olds) chose the same-category item about 70% of the time, significantly above chance. A second group of infants was given the same sequence, except that instead of demonstrating the function of the objects, the experimenter called them each by the same name. The 18-month-olds showed above-chance selection of the same-category object (roughly 60%), but the 14-month-olds did not.

These results suggest, first, that rich matches are easier than sparse matches for infants. The 14-month-olds did far better when the overall match was very strong, consisting of both object and relational commonalities, than when given a pure object match. This finding is consistent with the claim that early learning is conservative, and more importantly, with the

---

[8]Booth and Waxman's (2002) categories consisted of closely similar, but not identical, objects; there were small differences in color and shape. This probably made the categories more challenging to the 14-month-olds.

claim that relational learning can be bootstrapped by experience. Infants at this age would not succeed at a purely relational comparison (e.g., to learn a common function across a set of completely different objects), but they *can* learn a rich literal category that includes relational as well as property information. As countless studies have shown, once relational information is present, even if it is initially bound to particular object properties, it can be abstracted away via further comparisons (e.g., Gentner et al., 2003; Gick & Holyoak, 1983).

A second implication concerns the role of language. Although language comes to act as an invitation to compare, the results here suggest (not surprisingly) that rich overall similarity operates earlier in development as an incitement to compare. It is possible that common language comes to signal a comparison opportunity through the child's experience that highly similar objects have the same names.

GENERAL DISCUSSION

Relational categories are an important aspect of human cognition. My central thesis here is that these categories can be learned—although not by simple association models. I have suggested that comparison processes, either spontaneous or invited by language, drive much of this learning process.

This research suggests several conclusions. First, it supports the career of similarity thesis: Children begin with highly concrete overall similarity matches[9] and gradually become able to appreciate partial matches. Second, importantly, these early matches can involve relational as well as object commonalities. Third, among partial matches there is a relational shift from an early ability to match objects and object properties to a later ability to perceive purely relational commonalities. Fourth, this development is driven in large part by changes in domain knowledge. Fifth, by the second year of life, comparison processes can be invited not only by high similarity and close spatiotemporal juxtaposition, but also by the presence of common linguistic labels. The first of these represents alignment through experiential juxtaposition; the second, alignment through symbolic juxtaposition.

An important aspect of this proposal is that the increase in the sophistication of children's concepts does not result from global changes in logical processes or processing capacity. Such changes may occur, but they are not

---

[9]Early similarity is often described as "holistic." My sense of what this means is that early in development, alignment can only succeed with very strong overall similarity, in part because the infant's representations are idiosyncratic, lacking a uniform set of dimensions and properties. As infants' knowledge becomes more stable, they become able to match things that are only partially alike.

necessary to explain the relational shift. Rather, the shift comes about through gains in relational knowledge (sometimes gained via comparison). Numerous simulations have demonstrated that the relational shift can be modeled by applying the same structure-mapping processes to knowledge that varies in relational depth (e.g., Gentner, Rattermann, Markman, & Kotovsky, 1995; Loewenstein & Gentner, in press). The structure-mapping process grades naturally from highly concrete, literally similar comparisons to purely relational comparisons. Thus it can span the developmental course from overall similarity to relational similarity and abstract mappings.

Correspondence and Coherence

The contrast between *object categories* (defined chiefly by intrinsic features) and *relational categories* (defined chiefly by relations to other concepts) is related to the distinction between correspondence-based concepts (defined by reference to things in the world) and coherence-based concepts (defined by their relations with other concepts). Like the distinction between object categories and relational categories, this distinction is actually a continuum, but here too it is useful to contrast the end points. The correspondence-based view figures prominently in theories of concepts that conceive of word meaning as pointers to the world (e.g., Frege, 1892/1980; Russell, 1905/1956). The coherence-driven view is epitomized in Saussure's writings on language; for example, in the idea that "Language is a system of interdependent terms in which the value of each term results solely from the simultaneous presence of the others . . ." (Saussure, 1916/1966, p. 114). It seems obvious that both coherence and correspondence enter into human conceptual structure (see Markman, 1999). What is more interesting is the way they enter in. I suggest that concrete object concepts are heavily correspondence driven. They arise naturally from the way our perceptual capacities operate on the experiential world. Relational terms, like verbs and relational nouns, are relatively more coherence driven; there is a greater role for cultural and linguistic structures in determining the way information is organized into concepts.

The Role of Language

A constant theme in this chapter has been the importance of relational language in driving the development of relational category knowledge (Gentner, 2003; Gentner & Loewenstein, 2002). In this chapter I focused chiefly on the role of common language in inviting comparison, thereby promoting the highlighting of relational commonalities and a more uniform encoding of exemplars through rerepresentation. By fostering uniform relation representation, common relational language promotes transfer to new situations (Clement et al., 1994; Forbus, Gentner, & Law, 1995). As children gradually shed the concrete details of their initial representation—learning, for example, that taxis do not have to be yellow, nor islands sandy—they become able to transfer their relational concepts more broadly.[10]

Summary

Learning relational categories, and the relational information that belongs to object categories, is a challenge to learners. Relations are not pre-individuated by our cognitive systems. They can be encoded in dozens of different ways, and children have to learn the ways that work in their physical, cultural, and linguistic environment. But this learning can be achieved via general learning mechanisms available to humans; in particular, by structure-mapping processes. These processes are used in concert with other general processes such as associative learning and attentional mechanisms, and are guided by linguistic labels and social interactions that augment experiential knowledge and serve to invite comparison when intrinsic similarity is not enough. Progressive alignment promotes representational uniformity, and increases the likelihood that the learner will encode new relational situations in the same way across different situations. This process, which Gentner and Rattermann (1991) referred to as "the gentrification of knowledge," entails some loss of the child's immediate perception of the world. But the resulting gains in representational uniformity are important in achieving stable conceptual structure and a systematic and portable set of relational abstractions.

ACKNOWLEDGMENTS

This research was supported by NSF grant SBR-95-11757 and by NSF-ROLE award 21002/REC-0087516. The computational research was supported by ONR contract N00014-92-J-1098. I thank Melissa Bowerman for extremely helpful comments on an earlier draft, and Ken Forbus, Jeff Loewenstein, Ken Kurtz, Art Markman, Mary Jo Rattermann, Phillip Wolff, and the Analogy and Similarity group at Northwestern University for discussions of these

---

[10]This gradual abstraction need not entail losing the initial concrete representations. My assumption is that human representations are pluralistic; that, for example, we retain the concrete notion of taxis as yellow cabs along with the more abstract taxi concept that allows such uses as "water taxi."

issues. I also thank Kathleen Braun for assistance on the research and Jonathan Cohen for help in preparing the manuscript.

REFERENCES

Ahn, W. K. (1998). Why are different features central for natural kinds and artifacts?: The role of causal status in determining feature centrality. *Cognition, 69*, 135–178.

Ahn, W. K., Gelman, S. A., Amsterlaw, J. A., Hohenstein, J., & Kalish, C. W. (2000). Causal status effect in children's categorization. *Cognition, 76*, 35–44.

Asmuth, J. A., & Gentner, D. (2004). *Context sensitivity of relational nouns*. Unpublished manuscript, Northwestern University.

Au, T. K., Dapretto, M., & Song, Y. (1994). Input vs. constraints: Early words acquisition in Korean and English. *Journal of Memory and Language, 33*(5), 567–582.

Baldwin, D. A. (1989). Priorities in children's expectations about object label reference: Form over color. *Child Development, 60*, 1289–1306.

Barr, R. A., & Caplan, L. J. (1987). Category representations and their implications for category structure. *Memory & Cognition, 15*, 397–418.

Bassok, M. (1990). Transfer of domain-specific problem-solving procedures. *Journal of Experimental Psychology: Learning, Memory and Cognition, 16*, 522–533.

Booth, A. E., & Waxman, S. R. (2002). Object names and object functions serve as cues to categories for infants. *Developmental Psychology, 38*, 948–957.

Brooks, L. R. (1987). Decentralized control of categorization: The role of prior processing episodes. In U. Neisser (Ed.), *Concepts and conceptual development: The ecological and intellectual factors in categorization* (pp. 141–174). Cambridge, England: Cambridge University Press.

Brown, R. (1958). *Words and things: An introduction to language*. New York: The Free Press.

Callanan, M. A. (1990). Parents' descriptions of objects: Potential for children's inferences about category principles. *Cognitive Development, 5*, 101–122.

Carey, S. (1992). The origin and evolution of everyday concepts. In R. N. Giere & H. Feigl (Eds.), *Cognitive models of science: Minnesota studies in the philosophy of science* (pp. 89–128). Minneapolis, MN: University of Minnesota Press.

Caselli, M. C., Bates, E., Casadio, P., Fenson, J., Fenson, L., Sanderl, L., & Weir, J. (1995). A cross-linguistic study of early lexical development. *Cognitive Development, 10*, 159–199.

Chen, Z., & Klahr, D. (1999). All other things being equal: Acquisition and transfer of the Control of Variables Strategy. *Child Development, 70*(5), 1098–1120.

Clark, E. V. (1973). What's in a word? On the child's acquisition of semantics in his first language. In T. E. Moore (Ed.), *Cognitive development and the acquisition of language* (pp. 65–110). New York: Academic Press.

Clark, E. V. (1993). *The lexicon in acquisition*. Cambridge, England: Cambridge University Press.

Clement, C. A., Mawby, R., & Giles, D. E. (1994). The effects of manifest relational similarity on analog retrieval. *Journal of Memory and Language, 33*, 396–420.

Croft, W. (2001). *Radical construction grammar*. Oxford: Oxford University Press.

Dunbar, K. (1993). Concept discovery in a scientific domain. *Cognitive Science, 17*, 391–434.

Earles, J. L., & Kersten, A. W. (2000). Adult age differences in memory for verbs and nouns. *Aging Neuropsychology & Cognition, 7*(2), 130–139.

Falkenhainer, B. (1990). A unified approach to explanation and theory formation. In J. Shrager & P. Langley (Eds.), *Computational models of scientific discovery and theory formation* (pp. 157–196). Los Altos, CA: Kaufmann.

Falkenhainer, B., Forbus, K. D., & Gentner, D. (1989). The structure-mapping engine: Algorithm and examples. *Artificial Intelligence, 41*, 1–63.

Forbus, K. (2001). Exploring analogy in the large. In D. Gentner, K. J. Holyoak, & B. Kokinov (Eds.), *The analogical mind: Perspectives from cognitive science* (pp. 23–58). Cambridge, MA: MIT Press.

Forbus, K. D., Gentner, D., & Law, K. (1995). MAC/FAC: A model of similarity-based retrieval. *Cognitive Science, 19*, 141–205.

Frege, G. (1980). On sense and meaning. In P. T. Geach & M. Black (Eds.), M. Black (Trans.), *Translations from the philosophical writings of Gottlob Frege* (3rd ed.). Oxford, England: Basil Blackwell. (Original work published 1892)

Gelman, R., Spelke, E. S., & Meck, E. (1983). What preschoolers know about animate and inanimate objects. In D. Rogers & J. A. Sobaoda (Eds.), *The acquisition of symbolic skills* (pp. 297–326). New York: Plenum.

Gelman, S. A. (1988). The development of induction within natural kind and artifact categories. *Cognitive Psychology, 20*, 65–95.

Gentner, D. (1981). Some interesting differences between verbs and nouns. *Cognition and Brain Theory, 4*, 161–178.

Gentner, D. (1982). Why nouns are learned before verbs: Relativity vs. natural partitioning. In S. A. Kuczaj (Ed.), *Language development: Syntax and semantics*. Hillsdale, NJ: Lawrence Erlbaum Associates.

Gentner, D. (1983). Structure-mapping: A theoretical framework for analogy. *Cognitive Science, 7*, 155–170.

Gentner, D. (1988). Metaphor as structure mapping: The relational shift. *Child Development, 59*, 47–59.

Gentner, D. (1989). Mechanisms of analogical learning. In S. Vosniadou & A. Ortony (Eds.), *Similarity and analogical reasoning* (pp. 199–241). London: Cambridge University Press.

Gentner, D. (2002). Analogy in scientific discovery: The case of Johannes Kepler. In L. Magnani & N. J. Nersessian (Eds.), *Model-based reasoning: Science, technology, values* (pp. 21–39). New York: Kluwer Academic/Plenum.

Gentner, D. (2003). Why we're so smart. In D. Gentner & S. Goldin-Meadow (Eds.), *Language in mind: Advances in the study of language and cognition* (pp. 195–235). Cambridge, MA: MIT Press.

Gentner, D. (in press). Nouns and verbs, revisited. *APA PsycEXTRA*.

Gentner, D., & Boroditsky, L. (2001). Individuation, relativity and early word learning. In M. Bowerman & S. Levinson (Eds.), *Language acquisition and conceptual development* (pp. 215–256). New York: Cambridge University Press.

Gentner, D., & France, I. M. (1988). The verb mutability effect: Studies of the combinatorial semantics of nouns and verbs. In S. L. Small, G. W. Cottrell, & M. K. Tanenhaus (Eds.), *Lexical ambiguity resolution: Perspectives from psycholinguistics, neuropsychology, and artificial intelligence* (pp. 343–382). San Mateo, CA: Kaufmann.

Gentner, D., & Klibanoff, R. S. (2001). *On acquiring gift: The acquisition of relational nouns.* Unpublished manuscript, Northwestern University.

Gentner, D., & Kurtz, K. J. (in press). Learning and using relational categories. In R. Goldstone & W. Ahn (Eds.), *Categorization inside and outside the lab: A Festschrift in honor of Dr. Douglas Medin.*

Gentner, D., & Loewenstein, J. (2002). Relational language and relational thought. In J. Byrnes & E. Amsel (Eds.), *Language, literacy, and cognitive development* (pp. 87–120). Mahwah, NJ: Lawrence Erlbaum Associates.

Gentner, D., Loewenstein, J., & Thompson, L. (2003). Learning and transfer: A general role for analogical encoding. *Journal of Educational Psychology, 95*(2), 393–408.

Gentner, D., & Markman, A. B. (1997). Structure mapping in analogy and similarity. *American Psychologist, 52*, 45–56.

Gentner, D., & Medina, J. (1998). Similarity and the development of rules. *Cognition, 65*, 263–297.

Gentner, D., & Namy, L. (1999). Comparison in the development of categories. *Cognitive Development, 14,* 487–513.

Gentner, D., & Namy, L. (2004). The role of comparison in children's early word learning. In D. G. Hall & S. R. Waxman (Eds.), *Weaving a lexicon* (pp. 597–639). Cambridge, MA: MIT Press.

Gentner, D., & Rattermann, M. J. (1991). Language and the career of similarity. In S. A. Gelman & J. P. Byrnes (Eds.), *Perspectives on language and thought: Interrelations in development* (pp. 225–277). London: Cambridge University Press.

Gentner, D., Rattermann, M. J., & Forbus, K. D. (1993). The roles of similarity in transfer: Separating retrievability and inferential soundness. *Cognitive Psychology, 25,* 524–575.

Gentner, D., Rattermann, M. J., Markman, A. B., & Kotovsky, L. (1995). Two forces in the development of relational similarity. In T. J. Simon & G. S. Halford (Eds.), *Developing cognitive competence: New approaches to process modeling* (pp. 263–313). Hillsdale, NJ: Lawrence Erlbaum Associates.

Gentner, D., & Toupin, C. (1986). Systematicity and surface similarity in the development of analogy. *Cognitive Science, 10,* 277–300.

Gick, M. L., & Holyoak, K. J. (1980). Analogical problem solving. *Cognitive Psychology, 12,* 306–355.

Gick, M. L., & Holyoak, K. J. (1983). Schema induction and analogical transfer. *Cognitive Psychology, 15,* 1–38.

Gopnik, A., & Choi, S. (1995). Names, relational words, and cognitive development in English and Korean speakers: Nouns are not always learned before verbs. In M. Tomasello & W. E. Merriman (Eds.), *Beyond names for things: Young children's acquisition of verbs* (pp. 63–80). Hillsdale, NJ: Lawrence Erlbaum Associates.

Goswami, U., & Brown, A. L. (1989). Melting chocolate and melting snowmen: Analogical reasoning and causal relations. *Cognition, 35,* 69–95.

Graesser, A., & Hopkinson, P. (1987). Differences in interconcept organization between nouns and verbs. *Journal of Memory and Language, 26,* 242–253.

Halford, G. S. (1987). A structure-mapping approach to cognitive development. *International Journal of Psychology, 22,* 609–642.

Halford, G. S. (1993). *Children's understanding: The development of mental models.* Hillsdale, NJ: Lawrence Erlbaum Associates.

Hall, D. G., & Waxman, S. R. (1993). Assumptions about word meaning: Individuation and basic-level kinds. *Child Development, 64*(5), 1550–1570.

Holyoak, K. J., & Thagard, P. R. (1995). *Mental leaps: Analogy in creative thought.* Cambridge, MA: MIT Press.

Huttenlocher, J., & Lui, F. (1979). The semantic organization of some simple nouns and verbs. *Journal of Verbal Learning and Verbal Behavior, 18,* 141–162.

Imai, M., Gentner, D., & Uchida, N. (1994). Children's theories of word meaning: The role of shape similarity in early acquisition. *Cognitive Development, 9,* 45–75.

Keil, F. C. (1994). The birth and nurturance of concepts by domains: The origins of concepts of living things. In L. A. Hirschfeld & S. A. Gelman (Eds.), *Mapping the mind* (pp. 234–254). New York: Cambridge University Press.

Keil, F. C., & Batterman, N. (1984). A characteristic-to-defining shift in the development of word meaning. *Journal of Verbal Learning & Verbal Behavior, 23,* 221–236.

Kersten, A. W., & Earles, J. L. (in press). Semantic context influences memory for verbs more than memory for nouns. *Memory & Cognition.*

Kotovsky, L., & Gentner, D. (1996). Comparison and categorization in the development of relational similarity. *Child Development, 67,* 2797–2822.

Kurtz, K. J., & Gentner, D. (2001). Kinds of kinds: Sources of category coherence. *Proceedings of the 23rd Annual Conference of the Cognitive Science Society,* 522–527.

Kurtz, K. J., Miao, C., & Gentner, D. (2001). Learning by analogical bootstrapping. *Journal of the Learning Sciences, 10*(4), 417–446.

Landau, B., Smith, L. B., & Jones, S. S. (1988). The importance of shape in early lexical learning. *Cognitive Development, 3,* 299–321.

Langacker, R. W. (1987). Nouns and verbs. *Language, 63,* 53–94.

Loewenstein, J., & Gentner, D. (2001). Spatial mapping in preschoolers: Close comparisons facilitate far mappings. *Journal of Cognition and Development, 2*(2), 189–219.

Loewenstein, J., & Gentner, D. (in press). Relational language and the development of relational mapping. *Cognitive Psychology.*

Loewenstein, J., Thompson, L., & Gentner, D. (1999). Analogical encoding facilitates knowledge transfer in negotiation. *Psychonomic Bulletin & Review, 6*(4), 586–597.

Loewenstein, J., Thompson, L., & Gentner, D. (2003). Analogical learning in negotiation teams: Comparing cases promotes learning and transfer. *Academy of Management Learning and Education, 2*(2), 119–127.

Markman, A. B. (1999). *Knowledge representation.* Mahwah, NJ: Lawrence Erlbaum Associates.

Markman, A. B., & Gentner, D. (1993). Structural alignment during similarity comparisons. *Cognitive Psychology, 25,* 431–467.

Markman, A. B., & Gentner, D. (2000). Structure-mapping in the comparison process. *American Journal of Psychology, 113*(4), 501–538.

Markman, A. B., & Stilwell, C. H. (2001). Role-governed categories. *Journal of Experimental & Theoretical Intelligence, 13,* 329–358.

Markman, E. M. (1989). *Categorization and naming in children: Problems of induction.* Cambridge, MA: MIT Press.

Medin, D. L., Goldstone, R. L., & Gentner, D. (1993). Respects for similarity. *Psychological Review, 100*(2), 254–278.

Morimoto, Y. (1999). Loan words and their implications for the categorial status of verbal nouns. In S. S. Chang, L. Liaw, & J. Ruppenhofer (Eds.), *Proceedings of the twenty-fifth annual meeting of the Berkeley linguistics society, Feb. 12–15, 1999: General Session and Parasession on Loan Word Phenomena (BLS 25)* (pp. 371–382). Berkeley: Berkeley Linguistics Society.

Murphy, G. L., & Medin, D. L. (1985). The role of theories in conceptual coherence. *Psychological Review, 92,* 289–316.

Namy, L. L., & Gentner, D. (2002). Making a silk purse out of two sow's ears: Young children's use of comparison in category learning. *Journal of Experimental Psychology: General, 131,* 5–15.

Namy, L. L., Smith, L. B., & Gershkoff-Stowe, L. (1997). Young children's discovery of spatial classification. *Cognitive Development, 12,* 163–184.

Nersessian, N. J. (1992). How do scientists think? Capturing the dynamics of conceptual change in science. In R. N. Giere & H. Feigl (Eds.), *Minnesota studies in the philosophy of science* (pp. 3–44). Minneapolis, MN: University of Minnesota Press.

Oakes, L. M., & Madole, K. L. (2003). Principles of developmental change in infants' category formation. In D. H. Rakison & L. M. Oakes (Eds.), *Early concept and category development: Making sense of the blooming, buzzing confusion* (pp. 132–158). New York: Oxford University Press.

Oakes, L. M., & Ribar, R. J. (in press). A comparison of infants' categorization in paired and successive presentation familiarization tasks. *Infancy.*

Pae, S. (1993). *Early vocabulary in Korean: Are nouns easier to learn than verbs?* Unpublished doctoral dissertation, University of Kansas, Lawrence.

Pavlicic, T., & Markman, A. B. (1997). The structure of the verb lexicon: Evidence from a structural alignment approach to similarity. *Proceedings of the 19th Annual Conference of the Cognitive Science Society,* Stanford, CA.

Rattermann, M. J., & Gentner, D. (1998a). More evidence for a relational shift in the development of analogy: Children's performance on a causal-mapping task. *Cognitive Development, 13,* 453–478.

Rattermann, M. J., & Gentner, D. (1998b). The effect of language on similarity: The use of relational labels improves young children's performance in a mapping task. In K. Holyoak, D. Gentner, & B. Kokinov (Eds.), *Advances in analogy research: Integration of theory & data from the cognitive, computational, and neural sciences* (pp. 274–282). Sofia, Bulgaria: New Bulgarian University.

Rattermann, M. J., & Gentner, D. (2001). *The effect of language on similarity: The use of relational labels improves young children's analogical mapping performance.* Unpublished manuscript, Northwestern University.

Rehder, B., & Hastie, R. (2001). Causal knowledge and categories: The effects of causal beliefs on categorization, induction, and similarity. *Journal of Experimental Psychology: General, 130,* 323–360.

Ross, B. H. (1987). This is like that: The use of earlier problems and the separation of similarity effects. *Journal of Experimental Psychology: Learning, Memory, and Cognition, 13*(4), 629–639.

Ross, B. H. (1999). Postclassification category use: The effects of learning to use categories after learning to classify. *Journal of Experimental Psychology: Learning, Memory, and Cognition, 25*(3), 743–757.

Ross, B. H., Perkins, S. J., & Tenpenny, P. L. (1990). Reminding-based category learning. *Cognitive Psychology, 22,* 460–492.

Russell, B. (1956). On denoting. In R. C. Marsh (Ed.), *Logic and knowledge* (pp. 39–56). London: Routledge. (Original work published 1905)

Samuelson, L. K., & Smith, L. B. (2000). Grounding development in cognitive processes. *Child Development, 71*(1), 98–106.

Saussure, F. de. (1966). *Course in general linguistics* (C. Bally & A. Sechehaye, Eds., Baskin, Trans.). New York: McGraw Hill. (Original work published 1916)

Shatz, M. (1994). *A toddler's life: Becoming a person.* New York: Oxford.

Siegler, R. S. (1989). Mechanisms of cognitive development. *Annual Review of Psychology, 40,* 353–379.

Sloman, S. A., Love, B. C., & Ahn, W. K. (1998). Feature centrality and conceptual coherence. *Cognitive Science, 22,* 189–228.

Smith, L. B. (1983). Development of classification: The use of similarity and dimensional relations. *Journal of Experimental Child Psychology, 36,* 150–178.

Smith, L. B. (1989). From global similarities to kinds of similarities: The construction of dimensions in development. In S. Vosniadou & A. Ortony (Eds.), *Similarity and analogical reasoning* (pp. 146–178). New York: Cambridge University Press.

Sobin, N. (1982). Texas Spanish and lexical borrowing. In J. Amastae & L. Elias-Olivares (Eds.), *Spanish in the United States: Sociolinguistic aspects* (pp. 166–181). Cambridge: Cambridge University Press.

Talmy, L. (1975). Semantics and syntax of motion. In J. Kimball (Ed.), *Syntax and semantics* (Vol. 4, pp. 181–238). New York: Academic Press.

Tardif, T. (1996). Nouns are not always learned before verbs: Evidence from Mandarin speakers' early vocabularies. *Developmental Psychology, 32*(3), 492–504.

Tardif, T., Gelman, S. A., & Xu, F. (1999). Putting the noun bias in context: A comparison of English and Mandarin. *Child Development, 70*(3), 620–635.

Tversky, A. (1977). Features of similarity. *Psychological Review, 84*(4), 327–352.

Waxman, S. R. (1990). Linguistic biases and the establishment of conceptual hierarchies: Evidence from preschool children. *Cognitive Development, 5,* 123–150.

Waxman, S. R., & Klibanoff, R. S. (2000). The role of comparison in the extension of novel adjectives. *Developmental Psychology, 36,* 571–581.

Yan, J., Forbus, K., & Gentner, D. (2003). A theory of rerepresentation in analogical matching. In R. Alterman & D. Kirsh (Eds.), *Proceedings of the 25th Annual Meeting of the Cognitive Science Society,* 1265–1270.

Chapter 11

Demystifying Theory-Based Categorization

Woo-kyoung Ahn
Yale University

Christian C. Luhmann
Vanderbilt University

When cognitive psychologists first started studying concept learning, they relied on artificial stimulus materials that were not meaningful to participants in their studies. The idea was that if we want to study how people acquire novel concepts, we should use completely novel categories, thus controlling for the influence of people's already possessed concepts. In the last 20 years or so, however, many researchers have argued that this practice misses one of the most important components of concept-learning processes. Concepts are not represented in isolation, but are instead linked to and defined in relation to other concepts. In order to understand the concept of "shoes," for instance, we need to understand the concept of legs and walking. Therefore, it is no surprise that people have a strong tendency to apply their existing knowledge when learning a new concept because that new concept must be embedded in a complex network of existing knowledge. This emphasis on the influence of existing knowledge on concept learning has been called a theory-based approach to concept learning. The name theory-based is derived from the idea that our existing knowledge is represented like scientific theories such that concepts are causally related to each other and there are explanations underlying what we can directly observe. Unfortunately, the mechanism underlying theory-based categorization had not been explicitly articulated.

Recently, various attempts have been made to formalize background knowledge and the different ways in which this knowledge can influence concept learning (Heit, 1998; Rehder, 1999). The purpose of this chapter is to describe one such attempt, called the causal status hypothesis (Ahn, 1998), and to argue that this mechanism can account for numerous findings in children's conceptual representations that have been grossly described under the blanket of children's theory use. We first explain the causal status hypothesis, followed by illustrations of how this mechanism can provide parsimonious accounts for many important theory-based effects found in children's concept learning. Finally, we describe a series of recent studies showing that this mechanism is a primary process in adult categorization, suggesting that it might be developmentally privileged as well.

CAUSAL STATUS HYPOTHESIS: GENERAL INTRODUCTION

Concepts are connected to each other in many complex ways that resemble theories. For example, our concept of "boomerang" is connected with other concepts such as "throwing," "air," "speed," and so on, all of which are intricately connected as in a scientific theory. Furthermore, features within a concept exist in a rich structure, rather than as a set of independent features (Carey, 1985; Gelman & Kalish, 1993; Murphy & Medin, 1985; Wellman, 1990). In particular, features in concepts tend to be *causally* related. For instance, Kim and Ahn (2002a) found that more than 76% of symptom relations that clinicians drew for mental disorders could be classified as either causal or as implying causality. Ahn, Marsh, Luhmann, and Lee (2002) found that 58% of feature relations that laypeople recognized in sample natural kinds and artifacts were causal. As shown in Fig. 11.1, for instance, the most frequent label undergraduate participants in Ahn et al.'s study provided for relations among features in the category furniture was "causes" (e.g., having cushions causes furniture to be comfortable). Given that features in a concept are causally related to each other, the causal status hypothesis states that people regard cause features as more important and essential than effect features in their conceptual representations. (See also Gelman & Hirschfeld, 1999; Gelman & Kalish, 1993; Kahneman & Miller, 1986, for similar proposals.)

Ahn, Kim, Lassaline, and Dennis (2000) reported a number of tests of the causal status hypothesis. Participants in their Experiment 1 learned three characteristic features of a novel category (e.g., animals called "roobans" tend to eat fruit, have sticky feet, and build nests in trees). The Control group received no further information about the target category, and the Causal group was told that one feature tends to cause a second feature, which in turn tends to cause a third feature (e.g., eating fruit tends to cause roobans to have sticky feet, and having sticky feet tends to allow roobans to build nests in trees). Finally, all participants rated the membership likelihood of three transfer items, each of which had two features char-

FURNITURE

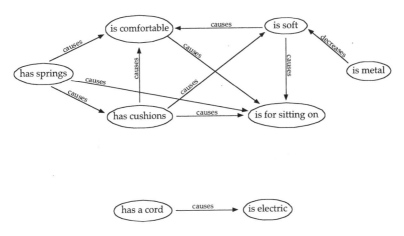

FIG. 11.1. An averaged lay-theory of furniture as extrapolated from Ahn et al. (2002).

acteristic of the target category and one noncharacteristic feature (e.g., an animal that likes to eat worms, has feet that are sticky, and builds nests in trees). For the Control group, likelihood ratings remained constant regardless of which feature the exemplar animal was missing. In the Causal condition, however, when an exemplar was missing the target category's fundamental cause in the causal chain, the mean likelihood of being a target category member was lower than when an object was missing its intermediate cause in the causal chain, which in turn was lower than when an object was missing its terminal effect. That is, the deeper a feature was in a causal chain, the more central it was in a categorization judgment.

In a further test of the causal status hypothesis, Ahn, Kim et al.'s (2000) Experiment 3 examined whether people prefer to free-sort objects based on cause features rather than effect features. Participants received a triad of objects, consisting of a target (e.g., Jane who is depressed because she has low self-esteem) and two options (e.g., Susan who is depressed because she has been drinking; Barbara who is defensive because she has low self-esteem), and were asked to choose an option that they would like to categorize with the target. As in the previous examples, one option (Susan) had the same effect as the target but a differing cause (Matching-Effect), and the other option (Barbara) had a matching cause but a differing effect (Matching-Cause). If the causal status effect occurs, matching on a cause feature would be considered more important than matching on an effect feature and consequently, participants would prefer the Matching-Cause case to the Matching-Effect case. In order to ensure that preference for the

Matching-Cause case was not due to any a priori salience of features that were chosen as causes, a control condition was employed in which all features and tasks were identical to those used in the experimental condition, except that the causal relations among features were explicitly denied (e.g., Jane is depressed. Jane has low self-esteem, which is NOT the reason why she is depressed.). Participants in this Non-Causal Condition showed no preference for either of the options. However, when causal relations were specified, 73.6% of responses were to prefer the Matching-Cause.

Why the Causal Status Effect?

Why should a cause feature be more central than its effect? Does the causal status effect stem from a rational basis so fundamental that we should expect it even from young children?

It would not be an exaggeration to assert that the most critical cognitive capacity an adaptive system should be equipped with is an ability to predict future events. The more one can infer future circumstances, the more one can be prepared for possible environments, resulting in a greater likelihood to survive. Indeed, one of the reasons why we possess concepts is so that we can infer or predict nonobvious properties (e.g., "is dangerous") based on category membership information (e.g., wolf). Thus, a "good" category is considered to be the one that allows rich inductive inferences (e.g., Anderson, 1990).

In particular, the more that underlying causes are revealed, the more inductive power the concept seems to gain. For instance, discovering a cause of a symptom such as nausea (e.g., Is it caused by bacteria or pregnancy?) allows doctors to determine the proper course of treatment, and also to make a better prognosis of the condition (e.g., Will it lead to a fever, or to a new baby?). In contrast, merely learning the effect of the symptom (e.g., nausea usually causes a person to throw up) does not necessarily help us come up with a treatment plan. Similarly, understanding the motive of a person's nice behavior (e.g., does he want a promotion or is he genuinely nice?) would allow us to predict many more behaviors of the person than would discovering the consequence of the person's nice behavior (e.g., people were impressed).

CONTENT-BASED VERSUS STRUCTURE-BASED APPROACH

By definition, the causal status hypothesis states that the determinant of feature centrality is not the specific content of features but rather the causal role that a feature plays. That is, the critical determinant is the position a feature takes in a conceptual structure.

This structure-based approach contrasts with what we have termed the content-based approach (Ahn & Kim, 2000), in which the focus lies on which specific feature is central in which type of concept. One example of this approach is a prominent debate in the developmental literature about whether young children categorize objects based on perceptually salient dimensions, such as overall shape, or, alternatively, based on what are known as "conceptual" dimensions, such as functions, intentions, and nonobvious inside features (e.g., Gelman & Koenig, 2003). For instance, Landau, Smith, and Jones (1988) presented 2- and 3-year-old children with a small, blue, wooden, inverted U-shaped object, and told the children that the object was a "dax." When asked to select other objects that were also daxes, children preferred objects with the same shape to those with the same size or material (behavior known henceforth as a shape bias). For other types of categories, such as biological kinds, internal properties are shown to be more central than overall shape (e.g., Gelman, 1988). In general, one camp argues that early in conceptual development children form concepts that are primarily based on perceptual features, whereas the other camp argues that even young children's concepts include more abstract information about causation, intentions, and other properties that are not directly observable. Thus, there are two sets of features differing in content (perceptual and conceptual ones) that are seen as core to children's concepts and it is this distinction in content that is the focus of debate.

Unlike this traditional content-based approach, we advocate the structural approach. That is, we are more concerned with how concepts are structured and how the mind handles various components of concepts, rather than what concepts actually contain as their content matter. In this chapter, we show that various developmental findings can in fact be explained in terms of the structural approach (the causal status hypothesis, in particular). Furthermore, we demonstrate that the structural approach can provide a more parsimonious account for the developmental debate pertaining to the bases of children's conceptual representations.

ACCOUNT OF DEVELOPMENTAL FINDINGS IN TERMS OF CAUSAL STATUS HYPOTHESIS

In essence, the hypothesis we entertain in this chapter is that the causal status effect is a processing bias that takes place in all domains across (almost) all developmental stages. How can this view account for variances, such as developmental differences or domain differences? Although the process might be uniform, the input to the system might differ, resulting in different outcomes.

For instance, two different experts might weigh features differently because of differences in their causal background knowledge rather than differences in their processing bias. Consider Fig. 11.2 showing the two radically different theories that expert clinical psychologists in Kim and Ahn's
(2002a) study drew about schizotypal personality disorder. The symptom
"Excessive social anxiety" is a cause of all other symptoms for the first ex-

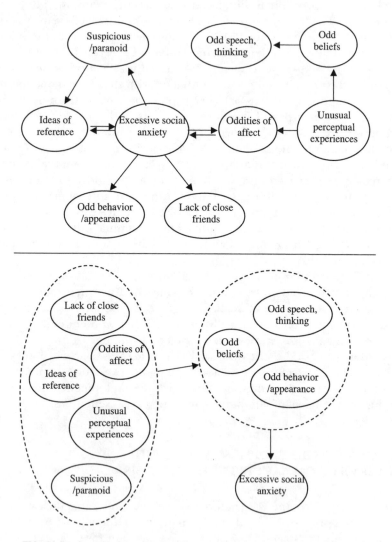

FIG. 11.2. Sample data showing disagreement in theories for schizotypal
personality disorder in Kim and Ahn (2002a). Reprinted with permission
from the authors and the American Psychological Association, Inc. Copyright
2002.

pert, but the same symptom is an effect of other symptoms for the second expert. Although clinicians' theories were idiosyncratic, Kim and Ahn found that within a given clinician's theory the causal status effect held. Therefore, the apparently different outcomes result from differences in the input (i.e., causal background knowledge) operating on the same processing mechanism. If a person does not know any causal relations among features, one has no way of weighting features based on their causal status and would rely on other factors (e.g., perceptual saliency, base rates, etc.). This may be the case with novices or with young children and domains in which they are lacking extensive causal knowledge (e.g., astrology).

Natural Kinds Versus Artifacts

Previous studies (e.g., Barton & Komatsu, 1989; Gelman, 1988; Keil, 1989; Rips, 1989) have shown that different features are central for natural kinds and artifacts: In natural kinds internal or molecular features are more conceptually central than functional features, but in artifacts functional features are more conceptually central than internal or molecular features.

In Gelman's (1988) study children first learned a feature novel to them for each type of category (e.g., this rabbit has a spleen inside) and were asked whether this feature is generalizable to another instance of the same category. The second graders in this study responded that features referring to substance and internal structure (e.g., "has a spleen inside," p. 74) were more generalizable for natural kinds, whereas functional features (e.g., "you can loll with it," p. 75) were more generalizable for artifacts.

Keil (1989) demonstrated a similar phenomenon using a transformation task. In this study, children learned, for instance, a story that a raccoon was dyed and painted with a white stripe to look like a skunk, or a story that a coffeepot was transformed into a bird feeder by changing its parts. Fourth graders as well as adults in this study judged that changes in perceptual appearance did not matter for natural kinds' identity, but these changes did matter for artifacts' identity. Presumably, a perceptual change in an artifact is directly related to the function it performs, and, therefore, perceptual changes were judged to matter for artifact category membership. However, a new discovery about the origin of an artifact (e.g., a key that was, in fact, made of pennies) did not affect category membership.

It is tempting to take the content-based approach based on these findings and conclude that there is something inherently special about molecular features for natural kinds and functional features for artifacts (e.g., Barton & Komatsu, 1989). In contrast, we argue that the mechanism underlying this phenomenon is the causal status effect. That is, in natural kinds, internal/molecular features tend to cause functional features (e.g., cow DNA determines whether or not cows give milk) but in artifacts, functional features determine compositional structure (e.g., chairs are used for sitting, and for that reason, they are made of a hard substance). In particular, Dennett (1987) dubbed the latter pattern in artifacts as the "design stance": A designer intentionally creates an artifact to fulfill a function and this intended function constrains its form, actual function, and the material it can be made from.

To test this structure-based hypothesis, Ahn (1998) examined the real-life categories used in previous studies (Barton & Komatsu, 1989; Malt & Johnson, 1992). Participants were asked to draw causal relations among features within a category. At the same time, they judged the centrality of features as measured by the degree to which a feature impacts categorization when that feature is missing. It was found that across natural and artifactual kinds, the more features any particular feature caused, the more influential the causal feature was in categorization. In addition, Ahn (1998) directly manipulated the causal status of features using artificial stimuli, and showed that when a compositional feature caused a functional feature, a compositional feature was more influential in categorization of both natural and artifactual kinds, whereas the opposite was true when the causal direction was reversed. These results suggest that the more fundamental determinant of feature centrality is not content but rather the structural roles played by specific features.

Given our emphasis on structure rather than content, it is preposterous that Sloman and Malt (2003) interpreted our position in a content-based manner: "So, one essentialist view is that, by virtue of its causal centrality, the intended function of an artifact is treated as its essence (Ahn et al., 2001)." Our claim is that the intended function can serve as an essence of an artifact because of its causal centrality, but that is not to claim that the intended function is always necessarily the essence of an artifact. Although most real artifacts in our culture probably are created with a certain function intended by the creator, artifacts can also be created by accident. For instance, an artist, after having randomly painted dots, might decide to call it "raindrops on a pond" even though that was not her initial intention. An essence of an artifact (or any category for that matter) is the deepest cause in that category, whether it is the intended function or something else.

Our intention, however, is not to dismiss domain differences. There appears to be a general pattern in the world as to which properties serve as cause features in which domain. For instance, as we alluded to earlier, intended function appears to frequently serve as cause for artifacts. Due to the frequency of this pattern, people might hold a default assumption about a given domain in the absence of specific causal theories. For instance, when confronted with an object that looks like an artifact, a typical assumption that people would make is that it is most likely created with a certain intended function. When confronted with an object that looks like an animal, adults would assume that it originated from the same kind of animal. However, such default assumptions can certainly be overridden by more specific causal theories about a category (Ahn, 1998). As a result, we cannot make a sweeping generalization that a specific type of property (e.g., intended function) is essential in all categories in a certain domain. In the next section, we examine more examples of this.

Form Versus Function Debate

Within the domain of artifacts, there has been debate on whether children prefer form or function of artifacts as a basis of extending novel names. For instance, children are taught that a novel artifact is named "Figley" and then asked which object they prefer to call "Figley," an object that shares the same perceptually salient feature but does not perform the same function, or an object that looks different but performs the same function. The results from studies using this paradigm are still controversial. We describe two representative studies from recent literature, and argue why these results are more parsimoniously described by the causal status hypothesis.

The strongest evidence supporting the perceptual camp is described in Smith, Jones, and Landau (1996). Three-year-old children learned the names of novel artifacts, and were asked whether the same name applied to test objects. There were four test objects, constructed by replacing the bases and parts of the target objects with contrast objects. Across two experiments, it was found that children extended the novel names to test objects that share the same perceptual dimensions that were salient in that experiment. That is, when parts were salient, children extended the names to test objects that shared the same part, whereas when bases were salient, they extended names to test objects that shared the same base. In two other experiments, Smith et al. taught participants novel functions of the same novel objects. Adult participants' naming was based on this functional information rather than perceptual salience. However, the responses of 3-year-old children remained based on the perceptually salient dimensions, and were not shifted by functional information.

Kemler Nelson, Frankenfield, Morris, and Blair (2000), however, argued that in order for functional information to be used by young children, it has to be compelling and nonarbitrary. That is, the function of an artifact should be based on principles of causality that are familiar to young children. For instance, consider an exemplar of "Amlas" in Smith et al.'s (1996) study. Its object-part biasing function was described to be, "A toy dog sits in." This function, however, might not have been used as a basis for naming due to its arbitrariness (e.g., a toy dog can sit almost anywhere). To test their hypothesis, Kemler Nelson et al. used either plausible or implausible functions. When a function was plausible, it provided a compelling explanation for why the objects had the structures they did. Drawing an analogy to real-life artifacts, "used for sitting" would be a plausible function for chairs because it explains why chairs have seats placed at a certain height, and backs attached to seats, and so on, whereas "used to prop a door" would be a possible but implausible function for chairs because it does not explain many structural components of chairs. Kemler Nelson et al. taught 4-year-olds labels of novel artifacts and examined whether they extended these labels to functional but perceptually similar objects or dysfunctional but perceptually less similar objects. They found preference for functional objects in the plausible function condition but not in the implausible function condition. Note, however, that this study still provides no theoretical reason as to why causal relations between functions and structure have to be compelling.

The causal status hypothesis provides a natural account in these described situations. Unless children can understand that the object was created to perform a certain function, that is, the parts and shape of an object are constrained by the intended function, the functional feature would not have a high causal status. Consequently, functions would be less likely to be conceptually central. Once again, what is critical here is not whether any feature is "functional" per se, but rather the features' causal status.

Even in adult categorization literature, the form–function debate remains controversial. For instance, although Barton and Komatsu (1989) found that physical appearance matters much less than functional features in artifact categorization, Malt and Johnson (1992) found that the physical appearance of objects is more important than functional features in artifact categories. At the surface level, these two studies seem contradictory to each other. However, in the framework of the causal status theory, they are not necessarily conflicting because the particular physical features chosen as the stimulus materials in each study could have varied with respect to causal status. Malt and Johnson used a set of complex physical features, some of which seem causally connected to other features, and some not. For example, a taxi's physical feature was "has a meter for fare, two seats, and is painted yellow" and its function was "to provide private land travel for 1–4 people at a time when their own cars are unavailable and they are willing to pay a variable amount of money depending upon their specific destination(s)." Of the features that were classified as physical in Malt and Johnson, "has a meter for fare" seems to determine the taxi's function whereas "painted yellow" does not. Based on this observation, the causal status hypothesis can explain the apparent discrepancy in the following way. The physical features used in Barton and Komatsu were not causal, whereas at least some of the physical features used in Malt and Johnson appear to be more causal. In order to test this hypothesis, Ahn (1998, Experiment 2) examined the physical features used in Malt and Johnson. Participants received all the physical features used in Malt and Johnson and assessed conceptual centrality of each individual feature ("would X still be X if it were in all ways like X except that it does not have property Y?") and causal centrality of that feature by drawing causal relations among the features within a target category. The results showed that not all physical features were equally conceptually central, and more importantly, that the conceptual centrality of physical features correlated with their causal centrality.

Again, these studies demonstrate that the form–function debate should be considered from a new perspective. Dichotomizing features based on their content (i.e., forms vs. functions) does not aid in providing a clear picture of how people assess feature importance. Looking at the causal status of features, apart from their content, allows for a more coherent interpretation of the studies described thus far.

Appreciation for Intentionality

Recently, several developmental studies demonstrated that even young children appreciate intentionality over appearance for naming external representations such as drawings. Bloom and Markson (1998) asked 3- and 4-year-old children to draw, for instance, a balloon and a lollipop. As one might expect, these drawings looked almost identical. Later, when the children were asked to name these drawings, the children named the pictures on the basis of what they had intended to depict. Similarly, Gelman and Ebeling (1998) showed that when the same picture was produced either intentionally or accidentally (e.g., drawings had been intentionally created to be a bear vs. spilled paint), intentional representation led to higher rates of naming responses (e.g., "bear") than did accidental representation. Clearly, the intention behind a drawing is a causal factor of the drawing's appearance. Thus, appreciation for the drawer's intention when naming drawings can be construed as an example of the causal status effect.

Is this effect limited to the naming of artwork or visual representations? Even 3-year-old children are familiar with paintings, and therefore have had firsthand experience with intentions behind drawings. Gelman and Bloom (2000) examined whether children would also be influenced by creator's intent when naming mundane artifacts such as tools and clothing. Participants in this study (3-year-olds, 5-year-olds, and adults) were presented with real artifacts (e.g., newspaper folded into the shape of a hat). They were told that the object was either intentionally created (e.g., "Jane went and got a newspaper. Then she carefully bent it and folded it till it was just right. Then she was done. This is what it looked like." [p. 94]) or accidentally created (e.g., "Jane was holding a newspaper. Then she dropped it by accident, and it fell under a car. She ran to get it and picked it up. This is what it looked like." [p. 94]). When told the object was intentionally created, participants in all age groups were more likely to name the object as the transformed object (e.g., hat in the just given example). However, when told the object was accidentally created, they were more likely to name it by its material composition (e.g., newspaper). Again, the cause of an object's existence (i.e., intent) derived naming of the object.

Apparently conflicting results to the aforementioned studies were obtained in Matan and Carey (2001). Participants were asked to judge whether an artifact that was originally made for one purpose (e.g., making tea) and was actually being used for another purpose (e.g., watering flowers) should be named as the object originally intended (e.g., a teapot) or as the object actually used (e.g., a watering can). Consistent with the previous studies, 6-year-olds and adults named the object based on its original intended function. However, unlike the three studies described earlier in this section that showed even 3-year-olds are sensitive to the original intent (e.g., Gelman & Bloom, 2000), 4-year-olds in Matan and Carey's study virtually never named objects based on their intended function.

There are two interrelated differences that might explain the discrepancy. First, in studies showing the importance of creator's intent, the intent of the creator was that the object be a certain kind (e.g., intent to draw a lollipop). In contrast, in Matan and Carey's (2001) study, the intent was about the function rather than the kind. As reviewed in the previous section, function alone does not consistently determine artifact naming in children's categorization. It is when the function's causal status is plausible and explicit that the function predominantly constrains naming. However, participants in Matan and Carey's study were presented only with ambiguous unidentifiable objects (e.g., a spout sticking out from behind a wall, which could be interpreted as belonging to either a teapot or a watering can), which made it difficult for them to clearly grasp the causal status of the intended function (i.e., that the form and materials of the object are caused by the intended function). (See also Chaigneau & Barsalou, 2002.) Older children and adults might have a default theory about artifacts, which includes the notion that the functions intended by designers of artifacts— and not the functions inflicted by the users—cause what the artifacts look like and what they are made of (i.e., Dennett's design stance, 1987). Younger children, on the other hand, might need more specific instantiations of such relations for a given object in order to allow intended function to override actual function in naming artifacts.[1]

Although learning about abstract causal structures underlying the design stance may come later in development (approximately 6 years old ac-

---

[1]It has been found that young children have "promiscuous" teleological belief—a tendency to believe that everything, even natural kinds such as mountains, has a purpose (Kelemen, 1999). Note that this promiscuous teleology is different from design stance (the belief that intended function causes what an artifact looks like or is made of).

cording to Matan & Carey, 2001), recent studies present evidence supporting the idea that even infants prefer to categorize events based on an agent's goal rather than mere perceptual information when the goal information is concrete. For instance, Gergely, Nádasdy, Csibra, and Bíró (1995) presented 12-month-old infants with a scene, in which a small disc and a large disc were separated by a block wall. The small disc moved toward the large disc and then jumped over the block, and moved to the large disc. In the test phase, the block was removed. In one condition, the small disc repeated the same jumping action, and in the other condition, the small disc moved directly toward the large disc without jumping. Infants looked longer at the less optimal event where the small disc repeated the same jumping action even though that event should be more perceptually familiar to them. Presumably, the original scene gives viewers an impression that the goal of the small disc is to be by the large disc, which requires it to jump over the block. It does not need to jump when the block is removed so the infants look at the jumping disc longer because its behavior is no longer consistent with the imagined goal. Therefore, the results suggest that even infants are sensitive to the goal of an agent.

Woodward (1998) presented similar findings from even younger infants (as young as 6 months old). In this study infants were habituated to an event in which a hand and arm moved to grasp one of two toys. In the test events, the position of the two toys was reversed and infants saw the hand and arm reaching for the same toy (i.e., along a different path than in the habituation sessions) or a different toy (i.e., along the previously used path). Infants looked longer at the same path event; that is, when the goal was changed. Again, an agent's goal is the cause of the agent's behavior, and these two studies are consistent with the causal status hypothesis: Participants categorize events based on the causal factor—goal—rather than the effect—behavior.

The causal relations between an agent's goal and the agent's behavior appear to be acquired very early on (compared to more abstract causal relations, say, design stance) because infants themselves carry out such causal actions. They, themselves, intend to perform a certain behavior and that intention leads to a certain action. Searle (1983) described how an ascription of intentional cause can be acquired without multiple observations: "For example, suppose I am thirsty and I take a drink of water. If someone asks me why I took a drink of water, I know the answer without any further observation: I was thirsty. Furthermore, in this sort of case it seems that I know the truth of the counterfactual without any further observations or any appeal to general laws . . ." (Searle, 1983, p. 118).

To summarize, we propose that intentionality behind the creation of an object is more conceptually central than the object's appearance because intentionality determines what the object looks like. If this causal status of intentionality is not obvious to a categorizer, intentionality may not be as conceptually central. In situations where the causal role of intentionality is most prominent (e.g., intention or goal of an actor), even young infants categorize events based on that dimension.

EVIDENCE FOR THE PRIMACY OF THE CAUSAL STATUS EFFECT

Primacy in Development

Thus far, we have illustrated how a large number of findings in children's categorization can be explained in terms of the causal status hypothesis. Yet, none of these tests with children directly tested the causal status hypothesis by holding the content constant and manipulating the causal status of features only. Ahn, Gelman, Amsterlaw, Hohenstein, and Kalish (2000) provided direct evidence of the causal status effect in 7- to 9-year-old children. In this study, adults and children learned descriptions of novel animals, in which one feature caused two other features. When asked to determine which transfer item was more likely to be an example of the animal they had learned, both adults and children preferred an animal with a cause feature and an effect feature than an animal with two effect features. Thus, children in this age group do indeed show the causal status bias. The paradigm used in this study would be difficult to use with younger children because participants had to learn novel features of an animal along with the causal relations among them, followed by a choice task between two transfer items. At this point, it remains to be seen whether direct evidence of the causal status effect can be obtained from children younger than 7 years.

Primacy in Categorization Processes

As discussed, the causal status hypothesis posits that children possess abstract beliefs about the implications of causal structure. This suggestion has met with implicit resistance. As addressed in Keil, Smith, Simons, and Levin (1998), one reason for this is that theory-based reasoning has traditionally been thought of as a slow, reflective process (e.g., Sloman, 1996; Smith & Sloman, 1994). Perhaps because of this, theory-use has also been assumed to be difficult and thus less readily available to children. This assumption is manifested in the notion of a concrete to abstract developmental shift (e.g., Werner & Kaplan, 1963) and in the claim that perceptually based categorization arises before categorization of conceptual features (e.g., Smith & Kemler Nelson, 1984). Keil et al. (1998) argued that this assumption is unwarranted. In the following, we present more direct evidence that theory-based categorization, and the causal status hypothesis in particular, is not a slow, deliberative process. (See Luhmann, Ahn, & Palmeri, 2002, for more detailed descriptions of this study.)

Experiment 1. Our stimuli consisted of four fictional animals (see Fig. 11.3). Each animal was described as possessing three features (e.g., A, B, and C). The features were described as having a causal chain structure such that feature A causes feature B and feature B causes feature C. In order to ensure that the three features' saliency did not vary in the absence of causal information, we removed the explicit causal information from the animal descriptions and asked a separate set of subjects to rate the likelihood of category membership of items missing a single feature (e.g., Fig. 11.4). The results of this pretest showed no significant differences between the ratings of items missing the first feature, items missing the second feature, and items missing the third feature (all $ps > .4$), confirming that the features were equated for a priori strength.

To allow for speeded responses, subjects in the main experiment were required to learn and memorize the four animals, their features, and the causal relations between the features. First, subjects were given the oppor-

Kehoes
have a small heart
have a low body temp
hibernate in winter

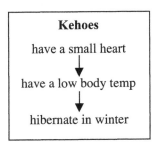

FIG. 11.3. A sample animal with causal links, from Luhmann, Ahn, and Palmeri (2002) "Theories and Similarity: Categorization Under Speeded Conditions." Reprinted with permission from Luhmann, Ahn, and Palmeri and Lawrence Erlbaum Associates.

Kehoe?
does not have a low body temp
has a small heart
hibernates in winter

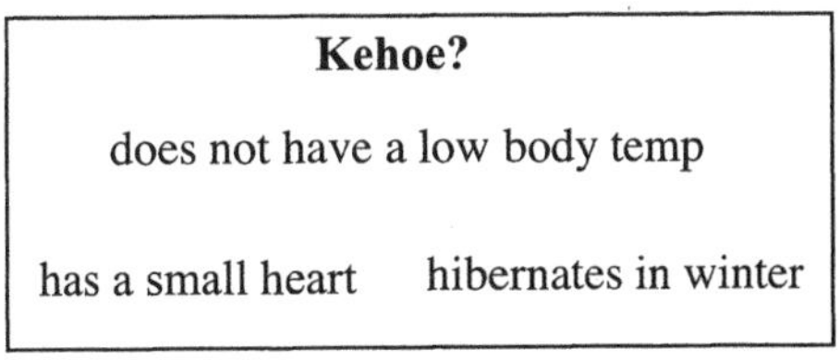

FIG. 11.4. A sample item from Experiment 1, from Luhmann, Ahn, and Palmeri (2002) "Theories and Similarity: Categorization Under Speeded Conditions." Reprinted with permission from Luhmann, Ahn, and Palmeri and Lawrence Erlbaum Associates.

tunity to study the description of each animal at the beginning of the experiment. While studying each description, subjects were instructed to "write about how you think each feature causes the next," in an attempt to force subjects to think causally about the features (instead of as a simple ordered list). To help subjects further learn the items, they were then presented with six trial blocks, during which they were prompted with the name of one of the animals and were required to select (using a mouse-click) in the appropriate causal order the features of that animal from an array containing the features of all four animals. In the first two blocks responses were unspeeded, whereas in the last four blocks responses had 5-second deadlines so that the novel causal background knowledge would be sufficiently internalized. In addition, on half of the blocks subjects were asked for the causal relations in the forward order (e.g., A, B, C), and in the other half in the backward order (e.g., C, B, A).

Once subjects completed these six blocks they proceeded to the experimental transfer task. Subjects were presented with items missing a single feature and were asked to rate the likelihood that the item belonged to its target category on an 8-point scale (with 1 labeled as "Definitely Unlikely" and 8 labeled as "Definitely Likely"). There were four blocks of trials in the transfer task. In two of the blocks subjects were instructed to answer as quickly as possible. In the other two blocks they were told to take as much time as needed. The reaction times in the speeded blocks ($M = 1560$ms) were indeed significantly faster than the times in the unspeeded blocks ($M = 3202$ms), $p < .05$, Tukey's HSD.

For the unspeeded trials we expected to find results similar to those of Experiment 1 of Ahn, Kim et al. (2000). That is, items missing the terminal effect feature should be rated as more likely category members than those missing the initial cause feature. The critical question was whether this causal status effect would disappear during the speeded trials.

The results for subjects' categorization responses are summarized in Fig. 11.5. A 2 (speed condition: speeded vs. unspeeded) × 3 (item type: missing first feature vs. missing second feature vs. missing third feature) repeated measures ANOVA was performed on subjects' responses. We observed a significant main effect of item type, $p < .0001$. Planned comparisons showed that in both the speeded and unspeeded conditions items missing the third feature were rated significantly higher than those missing the first or second features ($ps < .05$). The difference between items missing the first feature and those missing the second feature was not significant ($ps > .05$), possibly because the second feature also served as a cause of another feature, making the difference between the first and the second feature less pronounced (see also Kim & Ahn, 2002b). In addition, we observed no main effect of speed, and the speed × item type interaction was also not significant, $p > .05$. Overall, these results demonstrate

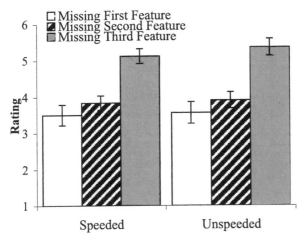

FIG. 11.5.   Results from Experiment 1, from Luhmann, Ahn, and Palmeri (2002) "Theories and Similarity: Categorization Under Speeded Conditions." Reprinted with permission from Luhmann, Ahn, and Palmeri and Lawrence Erlbaum Associates.

that the causal status effect occurs even when time for lengthy reflection is not allowed.

Experiment 2.   In Experiment 1, subjects were simply asked to respond as quickly as possible to the "speeded" items. Given this freedom, some subjects responded very quickly but others responded significantly more slowly. Although the speed manipulation we used in Experiment 1 is naturalistic in that subjects carried out what they thought to be a rapid decision-making process, forcing subjects to respond within a specific deadline ensures uniform time pressure across all subjects and items. Therefore, in Experiment 2, we imposed stricter control over subjects' response times by enforcing deadlines on subjects' responses.

One methodological complication with establishing appropriate response deadlines is that it is difficult to determine beforehand whether a particular deadline is short enough to challenge the categorization system but not so short as to make accurate responses impossible. That is, if the speeded condition does not show the causal status effect, it may be because theory-based reasoning does not take place during rapid categorization, or because the deadline is too short to produce any reasonable responses.

For this reason, we also tested whether similarity information could be used under similar deadlines. By testing both kinds of knowledge, the casual status effects can be compared to similarity-based categorization at each deadline. In this way it can be inferred whether any breakdown of the causal status effect is due to the inability to complete the processes necessary for theory-based categorization or if reasonable responses at that deadline are impossible for both kinds of categorization.

There were two conditions in Experiment 2, one representing a theory-based situation and the other representing a similarity-based situation. The condition representing a theory-based situation was the Causal condition, where subjects were given the same stimuli and accompanying causal information as used in Experiment 1. The condition representing a similarity-based situation was the Base-Rate condition, where subjects were provided with information about relative base rates of each feature within a category. More specifically, each category was described as having three features (e.g., A, B, and C) such that 100% of category members possessed feature A, 80% possessed feature B, and 60% possessed feature C. It was thought that these base rates (or a measure also known as category validity; Rosch & Mervis, 1975) would serve as a similarity-based determinant for feature weighting because similarity is frequently calculated based on how many attributes an item has in common with other members of the category (e.g., Tversky, 1977). Paralleling the results of Experiment 1, items in the Base-Rate condition missing the third (60%) feature should be rated as better category members than those missing the first (100%) feature. Using this condition as a point of comparison, and with the addition of strict response deadlines, we hoped to provide a more rigorous test of the causal status effect under speeded conditions.

The learning phase for the Causal condition was identical to that used in Experiment 1. Subjects in the Base-Rate condition did not have to generate explanations but instead categorized exemplars into one of the four animal categories. For this task, each exemplar always possessed the first feature of its category, possessed the second feature on 80% of the trials, and the third feature 60% of the time (thus mirroring the stated base rates). Feedback was given after each trial during the learning phase.

Blocks of 30 such trials alternated with blocks of a "selection task" like that used in the Causal condition. The directions for the selection task instructed those subjects in the Base-Rate condition to select features in an order (forward or backward) dictated by their base rate percentages rather than their position in the causal chain.

The transfer phase for both conditions was nearly identical to that used in Experiment 1 except for a modified speed manipulation. Instead of an instruction to respond quickly, Experiment 2 employed a signal-to-respond technique (Lamberts, 1998). Thus, every trial presented the feature triad (e.g., Fig. 11.4) for a set amount of time (see following). Subjects responded to the item once the presentation was completed and the item disappeared from the screen. If a response was made more than 300ms after the disappearance of the triad, subjects were told to respond more rapidly. There were four blocks of trials. Each block used one of four durations (5000ms, 2250ms, 1500ms, and 750ms) for the presentation of the triads.

The results from the categorization task can be seen in Figs. 11.6 and 11.7. A 2 (knowledge condition: Causal vs. Base-Rate) × 4 (speed condition: 5000ms vs. 2250ms vs. 1500ms vs. 750ms) × 2 (item type: missing first feature vs. missing third) ANOVA was performed with repeated measures on the latter two factors. Neither the main effect of nor any interaction with the knowledge condition (feature frequency vs. causal) was found to be significant. The main effect of item type was found to be significant, $p < .0001$.

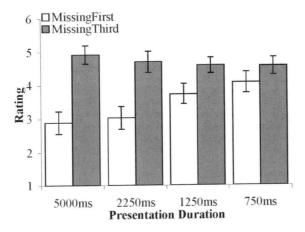

FIG. 11.6. Results from the Causal Condition, Experiment 2, extrapolated from Luhmann, Ahn, and Palmeri (2002).

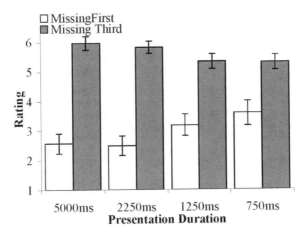

FIG. 11.7. Results from the Base Rate Condition, Experiment 2, extrapolated from Luhmann, Ahn, and Palmeri (2002).

Planned comparisons were conducted to determine whether a significant effect of item type was present at each of the response deadlines for each of the knowledge conditions. For simplicity, we include only those comparisons between items missing the first feature and those missing the third, the difference CSH predicts to be the largest. For both knowledge conditions and at all response deadlines the items missing the third feature were rated as significantly better category members than those items missing the first feature (all $p < .05$).

Experiment 3. Experiment 3 used faster response deadlines (1500 ms, 750ms, 500ms, and 300ms). The other aspects of the method were identical to that of Experiment 2.

The results from the categorization task can be seen in Figs. 11.8 and 11.9. A 2 (knowledge condition: Causal vs. Base-Rate) × 4 (speed condition: 1500ms vs. 750ms vs. 500ms vs. 300ms) × 2 (item type: missing first feature vs. missing third) ANOVA was performed with repeated measures on the latter two factors. We observed a significant main effect of item type, $p < .0005$, that did not interact with knowledge condition, demonstrating that both background conditions had the predicted effect on categorization behaviors. Planned comparisons were carried out to determine at what response deadlines the background information had an effect on categorization (items missing the second feature were again excluded). For the Base-Rate condition, items missing the first (100%) feature significantly differed from items missing the third (60%) feature in the

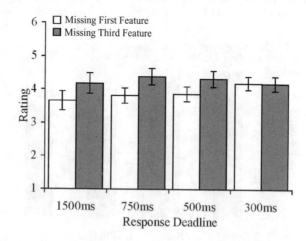

FIG. 11.8. Results from the Causal Condition, Experiment 3, from Luhmann, Ahn, and Palmeri (2002) "Theories and Similarity: Categorization Under Speeded Conditions." Reprinted with permission from Luhmann, Ahn, and Palmeri and Lawrence Erlbaum Associates.

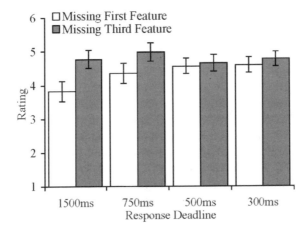

FIG. 11.9. Results from the Base Rate Condition, Experiment 3, from Luhmann, Ahn, and Palmeri (2002) "Theories and Similarity: Categorization Under Speeded Conditions." Reprinted with permission from Luhmann, Ahn, and Palmeri and Lawrence Erlbaum Associates.

1500ms condition, $t(29) = 3.43$, $p < .005$, and the 750ms condition, $t(29) = 2.41$, $p < .05$, but not in the 500ms, $t(29) = .3$, $p > .05$, or 300ms, $t(29) = 1.59$, $p > .05$, conditions. In the Causal condition, items missing the first (initial cause) feature differed from those missing the third (terminal effect) feature in the 1500ms condition, $t(29) = 2.22$, $p < .05$, the 750ms condition, $t(29) = 2.86$, $p < .01$, and the 500ms condition, $t(29) = 2.06$, $p < .05$, but not the 300ms condition, $t(29) = .81$, $p > .05$.

Discussion. These results support the idea that theory-use is as fast as, if not faster than, comparable similarity-use. In particular, subjects in Experiment 3 were able to categorize according to their theory even when allowed only 500ms to view the exemplar and make a response. Furthermore, our results indicate that the base-rate information, which has been considered a key determinant of similarity (Rosch & Mervis, 1975), did not result in differential responses under this deadline. The results taken together provide strong evidence that the causal status effect cannot be slower than the frequency effect.

Given the speed in which the causal status effect was obtained, it seems unlikely that people start reasoning about feature centrality as they encounter each transfer item. It is more likely that people developed notions about feature centrality as they were learning causal relations in a category and simply retrieved this precompiled knowledge when categorizing novel items. If this processing account is correct, it suggests that theory-based categorization does not necessarily have to be cognitively demanding. Thus, it becomes even more likely that the causal status effect would be obtained even among young children as long as they have well-learned causal knowledge.

CONCLUSION

One dominant line of theory is that children's initial concepts are concrete and perceptually based, and only later do they acquire the more conceptually based categories that adults have (e.g., Inhelder & Piaget, 1964). Presumably because of this tradition, most debate on children's conceptual representations is framed in terms of the use of perceptual versus non-perceptual features. In this chapter, we offer a new perspective on these issues. We propose that recent findings favoring either the perceptual camp or the non-perceptual camp can both be interpreted in terms of causal structures in concepts, and we provided several examples in this chapter. We presented several arguments for the advantages of this structure-based approach. The causal status hypothesis provides a more parsimonious account for various phenomena without having to resort to ill-defined concepts, such as domains. Furthermore, the causal status hypothesis can provide precise predictions about novel domains once we know the causal structure of concepts, whereas the content-based approach is merely descriptive and fails to provide predictions about novel domains. In most existing studies, however, the content effect has been confounded with the causal status effect. When they are pitted against each other, evidence favors the causal status effect.

Unfortunately, no existing study compares the content effect against the causal status effect among children younger than 7. Therefore, it is difficult to determine how developmentally primary the causal status effect is. One possible reason to believe the causal status effect would not be present in young infants is the idea that theory-based reasoning is deliberate and slow: After all, those tasks that adults need time to complete (e.g., long division) are not usually readily available to children. Our recent study, however, found that the causal status effect occurs as rapidly as the similarity-based effect in adult categorization. These results cast doubt on the possibility that the causal status effect is too analytic to be used by very young children. Instead, it further opens up a door to the possibility that children would use this process, however rudimentarily, early in life.

REFERENCES

Ahn, W. (1998). Why are different features central for natural kinds and artifacts? The role of causal status in determining feature centrality. *Cognition, 69,* 135–178.

Ahn, W., Gelman, S. A., Amsterlaw, J. A., Hohenstein, J., & Kalish, C. W. (2000). Causal status effect in children's categorization. *Cognition, 76,* B35–B43.

Ahn, W., Kalish, C., Gelman, S. A., Medin, D. L., Luhmann, C., Atran, S., Coley, J. D., & Shafto, P. (2001). Why essences are essential in the psychology of concepts. *Cognition, 82,* 59–69.

Ahn, W., & Kim, N. S. (2000). The role of causal status of features in categorization: An overview. In D. L. Medin (Ed.), *Psychology of learning and motivation* (Vol. 40, pp. 23–65). New York: Academic Press.

Ahn, W., Kim, N. S., Lassaline, M. E., & Dennis, M. J. (2000). Causal status as a determinant of feature centrality. *Cognitive Psychology, 41,* 1–55.

Ahn, W., Marsh, J., Luhmann, C., & Lee, K. (2002). Effect of theory-based feature correlations on typicality judgments. *Memory and Cognition, 30,* 107–118.

Anderson, J. R. (1990). *The adaptive character of thought.* Hillsdale, NJ: Lawrence Erlbaum Associates.

Barton, M. E., & Komatsu, L. K. (1989). Defining features of natural kinds and artifacts. *Journal of Psycholinguistic Research, 18,* 433–447.

Bloom, P., & Markson, L. (1998). Intention and analogy in children's naming of pictorial representations. *Psychological Science, 9,* 200–204.

Carey, S. (1985). *Conceptual change in childhood.* Cambridge, MA: Plenum.

Chaigneau, S. E., & Barsalou, L. W. (2002). Testing the roles of design history and affordances in the HIPE theory of function. In W. D. Gray & C. Schunn (Eds.), *Proceedings of the Twenty-Fourth Annual Conference of the Cognitive Science Society* (p. 30). Mahwah, NJ: Lawrence Erlbaum Associates.

Dennett, D. C. (1987). *The intentional stance.* Cambridge, MA: MIT Press.

Gelman, S. A. (1988). The development of induction within natural kind and artifact categories. *Cognitive Psychology, 20,* 65–95.

Gelman, S. A., & Bloom, P. (2000). Young children are sensitive to how an object was created when deciding what to name it. *Cognition, 76,* 91–103.

Gelman, S. A., & Ebeling, K. S. (1998). Shape and representational status in children's early naming. *Cognition, 66,* B35–B47.

Gelman, S. A., & Hirschfeld, L. A. (1999). How biological is essentialism? In D. L. Medin & S. Atran (Eds.), *Folkbiology* (pp. 403–446). Cambridge, MA: MIT Press.

Gelman, S. A., & Kalish, C. W. (1993). Categories and causality. In R. Pasnak & M. L. Howe (Eds.), *Emerging themes in cognitive development* (Vol. 2, pp. 3–32). New York: Springer Verlag.

Gelman, S. A., & Koenig, M. A. (2003). Theory-based categorization in early childhood. In D. Rakison & L. Oakes (Eds.), *Early category and concept development: Making sense of the blooming, buzzing confusion* (pp. 330–359). London: Oxford University Press.

Gergely, G., Nádasdy, Z., Csibra, G., & Bíró, S. (1995). Taking the intentional stance at 12 months of age. *Cognition, 56,* 165–193.

Heit, E. (1998). Influence of prior knowledge on selective weighting of category members. *Journal of Experimental Psychology: Learning, Memory, & Cognition, 24,* 712–731.

Inhelder, B., & Piaget, J. (1964). *The early growth of logic in the child.* New York: W. W. Norton & Company.

Kahneman, D., & Miller, D. T. (1986). Norm theory: Comparing reality to its alternatives. *Psychological Review, 93,* 136–153.

Keil, F. (1989). *Concepts, kinds, and cognitive development.* Cambridge, MA: MIT Press.

Keil, F. C., Smith, W. C., Simons, D. J., & Levin, D. T. (1998). Two dogmas of conceptual empiricism: Implications for hybrid models of the structure of knowledge. *Cognition, 65,* 103–135.

Kelemen, D. (1999). Functions, goals and intentions: Children's teleological reasoning about objects. *Trends in Cognitive Sciences, 12,* 461–468.

Kemler Nelson, D. G., Frankenfield, A., Morris, C., & Blair, C. (2000). Young children's use of functional information to categorize artifacts: Three factors that matter. *Cognition, 77,* 133–168.

Kim, N. S., & Ahn, W. (2002a). Clinical psychologists' theory-based representations of mental disorders affect their diagnostic reasoning and memory. *Journal of Experimental Psychology: General, 131,* 451–476.

Kim, N. S., & Ahn, W. (2002b). The influence of naïve causal theories on lay concepts of mental illness. *American Journal of Psychology, 115,* 33–65.

Lamberts, K. (1998). The time course of categorization. *Journal of Experimental Psychology: Learning, Memory, & Cognition, 24,* 695–711.

Landau, B., Smith, L. B., & Jones, S. S. (1988). The importance of shape in early lexical learning. *Cognitive Development, 3,* 299–321.

Luhmann, C. C., Ahn, W., & Palmeri, T. J. (2002). Theories and similarity: Categorization under speeded conditions. In W. D. Gray & C. D. Schunn (Eds.), *Proceedings of the 24th Annual Conference of the Cognitive Science Society,* 590–595. Mahwah, NJ: Lawrence Erlbaum Associates.

Malt, B. C., & Johnson, E. C. (1992). Do artifact concepts have cores? *Journal of Memory and Language, 31,* 195–217.

Matan, A., & Carey, S. (2001). Developmental changes within the core of artifact concepts. *Cognition, 78,* 1–26.

Murphy, G. L., & Medin, D. L. (1985). The role of theories in conceptual coherence. *Psychological Review, 92,* 289–316.

Rehder, B. (1999). A causal-model theory of categorization. *Proceedings of the Twenty-First Annual Conference of the Cognitive Science Society,* 595–600.

Rips, L. J. (1989). Similarity, typicality, and categorization. In S. Vosniadou & A. Ortony (Eds.), *Similarity and analogical reasoning* (pp. 21–59). New York: Cambridge University Press.

Rosch, E., & Mervis, C. B. (1975). Family resemblances: Studies in the internal structure of categories. *Cognitive Psychology, 7,* 573–605.

Searle, J. R. (1983). *Intentionality.* New York: Cambridge University Press.

Sloman, S. A. (1996). The empirical case for two systems of reasoning. *Psychological Bulletin, 119,* 3–22.

Sloman, S. A., & Malt, B. (2003). Artifacts are not ascribed essences, nor are they treated as belonging to kinds. Conceptual representation [Special issue]. *Language & Cognitive Processes, 18*(5–6), 563–582.

Smith, E. E., & Sloman, S. A. (1994). Similarity- versus rule-based categorization. *Memory & Cognition, 22,* 377–386.

Smith, J. D., & Kemler Nelson, D. G. (1984). Overall similarity in adults' classification: The child in all of us. *Journal of Experimental Psychology: General, 113,* 137–159.

Smith, L. B., Jones, S. S., & Landau, B. (1996). Naming in young children: A dumb attentional mechanism? *Cognition, 60,* 143–171.

Tversky, A. (1977). Features of similarity. *Psychological Review, 84,* 327–352.

Wellman, H. M. (1990). *The child's theory of mind.* Cambridge, MA: MIT Press.

Werner, H., & Kaplan, B. (1963). *Symbol formation: An organismic-developmental approach to language and the expression of thought.* New York: Wiley.

Woodward, A. L. (1998). Infants selectively encode the goal object of an actor's reach. *Cognition, 69,* 1–34.

Chapter 12

Can Our Experiments
Illuminate Reality?

Brian MacWhinney
Carnegie Mellon University

The chapters by Ahn and Luhmann, Bowerman, Gentner, and Gershkoff-Stowe present a detailed picture of current research on the many processes involved in children's concept learning. In this chapter, I first summarize and critique the findings of these authors. Then I discuss possible future directions in the study of children's categorization. In particular, I argue that we should now begin to study actual instances of real concept learning in homes and schools.

Ahn and Luhmann present a common sense analysis of artificial concept learning that emphasizes the role of prediction from properties and goals to concept membership. The basic idea is that we can best categorize results by looking at their causes. Good categories are those that maximize the probability of a result, given a cause or p(result|cause). Bayesian theory views the ongoing updating of this cue validity as involving the modification of the subjective probability of p(result|cause) on the basis of new evidence. This same traditional cue validity model also sits at the root of the Competition Model—a model that has been used to account for the learning of grammar, morphology, and concept learning (MacWhinney, 1987).

Ahn and Luhmann's work focuses primarily on the role of causes in the prediction of novel categories. For example, when given Jane who is depressed because she has low self-esteem, Susan who is depressed because she has been drinking, and Barbara who is defensive because she has low self-esteem, subjects tend to group together Jane and Barbara because they both have low self-esteem, rather than Jane and Susan because they are depressed. The basic idea here is that we focus more on causes than symptoms. After all, we have learned that a given underlying cause can produce a variety of effects that change over time. To form a consistent concept, it is best to focus on the causes, rather than the effects.

However, one might note that the shape of the novel concept learning task in the studies reported by Ahn and Luhmann, as well as those used in similar studies by Gelman, Keil, Rips, and others, tends to emphasize the salience of causes, perhaps more than in our natural experiences with concept learning. In these studies, causes are directly presented to the subject. There is no process of causal inference or discovery. Ahn and Luhmann conclude from their studies that "theory use is as fast as, if not faster than, comparable similarity use." This may well be generally true for studies of this type. However, in the natural world, the situation seems to be reversed. In nature, we are typically confronted with results from which we have to infer causes. We may see that Jane drinks too much or that Frank yells at his children. It takes awhile before we learn that they both have been having trouble at their jobs. We may notice that both lizards and snakes like to sit on rocks in the middle of the day. It takes awhile to learn that they do this because they are both cold-blooded.

Ahn and Luhmann suggest that their causal status hypothesis can be used to provide a natural resolution of the form versus function debate in the child categorization literature. However, the resolution they present seems to me biased in favor of the causal status account. They noted that children only make clear use of function in acquiring new categories, when the causal basis of the function is plausible. But in other studies (Kemler Nelson, Frankenfield, Morris, & Blair, 2000), the experimenter makes sure that the child is fully aware of the functions of the objects. This full disclosure of cause short-circuits the normal process of discovery of causal structures that is involved in concept learning. Although I thoroughly agree with Ahn and Luhmann that categorization is designed to maximize p(result|cause), it seems to me that the normal process of concept formation does not follow the royal road of immediate causal discovery provided by this experimental literature. Instead, if we take a close look at interactions between mothers and children or teachers and their students, we will see a complicated discourse designed to explore the uses of concepts in various contexts precisely with an eye toward elucidating causes. Thus, it should not be surprising to find that the initial stages of concept learning involve considerable attention to perceptual attributes.

However, Ahn and Luhmann also point to another view of concept learning that seems to tap more directly into early causal learning. This view points to a direct mapping between a new concept and a first-person intention. For example, Searle said that he knows immediately that he takes a drink of water because he is thirsty. If we see a horse drinking water, we can infer the cause directly by relating the horse to our own first-person perspective. I am not suggesting that all new categories are acquired through a mapping to first-person perspective. However, the idea that this type of embodied mapping stimulates concept coherence and productivity is certainly worth pursuing. Moreover it seems to me that the use of first-person perspective for causal discovery fits in well with an extended version of Ahn and Luhmann's causal status hypothesis.

Causal induction also figures prominently in Gentner's account of the acquisition of relational categories, such as *gift, robbery,* or *loan.* Gentner's account of the learning of relational categories focuses on the fact that category labels trigger a process of structural alignment. When a child hears two very different objects being described by the same term, the sharing of a label triggers a "cue search" process. Gentner thinks of this search as involving the alignment of two items. The technique of Namy and Gentner (2002) specifically involves the alignment of two objects, just as required by the model. One might argue that Gentner's structural alignment model overemphasizes pairwise similarities without providing a role for larger group alignment of the type one would find in neural network models. However, in defense of Gentner's position, I would note that there is evidence from the adult literature suggesting that learners often try to focus on a small set of exemplars and hypotheses, perhaps because of working memory limitations. From this viewpoint, Gentner's emphasis on pairwise alignment seems motivated. However, one must keep in mind that here, as in the case of Ahn and Luhmann, the particular experimental method being used emphasizes the presentation of pairs of objects or relations to be aligned.

Gentner also emphasizes the difficulties children face in discovering causal and functional properties underlying relational categories. However, instead of viewing perceptual features as a stable initial organizational system, she believes that they are only important to the extent that they induce structural alignment. Citing the results of Samuelson and Smith (1998), she notes that children's use of perceptual features as a basis for word learning may in fact be highly adaptive. When children lack knowledge about a concept, perceptual commonalities may serve as the initial "hook" that encourages them to engage in comparison and extract deeper relational commonalities. Note that the emphasis here is on structural alignment as the sole target with perceptual features only serving to direct the learner's attention. However, Gentner would probably agree that perceptual features serve additional roles in terms of allowing for the storing of episodic memories of objects and providing rich features for later support of structural alignment. Thus, what is at issue here is the microgenesis of the transition from initial perceptual alignment to deeper causal alignment. That is a worthy topic for future investigation.

The new work of Gentner and Klibanoff seeks to induce structural alignment in 3- to 6-year-olds. Inventing words such as *blick* with a meaning like "cutter," they were able to teach 4-year-olds, but not 3-year-olds, to relate cutting paper to chopping down a tree. One possible account of this finding is that the older children were quicker to map *blick* onto the concept of cutting. In this account it is the verbal and conceptual mediation and not the deep structural alignment that facilitated success in this task. Manipulations that overtly vary the ease of mapping a new action to an existent English word might control for this effect, although one would then worry about the status of actions that cannot be described by English words. Perhaps the children could be tested by a probe recognition technique to determine the degree to which they activated the word *cut* during the relevant set of *blick* stimuli.

More generally, we have only this one study in this new line of research to defend Gentner's general claim that relational categories can be learned by the general learning mechanism of progressive structural alignment, as triggered by label similarity. Even without further work, I would wonder a bit about the extent to which this general claim is falsifiable. It would seem difficult to deny that concept learning is facilitated by the presence of verbal labels. Theories might differ in the way they see this facilitation as operating mechanistically, but it would be difficult to deny the overall effect. Similarly, it would be difficult to imagine that pointing out the similarities between two objects would fail to help concept formation. We would only expect this type of manipulation to fail when the similarities involve entities and relations that are outside of the experience of the child. So, it is not clear to me yet how the theory can be tested. This is unfortunate, because it seems largely true.

Bowerman takes a rather different approach to the word-learning problem. Decrying the uniformity of the "cognitivist climate of the last 40 years," (p. 211, this volume) she suggests that it is worth pursuing the idea that children induce categories from the linguistic input. The fact that languages differ so markedly in their structuring of verbs and classifiers opens up great opportunities for cross-linguistic research on early word learning. Surveying a continually growing literature, Bowerman shows that children are indeed sensitive to the details of the meanings of the target language in areas such as spatial relations, clothing, dressing, and a variety of causative actions.

Bowerman presents detailed analyses of target linguistic structures and a view of the child as soaking up every detail of the linguistic input, unguided by universalist biases. Given the child's remarkable sensitivity to the input, the challenge is to explain the fact that children still make some errors. For example, English-speaking children may say that they are *opening* some

Lego blocks, rather than *taking apart* some Lego blocks. She refers to several mechanisms that could be operative here. First, there is a cue strength tuning process that can increase attention to dimensions such as the sharpness of the instrument used for English *cut*, as opposed to Spanish *cortar*. This process may well tap into the types of comparisons that Gentner has described in the theory of structural alignment. Second, there is a process of competition (MacWhinney, 1987) that eventually leads the child to extend *take apart* into the semantic area previously occupied by *open*. The final stages of fine-tuning of this competition appear to involve what Bowerman, Brown (1958), MacWhinney, and others have called cue search. In this process, the detection of errors in the use of terms triggers a search for dimensions that can predict correct usage. For example, a child may come to realize that you can only *open* something that you can also *close*. As a result, errors involving opening things like nuts and oranges will drop out relatively early. However, some errors involving the separation of assemblies such as Legos may remain for still further cue search.

Gershkoff-Stowe applies dynamic systems theory to conceptual development. According to her view, self-organizing processes centered around the child's actions shape cognitive development across multiple times scales within particular contexts. Here, Gershkoff-Stowe focuses on the ways in which children use repeated grouping and touching of objects to group them dynamically into categories. She finds that the sooner children begin manipulating the objects, the sooner they begin to group them into categories. Of course, one could argue that this is a simple "time on task" effect. However, the point is that children are engaged here in self-defined dynamic interactions with these objects that allow them to construct new categories. It is not the mere exposure to objects across a period of time that is important. It is what children do with the objects, both physically and cognitively, that shapes the emergence of the relevant categories.

In a second study (Namy et al., 1997), children further benefit from opportunities to compare and contrast between object classes, using a shape sorter. In effect, this study can be viewed as a dynamic externalization of what Gentner calls structural alignment or what others call cue search. In a final study, Gershkoff-Stowe shows how dynamic pressures shape categorization across multiple time scales. Children begin categorization in this experiment with a long-term shape bias. When confronted with evidence of the importance of the function of the object, children then demonstrate flexibility within the shorter time frame of the experiment.

Together, these four chapters illustrate the extent to which we now have a clear set of cognitive mechanisms that, in principle, should be sufficient for the acquisition of a conceptual world. We have clear ideas about structural alignment, causal status prediction, cue validity, cue search, competition, flexibility, and dynamic systems. We can use these concepts to predict the outcomes of carefully controlled experiments. But can we extend this thinking to the study and exegesis of concept learning in real-life situations?

In a sense this extension has already begun. The task used by Gershkoff-Stowe is a dynamic one similar to what children do in real play sessions. However, this task alone does not tell us much about the extraction of real categories. Providing another clue, Bowerman reports, at the conclusion of her chapter, an interaction between M and C (7;11). M describes a box with some broken toys and two scraps of felt as having "some other broken things" and C observes disdainfully that, "I wouldn't call felt broken, I would call it ripped." Presumably, M's use of "broken" is licensed by the fact that she includes the quantifier "other," which forces a comparison of a subset of the objects in the box to some previous set of objects. Why does C decide to ignore this interpretation of "other" and correct M (who is presumably an adult) at this point? Having access to a full video record of the interaction along with preceding context would certainly help us delineate the level at which C is constructing a cue search to delineate precise lexical borders or perhaps simply joking with M.

Fortunately, we now have a unique new opportunity to explore these issues. Over the last two years, researchers have begun to contribute large amounts of digitized video records of conversational interactions in the home and in the classroom. These sources are now directly accessible over the web through the servers of the Child Language Data Exchange System (CHILDES) at http://childes.psy.cmu.edu/data/ and TalkBank at http://talkbank.org/data/. Interactions of children in the home are at the CHILDES site, and interactions in classrooms are at the TalkBank site in the "classroom" data folders. In the following comments, I specifically refer to the "browsable" audio and video files at those sites. Browsable corpora include either audio or video recordings that are directly linked to the transcripts. By using QuickTime technology through your web browser, you can watch the video or listen to the audio and read the transcript concurrently. When you hit on a segment that reveals important aspects of concept learning, you can pause and repeat the playback. There are also facilities for commenting on segments of the interactions and sharing these comments with colleagues across the web.

Even at this early stage, the quantity of browsable data is so great that researchers interested in tracking out the naturalistic contexts of concept development would benefit from a set of guideposts and suggestions. Having now spent perhaps 100 hours reviewing these new resources, let me present three illustrations of how these data can teach us about the real world dynamic process of concept and word learning.

1. Consider first the case of the learning of the numerical interpretation of the word *dependable* in a seventh grade classroom in Nashville. The rele-

vant video was included in a *Journal of the Learning Sciences* special issue that is duplicated in the "JLS" folders on TalkBank. The class is discussing the performance of two types of batteries. Type A has a large number of long-lasting batteries, but also many failures. Type B has almost no failures, although fewer batteries were tested. In the lively discussion, several students focus only on the fact that type A has more successes, judging that therefore it is more "dependable." A dispute arises when one of the students points out that dependability is not just about successes, but also about lack of failures. This interaction not only illustrates the lateness of a full acquisition of the notion of dependability, but also some remarkable aspects of the social dynamics involved in the shifting of definitions in public spaces.

2. As a second example, consider the acquisition of the word *alert* by Mark MacWhinney at age 5 years, 4 months in the boys85.cha file on the CHILDES website. When the taping begins, the Father (Brian MacWhinney) is questioning the form *alerd bean* used by Mark. His older brother Ross then corrects Brian, saying that Mark was saying *alert*, not *alerd*. Eventually, it requires the collaborative participation of the whole family to figure out what Mark meant to say and where he learned it. For the details, please just go to the website and replay this interaction.

3. As a final example, consider the treatment of the phrase "when Ella was very small" in Michael Forrester's recordings from his daughter Ella at 28 months. Failing to use the conjunction "when" as a temporal delimiter, Ella then protests against her father's description of her as a "tiny, tiny baby."

What do we learn from examination of materials such as this? Perhaps the most immediate and obvious lesson is that current research on concept development fails to prepare us for the obvious fact that most conceptual learning is embedded in rich social contexts. These contexts are important not only for the way they present information, but also in the ways in which they provide for the dynamic sharpening of category boundaries. Through conversation, the borders of categories are explored, discussed, and refined. In effect, one of the major goals of conversation is the sharpening of shared categories.

This is not to say that concepts such as structural alignment, competition, dynamic exploration, causal prediction, and cue search are irrelevant to this social process. On the contrary, we can study real interactions to see exactly how children instantiate these processes. We use conversation to learn about causes, to resolve competitions, to align comparisons, and to search for cues. By studying these processes in their real, natural context we can make our understanding of the actual growth of the conceptual world far more accurate and precise.

REFERENCES

Brown, R. (1958). How shall a thing be called? *Psychological Review, 65,* 14–21.

Kemler Nelson, D., Frankenfield, A., Morris, C., & Blair, C. (2000). Young children's use of functional information to categorize artifacts: Three factors that matter. *Cognition, 77,* 133–168.

MacWhinney, B. (1987). The Competition Model. In B. MacWhinney (Ed.), *Mechanisms of language acquisition* (pp. 249–308). Hillsdale, NJ: Lawrence Erlbaum Associates.

Namy, L., & Gentner, D. (2002). Making a silk purse out of two sow's ears: Young children's use of comparison in category learning. *Journal of Experimental Psychology: General, 131,* 5–15.

Namy, L., Smith, L., & Gershkoff-Stowe, L. (1997). Young children's discovery of spatial classification. *Cognitive Development, 12,* 163–184.

Samuelson, L., & Smith, L. B. (1998). Memory and attention make smart word learning: An alternative account of Akhtar, Carpenter, and Tomasello. *Child Development, 69,* 94–104.

Chapter 13

Knowledge, Categorization, and the Bliss of Ignorance

Frank C. Keil
Yale University

This symposium is concerned with a question that has a long history in philosophy and the cognitive sciences. What degree of primacy should we grant to perceptual properties and relations in the development of the representational states that enable categorization?

One view of the developmental process is to resist any movement along the path to high-level cognition and knowledge, trying to maintain a pivotal role for perception and perceptual primitives. Categorization is first and foremost a product of perception and all other facets are optional add-ons, much like unneeded and unwanted accessories that auto dealers add on to make more of a profit. Such accounts tend to also distinguish between fast and slow categorization where fast, immediate, on-the-fly categorization is based on perceptual features. Slow, reflective categorization may be allowed to involve more components of higher level cognition, but that form of categorization is often marginalized to the work of philosophers and a few other unfortunate souls who are lost in thought instead of action.

A second view is to embrace more fully the influence of high-level cognition on adult categorization and then to figure out some way for the perceptually based categorization of children to metamorphose into that adult form. Very often, language is seen as the means behind the transformation, an old theme going back to Vygotsky in psychology and centuries earlier in philosophy (Vygotsky, 1962). In addition to language, other proposals for a mechanism behind such a shift include the emergence of metacognitive awareness, a shift from a processing of properties to relations (or, in slightly more formal terms, from 1-place predicates to n-place ones), or the emergence of logical thought.

A third alternative rejects the premise that infants are atheoretical, perceptually bound creatures. This alternative is usually (but not necessarily) cast in nativist terms in which babies come into the world knowing certain theories. Those theories typically include a naïve mechanics and a crude naïve psychology. By those accounts, somewhere in the language of thought of infants, if we look hard enough, we will find mental representations pretty much like those of adults. The representations are propositional, connected through chains of inferences that work like theories. This "rich interpretation" approach finesses many problems of developmental change and learning by making them unnecessary but does argue for a great deal of high-level cognition in the young infant.

I make the following arguments:

1. None of these three views is correct.

2. They are incorrect largely because of misunderstandings of the adult end state, that is, of the sorts of mental representations and information that guide categorization.

3. The end state is misunderstood at least in part because people tend to grossly overestimate the nature and detail of their explanatory knowledge. They think they have a much more vivid mechanistic understanding of world around them than they actually do; and this illusion is especially strong for explanatory knowledge as opposed to many other forms.

4. Although this adult illusion of explanatory depth does raise questions about the most popular "concepts-as-theories" views of concepts, categorization nonetheless does require a form of high-level cognition that tracks causal patterns and seeks out explanatory coherence. In that sense it seems to go beyond association and perception or at least requires of association and perception a way of tracking and using such relations.

5. A critical problem is how to track causal patterns in a world that has tremendous causal complexity and depth . . . that is, how to sparsely encode patterns in a manner that is useful but that is not computationally overwhelming. I suggest that we do so in an effective manner, which we also use to rely on the division of cognitive labor that exists in all cultures; that is, that our categorization is influenced not only by judgments of how the world is structured by also by how knowledge of that structure is clustered in other minds.

6. Finally, I argue that when our ability to track causal patterns is understood in this way, there is a good deal of developmental continuity, potentially right down to infancy, although my own data go no younger than preschool.

THE TROUBLE WITH THEORIES

Our views of the development of categorization are colored by the recent concepts-as-theories view in cognitive science (Gelman & Koenig, 2002; Murphy & Medin, 1985). This view argues that those mental representations responsible for categorization, namely concepts, are embedded in larger sets of beliefs that influence concept structure and use. Not only adults, but also children and even infants have been called intuitive scientists who reason about the world with detailed theories that they use to interpret patterns and relations in their physical and social worlds. At one level of description the case is a compelling one. The kinds of information that adults and children use seem to intrinsically involve not only a sense of causality but also structured causal relations and inferences that arise from that interconnected structure. The idea originally came from the philosophy of science, perhaps most dramatically from Kuhn's writings about scientific revolutions, where concepts such as mass or light changed dramatically as a function of changes in other related concepts (Kuhn, 1970, 1991). This theme has been extended into developmental work, with, for example, studies on how the concepts of heat and temperature became differentiated in development (Wiser & Carey, 1983). Thus, patterns of conceptual change in both the history of science and in development seemed to highlight the theory-dependent nature of concepts, and, by implication, categorization (Keil, 1989).

This idea spread to the study of adult concepts as the inadequacies of prior views became more apparent. The initial appeal of probabilistic views invoking either prototypes or exemplar sets became more limited as the influences of theory-like constructs became more evident. A somewhat more neutral way to describe those influences is in terms of "background knowledge" (Heit, 2001a); but that view can be rapidly trivialized if it is interpreted to mean that prior learning influences present and future learning, a truism that is intrinsic to any theory of concepts and categorization. The structured nature of that knowledge and its manner of influence must be specified.

It is possible to develop simulations that are prototype- or exemplar-based and that also incorporate prior knowledge. Thus, one might integrate prior exemplars into the set that is used in a learning experiment (Heit & Bott, 2000; Heit, 2001b). In this manner prior knowledge might influence learning in a way that looked like theoretical influences but that could be modeled in terms of a network model adhering to basic similarity principles. One problem is explaining which exemplars of prior knowledge are chosen as relevant to the learning task at hand. There has been some success with models that try different sets of exemplars and then, over time, favor those that give the most predictive success; and indeed, in some tasks the influence of prior knowledge has been shown to increase over time as better subsets of that knowledge are selected (e.g., Heit & Bott's "Baywatch" model). This selection problem, however, rapidly becomes computationally explosive in more real-world settings and seems implausible without further constraints on how relevant knowledge is selected. One way to guide selection is to consider the organization of prior knowledge into a limited number of high-level domains, a point returned to shortly.

In short, what we already know clearly influences what we learn next. That influence may help us weight certain features or feature types, discount or enhance certain correlations, guide induction about new properties and relations, or help us adopt thresholds and criteria in later categorization. This much is now widely agreed on and frames the remaining vigorous debates about the sorts of mental representations and processes responsible (e.g., Hampton, 2001). The notion of theories remains appealing to many because of the sense that we do develop mental models of how the world works, models that simulate some aspect of reality. When people overrule some feature correlations and not others, they don't merely cite exemplars from prior knowledge, they also describe how some correlations make more sense than others (Murphy, 2002). In categorizing birds, we weight very heavily wings and their role in enabling flight and any other features that enable those wings. We may use a very simple concept of the wings as supporting the bird on a cushion of air ignoring and/or misunderstanding the real aerodynamic principles (Murphy, 2002); but that concept guides our evaluation of features and feature relations in ways that seem to go far beyond reference to past exemplars.

Another argument for theory-like influences can be made from work on ad hoc categories (Barsalou, 1983). People adeptly classify objects for which they have never before considered the relevant category, whether it be things to take on a winter picnic, magazine subscriptions for a Cuban refugee, or politically correct restaurants. It appears in these cases that we set up goals and then define category structures around the causal consequences of trying to attain that goal. One can consider more familiar categories as being similarly influenced by goal-like structures, but where the goal might be a self-serving teleological one of flight for a bird or the human-serving one of an artifact such as an airplane (Keil, 1989).

The philosophy of science offers the most compelling arguments for the linkage between theories, concepts, and categorization. Theories define the nature of scientific inquiry and elucidate the concepts that comprise them. Whereas science has gradually evolved from folk understandings of the world, and whereas it is very much aware of its incomplete nature, it makes apparent sense to consider a smooth continuum from the theories of science to those of the layperson and to assume a similar embedding of the layperson's concepts within its theories. We know that theories in science attempt to pick up on regularities, often propose mechanisms that explain those regularities, and survive or perish based on their ability to make predictions. This borrowing of the obvious utility of theories in science, combined with the appeals to theories by laypeople, supports the idea of the concepts-as-theories approach for all of us. The actual canonical format of theories remains less clear however. The nomological–deductive model of science, in which a set of axiom-like principles are set forth and their deductive consequences explored, has not fared well as a model of theories in the natural science (e.g., Salmon, 1990). We have a sense that theories respect certain principles of coherence (e.g., Thagard & Verbeurgt, 1998), that they give some insight into mechanism (e.g., Ahn & Kalish, 2000), and that they are likely to contain a propositional structure capable of driving logical or quasilogical inferences (the extent of that propositional structure as opposed to other more image-like mental model structures, however, remains controversial).

But the concepts-as-theories point of view may be misleading in several respects. First, the analogy of theories in science to theories in a person's naïve sense-making of the world is suspect. Although science may strive for coherent tightly linked propositional structures, the individual scientist does so to a much lesser extent. Thus, the scientist as an individual in daily practice often operates on hunches, highly incomplete knowledge structures, and a good deal of serendipity and opportunism (Dunbar, 1995). If the individual scientist's theories are therefore not nearly as theory-like as they might seem, then the layperson's might be expected to be even weaker and more fragmentary. If so, why is it not more obvious that we have such weak theories? From time to time, the popular press does put out reports of the public's scientific illiteracy (e.g., Bodmer, 1985; Herbert, 1995); but even then we might assume that people have fairly well worked out theories, just ones that are often wrong.

In fact, we may assume we understand the world in far greater fidelity and clarity than we really do; we may be under the sway of an "illusion of explanatory depth." In a recent series of 12 studies, we documented such illusion in several adult populations (Rozenblit & Keil, 2002). Those studies typically have several steps:

1. We ask people to rate their own knowledge of how various artifacts and natural systems work.
2. Having offered such ratings, they are then asked to provide explanations for a subset of those rated.
3. They then re-rate their understanding in light of the quality of the explanations they offer.

4. They then are asked critical diagnostic questions that only an expert would know and again are asked to re-rate their understanding in light of their answer to the diagnostic question.

5. They are given a brief expert explanation and are again asked to re-rate their knowledge relative to the expert explanation.

These tasks ask people to evaluate long-held beliefs that they bring with them to the experiment, not recently learned information. The general result is a major drop in the ratings over successive re-ratings. Participants are routinely shocked at the shallow level of their knowledge and frequently say so. Moreover, it appears that the less educated the participants, the larger the drop may be.

This knowledge, which presumably corresponds most closely to intuitive theories, seems to be grossly miscalibrated such that people think they understand the world in far more detail than they do. The effect is much like that of "change blindness" blindness (Levin, Momen, Drivdahl, & Simons, 2000) in which people are grossly miscalibrated in terms of how much they think they will remember from visually presented scenes. The effect also shows a strong specificity to explanatory understanding as opposed to other kinds of knowledge. Ask participants how well they understand facts, such as the capitals of foreign countries, and although their mean ratings are the same as for the devices and phenomena, they show almost no drops in ratings over successive rating trials. Ask about more complex knowledge structures, such as those of procedures, and again people are well calibrated, showing no drops at all. Similarly, when rating their knowledge of narratives, such as the plots of familiar movies, people are accurate and indeed may be a bit conservative as to the depth of detail that they know. With narratives, it seems that the act of retelling the narrative often reminds the participant of other details.

There are, therefore, distinctive properties of explanatory understanding that make it especially likely to create an illusion of having much deeper knowledge than actually exists. Several factors seem to converge to make an especially strong illusion of knowing for our intuitive theories.

One factor is confusion between environmentally represented relations that can be recovered in real time from a system and those that are mentally represented. Many artifacts and natural systems can be understood when they are present and available for examination. One can figure out relations of their constituents and either see or infer causal interactions. This ability is confused with having mentally internalized those relations. For example, when a bicycle derailleur is in front of me, I may be able to figure out a variety of relations that explain its function, and when asked later how well I know that function, I may confuse my ability to explain it when present with a mental representation of its operations. (Our tasks make it clear that people are evaluating their internally represented knowledge, not how well they would do with an object present.) Indeed, the more salient and more visible an entity's parts, the larger the illusion of knowing. People tend to realize their more limited understandings of black box systems.

A second factor concerns the hierarchical nature of most complex systems and the iterative nature of explanation (Miyake, 1986). As was brilliantly observed by Herb Simon many years ago, much of the artificial and natural world can be understood as hierarchically organized sets of stable subassemblies with lawful principles governing their interactions (Simon, 1997, 2000). This kind of organization enables more reliable construction of complex structures. It also enables one to represent relations among high-level units and to avoid having to unpack them further. I may, for example, know that a computer has functional parts such as a disk drive, a CPU, a display, and keyboard, and know something about the functional properties of these units, but have little or no idea of how they themselves are made up of smaller functional units. Similarly, I may have some sense of what the kidney and the heart do while having very little sense of their internal organization and the necessary functional subcomponents. The illusion may occur when people get a surge of understanding at one level and confuse it with having an understanding at a deeper level. We have all had rushes of insight only to be later caught up short when we subsequently realize that we don't understand the next level down at all. This is all too often painfully revealed to us by a series of relentless "why" questions from a young child; indeed it is impressive just how few steps of such questions are needed to show up our ignorance.

There are other factors that also contribute to the especially strong illusion for explanations. One involves the rarity of actually giving explanations such that we cannot usually examine our past successes and failures. Another factor involves the indeterminacy of the end states of explanations and the corresponding difficulty of knowing what it means to have a successful complete explanation. Consider the difference here between procedural and explanatory knowledge. If asked how well one knows the procedure for making a long distance call to Europe, it is clear what it means to succeed; but what does it mean to have a successful explanation for why water is transparent to light? For many of us, we have little idea of what success looks like in any detail.

The adult studies, with a range of adult populations, reveal a consistent tendency to see ourselves as having much more detailed mechanistic understandings of the world than we really do. This tendency is also present at least by the age of 5 and probably quite a bit younger. If one adapts the tasks just described so as to make them more child-friendly, the same drops of re-rating occur. Children tend to rate their understanding higher than adults, perhaps also reflecting a higher level of optimism in young children in general (Lockhart, Story, & Chang, 2002); but, above and beyond this general overconfidence, they also show a clear selectivity in their understanding, dropping over time for explanatory understanding but not for knowledge of procedures, where they in fact re-rate their knowledge a bit higher over successive trials (Mills & Keil, 2004).

It is tempting to interpret these results as a fatal blow for the concepts-as-theories view. People seem to vastly overestimate their understandings of the world, such that their true intuitive theories hardly seem to deserve the status of theories at all, and children seem to be even worse. Perhaps we think of our concepts as deeply enmeshed in theories when in fact there is no neat set of beliefs in which to embed them. In one sense this interpretation is correct. If the concepts-as-theories view requires that we have rich mechanistic understandings of the world that can be stated in explicit terms by their owners, the view is plainly false. If intuitive theories are to be considered detailed mental models of the world, then we also do not have them.

Yet consider, for a moment, the implausibility of the strong claim that we do have fully accurate causal understandings of everyday phenomena. Unlike many other kinds of knowledge, causal understanding is quite often indefinitely deep. Ask how a helicopter flies, why there are tides, or how the kidney filters blood and the route to a full explanation is a very long one. It is not feasible for most of us to have such deep knowledge in most areas. The network of causal relations that pertain to objects and properties in the world around us is truly massive. The same properties can enter into many different causal relationships both in terms of ones that help create the presence or endurance of the property and in terms of those that describe its consequences. For example, the property of being magnetic arises from properties of an element's or compound's atomic and molecular structure. That story in detail is a very complex one that is still not fully understood by physicists. Being magnetic also has an extraordinary range of causal consequences ranging from all the uses of magnetic properties in artifacts to phenomena such as the aurora borealis. We do not grasp all of these causal links and of course cannot anticipate uses in yet-to-be-invented artifacts.

It is often noted that visual scenes have far more information inherent in them than is fully neurally codable, leading to analyses in which human vision performs sparse encodings and the biological analogue to compression algorithms (Seul, O'Gorman, & Sammon, 1999). Whatever complexity exists for visual features, it is far greater for causal and relational complexity. Consider a city street scene and all the causal patterns at work as well as the likely past and future ones. The list is nearly endless. This point is hardly controversial (Wilson & Keil, 1998). For causality as well there must be sparse encodings, but unlike those in some areas of vision these are not fully reversible compressions; that is, some real information is never encoded; instead a higher level "gist" is extracted, one that irretrievably misses details and may well include distortions as a result.

The causal patterns associated with explanatory understanding are not the same as those associated with "scripts," which are summary representations of highly repetitive causal patterns (Schank & Abelson, 1977). Scripts are often merely prototypes for events with none of the relevant explanatory understanding; indeed, that lack of such an explanatory component may have been a primary reason for their disappearance from the literature. The venerable restaurant script, for example, describes sequences concerning clients, waiters, and food service but contains no information about why people eat in restaurants, why they pay for their services, or why they usually don't attempt to cheat. The contrast with scripts is important because sparse encodings of causal relations must not be equated with encodings of surface event sequences that are often much closer to procedural knowledge than to explanatory knowledge.

It is therefore apparent that we are unable to track the full causal complexity of the world and do not remotely approach full explanatory understanding of most things that we encounter. Why then assume that we track causal patterns at all? Perhaps we simply notice feature frequencies and correlations and, because correlations often indicate causation, use that correlational information as our touchstone for inferences. The reasons for thinking we do a good deal more are several, but roughly come down to two points. First, without some biases to prefer some causal patterns over others, we would lack critical guidance in choosing among which feature frequencies and correlations to monitor. Second, often the most parsimonious explanation of our behavior comes from assuming that we track and use causal patterns. (There are nuances that try to capture causal inferences through more complex conditional correlational matrices [Cheng, 2000; Glymour, in press; Pearl, 2000]. Those mechanisms may sometimes be ways in which we come to infer cause and mechanism but they do not substitute for our representations of causality itself.)

The influences of causal patterns are often the most dramatic in studies on categorization. Consider for example, studies by Lin and Murphy (1997) in which having been taught a new category of artifact with several exemplars, participants generalized to quite different new cases depending on the causal interpretation applied to the original category (e.g., a kind of horse feeder, a kind of seed fertilizer). This study is particularly interesting because it shows how judgments of visual similarity are influenced by prior adoption of one or another explanatory scheme. Thus, the same stimuli sequences in learning trials can have dramatically different cognitive consequences when they are framed in different causal manners. How can such effects be understood in the face of the apparent paucity of true theory?

Skeletons in the Mind's Closet

Two themes are relevant to ways in which we might be guiding categorization and other aspects of reasoning through reference to high-level causal patterns while not having intuitive theories in the traditional sense: implicit understanding and skeletal systems of interpretation. The implicit theme, as is developed in more detail in studies described shortly, is simply that we may know a good deal about the causal patterns associated with various categories and phenomena without being able to articulate their nature, especially at earlier points in development. The skeletal theme echoes a notion that is now seen in many different ways in the literature. References to "framework theories" (Wellman, 1990), skeletal beliefs (Gelman & Brenneman, 1994), core theories (Spelke, 2000), interpretative frames (Hunt & Minstrell, 1994), and "modes of construal" (Keil, 1992, 1995), all converge on an idea of adults and children constraining their understandings without fully predetermining them. The trick lies in not allowing these two themes to become fudge factors for cases where one cannot find a traditional theory. I illustrate ways in which quite precise patterns of results support this perspective over others and how it leads to certain kinds of experiments and predictions, and finally to a different way of understanding categorization, its development, and how "high-level" cognition is involved.

One way to address the problem of what it means to have a sparse theory is to step back for a moment from considerations of the representational formats of the theory and to ask what sorts of information seem to be used. This strategy has often been used to great effect in studies of perception and perceptual development. Consider the case of depth perception. For years, most researchers did not ask about the internal representational and computational states and processes responsible for the ability to see objects in depth. Instead, they asked about the sorts of information that might help specify the layout of objects in depth and asked which ones are used in what contexts. Motion parallax cues, binocularity disparity cues, pictorial cues, and convergence cues have all been considered, among others, with some striking developmental patterns suggesting clear sequences in what sort of information is used to specify depth at what ages (Kellman & Banks, 1997). That work may now constrain models of internal representational and computational states, but it was not the point of departure for research.

The same strategy can be taken with respect to the kinds of information that is encoded and used in categorization and reasoning. With respect to sparse theories, we can therefore ask what sorts of information is used that might powerfully constrain explanations. There are now several such kinds for which there is considerable evidence. A few examples here will suffice to make the more general point and motivate the next section of this chapter.

One pattern concerns causal status, or, roughly, that the first element in causal sequence has a priority in weighting features for a concept (Ahn, Kim, Lassaline, & Dennis, 2000; Ahn & Luhmann, chap. 11, this volume). Even when features co-occur equally, the first one in a chain has an enhanced role and people attend to and use that piece of information to guide their judgments. This bias seems to extend to quite young children as well (Ahn, Gelman, Amsterlaw, Hohenstein, & Kalish, 2000), suggesting that a preference for early members in causal chains may be relatively constant over much of development. Even when early and late members have the same predictive value, the earlier occurring element intuitively seems more basic or primary.

Another pattern concerns causal diversity. If one considers cases where a single cause has a cascading downward set of branching causal consequences, terminal elements that are further apart in that tree structure are considered stronger evidence for the original cause than adjacent ones. People keep track of the hierarchical structure of a causal system, even when it is not presented as such, and then use that information to guide judgments about the likely causal agents in a situation (Kim & Keil, 2003). For example, if getting Lyme tick disease is seen as having a certain set of branching causal consequences, such as neurological and skeletal problems, one is more confident about the cause of a Lyme vaccine with more distantly related terminal effects such as a neural and skeletal problem than with two terminal effects of the same type, such as two neural effects or two skeletal effects. Thus, in constructing hunches about how a system works and what causes are in play, causal diversity may play a role. Moreover, this effect may occur even when people are not explicitly aware of the causal hierarchy that is involved.

A third pattern is causal relevancy, knowing what kind of properties are likely to be causally relevant in a domain. This requires both a classification of properties into types (e.g., color properties, shape properties, etc.) and then noting how they vary across categories. We have done a series of studies in this area and have found that people are quite sensitive to variations in causal relevancy and use them to guide category judgments (Keil, Smith, Simons, & Levin, 1998). In more recent work we have shown how such information constrains which explanations one would prefer. Thus, if one is trying to learn about a new kind of unfamiliar carpenter's tool and is presented with two explanations about its key properties, one of which puts great emphasis on its color, its surface markings, and the kind of stuff it is made out of, whereas another explanation puts emphasis on its shape, its size, and the strength of its material, people will tend to judge the second explanation as better even when they know nothing about the details. They show roughly the opposite pattern of judgments for explanations about the nature of novel animals. Moreover, this sort of constraint on explanation is also present in fourth graders and probably younger children in a less verbally laden version of the task.

In these examples people encode a wide variety of causal patterns and use them to constrain judgments about category membership and about the quality of explanations. There are several other sorts of causal patterns they also seem to encode, ones that seem to capture quite abstract schemas. For example, one that we've encountered in many studies involves classifying phenomena that are governed by monotonic relations between forces and consequences and those that are not, which often captures a division between mechanical causal systems and social causal ones. How such patterns are mentally represented is not clear; that they are represented in some form and used is now very clear.

In a similar manner we seem to quickly encode relations of support, prevention, containment, and launching. There are fairly objective ways in which we can define these relations, and people seem sensitive to that information even though we are unclear as to how they pick up on it or store it. Moreover, this sensitivity does not mean that any relational structure is easily encoded. We know that other relations that may be equally simple on formal grounds are far more elusive. For example, people may be much less able to spontaneously notice interaction effects as opposed to main effects if we are to see the world in ANOVA terms.

In all of these cases, the tracking of causal patterns often seems to occur outside awareness. Thus, participants may be unaware of a hierarchical structure or causal diversity in an explicit sense while nonetheless giving responses showing that they are indeed sensitive to that information. Just as in the case of depth perception, information can be used heavily to guide thought and action without being explicitly invoked. My argument here is that causal information is just as real as distance or velocity information and is just as likely to be encoded in ways that often do not reach explicit awareness.

Two interrelated phenomena are at work here. First, there are several examples of ways in which adults, and children, are sensitive to what we would normally call "higher order causal patterns" and use them to guide their reasoning. Second, certain constellations of these patterns become associated with domains of thought or large-scale categories. Hand tools, furniture, living things, and thinking creatures are understood as having certain causal patterns that are largely distinctive to one of those domains. Thus, when presented with a novel member of one of these high-level categories, an individual is able to make inferences about more detailed causal patterns that govern members of those categories. By way of example, consider studies on contingently interacting "creatures" and how children as young as 10 months take social contingency of sounds as a cue to the attentional states of a featureless blob of fur (Johnson, 2000). Sometimes through picking up on a causal pattern, such as socially contingent responding, sometimes on the basis of a perceptual pattern, such as the human face, quite young children rapidly erect a way of causally construing the entity in front of them and of seeing its similarity to other possible members of the same category. Similarity and categorization are therefore influenced by what causal interpretations are applied to a stimulus. Certain abstract causal patterns are linked here with quite large domains.

In this sense, adults, children, and probably quite young infants do indeed have "theories." They are not detailed mechanistic understandings of how things work or why a particular configuration of properties stably exists. They are, instead, much more schematic expectations about the kind of causal patternings that are expected to be present in a large domain. They may not be expressible in language and may often occur outside of awareness but are nonetheless powerful guides to how we make sense of entities' behaviors and how we categorize them. The concepts-as-theories view is correct in its assertion that concepts and those behaviors that depend on concepts, categorization, induction, and conceptual combination, critically rely on internalized understandings of domain specific principles and causal patterns; but it is wrong in thinking this knowledge has to be either explicit or concretely detailed.

This sparser view of concepts-as-theories remains compatible with research findings showing how tracking of causal structure influences categorization and thought. Consider, for example, the causal status effect (see also Ahn & Luhmann, chap. 11, this volume). The position of properties in causal chains heavily influences their perceived importance in thought. But the actual chains that we mentally represent are likely to be far less detailed than we think. For example, a person might believe that something inside a living thing, called DNA, is responsible for a wide array of surface effects and is therefore more causally central. That person might further believe that intentions of agents are the initial causes for phenomenal properties of artifacts and thereby are more conceptually central for artifacts (Ahn, 1998). In this manner, the causal status effect might have a powerful influence on the conceived centrality of properties while not reflecting very much at all of the detailed causal relationships among features.

More detailed causal understandings may also have impacts in several ways. First, in tasks where specific causal relations are taught, those relations appear to immediately influence such factors as feature weighting (Ahn & Luhmann, chap. 11, this volume; Kim & Keil, 2003). Second, in domains where people have specific areas of expertise, they may well have somewhat more detailed knowledge that influences judgments. Finally, people often construct more detailed ad hoc theories on-the-fly with particular situational support; and when they do, any causal chains so constructed might well influence judgments of feature centrality and thereby of categorization.

One implication of causal knowledge as sparse and skeletal in nature is that much of cognitive development proceeds from the abstract to the concrete. Children fill in more and more mechanistic details with more and more experience. This sort of developmental patterns seems to run contrary to almost a century of research claiming the opposite (e.g., Vygotsky, 1962; Werner & Kaplan, 1963). It is still often said that childhood is a period of being hopelessly concrete followed by a time of more abstract awareness. The two trends, however, are not contradictory, for several reasons. First, much of the developmental change from "concrete to abstract" comes in terms of explicit discussion of entities. It is true that children find it easier to talk about basic-level categories as opposed to superordinates as well as about simple properties as opposed to relations. But such an ability to explicitly describe does not equal the ability to respond systematically to the same kind of information. Only upper level psychology majors and some artists may be able to describe explicitly the different cues that specify depth, but they are all clearly used by preverbal infants. There is an interesting research program concerning why some sorts of categories, properties, and relations are more easily expressible than others; but that program is not at all the same as that which asks how people might be sensitive to that information and use it to guide thought and action.

A second factor suggesting a concrete to abstract shift may be the stronger tendency in younger children to default to the most immediately available concept in the case of ignorance, much as adults do. Thus, for many years there were claims of a syntagmatic to categorical shift in development, in which a child's first associations to words were the next thematically related element in discourse (e.g., "barks" to "dog," instead of "cat"). Later work, however, suggests that with sufficiently low frequency words, even adults will respond in the same manner (Cole & Means, 1981). Thus, under various conditions of cognitive load, it is quite possible to see a shift toward apparently more concrete thought.

Categorizing Knowledge and Categorizing the World

There is an extensive research program ahead that seeks to better understand the sorts of patterns people use in interpreting causal structures and how those interpretations vary across domains and contexts. One particularly interesting demonstration involves cases where people judge the clustering of knowledge in other minds. This is firstly a problem of categorization of knowledge; but it is also, and more interestingly for our purposes here, a problem of one's views about the clustering of causal underpinnings of stable categories and phenomena. Moreover, it illustrates the implicit nature of this knowledge.

All cultures have divisions of labor as specialized groups develop different areas of expertise. These divisions of physical labor are related to divisions of cognitive labor. The doctor/healer is assumed to have a different form of expertise from the mechanic/fixer. Moreover, as is revealed vividly by the illusion of explanatory depth studies, most of our knowledge is surprisingly shallow. Indeed, our knowledge has to be shallow because of the inherent complexity and depth of the causal structures governing phenomena around us (Wilson & Keil, 2000). We must rely on others' expertise to gain any traction in making sense of the world. Indeed, we seem to do this every time we utter commonplace words. Thus, the use of language terms, especially those for natural kinds such as "gold," "tiger," or "water," relies critically on presumed expertise in others (Putnam, 1975). When I call a certain pile of stuff "gold," I am assuming that some group of experts could back me up or at least tell me if I really am right. If I point to something that looks and feels like gold and call it gold, and a skeptic asks how I really know it is gold and am not being fooled by a sophisticated form of fool's gold, I will declare that the question can be decided by an expert. Ask me further about how an expert might help and I am likely to say that the internal molecular structure of gold is unique and that an expert can tell if this stuff has that structure and therefore is really gold.

A great deal of cognition is going on in these cases of deference to authority, and much of it has powerful implications for categorization. In particular, how does one know how to identify the relevant experts? What aspects of an entity are relevant to an area of supporting expertise? Why, for example, does one defer to an expert on gold's internal microscopic structure and not to one on gold's value in the financial markets? What does an expert have to know to be a likely authority on the question at hand?

There are many ways to go about addressing these problems, but one that has proven quite effective involves asking adults and children about how knowledge is clustered in the minds of others. One way to do this is to describe one phenomenon that a person understands well and ask which of two other phenomena that person is also likely to understand.

Consider the following example:

Henry knows all about why water is transparent to light and mercury is not.

Because he knows all about the transparency of water, which of the following is he more likely to know a lot about?

A. Why gold conducts electricity better than iron.
   or
B. Why gold prices rise in times of high unemployment.

Most adults will pick an item like A as their choice instead of an item like B. That they do so with a good deal of consensus is quite remarkable. First, they do so often without seeming to have any knowledge of how to answer these questions. Thus, most adults have no clue of how to explain why water is transparent to light, or why one metal conducts better than another, or how gold prices are related to other economic indicators. How, then, do they seem to achieve both consensus and confidence about the relevant expert?

Intuitively, it seems that the initial problem in this example is one of physics, in particular in the sub-area of electromagnetism, and that example A is in that same sub-area whereas example B is a problem of economics. If so, then one might speculate that a college education and explicit instruction on the nature of economics, physics, and chemistry is the source of insight. Perhaps in such courses the relations between transparency and conductivity and molecular structure are discussed on the one hand and between prices and unemployment in the other. If so, then college students who have taken the relevant courses should do well in such tasks whereas those who have not should do poorly. This is not the case. All college students do quite well and do so across a range from highly selective universities to ones that have open admissions and in a manner that is independent of their majors.

More importantly for our purposes, with some simplifications of the terms, much younger participants can also do quite well in these tasks, not just high school or middle school students, but kindergartners as well, and, in a more modified version of the task, preschoolers. Yet no one seriously thinks that young elementary school children have received instruction in the nature of the natural and social sciences, or indeed that they have ever heard anything whatsoever about those disciplines as such. What then, do they know that enables them to cluster knowledge in the minds of others in ways that seem to reflect major disciplines of the natural and social sciences? The answer is related to how the intuitive understandings of causal patterns described earlier are used effortlessly to constrain judgments and to influence categorization. To see how this could be so, consider the task in more detail.

To develop a task that would work with young elementary school children we needed stimuli that would describe phenomena that made sense to a young child but which at the same time tapped into principles central to an academic discipline. We asked participants in various majors, who were also naïve as to the purpose of the experiment, to list examples of phenomena that captured core aspects of major disciplines and which would be easily understandable, as phenomena, by young children. In one series of studies we gave them the following disciplines and subdisciplines: physics, chemistry, cellular biology, evolutionary biology, cognitive psychology, social psychology, economics, and political science. These can be understood as being arrayed in a hierarchical tree structure of the disciplines, starting with the natural and social sciences, broken down next into the physical, biological, behavioral, and sociological sciences, and finally into the eight categories corresponding roughly to the eight academic departments or large sections of departments.

There are several reasons why we picked these divisions in particular and why we avoided the humanities and engineering. The most relevant reason here is that we wanted areas that at least pretend to have core disciplinary principles and that have a large community of scholars with which they are associated.

From this tree of disciplines, we used our experts' descriptions to develop a set of phenomena at each of the bottom levels, for example, six problems in physical mechanics, six problems in chemistry, and so on. They were edited to make the descriptions as verbally simple as possible and also with an eye toward reducing cues arising from typical word co-occurrence patterns. More will be said about that second point shortly. Each description was also accompanied by a picture that served as a cue to the phenomenon but that on its own did not provide information that would bias clusterings, as revealed by a later test of clustering on the basis of pictures alone.

A specific example of the stimuli used with children should make things clearer:

This expert knows all about why people make a shopping list when they are going shopping later (cognitive psychology).
Would they know more about
(Y) why you can't remember things from when you were a baby (cognitive psychology),
or would they know more about
(Z) why a big, heavy boat takes a really long time to stop (physics)?

This particular comparison is what we call a "far" comparison, in that it took disciplines that were only joined at a fairly high node in the hierarchical tree structure of the disciplines. By contrast, a near comparison might pit a problem in biology against one in physics, or a problem in cognitive psychology against one in social psychology.

Children engaged in a pretest discussion of the notion of experts, using familiar examples such as doctors. They then heard triads of the sort just shown and also were shown pictures that accompanied each sentence and that served as memory cues. The pictures on their own (e.g., a written list, a big boat next to a small boat, and a baby) were not informative as to the relevant discipline and on their own were not sorted into discipline-based categories.

This "who knows what" task was immediately obvious to even the 5-year-olds. They clearly understood the idea of expertise and that knowledge was not distributed evenly in other minds. Even though adults may all know a great deal more than the children know, the children still saw different groups of adults with different areas of expertise. Moreover, expertise meant that an expert knew things that were clustered in sets of related beliefs. Even more important, children usually appealed to their notions of causal patterns in the world to solve these questions about clustering of knowledge in other minds. Put simply, they took the questions we posed them as decidable on the basis of what phenomena in the world were likely to arise from a common or closely related set of principles. They therefore seemed to approach the task as most adults do. If asked what else George knows by virtue of knowing x, they tended to think about the sorts of causal patterns that give rise to x and assumed that if George really knew those principles he would also know about other phenomena that were governed by similar principles. As adults, we say something like, "Oh, George knows mechanics" and therefore infer that he will understand other phenomena governed by mechanics. Young children certainly don't think explicitly of the term "mechanics," but they do seem to be able to implicitly grasp that domain.

Even kindergartners were well above chance levels in deciding how to cluster far comparisons across the disciplines. These included cases such as physics versus cognitive psychology, molecular biology versus economics, and chemistry versus social psychology. It was quite apparent to them, across most stimuli instances, how to cluster knowledge. With the near comparisons, such as physics versus chemistry, and economics versus political science, there were major developmental changes during the elementary school years and not until the fourth grade was there clear above-chance performance on all the near items. There are much more detailed stories about these patterns of change and how some, such as cognitive versus social psychology, are much slower to change than others, but those details are beyond the scope of this chapter. It suffices here to show that children as young as 5 years are able to make decisions about the cognitive division of labor that appear to be based on a sense of the causal principles and patterns that underlie basic academic disciplines. They seem to know something about why it is that disciplines such as physics, biology, and psychology were set up as such.

How could these children be solving these problems? Indeed, how do adults do it when they seem to know so little about how to explain the phenomena, often apparently nothing at all? In many cases adults who are confident about how to cluster these items do not refer to academic disciplines; they often are at a loss for words in explaining how they arrived at their judgments. In other cases, they refer to underlying relations that are shared, such as that both items involve something to do with objects and their motion, or the exchange of goods. Children make similar comments, sometimes very informative ones. For example, with several of the physical mechanics items, a monotonic relation between forces and consequences is at work and the children pick up on it and sometimes mention it.

We are embarking on several follow-up studies to better understand how it is that children make these judgments. Their comments suggest use of simple schemas that are abstract enough to cover many central instances of a disciplinary category. Based on analyses of their transcripts, we came up with some possible schema that they might be using for each comparison. For mechanics, a critical component seemed to be bounded objects in motion. For social psychology, it seemed to be dyadic interactions; for economics, exchanges of goods involving prices. Using these sorts of schemas it is possible to develop "−schema/+discipline" stimuli that are, for adults at least, still in the discipline, but nonconforming with the schema, and other stimuli that, for adults, seem to conform with the schema but still be outside the discipline (+schema/−discipline). With the bounded objects in motion schema, the −schema/+discipline case might be a case of static mechanics, such as "why building cranes get narrow and narrow up to the top." The +schema/−discipline case would involve examples such as "why you can't see bullets whizzing by," which are really in the discipline of cognitive psychology. We see a strong developmental trend with younger children being more likely to reject −schema/+discipline cases and to accept +schema/−discipline ones. Even in these cases, however, they never fully reject the −schema/+discipline cases or fully accept the +schema/−discipline cases, suggesting that they are using multiple schemas or that we haven't homed in on quite the right schema for particular domains. It would seem, however, that the young children must use some sort of high-level schema that enables them to see similarities between domains that are quite different at a lower level and for which they have little or no knowledge of specific mechanisms.

Because the academic disciplines as we know them today are in many cases not even 100 years old, why should we expect young children to do well on this task at all? If such expertise clusterings were not apparent in the university of 1800, why should they be to young children? The answer involves the difference between having a general template for academic disciplines and seeing local similarities. In other work, we have shown that many college-educated adults have difficulty sorting knowledge into discipline-based categories when other ways of sorting are in direct competition with the discipline-based manner. The triad tasks used here are carefully set up so that none of the competing information is at work. I have little doubt that these triad tasks would have been sorted in the same manner by adults of 1700, or even 1000 BC, as adults of today. We hope shortly to engage in cross-cultural studies with very traditional peoples to further explore the generality of these intuitions.

We have also discounted one model that would explain children's success at clustering knowledge on the basis of word co-occurrence patterns in discourse. There has been a surge of interest in recent years in new techniques for modeling co-occurrence patterns of words in text, with a major improvement in the ability to track not just how often two words occur together in a specified size of coherent text, but also to track how often each of those words occur in text with a third word, which then provides a link between the first two. One of the most successful approaches treats these co-occurrence patterns as vectors in a relatively low dimensional space (e.g., approximately 400 dimensions) that are then used to measure the conceptual similarity of passages of text (Landauer, Foltz, & Laham, 1998). It might be that young children are using that kind of analysis to solve the knowledge clustering problems. To explore this possibility, we selected words in the construction phase of our stimuli so that they intuitively would not be likely to fit such patterns and thereby supply clues as to how to cluster "why" statements. We then submitted all the sentences to the Latent Semantic Analysis (LSA) program (Landauer et al., 1998) and received outputs that indeed showed us that the program was at chance levels in sorting the why statements into discipline-based categories. These were the same statements that children as young as 5 sorted at above chance levels into discipline-based categories.

It may well be that if the stimuli contained words that LSA did cluster in a disciplinary manner, the clustering in triad tasks would be even more discipline based. Thus frequency-based information might well enhance ability in this task. But the critical point here is that the children seem to be able to do quite well without it. Put differently, they seem to be looking through the words at the real-world situation described by those words rather than using the words' statistical properties in discourse as the point of departure for their reasoning.

The division of cognitive labor tasks seem to be solved at all ages by reference to conceptions of the meaningful causal clusters that exist in the world and the assumption that one who really understands one phenomenon arising from those clusters is likely to understand other phenomena arising from the same cluster, presumably because they understand how the principles of that cluster generate surface phenomena. Moreover, those sparse, theory-like relations that people do seem to track in the world around them seem to be the same ones that people use to solve the division of cognitive labor problem.

Children are not just like adults, however. They have more difficulty telling apart more closely related disciplines. Moreover, they can be more easily fooled by distracters that seem to involve similar schemas. In addition, if one pits clustering knowledge by discipline against other ways such as clustering by goals, younger children prefer the goal-clustering basis. Indeed, in such cases of competing bases for knowledge clusters, a clear preference for a disciplinary base does not really appear until adolescence, and even then, not for everyone. So while, in a simpler version of the task, even preschoolers can show sensitivity to discipline-based ways of clustering knowledge (Lutz & Keil, 2002), they don't do so with a strong preference over other alternatives until several years later (Danovitch & Keil, 2004).

Categories and Development

From early in infancy we are sensitive to many of the causal patterns that reliably occur around us. We obviously cannot track all of these or even do so in specific domains in any detail. We do manage to track the causal gist in a way that seems to do several things at once. First, it helps constrain the features and feature relations we think are most central to a category. Second, it helps us decide how to cluster knowledge in the minds of others and, in doing so, be able to shift some of the burden of knowing to other minds yet feel confident that we have shifted the burden in a sensible and reliable manner that we could turn to when pressed for further information. We have a fair degree of confidence that we know what experts to defer to in what contexts. Different experts know different things and one important way those differences are organized is by mirroring the ways in which natural phenomena are clustered by adherence to common sets of principles, usually of a causal nature.

I doubt that young infants think in ways that rely on the division of cognitive labor, but by age 3 or 4 years, they definitely do, and their judgments of who knows what reflect their understandings of the world, understandings that influence their concepts and categorization as well. I am not at all sure what happens earlier, but I suspect that the ability to link certain abstract causal patterns to high-level categories is very early emerging. The Gibsonian idea of affordances may be one way in which infants manifest an ability to sense the causal consequences of various objects in the world around them, at least in terms of their actions on them. When babies see an object as a potential container, or supporter, or blocker, those sorts of relations powerfully influence how they understand the object, and presumably the similarity relations they see and the categories they apprehend. Those affordance-based relations may be the steppingstone out of which other causal patterns are noticed and become the basis for more sophisticated reasoning about objects.

The concepts-as-theories notion is therefore amended here to make the theories sparse, often implicit, gists of broad domains of causal patterns. These patterns are linked in various configurations to large-scale domains and to hunches about how pieces of knowledge map onto those domains. The illusion of explanatory depth may be a mechanism through which people feel they know enough at this high level by giving them the impression they know a good deal more when in fact it is only indirectly known through revisiting the phenomena and through sophisticated chains of reliable deference to those who do know. We do not want or need to be obsessional explanation seekers in a world that is indefinitely complex. We want to find the level of causal understanding that will constrain our reasoning and categorization yet not pose an excessive burden of its own. The illusion of explanatory depth may be a way of helping us stop and rely on other factors that do not involve our internally representing causal relations, especially the division of cognitive labor and reacquiring information from the actual object or phenomenon itself.

The largest problem remaining concerns the specification of what we do know that is good enough. I suggested that some structural properties of causal systems are tracked, such as causal status, causal relevancy, and causal diversity. In addition, there may a relatively small set of causal/perceptual relations of the sort that Mandler called "image schema" that capture relations like containing, launching, blocking, preventing, and supporting (Mandler, 2004). Others might include some sense of the ways that a thing's essence or vital force is causally linked to surface phenomena, a route that is very different for, say, biological phenomena, than it is for other natural or artificial phenomena (Gelman, 2003).

What develops are several things: (a) a grasp of more concrete mechanisms, (b) more access to implicit or nonverbal information, (c) an ability to more strongly override mere correlation or high typicality, (d) a more richly articulated and systematic set of schematic expectations, and (e) a way to stitch together local fragments of specific causal patterns with the higher order abstract relations. In the aggregate these factors can make young children's categorization behavior look quite different from that of adults. These differences, however, should not mask what may be much more powerful continuities in how both children and adults track and use abstract causal patterns to categorization.

This chapter started with three views of cognitive development, arguing that each had limitations. The views can be summarized as follows:

1. Perception-based cognition as dominant throughout development.
2. Cognition as metamorphosizing from perception-based forms to high-level theory-based forms.
3. Cognition as containing a theory-based format from the start.

This chapter has offered arguments and described studies that illustrate problems with each of these views.

The perception-throughout-development view seems problematic for several reasons. First, it is normally associated with development proceeding from concrete to abstract forms, yet there are now many examples of cognitive development proceeding in opposite directions, whether it be in language acquisition or the understanding of biology. Moreover, its characterization of the endstate of adult cognition as dominated by perception and association is also problematic given recent demonstrations that high-level thought about abstract causal relations can occur in the first moments of cognition, sometimes even faster than more perceptually based similarity computations (Ahn & Luhmann, chap. 11, this volume).

The second view, of cognition as metamorphosizing from perceptual and associative formats to more theory-laden and complex relational forms is also problematic. Its older versions, as championed by Piaget, Bruner, and others, have long been challenged on the grounds that stagelike changes in representational or computational capacities are extremely hard to document. Moreover, recent demonstrations of preschoolers' sensitivities to abstract causal relations, to potential essences, and to the division of cognitive labor further make the point. There remains an active debate on the potential power of the emergence of language to transform thought, perhaps by providing a relational "glue" between previously unassociated domains or perhaps by providing new sorts of quasilogical operators, such as forms of quantification (Carey, 2002; Spelke, 2003). These views of the transforming power of language in development are controversial (Bloom & Keil, 2001), but even if they are borne out, they in no way make the case for the preverbal infant as either a perceptually driven or largely associative creature.

The third view, of the infant as a little theorist from the start, seems to be the only other alternative and therefore the most reasonable, having raised problems with the first two views. But it too is problematic in more subtle ways having to do with the idea of young children as having detailed theories of the world around them. The image of the child, and perhaps even the infant, as a little scientist runs into trouble once one looks carefully at what those "theories" are actually like. Not just children, but also adults have far coarser understandings of causal relations and mechanism than they think. This illusion of explanatory depth helps create a false impression of having richly detailed theories when in fact we have something much closer to crude gists. It therefore appears that the whole notion of theory-laden cognition needs to be revised.

The shallowness of explanatory understanding should not be interpreted as indicating that children and adults alike have cognitions that are largely perceptual and associative in nature. This chapter has discussed several examples of how children and adults are sensitive to causal relations and how those sensitivities have strong influences on categorization and cognition. Unlike the first and second views, the view of development proposed here grants abstract thought and sensitivity to causal structure to very young children and possibly infants. Unlike the third view, however, it is reluctant to ascribe rich and explicit theories to children and rarely even to adults. Instead, the view proposed here sees considerable developmental continuity in the ways in which children and adults are sensitive to high-level causal patterns and sees much of development consisting of the child's working out more mechanistic details.

ACKNOWLEDGMENTS

Preparation of this chapter and much of the research reported on was supported by NIH grants R01-HD23922 and R37-HD23922 to Frank Keil. Many thanks to Woo-Kyoung Ahn for most helpful comments on an earlier draft of this chapter.

REFERENCES

Ahn, W. (1998). Why are different features central for natural kinds and artifacts? The role of causal status in determining feature centrality. *Cognition, 69*, 135–178.

Ahn, W., Gelman, S. A., Amsterlaw, J. A., Hohenstein, J., & Kalish, C. W. (2000). Causal status effect in children's categorization. *Cognition, 76*, B35–B43.

Ahn, W., & Kalish, C. (2000). The role of covariation vs. mechanism information in causal attribution. In F. Keil & R. Wilson (Eds.), *Cognition and explanation* (pp. 199–226). Cambridge, MA: MIT Press.

Ahn, W., Kim, N. S., Lassaline, M. E., & Dennis, M. J. (2000). Causal status as a determinant of feature centrality. *Cognitive Psychology, 41*, 1–55.

Barsalou, L. W. (1983). Ad hoc categories. *Memory & Cognition, 11*, 211–227.

Bloom, P., & Keil, F. (2001). Thinking through language. *Mind & Language, 16*, 351–367.

Bodmer, W. (1985). *The public understanding of science*. London: Royal Society.

Carey, S. (2002). The origin of concepts: Continuing the conversation. In N. L. Stein, P. J. Bauer, & M. Rabinowitz (Eds.), *Representation, memory, and development: Essays in honor of Jean Mandler* (pp. 43–52). Mahwah, NJ: Lawrence Erlbaum Associates.

Cheng, P. W. (2000). Causality in the mind: Estimating contextual and conjunctive power. In F. C. Keil & R. Wilson (Eds.), *Cognition and explanation* (pp. 227–253). Cambridge, MA: MIT Press.

Cole, M., & Means, B. (1981). *Comparative studies of how people think: An introduction*. Cambridge, MA: Harvard University Press.

Danovitch, J. H., & Keil, F. C. (2004). Should you ask a fisherman or a biologist?: Developmental shifts in ways of clustering knowledge. *Child Development, 75*(3), 918–931.

Dunbar, K. (1995). How scientists really reason: Scientific reasoning in real-world laboratories. In R. J. Sternberg & J. Davidson (Eds.), *The nature of insight* (pp. 365–395). Cambridge, MA: MIT Press.

Gelman, R., & Brenneman, K. (1994). First principles can support both universal and culture-specific learning about number and music. In L. A. Hirschfeld & S. A. Gelman (Eds.), *Mapping the mind: Domain specificity in cognition and culture (pp. 369–390). New York: Cambridge University Press.

Gelman, S. A. (2003). The essential child. New York: Oxford University Press.

Gelman, S. A., & Koenig, M. A. (2002). Theory based categorization in early childhood. In D. H. Rakison & L. M. Oakes (Eds.), Early category and concept development: Making sense of the blooming buzzing confusion (pp. 330–359). London: Oxford University Press.

Glymour, C. (in press). Mental notes: Bayes nets and graphical causal models in psychology. Cambridge, MA: MIT Press.

Hampton, J. A. (2001). The role of similarity in natural categorization. In U. Hahn & M. Ramscar (Eds.), Similarity and categorization (pp. 13–28). London: Oxford University Press.

Heit, E. (2001a). Background knowledge in models of categorization. In U. Hahn & M. Ramscar (Eds.), Similarity and categorization (pp. 155–178). London: Oxford University Press.

Heit, E. (2001b). Putting together prior knowledge, verbal arguments, and observations in category learning. Memory & Cognition, 29, 828–837.

Heit, E., & Bott, L. (2000). Knowledge selection in category learning. In D. Medin (Ed.), Psychology of learning and motivation: Vol. 39. Advances in research and theory (pp. 163–199). San Diego, CA: Academic Press.

Herbert, B. (1995, March 1). A nation of nitwits. New York Times, p. A15(N).

Hunt, E., & Minstrell, J. (1994). A cognitive approach to the teaching of physics. In K. McGilly (Ed.), Classroom lessons: Integrating cognitive theory and classroom practices (pp. 51–74). Cambridge, MA: MIT Press.

Johnson, S. C. (2000). The recognition of mentalistic agents in infancy. Trends in Cognitive Science, 4(1), 22–28.

Keil, F. C. (1989). Concepts, kinds and cognitive development. Cambridge, MA: MIT Press.

Keil, F. C. (1992). The origins of an autonomous biology. In M. R. Gunnar & M. Maratsos (Eds.), Modularity and constraints in language and cognition: Vol. 25. The Minnesota Symposia on Child Psychology (pp. 103–137). Hillsdale, NJ: Lawrence Erlbaum Associates.

Keil, F. C. (1995). The growth of causal understanding of natural kinds: Modes of construal and the emergence of biological thought. In D. Sperber, D. Premack, & A. J. Premack (Eds.), Causal cognition: A multidisciplinary debate. 6th Symposium of the Fyssen Foundation (pp. 234–267). New York: Clarendon Press/Oxford University Press.

Keil, F. C., Smith, C. S., Simons, D., & Levin, D. (1998). Two dogmas of conceptual empiricism. Cognition, 65, 103–135.

Kellman, P. J., & Banks, M. S. (1997). Infant visual perception. In R. Siegler & D. Kuhn (Eds.), Handbook of child psychology: Vol. 2. Cognition, perception, & language (5th ed., pp. 103–146). New York: Wiley.

Kim, N. S., & Keil, F. C. (2003). From symptoms to causes: Diversity effects in diagnostic reasoning. Memory & Cognition, 31(1), 155–165.

Kuhn, T. (1970). The structure of scientific revolutions (2nd ed.). Chicago: The University of Chicago Press.

Kuhn, T. (1991). The road since structure. In A. Fine, M. Forbes, & L. Wessels (Eds.), PSA 1990 (Vol. 2, pp. 3–13). East Lansing, MI: Philosophy of Science Association.

Landauer, T. K., Foltz, P. W., & Laham, D. (1998). Introduction to latent semantic analysis. Discourse Processes, 25, 259–284.

Levin, D. T., Momen, N., Drivdahl, S. B., & Simons, D. J. (2000). Change blindness blindness: The metacognitive error of overestimating change-detection ability. Visual Cognition, 7, 397–412.

Lin, E. L., & Murphy, G. L. (1997). The effects of background knowledge on object categorization and part detection. Journal of Experimental Psychology: Human Perception and Performance, 23, 1153–1169.

Lockhart, K. L., Chang, B., & Story, T. (2002). Young children's beliefs about the stability of traits: Protective optimism? *Child Development, 73,* 1408–1430.

Lutz, D., & Keil, F. (2002). Early understanding of the division of cognitive labor. *Child Development, 73*(4), 1073–1084.

Mandler, J. M. (2004). *Foundations of mind: The origins of conceptual thought.* New York: Oxford University Press.

Mills, C. M., & Keil, F. C. (2004). Knowing the limits of one's understanding. The development of an awareness of an illusion of explanatory depth. *Journal of Experimental Child Psychology, 87,* 1–32.

Miyake, N. (1986). Constructive interaction and the iterative process of understanding. *Cognitive Science, 10*(2), 151–177.

Murphy, G. (2002). *The big book of concepts.* Cambridge, MA: MIT Press.

Murphy, G., & Medin, D. (1985). The role of theories in conceptual coherence. *Psychological Review, 92,* 289–316.

Pearl, J. (2000). *Causality.* New York: Oxford University Press.

Putnam, H. (1975). The meaning of 'meaning.' *Mind, language, and reality* (pp. 215–273). Cambridge, England: Cambridge University Press.

Rozenblit, L., & Keil, F. C. (2002). An illusion of explanatory depth. *Cognitive Science, 26,* 521–562.

Salmon, W. C. (1990). *Four decades of scientific explanation.* Minneapolis, MN: University of Minnesota Press.

Schank, R. C., & Abelson, R. (1977). *Scripts, plans, goals, and understanding.* Hillsdale, NJ: Lawrence Erlbaum Associates.

Seul, M., O'Gorman, L., & Sammon, M. J. (1999). *Practical algorithms for image analysis: Description, examples, and code.* Cambridge, England: Cambridge University Press.

Simon, H. A. (1997). *The sciences of the artificial* (3rd ed.). Cambridge, MA: MIT Press.

Simon, H. A. (2000). Discovering explanations. In F. C. Keil & R. A. Wilson (Eds.), *Explanation and cognition* (pp. 21–59). Cambridge, MA: MIT Press.

Spelke, E. S. (2000). Core knowledge. *American Psychologist, 55*(11), 1233–1243.

Spelke, E. S. (2003). What makes humans smart? In D. Gentner & S. Goldin-Meadow (Eds.), *Advances in the investigation of language and thought* (pp. 277–311). Cambridge, MA: MIT Press.

Thagard, P., & Verbeurgt, K. (1998). Coherence as constraint satisfaction. *Cognitive Science, 22,* 1–24.

Vygotsky, L. S. (1962). *Thought and language.* Cambridge, MA: MIT Press.

Wellman, H. M. (1990). *The child's theory of mind.* Cambridge, MA: MIT Press.

Werner, H., & Kaplan, B. (1963). *Symbol formation: An organismic developmental approach to language and the expression of thought.* New York: Wiley.

Wilson, R. A., & Keil, F. C. (1998). The shadows and shallows of explanation. *Minds & Machines, 8,* 137–159.

Wiser, M., & Carey, S. (1983). When heat and temperature were one. In D. Gentner & A. Stevens (Eds.), *Mental models* (pp. 267–297). Hillsdale, NJ: Lawrence Erlbaum Associates.

Chapter 14

A Parallel Distributed Processing Approach to Semantic Cognition: Applications to Conceptual Development

Timothy T. Rogers
University of Wisconsin–Madison

James L. McClelland
Carnegie Mellon University

Although conceptual development in infancy is a wide and varying field of study that encompasses many different points of view, there are, broadly speaking, two sets of empirical findings that are relevant to understanding the competencies that emerge over the first year of life. First, infants as young as 3 to 4 months are sensitive to visual similarities existing across discriminably different stimulus events, and can capitalize on these to guide their behavior in preferential-looking and dishabituation studies. In some cases, this perceptual learning skill is sufficient for very young infants to discriminate natural semantic categories, on the basis of the visual similarity and variability of the stimulus items encountered during habituation and test (e.g., Eimas & Quinn, 1994). However, at the youngest testable ages, infant behavior in this respect seems to be strongly linked to the visual structure of the specific items encountered during habituation and test, and does not appear to reflect stored knowledge about the conceptual relationships that may exist among stimulus items (Mareschal, French, & Quinn, 2000; Quinn & Johnson, 1997). Thus several researchers have suggested that very young infants are capable of forming "perceptual categories" to guide their expectations in looking tasks.

The second set of findings suggests that, toward the end of the first year of life, infants are less bound to the immediately observed perceptual properties of objects, and are sometimes able to respond to objects on the basis of somewhat abstract properties that are not directly apparent in the situation. In a series of studies employing several related methods, Mandler and her collaborators (e.g., Mandler & Bauer, 1988; Mandler, Bauer, & McDonough, 1991; Mandler & McDonough, 1993, 1996; Mandler, 1997, 2000) and other investigators (e.g., Pauen, 2002a, 2002b) argued that preverbal children's choices of replicas of objects to touch, to play with, and to use in imitations of actions performed by others, suggest that at the earliest testable ages (about 7 months) infants treat objects that share certain informative but abstract properties (such as self-initiated movement) as similar to one another, even if the objects happen to differ in many other perceptible respects. Moreover, infants at this age seem to be sensitive predominantly to very general conceptual distinctions among perceptually varying items, and only later come to honor finer distinctions when perceptual and conceptual relations do not happen to coincide (e.g., Mandler & Bauer, 1988; Mandler & McDonough, 1993; Mandler, 2002). There is considerable dispute regarding the interpretation of these data—specifically, whether they can be explained solely with reference to perceptual learning mechanisms; whether or not confounding factors have been adequately controlled; and whether or not the infant behavior really reveals the first emergence of conceptual knowledge structures. But whichever position one takes on these issues, the data raise two important questions about conceptual development in infancy. First, how do infants come to construe semantically related items as similar to one another when they have few (or perhaps no) directly perceived properties in common? Second, why are coarse-grained conceptual distinctions available before finer-grained distinctions?

Other investigators have offered answers to one or both of these questions. These answers come with somewhat different slants on the empirical evidence, and both the evidence itself and the theories are the subject of considerable current discussion, as witnessed by the other articles in this volume. Here, we would like to raise the possibility that a process not considered by any of these investigators needs to be added to the mix of possible bases for the characteristics of children's earliest conceptual abilities. Specifically, we suggest that the learning mechanisms that give rise to infants' earliest concepts are strongly sensitive to patterns of *coherent covariation* among the directly perceived properties of objects and events. This sensitivity influences the first conceptual distinctions that emerge in infancy, as well as determining which properties of objects infants will weight in particular semantic tasks. Our goal is first to show that children's initial conceptual distinctions may reflect the effects of coherent covariation, and second, that the importance infants assign to particular cues may reflect the fact that these cues vary coherently with others, and thereby come to *acquire* salience.

The mechanism that supports these effects derives from our assumptions about the nature of the representations and processes that subserve cognition generally, and semantic cognition in particular: namely, the assumptions inherent in the parallel distributed processing (PDP) framework. Accordingly, we make our arguments with reference to a simple PDP model of semantic cognition first described by Rumelhart (Rumelhart, 1990; Rumelhart & Todd, 1993). This model has strongly influenced our thinking about the acquisition of conceptual knowledge, and we believe that the principles that govern its behavior can shed light on many different aspects of semantic cognition (Rogers & McClelland, 2004). In this chapter we focus on properties of the model that may help to explain how infants are able to represent conceptual similarity relations among perceptually varying stimulus items, and why they are first sensitive to coarse conceptual distinctions. The principles we emphasize will not and cannot refute the possibility that factors raised by other investigators are also at work. However, if we are able to establish that these principles can play a role in shaping children's conceptual distinctions and in determining what cues they are sensitive to, our account raises questions about the degree to which it is necessary to invoke some of the proposals that have been offered by others.

A BRIEF SURVEY OF THE LANDSCAPE

Though most theorists may agree that infant abilities in semantic tasks change in some fashion over the course of the first year of life, there is a diversity of opinion on how best to characterize the underlying cause of the observed differences. It is difficult to do justice to the richness of the literature in this regard; however, it will be useful for us to briefly survey some of the stances others have taken on this issue, to set the stage for our later consideration of the PDP approach. Painting with broad strokes, we here outline four positions regarding the nature of the knowledge that permits older infants to treat items from the same conceptual domain as similar, even if they do not share directly perceived properties. We should note that these positions need not be considered all mutually exclusive of one another—in some cases they are complimentary, and in other cases not.

Perceptual Enrichment

One possibility offered by several researchers (e.g., Mareschal, 2000; Quinn & Eimas, 1997a, 1997b; Quinn & Johnson, 1997) is that older infants come to discern conceptual relationships on the basis of learned associations among directly perceived properties of items across different episodes and situations. For example, older infants, on the basis of their encounters with particular dogs, cats, birds, and other animals, have learned to associate the various perceptual properties that co-occur together in these encounters—including some properties that may be directly observable in static photographs and toy replicas (such as eyes, legs, and fur) as well as some that are not (such as patterns of movement and behavior). Capitalizing on this stored knowledge, older infants in experiments like Mandler's make inferences about properties of the stimulus objects that cannot be directly observed in the experiment, but which have been directly observed on past occasions. On this view, semantically related items come to be associated with similar sets of properties, and as children gain experience they can come to exploit conceptual similarity relations on this basis.

Investigators who adopt this perspective emphasize studies of perceptual categorization in infancy, which have convincingly demonstrated that by 3 to 4 months of age infants are sensitive to visual similarities among discriminably different stimulus items, and can employ these similarities to direct their expectations in preferential looking and dishabituation procedures (e.g., Behl-Chada, 1996; Eimas & Quinn, 1994; Younger & Fearing, 2000). For example, when young infants are habituated with a series of cat photographs, habituation generalizes to novel cat photos, but not to photographs of dogs (Quinn, Eimas, & Rosenkrantz, 1991). A series of related studies has demonstrated that infant behavior in this respect depends on the visual similarity and variability of the specific items viewed during habituation, and it has been noted that it is not necessary to assume they reflect any prior knowledge about the classes to which the stimuli belong (Mareschal et al., 2000). Nevertheless these studies are viewed as being important for understanding conceptual development, because they demonstrate that in many cases the visual similarities apparent from photographs of real objects can be sufficient to allow the discrimination of semantic categories. The suggestion is that the same perceptual-learning mechanisms observed in such experiments, operating over a much longer interval, may be sufficient to explain the ultimate acquisition of conceptual representations (Quinn & Eimas, 1997b, 2000; Quinn, 2002) through day-to-day perceptual experience.

Advocates of the perceptual-enrichment view have tended to focus on understanding the perceptual-learning skills of very young infants, and on putting forth the argument that within-experiment perceptual learning could be the basis of successful discrimination of both fairly broad semantic categories (such as mammals vs. furniture; see Behl-Chada, 1996; Quinn & Johnson, 1997; Younger & Fearing, 2000) and somewhat narrower categories (such as cats vs. dogs as previously cited), based on the perceptual structure of the items encountered during the experiment (Quinn & Eimas, 2000). There has been less detailed emphasis on understanding how infant behavior changes with increasing age, and less acceptance of claims by others that performance in various tasks is conceptually rather than perceptually based.

Initial Salience of Particular Perceptual Properties

A related possibility put forward by Rakison and colleagues is that when infants first appear to demonstrate knowledge of conceptual relationships, they are in fact relying on certain directly observed perceptual properties that are particularly salient (Rakison, 2003). For example, the 12-month-olds in Mandler's experiments may tend to treat toy replicas of animals as similar to one another, and as different from artifacts, because the animals all share legs where most artifacts do not, and legs are especially salient to infants at this age. Specifically, Rakison proposed that movement is inherently salient even to very young infants. Large external parts, such as legs and wheels, attract infants' attention because they have a propensity to move, and through perceptual learning mechanisms, these parts themselves come to be salient to the infant. Thus around the end of the first year of life, infants assess similarity based mainly on whether or not objects share the same large external parts, and whether they are seen to exhibit the same patterns of movement (though if neither of these cues is available, they may rely on other information). Subsequent conceptual development arises from a process of association-based enrichment, as children learn the correlations among these salient properties.

The idea that observed patterns of motion might provide the initial impetus for discriminating animate from inanimate objects was proposed in earlier work by Mandler (1988, 1992), and the hypothesis received some support from Bertenthal's (1993) finding that, even at 3 months of age, infants discriminate mechanical from biological patterns of motion. Rakison has extended the notion that movement patterns form the first basis for conceptual distinctions by raising the possibility that children might notice that items with one kind of large external part (legs) tend to move in one way, whereas items with another kind of large external part (wheels) tend to move in a different way. Such correlations among highly salient properties, which Rakison suggested are shared among category members at a fairly superordinate level (animals have legs and move in one way, vehicles have wheels and move in another), would lead to an early emergence of relatively broad category distinctions; once these sets of salient properties became associated with other properties that are less salient initially, the infant would be able to treat diverse members of a superordinate category the same way, even if none of the highly salient features were actually present in the test stimulus (see Rakison, 2003).

Evidence for Rakison's view stems from experiments that follow up on some of Mandler's own work, in which semantic domain (e.g., animal or artifact) is pitted against the external parts possessed by the objects (e.g., whether or not they have legs or wheels). Across a set of such studies, Rakison and colleagues found that 14-month-old infants discriminate wheeled objects from objects with legs, but do not otherwise discriminate animals from artifacts (Rakison & Butterworth, 1998a, 1998b; Rakison & Poulin-Dubois, 2001; Rakison & Cohen, 1999). For example, when confronted with hybrid objects, such as truck bodies with animal legs or cows with wheels, the infants appear to treat artifacts with legs as no different from normal animals, and animals with wheels as no different from wheeled artifacts. The main factor determining their selection of objects to touch or to use for imitation appears to be whether the object has wheels or legs. Thus, Rakison suggested that wheels and legs are among the set of properties that infants find especially salient at 14 months of age. When tested with normal animals and vehicles, infants may appear to be discriminating items on the basis of their semantic relationships, but in fact they are attending only to particular salient properties, according to Rakison (2003).

Rakison also suggested that the salience of external parts and patterns of motion may provide an explanation of why broad semantic distinctions are the first to appear in development. The initial salience and availability of certain object properties makes these easier to attend to and learn about than other, less salient properties that happen to differentiate more fine-grained categories. The abilities Rakison specifically attributed to infants at birth include the capacity to discern that an object is composed of multiple parts, and an initial predisposition to find movement salient. As in the perceptual-enrichment view, infants first discern broad semantic distinctions because they first acquire the associations among properties shared by items in the same semantic domain—in this case, external parts and patterns of movement. However, in Rakison's view, the reason these associations are the first to be learned is that these are the attributes that are available and salient to the infant at birth (Rakison, 2003).

Other studies have indicated that infants can discriminate animate from inanimate objects, even when they share similar large external parts, and are not observed to be moving. For example, Pauen (2002a) found that 11-month-olds reliably discriminate toy animals from toy furniture in an object examination paradigm, even when the replicas are stylized in such a way that items in both categories have similar-looking "legs," similar textures, and similar salient parts (e.g., the "eyes" on the animals are physically the same as the "knobs" on the furniture, etc.). In fact, infants in this experiment were just as likely to discriminate animals from furniture as was a second group of 11-month-olds who were tested with realistic toy replicas that were perceptually quite different from one another.

A key factor contributing to the difference between Rakison's and Pauen's results may be that Pauen did not pit two highly salient and informative cues (such as legs and wheels) against other factors that may be weaker. When faced with some items that have wheels and others that have legs, infants may tend to group items on the basis of these features to the exclusion of other informative similarities and differences. Indeed, Rakison has found in other experiments that infants are capable of discriminating animals and vehicles when the salient external features (legs and wheels) are completely removed, indicating some knowledge of other properties that discriminate the domains. However, Pauen's data demonstrate that 11-month-old infants are capable of discriminating animals from artifacts when there are no obvious single features that differentiate the domains—a finding that is difficult to attribute to the greater salience of certain individual properties over others. Thus her findings appear to be consistent with the two approaches considered later, in which children rely on their emerging conceptual knowledge at least in some tasks.

Conceptual Versus Perceptual Knowledge

According to the approach taken by Mandler (e.g., Mandler, 1992, 1994, 1997, 2000a, 2000b), the competencies exhibited by older preverbal infants reflect a form of knowledge representation that is qualitatively different from that apparent earlier in life. Specifically, Mandler distinguished between two forms of knowledge possessed by infants: perceptual and conceptual knowledge. Perceptual knowledge encompasses knowledge about what things look like, and on the basis of the dishabituation studies described earlier, is available to infants by at least 3 months of age. Conceptual knowledge encompasses knowledge about object kinds: It allows infants (as well as older children and adults) to understand that different objects are of the same kind, regardless of whether they are perceptually similar. On this view, the ability of 7- to 9-month-old infants to treat perceptually disparate items as similar to one another (and perceptually similar items from different domains as distinct) provides the earliest evidence for an influence of conceptual knowledge on behavior. As discussed earlier, Mandler's claims have sometimes been controversial because of uncertainties about whether perceptual factors could account for some aspects of her results; however, the findings of Pauen's (2002a, 2002b) recent studies seem to support Mandler's claim that children in the second half of the first year of life show sensitivity to conceptual distinctions in object examination tasks.

According to Mandler, early conceptual representations are built on representational primitives that she called image-schemas (Lakoff, 1987). Image-schemas are structures that capture knowledge about relatively abstract spatiotemporal characteristics of objects and events, such as containment, self-initiated movement, and contingency. Mandler differentiated image-schemas from perceptual representations precisely because they capture similarities among inputs that may be superficially quite different. For example, a dog and a bird may move in ways that are perceptually quite distinct, but in both cases the movement is self-initiated. An image-schema for self-initiated movement thus permits infants to represent an element of similarity across these perceptually distinct events. Accordingly, initial concepts are built from such primitives, when infants notice and represent relationships among them. For example, the initial concept animal might be built from image-schemas such as *moves-by-itself, moves-irregularly, moves-contingently, interacts-at-a-distance*, and so on. Infants arrive at the concept *animal* when they realize that self-moving objects also happen to be those that behave contingently, show irregular patterns of motion, interact with objects at a distance, and so on. That is, the initial animal concept results from noticing and representing the relationships among these image-schematic primitives. The further ability to discriminate replicas of animals from artifacts, even when these are completely static, similarly arises when infants "notice" that things that move by themselves also tend to have limbs on the bottom, faces, and other directly observable properties. On the basis of such knowledge, infants understand that different self-moving, contingently interacting objects are of the same kind, and that such items tend to have certain observable external parts. Subsequently, they no longer need to observe an object in motion, or behaving contingently, to "categorize" it as such.

It is not fully clear to us whether Mandler believes that the set of image-schemas children first apply are predetermined by innate characteristics of their perceptual or conceptual systems, or whether she believes that they are discovered through the application of some sort of very general purpose mechanism of acquisition. Relatedly, it is not clear how early in life the first image-schemas are available to differentiate concepts. Mandler believes that the data from infants under about 7 months cannot shed light on these matters, because the looking-tasks with which very young infants are tested only tap perceptual representations, and not conceptual or image-schematic knowledge. Thus it is difficult to know whether young infants possess conceptual knowledge, but do not express it in laboratory tasks, or whether this knowledge first emerges at about 7 months.

In any case, Mandler's view is that by 7 to 9 months children conceptualize all instances of self-initiated movement as effectively the same, and from this knowledge the early distinction between animate and inanimate things falls out. Thus on this view, the competencies displayed by infants at this age reveal the presence of knowledge structures that, though they may or may not be abstracted from perceptual experience, are qualitatively different from perceptual representations in that they allow the infant to ignore irrelevant perceptual variability and to zero in on the more abstract commonalties and differences that reliably discriminate kinds. Items that have different overall shapes, parts, colors, and textures may be treated as similar to one another if they exhibit the same motion characteristics, or if they share other observable properties that have been incorporated into the infant's image-schemas. Conversely, items with similar outward appearances may be treated differently if they engage different image-schemas. The first image-schemas available to infants describe patterns of motion, and hence the first concepts represented discriminate animate from inanimate objects. Further conceptual development, and the progressive differentiation of concept representations, arises from a continuing process that yields new image-schemas as well as new knowledge about the relationships among image-schemas, although the precise mechanism by which this process occurs is not spelled out.

Emergence of an Initial Domain Theory

A fourth possibility derives from the theory-theory approach to cognition (Carey, 1985; Gelman & Williams, 1998; Gopnik & Meltzoff, 1997; Keil, 1989). On this view, different entities are construed as being the same kind of thing when they are understood to share certain "core" properties—that is, nonobservable characteristics that are causal in the sense that they give rise to the item's observable attributes and behaviors. For example, the concept "animal" might include such core properties as agency, rationality, and goal-directedness (e.g., Gergely, Nadasdy, Csibra, & Biro, 1995). Core properties in the theory-theory tradition serve a function similar to that of Mandler's image-schemas—that is, they permit infants (and older children and adults) to conceive as similar items that may differ in many peripheral respects. If the core properties of animacy include agency and goal-directedness, for example, then any items attributed these characteristics will be understood to be the same kind of thing, regardless of how perceptually dissimilar they may be. However, where Mandler stressed that new image-schemas and conceptual representations may be discovered by the infant through development, theory theorists often emphasize that some important core properties cannot be acquired through experience, and must be specified innately (e.g., Carey & Spelke, 1994, 1996).

In principle this addresses the question of why certain very broad distinctions are apparent early in life; they are based, in this view, on initially available core properties, rather than on less essential properties that must be learned. However, this stance still raises questions about how young children happen to know that a given object with particular directly-observable properties also possesses certain crucial but nonobservable core properties. One answer (Carey & Spelke, 1994; Gelman, 1990) is that there are initial tendencies to associate certain perceivable properties (e.g., legs) with certain core properties (e.g., agency). Under this position, one can see how the results reported by Rakison might be explained. Specifically, the 12-

month-old's judgments would rely on certain directly perceived object properties (legs again), which by virtue of an innate mechanism have been associated with the relevant core properties (e.g., agency). Learning could then allow the infant to associate the non-core properties of objects (such as their surface features) with their core properties, allowing subsequent judgments to be based on nonobservable properties.

THE ESSENCE OF OUR ARGUMENT

The positions we have reviewed offer different answers to what is effectively the same question: On what basis do infants come to conceive of different objects as being of the same kind? For Quinn, Johnson, Mareschal, and colleagues, the answer is that conceptually related items come to be associated with similar constellations of attributes on the basis of perceptual learning. For Rakison, conceptually related items share certain inherently salient perceptual properties, including large external parts and patterns of movement. According to Mandler, an understanding of conceptual relations arises from descriptions of objects provided by image-schematic knowledge structures, most of which emerge from a process of perceptual analysis. According to Carey, conceptual relations are determined by nonobservable core causal properties, at least some of which cannot be acquired from perceptual learning and must be innate.

To these ideas we would like to add one further suggestion: Perhaps infants treat objects as being of the same kind because they are sensitive to patterns of experienced coherent covariation of properties across objects. This proposal appears to be distinct from the proposals that have been offered by the investigators whose work we have just reviewed. Although many of them discuss the idea that correlational learning plays a role in category formation, none of these accounts really consider anything beyond the role of pair-wise correlations.

Many of the arguments that have been offered by protagonists of other approaches are explicitly or implicitly sensitive to the concern expressed by some proponents of theory theory (e.g., Gelman & Williams, 1998; Keil, 1989; Murphy & Medin, 1985), that correlation-based learning mechanisms are too underconstrained to provide a basis for concept acquisition. The reason is that there are simply far too many spurious or uninformative pairwise correlations in the world for such correlations to provide a good basis for concept learning. For example, Keil, Carter Smith, Simons, and Levin (1998) pointed out that although virtually all washing machines are white in color, being white is not critical to the concept *washing machine*. By contrast, all polar bears are white, and in this case, "whiteness" seems to be more important to the concept *polar bear*. How do people know that the former pairwise correlation (between whiteness and washing machines) is not particularly important, whereas the latter correlation (between whiteness and polar bears) is?

On the basis of such arguments, investigators who may otherwise have little common ground often agree that infants must begin life with what R. Gelman (Gelman, 1990; Gelman & Williams, 1998) called *enabling constraints*—that is, an initial state that constrains to which among the blizzard of correlations yielded up by the environment infants will become sensitive. Thus, for example, Rakison addressed this critique by suggesting that children initially learn about correlations among highly salient properties—effectively giving some correlations a privileged status relative to others. Similarly, Mandler promoted image-schemas as providing descriptors that shine through the welter of detail captured directly by perception; and Carey explicitly contended that innate knowledge provides the necessary guidance to bootstrap concept acquisition in the face of an overwhelming amount of irrelevant perceptual information. What we would like to suggest is that such a bias for the rapid learning of certain correlations over others *can itself arise* from higher order patterns of coherent covariation among stimulus properties—so that the properties that first become useful, informative, or salient to infants, and that are easiest to associate with one another, are just those that participate in the strongest patterns of coherent covariation across many different events and situations. In the remainder of the chapter, we focus on demonstrating how this can be, by considering a simple computational model of semantic memory.

THE RUMELHART MODEL

The model we focus on was first put forward by Rumelhart (Rumelhart, 1990; Rumelhart & Todd, 1993), to demonstrate that the semantic content captured by propositional spreading-activation models such as Collins and Quillian's (1969) could also be coded in the distributed representations acquired by a feed-forward PDP network trained with backpropagation. To that end, Rumelhart constructed a network whose architecture reflects the structure of a simple proposition, as shown in Fig. 14.1. The first term of the proposition is coded with local representations in the *Item* layer; different relations are coded with local representations in the *Relation* layer; and the various completions of a given proposition are represented by individual units in the layer labeled *Attribute*. When presented with a particular *Item* and *Relation* pair in the input, the network must turn on the attribute units in the output that correctly complete the proposition. For example, when the units corresponding to *robin* and *can* are activated in the input, the network must learn to activate the output units *move*, *grow* and *fly*. The particu-

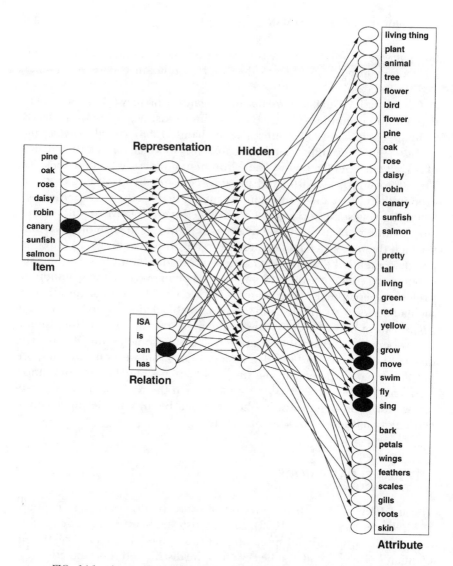

FIG. 14.1. A connectionist model of semantic memory adapted from Rumelhart and Todd (1993). The entire set of units used in the network is shown. Input units are shown on the left, and activation propagates from the left to the right. Where connections are indicated, every unit in the pool on the left is connected to every unit in the pool to the right. Each unit in the *Item* layer corresponds to an individual item in the environment. Each unit in the *Relation* layer represents contextual constraints on the kind of information to be retrieved. Thus, the input pair *robin can* corresponds to a situation in which the network is shown a picture of a robin, and asked what it can do. The network is trained to turn on all those units that represent correct completions of the input query. In the example shown, the correct units to activate are grow, move, and fly. Based on the network depicted in Rumelhart and Todd (1993), Figure 1.9, page 15.

lar items, relations, and attributes used by Rumelhart were taken directly from the corpus of propositions used by Quillian (1968) (indeed, though we have left them out in our work, Rumelhart included item input units for general as well as specific concepts in their model). Hence, when the network had learned to correctly complete all of the propositions, it had encoded the same information stored in the propositional spreading-activation model.

The network consists of a series of nonlinear processing units, organized into layers, and connected in a feed-forward manner as shown in the illustration. Patterns are presented by activating one unit in each of the item and relation layers, and allowing activation to spread forward through the network, subject to the constraints imposed by the weights and the sigmoid activation function of the units. In order to perform correctly, the network must find a configuration of weights that will produce the correct states across output units for a given pair of inputs—when it has done so, it can be said to "know" the domain (insofar, of course, as this is reflected in the training materials).

To find an appropriate set of weights, the model is trained with backpropagation (Rumelhart, Hinton, & Williams, 1986). First, an item and relation are presented to the network, and activation is propagated forward to the output units. The observed output states are then compared to the desired values, and the difference is converted to a measure of error. The partial derivative of the error with respect to each weight in the network is computed in a backward pass, and the weights are adjusted by a small amount to reduce the discrepancy.

Although the model's inputs are localist, each individual *Item* unit projects to all of the units in the layer labeled *Representation*. The activation of a single item in the model's input, then, generates a distributed pattern of activity across these units. The weights connecting item and representation units evolve during learning, so the pattern of activity generated across the *Representation* units for a given item is a learned internal representation of the item. Though the model's input and target states are constrained to locally represent particular items, attributes, and relations, the learning process allows it to derive distributed internal representations that do not have this localist character.

Because each item is represented locally in the input, the model is initially given no information about how the objects in its virtual world are related to one another. For example, the *pine* and *oak* inputs are no more similar to one another than each is to the *salmon* input. Due to the small, random values of the weights from these units to the *Representation* units, the patterns initially all have very similar internal representations, with only sight random differences. However, as the model learns to complete particular propositions, these representations gradually change, and as we see later, items with different attributes come to be differentiated, whereas items with many shared attributes continue to be represented by similar patterns of activity across the *Representation* units (Rumelhart & Todd, 1993). Thus, the connections that link *Item* and *Representation* units, once the model has been trained, can be viewed as encoding a set of semantic similarity relationships among a set of otherwise arbitrary markers. The connections in the rest of the network then reflect the learned mappings between these internal representations, in combination with input from the relation context, and explicit object properties.

An important departure from other representational schemes (including those used in some other connectionist approaches) is that the internal representations acquired by the Rumelhart network are not semantic features or in any other way directly interpretable semantically. Individual units in the model's *Representation* layer do not encode the presence or absence of explicit, intuitive object properties. Rather, these distributed representations are abstracted from the featural decomposition of objects represented in the output layer. The network's representations capture the similarities existing among different kinds of objects, not the actual semantic properties themselves which can only be activated from the combined effects of the units in the distributed representation working in concert with units in other parts of the network. The similarities that the network acquires through learning provide a basis for semantic generalization and induction: Items with similar internal representations will tend to generate similar outputs. To demonstrate this, Rumelhart and Todd (1993) trained a network like the one shown in Fig. 14.1 to correctly complete propositions about a variety of plants and animals. When it had learned the correct responses for the items and relations in its environment, they examined its generalization behavior using a procedure often employed in the connectionist literature (see, e.g., Miikkulainen, 1993). They added a new input node to represent a novel kind of bird (a *sparrow*), and used the backpropagation of error to assign a representation to the item based solely on the information that it was a kind of bird. Specifically, they turned on the *sparrow* and *isa* units in the input, and propagated activity forward to the output units. They then calculated error on just the "Bird" output unit, and used backpropagation to find an appropriate pattern of activity for the sparrow. Once a suitable representation had been found, they stored the pattern by adjusting only the weights connecting the sparrow unit to the *Representation* units. Using this procedure, the model found a representation for the new object that allowed it to activate the output property "Bird" with the *isa* relation, given the weights forward from the *Representation* units that encode its knowledge of the entire domain. Thus, the network's ability to assemble an appropriate representation relied on the information stored in its weights.

Once they had established a representation for sparrow based on the information that a sparrow is a bird, Rumelhart and Todd (1993) queried it about the sparrow in all four relation contexts. Although the network had derived its internal representation solely from the information that the sparrow is a kind of bird, it strongly activated all the properties shared by the familiar birds: *has wings, has feathers, can grow, can fly, isa animal,* and so on. However, properties unique to individual birds (such as *is red* or *can sing*) were not strongly activated. Examining the model's internal representations, the authors found that the network had come to represent the sparrow with a pattern of activity similar (but not identical) to those generated by the robin and canary inputs. This similarity led the model to attribute to the sparrow the properties shared by the robin and canary, but not their idiosyncratic properties.

The Rumelhart model, together with a range of related work (McClelland, McNaughton, & O'Reilly, 1995; McClelland & Rumelhart, 1986; McClelland, St. John, & Taraban, 1989; Rumelhart, Smolensky, et al., 1986), suggest a general framework for understanding semantic cognition that is quite different from propositional theories, and from other theories that assume a mechanism of categorization as the vehicle for semantic knowledge storage, generalization, and retrieval. According to this view, semantic representations of objects consist of patterns of activity across a set of units in a connectionist network, with semantically related objects represented by similar patterns of activity. In a given semantic task, these representations may be constrained both by incoming information about the object (in the form of a verbal description, a visual image, or other sensory information) and by the context in which the semantic task is performed. In turn, the instantiation of the representation in unit activation states allows the system to correctly complete the semantic task. On this view, all semantic knowledge is stored in and processed by the same set of hardware elements (the weights and units respectively). Generalization of stored knowledge to new items and situations results as a natural consequence of the similarities among object representations in a given context and not from the operation of a categorization mechanism, or by inference across a stored system of propositions. Obviously, the Rumelhart model's behavior in this respect depends on the state of its weight matrix at any given point during learning. The accumulation of small weight changes in the network as it learns leads its internal representations of objects to evolve in interesting ways, with consequences for the network's ability to perform various semantic tasks at different points throughout training. In the simulations to come, we show that the gradual weight changes that occur when the network is exposed to a set of propositions about a subdomain of conceptual knowledge, the resulting progressive differentiation of its internal representations, and the consequent change over time in its generalization and induction behavior, together suggest a mechanism that may help to explain how infants acquire conceptual representations on the basis of perceptual experience.

Progressive Differentiation and Feature Selection in the Rumelhart Model

We begin by considering how internal representations in the Rumelhart model change over time as a consequence of learning the Collins and Quillian corpus of propositions. This aspect of the model's behavior was previously considered in a simulation reported in McClelland et al. (1995), and other investigators interested in differentiation of perceptual and conceptual representations in infancy have also presented similar simulations (Miikkulainen & Dyer, 1991; Quinn & Johnson, 1997; Schyns, 1991). Here we replicate the progressive differentiation simulation of McClelland et al. as a starting point, then go on to consider the implications of this pattern for issues raised in the introduction.

We trained the network shown in Fig. 14.1 with the same corpus of propositions used by Rumelhart and Todd (1993). The weights were initialized to small random values selected from a uniform distribution with a mean of zero and variance of 0.5. With each pattern presentation, a single unit was activated in each of the *Item* and *Relation* layers, and weights were adjusted by a small amount (learning rate = 0.1) to reduce the sum-squared-error across output units. The network processed each input-relation pair once in each training epoch, but the order of patterns within an epoch was randomized. In this simulation, the simplest version of the back-propagation algorithm was used; the model was trained without noise, weight decay, or momentum. Weights were updated after every epoch, based on weight error derivatives calculated after processing each pattern. To ensure that the model's output responses relied entirely on input from other units in the network, we assigned to all units in the model a fixed, untrainable bias of −2. Thus, in the absence of input, each unit's state would rest at approximately 0.19, slightly below its midrange. We trained the network for 1500 epochs, at which point each output unit was within 0.05 of its target activation (0 or 1) on every pattern. To see how internal representations develop in the network, we stopped training at different points during learning and stepped through the eight items, recording the states of the representation units for each.

In Fig. 14.2 we show the activations of the representation units for each of the eight item inputs at three points in learning. Each pattern of activation at each time point is shown using eight bars, with each representing the activation of one of the representation units. Initially, and even after 50 epochs of training as shown, the patterns representing the items are all very

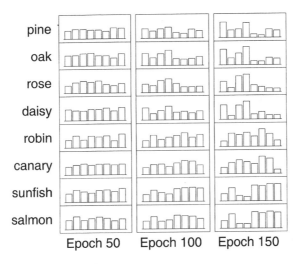

FIG. 14.2.   Learned internal representations of eight items at three points during learning, using the network shown in Fig. 14.1. The height of each vertical bar indicates the degree of activation for one of the eight units in the network's Representation layer, in response to the activation of a single *Item* unit in the model's input.

similar, with activations hovering around 0.5. At epoch 100, the patterns corresponding to various animal instances are similar to one another, but are distinct from the plants. At epoch 150, items from the same intermediate cluster, such as *rose* and *daisy*, have similar but distinguishable patterns, and are now easily differentiated from their nearest neighbors (e.g., *pine* and *oak*). Thus, each item has a unique representation, but semantic relations are preserved in the similarity structure across representations.

The arrangement and grouping of the representations shown in Fig. 14.3 reflects the similarity structure among the internal representations, as determined by a hierarchical clustering analysis using Euclidean distance as the measure of similarity between patterns. At 50 epochs the tree is very flat and any similarity structure revealed in the plot is weak and random. By epoch 100 the clustering analysis reveals that the network has differentiated plants from animals: All the plants are grouped under one node, whereas all the animals are grouped under another. At this point, more fine-grained structure is not yet clear. For example, oak is grouped with rose, indicating that these representations are more similar to one another than is oak to pine. By epoch 150, the network has learned the correct similarities, and we can see that the learned distributed representations fully capture the hierarchical relations among the input items. The degree of semantic relatedness among the eight items is reflected by the degree of similarity in the patterns of activity that represent each item when the model has finished

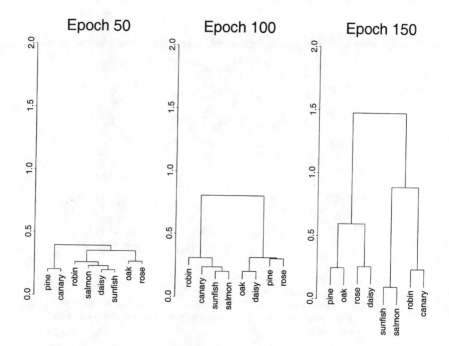

FIG. 14.3. Hierarchical cluster plot of the learned internal representations at three points during training. The clustering algorithm recursively links a pattern or a previously linked group of patterns to another pattern or previously formed group. The process begins with the pair that is most similar, whose elements are then replaced by the resulting group. These steps are repeated until all items have been joined in a single superordinate group. Similarity is measured by the Euclidean distance metric. The results show that the network is first sensitive to broad semantic distinctions, and only gradually picks up on more specific ones.

learning. Moreover, the model first discovers fairly broad conceptual distinctions, and only later comes to represent more subtle ones.

In order to better visualize the process of conceptual differentiation that takes place in this model, we performed a multidimensional scaling of the internal representations for all items at 10 different points during training. Specifically, the *Representation* layer activation vector for each item at each point in time was treated as a vector in an 8-dimensional space. The Euclidean distances between all vectors at all points over development were calculated. Each vector was then assigned a 2-d coordinate, such that the pairwise distances in the 2-d space were as similar as possible to the distances in the original 8-d space.

The solution is plotted in Fig. 14.4. The lines trace the trajectory of each item throughout learning in the 2-dimensional compression of the representation state space. The labeled end points of the lines represent the final

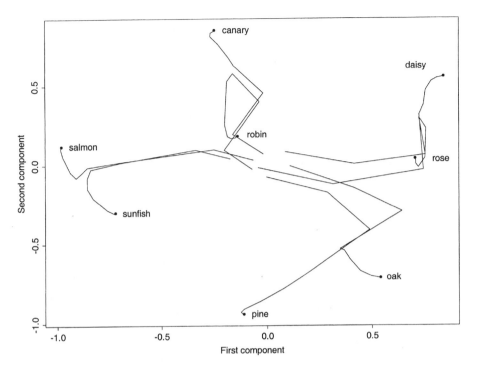

FIG. 14.4. Trajectory of learned internal representations during learning. The Euclidean distance matrix for all item representations was calculated at ten different points throughout training. A multidimensional scaling was performed on these data to find corresponding points in a two dimensional space that preserve, as closely as possible, the pairwise distances among representations across training. Thus, the proximity of two points in the figure approximates the actual Euclidean distance between the network's internal representations of the corresponding objects at a particular point in training. The lines indicate the path traversed by a particular item representation over the course of development.

learned internal representations after 1500 epochs of training. The figure shows that the items, which initially are bunched together in the middle of the space, soon divide into two global clusters (plant or animal) based on animacy. Next, the global categories split into smaller intermediate clusters, and finally the individual items are pulled apart.

Discussion of Differentiation Results

Our simulation replicates results described previously by others (McClelland et al., 1995; Quinn & Johnson, 1997) showing that when a backpropagation network is trained on a set of training patterns with a hierarchical similarity structure, it will exhibit a pattern of progressive differentiation. One interesting aspect of this process is the tendency for the different levels to differentiate in relatively discrete stages, first completing differentiation at the most general level before progressing to successively more fine-grained levels of differentiation. This tendency to exhibit stagelike learning is a feature of connectionist models that has been considered extensively elsewhere (McClelland, 1989; Plunkett & Sinha, 1992; McClelland, 1994). Our present task is to try to provide the reader with a mechanistic understanding of the progressive differentiation process, drawing on insights expressed in the papers just cited (see also McClelland & Rumelhart, 1988), to explain how stagelike progressive differentiation works in the present case.

With the training set used here, very early in learning, the network comes to represent all the animals as similar to one another, and as quite distinct from the plants. Only later does it come to learn to differentiate the patterns at an intermediate level, and only after that does it learn to differentiate the items from each other at the subordinate level. Why does this occur? To begin to gain an intuitive understanding of this, let us consider how the network learns about the following four objects: the oak, the pine, the daisy, and the salmon. Early in learning, when the weights are small and random, all of these inputs produce a similar meaningless pattern of activity throughout the network. Because oaks and pines share many output properties, this pattern results in a similar error signal for the two items, and the weights leaving the *oak* and *pine* units move in similar directions. Because the salmon shares few properties with the oak and pine, the same initial pattern of output activations produces a different error signal, and the weights leaving the *salmon* input unit move in a different direction. What about the daisy? It shares more properties with the oak and the pine than it does with the salmon or any of the other animals, and so it tends to move in a similar direction as the other plants. Similarly, the rose tends to be pushed in the same direction as all of the other plants, and the other animals tend to be pushed in the same direction as the salmon. As a consequence, on the next pass, the pattern of activity across the representation units will remain similar for all the plants, but will tend to differ between the plants and the animals.

This explanation captures part of what is going on in the early stages of learning in the model, but does not fully explain why there is such a strong tendency to learn the superordinate structure first. Why is it that so little intermediate level information is acquired until after the superordinate level information? Put another way, why don't the points in similarity space for different items move in straight lines toward their final locations? Several factors appear to be at work, but one is key:

For items with similar representations, coherent covariation of properties across these items tends to move connections coherently in the same direction, whereas idiosyncratic variation tends to move weights in opposing directions that cancel each other out.

To see how this happens in the model, let's consider the fact that the animals all share some properties (e.g., they all can move, they all have skin, they are all called animals). Early in training, all the animals have the same representation. When this is so, if the weights going forward from the representation layer "work" to capture these shared properties for one of the animals, they must simultaneously work to capture them for all of the others. Similarly, any weight change that is made to capture the shared properties for one of the items will produce the same benefit in capturing these properties for all of the other items: If the representations of all of the items are the same, then changes applied to the forward-projecting weights for one of the items will affect all of the other items equally, and so the changes made when processing each individual item will tend to cumulate with those made in processing the others. On the other hand, weight changes made to capture a property of an item that is not shared by others with the same representation will tend to be detrimental for the other items, and when these other items are processed the changes will actually be reversed. For example, two of the animals (canary and robin) can fly but not swim, and the other two (the salmon and the sunfish) can swim but not fly. If the four animals all have the same representation, what is right for half of the animals is wrong for the other half, and the weight changes across different patterns will tend to cancel each other out. The consequence is that:

Properties shared by items with similar representations will be learned faster than the properties that differentiate such items.

The preceding paragraph considers the effects of coherent covariation in the weights forward from the representation later in the Rumelhart network. What about the weights from the input units to the representation layer? As previously stated, items with similar outputs will have their representations pushed in the same direction, whereas items with dissimilar outputs will have their representations pushed in different directions. The question remaining is why the dissimilarity between, say, the fish and the birds, does not push the representations apart very much from the very beginning. The answer is somewhat complex, but understanding it is crucial, as it is fundamental to understanding the progressive nature of the differentiation process.

The key to this question lies in understanding that the magnitude of the changes made to the representation weights depends on the extent to which this will reduce the error at the output level. The extent to which change in the representation weights will reduce the error at the output in turn depends on whether the forward weights from the representation layer to the output are able to make use of any changes in the activations of the representation units. Their ability to make use of such changes depends on them already being at least partially organized to do so. Put in other words, we can point out a further very important aspect of the way the model learns:

> Error backpropagates much more strongly through weights that are already structured to perform useful forward-mappings.

We can illustrate this by observing the error signal propagated back to the representation units for the canary item, from three different kinds of output units: those that reliably discriminate plants from animals (such as *can move* and *has roots*), those that reliably discriminate birds from fish (such as *can fly* and *has gills*), and those that differentiate the canary from the robin (such as *is red* and *can sing*). In Fig. 14.5, we show the mean error reaching the *Representation* layer throughout training, across each of these types of output unit when the model is given the canary as input (middle plot). We graph this alongside measures of the distance between the two bird representations, between the birds and the fish, and between the animals and the plants (bottom plot); and also alongside of measures of activation of the output units for *sing, fly* and *move* (top plot). We can see that there comes a point at which the network is beginning to differentiate the plants and the animals, and is beginning to activate *move* correctly for all of the animals. At this time the average error information from output properties like *can move* is producing a much stronger signal than the average error information from properties like *can fly* or *can sing*. As a consequence, the information that the canary can move is contributing much more strongly to changing the representation weights than is the information that the canary can fly and sing. Put differently, the knowledge that the canary can move is more "important" for determining how it should be represented than the information that it can fly and sing, at this stage of learning. (The error signal for *can move* eventually dies out as the correct activation reaches asymptote, as there is no longer any error signal to propagate once the model has learned to produce the correct activation.)

The overall situation can be summarized as follows. Initially the network is assigning virtually the same representation to all of the items. At this point, the network is easily able to learn only what is shared across everything—the *is living, can grow,* and *isa living thing* outputs. All other output properties have their effects on the forward weights almost completely cancelled out. However, because the plants have several properties that none

Canary

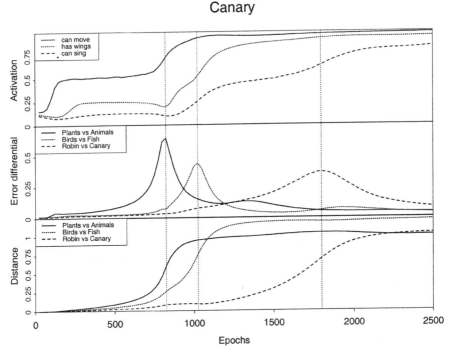

FIG. 14.5. Bottom: Mean distance between plant and animal, bird and fish, and canary and robin internal representations throughout training. Middle: Average magnitude of the error signal propagating back from properties that reliably discriminate plants from animals, birds from fish, or the canary from the robin, at different points throughout training when the model is presented with the canary as input. Top: Activation of a property shared by animals (can move), birds can fly, or unique to the canary (can sing), when the model is presented with the input canary *can* at different points throughout training.

of the animals have and vice versa, weak error signals from each of these properties begin to accumulate, eventually driving the representations of plants and animals apart. At this point, the common animal representation can begin to drive the activation of output units that are common to all animals, and the common plant representation can begin to drive activation of outputs common to all plants. The weights so structured in turn allow these coherently varying properties to exert much stronger influences on the representation units than those exerted by the properties that differ between the birds and the fish. The result is that the individual animal representations stay similar to one another, and are rapidly propelled away from the individual plant representations. Very gradually, however, the weak signals backpropagated from properties that reliably discriminate birds from fish begin to cumulate, and cause the representations of these subgroups to differentiate slightly, thereby providing a basis for exploiting this coherent covariation in the forward weights. This process eventually propagates all the way down to the subordinate level, so that idiosyncratic properties of individual items are eventually mastered by the net. In short, there is a kind of symbiosis of the weights into and out of the representation units, such that both sets are sensitive to successive waves of coherent covariation among output properties. Each "wave" of properties only becomes salient or "important" to the network after the prior stage of differentiation has occurred.

ADAPTING THE RUMELHART FRAMEWORK
TO ACCOMMODATE PREVERBAL LEARNING

With this background in place, we are ready to turn to the specific details of our use of the Rumelhart model as a vehicle for illustrating the key points of our argument. To launch our discussion of these issues, consider the following abstract formulation of the Rumelhart model architecture. Here we envision that the two parts of the input represent a perceived object (perhaps foregrounded for some reason to be in the focus of attention) and a context provided by other information available together with the perceived object. Perhaps the situation is analogous to one in which a young child is looking at a robin on a branch of a tree, and, as a cat approaches, sees it suddenly fly away. The object and the situation together provide a context in which it would be possible for an experienced observer to anticipate that the robin will fly away; and the observation that it does would provide input allowing a less experienced observer to develop such an anticipation. Conceptually speaking, this is how we see learning occurring in preverbal conceptual development. An object and a situation or context afford the basis for implicit predictions (which may initially be null or weak), and observed events then provide the basis for adjusting the connection weights underlying these predictions, thereby allowing the experience to drive change in both underlying representations and predictions of observable outcomes.

With this scenario in front of us, we can consider the wide range of different contexts in which the child might encounter an object. Some such contexts will be ones in which the child is watching the object and observing what others might do with it (pick it up, eat it, use it to sweep the floor, etc.); another (as in the given example) might be one in which the child is simply observing the object itself, watching the things that it does in various different situations. Several contexts will be ones in which someone engages the child in language-related interactions concerning the object.

Some such encounters may involve naming, as when an adult points to an object and says to a child "Look, Sally, it's a bunny rabbit." Others may include indicating for the child the various parts of the object ("OK, Sally, let's pat the Bunny's tail. Can you see the tail? Here it is!"). Each encounter with a particular object in a given context will give rise to certain observed consequences, and we suggest that the child learns to assign a conceptual representation to each object based on the consequences observed in different situations. The contexts or situations include linguistic ones as well as nonlinguistic situations in which the child observes the object either alone or in interaction with other objects. We suggest that conceptual development arises from the learning that occurs across many such situations.[1] We can now consider how our modeling framework allows us to capture aspects of this learning process, and in particular how useful conceptual representations can be acquired on the basis of such learning. The presentation of the "object" corresponds to the activation of the appropriate pattern of activity over the input units in the Rumelhart model; the context can be represented via the activation of an appropriate pattern over the context units; the child's expectations about the outcome of the event may be equated with the model's outputs; and the presentation of the actual observed outcome is analogous to the presentation of the target for the output units in the network.

On this view, the environment provides both the input that characterizes a situation as well as the information about the outcome that then drives the process of learning. In the given example, the item input corresponds to the visual appearance of the object, and the context input provides the additional source of information that constrains the child's predictions about what will happen next, which take the form of a pattern of activation across the output units. The weights and representations that mediate between the inputs and the outputs constitute the state of knowledge that allows the system to anticipate the outcome of the event, by activating the units that correspond to the predicted conclusion; but the environment contributes again by providing the actual observed event outcome, thereby yielding information the system can use to determine whether its predic-

---

[1] Scholars of philosophy and other students of Quine (1960) might observe that it is not a trivial matter for the child to determine what is being named when a name is given, and the argument can be extended to noting that it isn't at all clear what particular aspects of a situation are the ones that support the appropriate predictions of outcomes that might be expected to arise from it. Attentional foregrounding and characteristics of perceptual systems can influence these processes. Elsewhere we have argued as well that gradual learning in connectionist networks can sort out ambiguities that arise in individual cases (St. John & McClelland, 1990). For example, a naïve listener may not know what aspects of an event are picked out by the words "cat" and "dog" in a sentence like "The dog is chasing the cat"; but over many other sentence-event pairs (e.g., events described with sentences "The dog is chewing the bone," "The cat is drinking the milk," etc.) some of these ambiguities will naturally sort themselves out.

tions were accurate or not. This outcome information will consist sometimes of verbal, sometimes of nonverbal information, and in general is construed as information filtered through perceptual systems, no different in
any essential way from the information that drives the *Item* and *Context* units
in the network. What this means is that this information is provided by
nonconceptual (perceptual, motor feedback, etc.) systems and serves as input that drives the learning that results in the formation of conceptual representations. It will, of course, be obvious that this is a drastic simplification
of perceptual, motoric, attentional, and other processes, but we believe the
resulting model is useful in that it brings out some of aspects of the processes that may underlie conceptual development.

We can also see that there is a natural analog in the model for the distinction drawn between the perceptual information available from an item
in a given situation, and the conceptual representations that are derived
from this information. Specifically, the model's input, context, and targets
code the "perceptual" information that is available from the environment
in a given episode, and the intermediating units in the *Representation* and
Hidden layers correspond to the "conceptual" representations that allow the
semantic system to accurately perform semantic tasks.

SIMULATING CONCEPTUAL DIFFERENTIATION
IN INFANCY

To explore these ideas more fully, we conducted simulations with an alternative implementation of the Rumelhart model, designed to illustrate
how forces of coherent covariation can lead the model to represent semantically related items as similar, even when they have no directly perceived properties in common, and share only a few unobserved and abstract characteristics.

The alternative implementation is depicted in Fig. 14.6. It differs from
the model shown earlier, in two respects. First, we have expanded the training corpus to accommodate a somewhat broader range of items. Specifically, we added two new birds, fish, flowers, and trees to the set of items
from the original network, and an additional set of five different land animals. Thus there are 21 items in total in the new implementation: 13 animals from three categories (birds, land animals, and fish), and 8 plants
from two categories (trees and flowers). To allow differentiation of the individual items, and to capture the properties of the land animals, several additional property units were required, as indicated in the figure. In this case
we construe these properties not as verbal propositions but as directly observable properties of objects in the environment. Additionally, because
these simulations are meant to address preverbal conceptual learning, the

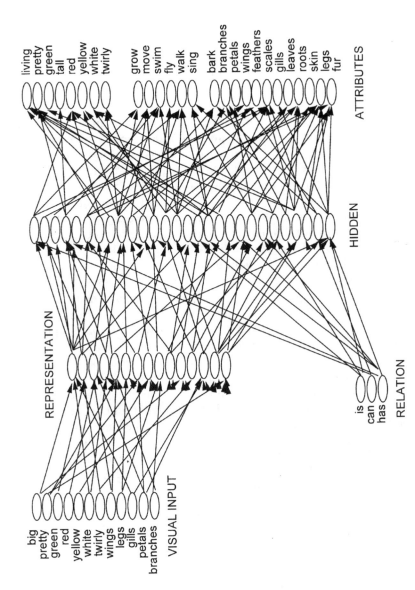

FIG. 14.6. Base architecture used for our simulation of conceptual differentiation in infancy.

361

model was not trained to name objects in either simulation—they were exposed to only the *is*, *can*, and *has* patterns. Though we believe that experience with spoken language may play some role in concept acquisition prior to the infant's ability to produce speech, it will be useful to see that the progressive differentiation of representations in the model does not depend on its being trained to name objects, or to explicitly categorize them in other ways that rigidly express taxonomic relations.

Although we have extended the training corpus, the reader will note that we have not gone all the way to producing a fully realistic training environment. First of all, there are many more kinds of things in the world that are not included in this training corpus, and indeed many more examples of each of the kinds that we are actually using. Second, though the properties are in some sense correctly assigned to the items, it is also true that the set of properties is far from complete, and it is not at all clear that those properties that are included are necessarily the most salient, informative, or likely to be available from the environment. As one example, in retaining the properties from the Rumelhart training set we retain the property *has skin*, which was originally used in Collins and Quillian (1969). However, this property is likely not to be as salient or available as, for example, the missing property *has eyes*. Other properties that some researchers have indicated as being important to discriminating animate from inanimate objects— contingent movement, action at a distance, wheels, surface textures, and the like—are not represented. Many readers may wonder what insights can come from a model based on such inherently incomplete and even somewhat inaccurate training data. Our response to this question is as follows.

The fundamental force that drives learning in our network is not the particular set of properties we have chosen, but the patterns of covariation that occur among the properties used in the model's training environment. To see this, imagine that we completely relabeled all of the input and output units with completely arbitrary symbols, such as I1–I21 (for the 21 different items) R1–4 (for the four different relation types) and A1–A34 for the 34 different attributes. None of this would have the slightest consequence for the process of learning in the network, which depends only on the degree of overlap in the properties shared across the range of items. Thus, we may agree that *has skin* is not really a salient feature of animals, but we might also agree that animals do nevertheless share some other salient attribute (e.g., *has eyes*). Again, the crucial point is that it is not the identity of the properties themselves but their patterns of covariation that is essential to the model's behavior.

In Fig. 14.7 we show the degree to which different items in the corpus tend to share the same output attributes, assessed across all contexts. It is apparent that the individual trees all have very similar sets of attributes, as do the flowers, the birds, the fish, and the land animals; that there is consid-

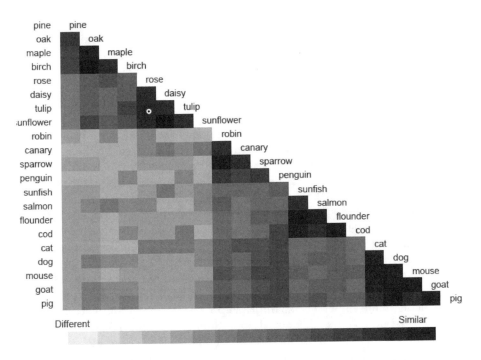

FIG. 14.7. Matrix indicating the similarities among the different items in their attribute structures. The shading indicates the degree to which two items have similar attributes, with dark colors signifying items with higher degrees of similarity. The measure of similarity is obtained by concatenating the output patterns for the is, *can*, and *has* contexts into a single vector for each item, with 1's for attributes that are present and 0's for attributes that are absent, then computing the normalized dot-product among the item representations.

erable similarity between the trees and the flowers and among the three types of animals; and that there is very little similarity between the various plants on the one hand and the various animals on the other. In the model, it is the structure present in this similarity matrix, rather than the particular sets of item, relation, and attribute labels used, that govern the models' learning and performance.

The second departure from the original Rumelhart model is that the new implementation was provided with distributed "perceptual" input representations, rather than localist proposition-like inputs. In place of the *Item* units employed in the original Rumelhart implementation (with one unit standing for each item), we instead construed the input units as representing the subset of perceptual attributes that are apparent from an item's visual appearance—for example, features such as *red*, *big* and *legs*. A particular item is presented to the model by instantiating a pattern of activation across this set of "perceptual" input units. The model might be shown a picture of a robin, for instance, by activating input units corresponding to *red*, *legs*, and *wings*. Each item in the training corpus is represented with a different pattern of activity across input features, rather than by the activation of a single input unit. The extent of feature overlap in these input representations provides a model analog of "visual" similarity in the input. The instantiation of a particular input pattern gives rise to a pattern of activity across *Representation* and *Hidden* units, which correspond to internal "conceptual" representations just as in the localist implementation.

We emphasize that the particular attributes that are included in the training corpus were not chosen with the goal of addressing infancy findings per se. Rather, we have employed this expanded corpus to investigate a wide range of different issues related to semantic cognition (Rogers & McClelland, 2004). Accepting that the particular perceptual properties to which infants are sensitive may not be precisely those that are expressed by the labeled attributes in the model, recall that it is the pattern of property covariation across items in the training corpus that determines the model's behavior. The units in the network could be relabeled to better express the particular kinds of perceptual information to which real infants are actually exposed, but of course this would not influence the behavior of the model. Addition or deletion of properties, alternations of the assignments of particular properties to particular objects, and manipulations of salience could alter the results, but only insofar as these alterations removed certain key properties of the training corpus, namely the presence of the particular pattern of coherent covariation of properties that gives rise to the item similarity structure seen in Fig. 14.7.

Choosing Input Representations

In generating "visual" input patterns for the 21 items in the distributed-inputs implementation, one is immediately faced with the question of which attributes to include in the input. We have argued that, in principle, all of the properties included in the training corpus are potentially observable, at least in certain circumstances; for example, the property *can move* can be considered "perceptual" information available from the input whenever one is directly observing a moving object. In other situations, this information is not available directly from perception, but must be inferred, for example, when one observes a stationary cat. Ought the property be coded then in the input, the output, or both? In fact we don't think there is a categorical distinction between those properties that are available as the basis for making predictions, and those that should be predicted. In recurrent networks, where a given unit can be at once both an input and an output unit, all attributes can serve both as inputs and as targets (see, e.g., Rogers et al., 2004). For simplicity we've stayed with the feed-forward architecture, however, so we must adopt a specific policy on the allocation of attributes to input and output.

The policy chosen reflects our primary aim in the current simulation, which is to investigate how the model comes to represent semantically related items as similar, even when they have few or no directly perceived properties in common. To this end, we employed as "perceptual" input attributes the complete set of *is* properties from the training corpus (*big, pretty, green, red, yellow, white,* and *twirly*) and a subset of the *has* properties (*wings, legs, gills, petals,* and *branches*). Note that these properties are also included as output attributes, along with the remaining *has* properties and the *can* properties for all 21 instances.

This choice accomplished three ends. First, the set of attributes chosen was intended to correspond at least approximately to those that might be directly observable in almost any encounter with the item or a picture of it, and thus could provide a simple analog to the visible properties of real-world objects that are likely to be seen regardless of the task or situation. We do not intend to suggest by this that the specific attributes we have chosen correspond to the actual visual attributes of real objects. We simply note that, of the complete set of perceptual properties that one could potentially observe in an object, a relatively small subset are likely to be frequently visible (e.g., outside parts and colors), whereas others are likely to be perceived only in certain limited circumstances (e.g., inside parts or particular behaviors). In the model, the complete range of potentially observable attributes is coded in the model's output attributes, and the subset of attributes that are treated as observable in all contexts and situations are coded in the distributed input.

Second, to the extent that the set of attributes used are the ones that are available in a picture or a scale replica of the object, they provide patterns that can be used as inputs in simulation analogs of experimental tests performed on children, which commonly use pictures or scale replicas as stimuli. Third, and of central importance for the key points we wish to make, the "perceptual" similarities expressed by this subset of attributes fail to specify any superordinate similarity structure beyond the intermediate category level. As shown in Fig. 14.8, items from the same intermediate categories (birds, fish, mammals, flowers, and trees) are "perceptually" similar to one another, but no global similarity between the trees and flowers, or between the birds, fish, and mammals, is available in this subset of properties. Thus the "perceptual" similarities captured by our choice of input patterns provides no impetus for the distributed-inputs simulation to develop a superordinate distinction between plants on the one hand and animals on the other. Yet as we see later the model does still learn to differentiate the

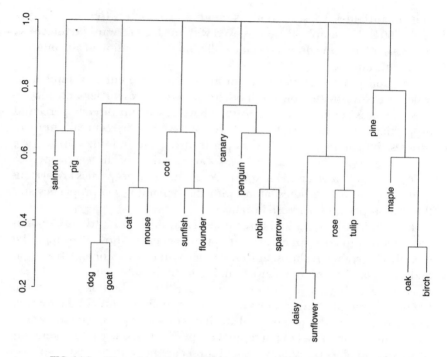

FIG. 14.8.   Hierarchical cluster plot of the similarities expressed by the overlap of input features used in the distributed-inputs implementation.

inputs on this basis, since the superordinate structure is still present in the
set of target attributes.

Simulation Details

The network was trained as described previously with each pattern appearing once in every training epoch, without momentum or weight decay, and
with output units assigned a fixed, untrainable bias weight of −2. However,
we adopted the following slight changes to the training procedure in this
simulation. First, a small amount of noise selected from a Gaussian distribution with a mean of zero and a variance of 0.05 was injected into the inputs
of all the hidden units throughout training. Second, the model was trained
with a learning rate of 0.005 instead of 0.1; with the larger training corpus
and the noisy hidden units a larger learning rate occasionally prevented the
model from completely mastering the training corpus. Third, weights were
updated after every 10 pattern presentations (rather than at the end of
each epoch). The order in which patterns were presented to the network
was determined randomly in each epoch. Finally, because the model's in-

ternal representations in the early epochs of training can be influenced by the particular configuration of random weights with which it is initialized, the results we describe here are averaged across five network runs trained with different random starting weights.

Differentiation of Representations for Familiar Items

To see how the model's internal "conceptual" representations for the familiar items in the training corpus change over development, we stopped training after every 125 epochs, and stepped through all 21 items, recording the patterns of activation across *Representation* units. Figure 14.9 shows hierarchical cluster plots of the distances among representations at three different points during learning, averaged across the five training runs. Again, items differentiated in a coarse-to-fine manner.

Note that at epoch 1000, the model behaves in a manner analogous to the 7- to 9-month-old infants described in Mandler's (2000) experiments. That is, it "groups together" items that share the few properties that reliably discriminate broad semantic domains—properties such as *can move, has skin, has roots,* and *has leaves.* The model may appear as though it is "using" these attributes as its basis for grouping items, even though none of these useful properties is coded in the input. In fact, there are no properties shared by all plants or all animals represented in the input; but nevertheless the model first differentiates its internal representations with respect to this global semantic distinction. Thus the weights that project from the *Input* to the *Representation* layer effectively serve the function that Mandler attributed to image-schemas, and that Carey (2000) attributed to core causal properties: They allow the model to "group together" a set of items that have disparate visual appearances, on the basis of a few abstract shared properties that are not directly represented in the input.

The model shows a progressive pattern of differentiation for the same reason outlined earlier. Initially all items are represented as similar to one another by virtue of the initial small random weights, and the model reduces error by learning to activate output units shared by all items in the environment (e.g., *can grow*). However, plants and animals, because they have few properties in common in the output, generate quite different error signals, and these gradually lead the model to distinguish them slightly. As the plants and animals slowly come to receive different internal representations, a kind of "feedback" loop arises in the learning mechanism: The weights projecting forward from the *Representation* layer are able to use the dimension of variability that separates plants and animals to reduce error on the sets of output properties shared across items in each domain. Consequently the error derivatives that come back from these properties to the *Representation* units grow increasingly large, propelling the plant and animal

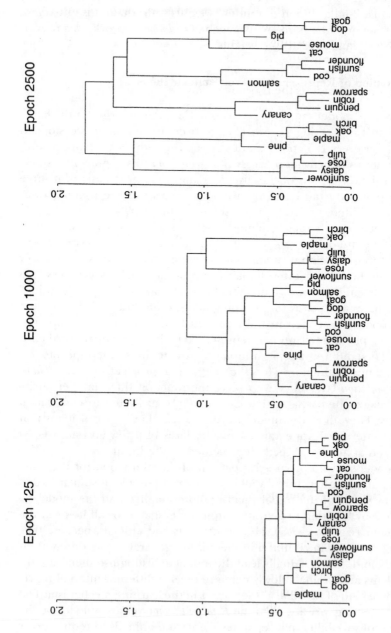

FIG. 14.9. Hierarchical cluster plot of the internal representations acquired by the model at three different points in learning. The distance matrices were generated by calculating the mean pairwise Euclidean distances among representations across five different network runs in each implementation.

representations further apart. This in turn gives the forward weights even more information to work with, and they adjust to capitalize still further on the growing distinction represented between plants and animals.

Over the course of learning, the constellation of output properties that reliably discriminate plants from animals effectively becomes more "salient" to the model, in the sense that only these properties generate a coherent error signal across the training corpus in the early epochs of learning. That is, the property *can move* is not initially predisposed to be any more salient or informative than any other attribute, but as the model begins to learn, the coherent covariation between *can move* and other attributes that reliably discriminate animate from inanimate objects in the training environment lead these properties to dominate learning in the model in the early epochs of training. As a consequence, these properties more strongly constrain the model's internal representations—leading the model to discover an early weight configuration that "filters" input similarities in such a way that differences between items in the same domain are minimized, and differences between items in different domains are emphasized.

As the network masters properties that vary coherently across domains, and as the smaller weight changes that accumulate across other output units very gradually allow the model to differentiate more fine-grained categories such as *bird* and *fish*, the dynamics shift to favor learning about the properties that vary coherently with these intermediate categories. That is, as the representations of different birds and fish pull apart from one another, properties such as *can fly* and *can swim* begin to produce coherent error signals that produce large derivatives and therefore large weight changes, at which point this learning comes to strongly influence representational change in the model. The consequence of these dynamics is that different sets of properties dominate the learning that drives representational change in the model at different points during training.

Simulating the Object-Examination Experiment

With these ideas in hand, we can begin to see how the model provides a basis for understanding the phenomena reviewed in the introduction: the ability of older infants to treat perceptually disparate stimuli as similar to one another on the basis of properties not present in the input available at the time of test. The explanation offered by the model is similar in some respects to that suggested by other investigators: Properties that reliably discriminate broad semantic domains are more important in determining the model's behavior early in development than are other properties, and items that share these properties are represented as conceptually similar, even if they differ in many other respects. What sets our account apart from that offered by others is the basis for the importance of these properties. In the case of our model, the salience of properties like movement emerges as a consequence of the sensitivity of the learning mechanism to coherent covariation.

To provide a concrete illustration of how these phenomena in the model might explain data from infant experiments, we conducted a simulation of the object-examination task conducted by Mandler and Mc-Donough (1993). In this experiment, infants were allowed to play with a series of toy objects belonging to the same semantic category. After habituation, they were presented with two new test objects in succession: first, a novel item from the same semantic category, and second, a novel item from a different category; the authors measured the amount of time the infant spent examining each. If the infants construe the same-category item as novel, they should spend more time examining it, relative to the last trial of habituation. If they further construe the different-category item as novel, they should spend still more time examining it, relative to the last trial of habituation.

Three different experimental conditions are of particular interest in this experiment. First, the authors habituated 9- and 11-month-olds to items from the same broad semantic domain (e.g., a series of animals, or a series of vehicles), which had broadly different overall shapes. In this case, infants of both ages failed to dishabituate to the same-category item, but successfully dishabituated to the different-category item—indicating that they could "group together" items from the same general category, even though they were perceptually fairly dissimilar, and could construe these as different from an out-of-category item. In the second condition, the authors habituated 9- and 11-month-olds to a set of items from the same intermediate category (e.g., a series of dogs), and then tested them with an item from a different category, but within the same broad domain (e.g., a fish). In this case, the different-category test item had a fairly different shape and some different parts from the habituation items; but nevertheless, 9-month-olds did not dishabituate to this test item—indicating that they did not construe the dogs and fish as different, despite their perceptual differences. In contrast, 11-month-olds dishabituated to the out-of-category item, indicating successful discrimination of the different kinds of animal. Finally in the third condition, the authors habituated 9- and 11-month-olds to a series of toy birds modeled with their wings outspread, and then tested them with a novel bird (also with wings outspread) or with a toy plane. Even though all habituation and test items had a similar overall shape, infants at both ages dishabituated to the different-category item, indicating successful discrimination of the categories despite perceptual similarities. Thus, in summation, infants at 9 months discriminated items from broadly different semantic categories, both when the habituation and test items had variable shapes and parts, and when they had a grossly similar overall shape; but they failed to discriminate dogs from fish, despite perceptual differences among these items. Eleven-month-olds, in contrast, discriminated both the broader and more specific categories in all conditions.

We find the Mandler and McDonough (1993) findings (and the similar findings of Pauen, 2002b) to be of particular interest because they indicate an early ability to discriminate broad conceptual domains for both perceptually similar and perceptually disparate items; and because of a developmental change between the ages of 9 and 11 months in the ability to differentiate subcategories within the same conceptual domain (i.e., dogs and birds). Infants at both ages were tested with the same stimulus items, hence the different patterns of behavior cannot be explained solely with reference to the perceptual structure of the stimulus materials themselves. Although it remains possible to attribute some aspects of the findings to perceptual rather than semantic similarities, the developmental change indicates differences in the representations and/or processing by infants at different ages—changes that are consistent with the developmental processes that operate in the Rumelhart model.

In the model analog of the experiment, we "habituate" the model with novel stimulus items that are perceptually similar to one another, and that belong to one of the four categories with which the model is familiar (birds, fish, trees, and flowers). We then test the model with novel test items that include a *semantically related* item from the same category that has few attributes in common with the habituation items, and that is therefore "perceptually dissimilar"; and a *semantically distinct* item from a different category that shares many perceptual attributes with the habituation items (and is therefore "perceptually similar" to these). We then measure the similarities among the model's internal representations to determine which of the test items the model construes as "novel" with respect to the habituation items, at different stages of learning.

Representing Test Items in the Distributed Implementation.   To present the model with a novel item, we simply apply a previously unseen pattern of activity across the input units, which corresponds to the directly observed visual properties of the novel item. We can then inspect the resulting pattern of activity across *Representation* units to determine what "conceptual" representations the model assigns to the item. To simulate the experiment, we needed to create input patterns that allow us to manipulate the "visual similarity"—the degree of overlap in directly perceived features—of the habituation and test items. Specifically, we created a set of *habituation* items that had many input attributes in common, and which belong to the same category; a semantically related test item that belongs to the same category but that has few properties overlapping with the habituation items; and a semantically distinct test item that shares many perceptual properties with the habituation stimuli, but that belongs to a different category. Input patterns with these properties are shown in Fig. 14.10. There are four "categories" of items represented. In each category, items 1 to 4 share many perceptible attributes in common. The fifth item in each case has few directly perceived attributes in common with its category neighbors, but in all cases it shares one especially useful and informative property with them. For example, bird-5 shares the property *wings* with the other birds, but otherwise has no perceptible attribute in common with them.

For each of the four categories, there is one "perceptually similar" out-of-category item from the contrasting domain, and one from the contrasting category in the same domain. For example, trees 1 to 4 have many proper-

	pretty	big	green	red	yellow	white	twirly	branches	petals	wings	gills	fur
tree1	0	1	1	1	1	0	0	1	0	0	0	0
tree2	0	1	1	0	1	1	0	1	0	0	0	0
tree3	0	1	1	0	1	0	0	1	0	0	0	0
tree4	0	1	1	0	0	0	0	1	0	0	0	0
tree5	0	0	0	1	0	1	1	1	0	0	0	0
flower1	1	0	0	1	0	1	1	0	1	0	0	0
flower2	1	0	0	0	1	1	1	0	1	0	0	0
flower3	1	0	0	0	0	1	1	0	1	0	0	0
flower4	1	0	0	0	0	1	0	0	1	0	0	0
flower5	0	1	1	0	1	0	0	0	1	0	0	0
bird1	1	0	1	1	0	0	1	0	0	1	0	0
bird2	1	0	0	1	1	1	0	0	0	1	0	0
bird3	1	0	0	1	0	1	0	0	0	1	0	0
bird4	1	0	0	0	0	1	1	0	0	1	0	0
bird5	0	1	1	0	1	0	0	0	0	1	0	0
fish1	0	1	1	0	0	1	0	0	0	0	1	0
fish2	0	1	1	1	1	0	0	0	0	0	1	0
fish3	0	1	1	0	1	0	1	0	0	0	1	0
fish4	0	1	1	0	1	0	0	0	0	0	1	0
fish5	1	0	0	1	0	1	1	0	0	0	1	0

FIG. 14.10. Attributes of 20 novel items used to simulate Mandler and McDonough's (1993) infant-preference experiment. Associated with each category are four perceptually similar exemplars that constitute habituation items, one perceptually dissimilar exemplar employed as a test item, and two perceptually similar out-of-category test items: one from the contrasting category in the same domain, and one in the opposite domain.

ties that overlap with bird-5, and many that overlap with flower-5. In this sense, both bird-5 and flower-5 are "perceptually" more similar to trees 1 to 4 than is tree-5. This construction allows us to pit perceptual feature overlap in the input against semantic relatedness in our analog of the preference task: We "habituate" the network with four similar items from the same category (e.g., trees 1–4), and then "test" it with a perceptually dissimilar item from the same category (e.g., tree-5) and a perceptually similar item from the contrasting category (flower-5) or domain (bird-5).

Figure 14.11 shows the similarities among some of the habituation and test items that are apparent from the overlap in attributes shown in Fig. 14.10. In each case the "habituation" items are those labeled 1 to 4 in the tree. As is apparent from the figure, the fifth category member is less similar to the four habituation items than is the test item from the contrasting cate-

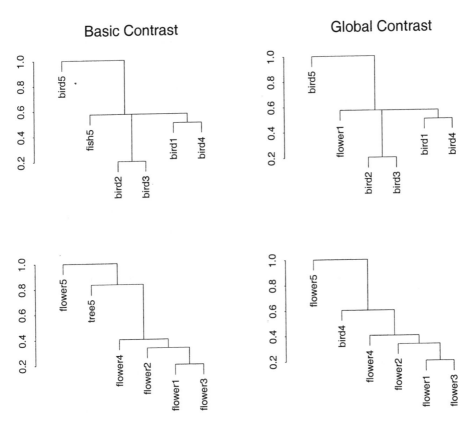

FIG. 14.11. Hierarchical cluster plot of the perceptual similarities for some of the novel habituation and test items used in the simulation. In each case, the fifth category item is less similar to its category coordinates than is an out-of-category test item.

gory or domain. Using this set of patterns we can investigate changes in the model's ability to discriminate both broad and more specific conceptual categories as it learns.

Habituation and Test Procedure

To simulate the familiarization-preference procedure, we present the model with four familiarization items (e.g., birds 1–4), a semantically related item (e.g., bird-5), and a semantically distinct item (e.g., fish-5 or tree-5) in sequence, and record the internal representations it derives for each. We then calculate the distance between the centroid of the representations for the four habituation items, and each of the two test items. To map from these distances to an analog of the infant behavior, we adopt the following assumption: We assume that the model construes as more novel, and therefore tends to choose whichever test item gives rise to a representation that has the largest distance from the centroid of the habituation items; and that the likelihood of choosing one object over another increases with the discrepancy in their respective distances from the habituation centroid. Consistent with this assumption, we use the following formula to determine the likelihood of choosing the target item given the relevant mean distances:

$$p_b = \sigma(s(d_b - d_w))$$

In this formula, p_b is the probability of choosing the between-category test item, σ is the logistic function, d_b is the mean distance from the between-category test to the four habituation items, d_w is the mean distance from the within-category test item to the four habituation items, and s is a scaling parameter that determines the degree to which the model is sensitive to the difference $d_b - d_w$. The probability of choosing the within category test item, p_w, is just $1 - p_b$. Intuitively, the equation indicates that when the between- and within-category items are equally distant from the habituation items, the model is equally likely to choose to manipulate either, but as one test item gets further from these relative to the other, the likelihood of choosing it for examination increases.

Simulation Details

The model was trained just as described in the previous section. Training was halted every 125 epochs, the weights were stored, and the simulation of the habituation experiment was begun. For each of the 20 test items shown in Fig. 14.10, the model generated an internal representation, simply by presenting the appropriate pattern across the input units and observing the subsequent pattern of activity arising across *Representation* units.

To test the network's tendency to choose a between-category test item, at both the global and intermediate (i.e., basic) levels, the distances among its internal representations of habituation and test items were calculated. Specifically, the centroid was determined for each set of four habituation items (birds 1–4, fish 1–4, flowers 1–4, or trees 1–4), and the distance between this centroid and each of the corresponding test items was calculated. These distances were then entered into the formula just shown to determine the probability that the model "preferred" the different-category item. Each category (e.g., the bird category) had one perceptually dissimilar same-category test item (e.g., bird-5); one perceptually similar global different-category test item (e.g., flower-1 or tree-4); and one perceptually similar, intermediate-level different-category test item from the contrasting category in the same domain (e.g., fish-5). This yielded four comparisons testing intermediate category differentiation, and four testing global category differentiation. The simulation was run five times with different starting weights, yielding 20 data points in total for each level of contrast. The data we report are averaged across these trials.

Note that the model was never trained with the items used in the habituation procedure, and no weight changes were made during the habituation process. The representations the model generates for these items simply reflect knowledge the model has accumulated on the basis of learning in the normal training environment.

Results

Figure 14.12 shows the similarities among the representations the model generates for one set of habituation and test items (the bird category), at three different points throughout learning. During the very early epochs of training all items are represented as quite similar to one another, although the organization of items does reflect to some extent the degree of overlap in the perceptual properties from which the internal representations are derived. For instance, bird-5 is represented as less similar to the other birds than either flower-1 or fish-5. The reason is that at this point, there is no information accumulated in the network's weights that allows it to map reliably between parts of the representation space and any of the directly perceived attributes that generate the error signal that the network is using to find internal representations. Items with similar sets of directly observed attributes thus generate similar, weak error derivatives at the *Representation* units, and the network finds similar internal representations for these, regardless of their semantic relationships to one another. However, as the model learns more about the coherent covariation among properties in the extended training corpus, this picture begins to change: The model first differentiates the global different-category test item (the flower) from the

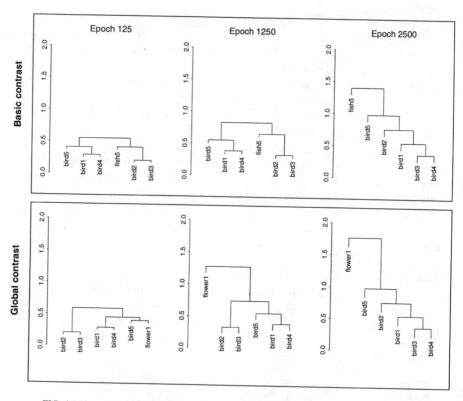

FIG. 14.12. Hierarchical cluster plot of the representations generated by the distributed-inputs model, for novel habituation and test items from the *bird* category at
three different points during training.

five birds, and later comes to differentiate the intermediate-level different-
category item (the fish) from the birds—even though both of these test
items share more "perceptual" properties with birds 1 to 4 than does bird-5.

Figure 14.13 shows the proportion of times the model chose the different-category test item over the same-category test item throughout early
training, for between-domain test items (e.g., tree or flower vs. bird, a
global discrimination) or for intermediate-level between-category test items
(e.g., tree vs. flower or bird vs. fish). Early in learning, all items are represented as similar to one another, so same- and different-category test items
(at both the global and intermediate levels) are equally distant from the habituation centroid. Consequently, the likelihood of choosing the between-
category item is near chance. As training proceeds, this likelihood begins to
change: The model first begins to reliably choose the different-category test
item from the contrasting global domain, and later begins to choose the local between-category test item. Like infants, the model's ability to differenti-

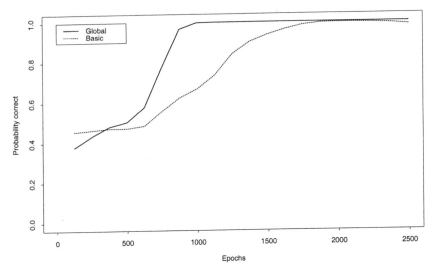

FIG. 14.13. Average likelihood of "preferring" the semantically unrelated test item throughout early epochs of learning, for "global" and "basic" semantic contrasts, in a model analog of the object examination task.

ate items on conceptual grounds emerges first for broad semantic distinctions, and only later for more specific ones.

Finally, it is worth noting that, in generating its internal representations of the novel items after learning, the model seems to lend special weight or importance to the properties that covary coherently together in its training environment. This is reflected in the fact that the model continues to group the same-category item with the habituation items through learning—even though it shares very few of its properties with these. For instance, of the four features that describe bird-5 (shown in Fig. 14.10), only one is consistently shared by the four other birds seen during habituation. By contrast, the test item fish-5 shares five of its six properties with at least half of the birds seen during habituation. Considering just the overlap in features, then, fish-5 is more similar to the habituation items than is bird-5 (as is clear from Fig. 14.11). However, the one property that bird-5 does have in common with the four habituation birds—*wings*—happens to covary coherently with many other properties in the model training corpus. By contrast, the five properties that fish-5 shares with the habituation birds are all somewhat idiosyncratic in the training corpus, and do not covary coherently together with anything else. As a consequence of the dynamics of learning described earlier, the coherently covarying property comes to contribute more strongly to representational change than do the various idiosyncratic properties—so that the network treats as similar those items that share the coherent property, even if they do not have many other attributes in common, and treats as different items that differ for the coherent property, even if they share many idiosyncratic attributes. In this sense, the model's sensitivity to coherent covariation leads it to treat some properties as more "important" for semantic representation than others; that is, these properties come to have an acquired salience for the model.

DISCUSSION

There are several points we would like to make on the basis of the preceding simulations. To begin, one of our aims has been to support the idea that the Rumelhart model, as simple as it is, might nevertheless provide some insight into the acquisition of semantic knowledge from different kinds of perceptual experience across a range of events and situations; and might specifically have relevance to understanding aspects of the early conceptual development of preverbal infants. On the present construal of the model, both the input and output attributes can be viewed as coding various aspects of similarity and difference among objects encountered in the environment, as detected by perceptual processes across different events and situations. In any given situation, such perceptual similarities may not yield much information about which objects should be treated as the same kind of thing. However, repeated encounters with a range of objects across a variety of contexts leads to a state of knowledge in which some attributes exert particularly strong constraints on the semantic system's internal representations, allowing it to treat items that share these properties as similar even when they differ in many other respects.

The key factor contributing to this state of knowledge is the influence of coherent covariation on the learning processes that govern weight changes in the system. The ease with which the system can learn that a particular item has a certain property depends on the degree to which the property is shared by other items with similar internal representations. However, the similarities represented by the model at any point in time themselves depend on the mappings it has learned between internal representations and particular output properties. At a particular time the model treats as salient those properties that are shared by items within the clusters of objects that it has learned to differentiate at that time. As we have seen, such properties are easiest for the system to acquire, and thus dominate the representational change that occurs as the system learns. Once these properties have been mastered, representational change slows dramatically until, on the basis of minute weight changes accumulating from other properties, the system finds a new organization of its internal representations that renders a new set of properties coherent. Such properties become easier to learn and propel new, rapid representational change until they are mastered. Thus, coherent covariation among stimulus attributes at different granularities spurs successive waves of differentiation, with different stimulus properties acquiring salience at different points during development. It is this changing sensitivity to patterns of coherent covariation that we propose to add to the repertoire of possible mechanisms that may contribute to the process of conceptual development.

It is important to acknowledge a key point that must be treated as an essential presupposition of our analysis. The mechanism we have described depends on the following proposition being true:

> The conceptual distinctions to which children are first sensitive are just the ones that reflect the strongest patterns of coherent covariation present in the child's perceptual experience.

We anticipate this presupposition will be viewed by our critics as revealing a fatal flaw in our reasoning. To the contrary, we suggest the assumption in itself does not preclude a role for other contributing factors to concept development, including additional assumptions similar to those that other investigators have offered. In other words, we believe that more than one of the alternative positions can be partially correct; and indeed we believe it is likely that all of them have at least some partial validity. This validity stems in part from the fact that the child's perceptual experience reflects not just the structure present in the world, but the ways in which this structure is filtered by the child's perceptual system. Consider, first, the suggestion of Rakison that some kinds of perceptual information may be more salient than others. This idea is a very old one, and is almost certain to have some validity. For example, it is clear that the brain has specialized mechanisms for motion detection (e.g., Zeki, 1978), and that motion strongly engages attention. The training materials used in our modeling efforts could not be justified without accepting that they presuppose a selection of certain properties for inclusion, and that the basis for inclusion reflects assumptions about the availability and salience of information in the input. That is, the model's behavior depends on the particular training patterns to which it is exposed, and these training patterns incorporate implicit or explicit assumptions about which properties of objects are available or salient in the input, and which are not.[2]

---

[2]As a side point it should perhaps be noted that it is easy to manipulate salience explicitly in connectionist networks, for example, by introducing a scalar "salience" parameter that determines the strength with which each property can drive learning in the network. Rather than do this, our model might be seen instead as relying on the extreme approximation of a binary choice of salience values—salience of 1 for those properties included in the training set, salience of 0 for all others.

Consider, second, the suggestion of Mandler that conceptual knowledge emerges from a process that generates conceptual descriptors, which represent certain stimulus events as similar despite differences in perceptual details. For example, as we have seen, different instances of self-initiated movement, in Mandler's view, come to be treated as conceptually the same, even though they may be quite distinct perceptually: A flounder and a gazelle seem to move in very different ways, but somehow the fact that they are both self-propelled becomes apparent to infants, and provides the basis for forming the concept *animal*. For Mandler, the problem of understanding how infants arrive at this realization is solved by supposing that there exists a process that yields up descriptions of the flounder's movement and the gazelle's movement that have something in common. Our analysis, like Mandler's, also depends on the assumption that different kinds of animal movement share some common representational element. We include a unit in the model that corresponds to the attribute *can move*—an attribute shared by all animals and none of the plants. To use such a unit in our simulations is essentially to specify that all forms of animal movement overlap in some perceptually detectable way, thereby providing a basis for seeing them as having something in common. Similar points can be made about all of the attributes in our training set.

It is important to realize, however, that in imbuing the network with these perceptual skills, we have not predisposed it to assign special weight or salience to some attributes rather than others. The network must still discover the category structure inherent in its inputs, and must still determine which of the attributes are "important" for organizing its internal representations. To see this, consider what happens when the Rumelhart network is exposed to three different events—a red robin, flying; a white goat, walking; and a red rose, growing. The target representations we have used "build in" similarities and differences between experiences with these different events. The *move* attribute unit in the model encodes a degree of similarity between the goat's walking and the robin's flying, whereas the *walk* and *fly* units code a degree of difference between these as well. The *red* unit codes an aspect of similarity between the robin and the rose, which differentiate both from the goat. All of these elements of similarity and difference are coded in target patterns provided for the model's attribute units. However, feedback from the environment does not indicate which of them the model should use to "group together" the different items in its internal conceptual representations. In fact, on the basis of their movement patterns and colors, there is no perceptual basis provided by the environment for determining which two items are of the same "kind" in this example. What this will depend on, instead, is the fact that moving covaries coherently with other properties across all items in the training corpus, whereas being red does not—thus the learning process will issue a greater salience to movement.

At issue is the young infant's (and the model's) capacity to "choose" which of the many different kinds of detectable similarities and differences among stimulus objects should be used to determine which items are of the same kind. Although the model "builds in" an initial ability to detect various elements of similarity and difference between experiences (and could be further augmented to reflect differential salience as previously noted), there is nothing in the initial state as we have specified it for these simulations that inherently lends more weight or importance to (for example) the *move* attribute relative to others. Hence, the model has no "built in" basis to represent as similar two items that share the capacity to *move* than two items that share the attribute *is red*. The competencies exhibited by infants at 9 months of age in the studies previously described above—their ability to zero in on such properties as self-initiated movement, or movement-enabling parts such as legs and wheels, and to employ these as the basis for representing objects as similar to one another—are not given to the network in its initial state.

There remains, in our view, a fundamental unresolved question: To what extent does our use of units to detect aspects of similarity across various different kinds of events amount to building in domain-specific knowledge? This is where we anticipate that the opinions of other investigators will differ, with Carey, Spelke, and some of the other theory-theorists lining up behind the view that it does, and others whose perspectives we have considered perhaps leaning toward the view that it does not. We would like to adopt a somewhat agnostic position on this point, and simply contend that children's perceptual processing systems can act as "filters" that influence the degree to which distinct events will be perceived as similar or different. We resist the assertion that different perceptual filtering systems are brought to bear on different "kinds" of things. To be sure, different "kinds" of things draw on different types of information at some point fairly early in the life span (e.g., movement may be important for some things, shape and color for others); and different types of information may be filtered in different ways from birth. We do not deny that such filtering can influence the knowledge infants acquire about different kinds of things. However, we do not accept the idea that perceptual filtering systems are wired up in advance to apply different filters to the very same type of information, depending on what "kind" of object or event is being processed by the filter.

The principles illustrated by the Rumelhart model do not and cannot refute other claims about the factors that may potentially contribute to conceptual development. However, accepting that the mechanism we have identified may be a contributing factor, our simulations have implications for each of the other viewpoints we reviewed earlier.

In agreement with advocates of perceptual enrichment, the PDP framework suggests that conceptual knowledge acquisition is spurred by domain-general learning that is based on perceptual experience. Our further point here is that the sensitivity of correlation-based learning mechanisms to coherent covariation among stimulus properties, and the resultant influence on acquired feature salience, provides a previously unrecognized mechanism by which such domain-general perceptual learning can give rise to internal representations that capture similarity structure different from that which is available directly from the perceptual input provided by test stimuli.

Rakison's claim that certain directly observed properties are especially salient to 12-month-old infants is not inconsistent with our theory; and indeed, nothing in our approach refutes the possibility that some attributes are initially and inherently more salient to infants than others. However, our simulations also demonstrate that coherent covariation can lead certain properties to have an *acquired* salience. Thus, the empirical demonstration that infants in semantic tasks are most sensitive to large, external parts, or to patterns of motion, need not reflect a learning-independent perceptual salience of these properties—this salience might emerge as a consequence of domain-general learning over the first year of life. If so, this might explain why 12-month-olds are inclined to emphasize external parts such as legs or wheels as a basis for grouping objects (Rakison & Poulin-Dubois, 2001). Note that, under this account, there is nothing special about external parts; any properties that varied coherently across domains could potentially provide the basis for differentiating concepts, including overall shape and structural characteristics that are likely to covary coherently with other properties.

We also suggest that the PDP framework has similarities with some aspects of Mandler's ideas about the emergence of conceptual representations from perceptual experience. The state of knowledge captured by the network at a fairly early point is similar in many respects to that attributed by Mandler to 7- to 9-month-old infants. That is, the model treats as similar perceptually varying items that happen to share characteristics such as self-initiated movement that are not directly available in stimuli used in experiments. For example, our model first represents animals as similar to one another and as distinct from plants, despite the fact that there are no input properties held in common between the birds and the fish, and many input and target properties that differentiate these items. One might argue that the model's "conceptual" and "perceptual" representations capture different information about the similarities among objects, as Mandler suggested—immediately available perceptual similarities are captured in the input, and conceptual similarities are captured in the internal representations. Moreover, the learning process captured by our model provides a new mechanistic basis for the extraction of conceptual representations from perceptual experience, different from but not inconsistent with the conceptual discovery process that Mandler attributes to infants.

Finally, Carey (2000) suggested that the conceptual distinctions made by infants early in life cannot be acquired and must reflect initial domain-specific knowledge about non-obvious "core" conceptual attributes. We have addressed some of Carey's ideas in detail in related work (see Rogers & McClelland, 2004), but for the time being we should point out that there is one sense in which, on our view, infants are biologically prepared to acquire concepts. The influence of coherent covariation on concept development depends on the infant's initial ability to detect elements of similarity and difference among particular events. Without such a facility, there can be no basis for patterns of covariation to influence knowledge acquisition. The theory thus assumes that, among the many various elements of similarity to which infants are initially sensitive, there exist some that vary coherently across semantic domains. Our simulations suggest that it may not be necessary to attribute to infants initial domain-specific predispositions to lend special salience, weight, or attention to specific core properties, as this salience may emerge as a consequence of coherent covariation.

We close with a final thought on what will perhaps be viewed as the most difficult contention of our theory: the assumption that "perceptual" input contains elements that remain invariant from one event to another, despite discriminable differences in the particular instantiations of such common elements across different events. This assumption amounts to the claim that, although there may be differences, say, between the specific legs of one animal and another, there is also at least some perceptually given element of similarity. Our network assigns internal representations to objects on the basis of coherent covariation tabulated across such presumed elements of similarity, and the results described here may suggest to some readers that the model depends strictly on this literal overlap for its success in discovering the category structure of the domain.

Although our simulations do not illustrate it, other work has shown that PDP networks can sometimes discover patterns of coherent covariation among items that have no direct feature overlap of any kind. Such a situation is illustrated in the simulations of Hinton (1986, 1989), in a network with an architecture similar to the Rumelhart model. Hinton trained his network with a corpus of information about the relationships among individuals in two different families, one English and one Italian. When given an individual's name and a relationship as input (e.g., *Colin* and *father*), the model was trained to activate the name of the appropriate individual in the output (e.g., Colin's father *James*). Each person was represented with a localist unit in the model, both at the input and the output level, so there was no direct overlap of any kind for the various individuals in the two families. Even so the network discovered internal representations that captured the position of each individual within the respective family tree—for example, assigning near identical internal representations to the English and Italian "grandchildren"; near identical representations to the English and Italian "uncles," and so on. Although there was no direct overlap in the input and output representations for, say, the English and Italian grandfathers, the network's internal representations discovered the higher order commonalties across the two different families—that is, it discovered that both grandfathers entered into a similar set of relationships with others in their respective families, and on this basis came to represent the individuals as similar. This and other work (e.g., Altmann & Dienes, 1999) is consistent with the idea that coherent covariation can be discovered by networks even in the absence of any overlap of the input and output patterns of activation. Although direct feature-overlap for different items may not be necessary for coherent covariation to exert an influence on the acquisition of internal representation, we believe such overlap is in fact made available by our perceptual systems, at least for some covarying attributes of objects if not for all of them. In either case, the fundamental point remains the same: The ability of networks to exploit such covariation plays a crucial role in the early emergence of semantic categorization abilities and in the global-to-local differentiation of such categories as a gradual result of experience, beginning in infancy and continuing throughout life.

REFERENCES

Altmann, G. T. M., & Dienes, Z. (1999). Rule learning by seven-month-old infants and neural networks. *Science, 284,* 875. (With reply by G. Marcus)

Behl-Chada, G. (1996). Basic-level and superordinate-like categorical representations in infancy. *Cognition, 60,* 105–141.

Bertenthal, B. (1993). Infants' perception of biomechanical motions: Intrinsic image and knowledge-based constraints. In C. Grandrud (Ed.), *Visual perception and cognition in infancy* (pp. 175–214). Hillsdale, NJ: Lawrence Erlbaum Associates.

Carey, S. (1985). *Conceptual change in childhood.* Cambridge, MA: MIT Press.

Carey, S. (2000). The origin of concepts. *Cognition and Development, 1,* 37–42.

Carey, S., & Spelke, E. (1994). Domain-specific knowledge and conceptual change. In L. A. Hirschfeld & S. Gelman (Eds.), *Mapping the mind: Domain specificity in cognition and culture* (pp. 169–200). New York: Cambridge University Press.

Carey, S., & Spelke, E. (1996). Science and core knowledge. *Journal of Philosophy of Science, 63,* 515–533.

Collins, A. M., & Quillian, M. R. (1969). Retrieval time from semantic memory. *Journal of Verbal Learning and Verbal Behavior, 8,* 240–247.

Eimas, P. D., & Quinn, P. C. (1994). Studies on the formation of perceptually based basic-level categories in young infants. *Child Development, 65*(3), 903–917.

Gelman, R. (1990). First principles organize attention to and learning about relevant data: Number and the animate/inanimate distinction as examples. *Cognitive Science, 14,* 79–106.

Gelman, R., & Williams, E. M. (1998). Enabling constraints for cognitive development and learning: A domain-specific epigenetic theory. In D. Kuhn & R. Siegler (Eds.), *Handbook of child psychology: Vol. 2. Cognition, perception and development* (5th ed., pp. 575–630). New York: Wiley.

Gergely, G., Nadasdy, Z., Csibra, G., & Biro, S. (1995). Taking the intentional stance at 12 months of age. *Cognition, 56,* 165–193.

Gopnik, A., & Meltzoff, A. N. (1997). *Words, thoughts, and theories.* Cambridge, MA: MIT Press.

Hinton, G. E. (1986). Learning distributed representations of concepts. *Proceedings of the 8th annual conference of the Cognitive Science Society,* 1–12.

Hinton, G. E. (1989). Learning distributed representations of concepts. In R. G. M. Morris (Ed.), *Parallel distributed processing: Implications for psychology and neurobiology* (pp. 46–61). Oxford, England: Clarendon Press.

Keil, F. (1989). *Concepts, kinds, and cognitive development.* Cambridge, MA: MIT Press.

Keil, F., Carter Smith, W., Simons, D. J., & Levin, D. T. (1998). Two dogmas of conceptual empiricism: Implications for hybrid models of the structure of knowledge. *Cognition, 65*(2–3), 103–135.

Lakoff, G. (1987). *Women, fire, and dangerous things: What categories reveal about the mind.* Chicago: University of Chicago Press.

Mandler, J. M. (1988). How to build a baby: On the development of an accessible representational system. *Cognitive Development, 3,* 113–136.

Mandler, J. M. (1992). How to build a baby II: Conceptual primitives. *Psychological Review, 99*(4), 587–604.

Mandler, J. M. (1994). From perception to conception. In P. van Geert & L. Mos (Eds.), *Annals of theoretical psychology* (Vol. 10, pp. 43–57). New York: Plenum.

Mandler, J. M. (1997). Representation. In D. Kuhn & R. Siegler (Eds.), *Handbook of child psychology: Vol. 2. Cognition, perception and development* (5th ed., pp. 255–308). New York: Wiley.

Mandler, J. M. (2000a). Perceptual and conceptual processes in infancy. *Journal of Cognition and Development, 1,* 3–36.

Mandler, J. M. (2000b). What global-before-basic trend? Commentary on perceptually based approaches to early categorization. *Infancy, 1*(1), 99–110.

Mandler, J. M. (2002). On the foundations of the semantic system. In E. M. Forde & G. Humphreys (Eds.), *Category specificity in mind and brain* (pp. 315–340). East Sussex, England: Psychology Press.

Mandler, J. M., & Bauer, P. J. (1988). The cradle of categorization: Is the basic level basic? *Cognitive Development, 3,* 247–264.

Mandler, J. M., Bauer, P. J., & McDonough, L. (1991). Separating the sheep from the goats: Differentiating global categories. *Cognitive Psychology, 23,* 263–298.

Mandler, J. M., & McDonough, L. (1993). Concept formation in infancy. *Cognitive Development, 8,* 291–318.

Mandler, J. M., & McDonough, L. (1996). Drinking and driving don't mix: Inductive generalization in infancy. *Cognition, 59,* 307–355.

Mareschal, D. (2000). Infant object knowledge: Current trends and controversies. *Trends in Cognitive Science, 4,* 408–416.

Mareschal, D., French, R. M., & Quinn, P. C. (2000). A connectionist account of asymmetric category learning in early infancy. *Developmental Psychology, 36*(5), 635–645.

McClelland, J. L. (1989). Parallel distributed processing: Implications for cognition and development. In R. G. M. Morris (Ed.), *Parallel distributed processing: Implications for psychology and neurobiology* (pp. 8–45). New York: Oxford University Press.

McClelland, J. L. (1994). Learning the general but not the specific. *Current Biology, 4,* 357–358.

McClelland, J. L., McNaughton, B. L., & O'Reilly, R. C. (1995). Why there are complementary learning systems in the hippocampus and neocortex: Insights from the successes and failures of connectionist models of learning and memory. *Psychological Review, 102*, 419–457.

McClelland, J. L., & Rumelhart, D. E. (1986). A distributed model of human learning and memory. In J. L. McClelland, D. E. Rumelhart, & the PDP Research Group (Eds.), *Parallel distributed processing: Explorations in the microstructure of cognition* (Vol. 2, pp. 170–215). Cambridge, MA: MIT Press.

McClelland, J. L., & Rumelhart, D. E. (1988). *Explorations in parallel distributed processing: A handbook of models, programs, and exercises.* Cambridge, MA: MIT Press.

McClelland, J. L., St. John, M. F., & Taraban, R. (1989). Sentence comprehension: A parallel distributed processing approach. *Language and Cognitive Processes, 4*, 287–335.

Miikkulainen, R. (1993). *Subsymbolic natural language processing: An integrated model of scripts, lexicon, and memory.* Cambridge, MA: MIT Press.

Miikkulainen, R., & Dyer, M. G. (1991). Natural language processing with modular PDP networks and distributed lexicon. *Cognitive Science, 15*, 343–399.

Murphy, G. L., & Medin, D. L. (1985). The role of theories in conceptual coherence. *Psychological Review, 92*, 289–316.

Pauen, S. (2002a). Evidence for knowledge-based category discrimination in infancy. *Child Development, 73*(4), 1016.

Pauen, S. (2002b). The global-to-basic shift in infants' categorical thinking: First evidence from a longitudinal study. *International Journal of Behavioural Development, 26*(6), 492–499.

Plunkett, K., & Sinha, C. (1992). Connectionism and developmental theory. *British Journal of Developmental Psychology, 10*(3), 209–254.

Quillian, M. R. (1968). Semantic memory. In M. Minsky (Ed.), *Semantic information processing* (pp. 227–270). Cambridge, MA: MIT Press.

Quine, W. V. O. (1960). *Word and object.* Cambridge, MA: MIT Press.

Quinn, P. C. (2002). Early categorization: A new synthesis. In U. Goswami (Ed.), *Blackwell handbook of childhood cognitive development* (pp. 84–101). Malden, MA: Blackwell.

Quinn, P., & Eimas, P. (1997a). Perceptual organization and categorization in young infants. In C. Rovee-Collier & L. P. Lipsitt (Eds.), *Advances in infancy research* (Vol. 11, pp. 1–36). Norwood, NJ: Ablex.

Quinn, P., & Eimas, P. (1997b). A reexamination of the perceptual to conceptual shift in mental representations. *Review of General Psychology, 1*, 271–287.

Quinn, P., & Eimas, P. D. (2000). The emergence of category representations during infancy: Are separate perceptual and conceptual processes really required? *Journal of Cognition and Development, 1*, 55–61.

Quinn, P., Eimas, P., & Rosenkrantz, S. (1991). Evidence for representations of perceptually similar natural categories by 3-month-old and 4-month-old infants. *Perception, 22*, 463–475.

Quinn, P. C., & Johnson, M. H. (1997). The emergence of perceptual category representations in young infants: A connectionist analysis. *Journal of Experimental Child Psychology, 66*, 236–263.

Rakison, D. (2003). Parts, categorization, and the animate-inanimate distinction in infancy. In L. M. Oakes & D. H. Rakison (Eds.), *Early concept and category development: Making sense of the blooming, buzzing confusion* (pp. 159–192). New York: Oxford University Press.

Rakison, D., & Butterworth, B. (1998a). Infant attention to object structure in early categorization. *Developmental Psychology, 34*(6), 1310–1325.

Rakison, D., & Butterworth, B. (1998b). Infants' use of parts in early categorization. *Developmental Psychology, 34*(1), 49–62.

Rakison, D., & Cohen, L. B. (1999). Infants' use of functional parts in basic-like categorization. *Developmental Science, 2*, 423–432.

Rakison, D., & Poulin-Dubois, D. (2001). The developmental origin of the animate-inanimate distinction. *Psychological Bulletin, 127*, 209–228.

Rogers, T. T., Lambon Ralph, M. A., Garrard, P., Bozeat, S., McClelland, J. L., Hodges, J. R., & Patterson, K. (2004). The structure and deterioration of semantic memory: A neuropsychological and computational investigation. *Psychological Review, 111*(1), 205–235.

Rogers, T. T., & McClelland, J. L. (2004). *Semantic cognition: A parallel distributed processing approach.* Cambridge, MA: MIT Press.

Rumelhart, D. E. (1990). Brain style computation: Learning and generalization. In S. F. Zornetzer, J. L. Davis, & C. Lau (Eds.), *An introduction to neural and electronic networks* (pp. 405–420). San Diego, CA: Academic Press.

Rumelhart, D. E., Hinton, G. E., & Williams, R. J. (1986). Learning representations by back-propagating errors. *Nature, 323*(9), 533–536.

Rumelhart, D. E., Smolensky, P., McClelland, J. L., & Hinton, G. E. (1986). Schemata and sequential thought processes in PDP models. In J. L. McClelland, D. E. Rumelhart, & the PDP Research Group (Eds.), *Parallel distributed processing: Explorations in the microstructure of cognition* (Vol. 2, pp. 7–57). Cambridge, MA: MIT Press.

Rumelhart, D. E., & Todd, P. M. (1993). Learning and connectionist representations. In D. E. Meyer & S. Kornblum (Eds.), *Attention and performance 14: Synergies in experimental psychology, artificial intelligence, and cognitive neuroscience* (pp. 3–30). Cambridge, MA: MIT Press.

Schyns, P. G. (1991). A modular neural network model of concept acquisition. *Cognitive Science, 15*, 461–508.

St. John, M. F., & McClelland, J. L. (1990). Learning and applying contextual constraints in sentence comprehension. *Artificial Intelligence, 46*, 217–257.

Younger, B., & Fearing, D. (2000). A global-to-basic trend in early categorization: Evidence from a dual-category habituation task. *Infancy, 1*, 47–58.

Zeki, S. M. (1978). Functional specialization in the visual cortex of the rhesus monkey. *Nature, 274*, 423.

Chapter 15

Abstraction as Dynamic Interpretation in Perceptual Symbol Systems

Lawrence W. Barsalou
Emory University

INTRODUCTION

If a scientific construct's centrality reflects the variety of forms it takes, then abstraction is a central construct in cognitive science, taking at least the following six senses:

Sense 1: Abstraction as categorical knowledge. Abstraction can simply mean that knowledge of a specific category has been abstracted out of the buzzing and blooming confusion of experience. Just about any account of knowledge is comfortable with this sense, including rule-based, prototype, exemplar, connectionist, and embodied theories.

Sense 2: Abstraction as the behavioral ability to generalize across instances. Another relatively uncontroversial sense is that people can summarize the properties of one or more category members *behaviorally*. All theories agree that people state generics, such as "Bats live in caves," and state quantifications, such as "Some birds fly." Behaviorally, people clearly produce abstractions.

The material in this chapter was first presented at the Workshop on Abstraction, supported by the Cognitive Science Program, French Ministere de la Recherche, CNRS, Gif sur Yvette, France, September 2001. This research was supported by National Science Foundation Grants SBR-9905024 and BCS-0212134 to Lawrence W. Barsalou. Address correspondence to Lawrence W. Barsalou, Department of Psychology, Emory University, Atlanta, GA 30322 (barsalou@emory.edu, http://userwww.service.emory.edu/~barsalou/).

Sense 3: Abstraction as summary representation. Much more controversial are the cognitive bases of the behavioral abstractions in Sense 2. According to some theories, behavioral abstractions reflect underlying summary representations of category instances in long-term memory. On these views, when people generalize behaviorally, they read out an underlying summary representation, such as a declarative rule, a statistical prototype, or a connectionist attractor. Notably, however, the summary representations in Sense 3 are not necessary to produce the behavioral abstractions in Sense 2. In exemplar models, only exemplars are stored in memory—no summary representations—and behavioral abstractions result from scanning and summarizing exemplars online (e.g., Hintzman, 1986).[1]

Sense 4: Abstraction as schematic representation. Another controversial sense is that schematic representations describe categories in memory. According to this sense, summary representations are sparser than exemplars, abstracting critical properties and discarding irrelevant ones (e.g., Biederman's, 1987, geons). Alternatively, properties may be distorted in various ways to idealize or caricature a category, thereby increasing its distinguishability relative to other categories (e.g., Posner & Keele, 1968; Rhodes, Brennan, & Carey, 1987; also see Barsalou, 1985; Palmeri & Nosofsky, 2001).

Sense 5: Abstraction as flexible representation. Another controversial sense of abstraction is that summary representations can be applied flexibly to a wide variety of tasks, including categorization, inference, language comprehension, reasoning, and so on. According to this sense, increasing abstractness allows a representation to become increasingly flexible (e.g., Winograd, 1975).

Sense 6: Abstraction as abstract concepts. Finally, abstraction can refer to the concreteness of concepts, ranging from concrete (e.g., *CHAIR*) to abstract (e.g., *TRUTH*).[2] As concepts become increasingly detached from physical entities, and more associated with mental events, they become increasingly abstract (e.g., Barsalou, 1999; Barsalou & Wiemer-Hastings, in press; Paivio, 1986; Wiemer-Hastings, Krug, & Xu, 2001).

---

[1]A classic problem for this view is why these abstractions do not subsequently become stored in memory along with exemplars. To the extent that abstractions require deep processing to produce, they should become well established in memory (e.g., Hyde & Jenkins, 1969).

[2]Italics will be used to indicate concepts, and quotes will be used to indicate linguistic forms (words, sentences). Thus, *CHAIR* indicates a concept, and "chair" indicates the corresponding word. Within concepts, uppercase words will represent categories, whereas lowercase words will represent properties of categories (e.g., *CHAIR* vs. *seat*) and relations between properties (e.g., *above* for the relation of a *CHAIR's seat* to its *back*).

As these senses illustrate, abstraction is a central construct in cognitive science. The focus here, however, is on the most controversial sense, namely, Sense 3. From here on, "abstraction" will mean *summary representations* in long-term memory.

The first of the five remaining sections describes three properties of abstractions. The second section reviews existing approaches and problems that they encounter for these properties. The third and fourth sections present the DIPSS theory of abstraction (Dynamic Interpretation in Perceptual Symbol Systems). The fifth section shows how DIPSS can be applied to various abstraction phenomena in categorization, inference, background knowledge, and learning. The final section revisits the other five senses of abstraction, and applies DIPSS to them.

PROPERTIES OF ABSTRACTIONS

Three properties of abstractions appear central to their nature: interpretation, structured representation, and dynamic realization.

Interpretation

In a classic paper, Pylyshyn (1973) argued that cognition is inherently an interpretive process. Addressing the nature of mental imagery, Pylyshyn argued that cognitive representations are not like the holistic bit-mapped recordings in cameras, video recorders, and audio recorders. Many perception researchers would agree (e.g., Hochberg, 1998). Rather than being recordings, Pylyshyn argued, cognitive representations are interpretations of experience. To produce an interpretation, concepts in memory type the components of sensorimotor experience to produce type–token propositions. On walking into a living room, for example, the concepts for *SOFA*, *RUG*, and *LAMP* become bound to particular objects, thereby creating type–token propositions of the sort, *SOFA*(object-98), *RUG*(object-32), and so on. Such propositions essentially make claims about the world that can be true or false, such as the belief that object-98 is a *SOFA* (e.g., Church, 1956).

A given component of experience can be interpreted in infinite ways. Thus object-98 could be interpreted alternatively as *FURNITURE*(object-98), *CONTEMPORARY SOFA*(object-98), *PLACE TO CRASH*(object-98), *PLACES THE DOG CAN'T SIT*(object-98), and so forth. Not only are there infinite true interpretations of an individual, there are infinite false ones as well, with each interpretation providing a different spin on how to think about it.

Once a type–token proposition is constructed to interpret an entity or event, the proposition provides a wealth of inferential knowledge. Once something is interpreted as a *SOFA*, inferences follow that it's soft, comfortable, and heavy, extending the object's interpretation. If the object were interpreted instead as *A PLACE THE DOG CAN'T SIT*, different inferences would follow. All such inferences constitute propositions linked to the type–token mappings that triggered them.

On this view, propositions underlie representations of the world, not bit-mapped recordings (also see Barsalou, 1999; Dretske, 1995; Haugeland, 1991). A representation of a chair is not a holistic recording of it, but a set of propositions that interpret it. Most importantly for our purposes, Pylyshn assumed that abstractions underlie this process. The types in his type–token propositions are abstractions for properties, objects, events, relations, and so forth. Once a concept has been abstracted from experience, its summary representation enables the subsequent interpretation of later experiences. Thus abstractions are linked closely to interpretation.

Structured Representation

When concepts interpret experience, they typically do not do so individually. Instead they become organized into structured representations that capture relations between individual type–token propositions. Rather than *SOFA*(object-98) and *RUG*(object-32) being independent, a spatial concept, such as *on*, might organize them into a structured proposition, such as:

$$on(\textit{upper-region} = SOFA[\text{object-98}], \textit{lower-region} = RUG[\text{object-32}])$$

Much empirical evidence demonstrates the extensive presence of structured representations in human knowledge. Perhaps the most direct evidence comes from work on concepts and categorization, where researchers have explicitly assessed the presence of such structure and found robust evidence for it (e.g., Goldstone & Medin, 1994; Markman & Gentner, 1997; also see Barsalou, 1992; Barsalou & Hale, 1993). Assigning exemplars to categories, judging the similarity of exemplars, and drawing categorical inferences all rely heavily on structured relations—not just on independent properties. Furthermore, the process of conceptual combination is essentially the process of combining individual concepts into structured representations (e.g., Hampton, 1997; Rips, 1995; Wisniewski, 1997).

Much additional evidence comes from research on analogy, where structured representations are strongly implicated in people's ability to extend relational systems from one domain to another (e.g., Gentner & Markman, 1997; Holyoak & Thagard, 1997). Similar evidence comes from the literature on language comprehension, where complex propositional structures provide the standard scheme for representing meaning (e.g., Graesser, Singer, & Trabasso, 1994; Kintsch & van Dijk, 1978). Fodor and Pylyshyn (1988) offered general theoretical arguments for the necessity of structured representations, and for the related constructs of productivity and systematicity.

Thus a second important property of abstractions is that they enter into complex interpretive systems. Rather than interpreting isolated components of experience, abstractions assemble into structured representations that interpret complex structure in the world.

Dynamic Realization

The abstractions that represent a category are notoriously difficult to pin down. In my own research, I have continuously experienced the slipperiness of abstractions, referring to it as *linguistic vagary* (Barsalou, 1993). Artificial intelligence researchers who program knowledge into intelligent systems chronically experience similar vagaries in articulating abstractions. Specifically, three problems arise in trying to specify the abstraction that represents a category:

Identifiability. What particular information should be included in an abstraction? Consider Schank and Abelson's (1977) attempt to specify the abstraction that underlies the restaurant script. Of everything that could possibly occur in a restaurant, what should be included in a summary representation? Only the most invariant properties across restaurant visits? What about important properties only true occasionally? What about differences between cultures and individuals? When is an abstraction complete? Specifying the content of an abstraction is an extremely challenging task.

Motivation. Why is a particular abstraction the correct one? Typically artificial intelligence researchers intuitively select the abstractions that best serve a specific application. Problematically, however, no principled account of how to do this exists, nor is it clear that such an account is possible.

Rigidity. How does one handle all of the exceptions that arise for an abstraction? When Schank and Abelson proposed the restaurant script, a common criticism was that it could not handle unexpected deviations and unusual restaurant visits. Schank and Abelson replied that different *tracks* through a script handle special cases, but the counter-reply was that infinitely many tracks are required to handle all the possibilities. Moreover, how does one handle cases never encountered, which people seem to do effortlessly? No compelling account of how abstraction can handle such variability exists.

Conclusion. One could view the identifiability, motivation, and rigidity problems for abstractions as a sign that we simply need a better methodology for discovering them. Alternatively there may be no correct abstractions to discover. Rather than a single abstraction representing a category, diverse abstractions may be constructed online to represent a category temporarily (Barsalou, 1987, 1989, 1993). If so, then studying the *skill* to construct temporary abstractions dynamically may be more fruitful than attempting to establish one particular abstraction that represents a category. In this spirit, I assume that a third important property of abstractions is their dynamic realization (this is clearly not a standard assumption in the literature).

THEORIES OF SUMMARY REPRESENTATION

Later sections develop a theory of dynamically realized abstractions. First, however, it is useful to briefly review existing theories, and the status of abstraction as a theoretical construct.

GOFAI Theories of Abstraction

Haugeland (1985) dubbed classic abstraction theories as "Good Old Fashioned Artificial Intelligence" (i.e., GOFAI), an approach that dominated the early history of the field, and that continues alongside other approaches currently. Classic examples can be found in Winograd (1972), Newell and Simon (1972), Schank and Colby (1973), Bobrow and Collins (1975), Schank and Abelson (1977), and Charniak and McDermott (1985).

GOFAI provides a powerful account of interpretation and structured representation. Through the mechanisms of argument binding and recursion, GOFAI implements these processes elegantly and powerfully. Simple interpretation results from binding a predicate to an individual, and structured representation results from binding higher order predicates to lower order ones. Thus, *SOFA(X)* and *RUG(X)* can be bound to object-98 and object-32, thereby interpreting those objects in particular ways. Similarly, *on(upper-region* = x, *lower-region* = y) can be bound to *SOFA*(object-98) and *RUG*(object-32), thereby forming a structured representation.

The problem that has bedeviled GOFAI theories for decades is dynamic realization. Identifying the content of the abstractions in GOFAI theories has constituted a daunting and sobering challenge. Clearly, adequate abstractions can be developed for specific tasks, yet few would argue that they offer definitive accounts of human knowledge. Motivating these accounts has also been difficult, given their reliance on programmer intuition. Perhaps most critically, these accounts are known for their brittleness. Although they work in some situations, they don't work in all, given the difficulty of handling exceptions and novel cases.

Another major problem for GOFAI concerns the basic nature of their symbols. On the one hand, connectionist theories argue that the discrete symbols in GOFAI representations don't exist—instead knowledge is distributed statistically across continuous neural-like processing units (e.g., McClelland, Rumelhart, & the PDP Research Group, 1986; Rumelhart, McClelland, & the PDP Research Group, 1986; Smolenksy, 1988). On the other hand, embodied theories argue that the arbitrary amodal symbols in GOFAI don't exist—instead simulations of sensorimotor processing represent knowledge (e.g., Barsalou, 1999; Glenberg, 1997; Mandler, 1992).

For all these reasons, accounts of human knowledge look increasingly less and less like GOFAI representations. Theorists find it increasingly implausible that knowledge takes this form.

Connectionist Theories of Abstraction

In GOFAI theories, abstractions are clear and explicit, spelled out in predicate calculus-like expressions. Connectionism offers a radically different approach, where abstractions are relatively fuzzy and implicit. In a network of neural-like processing units, an abstraction is an attractor for a statistically likely combination of properties. When a set of learned exemplars shares correlated properties, the network's weights evolve to recognize this pattern and its variants, establishing an attractor for the category. Within the dynamical system that constitutes the network's state space, activation prefers to follow trajectories toward learned attractors.

The active units that characterize an attractor implicitly represent an abstraction. When these units are distributed and course-coded, the content of an abstraction can be difficult to specify precisely, but this is the beauty of the approach: It is not necessary or even desirable to specify abstractions explicitly or precisely, thereby avoiding the brittleness of GOFAI abstractions.

Two properties of connectionist abstraction further allow it to avoid brittleness. First, many activation states around an attractor can each represent the same category. Depending on the current context, the representation of the category can vary dynamically (e.g., Smolensky, 1988). Second, as experience with a category changes, an attractor can adapt quickly. Connectionist learning algorithms offer powerful ways to revise abstractions as the input changes. For all these reasons, connectionist approaches offer a compelling account of dynamic realization.

Where connectionist theories struggle is with the first two properties of abstraction: interpretation and structured representations. Connectionist theories do offer a basic form of interpretation. When an attractor becomes active, it provides an interpretation of the input. Because the attractor represents multiple category instances, it is a type that can interpret tokens. Implicitly, the simultaneous activation of an attractor and its input constitute a type–token relation, albeit of a much different variety than in GOFAI theories. Furthermore, if the attractor represents information not found in the input, the attractor provides inferences via pattern completion (e.g., unseen parts, actions, contexts, etc.; Rumelhart, Smolensky, McClelland, & Hinton, 1986).

Although connectionist nets have basic interpretive ability, limitations become apparent as interpretations become increasingly complex and structured (e.g., Fodor & Pylyshyn, 1988). In a complex situation with many exemplars present, it becomes tricky to bind all of the active attractors to their respective instances. Furthermore, when arguments must be bound in structured relations, connectionist nets don't naturally accomplish this, at least not nearly as naturally or easily as in GOFAI. Connectionist theorists have offered various solutions. For example, a separate bank of units can be set aside for each argument in a relation, with its bound value being the currently active state (e.g., Miikkullainen & Dyer, 1991). A problem with this approach is its assumption that the set of arguments is finite, small, and known in advance—an unlikely possibility (Barsalou, 1993).

Another approach is to translate each element of a predicate calculus expression into a vector, superimpose all these individual vectors into a single vector, and then extract the string of symbols as needed later (e.g., Pollack, 1990; Smolensky, 1990; van Gelder, 1990). Technically, this algorithm can implement structured representations, although there are problems for it too (Barsalou, 1993). Problematically, this approach has not struck many researchers as psychologically plausible—it primarily seems like an engineering solution, mostly having computer science applications. Furthermore, this approach assumes implicitly that predicate calculus expressions—at some level of functionality—are the right way to think about knowledge. Given the troubled status of GOFAI representations as psychological accounts, their connectionist cousins could be viewed similarly.

Lack of a Viable Account

Abstraction in the classic sense has gone out of fashion—at the least, it has become a dubious construct. On the one hand, classic GOFAI theories that champion abstraction are falling by the wayside. On the other hand, abstraction plays a minimalist role in the theories replacing them. As we just saw, abstraction exists in connectionism, but in a much less powerful form. Simple interpretation arises naturally and elegantly, but complex structured interpretations do not.

Furthermore, the other reigning theories of knowledge—exemplar models and latent semantic analysis—similarly relegate abstraction to the periphery. In standard exemplar models, no abstractions exist—only exemplar representations (e.g., Brooks, 1978; Lamberts, 1995; Medin & Schaffer, 1978; Nosofsky, 1984). Furthermore the empirical literature has largely failed to support the existence of summary representations for categories (although see Nosofsky, Palmeri, & McKinley, 1994; J. Smith & Minda, 2002; Spalding & Ross, 1994). The message is that there is no need for summary representations in memory. When an abstraction is needed, it can be constructed online behaviorally and then discarded. In latent semantic analysis, the message is similar: From a large data base of low-level associative knowledge, it is possible to compute online abstractions as needed—it is not necessary to store them explicitly (Burgess & Lund, 1997; Landauer & Dumais, 1997).

All of these approaches do a great job capturing the dynamic realization of abstractions; indeed, they can all be viewed as reactions to the rigidity and brittleness of GOFAI theories. Where they fall down, though, is in handling structured representations. Some might say that we don't need to worry about structured representations, but throwing out babies with bath water appears applicable here. Researchers who study conceptual combination, language, and thought all know that structured representations are not only a signature property of human cognition, but are essential for adequate accounts of these phenomena. Thus it is important to search for theories of abstraction that not only explain dynamic realization but that also explain structured interpretation.

SIMULATORS AND SIMULATIONS IN PERCEPTUAL SYMBOL SYSTEMS

One tack would be to develop more plausible connectionist accounts of abstraction. Indeed, this is an important direction to explore. The theme of this article, however, is that an elegant and natural account of structured interpretation can be found elsewhere, namely, in theories of embodied cognition. Furthermore, these theories naturally exhibit dynamic realization, thereby offering the potential for a complete account.

This current section lays the groundwork for the embodied theory of abstraction in the subsequent two sections. Obviously a working computational model is desirable. The goal here, however, is to outline the mechanisms of such a model, and to show how this architecture implements the three properties of abstraction. First, simulators and simulations are defined (i.e., two of the basic constructs in perceptual symbol systems; Barsalou, 1999). The focus then turns to simulators for properties and relations, and the empirical evidence for them.

Simulators and Simulations

Sensorimotor Reenactment. The account of abstraction later relies on simulators and simulations, which more basically rely on the mechanism of sensorimotor reenactment. Damasio (1989) presented this mechanism in his convergence zone theory (also see Simmons & Barsalou, 2003, for further development of this approach). Sensorimotor reenactment has also been adopted widely in neural accounts of mental imagery (e.g., Farah, 2000; Jeannerod, 1995; Kosslyn, 1994). As Fig. 15.1 illustrates, this mechanism has two phases—storage and reenactment—each addressed in turn.

When a physical entity is perceived, it activates feature detectors in the relevant sensorimotor areas. During the visual processing of a chair, for example, some neurons fire for edges, vertices, and planar surfaces, whereas others fire for color, orientation, and direction of movement. The overall pattern of activation across this hierarchically organized distributed system represents the entity in visual perception (e.g., Palmer, 1999; Zeki, 1993). Analogous distributions of activation on other modalities represent how the entity might sound and feel, and also actions performed on it. A similar

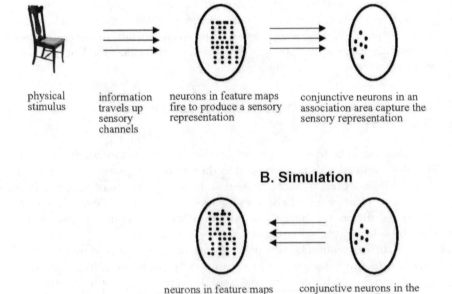

FIG. 15.1. Illustration of the storage (A) and simulation (B) of sensorimotor information in Damasio (1989) and Barsalou (1999).

account can be given for introspective states that arise while interacting with an entity. For example, patterns of activation in the amygdala and orbitofrontal areas represent emotional reactions to perceived entities. A tremendous amount of neuroscience research has documented the structure of feature maps across modalities and the states that arise in them.

One might be concerned that the neural activation of a feature map in Fig. 15.1 looks like a chair. Notably, however, feature maps in vision are often organized topographically. Indeed, many topographically mapped areas reside in the visual system alone, with others residing in the motor, somatosensory, and auditory modalities. Thus it is not unreasonable to assume that modality-specific representations take a somewhat topographic form. Most importantly, however, *nothing* in perceptual symbol systems, nor in the account to follow, depends on topographically mapped representations! If these representations were completely nontopographic, the theory would work identically. The important assumption is that sensorimotor representations exist, and that high-level cognitive processes reenact them to represent knowledge.

As Fig. 15.1 further illustrates, when a pattern becomes active in a feature map, conjunctive neurons in an association area capture the pattern's features for later use. Damasio (1989) referred to these association areas as "convergence zones," and assumed that they exist at multiple hierarchical levels, ranging from posterior to anterior in the brain. Most locally, posterior convergence zones near a particular modality capture patterns of activation within it. Thus association areas near the visual system capture patterns of activation there, whereas association areas near the motor system capture patterns of activation there. Further downstream in more anterior areas, higher level association areas, such as the temporal and frontal lobes, conjoin patterns of activation *across* modalities.

This architecture of feature maps and convergence zones has the functional capability to produce sensorimotor reenactment: Once a subset of conjunctive neurons in a convergence zone captures an activation pattern in a feature map, the conjunctive neurons can later reactivate the pattern in the absence of bottom-up sensory stimulation. While remembering a perceived object, for example, conjunctive neurons reenact the sensorimotor states that were active while encoding it. Similarly, when representing a concept, conjunctive neurons reenact the sensorimotor states characteristic of its instances. A given reenactment is never complete, and biases may enter into its reactivation, but at least some semblance of the original state is partially activated.

Although this basic mechanism is viewed widely as underlying mental imagery (e.g., Farah, 2000; Jeannerod, 1995; Kosslyn, 1994), the reenactments it produces need not be conscious mental images. As Barsalou (1999, 2003) suggested, *unconscious* reenactments may often underlie memory, conceptualization, comprehension, and reasoning. Whereas explicit attempts to construct mental imagery may typically create relatively vivid reenactments, other cognitive processes may typically rely on less conscious reenactments. In the account of abstraction to follow, the neural reenactment of sensorimotor mechanisms is the critical mechanism—*not* conscious mental images.

Simulators and Simulations. Barsalou (1999) developed a theory of concepts based on the neural reenactment of sensorimotor states. Figure 15.2 illustrates the basic constructs in this theory: *simulators* and *simulations.* As multiple instances of the same concept are encountered, they tend to activate similar neural states in feature maps (i.e., categories tend to have statistically correlated features; Rosch & Mervis, 1975). As a result, similar populations of conjunctive neurons tend to capture these states (Simmons & Barsalou, 2003, argued that these populations are localized topographically). Over time, conjunctive neurons integrate sensorimotor features across diverse category instances and across diverse settings, establishing a multimodal representation of a category. For the category *CAR*, visual information about how cars look is integrated, along with auditory information about how they sound, olfactory information about how they smell, motor information about driving them, somatosensory information about the feel of riding in them, and emotional information associated with acceleration, collisions, and so on. The result is a distributed system throughout the brain's association and modality-specific areas that establishes conceptual content for *CAR.* Barsalou (1999) referred to this distributed system as a *simulator.*

Once a simulator exists, it can reenact small subsets of its content as specific *simulations.* The entire content of a simulator is never activated at once; only a small subset becomes active on a given occasion (cf. Barsalou, 1987, 1989, 1993). As Barsalou (2003) proposed, the active subset is tailored to the agent's current context of action, providing goal-relevant inferences about objects, actions, mental states, and the background setting. Thus, on one occasion, the *CAR* simulator might produce a simulation of driving a car, whereas on others it might produce a simulation of fueling a car, of seeing a car drive by, and so forth. Although all the experienced content for a category resides implicitly in a simulator, only specific subsets are reenacted on a given occasion.

Once a simulation has been constructed, it can serve a wide variety of cognitive functions (Barsalou, 1999). For example, simulations can be used to draw inferences about physical instances of a category currently present in the environment. Alternatively, simulations can represent instances in their absence during memory, language, and thought.

A. Storage of Multiple Instances in a Simulator

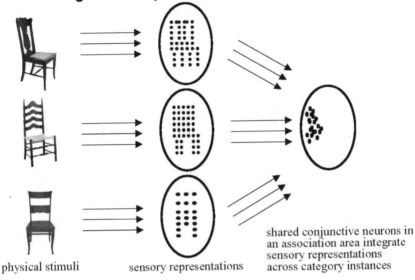

physical stimuli   sensory representations   shared conjunctive neurons in an association area integrate sensory representations across category instances

B. Simulation of Different Instances by a Simulator

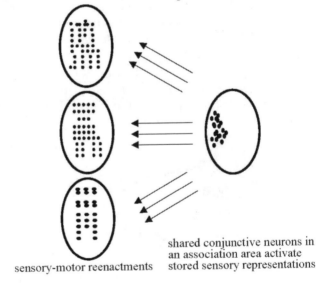

sensory-motor reenactments   shared conjunctive neurons in an association area activate stored sensory representations

FIG. 15.2. Illustration of simulators (A) and simulations (B) in perceptual symbol systems (Barsalou, 1999).

Property Simulators

In principle, an infinite number of simulators can be established in the brain, reflecting the considerable flexibility of selective attention. Barsalou (1999) argued that a simulator develops for any component of experience that attention selects repeatedly. Thus, if attention focuses repeatedly on chairs, a simulator develops for them. Simulators don't just develop for physical objects, however, they also develop for locations, events, actions, mental states, and so forth. Such flexibility is consistent with Schyns, Goldstone, and Thibaut's (1998) argument that new features can be learned creatively as they become relevant for categorization.

The theory of abstraction to follow rests on simulators for properties (this section) and simulators for relations (next section). Most basically, a property simulator constructs specific simulations of the forms that a property takes across different categories. As Fig. 15.3 illustrates, the simulator for *nose* stimulates the noses of *HUMANS, DOGS, FISH, JETS*, and so forth. The next seven subsections develop the construct of a property simulator in greater detail.

Multimodal Property Simulations.   Property simulators are multimodal. Although Fig. 15.3 only illustrates visual information for *nose*, a property simulator reenacts whatever information across modalities is relevant. Thus when the *nose* simulator simulates a human nose, the simulation might reenact blowing one's nose, how it feels, and how it sounds—not just how it looks.

Local Property Simulations.   Property simulators represent properties locally (Solomon & Barsalou, 2001). Rather than there being a single global representation of a property that represents it in different objects, many lo-

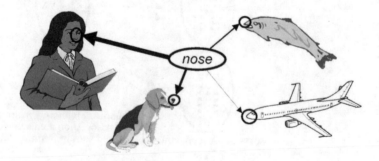

FIG. 15.3.   Illustration of the local simulations for different property forms that a property simulator produces, each framed in a background simulation of the respective object (Solomon & Barsalou, 2001). Increasing link thickness represents a simulation's dominance in the simulator.

cal representations of a property represent it collectively. Thus, *nose* may be represented by local representations of *human noses, dog noses, fish noses,* and so forth. Although Fig. 15.3 only shows one nose for each category, many local representations may exist for each (e.g., many different *human noses*).

Simulations of Background Contexts. Local property representations are simulated in the background contexts of their respective objects (or events). As Fig. 15.3 illustrates, the property of *human nose* is not simulated as an isolated detached nose. Instead it is simulated as a focal region in a background face (or possibly a background body). Attention plays a central role in highlighting properties against background simulations (Barsalou, 1993, 1999; Langacker, 1986; Talmy, 1983).

Dominance Orders of Local Simulations. Within a property simulator, local property simulations are ordered implicitly by dominance (decreasing link thickness in Fig. 15.3). On activating a property simulator, dominant simulations are more likely to run than less-dominant ones. Although many factors influence dominance, frequency is likely to be particularly important. The more often a particular property form is experienced, the more dominant it becomes. Because people experience *human nose* more often than other noses, this local form becomes particularly dominant. As a result, when people think of *nose*, they are most likely to simulate *human nose* first. As they continue thinking about *nose*, however, other less dominant senses may be simulated.

Interpreting Simulated Objects and Events. Not only can a property simulator simulate local properties in their absence, it can interpret regions of simulated entities (and of perceived entities) as containing the property. Consider Fig. 15.4. At the top, the simulator for *JET* has run one particular simulation. At the bottom, the simulator for *nose* has run four different simulations, with one of them corresponding to a region in the *JET* simulation at the top. As a result of this mapping, the simulated object is interpreted as having the property of a *nose.*

Solomon and Barsalou (2001) discussed factors that affect this interpretive mapping. First, the likelihood of a successful mapping increases as a local property form increasingly matches some region of the simulated object (e.g., if a simulated human nose matches some region of a simulated human). Second, the likelihood of a successful mapping increases as the position of the simulated property in its background simulation increasingly corresponds to the position of the matching region in the simulated object (e.g., if both are in the center of a face on top of a body). To the extent that the two simulations are alignable, the mapping is more likely to be correct. Third, the likelihood of a successful mapping increases as the simulated

FIG. 15.4. Illustration of a property simulator, with one of its local simulations construing a region of an object simulation, thereby creating a type–
token property mapping (Solomon & Barsalou, 2001).

function of the property corresponds to the function of the matching region in the object (e.g., if both sneeze, breathe, etc.). Assessments of function are likely to rely on the multimodal character of simulations (Barsalou,
Sloman, Chaigneau, in press).

Type–Token Interpretation. Once a property simulator interprets a region of a simulated object as a property instance, an implicit type–token relation exists. The region of the simulated object is established as a token of
the type that the property simulator represents. Mapping the *nose* simulator
into a region of a simulated object types the region as a *nose*. The result is an
implicit proposition that could be either true or false, and that carries inferences from the type to the token. For example, if an object region is interpreted as a *nose*, inferences about the region sneezing and breathing may

follow as further simulations from the *nose* simulator. In this manner, simulators produce the standard categorical inferences associated with type–token propositions (Barsalou, 1999).

Infinite Property Interpretations. In principle, an infinite number of property interpretations can be made of an entity. Given the continuous nature of a simulation, an infinite number of its regions (and groups of its regions) can be interpreted as properties. Furthermore, for a given region, an infinite number of simulators could interpret it truly or falsely. This open-ended character provides property interpretation with a dynamical character important in the later account of abstraction. This open-endedness also explains why enumerating a concept's properties exhaustively is impossible (Barsalou, 1993), as well as why people construct properties prolifically during learning (Schyns et al., 1998).

In summary, property simulators produce local simulations of properties that are multimodal, framed within the context of larger entities, and organized implicitly by dominance. When a local property simulation becomes active, it can interpret a region of a simulated or perceived entity, thereby establishing a type–token proposition that carries categorical inferences. An infinite number of such interpretations is possible.

Empirical Evidence for Property Simulators

Increasing evidence supports this account of property representation. Evidence for local property representations and dominance is reviewed first, followed by evidence for the modal character of these representations.[3]

Local Property Representations and Dominance. In Solomon and Barsalou (2001), participants verified a property first for one concept (e.g., *mane* for *HORSE*) and then, 15 to 25 trials later, verified the same property again for a different concept (e.g., *PONY-mane*). The key manipulation was the perceptual similarity of the first property sense to the second. Sometimes the two property forms were similar (e.g., *HORSE-mane* then *PONY-mane*) and sometimes they were not (e.g., *LION-mane* then *PONY-mane*). Of interest was whether only *HORSE-mane* would facilitate verifying *PONY-mane*, or whether *LION-mane* would facilitate it as well. If a single global representation underlies a property's meaning, then verifying *mane* for any concept earlier (e.g., *HORSE* or *LION*) should facilitate verifying it later for *PONY*. If local representations underlie a property's meaning instead, then only veri-

---

[3]This section only reviews evidence for property simulators. Barsalou (2003) provided a broader review of empirical results that support the presence of simulators across a variety of concepts and tasks.

fying *mane* for *HORSE* should produce a benefit; verifying *mane* for *LION* should not. Across several experiments, priming only occurred for similar local forms, ranging from 37 to 80 ms.[4]

This result indicates that local representations underlie properties. If a single representation underlies a property, the first property should facilitate it, regardless of the first property's similarity to the second. Limited facilitation indicates that a local form becomes active initially, and only facilitates similar forms later.

This finding also indicates that dominance organizes local property representations. Because a priming trial increases the accessibility of a local representation, an underlying dominance order is implied. Rather than being rigid, the dominance order of the local property representations within a simulator is malleable. A single trial can boost a local representation considerably.

An additional result also indicates the presence of dominance orders. When a property was verified for the first time, the dominant forms of properties were verified much more easily than less-dominant forms. For example, the dominant form of *mane* for *HORSE* was verified more easily than the less-dominant form for *LION*. Similarly, *HOUSE-roof* was easier than *CAR-roof*, and *HUMAN-nose* was easier than *AIRPLANE-nose*. These dominance effects were substantial. Nondominant senses were verified 173 ms slower than dominant ones (948 vs. 775 ms), and they exhibited many more errors (22% vs. 3%). Indeed, participants spontaneously noted that images of dominant forms came to mind while verifying nondominant forms, causing mistakes (imaging a human nose while verifying *AIRPLANE-nose*). These results indicate that local representations underlie the meaning of property words, and that dominance organizes them (also see Halff, Ortony, & Anderson, 1976; Wisniewski, 1998).

Modal Property Representations. Increasing evidence suggests that sensorimotor simulations underlie property representations. In Solomon and Barsalou (2004), some participants were asked to use imagery while verifying properties, whereas others received neutral instructions. If neutral participants spontaneously adopt amodal representations, their performance should differ from imagery participants. If, however, neutral partici-

---

[4]A potential concern is that concept similarity—not property similarity—underlies these effects. Limited facilitation may occur because the overall similarity of *HORSE* to *PONY* exceeds the overall similarity of *LION* to *PONY*, not because the local forms of *mane* are more similar for the first pair than for the second. To assess this possibility, Solomon and Barsalou (2001) included properties that were equally similar for all three concepts (e.g., *belly* was found to be equally similar for *HORSE*, *PONY*, and *LION*). However, property similarity—not concept similarity—continued to be the critical factor, given that *LION* facilitated *belly* as much as did *HORSE* when verifying it for *PONY*.

pants spontaneously run simulations to verify properties, their performance should mirror the performance of imagery participants. Regression analyses showed strong similarities in the detailed performance of both groups. Perceptual factors were most important for both, followed by expectancy factors, and then linguistic factors. This predicted equivalence is consistent with neutral participants adopting simulations spontaneously.

Furthermore, a perceptual variable, a property's size, was central in the performance of both neutral and imagery participants. The larger a property, the longer it took to verify. This finding is consistent with the interpretation that participants had to interpret a region of a simulation to verify the property in it. The larger the region to be processed, the longer the verification.

Kan, Barsalou, Solomon, Minor, and Thompson-Schill (2003) performed the Solomon and Barsalou (2004) experiment in an fMRI scanner. Under neutral conditions, activation occurred in the fusiform gyrus, an area that underlies visual imagery and high-level vision. These results corroborate Solomon and Barsalou's behavioral results, further implicating visual simulation in the verification of visual properties.

Pecher, Zeelenberg, and Barsalou (2003) found further evidence for modality-specific property representations. Perception research has shown that detecting a signal on a modality is faster when the previous signal was on the same modality than on a different one (e.g., Spence, Nicholls, & Driver, 2000). For example, verifying the presence of a tone is faster when the previous signal was a tone than when it was a light flash. Using linguistic materials and no imagery instructions, Pecher et al. demonstrated a similar phenomenon in the property verification task across six modalities (vision, audition, action, touch, taste, smell). When participants verified a property on the same modality as the previous trial, processing was 20 to 41 ms faster across experiments. For example, verifying *bland* (taste) for *CUCUMBER* was faster when *sour* (taste) had just been verified for *BUTTERMILK* than when *speckled* (vision) had just been verified for *BIRD EGG*. Further findings indicated that associative strength was not responsible for these effects. For a review of findings in this paradigm, see Barsalou, Pecher, Zeelenberg, Simmons, and Hamann (in press).

Finally, Martin and his colleagues performed an extensive program of fMRI research to localize property representations in the brain (for reviews, see Martin, 2001; Martin & Chao, 2001; Martin, Ungerleider, & Haxby, 2000). Across many experiments, they consistently found that properties are represented in modality-specific areas. Color properties reside in brain regions that process color; visual form properties reside in regions that process visual form; visual motion properties reside in regions that process visual motion; agentive action properties reside in regions that execute movements. Many reviews of the lesion literature reach similar conclusions (e.g., Damasio, 1989; Humphreys & Forde, 2001; McRae & Cree, 2002; Simmons & Barsalou, 2003; Warrington & Shallice, 1984).

Summary. The foregoing evidence is consistent with the account of property simulators presented earlier. A variety of local property representations, organized by dominance, underlies a property's meaning. Furthermore, these local representations are modality-specific, not amodal. Later we show how this account of properties lends itself to an account of abstraction.

Relation Simulators

Relation simulators will also be central to the later account of abstraction. Analogous to how a property simulator interprets a region of an object, a relation simulator interprets multiple regions and their configuration. For accounts that inspired this one, see Talmy (1983) and Langacker (1986).

Consider the *above* relation in Fig. 15.5a. Imagine that a child is told, "The jet is above the bird." While understanding this utterance, the child attends at some point to the spatial regions that contain the two objects. As a result, a memory of the regions, relative to spatial dimensions, is stored in memory, with the objects largely filtered out (i.e., in the dorsal stream). Further imagine that the upper region is of more interest and receives more attention (the bold regions in the middle of Fig. 15.5a), such that the memory represents the distribution of attention, as well as the spatial regions. Imagine that the child later hears "above" refer to other pairs of objects, as Fig. 15.5a illustrates. Over time, analogous to Fig. 15.3, multiple instances of the same spatial relation become stored together, establishing a simulator for *above*. As a result, it becomes possible to simulate different instances of *above*, each having a slightly different configuration of spatial regions (Fig. 15.5b). Furthermore, these simulations can be used to interpret spatial regions in perceptions and simulations. Just as a property simulator can be used to verify that a *HORSE* has a *mane*, a relation simulator can be used to verify that a *NOSE* is *above* a *MOUTH* in a face. As the bottom of Fig. 15.5b illustrates, mapping an *above* simulation into the regions of a perceived face can verify that the nose is above the mouth.

Empirical Evidence. Research in the attention and comprehension literatures supports the view that the meaning of a spatial relation is a simulation of spatial regions. In the attention literature, researchers present participants with a reference point, R, and tell them that another object, O, stands in some spatial relation to it (e.g., O is *above* R). O is then shown in many different positions around R, and the participant indicates how well each relation exemplifies *O is above R*. Sometimes the measure is simply a goodness rating; sometimes it's the time to find and process O.

A. Storage of Multiple Instances in the *above* Simulator

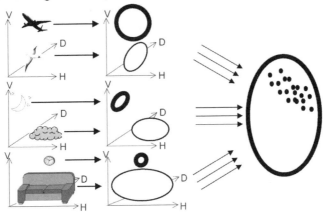

B. Simulation of Different Instances by the *above* Simulator

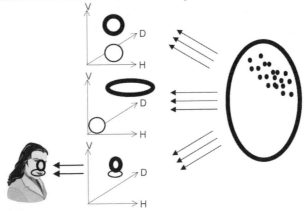

FIG. 15.5.   Illustration of simulators (A) and simulations (B) for the *above* relation. V, H, and D represent the vertical, horizontal, and depth dimensions, respectively.

Much work has shown that a prototypical configuration of spatial regions underlies the meaning of a spatial preposition (e.g., Carlson-Radvansky & Logan, 1997; Hayward & Tarr, 1995; Logan & Compton, 1996). For *above*, the ideal configuration is for the center of O to be aligned geometrically above the center of R, not too far away. On hearing "above," participants appear to construct a perceptual simulation of the ideal configuration. When the subsequent display matches this simulation, processing is optimal. As the display departs increasingly from the ideal simulation, processing efficiency falls off in a graded manner. Importantly, however, even non-ideal displays are categorized as instances of the spatial relation, as long as they satisfy the qualitative criteria that define it. This graceful degradation is consistent with the amount of work that a simulator must do to adjust its simulation. The greater the departure from ideal, the more transformation necessary to simulate the configuration. Analogous to property simulators, a family of simulations—not just one simulation—underlies a spatial relation. Although some simulations are preferred, a wide variety exists.

Additional research shows that function modifies ideal geometric simulations to optimize situated action (e.g., Carlson-Radvansky, Conventry, 1998; Covey, & Lattanzi, 1999). Consider the statement, "The toothpaste tube is above the toothbrush." If spatial geometry were the only factor affecting the ideal simulation of a spatial relation, then a picture of a toothpaste tube centered over a toothbrush should be verified fastest as instantiating *above*. Verification is fastest, however, when the toothpaste tube is positioned over the end of the toothbrush with the bristles. This shows that hearing "above" does not always trigger a single idealized geometric simulation. Instead the arguments of "above" help select a simulation that is currently most appropriate. Thus, "the toothpaste tube is above the toothbrush" activates a configuration of *above* regions that differs from "The mercury in the thermometer is above 90" and "The moon is above your face."

Summary. Together, all of these findings suggest that simulators represent spatial relations. A given relation simulator has a dominant simulation that may be a geometric ideal. However it contains other simulations as well, each tailored to a specific context. Once one of these simulations becomes active, it creates a perceptual representation that directs attention to relevant regions of space. If the simulation becomes bound to a perceived situation, it provides an interpretation, specifying that a particular spatial relationship holds between the attended regions. In all these ways, relation simulators parallel property simulators.

This discussion of relation simulators has only addressed spatial relations. Clearly, though, other types of relations exist, too, including temporal, causal, and intentional relations. Similar analyses can be applied to them. According to perceptual symbol systems, any type of relation focuses on multiple space–time regions, and attempts to establish a particular configuration between them. For example, temporal relations represent configurations of space–time regions that vary in time. Thus, *before* highlights two nonsimultaneous events in a simulation, focusing attention on the first. Similarly, causal relations focus attention on causal components of entities and on the event sequences they produce as effects. Thus focusing on *gasoline* and *spark plug firing* in a *CAR* simulation activates subsequent simulated events that follow from their joint presence (e.g., *combustion, engine operation, driving*). The causal potency of *gasoline* and *spark plug firing* is established by assessing the counterfactual simulation in which *gasoline* and *spark plug firing* are absent, and finding that the event sequence isn't simulated (cf. Pearl, 2000). Thus assessing a complex configuration of regions across multiple simulations is necessary for establishing a causal relation.

Interpretation and Structured Representation

We have seen how perceptual symbol systems implement interpretation. When a property simulator becomes bound to a region of a perception or a simulation, it interprets the region as an instance of the property. Similarly, when a relation simulator becomes bound to multiple regions, it interprets them as an instance of the relation. In each case, interpretation carries inferential capability. Because a simulator accrues information about many instances across situations, it captures the broad content of the property or relation. This broad content then provides a wealth of inferences about any new instance bound to the simulator. For example, if a perceived nose is partially occluded by a scarf, the *nose* simulator can infer the rest of the nose during the property interpretation. Similarly, the *nose* simulator could infer nasal passages, breathing, and sneezing, with each inference being carried in a simulation that goes beyond the information perceived. In this manner, perceptual symbol systems achieve the basic functionality of type–token interpretation.

Structured representation is essentially a more complex form of type–token interpretation, where structure is accomplished by embedding simulations in one another (Barsalou, 1999). To see this, consider Fig. 15.6A. The left side depicts a visually perceived scene. The right side depicts simulators for *BALLOON, CLOUD,* and *above.* The middle depicts an embedded set of simulations that, first, form a structured representation, and second, interpret complex structure in the scene. Specifically, the *BALLOON* and *CLOUD* simulators run simulations that become bound to the relevant regions of the perceived scene (as indicated by the lines running from these simulators to their simulations to their referents in the scene). Simultaneously, the *above* simulator runs a simulation whose regions become bound to the regions containing the balloon and the cloud. Finally, the *BALLOON* and *CLOUD* simulations are embedded in the respective regions of the *above* simulation. This embedded simulation is formally equivalent to the standard amodal proposition:

$$above \ (upper\text{-}region = \text{balloon-1}, \ lower\text{-}region = \text{cloud-1})$$

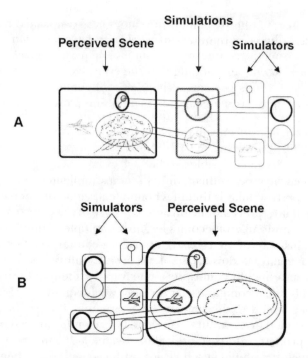

FIG. 15.6.   Illustrations of structured interpretation (A) and recursive interpretation (B) in perceptual symbol systems. In (B), only simulators and the perceived scene are shown; simulations are assumed to exist but are omitted for simplicity.

Regions of the *above* simulation constitute arguments in a relation that become bound to embedded *BALLOON* and *CLOUD* simulations. Whereas classic propositions capture this conceptual structure explicitly, perceptual symbol systems capture it implicitly in the relations between simulations.

As Fig. 15.6B illustrates, this approach further implements the recursive embedding found in amodal propositions, where an argument of a conceptual relation takes another conceptual relation as a value. Thus the recursive proposition,

above (*upper-region* = balloon-1, *lower-region* = *left-of* [*left-region* = jet-1, *right-region* = cloud-1])

is implemented by having a *left-of* simulator map its two regions onto the jet and the cloud in the perceived scene, with this simulation then being embedded in *above's* lower region.

As these examples illustrate, perceptual symbol systems implement structured representations naturally and powerfully. By embedding simulations in one another, binding arguments to values is accomplished readily—the hallmark of structured representations.

Holistic Simulations

One more piece of groundwork must be laid before returning to the issue of abstraction. Consider again the account of property verification depicted in Fig. 15.4. To verify that *JET* has a *nose*, a participant simulates *JET* and then attempts to map possible simulations of *nose* into the *JET* simulation. An unaddressed issue to this point is how the *JET* simulation arises. The possibility pursued here is that object simulators initially construct holistic simulations of instances from pre-attentive sensory representations.[5]

Holistic representations could include blob-like representations of an entity's global shape, extracted by low spatial frequency filters during visual processing (e.g., De Valois & De Valois, 1988; L. Smith, 1989). High spatial frequency information could further be captured at points in the image where such information exists (e.g., Morrison & Schyns, 2001). Holistic representations could also include primary axes, parsed subregions, and distributed configural features that capture direction and distance relations between subregions (e.g., Tanaka & Farah, 1993). Thus, the initial simulation of a *JET* could be a holistic representation of its basic shape, major axes, parsed subregions, and spatial frequency spectra.

Notably, no analytic properties of the sort described earlier exist in these early representations. These holistic simulations do not explicitly represent properties at the conceptual level—they only contain perceptual information. Instead such properties exist only after property simulators become explicitly bound to the holistic simulation (Fig. 15.4).

An additional possibility, though, is that some property and relation simulators become highly associated to particular category over time (e.g., the *wings* simulator becomes highly associated to the *JET* simulator). As a result, when holistic simulations of the category are produced, they quickly activate highly associated property and relation simulators, which fuse with the holistic simulation. Thus, the *wings* simulator might become active and run a simulation that enhances corresponding regions of the holistic *JET* simu-

---

[5]Holistic simulations are *not* bit-mapped recordings (cf. Hochberg, 1998). Much research on early vision demonstrates that pre-attentive sensorimotor representations are collections of features, not simply pixel-like representations. In early vision, for example, information about lines, surfaces, planes, orientations, and so on, are all extracted and coded as features. Thus early visual representations are interpretations themselves in the sense that detectors interpret subregions of the visual field as containing particular features. The difference is that these interpretations are pre-attentive and guide the formation of perceptual representations and experiences. In contrast, the interpretation in abstraction is attention driven and guides the learning of conceptual structures (simulators) in memory.

lation that is developing. As a result, the *JET* simulation becomes a mixture of holistic and analytic representations.

THE DIPSS THEORY OF ABSTRACTION

The previous sections have laid the groundwork for the DIPSS theory of abstraction (Dynamic Interpretation in Perceptual Symbol Systems). Again the goal is to account for the abstractions that represent categories such as *JET, BIRD*, and so forth.[6]

Loose Collections of Property and Relation Simulators

There are no static summary representations in DIPSS. Nor is there an attempt to construct a summary representation that perfectly describes all of a category's instances, or that provides a structurally coherent background theory. Instead the structural component of DIPSS is simply a loose collection of property and relation simulators. This collection is loose in two senses. First it's loose in the sense of being relatively unprincipled and open-ended. As Fig. 15.7A illustrates, a variety of property simulators develops to process the regions of a category's instances (and so do relation simulators, which are not shown). Thus simulators for *nose, wing, engine,* and *tail* develop to interpret the regions of *JETS* (and also to interpret other categories having similar properties). Typically, the property simulators that develop may be relatively unprincipled. A child learns those pointed out by speakers, and those that are functionally relevant in everyday activities. As attention is drawn to object regions via language and goal pursuit, simulators for them begin to develop. Although existing property words in a language may guide and constrain the properties learned, there is nothing particularly logical or systematic about the process.

Property simulators are also loose in the sense of the local simulations they contain. Although two people may have a simulator for the same property, its content may differ because of exposure to different category instances (Figs. 15.2 and 15.5). When different instances of a property become integrated in a simulator, they later produce different simulations, expectations, and inferences about the property. As a result, property infor-

---

[6]Although the focus here is on the interpretation of objects, the same basic approach applies to the interpretation of physical events, mental events, settings, and so on. One notable difference is that the interpretation of physical events and settings often utilizes category simulators—not just property and relation simulators. To interpret instances of *EATING*, for example, categories such as *MONKEY, BANANA,* and *FORK* are required. Thus the interpretive system for physical events and settings requires the presence of object simulators, along with property and relation simulators.

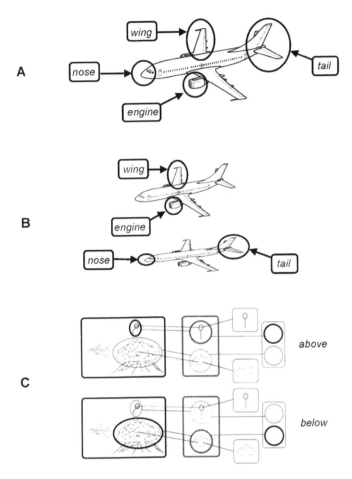

FIG. 15.7.   (A) Illustration of the loose collection of property simulators that can interpret a category's instances. (B) Illustration of property simulators being applied dynamically to a category's instances. (C) Illustration of relation simulators being applied dynamically to a scene.

mation is far from a neat and tidy system across the speakers of a language. What remains in common is a shared awareness that certain regions of category instances have names and are important for goal-directed activity.

Dynamic Application of Property and Relation Simulators

As we just saw, DIPSS's first assumption is that people possess loose collections of property and relation simulators used to interpret category instances. The second assumption is that these simulators are applied dynamically—they are not applied identically across instances or occasions. As Fig. 15.7B illustrates, the property simulators used to interpret an instance vary widely. Whereas *wing* and *engine* might interpret a jet on one occasion, *nose* and *tail* might interpret a jet on another. Similarly, as Fig. 15.7C illustrates, two people could use different relation simulators—*above* and *below*—to interpret the same situation. Although a relatively fixed stock of simulators may exist for a person, the particular ones used to interpret a perception or simulation may vary considerably.

Abstractions. The subset of property and relation simulators applied to an instance on a given occasion can be viewed as an abstraction. This subset types, interprets, and structures aspects of an instance, and classifies it implicitly as something that the abstraction covers. However, such abstractions are not the classic sort of summary representation, because once an instance drops from attention, its abstraction on that occasion becomes largely irrelevant. The next time this instance or another is processed, a different abstraction may be constructed dynamically to interpret it. Thus abstractions are temporary online constructions, derived from an underlying set of property and relation simulators used to interpret many category instances.

Interpretative Attractors. Although the abstractions constructed to interpret instances vary widely, they are not constructed randomly from the available set of property and relation simulators. Due to frequency and recency, some simulators may be more likely to be applied than others. Simulators used frequently in the past will have an advantage, as will simulators applied recently. Furthermore, associations between simulators will produce correlations in the simulators applied. Thus if *steering wheel* is used for *CAR*, it may bring in other simulators associated with driving (e.g., *gear shift* becomes more likely, and *trunk* becomes less so). Furthermore, particular simulators may be associated with particular situations (e.g., *engine* and *oil* are associated with auto maintenance, whereas *trunk* and *stereo* are associated with travel). As a result, being in a particular situation activates relevant property simulators that bias interpretation.

The presence of attractors does not imply rigid interpretation. Even though attractors exist, a wide variety of factors may inhibit them and facilitate other interpretive strategies. As a result, the interpretation process retains a highly dynamic quality.

Category Learning as Skilled Online Abstraction

Again, no static abstractions reside in DIPSS. Instead, a loose collection of property and relation simulators is available for interpreting the instances of a category. On a given occasion, a temporary online abstraction is constructed dynamically to interpret the current instance. Across occasions, both statistical attractors and dynamic variability characterize the abstractions formed. Thus abstraction is more of a skill than a structure. As people learn about a category, they learn to interpret the properties and relations of its instances. With increasing skill, a person can effectively process more regions of instances, and know the most appropriate regions to process in a particular context. What develops permanently is not a fixed summary representation, but a skill for interpreting instances effectively and efficiently.

Explaining Abstraction

DIPSS naturally explains the three properties of abstraction presented earlier: type–token interpretation, structured representation, and dynamic realization. Type–token interpretation results from the application of property and relation simulators to the regions of perceived and simulated entities. As a result, implicit type–token propositions are established that carry a wealth of inferences from simulators. Structured representation results from embedding simulations in one another. The classic mechanisms of argument binding and recursion follow naturally from this process. Once a complex simulation exists, it can be bound to relevant regions of the instance to establish a complex structured proposition. Finally, dynamic realization results from the online application of a loose collection of property and relation simulators to category instances. On a given occasion, a subset of simulators interprets an instance, producing a temporary online abstraction. Across occasions, the abstractions constructed vary widely. The diversity of the resulting abstractions explains the problems associated with classic theories. It is impossible to identify and motivate any single abstraction as *the* summary representation of a category, because infinitely many are possible. Furthermore, none of them need to provide a complete account of the category—instead each simply interprets those aspects of an instance that are relevant in the current situation.

APPLICATIONS

DIPSS can be applied to a wide variety of abstraction phenomena in categorization, inference, background knowledge, and learning.

Categorization

Holistic Versus Analytic Processing. Much work has found that category learning begins holistically and then becomes increasingly analytic (e.g., Kemler, 1983; L. Smith, 1989). Early in learning, relatively undifferentiated representations of instances are stored, with no particular dimensions dominating. Later in learning, however, attention focuses on the most diagnostic dimensions for categorization, and they come to control learning.

According to DIPSS, simulators for properties and relations do not exist initially to interpret a category's instances. As a result, holistic representations established in early sensory processing dominate categorization. With increasing experience, however, attention focuses on the diagnostic regions of instances, and simulators come to represent the content of these regions. During later categorization, these simulators draw attention to the corresponding regions of new instances, thereby causing their content to dominate categorization.

Dimension Weights in Exemplar Models.   Applications of exemplar models to learning data consistently find that some dimensions are weighted more than others (e.g., Lamberts, 1995; Medin & Schaffer, 1978; Nosofsky, 1984). These effects can be viewed as the result of simulators that represent dimensional values becoming differentially associated with categories. Thus if *shape* tends to take the form of *circle* in Category A, and *square* in Category B, then simulators for these values become associated with the categories.

What may be somewhat misleading about these learning paradigms is that they focus learners on a constant set of dimensions and values over the course of learning. As a result, learners apply simulators for them rigidly to instances. As DIPSS suggests, however, the construal of instances in everyday activity is typically much more dynamic. Rather than interpretation taking a rigid form across category instances, it varies widely as a function of experience and goals. Building such structure into category learning paradigms might yield more variable dimension weights than in previous studies. Instances are unlikely to be interpreted rigidly in everyday activity—their interpretation is probably much more dynamic.

Descriptive Inadequacy.   Many theorists have noted the difficulty of specifying the properties that define a category (e.g., Wittgenstein, 1953). In classic work, Putnam argued that whatever description a person has for a category, it will never be sufficient to fix the category's reference (e.g., Putnam, 1973, 1975; also see Fodor, 1998; Margolis & Laurence, 1999). If the description turns out to be inadequate, the reference for the category often doesn't change, suggesting that something besides the description establishes membership. For example, if *WATER* turns out not to have the property, H_2O, but to have some other property instead, the physical things classified as *WATER* nevertheless tends to remain the same. The property, H_2O, never fixed reference and was therefore an inadequate description of category members.

DIPSS provides a natural account of descriptive inadequacy. Descriptions of a category are abstractions that arise from applying property and relation simulators in the available pool. Because this pool develops haphazardly, and because descriptions are constructed dynamically, it's no surprise that these descriptions never fix the category adequately. DIPSS embraces descriptive inadequacy. Because abstraction is a skill that supports goal achievement in particular situations, its purpose is not to construct summary representations that fix category membership.

The remaining question, though, is what does fix a category's reference as descriptions about it vary? As changes in scientific theories produce changes in the lay understanding of *WATER*, why does the reference of *WATER* remain basically the same? DIPSS explains this as the result of pre-attentive holistic representations. Low-level sensory representations of *WATER* are likely to remain relatively constant, as analytic properties and relations about it change. As beliefs about *WATER* come and go, the perception of *WATER* remains basically the same. Because these perceptions tend to be highly accurate in fixing category membership, they play the central role in everyday categorization, regardless of the analytic properties that currently reign.

Analytic properties certainly influence categorization. For example, Biederman and Shiffrar (1987) taught people analytic properties for chicken genitalia that facilitated chick sexing. Similarly, Lin and Murphy (1997) found that learning the functions of artificial objects influenced visual categorization. As such findings illustrate, categorization is not determined solely by holistic representations, but can be influenced by property and relation simulators as well. Nevertheless, it doesn't follow that these simulators completely fix reference; they only contribute to it partially, working together with holistic representations.

Inference

Feature Listing. The feature listing task has often been assumed to access and describe the underlying summary representation of a category. On this view, participants access a feature list, semantic network, or schema for a category, and then read out the information as verbal features.

According to DIPSS, however, no such underlying abstractions exist. Instead, participants run one of many holistic simulations of a category, and then attempt to interpret it using property and relation simulators. Rather than reading out a summary representation for the category, feature listing simply reflects one of many possible temporary abstractions that can be constructed online for a particular instance. Measuring these abstractions can be informative and useful (e.g., Wu & Barsalou, 2004), but they should not be viewed as accessing anything like a summary representation that covers the category descriptively or that fixes its reference.

Conceptual Instability. Barsalou (1987, 1989, 1993) reported that participants exhibit tremendous variability in accessing category information. In the feature listing task, different people produced very different features for the same category (an average overlap of only 44%). When the same person produced features for the same category on two occasions, the average overlap was only 66%. DIPSS explains this variability naturally. When different people produce features for the same category, they construct different holistic simulations, which leads to considerable diversity in the properties and relations used to interpret them. Even when two people construct similar holistic simulations, they may interpret it with different property and relation simulators. Analogously, when the same person produces features on two occasions, different features result for the same two reasons. Thus conceptual instability is a natural outcome of the dynamic simulation and interpretation process.

Script Tracks. As described earlier, a classic problem for Schank and Abelson's (1977) script construct was that are infinitely many script tracks. It didn't seem possible to construct a single summary representation for them all. According to DIPSS, such variability is to be expected, and the interpretative system should be geared to handling it. Because restaurant visits take infinitely many forms, a dynamical interpretive system—such as a loose collection of property and relation simulators—is needed to interpret them. As long as none of the properties or relations in a restaurant visit is new, a novel configuration of existing property and relation simulators can be configured to interpret it. Thus script tracks are a natural and desirable—not problematic—outcome in DIPSS.

Verbal Overshadowing. Schooler and his colleagues have demonstrated that verbally describing a perceptual stimulus interferes with remembering it later, relative to not describing it (see Schooler, Fiore, & Brandimonte, 1997, for a review). For example, describing a perceived face makes it less memorable than not describing it. According to DIPSS, the words in a description activate property and relation simulators, which in turn activate prototypical simulations that become linked to the perceptual stimulus (as in Figs. 15.5B bottom, 15.6, and 15.7C). For example, describing a face as having "big eyes, a long nose, and a full mouth" causes simulations of these properties' prototypical forms to be linked with the corresponding regions of the face's holistic representation. Later, at retrieval, these simulations become active, fuse with the holistic representation, and distort it. When no description is made, the holistic representation alone remains and provides superior information about the presented face. The dynamic application of property and relation simulators to holistic representations naturally explains verbal overshadowing phenomena. More generally, the interpretive process in DIPSS can be viewed as the general basis of encoding effects in episodic memory.

Background Knowledge

Intuitive Theories. Many researchers agree with Murphy and Medin's (1985) claim that intuitive theories of some sort provide background knowledge for categories. The problem has been little success in formulating these theories, and little agreement on the form they should take. DIPSS both explains this quandary and provides a solution to it. Just as there is no single script for an event, there is no single intuitive theory for a category. According to DIPSS, the background knowledge for a category is the loose collection of property and relation simulators used to interpret its instances, along with the skill to apply them appropriately in different contexts.

On some occasions, this interpretive system might produce an online abstraction along the lines of an intuitive theory. For example, property and relation simulators could be configured to explain how biological mechanisms keep an organism alive. Notably, however, a different abstraction might be constructed on another occasion for another purpose (e.g., to explain the reproductive origins of an organism). Over time, a diverse number of explanatory accounts of a category's members may be constructed. Analogous to script tracks, there is no single intuitive theory. Instead there is simply a system that can produce theory-like abstractions (among others) dynamically during the interpretation of category instances. Thus, the same person might construct vitalist, mechanistic, and psychological theories of *ANIMALS* on different occasions (Gutheil, Vera, & Keil, 1998).

Dimensions and Multidimensional Spaces. Theorists have often noted that a category's instances can be arranged in a multidimensional space (e.g., Gärdenfors, 2000; Rips, Shoben, & Smith, 1973). Various problems, though, have confronted this approach (e.g., Tversky, 1977). First, a given multidimensional space never seems to capture all of a category's properties. Second, the multidimensional space for a category is malleable, changing as the set of judged instances changes, and as the task changes.

DIPSS explains both the ability to construct multidimensional spaces and the problems they encounter. Multidimensional spaces are possible when subsets of property simulators have a higher order organization. For example, the simulators for *round, square, triangular,* and so on, can be organized into the higher order property, *shape,* which generally focuses attention on the exterior form of an object. Similarly, the simulators for *red, blue, yellow,* and so on, can be organized into the higher order property, *color,* which generally focuses attention on the surface appearance of an object.

When the simulator for a dimensional value becomes bound to a category instance, it activates the dimension. When another category member is encountered, the active dimension biases interpretation toward one of its values. As a result, the dimension comes to organize the set of instances.

This account explains the problems for multidimensional spaces. As dimensions come to guide the interpretation of instances, other properties and relations remain idle, and therefore don't show up in multidimensional solutions. The interpretive bias toward a few dimensions inhibits the use of other property simulators. As the instances and the task change, the dimensions activated change, such that the resulting multidimensional space reflects the system's current interpretive bias. Again DIPSS views these phenomena as natural products of dynamic interpretation—not as problems. They simply reflect the facts that not all potential property and relation simulators are used at once to interpret a category, and that the subset of simulators applied varies widely.

Analogy.   When the same configuration of property and relation simulators can be applied to different categories, analogy becomes possible (cf. Gentner & Markman, 1997; Holyoak & Thagard, 1997). For example, a common configuration of simulators can be applied to holistic simulations of faces for *HUMAN, DOG,* and *FISH* to draw an analogy between them. Interpreting a given *HUMAN* face as having a *mouth,* a *nose,* and *eyes* results from applying the simulators for *mouth, nose,* and *eyes,* along with relation simulators, to a holistic simulation. Once this temporary abstraction has been constructed, the same configuration of simulators can be tried out on another holistic simulation, say a *DOG* face. If the configuration can be made to fit, an analogy is achieved.

The dynamic property of a simulator to produce different local simulations is central to analogy. The realization of a property or relation across two domains is rarely the same (e.g., different senses of *mouth* and *nose*). This variability is captured naturally by the idea that different simulations of a property reside in its simulator, one for each category. Furthermore, as an analogy is extended to new categories, the nature of the properties and relations that underlie it change, because the respective simulators acquire new local simulations (cf. Dietrich, 2000).

Learning

Novice Knowledge and Shallow Explanation.   Keil and his colleagues have shown that people are over-confident about their understandings of how things work (e.g., Rozenblit & Keil, 2002; Wilson & Keil, 1998). For example, people believe that they understand how a zipper works, how a flush toilet works, and how a jet engine works. When asked for explanations, however, people can only produce partial, superficial ones. DIPSS explains overconfidence as resulting from people's ability to run holistic simulations. The ability to run a complete simulation of an object functioning from start to finish creates the illusion of understanding (e.g., zipping up a zipper). Conversely, DIPSS explains the shallowness of explanations as the result of having an insufficient set of property and relation simulators to construct adequate abstractions. As people began producing an explanation, they use the available property and relation simulators to construct a temporary online abstraction that interprets relevant regions of the holistic simulation. To the extent that a coherent configuration of simulators can't be assembled that covers the holistic simulation, the explanation fails.

More generally, DIPSS assumes that, early in learning, novices have a relatively limited set of property and relation simulators at their disposal. Furthermore, such simulators may mostly interpret "exterior" properties of perceived and simulated events. Novices may often fail to have simulators for key 'internal' properties whose causal properties give entities their functionality. Novices may also fail to have simulators for key relations that link components and events in causal chains.[7]

Expertise.   With experience in a domain, learners acquire a much larger set of property and relation simulators. As a result, the depth and completeness of their explanations increases (cf. Chi, Feltovich, & Glaser, 1981). Experts can identify and interpret more critical regions in perceived events and simulations, and they can structure them in more sophisticated abstractions to form causal chains. By having greater ability to interpret and organize the regions of instances, experts also become better categorizers, moving their basic level down to the subordinate level (e.g., Gauthier, Skudlarski, Gore, & Anderson, 1999; Johnson & Eilers, 1998; Johnson & Mervis, 1997, 1998).

Theories of expertise generally assume that increased storage of exemplars, chunks, or rules speeds performance (e.g., Anderson, 1987; Logan, 1988; Newell, 1990). In DIPSS, the corresponding units are attractors for configurations of property and relation simulators. As an expert encounters instances in a domain, a configuration of simulators interprets each. Over time, the wide variety of configurations used to interpret most instances become well-established attractors and therefore highly accessible. As a result, relatively effortless performance becomes possible.

---

[7]Keil and Batterman's (1984) characteristic-to-defining shift may be a similar case. Initially during category learning, holistic simulations and simulators for exterior surface properties dominate categorization. Later, as simulators for internal causal properties are learned, they come to dominate.

Conceptual Change.   DIPSS explains conceptual change as the result of an evolving set of property and relation simulators. As new simulators are acquired, the ability to interpret instances changes. Sometimes this change may appear gradual, as old-style interpretations are fleshed out with additional properties and relations. Change may be abrupt, however, when a new property or relation simulator is added that affects the use of other simulators. For example, when children add the property *gasoline* and *combustion* to the interpretive system for *CARS*, their interpretations of *CARS*'s behavior may change qualitatively. New online interpretations may be constructed that vary considerably from previous ones. To the extent that configurations of property and relation simulators become linked to form attractors, a large set of simulators may rise in dominance, while another large set falls. The result is a mini-revolution in interpreting the category.

ABSTRACTION REVISITED

We began with six senses of abstraction. The DIPSS account of Sense 3—abstraction as summary representations—can now be brought to bear on the remaining five senses.

Sense 1: Abstraction as categorical knowledge. According to this sense, knowledge of a specific category is abstracted from experience. In DIPSS, this amounts to establishing property and relation simulators that can interpret regions of perceived instances and holistic simulations.

Sense 2: Abstraction as the behavioral ability to generalize across instances. According to DIPSS, when people behaviorally state a generic, such as "Birds have wings," they have simulated a variety of *BIRD* instances, used the *wing* simulator to interpret these simulations, and then used language to describe the temporary online abstraction.

Sense 3: Abstraction as summary representation. Once a temporary abstraction exists for a category, a record of it becomes established in memory, increasing the likelihood of constructing the abstraction again in the future. Nevertheless the abstraction far from dominates the interpretive system that created it—it does not become part of a single summary representation for the category. It simply changes the dynamic qualities of the interpretive system, with the system remaining flexible and unsettled, such that future abstractions vary widely, each tailored to the current situation.

Sense 4: Abstraction as schematic representation. According to this sense, summary representations are sparser than exemplars, abstracting critical properties and discarding irrelevant ones. DIPSS accomplishes this in three ways. First, the property and relation simulators that develop for a category never exhaust the simulators possible but instead constitute a relatively limited set. As a result, the interpretive system is schematic, only representing certain aspects of category instances. Second, the simulations that property and relation simulators construct typically contain far less information than the sensorimotor perceptions that produced them. Thus they are schematic in the sense of reenacting partial information and discarding details. Third, property and relation simulators are capable of producing idealized or caricatured simulations, thus being schematic in the sense of producing prototypical or diagnostic representations. Such simulations could result from the passive integration or averaging of information in a simulator, such that the most prototypical category information emerges as a dominant simulation (similar to Hintzman's, 1986, echo; also see Palmeri & Nosofsky, 2001).

Sense 5: Abstraction as flexible representation. According to this sense, summary representations can be applied flexibly to a wide variety of tasks. In DIPSS, this flexibility is not the result of a single abstracted representation, but of a dynamic interpretive system. As learning evolves, the set of property and relations simulators increases, as does skill in applying them to instances. The result is increased flexibility of interpretation, although attractors may produce ruts that work against flexibility to some extent.

Sense 6: Abstraction as abstract concepts. According to this sense, some concepts become increasingly detached from physical entities and increasingly associated with mental events (e.g., *truth*). In an extensive analysis, Wiemer-Hastings (2004) found that most abstract concepts refer to properties and relations—not to objects and events—suggesting that abstract concepts belong to interpretive systems. This fits well with Barsalou's (1999) proposal that abstract concepts pick out complex relational configurations of physical and mental states in background events.

For example, one sense of *truth* picks out a complex relation where one person makes a claim about the world to another person, who assesses whether the claim is accurate. For *truth* to apply in such situations, a speaker must make a claim, a listener must represent the claim, the listener must compare this representation to the world, and the representation must be accurate. When this complex relation exists, *truth* is a valid interpretation of the speaker's claim (also see Barsalou & Wiemer-Hastings, in press).

In general, abstract concepts often appear to capture complex configurations of physical and mental events in this manner. Analogous to relation simulators, abstract concepts interpret multiple regions of simulated and perceived events, and can thus be viewed as belonging to the loose collections of simulators that constitute interpretive systems. What distinguishes abstract concepts, perhaps, is the complexity of the relational information they capture, along with their frequent inclusion of mental states.

CONCLUSION

Although abstraction has gone out of fashion, it will not go away. Interpretation and structured representations are hallmarks of human cognition. The problem has been explaining these phenomena with mechanisms that are psychologically plausible and well suited for the job. Dynamic interpretation in perceptual symbol systems appears to offer promise in these regards. Although empirical evidence and computational models are necessary to realize this promise, the first step is to sketch its solution to the problem. It is hoped that this chapter has accomplished this goal.

REFERENCES

Anderson, J. R. (1987). Skill acquisition: Compilation of weak-method problem situations. *Psychological Review, 94,* 192–210.

Barsalou, L. W. (1985). Ideals, central tendency, and frequency of instantiation as determinants of graded structure in categories. *Journal of Experimental Psychology: Learning, Memory, and Cognition, 11,* 629–654.

Barsalou, L. W. (1987). The instability of graded structure: Implications for the nature of concepts. In U. Neisser (Ed.), *Concepts and conceptual development: Ecological and intellectual factors in categorization* (pp. 101–140). Cambridge, England: Cambridge University Press.

Barsalou, L. W. (1989). Intraconcept similarity and its implications for interconcept similarity. In S. Vosniadou & A. Ortony (Eds.), *Similarity and analogical reasoning* (pp. 76–121). Cambridge, England: Cambridge University Press.

Barsalou, L. W. (1992). Frames, concepts, and conceptual fields. In E. Kittay & A. Lehrer (Eds.), *Frames, fields, and contrasts: New essays in semantic and lexical organization* (pp. 21–74). Hillsdale, NJ: Lawrence Erlbaum Associates.

Barsalou, L. W. (1993). Structure, flexibility, and linguistic vagary in concepts: Manifestations of a compositional system of perceptual symbols. In A. C. Collins, S. E. Gathercole, & M. A. Conway (Eds.), *Theories of memory* (pp. 29–101). London: Lawrence Erlbaum Associates.

Barsalou, L. W. (1999). Perceptual symbol systems. *Behavioral and Brain Sciences, 22,* 577–660.

Barsalou, L. W. (2003). Situated simulation in the human conceptual system. Conceptual representation [Special Issue]. *Language & Cognitive Processes, 18*(5–6), 513–562.

Barsalou, L. W., & Hale, C. R. (1993). Components of conceptual representation: From feature lists to recursive frames. In I. Van Mechelen, J. Hampton, R. Michalski, & P. Theuns (Eds.), *Categories and concepts: Theoretical views and inductive data analysis* (pp. 97–144). San Diego, CA: Academic Press.

Barsalou, L. W., Pecher, D., Zeelenberg, R., Simmons, W. K., & Hamann, S. B. (in press). Multi-modal simulation in conceptual processing. In W. Ahn, R. Goldstone, B. Love, A.

Markman, & P. Wolff (Eds.), *Categorization inside and outside the lab: Festschrift in honor of Douglas L. Medin.* Washington, DC: American Psychological Association.

Barsalou, L. W., Sloman, S. A, & Chaigneau, S. E. (in press). The HIPE theory of function. In L. Carlson & E. van der Zee (Eds.), *Representing functional features for language and space: Insights from perception, categorization and development.* Oxford, England: Oxford University Press.

Barsalou, L. W., & Wiemer-Hastings, K. (in press). Situating abstract concepts. In D. Pecher & G. R. Zuaan (Eds.), *Grounding cognition: The role of perception and action in memory, language, and thought.* New York: Cambridge.

Biederman, I. (1987). Recognition-by-components: A theory of human image understanding. *Psychological Review, 94,* 115–147.

Biederman, I., & Shiffrar, M. M. (1987). Sexing day-old chicks: A case study and expert systems analysis of a difficult perceptual-learning task. *Journal of Experimental Psychology: Learning, Memory, & Cognition, 13,* 640–645.

Bobrow, D. G., & Collins, A. M. (Eds.). (1975). *Representation and understanding: Studies in cognitive science.* New York: Academic Press.

Brooks, L. R. (1978). Nonanalytic concept formation and memory for instances. In E. Rosch & B. B. Lloyd (Eds.), *Cognition and categorization.* Hillsdale, NJ: Lawrence Erlbaum Associates.

Burgess, C., & Lund, K. (1997). Modelling parsing constraints with high-dimensional context space. *Language and Cognitive Processes, 12,* 177–210.

Carlson-Radvansky, L. A., Covey, E. S., & Lattanzi, K. M. (1999). "What" effects on "where": Functional influences on spatial relations. *Psychological Science, 10,* 516–521.

Carlson-Radvansky, L. A., & Logan, G. D. (1997). The influence of reference frame selection on spatial template construction. *Journal of Memory and Language, 37,* 411–437.

Charniak, E., & McDermott, D. (1985). *Introduction to artificial intelligence.* Reading, MA: Addison-Wesley.

Chi, M. T. H., Feltovich, P. J., & Glaser, R. (1981). Categorization and representation of physics problems by experts and novices. *Cognitive Science, 5,* 121–152.

Church, A. (1956). *The problem of universals.* Notre Dame, IN: University of Notre Dame Press.

Coventry, K. R. (1998). Spatial prepositions, functional relations, and lexical specification. In P. Oliver & K. P. Gapp (Eds.), *Representation and processing of spatial expressions* (pp. 247–262). Mahwah, NJ: Lawrence Erlbaum Associates.

Damasio, A. R. (1989). Time-locked multiregional retroactivation: A systems-level proposal for the neural substrates of recall and recognition. *Cognition, 33,* 25–62.

De Valois, R., & De Valois, K. (1988). *Spatial vision.* New York: Oxford University Press.

Dietrich, E. (2000). Analogy and conceptual change, or you can't step into the same mind twice. In E. Dietrich & A. Markman (Eds.), *Cognitive dynamics: Conceptual change in humans and machines* (pp. 51–77). Cambridge, MA: MIT Press.

Dretske, F. (1995). *Naturalizing the mind.* Cambridge, MA: MIT Press.

Farah, M. J. (2000). The neural bases of mental imagery. In M. S. Gazzaniga (Ed.), *The cognitive neurosciences* (2nd ed., pp. 965–974). Cambridge, MA: MIT Press.

Fodor, J. A. (1998). *Concepts: Where cognitive science went wrong.* New York: Oxford University Press.

Fodor, J. A., & Pylyshyn, Z. W. (1988). Connectionism and cognitive architecture: A critical analysis. *Cognition, 28,* 3–71.

Gärdenfors, P. (2000). *Conceptual spaces: The geometry of thought.* Cambridge, MA: MIT Press.

Gauthier, I., Skudlarski, P., Gore, J. C., & Anderson, A. W. (2000). Expertise for cars and birds recruits brain areas involved in face recognition. *Nature Neuroscience, 3,* 191–197.

Gentner, D., & Markman, A. B. (1997). Structure mapping in analogy and similarity. *American Psychologist, 52,* 45–56.

Glenberg, A. M. (1997). What memory is for. *Behavioral and Brain Sciences, 20,* 1–55.

Goldstone, R. L., & Medin, D. L. (1994). The course of comparison. *Journal of Experimental Psychology: Learning, Memory, and Cognition, 20,* 29–50.

Graesser, A. C., Singer, M., & Trabasso, T. (1994). Constructing inferences during narrative text comprehension. *Psychological Review, 101,* 371–395.

Gutheil, G., Vera, A., & Keil, F. C. (1998). Do houseflies think? Patterns of induction and biological beliefs in development. *Cognition, 66,* 33–49.

Halff, H. M., Ortony, A., & Anderson, R. C. (1976). A context-sensitive representation of word meanings. *Memory & Cognition, 4,* 378–383.

Hampton, J. A. (1997). Conceptual combination. In K. Lamberts & D. Shanks (Eds.), *Knowledge, concepts, and categories* (pp. 133–159). Cambridge, MA: MIT Press.

Haugeland, J. (1985). *Artificial intelligence: The very idea of it.* Cambridge, MA: MIT Press.

Haugeland, J. (1991). Representational genera. In W. Ramsey, S. P. Stitch, & D. E. Rumelhart (Eds.), *Philosophy and connectionist theory* (pp. 61–89). Hillsdale, NJ: Lawrence Erlbaum Associates.

Hayward, W. G., & Tarr, M. J. (1995). Spatial language and spatial representation. *Cognition, 55,* 39.

Hintzman, D. L. (1986). "Schema abstraction" in a multiple-trace memory model. *Psychological Review, 93,* 411–428.

Hochberg, J. (1998). Gestalt theory and its legacy: Organization in eye and brain, in attention and mental representation. In J. Hochberg (Ed.), *Perception and cognition at century's end: Handbook of perception and cognition* (2nd ed., pp. 253–306). San Diego, CA: Academic Press.

Holyoak, K. J., & Thagard, P. (1997). The analogical mind. *American Psychologist, 52,* 35–44.

Humphreys, G. W., & Forde, E. M. E. (2001). Hierarchies, similarity, and interactivity in object recognition: "Category-specific" neuropsychological deficits. *Behavioral & Brain Sciences, 24*(3), 453–509.

Hyde, T. S., & Jenkins, J. J. (1969). Differential effects of incidental tasks on the organization of recall of a list of highly associated words. *Journal of Experimental Psychology, 82,* 472–481.

Jeannerod, M. (1995). Mental imagery in the motor context. *Neuropsychologia, 33,* 1419–1432.

Johnson, K. E., & Eilers, A. T. (1998). Effects of knowledge and development on subordinate level categorization. *Cognitive Development, 13,* 515–545.

Johnson, K. E., & Mervis, C. B. (1997). Effects of varying levels of expertise on the basic level of categorization. *Journal of Experimental Psychology: General, 126,* 248–277.

Johnson, K. E., & Mervis, C. B. (1998). Impact of intuitive theories on feature recruitment throughout the continuum of expertise. *Memory & Cognition, 26,* 382–401.

Kan, I. P., Barsalou, L. W., Solomon, K. O., Minor, J. K., & Thompson-Schill, S. L. (2003). Role of mental imagery in a property verification task: fMRI evidence for perceptual representations of conceptual knowledge. Invited article under review at *Cognitive Neuropsychology, 20,* 525–540.

Keil, F. C., & Batterman, N. (1984). A characteristic-to-defining shift in the development of word meaning. *Journal of Verbal Learning & Verbal Behavior, 23,* 221–236.

Kemler, D. G. (1983). Exploring and reexploring issues of integrality, perceptual sensitivity, and dimensional salience. *Journal of Experimental Child Psychology, 36,* 365–379.

Kintsch, W., & van Dijk, T. A. (1978). Toward a model of text comprehension and production. *Psychological Review, 85,* 363–394.

Kosslyn, S. M. (1994). *Image and brain.* Cambridge, MA: MIT Press.

Lamberts, K. (1995). Categorization under time pressure. *Journal of Experimental Psychology: General, 124,* 161–180.

Landauer, T. K., & Dumais, S. T. (1997). A solution to Plato's Problem: The latent semantic analysis theory of acquisition, induction, and representation of knowledge. *Psychological Review, 104,* 211–240.

Langacker, R. W. (1986). An introduction to cognitive grammar. *Cognitive Science, 10,* 1–40.

Lin, E. L., & Murphy, G. L. (1997). Effects of background knowledge on object categorization and part detection. *Journal of Experimental Psychology: Human Perception & Performance, 23,* 1153–1169.

Logan, G. D. (1988). Toward an instance theory of automatization. *Psychological Review, 95,* 492–527.

Logan, G. D., & Compton, B. J. (1996). Distance and distraction effects in the apprehension of spatial relations. *Journal of Experimental Psychology: Human Perception and Performance, 22,* 159–172.

Mandler, J. M. (1992). How to build a baby: II. Conceptual primitives. *Psychological Review, 99,* 587–604.

Margolis, E., & Laurence, S. (1999). Concepts and cognitive science. In E. Margolis & S. Laurence (Eds.), *Concepts: Core readings* (pp. 3–81). Cambridge, MA: MIT Press.

Markman, A. B., & Gentner, D. (1997). The effects of alignability on memory. *Psychological Science, 8,* 363–367.

Martin, A. (2001). Functional neuroimaging of semantic memory. In. R. Cabeza & A. Kingstone (Eds.), *Handbook of functional neuroimaging of cognition* (pp. 153–186). Cambridge, MA: MIT Press.

Martin, A., & Chao, L. (2001). Semantic memory and the brain: Structure and process. *Current Opinion in Neurobiology, 11,* 194–201.

Martin, A., Ungerleider, L. G., & Haxby, J. V. (2000). Category-specificity and the brain: The sensory-motor model of semantic representations of objects. In M. S. Gazzaniga (Ed.), *The new cognitive neurosciences* (2nd ed., pp. 1023–1036). Cambridge, MA: MIT Press.

McClelland, J. L., Rumelhart, D. E., & the PDP Research Group. (1986). *Parallel distributed processing: Explorations in the microstructure of cognition: Vol. 2. Psychological and biological models.* Cambridge, MA: MIT Press.

McRae, K., & Cree, G. S. (2002). Factors underlying category-specific semantic deficits. In E. M. E. Forde & G. Humphreys (Eds.), *Category-specificity in mind and brain* (pp. 211–249). East Sussex, England: Psychology Press.

Medin, D. L., & Schaffer, M. (1978). A context theory of classification learning. *Psychological Review, 85,* 207–238.

Miikkulainen, R., & Dyer, M. G. (1991). Natural language processing with modular PDP networks and distributed lexicon. *Cognitive Science, 15,* 343–399.

Morrison, D. J., & Schyns, P. G. (2001). Usage of spatial scales for the categorization of faces, objects, and scenes. *Psychonomic Bulletin & Review, 8,* 454–469.

Murphy, G. L., & Medin, D. L. (1985). The role of theories in conceptual coherence. *Psychological Review, 92,* 289–316.

Newell, A. (1990). *Unified theories of cognition.* Cambridge, MA: Harvard University Press.

Newell, A., & Simon, H. A. (1972). *Human problem solving.* Englewood Cliffs, NJ: Prentice-Hall.

Nosofsky, R. M. (1984). Choice, similarity, and the context theory of classification. *Journal of Experimental Psychology: Learning, Memory, and Cognition, 10,* 104–114.

Nosofsky, R. M., Palmeri, T. J., & McKinley, S. C. (1994). Rule-plus-exception model of classification learning. *Psychological Review, 101,* 53–79.

Paivio, A. (1986). *Mental representations: A dual coding approach.* New York: Oxford University Press.

Palmer, S. E. (1999). *Vision science: Photons to phenomenology.* Cambridge, MA: MIT Press.

Palmeri, T. J., & Nosofsky, R. M. (2001). Central tendencies, extreme points, and prototype enhancement effects in ill-defined perceptual categorization. *Quarterly Journal of Experimental Psychology. Section A, Human Experimental Psychology, 54,* 197–235.

Pearl, J. (2000). *Causality: Models, reasoning, and inference.* Cambridge, England: Cambridge University Press.

Pecher, D., Zeelenberg, R., & Barsalou, L. W. (2003). Verifying properties from different modalities for concepts produces switching costs. *Psychological Science, 14(2),* 119–124.

Pollack, J. (1990). Recursive distributed representations. *Artificial Intelligence, 46,* 77–105.

Posner, M. I., & Keele, S. W. (1968). On the genesis of abstract ideas. *Journal of Experimental Psychology, 77,* 353–363.

Putnam, H. (1973). Meaning and reference. *Journal of Philosophy, 70,* 699–711.

Putnam, H. (1975). The meaning of "meaning." In H. Putnam (Ed.), *Mind, language, and reality: Philosophical papers* (Vol. 2, pp. 215–271). New York: Cambridge University Press.

Pylyshyn, Z. W. (1973). What the mind's eye tells the mind's brain: A critique of mental imagery. *Psychological Bulletin, 80,* 1–24.

Rhodes, G., Brennan, S., & Carey, S. (1987). Identification and ratings of caricatures: Implications for mental representation of faces. *Cognitive Psychology, 19,* 473–497.

Rips, L. J. (1995). The current status of research on concept combination. *Mind & Language, 10,* 72–104.

Rips, L. J., Shoben, E. J., & Smith, E. E. (1973). Semantic distance and the verification of semantic relations. *Journal of Verbal Learning and Verbal Behavior, 12,* 1–20.

Rosch, E., & Mervis, C. B. (1975). Family resemblances: Studies in the internal structure of categories. *Cognitive Psychology, 7,* 573–605.

Rozenblit, L., & Keil, F. (2002). The misunderstood limits of folk science: An illusion of explanatory depth. *Cognitive Science, 26*(5), 521–562.

Rumelhart, D. E., McClelland, J. L., & the PDP Research Group. (1986). *Parallel distributed processing: Explorations in the microstructure of cognition: Vol. 1. Foundations.* Cambridge, MA: MIT Press.

Rumelhart, D. E., Smolensky, P., McClelland, J. L., & Hinton, G. E. (1986). Schemata and sequential thought processes in PDP models. In J. L. McClelland, D. E. Rumelhart, & the PDP Research Group (Eds.), *Parallel distributed processing: Explorations in the microstructure of cognition: Vol. 2. Psychological and biological models* (pp. 7–57). Cambridge, MA: MIT Press.

Schank, R. C., & Abelson, R. P. (1977). *Scripts, plans, goals, and understanding: An inquiry into human knowledge structures.* Hillsdale, NJ: Lawrence Erlbaum Associates.

Schank, R. C., & Colby, K. M. (Eds.). (1973). *Computer models of thought and language.* San Francisco: Freeman.

Schooler, J. W., Fiore, S. M., & Brandimonte, M. A. (1997). At loss *from* words: Verbal overshadowing of perceptual memories. *The Psychology of Learning and Motivation, 37,* 291–340.

Schyns, P. G., Goldstone, R. L., & Thibaut, J. P. (1998). The development of features in object concepts. *Behavioral and Brain Sciences, 21,* 1–54.

Simmons, K., & Barsalou, L. W. (2003). The similarity-in-topography principle: Reconciling theories of conceptual deficits. The organisation of conceptual knowledge in the brain: Neuropsychological and neuroimaging perspectives [Special Issue]. *Cognitive Neuropsychology, 20*(3–6), 451–486.

Smith, J. D., & Minda, J. P. (2002). Distinguishing prototype-based and exemplar-based processes in dot-pattern category learning. *Journal of Experimental Psychology: Learning, Memory, and Cognition, 28,* 800–811.

Smith, L. B. (1989). A model of perceptual classification in children and adults. *Psychological Review, 96,* 125–144.

Smolensky, P. (1988). On the proper treatment of connectionism. *The Behavioral and Brain Sciences, 11,* 1–74.

Smolensky, P. (1990). Tensor product variable binding and the representation of symbolic structures in connectionist systems. *Artificial Intelligence, 46,* 159–216.

Solomon, K. O., & Barsalou, L. W. (2001). Representing properties locally. *Cognitive Psychology, 43,* 129–169.

Solomon, K. O., & Barsalou, L. W. (2004). Perceptual simulation in property verification. *Memory & Cognition, 32,* 244–259.

Spalding, T. L., & Ross, B. H. (1994). Comparison-based learning: Effects of comparing instances during category learning. *Journal of Experimental Psychology: Learning, Memory, and Cognition, 20,* 1251–1263.

Spence, C., Nicholls, M. E. R., & Driver, J. (2000). The cost of expecting events in the wrong sensory modality. *Perception & Psychophysics, 63,* 330–336.

Talmy, L. (1983). How language structures space. In H. Pick & L. Acredelo (Eds.), *Spatial orientation: Theory, research, and application* (pp. 225–282). New York: Plenum.

Tanaka, J. W., & Farah, M. J. (1993). Parts and wholes in face recognition. *Quarterly Journal of Experimental Psychology: Human Experimental Psychology, 42,* 225–245.

Tversky, A. (1977). Features of similarity. *Psychological Review, 84,* 327–352.

van Gelder, T. (1990). Compositionality: A connectionist variation on a classical theme. *Cognitive Science, 14,* 355–384.

Warrington, E. K., & Shallice, T. (1984). Category specific semantic impairments. *Brain, 107,* 829–854.

Wiemer-Hastings, K. (2004). *Abstract concepts.* Manuscript in preparation.

Wiemer-Hastings, K., Krug, J., & Xu, X. (2001). Imagery, context availability, contextual constraint, and abstractness. *Proceedings of the 23rd Annual Conference of the Cognitive Science Society,* 1134–1139.

Wilson, R. A., & Keil, F. (1998). The shadow and shallows of explanation. *Minds & Machines, 8,* 137–159.

Winograd, T. (1972). *Understanding natural language.* San Diego, CA: Academic Press.

Winograd, T. (1975). Frame representations and the declarative-procedural controversy. In D. G. Bobrow & A. M. Collins (Eds.), *Representation and understanding: Studies in cognitive science.* New York: Academic Press.

Wisniewski, E. J. (1997). When concepts combine. *Psychonomic Bulletin & Review, 4,* 167–183.

Wisniewski, E. J. (1998). Property instantiation in conceptual combination. *Memory & Cognition, 26,* 1330–1347.

Wittgenstein, L. (1953). *Philosophical investigations* (G. E. M. Anscombe, Trans.). New York: Macmillan.

Wu, L., & Barsalou, L. W. (2004). *Perceptual simulation in property generation.* Manuscript under review.

Zeki, S. (1993). *A vision of the brain.* Oxford, England: Blackwell Scientific.

Chapter 16

Models of Categorization: What Are the Limits?

Robert Siegler
Carnegie Mellon University

INTRODUCTION

All three of the papers in this session present bold and innovative accounts of categorization. Barsalou portrays categorization as a process of dynamic interpretation of perceptual symbols, Rogers and McClelland as a process of detection of coherent variation, and Keil as a process of formation of implicit, skeletal theories. Each paper presents elegant programs of research that have yielded a great deal of data consistent with the underlying theoretical perspective.

There is also a fourth paper that was not presented in the session but that nonetheless seems directly relevant to all of the papers that were presented. This is Allen Newell's (1973) famous commentary "You Can't Play 20 Questions with Nature and Win." In that paper, Newell argued that even the most elegant empirical experiments fail to cumulate without an encompassing model to motivate and integrate them. To address this problem, he recommended that investigators who focus their empirical research on specific experimental tasks "construct a single system to perform them all . . . It must truly be a single system to provide the integration that we seek" (p. 305).

All three of the present papers reflect efforts in the direction Newell recommended; the investigators have generated broad, encompassing models that, to varying degrees of specificity, integrate findings from a range of experimental tasks. However, I can't help wondering whether Newell would

433

write the same prescription today as he did when he wrote the "20 Questions" article for an earlier Carnegie Cognition Symposium, 30 years ago almost to the day. Although Allan is no longer here to tell us what he thinks, much of my discussion is a kind of conversation with him regarding the present papers and broader issues concerning how to achieve his goal of helping psychological research to cumulate.

Contributions of the Papers

The proof of the value of these diverse approaches to categorization is that although I do not study categorization, reading them increased my understanding of phenomena of direct interest to me. (This may seem like a rather egocentric standard of scientific value, but I suspect that it's the one most scientists use most of the time.) There is a surprising degree of overlap between the data and conclusions regarding categorization reported in each of these papers and the data and conclusions that have emerged in the area of my own focus, strategy choice and discovery in children's mathematical and scientific thinking.

Barsalou. Larry Barsalou makes a compelling argument for the view that representations are often modality specific, reflecting the perceptual/ motor contexts in which the representations were formed. One of my favorite brain-imaging studies supports this perspective and illustrates its importance for understanding the development of arithmetic skills (Zago et al., 2001). The study involved PET scans of college students as they performed single-digit arithmetic problems. The college students, who were chosen for consistently retrieving answers to such problems, showed increased activity in a part of the brain associated with finger counting, including the right cerebellar cortex, but no increased activity in areas associated with linguistic processing. Given the importance of finger counting in development of basic arithmetic skills, these neural data support the view that the history of learning, including motor and perceptual activity during learning, influences the representations that are formed.

Other conclusions from Barsalou's research on adults' categorization also parallel conclusions that have arisen from research on children's mathematical and scientific thinking. For example, Barsalou emphasized that representations of a given object are not fixed but rather change with experience; work on children's representations of mathematical and scientific problems shows similar change. Thus, when 5-year-olds see a balance scale, they represent the amount of weight on the two sides of the fulcrum; when 8-year-olds see the same balance scale, they represent not only the amount of weight but also the distance of the weight from the fulcrum (Siegler, 1976). Similarly, the flexible adaptation of representations to context that

Barsalou observed in adult categorization is also present in children's strategy choices in arithmetic. For example, Siegler (1996) found that relative to a control group that was given equal incentive for speed and accuracy on subtraction problems, rewarding accuracy led to more accurate but slower performance and rewarding speed led to faster but less-accurate performance (but interestingly, not to changes in strategy use). Thus, Barsalou has successfully identified characteristics not only of adults' categorization but of a wide range of cognitive activity.

Rogers and McClelland. Like Barsalou, Rogers and McClelland have identified a number of characteristics of categorization that apply equally well to children's mathematical and scientific development. For example, their PDP model offers a well-specified account of why coarse-grain distinctions among categories become available sooner than fine-grain distinctions. This same phenomenon is seen in preschoolers' numerical understanding, where even 3-year-olds know that nine is a bigger number than one, but the knowledge of whether seven or eight is bigger does not emerge until 2 or 3 years later (Siegler & Robinson, 1982). The Rogers and McClelland model also offers an account of how initially nonsalient cues acquire salience, a major issue in understanding cognitive developmental phenomena such as the balance scale observations, alluded to earlier, regarding encoding of distance from the fulcrum.

Keil. Keil's fascinating findings regarding lack of explanatory depth attests to the wisdom of one of my favorite jokes. A public-spirited scientist decides to enlighten the citizens of a small Southern town by telling them about astronomy. To stir interest, he starts out with the question, "Who can tell me how the earth stays up rather than falling down?" An old lady raises her hand and answers "It sits on the back of a giant turtle." The scientist smiles a little at this opportunity to enlighten the benighted, and asks, "So what holds up the turtle?" This elicits a quick answer, "Another turtle." The scientist responds, "And what holds that up?"; the old lady, predictably enough, says, "Another turtle." Becoming increasingly agitated, the scientist says, "And what holds up that one? And the next one? And the next one?" The old lady just smiles and says, "You can save your breath, sonny; it's turtles all the way down."

Keil's findings provide an interesting perspective on recent research about the effects of asking people to explain answers to math and science problems that a more knowledgeable person or textbook says are correct. Such requests for explanations have been shown to deepen the learning of people of all ages from preschoolers (Siegler, 1995) to adolescents (Chi, de Leeuw, Chiu, & LaVancher, 1994) to adults (Renkl, 1997). Keil's findings help to explain why such questions are effective. Left to themselves, even educated adults fail to generate explanations of any depth for scientific and mathematical phenomena; therefore, asking them to explain why outcomes occurred can lead them to think more deeply about the phenomena than they would on their own, and therefore to learn more about them.

Keil's results also demonstrate that a characteristic that is usually viewed as unique to young children actually is shared by adults. This characteristic involves the superiority of understanding of static states relative to that of transformations. Piaget observed that this difference in understanding is a distinctive feature of preoperational children's thinking; Keil's observations indicate that it is characteristic of adults' thinking as well. The adults in his studies knew the static components of mechanical systems, but generated only vague and half-baked ideas about how movements of the system's components would generate its functioning. Contemporary research in developmental psychology has emphasized ways in which the thinking of infants and young children is more adult-like than had been realized; Keil's findings indicate that the thinking of adults also is more child-like than is commonly acknowledged.

Questions Raised by the Papers

As with almost all good research programs, these three raise at least as many questions as they answer. The high quality of these research programs is attested to by the complexity of the questions they raise; these are not easy questions for anyone to answer.

Barsalou. Barsalou's description of DIPSS provides a general sense of how the system works, but many of the specifics remain unclear. How does the system know which simulator to use in a given situation? How does the interpreter work? How is older and newer information integrated to form updated representations? These and a number of other aspects of the system's functioning are described in a rather vague way, which raises questions not only about the workings of particular components but of whether the components would work together as expected. In addition to recommending broad, encompassing models, Newell (1973) also recommended that psychologists generate complete processing models that specify the workings of the system on specific tasks; this advice seems particularly apropos here.

A second question raised by Barsalou's article concerns what it means to say that a representation is perceptual. Barsalou's example of DIPPS' representations of cars can be used to illustrate the point. People represent a variety of quite abstract concepts about cars: the roles of gasoline, engines, brakes, and so on. In what sense would a representation of such information be perceptual? Is information about the workings of engines represented differently in any important way if the information enters the cognitive system through the eyes or through the ears (reading vs. listening)? In the absence of evidence of a systematic influence on abstract understanding of the perceptual modality through which information enters the system, it is unclear what Barsalou means when he says that DIPSS is a perceptual symbol system, nor how the approach differs from ones based on general constructivist ideas, such as those of Bransford and Johnson (1973).

Rogers and McClelland. Rogers and McClelland's model of how infants and toddlers build simple concepts such as "animal" encodes a remarkably wide range of characteristics of the objects it encounters: scales, gills, skin, bark, life status, growth, and so on. However, it seems implausible that any child has ever existed who did not know the concept "animal" but who nonetheless encoded these and many other features that the model depicts children as encoding. Rogers and McClelland noted this problem and said that the particular features that are encoded may not be realistic, but that this does not affect the truth of the more general point that concepts such as "animal" arise out of the covariation of whatever features are encoded. This claim may be true, but it is not clear that the Rogers/McClelland model provides relevant evidence. Whether particular concepts could arise out of featural covariation depends entirely on which features are encoded. For example, if a child only encoded the color, size, and sounds of objects, it is far from clear that the concept "animal" would arise.

A second issue relevant to the plausibility of this model concerns the amount of experience that the model requires to learn. Rogers and McClelland noted that the initial model has not done much conceptual differentiation after 50 epochs, but that it shows considerably more differentiation later. This sounds fine until we stop to consider that each of the 50 epochs includes 8 objects, 4 relations per object, 34 properties per object per relation—a total of 54,000 trials over the 50 epochs. And that's the amount of experience needed for the model to reach the point at which conceptual differentiation is just beginning. The second model that Rogers and McClelland described is yet slower; in it, conceptual distinctions remain minimal after more than 350,000 trials. If children were not vastly faster categorizers, none of us would be around today to build simulation models.

Keil. Keil posited that cognitive development generally proceeds from the abstract to the concrete. This pattern certainly emerges sometimes, but it seems likely that development proceeds at least as often from a middling level of abstraction toward both more abstract and more concrete. To obtain a sense of why this seems likely, consider the following question. Which concept is likely to develop first: living thing; animal; mammal; medium size, four-legged, intentionally moving thing; dog, poodle, toy poodle, or Mookie? Although the answer is unknown, it seems more likely to be one of the concepts of middling generality, rather than a highly abstract concept such as "living thing," which would include both plants and animals.

Another challenge for Keil is to provide evidence or argument to support his claim that understanding of mechanical devices involves explanatory knowledge but understanding of narratives does not. Maybe people are just better at formulating explanations involving other people than they are at formulating explanations of mechanical devices. Alternatively, the key may be our access to our own mental life and ability to use that access to explain the actions of others. A third possibility is that living provides ample motivation for explaining the actions of other people, whereas interacting with physical and biological systems rarely requires deep explanations. Determining why people are better at explaining actions in narratives than actions of mechanical devices presents an interesting challenge, but defining one type of explanation as not involving explanatory knowledge seems more likely to discourage inquiry than to stimulate it.

Pushing the Limits: Pros and Cons of a Research Strategy

These investigators, particularly Barsalou and Rogers and McClelland, have taken to heart Newell's (1973) recommendation of proposing a single model that integrates results across a wide variety of experimental tasks. The basic logic of this approach is to push the limits of the range of phenomena that a model can explain. Thus, investigators try to show the applicability of this model to a variety of domains (language, memory, categorization, etc.), populations (age groups, ability levels, etc.), and experimental conditions (contextual framing, time limits, goals, etc.). In line with Newell's intent, such approaches have provided a needed centripetal force to counteract the centrifugal forces militating toward fragmentation of cognitive psychology into an infinite number of sub-areas with no core. However, it is less clear how well these efforts have promoted Newell's deeper goal: to help research findings cumulate into increasingly precise and refined mechanistic theories.

Although Newell (1973) didn't emphasize the point, theoretical progress requires discriminant as well as convergent validation of mechanisms. In other words, such progress requires establishing the boundary conditions of theories and their associated mechanisms—when the theories are applicable and when a given mechanism plays a dominant role, a subordinate role, or no role. The importance of such discriminant validity is seen in the fates of Hullian, Skinnerian, and Freudian theories. Because these theories became able to explain everything, they ultimately could explain nothing. To the degree that a theory becomes able to explain any data pattern that may arise, the theory stops being scientifically useful. I am unsure exactly how strongly this concern applies to DIPSS and PDP models, but it clearly applies to some degree.

In 1973, Newell proposed that pushing the limits of psychological theory meant proposing encompassing, integrative models that would account for a broad range of data with one or a small number of mechanisms. In 2003, pushing the limits of psychological theory may require setting a new goal: To identify the boundary conditions of the applicability of theories, and to add new mechanisms to account for phenomena beyond that boundary. Pursuing this path may move us toward Newell's deepest goal of truly unified theories of cognition.

REFERENCES

Bransford, J. D., & Johnson, M. K. (1973). Considerations of some problems of comprehension. In W. G. Chase (Ed.), *Visual information processing* (pp. 383–438). New York: Academic Press.

Chi, M. T. H., de Leeuw, N., Chiu, M.-H., & LaVancher, C. (1994). Eliciting self-explanations improves understanding. *Cognitive Science, 18*, 439–477.

Newell, A. (1973). You can't play 20 questions with nature and win: Projective comments on the papers of this symposium. In W. G. Chase (Ed.), *Visual information processing* (pp. 283–308). New York: Academic Press.

Renkl, A. (1997). Learning from worked-out examples: A study on individual differences. *Cognitive Science, 21*, 1–29.

Siegler, R. S. (1976). Three aspects of cognitive development. *Cognitive Psychology, 8*, 481–520.

Siegler, R. S. (1995). How does change occur: A microgenetic study of number conservation. *Cognitive Psychology, 28*, 225–273.

Siegler, R. S. (1996). *Emerging minds: The process of change in children's thinking.* New York: Oxford University Press.

Siegler, R. S., & Robinson, M. (1982). The development of numerical understandings. In H. W. Reese & L. P. Lipsitt (Eds.), *Advances in child development and behavior* (Vol. 16, pp. 241–312). New York: Academic Press.

Zago, L., Pesenti, M., Mellet, E., Crivello, F., Mazoyer, B., & Tzourio-Mazoyer, N. (2001). Neural correlates of simple and complex mental calculation. *NeuroImage, 13*, 314–327.

Author Index

441

D

Subject Index